COMPLEMENTARITY IN THE

Of the many expectations attending the creation of the first permanent International Criminal Court, the greatest has been that the principle of complementarity would catalyse national investigations and prosecutions of conflict-related crimes and lead to the reform of domestic justice systems.

Sarah M. H. Nouwen explores whether complementarity has had such an effect in two states subject to ICC intervention: Uganda and Sudan. Drawing on extensive empirical research and combining law, legal anthropology and political economy, she unveils several effects and outlines the catalysts for them. However, she also reveals that one widely anticipated effect – an increase in domestic proceedings for conflict-related crimes – has barely occurred. This finding leads to the unravelling of paradoxes that go right to the heart of the functioning of an idealistic Court in a world of real constraints.

SARAH M. H. NOUWEN is a university lecturer in law at the University of Cambridge. She is also a Fellow of the Lauterpacht Centre for International Law and of Pembroke College.

To Katy and Jan,

looking forward to many more discussions about topics of shared interest... kids included!

Sarah

CAMBRIDGE STUDIES IN LAW AND SOCIETY

Cambridge Studies in Law and Society aims to publish the best scholarly work on legal discourse and practice in its social and institutional contexts, combining theoretical insights and empirical research.

The fields that it covers are: studies of law in action; the sociology of law; the anthropology of law; cultural studies of law, including the role of legal discourses in social formations; law and economics; law and politics; and studies of governance. The books consider all forms of legal discourse across societies, rather than being limited to lawyers' discourses alone.

The series editors come from a range of disciplines: academic law; socio-legal studies; sociology; and anthropology. All have been actively involved in teaching and writing about law in context.

Series editors

Chris Arup *Monash University*, *Victoria*

Martin Chanock *La Trobe University*, *Melbourne*

Sally Engle Merry *New York University*

Susan Silbey *Massachusetts Institute of Technology*

Books in the Series

Diseases of the Will
Mariana Valverde

The Politics of Truth and Reconciliation in South Africa: Legitimizing the Post-Apartheid State
Richard A. Wilson

Modernism and the Grounds of Law
Peter Fitzpatrick

Unemployment and Government: Genealogies of the Social
William Walters

Autonomy and Ethnicity: Negotiating Competing Claims in Multi-Ethnic States
Yash Ghai

Constituting Democracy: Law, Globalism and South Africa's Political Reconstruction
Heinz Klug

The Ritual of Rights in Japan: Law, Society, and Health Policy
Eric A. Feldman

The Invention of the Passport: Surveillance, Citizenship and the State
John Torpey

Governing Morals: A Social History of Moral Regulation
Alan Hunt

The Colonies of Law: Colonialism, Zionism and Law in Early Mandate Palestine
Ronen Shamir

Law and Nature
David Delaney

Social Citizenship and Workfare in the United States and Western Europe: The Paradox of Inclusion
Joel F. Handler

Law, Anthropology and the Constitution of the Social: Making Persons and Things
Edited by Alain Pottage and Martha Mundy

Judicial Review and Bureaucratic Impact: International and Interdisciplinary Perspectives
Edited by Marc Hertogh and Simon Halliday

Immigrants at the Margins: Law, Race, and Exclusion in Southern Europe
Kitty Calavita

Lawyers and Regulation: The Politics of the Administrative Process
Patrick Schmidt

Law and Globalization from Below: Toward a Cosmopolitan Legality
Edited by Boaventura de Sousa Santos and Cesar A. Rodriguez-Garavito

Public Accountability: Designs, Dilemmas and Experiences
Edited by Michael W. Dowdle

Law, Violence and Sovereignty among West Bank Palestinians
Tobias Kelly

Legal Reform and Administrative Detention Powers in China
Sarah Biddulph

The Practice of Human Rights: Tracking Law Between the Global and the Local
Edited by Mark Goodale and Sally Engle Merry

Judges Beyond Politics in Democracy and Dictatorship: Lessons from Chile
Lisa Hilbink

Paths to International Justice: Social and Legal Perspectives
Edited by Marie-Bénédicte Dembour and Tobias Kelly

Law and Society in Vietnam: The Transition from Socialism in Comparative Perspective
Mark Sidel

Constitutionalizing Economic Globalization: Investment Rules and Democracy's Promise
David Schneiderman

The New World Trade Organization Knowledge Agreements: 2nd Edition
Christopher Arup

Justice and Reconciliation in Post-Apartheid South Africa
Edited by François du Bois and Antje du Bois-Pedain

Militarization and Violence against Women in Conflict Zones in the Middle East: A Palestinian Case-Study
Nadera Shalhoub-Kevorkian

Child Pornography and Sexual Grooming: Legal and Societal Responses
Suzanne Ost

Darfur and the Crime of Genocide
John Hagan and Wenona Rymond-Richmond

Fictions of Justice: The International Criminal Court and the Challenge of Legal Pluralism in Sub-Saharan Africa
Kamari Maxine Clarke

Conducting Law and Society Research: Reflections on Methods and Practices
Simon Halliday and Patrick Schmidt

Planted Flags: Trees, Land, and Law in Israel/Palestine
Irus Braverman

Culture under Cross-Examination: International Justice and the Special Court for Sierra Leone
Tim Kelsall

Cultures of Legality: Judicialization and Political Activism in Latin America
Javier Couso, Alexandra Huneeus, Rachel Sieder

Courting Democracy in Bosnia and Herzegovina: The Hague Tribunal's Impact in a Postwar State
Lara J. Nettelfield

The Gacaca Courts and Post-Genocide Justice and Reconciliation in Rwanda: Justice without Lawyers
Phil Clark

Law, Society, and History: Themes in the Legal Sociology and Legal History of Lawrence M. Friedman
Robert W. Gordon and Morton J. Horwitz

After Abu Ghraib: Exploring Human Rights in America and the Middle East
Shadi Mokhtari

Adjudication in Religious Family Laws: Cultural Accommodation: Legal Pluralism, and Gender Equality in India
Gopika Solanki

Water On Tap: Rights and Regulation in the Transnational Governance of Urban Water Services
Bronwen Morgan

Elements of Moral Cognition: Rawls' Linguistic Analogy and the Cognitive Science of Moral and Legal Judgment
John Mikhail

A Sociology of Constitutions: Constitutions and State Legitimacy in Historical-Sociological Perspective
Chris Thornhill

Mitigation and Aggravation at Sentencing
Edited by Julian Roberts

Institutional Inequality and the Mobilization of the Family and Medical Leave Act: Rights on Leave
Catherine R. Albiston

Authoritarian Rule of Law: Legislation, Discourse and Legitimacy in Singapore
Jothie Rajah

Law and Development and the Global Discourses of Legal Transfers
Edited by John Gillespie and Pip Nicholson

Law Against the State: Ethnographic Forays into Law's Transformations
Edited by Julia Eckert, Brian Donahoe, Christian Strümpell and Zerrin Özlem Biner

Transnational Legal Process and State Change
Edited by Gregory C. Shaffer

Legal Mobilization under Authoritarianism: The Case of Post-Colonial Hong Kong
Edited by Waikeung Tam

Complementarity in the Line of Fire: The Catalysing Effect of the International Criminal Court in Uganda and Sudan
Sarah M. H. Nouwen

COMPLEMENTARITY IN THE LINE OF FIRE

The Catalysing Effect of the International Criminal Court in Uganda and Sudan

SARAH M. H. NOUWEN

CAMBRIDGE
UNIVERSITY PRESS

CAMBRIDGE
UNIVERSITY PRESS

University Printing House, Cambridge CB2 8BS, United Kingdom

Published in the United States of America by Cambridge University Press, New York

Cambridge University Press is part of the University of Cambridge.

It furthers the University's mission by disseminating knowledge in the pursuit of education, learning and research at the highest international levels of excellence.

www.cambridge.org
Information on this title: www.cambridge.org/9781107646575

© Sarah M. H. Nouwen 2013

First published 2013

Printed in the United Kingdom by CPI Group Ltd, Croydon CR0 4YY

A catalogue record for this publication is available from the British Library

Library of Congress Cataloguing in Publication data
Nouwen, Sarah M. H.
Complementarity in the line of fire : the catalysing effect of the international criminal court in Uganda and Sudan / Sarah M. H. Nouwen.
pages   cm. – (Cambridge studies in law and society)
Summary: "This book follows as LAW" – Provided by publisher.
ISBN 978-1-107-01078-9 (Hardback)
1. Complementarity (International law)   2. International Criminal Court.   I. Title.
KZ7379.N68 2013
341'.04–dc23   2013000787

ISBN 978-1-107-01078-9 Hardback
ISBN 978-1-107-64657-5 African edition Paperback

In memory of
Heiltjen Nouwen-Kronenberg
7 February 1944 – 21 July 2007

... j'écris ton histoire. Et celle des tiens. Des miens désormais. Parce que tu m'as dit sans rancœurs ni haines le terrible des petites vies de rien, et de leurs théâtres intimes, que les mots sont de la chair, qu'il suffit de les écouter battre, bien au ras des émotions simples, et qu'ainsi tu m'as fait comprendre le métier d'écrire. Parce que avec du vif, sincère, sans fard, sans frime, ta vie dans tes paumes ouvertes, tu m'as dit aussi l'humanité nue. Pas l'idéale, celle des religions et des philosophies, ni la créature politique, mais celle qui a mal aux dents, qui essaie d'aimer à grande douleur et immenses espoirs, malgré son gros nez, malgré la maladie, les préjugés, malgré les gloires savoureuses et les bravos, la ballottée d'histoire, l'oubliée des guerres et des destinées jolies, la minuscule, celle qui trahit et tue, et celle qui a peur, l'innocente et l'héroïque ordinaire, celle qui veut enfermer l'univers dans son poing fermé et ne peut y tenir un papillon.

Michel Quint
Et mon mal est délicieux (Folio, Gallimard, Paris, 2004)

... I am writing your story. And the story of those dear to you. Dear to me now. Because with neither resentment nor hatred you told me about the awfulness of small lives with nothing, and their intimate dramas, you told me that words are made of flesh, that we only need to listen to them pulsate, right down next to simple emotions, and in this way you made me understand the craft of writing. Because with spontaneity, sincerity, without masquerading, without showing off, your life in your open palms, you also told me about naked humanity. Not the ideal one, of religions and philosophies, nor the political creature, but the one whose teeth ache, the one that tries to love with great pain and immense hope, despite its big nose, despite illness, despite prejudice, despite delicious glories and cheers, the one that is tossed about by history, forgotten by wars and pretty destinies, minuscule, the one that betrays and kills, and the one that is afraid, innocent and mundanely heroic, the one that wishes to trap the universe within its hand and cannot keep hold of a butterfly.

Translation by D. Roshd

CONTENTS

Foreword   page xv
Preface   xvii
List of abbreviations   xix
Map of ICC situation countries in July 2012   xxi

Prologue: in the line of fire   1

1   Complementarity from the line of fire   8
    The story of complementarity's catalysing effect in
    Uganda and Sudan   10
    Complementarity's double life   14
    The *dramatis personae* of complementarity's catalysing effect   21
    Assumptions underlying the expectation of a catalysing effect   24
    Normative, theoretical and methodological perspective   26
    The choice of a line-of-fire perspective   30
    The road ahead   33

2   The Rome Statute: complementarity in its legal context   34
    The key provisions setting forth complementarity   35
    Three popular assumptions   36
        An obligation to investigate or prosecute pursuant to the
        Rome Statute?   36
        An obligation to criminalise in domestic law?   40
        A prohibition on amnesties?   41
    The substance of complementarity: the criteria for
    inadmissibility   43
        The inadequacy of the shorthand description   43
        The 'same case' requirement: same person, same conduct,
        same incidents?   45
        Reasons to depart from the same-conduct test   51
        The requirement of an 'investigation'   59
        A decision not to prosecute   61
        Where domestic proceedings have been initiated:
        unwillingness and inability   62

Low punishment or a pardon is not a ground for
admissibility *per se* 66
The ICC is not a human rights court overseeing
compliance with fair trial rights 67
The procedural aspects of complementarity 70
Complementarity contains a primary right for *all* states 71
The Prosecutor must assess complementarity prior to
opening an investigation 71
The complementarity assessment is case-specific 72
Complementarity must be assessed irrespective of the
trigger mechanism 75
A state can directly influence the scope of the ICC's
investigation on grounds of complementarity 76
A state cannot force the Prosecutor to end an investigation 78
A state's jurisdiction to adjudicate is unaffected by ICC
intervention 78
The complementarity assessment is dynamic 79
The ICC does not have a conditional deferral procedure
like the ICTY and ICTR 83
Looking for a catalysing effect: the potentially confounding
and intervening variables 86
Other jurisdictional provisions: the triggers 86
Other jurisdictional provisions: a deferral requested by
the Security Council 90
Other jurisdictional provisions: the admissibility criterion
of gravity 90
No ICC proceedings because of the 'interests of justice' 91
The OTP's prosecutorial policy 92
The policy of positive complementarity 97
Conclusion: complementarity and its potential
catalysing effect 104

3   Uganda: compromising complementarity 111
The context for catalysis 114
The ICC in Uganda: a joint enterprise 114
Uganda and the ICC: a marriage of convenience 116
Compromised complementarity 120
The conflict in northern Uganda – and far beyond 124
Peace-making in the shadow of the ICC 129
Complementarity: the linchpin of the agreement 133
The ICC: sword of Damocles 136
Cracks in the marriage: the opening for complementarity's
catalysing effect 137

Effects catalysed   141
Promoting the study of local justice practices   141
Putting accountability and transitional justice on the peace-talks agenda   159
Stimulating a debate on transitional justice   162
Broadening the approach to the conflict to include a legal dimension   171
Stimulating the establishment of a Ugandan international crimes division   179
Increasing the attention paid to 'international standards'   187
Shaping the International Criminal Court Act?   194
Discouraging amnesties   206
Effects expected but not catalysed   228
Encouraging more trials, prosecutions and/or investigations?   228
Conclusion: complementarity's catalysing effect in Uganda   234

4   Sudan: complementarity in a state of denial   244
The context for catalysis   245
Sudan and the ICC: souring relations   247
Complementarity: less than a secondary response   252
Complementarity: the views of the ICID and the ICC   258
The Darfur conflict   261
Effects catalysed   266
Fostering interest in transitional justice   266
Triggering the establishment of domestic accountability mechanisms   279
Motivating the adoption of laws on international crimes   284
Putting accountability on the agenda of peace negotiations   291
Providing a boost for traditional justice   299
Effects expected but not catalysed   306
Broadening the approach from the military and political to the legal?   306
Discouraging immunities and amnesties?   316
Encouraging more trials, prosecutions and/or investigations?   320
Conclusion: complementarity's catalysing effect in Sudan   328

5   Paradoxes unravelled: explanations for complementarity's weak catalysing effect on domestic proceedings   337
Complementarity's normative character   338
Complementarity as primary right: confusion, ambiguity and misrepresentation   339
Complementarity as big idea: a responsibility to investigate and prosecute?   344

The normative paradox of complementarity 345
Pro-ICC ideology countering a political expectation
on states to conduct proceedings 352
A domestic context inhospitable to a responsibility
to conduct proceedings 361
Complementarity and the state's cost–benefit analysis 367
High cost of action: obstacles to domestic proceedings 369
ICC involvement has not reduced the costs
of domestic action 378
Low costs of inaction 385
Costs of inaction can be avoided by means other than
the invocation of complementarity 389
Paradoxes of complementarity: cost–benefit analyses
combined 392
Conclusion: unravelling the paradoxes 396

6   Complementarity in the line of fire 406

Epilogue: beyond complementarity in the line of fire 411

Bibliography 415
Literature and documents from states and international
organisations 415
Cases and procedural documents 465
Legal instruments 486
Index 494

FOREWORD

When in the summer of 1998 most of the world's states converged in Rome to negotiate a treaty to establish an international criminal court, they were divided between those who sought to defend the sovereign right of a state to deal with crimes within its jurisdiction, and others who wanted to see an international prosecutor with a free hand to pursue cases on the basis of the evidence alone.

Eventually a compromise emerged which was reflected in the concept of complementarity, now encapsulated in the Rome Statute's provisions governing the admissibility of cases before the ICC. Under those rules, states have the priority in the exercise of criminal jurisdiction over crimes, and the International Criminal Court (ICC) can intervene only in the face of inaction by states. Yet, as Sarah Nouwen demonstrates in this engaging book, this relatively simple idea has met with continuing resistance despite the apparent clarity of the language employed in the Rome Statute.

In this rigorously argued book, which should cure any sloppy thinking about complementarity, the reader will reap the benefit of a work which began life as a doctoral thesis. Readers will also gain insights from Dr Nouwen's intimate and respectful 'fly on the wall' account of how Ugandan and Sudanese officials and civilians alike have grappled with the diverse and often contradictory demands arising as a consequence of the intervention of the ICC in each of their countries.

Whilst the book has, to its credit, avoided an overtly political tone, its analysis and insights will nevertheless support critical reflection on the mechanics and politics of the application of the Rome Statute, especially in Africa, where the ICC has come under severe criticism for its exclusive focus on this continent, and for apparently disregarding the complexities and dilemmas of managing politically turbulent and fragile societies.

While African states and other commentators have maintained these criticisms of the Court, as Dr Nouwen observes, African states have also engaged in political calculations to avoid the costs and maximise benefits of cooperation with the ICC. These governments have sought—and often succeeded—in deflecting or co-opting the ICC as an instrument for dealing with local adversaries or for managing international critics, without themselves exercising criminal jurisdiction in relation to crimes committed by their nationals or on their territory. Thus emerges a central challenge, and irony, in relation to the ICC, that an institution that was intended to be a court of last resort has, with the encouragement of some states, become a court of first and, increasingly, only, instance.

In addition to its refreshing exposition of the concept of complementarity, this book thus poses a fundamental question about the identity of the ICC: will it establish itself, as envisaged by the Rome Statute, as a court that defers to the jurisdiction of states, or will it arrogate to itself the priority for dealing with international crimes?

If the ICC assumes the latter posture, it may either induce in states the sense that defiance is preferable to compliance with the orders of the Court. Besides inducing confrontation, a misapplication of complementarity may also deprive states of any incentive to deal with crimes at the national level, with states increasingly leaving to the ICC the responsibility for dealing with all such crimes. Both outcomes would cement a departure from the letter and spirit of the Rome Statute.

One can be confident that this book will therefore be indispensable reading for those seeking a thorough grounding in the tenets of the contested concept of complementarity. There will also be rich pickings in here for readers looking for an informed and nuanced exposition of the politics of the International Criminal Court in action, especially on the African continent.

Barney Afako

Barney Afako has assisted conflict resolution initiatives in Africa, including talks between the Government of Uganda and the Lord's Resistance Army, as well as the African Union panels on Darfur, and on Sudan and South Sudan. He sits as a Tribunal judge in London.

PREFACE

The photograph on the cover was taken by Olivier Chassot on 8 March 2009. A crowd welcomes Sudan's President Omar Al-Bashir to El-Fasher, the capital of North Darfur, four days after the International Criminal Court issued an arrest warrant against him on counts of crimes against humanity and war crimes committed during the conflict in Darfur. The poster with a cross on ICC Prosecutor Ocampo's face reads: 'Liar, liar, you agent'. The big white banner (not entirely visible) says: 'Welcome Omar Al-Bashir and his supporters'. The text on the big yellow banner (again not entirely visible) can roughly be translated as: 'We will sacrifice ourselves for you'. Other posters read: 'No to destabilising the country' and 'One line behind our leader'. The map on page xxi below was designed by the Scientific Response Unit (SRU) of the ICC's Office of the Prosecutor. All other photographs in the book were taken by the author.

Parts of Chapter 2 appear as a chapter titled 'Fine-Tuning Complementarity' in the *Research Handbook on International Criminal Law*, edited by Bartram S. Brown and published by Edward Elgar in 2011. Parts of Chapter 3 have been published in 'Complementarity in Uganda: Domestic Diversity or International Imposition?', in *The International Criminal Court and Complementarity: From Theory to Practice*, edited by Carsten Stahn and Mohamed M. El Zeidy, published by Cambridge University Press in 2011. Material from that chapter has also been used for a chapter titled 'The ICC and Complementarity Post Juba: Between International Imposition and Domestic Diversity', forthcoming in *The International Criminal Court and the Juba Peace Process or Global Governance and Local Friction*, edited by Pål Wrange.

In order to avoid already long footnotes getting even longer, references have been abbreviated. Full details of (a) literature and official documents, (b) cases and procedural documents and (c) legal instruments can be found in the bibliography. References to literature and official documents refer to the author (or alternatively the title) or document number and year. Orders, decisions, judgments and procedural documents (in italics) relate to ICC proceedings, unless specifically attributed to a different court. In the bibliography, they are organised by court, and, for the ICC, by situation or case. The abbreviated name indicates the relevant situation or case. All links to websites were effective on 17 October 2012.

The book aims to be up to date to July 2012.

ABBREVIATIONS

A&R Accords	A&R Agreement and its Annexure
A&R Agreement	Agreement on Accountability and Reconciliation
AC	Appeals Chamber
ASP	Assembly of States Parties
AU	African Union
AUPD	African Union High-Level Panel on Darfur
CAR	Central African Republic
CICC	Coalition for the International Criminal Court
CPA	Comprehensive Peace Agreement
DDDC	Darfur–Darfur Dialogue and Consultation
DDPD	Doha Document for Peace in Darfur
DPA	Darfur Peace Agreement
DPP	Director of Public Prosecutions
DRC	Democratic Republic of the Congo
EU	European Union
FPA	Final Peace Agreement
GoS	Government of Sudan
GoSS	Government of Southern Sudan
GoU	Government of Uganda
ICC	International Criminal Court
ICCPR	International Covenant on Civil and Political Rights
ICD	International Crimes Division
ICID	International Commission of Inquiry on Darfur
ICJ	International Court of Justice
ICTR	International Criminal Tribunal for Rwanda
ICTY	International Criminal Tribunal for the former Yugoslavia
IDP	internally displaced person
ILR	International Law Reports
INC	Interim National Constitution
JCCD	Jurisdiction, Complementarity and Cooperation Division
JEM	Justice and Equality Movement
JIC	Judicial Investigation Commission
JLOS	Justice Law and Order Sector
LJM	Liberation and Justice Movement
LRA	Lord's Resistance Army

NCP	National Congress Party
NGO	non-governmental organisation
NISS	National Intelligence and Security Service
NRA	National Resistance Army
NRM	National Resistance Movement
OHCHR	Office of the High Commissioner for Human Rights
OPCV	Office of Public Counsel for Victims
OTP	Office of the Prosecutor
PCA	Permanent Court of Arbitration
PCIJ	Permanent Court of International Justice
PSC	Peace and Security Council
PTC	Pre-Trial Chamber
RPE	Rules of Procedure and Evidence
RS	Rome Statute of the International Criminal Court
SCCED	Special Criminal Court on the Events in Darfur
SCSL	Special Court for Sierra Leone
SDHC	Special Division of the High Court (also referred to as War Crimes Court or War Crimes Division)
SLA	Sudanese Liberation Army
SLA/AW	Sudanese Liberation Army/Abdel Wahid section
SLM	Sudanese Liberation Movement
SPLA	Sudan People's Liberation Army
SPLM	Sudan People's Liberation Movement
STL	Special Tribunal for Lebanon
TC	Trial Chamber
UCICC	Ugandan Coalition for the International Criminal Court
UN	United Nations
UNAMID	AU/UN hybrid operation in Darfur
UNDP	United Nations Development Programme
UNHCHR	United Nations High Commissioner for Human Rights
UNSC	United Nations Security Council
UNSCR	United Nations Security Council Resolution
UNTS	United Nations Treaty Series
UPDF	Uganda People's Defence Forces
USAID	United States Agency for International Development
VCLT	Vienna Convention on the Law of Treaties
WCC	War Crimes Court (also referred to as Special Division of the High Court or War Crimes Division)

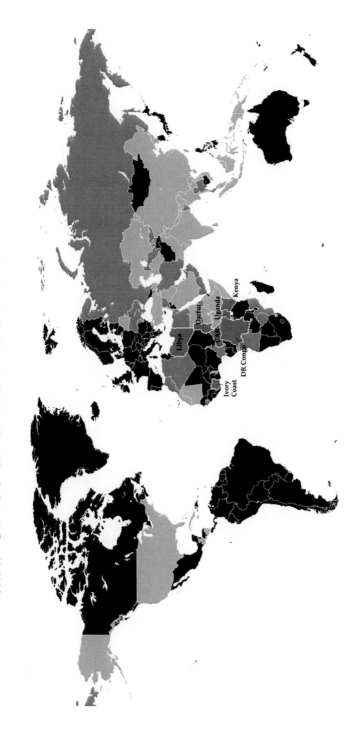

MAP OF ICC SITUATION COUNTRIES IN JULY 2012

Libya
Darfur
C.A.R.
Uganda
Kenya
DR Congo
Ivory Coast

PROLOGUE: IN THE LINE OF FIRE

In my eyes burns a fire that sees how much our lives have changed, a fire that sees and realizes how beauty can influence and transform even the most wretched of lives . . .

I was convinced that I could paint the war only by contrasting it with love . . . Hatred of war could exist only out of love for others.

Vamba Sherif[1]

The dashboard indicates 47 °C. I hold my breath, as if that will protect me in the confrontation that is about to come, open the door of the land-cruiser and plunge into one of Khartoum's busiest streets. Racing against the heat, I focus on my destination. The entrance of the Ministry of Justice is flocked with people; some go in, some go out, but most stay, standing, lingering and staring. Together, they make for a busy scene. The gentleman behind the desk seems to be in charge of making visitors wait while he is engaged on the phone. I pass the desk as if I know where I am going, respond to my Sudanese nickname 'hey you' with a smile, but do not halt my course.

The young man in the ante-chamber of the Advocate General's office slowly lifts his head from an otherwise empty desk. I point to the room of my interlocutor. '*Ma fi*', not there, he responds. '*Itfadali*', welcome, he continues, pointing me to the one free chair in the room. And down goes his head again. I assess the risk that I will never muster the energy to rise from the deep armchair, but then surrender to the heat and sink next to snoozing women.

Eyes go up when the Advocate General enters. He signs the documents that the colourfully dressed women present to him and turns to me. A young diplomat in Sudan, I have been assigned to report on the Government of National Unity's progress in implementing the

---

[1] Sherif 1999:317 and 314, respectively, translated from Dutch by Vamba Sherif.

Comprehensive Peace Agreement (CPA) that the previous government concluded with the Sudan People's Liberation Movement (SPLM). A lawyer by training, I frequent the Ministry of Justice to check whether draft legislation has materialised to give effect to the hundreds of provisions in the CPA. But first things first, my interlocutor reminds me: coffee. 'No sugar? How will you ever get fat and find a husband?' The senior legal official then takes great care to explain to me the legislative process, the stages of the various bills and the obstacles. Impressed by his generosity in time and insights, I wonder whether Sudanese diplomats encounter such hospitality and patience in any European Ministry of Foreign Affairs.

After two hours, drops of liquid running down the back of my ears suggest that it is time to go. But after all mine, the Advocate General asks the final question. 'Can you help the Ministry with some training in international law, in particular international criminal law? Now the situation in Darfur has been referred to the International Criminal Court, my staff must learn more about this. Especially about the principle of complementarity.'

Heat notwithstanding, I almost jump out of my seat. In his inaugural speech two years earlier, the first prosecutor of the world's first permanent international criminal court defined a successful court as one without cases. He could explain this counter-intuitive statement by reference to the principle of complementarity, according to which national justice systems, rather than the International Criminal Court (ICC), have the primary right to investigate and prosecute crimes within the Court's jurisdiction. In defining the Court's success by reference to complementarity, the ICC Prosecutor seemed to subscribe to the idea that complementarity is not just a rule in the Rome Statute that governs the admissibility of cases, but a cornerstone principle that reflects an ideal; namely, that the ICC acts as a court of last resort and that the crimes defined in the Rome Statute are ideally investigated, prosecuted and tried at the domestic level.

Could the United Nations Security Council, by referring the situation in Darfur to the ICC, have spurred the Sudanese justice system into action, signalling that something must be done about the prevailing impunity? Does Sudan intend to render ICC cases inadmissible by invoking complementarity? Can it, legally? Can it, practically? Can it, politically?

Back at the embassy, I make a case for funding a training programme in international criminal law. While my own Ambassador is supportive, colleagues from headquarters and other European states express reservations. Their argument is that as ICC states parties we should not be seen as undermining the Court by helping Sudan launch an admissibility challenge. I disagree: an admissibility challenge does not threaten the Court. Indeed, in line with the Prosecutor's argument in his opening address, the Court would be successful if it catalysed genuine Sudanese proceedings. If the Sudanese efforts are not genuine, this need not undermine the Court: the Statute leaves the final decision on admissibility to the ICC judges.

The training gets organised but the episode continues to intrigue me: will complementarity have a catalysing effect and, if so, what kind of effects will it catalyse? How will these effects be brought about? Who will be the key actors? Will the ICC and states parties support it, or will they focus on establishing the ICC? Will answers be different in situations in which not the Security Council, but a state refers a situation to the Court? What has happened, for instance, in Uganda, a state that referred a situation in its own country to the Court? A research project is born.

I leave the embassy and return to the University of Cambridge to embark on a new odyssey: a PhD. I peruse libraries, trying to understand what lawyers, and – sometimes almost forgotten – I myself, think that complementarity is, work in the ICC as a Visiting Professional to get to know the system from within, and spend many months in Uganda and Sudan searching for any catalysing effect and explanations. After the PhD, I work for the African Union on Sudan, and then return to Darfur, Khartoum and Uganda once again looking for and trying to understand complementarity's catalysing effect. Seven years after that first discussion in the Ministry of Justice, I now close this book containing the treasures from the quest for complementarity's catalysing effect in Uganda and Sudan.

However, it is not just my wanderings that led to this book. Along the way, thousands of people wrote part of the story, by sharing phone numbers, accommodation or insights, by helping to obtain a book, an appointment or a travel permit, by feeding, challenging and improving my assumptions, my writing, and, ultimately, myself. The painful reality is that, as a matter of fact, I was 'yet another student earning a PhD on [others'] backs',[2] searching for information – some Sudanese

---

[2] Discussion with a person from northern Uganda, Kampala, August 2008.

and Ugandan interviewees' last possession – against a backdrop of the rapacity of colonialism, of national elites and of armed groups. This inequality cannot be remedied by the gratuitous observation that I 'care'.[3] Access to education and knowledge production has become a personal cause that I will continue to pursue in the years to come. Here, I merely acknowledge that I am indebted to each and every person who made a contribution. I thank them, even if for reasons of confidentiality, security or, more pragmatically, space, I cannot mention everyone by name.

I particularly thank all the interviewees and informants, ranging from traditional leaders in Uganda and Sudan to activists in the international-criminal-justice movement in Western metropoles; from undercover Sudanese human rights activists to ambassadors in The Hague; from incumbent and former cabinet ministers in Kampala, Khartoum and Washington to parliamentary researchers and analysts in military intelligence services; from ICC officials in The Hague to spin doctors in peace negotiations in conflict zones; from Ugandan and Sudanese policemen, prosecutors and judges to UN and AU peacekeepers. They all contributed to this book by giving their time, insights and trust. Moreover, their wisdom, generosity and philosophies have taught me lessons far beyond the scope of this book. While they bear no responsibility for errors and may disagree with my evaluation, this work is partly theirs.

Roger O'Keefe could, if he wished, also claim this work to be partly his. Supervising the PhD thesis that led to this book, he scrutinised each and every word – indeed, character – with a legal and linguistic precision that will always remain an inspiration. So will his rigour in legal analysis, his depth of knowledge and his work ethic. If only PhD supervisors could remain supervisors for life.

Willing or not, Barney Afako was stalked until he became a *de facto* second supervisor. No one has shown me as many tints colouring law, politics and life as he has.

Several others will recognise their influence in this work. Wendy Hanson and Célina Korthals selflessly provided assistance in Uganda and proved indefatigable sparring partners in the development of arguments. Ali, Mohamed and Lyandro gave perspectives on Sudan and Uganda that cannot be captured in any book. Barney Afako,

[3] Wainaina 2005.

James Crawford, Robert Cryer, Simon De Smet, Chris Dolan, Bibi Eng, Jeff Handmaker, Wendy Hanson, Andrew Hillam, Christina Jones-Pauly, Warner ten Kate, Claus Kress, Zachary Lomo, Kevin Malseed, Frédéric Mégret, Dominic McGoldrick, Joe McIntyre, Juliette McIntyre, Moses Chrispus Okello, Surabhi Ranganathan, Ajay Ratan, Shamim Razavi, Hannah Richardson, Edward Thomas, Jérome Tubiana, Guglielmo Verdirame, Michael Waibel, Christopher Ward and Alexander Zahar read parts of previous versions of the book and gave feedback on argumentation and language. They are responsible for many improvements. Other inspiring scholars such as Tarak Barkawi, Kirsten Campbell, Anthony Cullen, Devon Curtis, Mark Drumbl, Sara Kendall, Gerben Kor, Martti Koskenniemi, Joanna Quinn, William Schabas, Immi Tallgren, Sari Wastell and Wouter Werner gave me confidence in this project when I lacked it. Katie O'Byrne helped me reach the finish with her meticulous copy editing.

Equally encouraging was Cambridge University Press. In the days when I could not even envisage a first draft of a PhD thesis, law editor Finola O'Sullivan already spoke of 'the book'. Combining professionalism with personal involvement, she and Nienke van Schaverbeke pushed for the book, but were also understanding and forgiving when the manuscript got delayed, again. At the same press, Richard Woodham made sure that a text became a book.

Financially, this research would not have been possible without contributions from various funds in Cambridge: the Bartle Frere Fund, the Isaac Newton Trust, Emmanuel College, Pembroke College, the Yorke Fund, the UAC of Nigeria Travel Fund and the Smuts Fund for Commonwealth Studies. The Arts and Humanities Research Council and the Gates Cambridge Trust made the most generous contributions to the research in Uganda and Sudan and financed the PhD studies. William Charnley at Mayer Brown, Pembroke College and the Lauterpacht Centre for International Law funded post-doctoral life.

Displacement was inherent in this research, and without those who gave me a sense of home I might not have survived the lines of fire – a few times all too literally. Shaza not only assisted in translations, forged contacts and advised on personal security ('the less you mention the word ICC, the better; as a Dutch person, you should not use the term at all'), but also cared for wounds after a fire incident and in other difficult moments. Neha, Abdul and Alex, the demands of high-level politics notwithstanding, paid daily visits to the hospital, where

Sister Prya reassured me that everything would be all right. Maarten put me together after a disorienting run through a minefield. Hildebrand conciliated in a confrontation with armed – and drunk – soldiers. Aziz got us home post-curfew hours, turning the car into an oasis of peace by playing Chopin under Darfur's stars. Abdi enhanced my security by transforming me into a Nyala local – the outfit remains a favourite. Rusoke was *always* there. All over the world, people invested in deep and long-lasting friendships, the temporariness of my stay notwithstanding.

The Refugee Law Project in Kampala, an NGO in Sudan (the name of which is withheld for security reasons), Judge Fulford's team at the ICC and Le Cocq & Partners in Rotterdam allowed me to be part of inspiring professional communities. In terms of physical homes, I thank Esther, Faisal, Fahd, Rose and Annelieke in Kampala, Steven in Gulu, Rose in Kitgum, Corina, Claude, Abdul, Alex, David, Neha and Reena in Khartoum, Sander and Abdi in Nyala, Aziz and his team in El-Fasher, Hans, Margaret and Diet in London, Bert and Marianne in France, Francesca in Brussels, Riet and Vokke in Voorburg, Marianne, George and Colet in Amsterdam, Maria in Utrecht, Laurien and Henri in Nijmegen, Anna and Raymond in Belfast, Sara in New York, Sandra in Washington, St Andrew's and Manchester, unique fellow nomad B all over the world, and, ultimately, my beloved Mr Darcy in Cambridge who opened the gate to inner peace. All gave me so much more than a bed.

After all the moves and living out of suitcases, William Charnley at Mayer Brown, Pembroke College and the Lauterpacht Centre for International Law gave me the enormous luxury of a concrete home in Cambridge, when welcoming me as Mayer Brown Research Fellow in Public International Law. Anita Rutherford and Karen Fachechi at the Lauterpacht Centre and the fellowship of Pembroke College offered me also the *idea* of home by allowing me to keep my cherished work and living spaces in the year that I went back to Sudan and Uganda. The Law Faculty and Squire Law Library of the University of Cambridge provided a desk, books and 24/7 access, and – even more valuable – most supportive experts, among whom Lesley Dingle, the always helpful international law librarian, and computer-rescuers Sarah Kitching, Andrew Gerrard and Steve Burdett. At the Lauterpacht Centre, Michael Waibel, as modest and kind as brilliant and exemplary, and Tara Grant, as generous and considerate as original and creative, were most encouraging officemates.

6

An inexhaustible source of inspiration also flowed from the office next door, from which James Crawford shared his passion for international law in the broadest sense and unconditionally supported this admittedly rather 'different' international legal research project. When I was running around in the wider world, seeking to give the research some practical relevance, James, working on heavyweight international law cases somewhere else in the wider world, would occasionally send an email with only one line – 'When are you finishing the book?' – getting me back to it by putting in the subject line 'important before urgent'. Later, he kept up my momentum by asking for chapters and returning them within a few hours, eradicating infestations of Dutchisms and quelling the manuscript's thirst for commas.

Cambridge provided not only a community of scholars but also of true friends. In addition to the already mentioned colleagues, I particularly thank Alfonso, Ana, Elselijn, Eva, Francesca, the Fuchs-Mtwebana family, Kate, Murray, Renaud and Virginie, Sandra, Sietse, Simon, Yseult, the housemates of 'the Mediterranean Institute', the Savino's dynasty, and Fenners' gym buddies. Other vital dimensions of the sense of belonging are rooted in the past. I remain indebted to friends, teachers and supervisors from de Kralingsche School, het Erasmiaans Gymnasium, Universities of Utrecht, Western Cape and Cape Town, Loyens & Loeff Paris, the Centre of International Studies in Cambridge, The Netherlands Ministry of Foreign Affairs in The Hague, New York and Khartoum, and close family friends and neighbours in and around the Avenue Concordia.

Last, yet essentially first, I thank my brother Raphaël and his dear Ilse for welcoming home their prodigal sister; my sister Laura for helping me to see things from a more relevant perspective; and my father Laurent, now accompanied by his beloved Noor, for exemplary perseverance and engagement with the world's suffering. I dedicate any good parts in this work to the memory of my mother, Heiltjen Nouwen-Kronenberg, whose complementarity continues to catalyse.

CHAPTER 1

COMPLEMENTARITY FROM THE LINE OF FIRE

> *As a consequence of complementarity, the number of cases that reach the Court should not be a measure of its efficiency. On the contrary, the absence of trials before this Court, as a consequence of the regular functioning of national institutions, would be a major success.*
>
> Luis Moreno-Ocampo, first Prosecutor of the
> International Criminal Court[1]

Great expectations have attended the creation of the world's first permanent International Criminal Court ('ICC' or 'the Court'). One of the greatest is that the ICC will contribute to ending impunity not only by investigating and prosecuting crimes within its jurisdiction, but also by inspiring, encouraging or even pressuring domestic justice systems to do the same. This expectation is tied to what has been called a, or the, 'defining feature', 'cornerstone'[2] or 'foundational principle'[3] of the Rome Statute that creates and governs the ICC: the principle of complementarity.[4]

As set forth in article 17 of the Statute, complementarity dictates that the Court may exercise its jurisdiction over a case only if the latter is not being, or has not been, genuinely investigated or prosecuted by a state.[5] In other words, in case of competing claims for jurisdiction, complementarity accords national criminal justice systems, rather than the international court, the primary right to investigate and prosecute war crimes, crimes against humanity and

---

[1] Moreno-Ocampo 2003a:2.
[2] See, *inter plurima alia*, *Decision on the Practices of Witness Familiarisation and Witness Proofing Lubanga*:[34], n. 38, *LRA Admissibility Decision (PTC)*:[34], *Prosecution Response to Libyan Admissibility Challenge*:[4], UN Doc. A/50/22 (1995):[29] and Holmes 1999:73.
[3] Coalition for the International Criminal Court 2011:29.
[4] Rome Statute of the International Criminal Court (RS), tenth preambular recital and arts. 1 and 17.
[5] RS, art. 17(1)(a), (b), (c). The text is reproduced in Chapter 2, 'The key provisions setting forth complementarity'.

genocide.[6] It was with reference to this principle that the Court's first Prosecutor in his inaugural address defined the Court's success by reference to the *absence* of trials before the ICC. His above-cited statement encapsulates the hope that there might be no need for ICC trials, since the existence of the Court would encourage states to use their primary right to investigate and prosecute.

States, non-governmental organisations (NGOs) and scholars, too, have expressed expectations that the principle of complementarity will have a catalysing effect at the domestic level.[7] The anticipated effect consists not only of domestic investigations and prosecutions of crimes within the Court's jurisdiction, but also reform of domestic justice systems in order to make such proceedings possible.[8]

---

[6] RS, art. 5. The amendment incorporating into the Statute the definition of the crime of aggression and the jurisdictional modalities for its prosecution has not yet entered into force (see RC/Res.4 (2010)). This book uses the term 'conflict-related crimes' to refer to offences for which the conduct is the same as the conduct of the crimes within the ICC's jurisdiction, but which are not necessarily criminalised domestically as genocide, crimes against humanity or war crimes as in the Rome Statute.

[7] For the expectation of, or hope for, a catalysing effect, see, *inter alia*, Akhavan 2003:716–17, Alvarez 2003:438–9, Ambos 2010:41, Becker 2004:481, Bekou and Cryer 2004:xii–xiii and xviii, Benvenuti 1999:39, Benzing 2003:596 and 632, Benzing and Bergsmo 2004:413–14, Bergsmo, Bekou and Jones 2010:795, Blumenson 2006:805, Bourdon 2000:330–1, Broomhall 2003:86, Burke-White 2003–2004:201–3, Cassese 2003:353, Charney 2001:122–3, Chesterman 2009:350, Chung 2007–2008:228, Cryer 1998:281, Cryer 2005b:96, 116–17, 143, 149, 164–5, 185–6 and 329, Cryer 2011:1102, Drumbl 2007:141 and 145, Dunofe and Trachtman 1999:405, Dupuy 2008:17, El Zeidy 2008b:299–300, Ellis 2002:223, Gordon 2011, Hall 2003:8, 22 and 24, Hernández 2000:100, International Center for Transitional Justice 2010:1, Jurdi 2010:74, Keppler 2013, forthcoming, Kleffner 2009:44 and 51, McCormack 2006:142, McGoldrick 2004a:45–6, McGoldrick 2004b:468 and 473, Miskowiak 2000:77, Nassar 2003:595, Nerlich 2009:347, Olásolo-Alonso and Rojo 2011:405–6 and 413, Rastan 2007:8, Rastan 2008:440, Rastan 2011:433, 449–50 and 459, Robinson 2010:91, Sarooshi 2004:940–1, Seils and Wierda 2005:3, Stigen 2008:14, 18, 264, 391, 401, 469, 473 and 488, Struett 2005:187, Wippman 2004:176, Yang 2003:621 and Yang 2005a:122–4. Specifically on complementarity's catalysing effect on domestic legislation, see UN Doc. S/2004/616 (2004):16, Bassiouni 2005:100, Cryer 2005b:171–2, Delmas-Marty 2009:97, Doherty and McCormack 1999, Hernández 2000:95, Lattanzi 2001, Mégret 2004:186, Kleffner 2003, Razesberger 2006:27, Schabas 2001:205, Stahn 2008:92, Stahn 2011b:250, Terracino 2007, Weschler 2000:96 and Yang 2005b:290. The questions how and when complementarity could have a catalysing effect have been most developed in Burke-White 2005:568 *et seq.*, Burke-White 2008b, Burke-White 2008c:299–301, Kleffner 2006 and Kleffner 2008:309–39.

[8] Apart from where it indicates otherwise, this book uses the term 'proceedings' in the meaning of 'criminal process', including both investigations and prosecutions. This

This book puts to a test this great expectation of a catalysing effect of complementarity. Has complementarity had a catalysing effect and, if so, what has it catalysed and why? What effects have been widely expected but have not been catalysed? Why not? Where did the assumptions underlying the expectation of a catalysing effect go wrong? Honing in on two states facing unresolved violent conflict and subject to ICC intervention, this book tells the story of complementarity's catalysing effect in Uganda and Sudan.

THE STORY OF COMPLEMENTARITY'S CATALYSING EFFECT IN UGANDA AND SUDAN

In Uganda and Sudan, complementarity did catalyse some widely anticipated effects. Crimes within the ICC's jurisdiction were incorporated into domestic law, even in Sudan, a state not party to the Rome Statute. Domestic courts specialising in international crimes proliferated. Some less predicted effects appeared, too: adultery – where committed 'within the framework of a methodical direct and widespread attack'[9] – was included in the list of crimes against humanity; mini ICCs mimicked the Court not just in subject-matter jurisdiction, but also in terms of budget, discourse and audience; 'traditional' practices were rediscovered, reframed and rebranded; lawyers asserted their relevance to the resolution of armed conflict; rebel movements demanded accountability instead of amnesty; the transitional-justice economy boomed and 'international standards' became a fetish.

But the ICC also catalysed processes that *went against* the encouraging effect on domestic proceedings that complementarity was expected to have: states *outsourced* the responsibility for investigations and prosecutions to the ICC; mediators took the topic of accountability *off* the peace-talks agenda because the ICC was already dealing with the issue; human rights activists' operational space was *reduced*, rendering the domestic promotion of international norms, including those related to accountability, more difficult. Notably, the one and only effect that is directly relevant for an invocation of complementarity before the Court, namely, the initiation of genuine domestic

is in line with RS, art. 17, which defines unwillingness (art. 17(2)) and inability (art. 17(3)) with reference to 'proceedings', these definitions applying to the phases of both investigation and prosecution (art. 17(1)(a) and (b)).

[9] See Chapter 4, 'Motivating the adoption of laws on international crimes'.

investigations and prosecutions of crimes within the ICC's jurisdiction, is for the most part yet to occur in Uganda and Sudan.

The book traces the processes that brought about these effects, or prevented expected effects from occurring, to reveal at least nine developments and paradoxes that are relevant beyond Uganda or Sudan.

For a start, complementarity has been living a double life. Legally, it is a technical admissibility rule in the Rome Statute determining when the ICC may proceed with the investigation or prosecution of a case within its jurisdiction. However, writers, diplomats, activists and legal practitioners have also conceptualised complementarity as a 'big idea' that entails more than its technical legal meaning. Complementarity as big idea includes 'responsibilities' and even obligations for states. In many of its manifestations, complementarity as big idea bears little resemblance to the admissibility rule. Consequently, complementarity's legal life differs remarkably from the rhetoric on complementarity as big idea. Cloaked in technical language, the legal concept of complementarity has been accessible and of interest only to specialists. The rhetorical concept, by contrast, lives in the assembly halls of international organisations, conference rooms, auditoria and other places where diplomats, politicians, ICC officials, NGOs and scholars take the floor, and has been recorded in policy statements, press releases and academic literature.

Secondly, the effects that complementarity has catalysed are often based more on the meaning of complementarity as mediated by influential actors, such as international NGOs or members of the United Nations Security Council, than on complementarity as set forth in article 17 of the Statute. Promoting normative agendas beyond the Rome Statute, NGOs, for instance, have advocated 'benchmarks' that states must meet for a successful complementarity challenge that go beyond the requirements of article 17. The Security Council, for its part, is believed to take complementarity into account when deciding on referrals of situations to the Court or possible requests for a deferral of ICC proceedings. These actors have not just boosted but also transformed complementarity's catalysing effect by ascribing a meaning to complementarity that differs from that in the Statute.

Thirdly, the ICC, in particular the Office of the Prosecutor (OTP), has itself at times employed the term 'complementarity' to promote a different concept. By using the term in its literal rather than legal meaning, namely, to describe an international court and domestic courts 'complementing' each other, it has advocated a division of labour according to which the former deals with the cases involving those bearing the greatest responsibility (the 'big fish') while the latter handle only the less serious cases (the 'small fry'). Even though such a division of labour is unrelated to complementarity in the sense of article 17, this interpretation has infiltrated domestic systems – separating the 'nile perch' from the 'tilapia' – and has thus *discouraged* domestic proceedings for the 'big fish'/the 'nile perch'.

Fourthly, catalysing effects have been strongest when the outcome of a government's comparison of the costs and benefits of ICC proceedings with those of taking domestic action (a so-called 'cost–benefit analysis') coalesced with pressure from the Security Council and norm entrepreneurs (that is, activists promoting the adoption of international norms at the domestic level). However, whilst references by national actors to international concepts such as 'transitional justice' or 'international standards' may be music to the ears of international donors, they do not necessarily sound in domestic practices and beliefs. Moreover, steps such as the adoption of domestic laws incorporating ICC crimes or the establishment of special courts – both the focus of international advocacy – are politically inexpensive, since they do not address the real obstacles to domestic proceedings. Once in place, their existence is cosmetic.

This leads to the fifth point, namely, that complementarity has insufficiently affected states' cost–benefit analyses to bring about a catalysing effect on domestic investigations and prosecutions. On the one hand, the obstacles to domestic proceedings are more ingrained than problems such as absence of laws, courts or 'capacity' – the areas that international assistance programmes focus on under the banner of 'positive complementarity'. Instead, a key obstacle is the reality of state institutions' being subordinated to patronage systems. Neither ICC intervention nor complementarity reduces the often insuperable loyalty costs that domestic proceedings would incur. On the other hand, the sovereignty and reputation costs of ICC proceedings have not been high enough to encourage domestic proceedings – indeed, some states have considered (partial) ICC intervention as beneficial. Even if considered high, the costs of ICC intervention can be avoided by means other than conducting domestic proceedings, particularly because of the ICC's greatest handicap: its lack of enforcement powers.

However, and sixthly, the obstacles to a catalysing effect on domestic proceedings do not exist only at the domestic level. The Court and its supporters have to some extent discouraged domestic proceedings. By merely referring to a state's duty to exercise criminal jurisdiction over international crimes in a preambular recital while at the same time establishing a court on the very assumption that states fail to investigate and prosecute, the Statute contains the seeds of the *normative paradox of complementarity*. Complementarity as big idea – in contrast to the admissibility rule – stresses the responsibility or even obligation of states to investigate and prosecute. However, the creation of the Court, and particularly the way the Statute has been implemented so far, may, by projecting the Court as an institution to take over from states the responsibility to investigate and prosecute conflict-related crimes, actually erode the pressure on states to discharge that responsibility. The normative paradox has been intensified by the OTP's policy of inviting states to refer situations on their own territory to the Court and the way the Court has dealt with such 'self-referrals'. The Rome Statute and the ICC have thus fostered a norm according to which crimes may not go unpunished, but weakened the idea that states have a domestic responsibility to this effect.

Seventhly, the idea of a state's responsibility or obligation to investigate or prosecute domestically has been further weakened by the emergence of a *pro-ICC ideology*. This ideology is based on three sometimes interrelated beliefs, namely, that (1) international courts mete out better justice than domestic systems; (2) international crimes, particularly those committed by those bearing the greatest responsibility, must be prosecuted as international crimes and, ideally, in international courts, because such crimes have been committed 'against humanity'; and (3), at a minimum, once the ICC is involved the fledgling Court must be seen to succeed. Whilst lacking a legal foundation, this ideology has been at times more powerful than complementarity and has thus thwarted the latter's catalysing effect.

Eighthly, the OTP has been double-faced with respect to encouraging domestic proceedings. In accordance with what it perceives to serve its institutional interests (legitimacy and, what it prioritises even more, effectiveness), it has encouraged domestic proceedings in those situations and cases in which cooperation is unlikely to be forthcoming, in which intervention would upset an international great power and in which it has not yet invested many resources. But it has discouraged domestic proceedings in situations and cases where it could count on essential cooperation, which have obtained the blessing – or at least a no objection certificate – from the world's great powers and in which it has invested its resources. The book reveals how this can lead to the *catalysing effect paradox*: the ICC is most keen to exercise its jurisdiction in precisely those cases where complementarity has the greatest chances of catalysing genuine domestic proceedings.

Finally, the explanation of this paradox is found in the fact that not just state institutions but also international institutions such as the ICC are subordinated to patronage networks, and thus, at times, 'unwilling' or 'unable' (in the lay sense of the terms) to investigate and prosecute. The only way for the ICC to liberate itself from this subordination is to take the reality of its dependence on cooperation, rather than a myth of total independence, as the starting point for its own perception of its success or failure. That will allow it actually to believe in the definition of the Court's success as pronounced in the Court's first prosecutor's inaugural address.

This is the story of complementarity's catalysing effect developed in this book. But, before we set off, some issues merit introduction: the difference between complementarity as admissibility rule and as big idea, the *dramatis personae* of complementarity's catalysing effect, the assumptions underlying the expectations of a catalysing effect, the book's normative, theoretical and methodological perspective, its line-of-fire approach and, finally, its structure.

COMPLEMENTARITY'S DOUBLE LIFE

Legally, 'complementarity' is a technical term of art for a priority rule set out in article 17 of the Rome Statute. According to this provision, the ICC may exercise its jurisdiction only if there are or have been no genuine domestic proceedings in that case. As Chapter 2 will elaborate, states and defendants may invoke this rule, and the OTP and Chambers must consider it.

A priority rule is necessary because the ICC's jurisdiction is concurrent with that of national jurisdictions.[10] Other international criminal

---

[10] The original version of *Admissibility Decision Katanga (TC)*:[45] is ambiguous in this respect ('Les auteurs du Statut entendaient bien faire de la Cour une juridiction complémentaire et non pas concurrente des juridictions nationales.') but the

tribunals, namely, the *ad hoc* international tribunals for the former Yugoslavia (ICTY) and Rwanda (ICTR), the Special Court for Sierra Leone (SCSL) and the Special Tribunal for Lebanon (STL), have concurrent jurisdiction, too, but a different priority rule: they enjoy primacy of jurisdiction, according to which they are, in broadly defined circumstances, empowered to oblige domestic justice systems to defer to the tribunal's competence.[11] In fact, neither primacy nor complementarity is absolute – both rules require certain criteria to be fulfilled for the international court to be allowed to exercise its jurisdiction in the event of a competing national claim. However, for a court with complementary jurisdiction these criteria are stricter than for a court with primary jurisdiction.[12] The mere fact that statutes have given the two jurisdictional arrangements contrasting labels suggests that they have different starting points: the international tribunal with primacy of jurisdiction can in principle exercise its jurisdiction when it wants, whereas the international court with complementarity jurisdiction must, in case of competing claims, grant domestic justice systems the first bite of the cherry.

Complementarity's other, more public, grandiose and eventful life has been that of a 'big idea'. Complementarity fits the garb of big idea as it reflects a shift in thinking as to where international crimes belong. In 1995, the Appeals Chamber of the ICTY ruled that international tribunals 'must be endowed with primacy over national courts' on the ground that '[o]therwise, human nature being what it is, there would be a perennial danger of international crimes being characterised as "ordinary crimes" ... or proceedings being "designed to shield the accused", or cases not being diligently prosecuted'.[13] But, in 1998, without an apparent change in human nature, the Rome Statute accorded states the primary right to investigate and prosecute

English version makes clear that 'concurrent' is employed here with the meaning of 'competing'. However, as Chapters 2 and 5 will argue, that reading is problematic for different reasons.

[11] ICTY Statute 1993, art. 9, ICTR Statute 1994, art. 8, SCSL Statute 2002, art. 8, STL Statute 2007, art. 4. Whereas the ICTY and ICTR have primacy with respect to all states, the SCSL and STL have primacy only with respect to Sierra Leone and Lebanon respectively. SCSL Statute, art. 1(2) and (3) grants the SCSL complementary jurisdiction for crimes committed by peacekeepers, subject to authorisation by the Security Council.

[12] See, more elaborately, Nouwen and Lewis 2013.

[13] ICTY, *Tadić Defence Motion Decision* (AC):[58].

genocide, crimes against humanity and war crimes. In the drafting negotiations, three conceptually different reasons were advanced for this shift.[14] Least dominant of those was the argument that complementarity protects the rights of the accused, namely, the right to be free from double jeopardy.[15] More often mentioned was the comparative practical advantage of domestic proceedings (domestic jurisdictions, at least those in the territory of which the crimes were committed, are closer to the evidence and, when combined, have more capacity than one international court).[16]

The principal argument for complementarity, however, was state sovereignty.[17] As Frédéric Mégret has argued, '[a]lthough crime is obviously something that societies are keen to eliminate, it is also curiously something about which they feel a strong sense of ownership, especially when competing claims for jurisdiction arise'.[18] Given states' protectiveness, they had to be convinced to ratify the Rome Statute – a consideration that did not concern the drafters of the ICTY and ICTR, since all states were bound to accept the jurisdiction of those tribunals by virtue of Security Council resolutions adopted pursuant to Chapter VII of the UN Charter. Complementarity earned its cornerstone status by seemingly reconciling international justice with state sovereignty and thus making agreement on the Statute possible.

---

[14] More elaborately on the rationales of complementarity, see Benzing 2003:595–600, Burke-White and Kaplan 2009:section 3 and Kor 2006.

[15] See UN Doc. A/CONF.183/C.1/SR.11 (1998):[28]. See also *Admissibility Decision Katanga (TC)*:[48].

[16] E.g. see UN Doc. A/50/22 (1995):[31] and UN Doc. A/51/22 (1996):[155].

[17] On complementarity as a principle protecting state sovereignty, see e.g. *Admissibility Decision Katanga (TC)*:[48] and [78], UN Doc. A/CN.4/SR.2357 (1994):[22] (Mr Yamada), UN Doc. A/C.6/52/SR.11 (1997):[65] (Mr Erwa), UN Doc. A/CONF.183/C.1/SR.8 (1998):[59], UN Doc. A/CONF.183/C.1/SR.12 (1998): [7] and [35], Scheffer 1998, Benzing 2003:595 and 631–2, Bergsmo 2000:99, Brown 1998:389, Burke-White and Kaplan 2009:264, Cassese 2003:351, Chesterman 2009:350, Clarke 2007:135, Cryer 2011:1117, Dascalopoulou-Livada 2008:57, El Zeidy 2002:879, El Zeidy 2008a:412, El Zeidy 2008b:25, 110, 158, 239 and 306, Gioia 2006:1096, Greppi 2008:63, Lattanzi 1999:53, Miskowiak 2000:50, Mégret 2004:186, Ntanda Nsereko 1999:114, Meron in Politi and Gioia 2008b:135, Sands 2003:75, Schiff 2008:79, 82, 92 and 248, Simpson 2004:55, Solera 2002:169, Stigen 2008:11, 17 and 87, Tallgren 1998:107, Turner 2005:6, Williams 2008: margin 1 and Zappalà 2009:221.

[18] Mégret 2005:739. See also de Tocqueville 2000:260 ('the man who judges the criminal is really the master of society'), McGoldrick 2004c:441 and Gioia 2006:1096.

However, as with other cornerstones, complementarity's name has become more famous than the provisions setting forth the principle. This has had at least two results. First, complementarity is generally known by its popular shorthand definition according to which the Court may not exercise jurisdiction 'unless a State is genuinely unable or unwilling to carry out prosecutions'.[19] Or, in the words of the ICC Registrar, '[t]he core test in article 17 to determine admissibility is whether a state with jurisdiction has the willingness or ability to investigate and prosecute a case'.[20] As Chapter 2 elaborates, this definition misrepresents the principle set forth in articles 17 and 20 of the Statute.

Secondly, as the 'foundational principle' of the Statute, complementarity is often invoked to found theories of how international criminal justice works or should work. Complementarity has been considered as a constitutional arrangement, a 'forum for managerial interaction',[21] and a 'model of global governance',[22] reflecting an ideal division of 'responsibilities' between domestic and international jurisdictions.[23] Refining how these relationships could and should be, academic literature has conceptualised complementarity as a 'tale of many notions',[24] distinguishing 'positive' from 'negative' or 'classical' complementarity[25] and 'proactive' from 'passive',[26] while also envisaging 'investigative' and 'informational' complementarity.[27] With the right adjective, almost everything seems to be classifiable as a 'model'[28] of 'complementarity'.[29]

The various proposed models are not merely alternative ways of understanding the role of a specific admissibility rule; the models attach to the principle legal consequences for states, so-called

---

[19] International Bar Association ICC Monitoring and Outreach Programme 2008:11. For another influential NGO, also involved in training people in international criminal justice, using the shorthand definition, see International Center for Transitional Justice 2010:1.

[20] Arbia and Bassy 2011:53.   [21] Stahn 2008:88.

[22] See e.g. Burchard 2011 and Burke-White 2005.   [23] See Stahn 2011b:237.

[24] For a 'tale of two notions', see Stahn 2008.

[25] See, *inter alia*, Akhavan 2005, Stahn 2008, Burke-White 2008a and Burke-White 2011.

[26] Burke-White 2008b.   [27] Burchard 2011:175.

[28] See Burke-White 2005:558 and Kleffner 2006:96.

[29] On the appeal of complementarity as a term for everything that has anything to do with the relationship between international and domestic proceedings, see also Cryer 2011:1098.

'complementarity obligations'.[30] These obligations go beyond the only legal consequence that stems from the Statute (admissibility or inadmissibility of cases before the Court).[31] And, even if at times difficult to found on the text of the relevant provisions in the Statute, these legal consequences have been advocated by the Registry, OTP and activists who promote the Court's work in domestic justice systems.

For instance, it has been argued that complementarity, or the Statute more generally, prohibits states from issuing amnesties for crimes within the Court's jurisdiction. Thus, whilst the Statute is in fact silent on amnesties, the OTP has briefed peace mediators that genocide, crimes against humanity and war crimes cannot be the subject of amnesties.[32] Even more commonly, it has been argued that the complementarity scheme reflects not just a state's primary *right* to investigate and prosecute crimes within the ICC's jurisdiction, but also its 'responsibility',[33] 'primary responsibility',[34] 'duty',[35] 'primary

---

[30] See Coalition for the International Criminal Court 2011:30 and RC/11 Annex V(c) (2010):[10], reflecting a debate on complementarity at the Review Conference.

[31] For a great exposé of how advocacy groups use complementarity for more than what the doctrine seems to support, see Mégret 2011.

[32] ICC-OTP 2010b:[49] and [80] and Moreno-Ocampo 2011:28.

[33] For the view that the Statute recognises or creates states' 'responsibility' to investigate and prosecute or to exercise their criminal jurisdiction, see e.g. UN Doc. A/CONF.183/C.1/SR.12 (1998):[7] and *Decision on Jurisdiction Challenge Mbarushimana*:[16]. See also Benvenuti 1999:39, Dupuy 2008:17, Miskowiak 2000:76, Stahn 2012b:184, n. 7 and Stigen 2008:401.

[34] For the view that the Statute recognises or creates states' 'primary responsibility' to investigate and prosecute or to exercise their criminal jurisdiction, see also *Admissibility Judgment Muthaura et al. (AC)*:[36] and *Admissibility Judgment Ruto et al. (AC)*:[37], Resolution RC/Res.1 (2010):[1] on complementarity, adopted by the Review Conference ('Recognizes the primary responsibility of States to investigate and prosecute the most serious crimes of international concern . . .'), ICC Weekly Update 2009:2, ICC-ASP/8/Res.9 Annex 4 (2010):[13], ICC-OTP 2003c:3, ICC-OTP 2003d:4, ICC-OTP 2009:1, ICC-OTP 2010a, ICC-OTP 2010b and ICC 2011:4. See also Boot 2002:610–11, International Center for Transitional Justice 2010:2, Eckert 2009:219, Kleffner 2003:87, Stigen 2008:370, Yáñez-Barnuevo 2000:50, Zahar and Sluiter 2008:489 and Pocar in Politi and Gioia 2008a:137.

[35] For the view that the Statute contains or recognises a duty for states to investigate and prosecute the crimes within the Court's jurisdiction, see, *inter alia*, *Dissenting Opinion Judge Pikis Arrest Warrant Ntaganda (AC)*:[31] and [41], former ICC Judge Politi 2011:145, the French cour d'appel in *Gaddafi*:491, ICC-OTP 2003d:5, Moreno-Ocampo 2008a:1, Moreno-Ocampo 2009b:4, Coalition for the International Criminal Court 2011:29, Ambos 2010:55, Burke-White 2003–2004:201, Burke-White 2008a:64, Burke-White 2008b:79, El Zeidy 2002:n. 402, Okumu-Alya 2006:25, Takemura 2007, Van der Vyver 2000:73 and Williams 2008:margin 1.

duty',[36] 'obligation'[37] or 'primary obligation'[38] to do so.[39] Some advocates have gone even further, arguing that complementarity entails a responsibility/duty/obligation not just to investigate and prosecute as such, but also to investigate or prosecute the same international crimes (as opposed to ordinary crimes) and in the same manner in terms of procedure (for instance, victim participation) and punishments (no death penalty) as the ICC.[40]

Illustrative of the power of some of these big conceptual ideas, the Court's first Prosecutor, following pioneering work by scholar William Burke-White,[41] conceptualised complementarity as one of the principles underpinning a 'Global Criminal Justice System' or 'Rome System', established by the Statute.[42] He explained this 'system' as follows:

> The goal of the Rome Statute is to end impunity for the most serious crimes of international concern and to contribute to the prevention of such crimes. To achieve its goal, the Rome Statute integrates sovereign States and an international criminal court in one legal system. The

---

[36] For the view that the Statute creates or recognises states' primary duty to investigate and prosecute the crimes within the Court's jurisdiction, see e.g. Mr Katanga's lead defence counsel, *Transcripts Admissibility Challenge Katanga*:12 (lines 24–5), Holmes 2002:673, Ryngaert 2009:148, and Zahar and Sluiter 2008:456.

[37] For the view that the Statute obliges states, or recognises the obligation of states, to investigate and prosecute the crimes within the Court's jurisdiction, see e.g. Ambos 2010:v, Deen-Racsmány 2007:n. 19, International Center for Transitional Justice 2010:2, Kleffner 2008:234–308 and Mégret 2004:197.

[38] For the view that the Statute obliges states, or recognises the 'primary obligation' to investigate and prosecute the crimes within the Court's jurisdiction, see e.g. UN Doc. A/CONF.183/C.1/SR.11 (1998):213, *Prosecutor's Libya Statement SC May 2012*:[6], Brubacher 2010:267, Brubacher 2013, forthcoming, and Bergsmo, Bekou and Jones 2010:793.

[39] For references to such 'implied' duties or obligations, see UN Doc. A/RES/60/147 (2006):3, nuanced Greenawalt 2009:122, Schiff 2008:190, and, more radically, Razesberger 2006:57 and 38.

[40] See e.g. UN Doc. S/2011/634 (2011):[32], in which the UN Secretary-General states in the context of complementarity: 'The specialized requirements of international criminal prosecutions must be more consistently mainstreamed into capacity-building at the national level. Efforts must be made to implement the full architecture of the Rome Statute, including rules of procedure and evidence, elements of crimes, witness assistance and reparations and gender advisers.'

[41] See Burke-White 2005, Burke-White 2008a and Burke-White 2008b.

[42] For the term 'Rome System', see Moreno-Ocampo 2008c:3. ICC-ASP/8/L.5/Rev.1 (2009):Annex IV refers to the 'Rome Statute System'.

Rome Statute incorporates detailed definitions of genocide, crimes against humanity and war crimes in one text, defining the prosecution and prevention of these crimes as a *national* and international *obligation*.[43]

Whereas, as Chapter 2 argues, complementarity as admissibility rule does not create any obligation on states, such an obligation is thus part of complementarity as big idea and has been actively promoted by the OTP and NGOs advocating 'implementation' of the Rome Statute at the domestic level.

To contribute to this system in which states play a role in prosecuting international crimes, the Prosecutor has promulgated a policy of so-called 'positive complementarity' which he has referred to as the 'second dimension' of complementarity (the first being complementarity as admissibility rule).[44] According to this policy, '[r]ather than competing with national systems for jurisdiction, [the OTP] will encourage national proceedings wherever possible'.[45] The Assembly of States Parties (ASP), in turn, has also adopted this idea, focusing on states' assisting other states in writing 'implementing legislation', capacity-building and creating physical infrastructure. Positive complementarity, as opposed to 'negative' or 'classical' complementarity (that is to say, complementarity as admissibility rule), is thus a programme of action.[46] Against this background of complementarity as big idea, whilst making little sense in respect of an admissibility rule, references by the ICC, the UN, activists and scholars to 'complying with',[47] 'implementing',[48]

---

[43] Moreno-Ocampo 2008b:2–3 (emphases added).

[44] Moreno-Ocampo 2011:23. See also ICC-OTP 2010b:[16].

[45] Moreno-Ocampo 2004c:1.

[46] In the words of the head of the OTP's Jurisdiction, Complementarity and Cooperation Division: 'We have talked enough about complementarity that there are enough people who understand it ... It is now time for action.' (International Center for Transitional Justice 2012). Some authors treat any catalysing effect of complementarity as prove of 'positive complementarity'. However, as the book will demonstrate, complementarity sometimes has a catalysing effect irrespective, or even in spite, of ICC action. The effects thus catalysed cannot be considered effects of 'positive', as opposed to normal, complementarity.

[47] Ambos 2010:v and 55.

[48] See e.g. UN Doc. S/2011/634:[32] ('the United Nations system is involved in a coordinated effort to assist national authorities to *implement complementarity* between the International Criminal Court and national-level jurisdictions' (emphasis added)).

'promoting',[49] 'strengthening',[50] 'integrating'[51] and 'furthering'[52] complementarity can at least be understood.

In most conceptualisations, complementarity as admissibility rule and complementarity as big idea are, even if different, linked to each other. This book shows, however, that in practice the developing case law on complementarity as admissibility rule and the external statements on complementarity as big idea are growing further and further apart. Moreover, by definition lacking a definition, complementarity as big idea, in particular the policy of positive complementarity, is used for different projects at different times.[53] Whereas sometimes the emphasis is on encouraging states to conduct proceedings domestically (i.e. on 'complementarity'), at other times the emphasis is on cooperation between a state and the ICC in the joint project of ending impunity (i.e. on 'positive' relations between the ICC and states). The latter, which in practice is a strategy of cooperation that has little to do with complementarity as such, can in fact have the opposite effect of the former. Which element is emphasised is determined by factors other than law.[54]

THE *DRAMATIS PERSONAE* OF COMPLEMENTARITY'S CATALYSING EFFECT

A provision in a legal document, complementarity by itself has not catalysed anything. The effects, both those encouraging and discouraging domestic proceedings, are the result of various actors' responses to that provision.

Evidently, a key international actor shaping complementarity's catalysing effect is the ICC itself. In fact, it is not so much the ICC as legal entity as its various organs – the Presidency, the Chambers (Appeals, Trial and Pre-Trial), the OTP and the Registry[55] – that,

---

[49] Human Rights Watch 2012:1 and International Center for Transitional Justice 2010:2.

[50] Coalition for the International Criminal Court 2011: executive summary.

[51] Open Society Justice Initiative 2010:2.

[52] Arbia and Bassy 2011:56, writing on behalf of the ICC Registry.

[53] See also Stahn 2011b:235.

[54] For a similar argument in a different context (namely, that of the international treatment of child soldiers), see Drumbl 2012:3: '[L]aw and policy do not always apply consistently. Their forward trajectory may ebb and flow depending on state power and politics.'

[55] RS, art. 34.

sometimes in opposing directions, shape complementarity's meaning. They do so through procedures prescribed in the Statute (for example, requests for arrest warrants, decisions on admissibility and assistance to domestic proceedings) but even more so through influential statements outside criminal proceedings, for instance those of the Prosecutor cited above. The legal developments inside the court room do not always match the statements made outside.

Facing the Court is the defendant, whom the Statute accords the procedural right to challenge admissibility on grounds of complementarity. To date, no defendant has successfully done so. Most have refrained from challenging admissibility, probably expecting a better outcome at the ICC than domestically – indeed, this is why, as this book goes to press, Saif Gaddafi opposes the Libyan government's admissibility challenge and argues for a high threshold for inadmissibility. Germain Katanga is hitherto the only defendant to challenge admissibility. He argued for a low threshold for inadmissibility, referring to a state's right and duty to investigate and prosecute domestically. But his case illustrates that a defendant does not stand much chance where the state where his crimes were committed and of which he is a national prefers ICC proceedings to a domestic trial. Little catalysing effect has come from defendants invoking complementarity.

Instead, the Court's most direct counterpart on issues of complementarity is the state, as represented by its government. Again, different branches of government – the executive, the legislative and the judicial – play different and sometimes opposing roles in influencing complementarity's catalysing effect. The division of power, not so much the constitutional as the actual, between the various branches of government is decisive for the outcome.

Within the state, several groups invoke complementarity: NGOs, opinion-makers, politicians, legal professionals and community leaders bring complementarity into play, whether it is to argue against ICC proceedings, to encourage domestic proceedings or to rally support for the ICC. Seldom do these actors operate purely 'locally' – most are connected with foreign NGOs, lobby groups, activists or professional networks that work internationally.

In practice, most catalysing effects are not the result of direct ICC-state interaction. Indeed, in neither Uganda nor Sudan has the government shown any intention to challenge complementarity before the Court. Instead, complementarity's catalysing effects have been mediated by norm entrepreneurs or Security Council members.

Norm entrepreneurs are activists, often foreigners working in cooperation with local actors, who promote the adoption of international norms (or what in their view should be international norms) at the domestic level.[56] Since their interventions are invariably conditioned by the choices a government makes on the basis of its own cost–benefit analysis, catalysis has been most evident, as Chapter 3 shows, where the interests of such norm entrepreneurs and the state have coincided. For the Ugandan government, there were reputational, institutional and financial incentives for accepting, and at times nominally adopting, the activities and agendas of norm entrepreneurs. Because of their more horizontal relationships with Ugandan actors, these organisations have been better placed than the ICC to potentiate the catalysing effect of complementarity in Uganda.[57] In Sudan, by contrast, the ICC's intervention has closed off space for norm entrepreneurs: ever since the Prosecutor requested an arrest warrant for the Sudanese President, NGOs and human rights activists have faced even greater difficulties than usual. In Sudan, but also to some extent in Uganda, it was Security Council members who, by seemingly considering a state's domestic accountability efforts, translated complementarity from a legal admissibility rule into a political consideration and hence spurred its catalysing effect.

Norm entrepreneurs are often connected with, or part of, international networks. One of the most influential international networks shaping complementarity's catalysing effect is the international-criminal-justice movement, a loose coalition of mainly Western NGOs, other NGOs funded by Western organisations and officials working in or on international criminal tribunals. The movement goes beyond, for instance, the Coalition for the International Criminal Court, an alliance of more than 2,500 civil society organisations, by also encompassing diplomats working within foreign ministries to support the ICC and lawyers working on international tribunals themselves. The latter may not belong to a formal network, but often share a belief in what is generally called 'international justice'. Whilst leaving open whether 'international justice' is defined as criminal justice meted out by international tribunals or the prosecution of international crimes, irrespective of whether the forum is domestic or international, the movement arrogates the term 'international justice' to the project of

[56] See Finnemore and Sikkink 1998:893.
[57] For a similar finding with respect to the DRC, see Baylis 2009.

the enforcement of international criminal law.[58] In Mark Drumbl's words: 'The architecture of justice involves courtrooms and jailhouses while the narrative of justice relates to individual culpability.'[59] In the absence of international architecture to house other conceptions of justice, for instance distributive (socio-economic) or restorative justice, the international-criminal-justice movement promotes only the limited concept of punitive justice at the domestic level.

The international-criminal-justice movement, in particular the NGOs, relies to a large extent on so-called 'donors': international and foreign governmental organisations and development agencies that provide money to allow other actors to implement certain agendas. The donors to the international-criminal-justice movement are often the same as the ones that provide development aid to countries in which the ICC intervenes. As the developments in Uganda reveal, availability of donor money spurs complementarity's catalysing effect, albeit often more in form than in substance.

Many of these actors, in particular international organisations and donors, are internally divided about how far their support to the ICC should reach. As the story about the Juba peace process will illustrate,[60] positions may differ strongly between, on the one hand, headquarters, legal advisors and human rights activists, and, on the other, field offices, diplomats and humanitarian aid workers. Whilst the international criminal justice movement and ICC-supporting donors have done much to promote the ICC, this has not necessarily included support for complementarity. Indeed, their pro-ICC ideology has at times undermined complementarity. Only those who have sought alternatives to the ICC or those who emphasised that the ICC is not a panacea have actively promoted complementarity.[61]

ASSUMPTIONS UNDERLYING THE EXPECTATION OF A CATALYSING EFFECT

Before the story of complementarity's catalysing effect in Uganda and Sudan unravels, the great expectations must be unpacked: *why would* complementarity have a catalysing effect? Most of the authors expecting a catalysing effect did not posit a precise causal pathway.

---

[58] See also, much more extensively, Drumbl 2007 and Nouwen 2012a:332.
[59] Drumbl 2009:38–9.   [60] See Chapter 3.
[61] See e.g. AU Doc. PSC/AHG/2(CCVII) 2009:[17] and [245].

Extrapolating from William Burke-White's and Jann Kleffner's pioneering writings on complementarity's potential catalysing effect,[62] one can identify broadly two types of assumptions underpinning that expectation. One type reveals a constructivist worldview that stresses the power of ideas: the expectation of complementarity's catalysing effect is based on assumptions as to the normative content of complementarity. The other reflects a rational-choice perspective: the expectation of complementarity's catalysing effect rests on assumptions based on political economy, focusing on the cost–benefit (which in practice can be a cost–cost) analysis engaged in by states and other rational actors.

As to the first, it was assumed that states would implement reforms out of a commitment to complementarity as the reflection of a political expectation on states or even a legal norm. Since complementarity accords states the primary right to investigate and prosecute, states were expected to consider this also their 'responsibility' (in some unspecified sense of the word)[63] or even their formal international legal obligation.[64] By '[r]ecalling that it is the duty of every State to exercise its criminal jurisdiction over those responsible for international crimes',[65] the Statute promotes this idea. So did the Court's first Prosecutor, stating in his first policy paper:

> It should . . . be recalled that the system of complementarity is principally based on the recognition that the exercise of national criminal jurisdiction is not only a right but also a duty of States. Indeed, the principle underlying the concept of complementarity is that States remain responsible and accountable for investigating and prosecuting crimes committed under their jurisdiction and that national systems are expected to maintain and enforce adherence to international standards.[66]

His conceptualisation of a 'Rome System' and formulation of the policy of positive complementarity have equally contributed to a normative expectation on states to investigate and prosecute domestically.

As to the second assumption underpinning the expectation of a catalysing effect, namely, the assumption based on the cost–benefit analysis engaged in by states and their actors, states were expected to

---

[62] See Kleffner 2006, Kleffner 2008:309–39, Burke-White 2005, Burke-White 2008b and Burke-White 2008c:299–301.

[63] See above nn. 33 and 34. See also for expectations of a catalysing effect on normative grounds, Alvarez 2003:438 and Bekou and Shah 2006:500.

[64] See above nn. 37 and 38.   [65] RS, sixth recital.   [66] ICC-OTP 2003d:3.

regard ICC proceedings as against their interests, chiefly their sovereignty and reputation. It was assumed that states would consider ICC intervention as a liability for their reputation and an encroachment on their sovereignty.[67] Reputational damage could ensue particularly from a finding of unwillingness or inability genuinely to investigate and prosecute.[68] It was expected that states would use complementarity in order to avoid or end ICC intervention and, in order to do so successfully, would conduct domestic proceedings for crimes within the ICC's jurisdiction and reform their justice systems accordingly.[69]

As the experiences in Uganda and Sudan will reveal, complementarity's catalysing effect has indeed to a large extent been driven by normative and rational-choice processes. To be sure, sovereignty and reputation considerations do play a role. However, whereas the Sudanese government has perceived ICC intervention as costly,[70] the Ugandan government has largely considered it as *beneficial* to its sovereignty and reputation, the ICC thus contributing to the outsourcing of domestic proceedings. Moreover, as Chapter 5 will argue, even in countries where sovereignty and reputation costs are considered high, complementarity has not catalysed domestic proceedings because there are other costs that are even higher and because some costs of ICC intervention can be circumvented.

NORMATIVE, THEORETICAL AND METHODOLOGICAL PERSPECTIVE

> *Theoretical approaches have their place and are, I suppose,*
> *essential but a theory must be tempered with reality.*[71]
> Jawaharlal Nehru

---

[67] On complementarity as a principle protecting state sovereignty, see above n. 17.

[68] See Akhavan 2003:716, Benzing and Bergsmo 2004:414, Brown 1998:431, Burke-White 2011:344, Charney 2001:122, Cryer 2005b:148 and 164, Cryer 2011:1102, Dunofe and Trachtman 1999:405, Mégret 2004:188, Mégret 2006:11, Schabas 2001:204, Stigen 2008:17 and 474, and Jensen 2006:169, the latter arguing that the ICC can hold a state 'accountable' for a failure to prosecute. For this argument, see also Condorelli 2008:163–4.

[69] See e.g. Akhavan 2003:716, Burke-White 2008b, Burke-White 2008c:299–301, Charney 2001:122–3, Ellis 2002:223, Kleffner 2006:8, Kleffner 2008:318–26 and Stahn 2008:97–8.

[70] See also, for a fine expression of Kenya's experience of ICC intervention as costly to its sovereignty and reputation, *Government of Kenya Admissibility Reply Muthaura et al*:[27].

[71] Nehru 1964:235.

The purpose of this book is empirical: it puts to a test the widespread expectation that complementarity would have a catalysing effect. It is not a primary aim of this book to evaluate whether the existence or otherwise of such effects is a good or bad thing. Such an evaluation depends on one's normative framework, which must answer fundamental questions as to who can be considered a victim of an international crime, at what level such crimes are best adjudicated and what values must be prioritised when a society tries to transition from conflict to something better. Answers to these questions merit separate treatises, as does an evaluative framework for complementarity's catalysing effect. And yet, since it is impossible to write a book devoid of any evaluation, the author's own normative commitment must be disclosed.

This commitment is to realism. Realism does not refer here to the international-relations theory according to which states are rational actors that primarily pursue survival and other national interests, if necessary through self-help. Instead, it describes a concern with what *actually is*. This is a realism that acknowledges the importance of big ideas and great ideals, but believes that they should start from what as a matter of fact *is*, for them not to become dangerous;[72] a realism that is idealistic precisely because it works towards ideals from a difficult *status quo*, as opposed to an idealism that proceeds on the basis of assumptions that do not reflect reality; a realism that believes in the transformative power of norms for good, *and* for bad (depending on the content of the norm, one's interests, position, motivations and perspective); a realism that recognises that societies, and the individuals that make them, long for accountability but first and foremost for security, food, jobs and, in particular, prospects; and a realism that admits that, ideally, people and societies obtain all of this, but that in reality difficult choices may have to be made and that criminal accountability is not necessarily the obvious first choice for everybody. Accordingly, this realism disagrees with those who see complementarity merely as a sacrifice of international justice to state sovereignty. States' primary right to deal with their pasts could be an avenue to

---

[72] See also Geuss 2008:10: 'A realist can fully admit that products of the human imagination are very important in human life, provided he or she keeps a keen and unwavering eye upon the basic motto *Respice finem*, meaning in this case not "The best way to live is to keep your mind on your end: death" but "Don't look just at what they say, think, believe, but at what *actually happens* as a result".'

more justice, both in quantitative terms (domestic justice systems combined have more resources, capacity and experience than the ICC) and in a qualitative sense (the promotion of a concept of justice that is meaningful for the society concerned and a prioritisation that reflects that society's needs).

A commitment to realism in this sense may amount to an anti-theory, arguing as it does that no theory will ever capture all dimensions of reality. Specifically with respect to complementarity's catalysing effect, the developments in Uganda and Sudan are too diverse, and too important, to be analysed from the perspective of only one predetermined theory. Constructivism, realism and neoliberal institutionalism, or, more specifically, norm emergence, promotion, compliance and translation, political economy, post-colonialism, legalism, transnational networking, political trial-ism, institution-building, development, religion, global constitutionalism, complexity, and many other -isms, theories and approaches can each *partially* explain complementarity's catalysing effect. Where particularly pertinent, the book will borrow from them. But it is not the aim of this book – yet others may well use its story precisely to that end – to apply or to improve upon any of these. Instead, this book seeks to identify, understand and explain complementarity's catalysing effect in Uganda and Sudan. No matter how little generalisable, that analysis ultimately amounts to a theory in itself, albeit only of complementarity's catalysing effect in these two states within a limited time frame.

The methodological approach to the research was realist, too, based as it was on 'grounded theory'.[73] The empirical parts of this book stem from process tracing: histories, archival documents, interview transcripts and other sources were examined in order to establish who did what, when and why.[74] Given the multitude of claims concerning complementarity's catalysing effect and the impact of the ICC more

---

[73] See Strauss and Corbin 1998. The essence of this research approach is that a researcher allows theory to emerge from data, while data collection is guided strategically by emergent theory. Nonetheless, no researcher can escape reflexity, namely, the fact that he or she is part of the studied world and that his or her orientations will be shaped by socio-historical locations, including the values and interests that these locations confer upon him or her (see Hammersley and Atkinson 1995:16–21). In the context of this research there were also more specific preconceptions, such as assumptions in the literature as to complementarity's catalysing effect on domestic proceedings and laws.

[74] See George and Bennett 2004:6–7, 206 and 207.

generally, process tracing is particularly relevant to overcome the key challenge of inferring causality: it was not enough to identify develop-ments that seem relevant or related to complementarity (correlation); rather, to the extent possible, it had to be verified whether the empirical association could be brought back to complementarity or had in fact been generated by a confounding factor.[75] Specific atten-tion has thus been paid to 'equifinality' – alternative paths by which an outcome could have occurred.[76] Moreover, complementarity is not a mechanical 'pushing and pulling' force that automatically catalyses certain effects; in order to establish causal relations, the role of ideas, rules and material conditions must also be assessed.[77]

As Chapter 2 will demonstrate, the commitment to realism has also influenced the choice of methods for the legal analysis of the Rome Statute. Of the three aspects of interpretation mentioned in the general rule on interpretation embodied in article 31(1) of the Vienna Convention on the Law of Treaties (VCLT),[78] this book primarily uses a term's ordinary meaning and context. In contrast to the ICC, it does not overly rely on the object and purpose of the treaty, the third aspect of the general rule on interpretation. It is never easy to reduce the often multiple and undefined motivations behind a treaty to the single object and purpose required by article 31. If one were to do so for the Statute, taking into account the preamble and the text of the Statute, one finds that the only evident object and purpose is to create a permanent international criminal court, complementary to national criminal jurisdictions, for the prosecution of the most serious crimes of concern to the international community as a whole, as defined in the Statute. The Court, by contrast, has stressed the aim of ending impun-ity and deterring crimes.[79] However, even if one reads ending impun-ity and deterrence into the object and purpose of the Statute (by considering as the object and purpose of the Statute the establishment of a permanent international criminal court with these aims), the Statute gives no guidance as to by which of diverse potential methods

---

[75] A confounding factor is a third variable which generates an empirical association between two variables that are actually independent.

[76] See George and Bennett 2004:207.   [77] Kurki 2008:12 and 32.

[78] The International Court of Justice (ICJ) has confirmed that VCLT arts. 31 and 32 reflect customary international law in, *inter alia*, *Sovereignty over Pulau Ligitan and Pulau Sipadan*:[37].

[79] See e.g. *Confirmation of Charges Lubanga*:[281] and *Decision Arrest Warrant Lubanga*:[47].

these aims should be pursued, other than that the Court is to function in accordance with its Statute. Recognising that the preamble's indefinite and multifarious ideals can be used to support a range of sometimes contradictory outcomes, this book relies, where possible, on the more determinate modes of interpretation.

Finally, realism compels disclosure of the fact that the methodological and ethical challenges in carrying out the research leading to this book were such that they deserve their own publication.[80] Two comments must suffice here. First, in terms of methods, data have been triangulated where possible by using different sources and methods for answering the same questions. Particular attention has been paid to factors that might obstruct truth-finding through interviewing, such as answers that are socially desirable, pedagogical or part of a survival strategy.[81] Repeat interviewing and alternative lines of questioning were used to verify the accuracy of answers. Secondly, with respect to ethics, in most instances this book does not reveal the interviewee's identity or the precise date and place of the interview in order to err on the safe side of people's security. This is the price verifiability must pay for research in the line of fire.[82]

THE CHOICE OF A LINE-OF-FIRE PERSPECTIVE

Complementarity could catalyse effects in all states in the world, whether or not party to the Rome Statute, whether or not facing armed conflict, whether or not subject to ICC intervention. But, in order to allow the detailed process tracing described above, including consideration of contextual factors and discernment of complex causal relations, this book presents an in-depth analysis of complementarity's catalysing effect in only two countries. The choice was for two so-called 'situation

---

[80] Some of these challenges have been considered in Nouwen 2010a. They are elaborated in Nouwen 2014b, forthcoming.

[81] Social desirability occurs when a respondent answers in a manner that he or she thinks will please the interviewer. Pedagogical answers reflect the interviewee's perception of how something should be, rather than of how it is. Answers inspired by a survival strategy reflect the interviewee's perception of which account will serve his or her interests.

[82] See also Schnabel 2005:33: '[A]ll potentially compromising information that could identify the respondents must be excluded from any published texts, even if such omissions would weaken the scientific value of the researcher's evidence and arguments.'

countries'[83] – that is, countries in which the ICC has opened investigations – because complementarity matters most in the line of fire: the Prosecutor's opening of an investigation implies that there is a reasonable basis to believe that crimes within the Court's jurisdiction have been committed and that they have not been genuinely investigated or prosecuted domestically. A catalysing effect is more relevant for states where crimes within the Court's jurisdiction have been committed than for states where they have not, and is particularly relevant for states where the commission of those crimes is not yet investigated or prosecuted.

Uganda and Sudan were selected on the ground that they were both 'firsts'. Uganda was the first situation to be referred to the Court by a state party, indeed through a 'self-referral', setting the example for the Democratic Republic of the Congo,[84] the Central African Republic[85] and Mali. The situation in Darfur, Sudan, was the first to be referred to the Court by the UN Security Council, to be followed by Libya. After the investigations for this book had commenced, the situation in Kenya became the first with respect to which the Prosecutor used his *proprio motu* powers to open an investigation, setting a precedent for Côte d'Ivoire. Study of a catalysing effect in such a scenario remains for other research.[86]

This book is not a comparative study, even though it tells the story of complementarity's catalysing effect in two states. The focus is on how the complementarity principle has played out in two different places, rather than to compare systematically the findings in these two states. Another parameter of the research is its focus on the effects specifically catalysed by complementarity. Whether the ICC spurs or hampers peace negotiations, deters crime, marginalises suspects, makes legislators adopt laws to cooperate with the Court or convinces armed forces to adjust their manuals, for example, may all implicate questions as to the catalysing effect of the Court, but any such effects are not necessarily related to complementarity. It may be that tribunals with primacy of jurisdiction, such as the ICTY and ICTR, have similar effects.[87] Whilst at times

---

[83] The term does not appear in the Rome Statute, but is widely used in academic literature and by the ICC, e.g. in Moreno-Ocampo 2007a:7. For a map of the ICC's situation countries in July 2012, see p. xxi.

[84] For research on complementarity's catalysing effect in the DRC see Burke-White 2005, Baylis 2009, Clark 2011 and Glasius 2011.

[85] See Glasius 2011.   [86] See Alai and Mue 2011.

[87] The association with complementarity and catalysing effects has become so strong that some writers consider *any* impact of the Court on the domestic justice system in a situation country a 'complementarity effect'. See e.g. Arbia and Bassy 2011.

31

difficult to differentiate, the effects of intervention by an international criminal tribunal *per se* are discussed only when relevant in the context of complementarity.

Focusing on the responses of two states in Africa to an international legal principle, there is a risk for the book to be misunderstood as 'ethnophilosophy', validly criticised by Paulin Hountondji,[88] 'culture talk'[89] as identified by Mahmoud Mamdani, or 'Meridionalism', to paraphrase Edward Said.[90] But this book suggests neither that all people in Africa have the same worldview nor a radical distinction between the worlds of the observer and of the observed, of the author and of the other. It is beyond the scope of this book (and would be rather repetitive) to highlight, with each observation, that Western states appear, for example, equally reluctant to prosecute nationals for conflict-related crimes if this could divide their societies.[91]

In light of the limitations of, and challenges to, the research underpinning this book, its arguments are presented with a degree of humility. Relevant information may have remained undisclosed despite flexibility and creativity in data collection. Moreover, since the Court began its operations only in 2003 and its investigations in Uganda and Sudan only in 2004 and 2005 respectively, any effects catalysed by complementarity may very well change. The study therefore purports to provide neither an exhaustive nor a definitive answer to the question of complementarity's catalysing effect in Uganda and Sudan. Moreover, complementarity's catalysing effect may be different in other states, particularly in states in which the ICC has not (yet) intervened. All this said, even if complementarity's catalysing effect were radically different elsewhere or to change in the future, the present story would remain one of complementarity's effect in two states during the Court's formative years.

---

[88] Hountondji 1983:38 coins the term 'ethnophilosophy' for 'the imaginary search for an immutable, collective philosophy, common to all Africans'. For an application of his critique with respect to Western promotion of 'traditional' justice in Uganda, see Branch 2011:Chapter 5.

[89] Mamdani 2004:219 distinguishes 'culture talk' (seeking 'the explanation for a deed in the culture of the doer') from 'political talk' (tending 'to explain the deed as a response to issues, to a political context of unaddressed grievances').

[90] Said 1995:5 describes Orientalism, *inter alia*, as a Western style for dominating, restructuring, and having authority over the Orient by making statements about it, authorising views of it, describing it, by teaching it, settling it and ruling over it.

[91] For some sobering observations on European practice in this respect, see Judt 2005:41–62.

THE ROAD AHEAD

This book analyses the effects that complementarity has catalysed and why and how it has done so, and identifies reasons why certain widely expected effects have not (or not yet) occurred in Uganda and Sudan. To that end, Chapter 2 first discusses what complementarity *is*. Both in that legal debate and in the subsequent chapters revealing how complementarity has been explained and interpreted in Uganda and Sudan, complementarity's meaning, like that of any legal principle, is ultimately ambiguous.[92] Indeed, as Chapters 3 and 4 will show, most of the effects catalysed by the principle derive from interpretations other than the one presented in the doctrinal analysis in Chapter 2. However, in order to have a starting point for research into complementarity's catalysing effect, Chapter 2 will present what is considered the most compelling legal interpretation of complementarity.

Against the background of the doctrinal analysis, the book tells the empirical story of complementarity's life in Uganda, in Chapter 3, and Sudan, in Chapter 4. Showing that complementarity's life in practice differs from that in doctrine, the book does not cry foul play, hypocrisy or conspiracy. As legal anthropologists or international lawyers who have reconciled themselves with Martti Koskenniemi's analysis of the indeterminacy of (international) law[93] will immediately react, 'of course': actors – whether politicians, ICC officials, community leaders or NGOs – invoke and use complementarity for their own political agenda. *That* they do is not surprising; this book's interest is in *how* they do so, with what effects and for whose benefit. The result is a story of ideas, agency, power and interests, their convergences and clashes.

The most striking empirical finding in Chapters 3 and 4 is that an increase in domestic proceedings for crimes within the Court's jurisdiction – the only action that can render a case inadmissible before the ICC – is barely observable in either state. In that light, Chapter 5 revisits the assumptions underpinning the expectations of a catalysing effect as set out in the beginning of the present chapter and identifies where they go wrong.

Chapter 6 concludes where Chapter 1 began, with a call for realism.

---

[92] Koskenniemi 2005. See also, more specifically with respect to the Rome Statute, Robinson 2011a:381–4 on 'Open-mindedness to Multiple Plausible Models'.
[93] Koskenniemi 2005.

CHAPTER 2

THE ROME STATUTE: COMPLEMENTARITY IN ITS LEGAL CONTEXT

> Emphasizing *that the International Criminal Court estab-*
> *lished under this Statute shall be complementary to national*
> *criminal jurisdictions* ...
>
> Rome Statute, tenth preambular recital

Complementarity exists by virtue of the Rome Statute. It is the Rome Statute that sets forth the substantive criteria that domestic proceedings must fulfil in order to render cases inadmissible before the ICC on grounds of complementarity and the procedures by which the principle is to be given effect. In theory, it is these provisions that ought to foster the principle's catalysing effect on domestic justice systems.

In practice, however, the principle has been popularly encapsulated in shorthand descriptions, for instance that the Court may not exer-cise jurisdiction 'unless a State is genuinely unable or unwilling to carry out prosecutions'.[1] The principle is discussed as if it existed separately from the Statute; the provisions that actually generate the principle are ignored.[2] As Chapters 3 and 4 will illustrate, it is frequently popular (mis)understandings of complementarity, rather than the legal principle, that infiltrate the domestic justice system and catalyse domestic changes.

This chapter distinguishes law from popular discourse and provides a legal analysis of those provisions of the Rome Statute that have a bearing on complementarity's catalysing effect. After introducing the key provisions setting forth the complementarity principle, the chap-ter addresses three popular assumptions concerning the Rome Statute that have fostered expectations of complementarity's catalysing effect. The chapter then goes into the depths of complementarity, discussing in turn its substance and the procedures by which it is given effect. It ends with a discussion of factors other than complementarity that

---

[1] International Bar Association ICC Monitoring and Outreach Programme 2008:11.
[2] See also Robinson 2010 and Robinson 2011b.

determine whether the Court exercises its jurisdiction and therefore have the potential to confound any inquiry into complementarity's putative catalysing effect: other jurisdictional provisions in the Rome Statute, the OTP's prosecutorial policy and its policy of 'positive complementarity'.

THE KEY PROVISIONS SETTING FORTH COMPLEMENTARITY

The principle of complementarity is embodied in the Rome Statute in a preambular recital, in the opening article and in a provision on the admissibility of cases. According to the preamble's tenth recital and article 1, the ICC 'shall be complementary to national criminal jurisdictions'. Without referring to the term 'complementarity', article 17, titled 'Issues of Admissibility', gives content to the principle as follows:

1. Having regard to paragraph 10 of the Preamble and article 1, the Court shall determine that a case is inadmissible where:
   (a) The case is being investigated or prosecuted by a State which has jurisdiction over it, unless the State is unwilling or unable genuinely to carry out the investigation or prosecution;
   (b) The case has been investigated by a State which has jurisdiction over it and the State has decided not to prosecute the person concerned, unless the decision resulted from the unwillingness or inability of the State genuinely to prosecute;
   (c) The person concerned has already been tried for conduct which is the subject of the complaint, and a trial by the Court is not permitted under article 20, paragraph 3;
   (d) ... [3]
2. In order to determine unwillingness in a particular case, the Court shall consider, having regard to the principles of due process recognized by international law, whether one or more of the following exist, as applicable:
   (a) The proceedings were or are being undertaken or the national decision was made for the purpose of shielding the person concerned from criminal responsibility for crimes within the jurisdiction of the Court referred to in article 5;

---

[3] RS, art. 17(1)(d) provides as a fourth ground of inadmissibility that '[t]he case is not of sufficient gravity to justify further action by the Court'. Gravity is an independent admissibility criterion, not an element of complementarity. Unless otherwise provided, the observations on the admissibility criteria in this book relate only to the criteria embodying complementarity.

(b) There has been an unjustified delay in the proceedings which in the circumstances is inconsistent with an intent to bring the person concerned to justice;

(c) The proceedings were not or are not being conducted independently or impartially, and they were or are being conducted in a manner which, in the circumstances, is inconsistent with an intent to bring the person concerned to justice.

3. In order to determine inability in a particular case, the Court shall consider whether, due to a total or substantial collapse or unavailability of its national judicial system, the State is unable to obtain the accused or the necessary evidence and testimony or otherwise unable to carry out its proceedings.

Article 17(1)(c) is to be read in conjunction with paragraph 3 of article 20 ('Ne bis in idem'),[4] which states:

No person who has been tried by another court for conduct also proscribed under article 6, 7 or 8 shall be tried by the Court with respect to the same conduct unless the proceedings in the other court:

(a) Were for the purpose of shielding the person concerned from criminal responsibility for crimes within the jurisdiction of the Court; or

(b) Otherwise were not conducted independently or impartially in accordance with the norms of due process recognized by international law and were conducted in a manner which, in the circumstances, was inconsistent with an intent to bring the person concerned to justice.

THREE POPULAR ASSUMPTIONS

Three popular assumptions concerning the Rome Statute have fostered expectations of complementarity's catalysing effect. These are a presumed obligation to prosecute, a putative obligation to criminalise the crimes in the Rome Statute in domestic law and a supposed prohibition on the use of amnesties. But to accept such assumptions is misguided. In fact, none of the three assumptions survives an analysis of the Rome Statute.

An obligation to investigate or prosecute pursuant to the Rome Statute?

One of the assumptions that underpin expectations of complementarity's catalysing effect is that the Rome Statute grants states the

---

[4] See also *Decision Arrest Warrant Lubanga*:[29]. Cf. *contra Judgment Lubanga Jurisdiction Challenge*:[23].

'responsibility', 'primary responsibility' or even 'obligation' or 'duty' to investigate or prosecute crimes within the Court's jurisdiction. Not only academic commentators and international-criminal-justice activists, but also organs of the ICC have made statements to that effect, referring to the principle of complementarity.[5] For instance, the ICC Prosecutor argued in his first policy paper:

> It should ... be recalled that the system of complementarity is principally based on the recognition that the exercise of national criminal jurisdiction is not only a right but also a duty of States. Indeed, the principle underlying the concept of complementarity is that States remain responsible and accountable for investigating and prosecuting crimes committed under their jurisdiction and that national systems are expected to maintain and enforce adherence to international standards.[6]

However, while states may be under an obligation to investigate or prosecute pursuant to *other* rules of international law, the principle of complementarity itself establishes no such legal duty.[7] The articles setting forth the principle, articles 17 and 20(3), provide that a case is inadmissible before the ICC if a state genuinely investigates or prosecutes the case, or has done so. By doing so, the Statute recognises each state's right to investigate and prosecute crimes within the Court's jurisdiction and grants it primacy. But articles 17 and 20(3) do not impose a 'responsibility', let alone an obligation on states. As admissibility rules regulating when the Court may exercise its jurisdiction, located in a part of the Statute entitled 'Jurisdiction, Admissibility and Applicable Law', these articles articulate obligations for the Court, not for states.

The Statute's only provision explicitly referring to a relevant duty of states is the sixth preambular recital, 'recalling that it is the duty of every State to exercise its criminal jurisdiction over those responsible for international crimes'. Considering the ordinary meaning of the text, the context and the treaty's object and purpose, it is apparent that this recital does not create an obligation.

With respect to the text, the generic wording of the provision militates against its creating an obligation for states parties domestically

---

[5] See Chapter 1, 'Complementarity's double life', especially nn. 33–39.

[6] ICC-OTP 2003d:5.

[7] See also *Admissibility Decision Katanga (TC)*:[80] ('Sans pour autant que soit méconnu le principe de complémentarité, un État peut s'il le juge opportun, déférer à la Cour une situation concernant son propre territoire, de la même manière qu'il peut décider de ne pas mener une enquête ou de ne pas engager des poursuites relatives à une affaire donnée.').

to investigate and prosecute the crimes within the Court's jurisdiction. It speaks of a duty of 'every State', whereas a treaty can impose obligations only on states parties.[8] It refers to a duty to prosecute 'international crimes', instead of only the international crimes within the Court's jurisdiction.[9] Moreover, it refers to a state's duty to 'exercise its criminal jurisdiction', which does not necessarily require a state to conduct domestic investigations and prosecutions.[10] Arresting and transferring an accused to the ICC is an exercise of criminal jurisdiction, too.[11] Finally, the text does not establish but merely 'recalls' a suggested pre-existing duty. As it is, in respect of only some of the crimes within the Court's jurisdiction do certain treaties[12] and perhaps, exceptionally, customary international law[13] impose obligations to criminalise and prosecute or extradite.[14]

---

[8] VCLT, art. 34.   [9] See also Bergsmo and Triffterer 2008:margin 17.
[10] See also Robinson 2010:94.
[11] See also *Admissibility Decision Katanga (TC)*:[79] and *Admissibility Judgment Katanga (AC)*:[85].
[12] For relevant provisions, see the Genocide Convention 1948, arts. V and VI, the four Geneva Conventions 1949, arts. 49, 50, 129 and 146, respectively, and their First Additional Protocol 1977, art. 85(1), the Cultural Property Convention 1954, art. 28, and its Second Protocol 1999, Chapter 4, the Convention on the Safety of United Nations and Associated Personnel 1994, arts. 9–16, the Chemical Weapons Convention 1992, art. 7(1), the Anti-Personnel Mines Convention 1997, art. 9, and Protocol II 1996, art. 14. See also the Great Lakes Pact Protocol for the Prevention and the Punishment of the Crime of Genocide, War Crimes and Crimes against Humanity and All Forms of Discrimination 2006, arts. 8–10.
[13] UN General Assembly resolutions (e.g. UN Doc. GA/RES/2840 (1971) and UN Doc. GA/RES/3074 (1973)) notwithstanding, state practice and *opinio juris* do not bear out the existence of obligations under customary law to investigate and prosecute customary international crimes such as crimes against humanity, some war crimes and certain treaty crimes (see also Cryer 2005b:109). The crime of genocide may be an exception: consider ICJ, *Reservations to the Convention on Genocide*:23, ICJ, *Application of the Convention on Genocide*:[31] and ICJ, *Armed Activities (DRC v. Rwanda)*:[64]. For some of the offences that constitute crimes against humanity, specific treaties contain an obligation to criminalise and prosecute (see the Apartheid Convention 1973 (arts. IV and V), the Torture Convention 1984 (arts. 4, 5 and 7) and the Enforced Disappearance Convention 2006 (arts. 4, 6 and 11)), but the definition of the crimes in the Statute and in the specific treaties diverge. Cf. *contra* International Law Commission 2011:24, where the then Special Rapporteur Galicki proposed an article in which an *aut dedere aut judicare* obligation was derived from the *jus cogens* character of certain international crimes.
[14] Kleffner 2008:26 argues that an independent obligation to prosecute the crimes in the Rome Statute flows from the obligation in human rights treaties to 'ensure' or 'secure' the human rights contained in those treaties in conjunction with the right

The context of the recital equally counts against its establishing a duty. Considering the lack of a pre-existing obligation to investigate and prosecute all the crimes within the Court's jurisdiction, it is evident that such a fundamental primary rule would have been included in the operative provisions had the states parties to the Statute intended to impose such an obligation. The fact that the reference is made in the preamble and only in the preamble shows that the parties had no intention to create an obligation to investigate and prosecute crimes within the Court's jurisdiction.[15] The recital merely reflects an aspiration, just like many of the other preambular considerations.

Finally, the Statute's object and purpose weighs against interpreting the sixth recital as creating an obligation. The Statute's object and purpose, not to be confused with some of the lofty aims the states parties express in the preamble,[16] is to create a permanent international criminal court, complementary to national criminal jurisdictions, and to regulate the conduct of the court and the obligations of states towards it. The Statute does not create obligations for states independent of the Court's operation. Neither does it provide for a mechanism by which the Court, or any other body, may compel domestic proceedings;[17] it provides only that if states do

---

to an effective remedy, at least as long as the rights were violated within the state's jurisdiction. However, practice is too equivocal to substantiate such an interpretation. Although some decisions of human rights courts indeed refer to such an obligation in case of certain human rights violations (most notably the rights to life and freedom from torture), there is insufficient evidence for the assertion that there is always a non-derogable obligation for the state to prosecute and punish all the crimes within the Court's jurisdiction. See also Cryer 2005b:103–5.

[15] Indeed, because of the absence of such a duty, Akhavan 2010b proposes an optional protocol obliging states parties to prosecute the crimes within the ICC's jurisdiction at the domestic level and granting the ICC jurisdiction to enforce this obligation.

[16] For such conflation, see e.g. *Admissibility Judgment Katanga (AC)*:[79] ('The aim of the Rome Statute is "to put an end to impunity" and to ensure that "the most serious crimes of concern to the international community as a whole must not go unpunished". This object and purpose of the Statute . . .') and ICC-OTP 2011b:[8] ('The Prosecutor's action will be guided by the object and purpose of the Statute, namely: the prevention of serious crimes of concern to the international community through the ending of impunity.').

[17] As was explicitly recognised by the ICC Appeals Chamber in *Admissibility Judgment Katanga (AC)*:[86] ('under the Rome Statute, the Court does not have the power to order States to open investigations or prosecutions domestically').

not investigate or prosecute crimes within the Court's jurisdiction the ICC is entitled to do so.[18] In sum, neither the sixth recital of the preamble nor any other provision in the Statute obliges states domestically to investigate or prosecute crimes within the Court's jurisdiction.

That said, complementarity could have a catalysing effect on normative grounds. States could *believe* that the rules embodying the principle of complementarity oblige them to investigate and prosecute Rome Statute crimes domestically. The Statute could also remind states of their obligations to investigate and prosecute international crimes pursuant to their participation in other treaties. Or states could interpret their primary right as a political expectation on them to investigate and prosecute crimes within the Court's jurisdiction. As subsequent chapters will demonstrate, the Court's organs, for their part, can both heighten and diminish such a political expectation.[19]

An obligation to criminalise in domestic law?

Another common assumption underpinning expectations of complementarity's catalysing effect is that the Rome Statute requires states parties to adopt 'implementing legislation' that makes the crimes within the ICC's jurisdiction crimes under domestic law.[20] However,

---

[18] Cf. *contra* Kleffner 2008:249–50. His argument, at 251, that the duty in preambular recital 6 is the legal principle, the exact contents of which should be determined with reference to the legal rules on complementarity as reflected in the admissibility criteria, turns the rules of interpretation upside down. Preambular recitals can be of assistance in interpreting the operative provisions of a treaty (see ICJ, *Asylum Case*:282 and ICJ, *Rights of Nationals*:196), but the operative part cannot be used to interpret open-textured recitals as legal obligations.

[19] So can the Assembly of States Parties. The Review Conference, in its first resolution, '[r]ecognize[d] the primary responsibility of States to investigate and prosecute the most serious crimes of international concern', and '[e]mphasize[d] the principle of complementarity as laid down in the Rome Statute and stresse[d] the obligations of States Parties flowing from the Rome Statute', while refraining from spelling out which 'obligations' were related to complementarity (RC/Res.1 (2010), operative paragraphs 1 and 2).

[20] See Chapter 1, nn. 7 and 48. See also the ICC Registrar in Arbia and Bassy 2011:65 ('Implementing legislation is not only crucial for fair trials at the ICC, however, it is also the anchor for domestic trials of international crimes, and thus for the principle of complementarity to be effective. For this purpose, it is also

the Rome Statute requires only that national law facilitate cooperation with the Court[21] and criminalise offences against the ICC's administration of justice.[22] It does not oblige states parties to criminalise genocide, crimes against humanity and war crimes in domestic law.[23] Of course, states parties are free to do so and, indeed, many have done so upon ratification of the Rome Statute.[24]

For those states that wish to avoid ICC intervention by taking advantage of complementarity, incorporation of the Rome Statute's crimes into domestic law is necessary only to the extent that existing domestic law does not cover all the conduct within the ICC's jurisdiction,[25] since it suffices for a successful admissibility challenge on the ground of complementarity to charge the relevant conduct as an ordinary crime.[26] Many of the *actus rei* of the crimes within the ICC's jurisdiction will already be criminalised in ordinary penal law, but conduct such as recruitment of child soldiers and treatment of prisoners of war, and modes of liability such as command responsibility, could well require criminalisation.[27]

A prohibition on amnesties?

A third popular assumption fostering expectations of complementarity's catalysing effect is that the Rome Statute bans amnesties.[28]

---

essential for implementing legislation to incorporate the Rome Statute crimes into national law. Without this, states could be left in the position of prosecuting only for some of the constitutive acts of the crimes, such as murder and rape. This could undermine the basis of national prosecutions, and may invite the ICC's Judges to take jurisdiction where this might not be needed.') and Newton 2011:320.

[21] RS, art. 88.   [22] *Ibid.*, art. 70(4)(a).

[23] See also *Prosecution Response to Libyan Admissibility Challenge*:[23].

[24] For an overview, see e.g. Amnesty International 2006, and, for a collection of implementing legislation, the database of the ICC Legal Tools project, at www.legal-tools.org.

[25] The review of domestic legislation may, of course, be an occasion for passing legislation to criminalise and establish broad jurisdiction over international crimes in general, as has been advocated by e.g. Amnesty International 2004a and Human Rights Watch 2001.

[26] See below, this chapter: 'The "same case" requirement: same person, same conduct, same incidents?'.

[27] For other examples, see Broomhall 2003:91.

[28] See Chapter 1, n. 32.

However, the Statute does not contain any prohibition on amnesties or any obligation on states that is irreconcilable with the use of amnesties.[29] This fits with the character of the Statute more generally, namely, to regulate only the conduct of the Court and the cooperation of states with the Court – the Statute is silent on what states should or should not do independently of the Court. For the Court, the implication of this silence on amnesties is that it is not legally bound to respect amnesty measures – amnesty laws usually derive their legal force solely from domestic law, which as such is not part of the ICC's applicable law.[30] For states, the Statute's silence means that use of amnesties does not amount to a violation of the Statute – they could of course be in violation of treaties that do oblige them to investigate, prosecute and punish.[31]

That said, the Rome Statute could have a discouraging effect on the use of amnesties. First, states parties could consider themselves politically obliged not to use amnesties for crimes within the Court's jurisdiction because they subscribe to its anti-impunity agenda. Secondly, states parties may realise that the ICC's existence has diminished the political value of domestic amnesties since the risk of prosecution on the international plane has increased. Finally, states could refrain from using amnesties because amnesties often obstruct domestic proceedings, thus inhibiting states from avoiding or ending ICC involvement by using their primary right to investigate and prosecute pursuant to the principle of complementarity.[32]

---

[29] The argument that amnesties are incompatible with the anti-impunity 'spirit' of the Statute is legally not convincing. The Statute does not recognise 'spirit' as a source of applicable law; nor does international law for that matter.

[30] See RS, art. 21. This does not prevent the Prosecutor from taking into account an amnesty in the context of considering the 'interests of justice' (see below on RS, art. 53(1)(c) and (2)(c)), or the Security Council when deciding whether or not to defer ICC proceedings pursuant to RS, art. 16 (see below).

[31] See n. 12 above.

[32] The precise impact of an amnesty law on an admissibility assessment pursuant to art. 17 will depend on the type of amnesty law and its application. If the result is that there are no investigations into a specific case, the case will be admissible on grounds of absence of domestic proceedings (art. 17(1)). If criminal investigations or prosecutions are followed by a decision not to prosecute on account of an amnesty law, the state is likely to be found unwilling or unable genuinely to prosecute (art. 17(1)(b)). See more elaborately, next section, and Dugard 1999, Robinson 2003 and Robinson 2006.

In sum, many of the great expectations of complementarity's cata-lysing effect discussed in Chapter 1 are based on popular but incorrect assumptions about what the Rome Statute requires states to do (investi-gate and prosecute, criminalise Rome Statute crimes in domestic law) or not to do (refrain from issuing amnesties). And yet, as Chapters 3 and 4 will reveal, in practice popular assumptions sometimes can have a stronger impact on complementarity's catalysing effect than the law itself.

THE SUBSTANCE OF COMPLEMENTARITY: THE CRITERIA FOR INADMISSIBILITY

The above-cited articles 17 and 20(3) give effect to the idea of complementarity referred to in the preamble and article 1 by way of an admissibility rule. This section will argue that careful reading of these provisions shows the inadequacy of the shorthand description according to which the complementarity assessment focuses on a state's willingness and ability. Rather, as the Court's early case law confirms, article 17(1)(a), (b) and (c) envisage two basic scenarios in which cases are admissible before the ICC. The first is where no relevant domestic proceedings have been initiated. According to the Court, relevant proceedings require domestic proceedings in relation to the same 'case', requiring identity in person, conduct, and possibly even factual incidents and mode of liability. Reasons will be advanced, however, to depart from this test. Other concepts pertaining to the question whether relevant domestic proceedings have been initiated are that of an 'investi-gation' and a 'decision not to prosecute'. The second scenario in which cases are admissible before the ICC is where domestic proceedings have been initiated but the state is unwilling or unable to conduct these genuinely. Only then does the question of domes-tic willingness and ability arise. Neither low punishment nor violation of fair trial rights is *per se* grounds for admissibility of cases before the Court.

The inadequacy of the shorthand description
Contrary to what the omnipresent shorthand description of comple-mentarity suggests – a case is inadmissible 'unless a State is genuinely

unable or unwilling to carry out prosecutions'[33] – precise reading of article 17 shows that ability and willingness are only of secondary importance to an admissibility assessment. Before mentioning ability and willingness, article 17(1) first provides that the Court shall determine that 'a case' is inadmissible where that case 'is being investigated or prosecuted', 'has been investigated' or 'has already been tried'. The references to ongoing and concluded proceedings reveal that, if there is no state investigating or prosecuting the case or no state which has done so, none of the criteria of inadmissibility can be satisfied. In the absence of ongoing or concluded national investigations or prosecutions, therefore, cases are admissible before the ICC without the need for any determination of a state's unwillingness or inability as defined in paragraphs 2 and 3 of article 17.[34] Only when domestic investigations or prosecutions are being or have been conducted is it necessary in any given case to determine whether the state concerned is or was willing and able to carry out these proceedings in a genuine fashion. In the words of the ICC Appeals Chamber:

> [I]n considering whether a case is inadmissible under article 17(1)(a) and (b) of the Statute, the initial questions to ask are (1) whether there are ongoing investigations or prosecutions, or (2) whether there have been investigations in the past, and the State having jurisdiction has decided not to prosecute the person concerned. It is only when the answers to these questions are in the affirmative that one has to look to the second halves of sub-paragraphs (a) and (b) and to examine the

---

[33] International Bar Association ICC Monitoring and Outreach Programme 2008:11. See also, *inter plurima alia*, Arsanjani and Reisman 2005 and Chapter 1, nn. 19 and 20.

[34] This has been consistently upheld by the ICC Chambers. See e.g. *Decision Arrest Warrant Lubanga*:[40], *Admissibility Judgment Katanga (AC)*:[78], *Decision Authorizing Kenya Investigation*:[53]–[54], *Judgment Admissibility Challenge Bemba (AC)*: [107]–[108], *Admissibility Decision Muthaura et al. (PTC)*:[44] and [66], *Admissibility Decision Ruto et al. (PTC)*:[48] and [70], *Admissibility Judgment Muthaura et al. (AC)*:[40], *Admissibility Judgment Ruto et al. (AC)*:[41], *Decision Confirmation of Charges Abu Garda*:[29] and *Authorisation Investigation Republic of Côte d'Ivoire*:[193] and [206]. See also *Admissibility Judgment Ruto et al. (Dissenting Opinion Judge Ušacka)*:[19] and [27] and *Admissibility Judgment Muthaura et al. (Dissenting Opinion Judge Ušacka)*:[19] and [27]. For the OTP's concurrence, see ICC-OTP 2003d:5, Moreno-Ocampo 2004c:2, ICC-OTP 2006c:5 and ICC-OTP 2003c:7–8 and 11. See also Robinson 2010 and Robinson 2011b. More implicitly, see *Decision Arrest Warrant Bashir (PTC)*:[50], *Decision on Summons for Abu Garda*:[4] and *Decision Summonses Banda and Jerbo*:[4].

question of unwillingness and inability. To do otherwise would be to put the cart before the horse. It follows that in case of inaction, the question of unwillingness or inability does not arise; inaction on the part of a State having jurisdiction (that is, the fact that a State is not investigating or prosecuting, or has not done so) renders a case admissible before the Court, subject to article 17(1)(d) of the Statute.[35]

Indeed, in the majority of ICC decisions addressing complementarity so far, the Court has not begun to assess states' willingness or ability to conduct genuine proceedings.[36] The Court reasoned that the cases before it were admissible in the simple *absence* of domestic proceedings – there was thus no willingness or ability in any specific procedures to assess.[37]

However, in order to reach the conclusion of domestic inaction, the Court had to engage with the meaning of three terms appearing in article 17 prior to any mention of willingness or ability. Whereas academic literature had brooded over how to measure willingness and ability, in practice the seemingly quotidian terms 'case' and, to a lesser extent, 'investigated' and 'decided not to prosecute' were the focus of the Court's early case law on admissibility.

The 'same case' requirement: same person, same conduct, same incidents?

In fact, many of the ICC's first suspects *were* subject to some form of domestic proceedings. The Court could nonetheless reach a finding of domestic inaction, and thus admissibility, by narrowly defining the word 'case' and then arguing that the domestic investigations did not cover the *same* case as that before the ICC.

---

[35] *Admissibility Judgment Katanga (AC)*:[78] (correcting *Admissibility Decision Katanga (TC)*, in which the Trial Chamber had employed the shorthand version of complementarity ([74]: '[A]ux termes du Statut, la Cour n'exercera sa juridiction que si les États compétents pour juger des crimes internationaux soit n'ont pas la volonté soit se trouvent dans l'incapacité de mener véritablement à bien une enquête et, le cas échéant, de poursuivre les auteurs de ces crimes.') and had assessed willingness without first assessing whether there were domestic proceedings in the same case).

[36] The exception being *Admissibility Decision Katanga (TC)*.

[37] This is likely to change when the Court considers the admissibility challenge by the Government of Libya. As the Prosecutor notes in *Prosecution Response to Libyan Admissibility Challenge*:[4]: 'This is the first time that a State has submitted an admissibility challenge providing concrete information that it is prosecuting the same case as that pending before the International Criminal Court.'

This approach was first adopted in *Lubanga*, when the Pre-Trial Chamber (PTC) assessed admissibility as part of a decision on whether to issue an arrest warrant. At that moment Thomas Lubanga was already detained in the Democratic Republic of the Congo (DRC). The DRC authorities had arrested him on charges of crimes against humanity, genocide, murder, illegal detention and torture. Domestic charges notwithstanding, the PTC found the case admissible on the ground of inaction.

The finding of inaction was based on the PTC's determination that the DRC proceedings did not involve the same case as the Prosecutor's. The PTC appeared to divide the concept of same case into two limbs: same *person* and same *conduct*. According to the PTC, it was 'a *conditio sine qua non* for a case arising from the investigation of a situation to be inadmissible that the national proceedings encompass[ed] both the *person* and the *conduct* which is the subject of the case before the Court'.[38] The DRC proceedings concerned the same person but, according to the Chamber, not the same conduct. Whilst the domestic charges included genocide and crimes against humanity, they did not include the one (and only) crime on the basis of which the ICC Prosecutor brought charges: the war crime of enlisting, conscripting and using child soldiers. Comparing the charges, the Chamber held that the 'DRC cannot be considered to be acting in relation to the specific case before the Court'.[39] Since it found that no other state with jurisdiction was acting or had acted 'in relation to such case',[40] the PTC considered Lubanga's case admissible before the ICC.[41]

Other Pre-Trial Chambers have adopted the same approach. In *Katanga*, the suspect had been detained in the DRC on the basis of a DRC arrest warrant charging him with crimes against humanity and genocide. The ICC Prosecutor brought charges of crimes against humanity and war crimes. Even though the charges seemed remarkably similar and without explicitly comparing them, the PTC concluded that 'the proceedings against Germain Katanga in … DRC

---

[38] *Decision Arrest Warrant Lubanga*:[31]. See also [37].
[39] *Ibid.*:[39].   [40] *Ibid.*:[40].
[41] The same reasoning was applied in the decision on an arrest warrant for Lubanga's co-suspect, Bosco Ntaganda. See *Decision Arrest Warrant Ntaganda (PTC)*: [31]–[41].

[did] not encompass the same conduct which [was] the subject of the Prosecution Application'.[42]

In the Darfur situation, the Prosecutor seemed to suggest an even narrower concept of 'same case'. Like Lubanga and Katanga, Ali Kushayb was in domestic detention when the PTC decided on the Prosecutor's request for a summons to appear. Sudanese investigations appeared to be ongoing into five separate incidents in five communities involving attacks accompanied by looting, burning houses, killing and forced disappearance. The ICC Prosecutor, for his part, accused Kushayb of having committed war crimes and crimes against humanity involving killing, rape, torture, persecution, forcibly displacing civilians, depriving civilians of their liberty, pillaging and destroying property. One of the incidents that the Prosecutor focused on was alleged to have taken place in the same locality as one of the incidents under domestic investigations.

But the Prosecutor pointed out that the domestic investigations into the incident had made 'no mention of rape or other inhumane treatment'.[43] The Prosecutor argued that the case was admissible before the ICC because the domestic investigations did 'not relate to the same conduct which [was] the subject of the case before the Court: the national proceedings [were] not in respect of the same *incidents* and address[ed] a significantly narrower range of *conduct*'.[44] In short, the Prosecutor submitted that the 'same conduct' test required domestic proceedings to involve not merely the same acts, generically speaking, but also the same *incidents*; that is, the same factual allegations.[45] Seemingly in further support of the argument for admissibility, the Prosecutor also averred that the Sudanese proceedings did 'not

---

[42] *Decision Arrest Warrant Katanga*:[20]. The PTC applied the same logic in the simultaneous *Decision Arrest Warrant Chui*:[21]. Katanga appealed and challenged the appropriateness of the same-conduct test. As will be discussed below, both the Trial Chamber and the Appeals Chamber found the case admissible, both on different grounds, but neither of which related to the same-conduct test.

[43] *OTP Application Harun and Kushayb*:[265].

[44] *Ibid.*:[267] (emphases added). See also [266].

[45] In the context of victim participation, *Decision VPRS 1–6 DRC*:[65] also used incidents as a factor when defining a 'case'. The OTP's description of the test is at times loose. For instance, with reference to Libya, *Prosecutor's Libya Statement SC May 2012*:[6] argued: 'This is the first time in the short history of the International Criminal Court that a State is requesting jurisdiction to conduct a national investigation against the same individual and for the same incidents under investigation by the International Criminal Court.' There was no reference to 'conduct'.

connect Ali Kushayb to Ahmad Harun',[46] suggesting that, in order to qualify as the same case, domestic proceedings must involve a similar mode of criminal responsibility as in the case before the ICC.

In its eventual decision to issue an arrest warrant for Ali Kushayb, the PTC did not engage with these alleged additional requirements, merely repeating the definition of a 'case' enunciated in *Lubanga*.[47] But, by concluding that the case appeared admissible, the PTC implied that the Prosecutor's formulation of the 'same-conduct' test as requiring the same incidents was correct.[48] The Prosecutor has subsequently maintained the same-incident test in arguing the admissibility of its cases.[49]

In the Kenya situation, the Appeals Chamber affirmed, but possibly also altered, the same-person–same-conduct test. The Kenyan Government's challenge focused on the same-person element of the test. Both the Pre-Trial Chamber and the Appeals Chamber dismissed its argument that the test should involve 'the same conduct in respect of persons *at the same level in the hierarchy being investigated by the ICC*',[50] and confirmed, for the purpose of challenging the admissibility of a case, that the same-person test requires exactly the same persons

---

[46] *Prosecutor's Darfur Statement SC June 2007*:6. See also, on behalf of the OTP, Seils 2007:2.

[47] *Decision Arrest Warrants Harun and Kushayb*:[24], this time defining the test negatively.

[48] When issuing the first public arrest warrant in the CAR situation (*Decision Arrest Warrant Bemba*), PTC III was equivocal as to on which ground it found the case admissible. On the one hand, it suggested that the case was admissible in the absence of domestic proceedings in the same case when it found that there was no evidence indicating that the accused had been investigated or prosecuted at the national level for the crimes charged by the ICC Prosecutor. On the other hand, the PTC seemed to refer to a decision not to prosecute and unwillingness or inability to conduct genuine proceedings when it observed that the CAR authorities seemed to have refrained from prosecuting Jean-Pierre Bemba because they believed he was immune from prosecution on account of his status as Vice-President. The Trial Chamber decided the case was admissible because of the absence of domestic proceedings (*Decision Admissibility Challenge Bemba (TC)*).

[49] See e.g. *OTP Response to Admissibility Challenge Katanga*:[15] ('[T]he incident with which the Accused is charged at the International Criminal Court ("the Bogoro incident") was not at any stage subject to actual investigation in the DRC for the purpose of satisfying the conditions set out in Articles 17(1)(a), 17(1)(b) or 17(1)(c) of the Statute.') and [59] ('The term "case" should ... be understood as being constituted by the underlying event, incident and circumstances – i.e. in the criminal context, the conduct of the suspect in relation to a given incident.').

[50] *Admissibility Challenge Government of Kenya*:[32].

(and not just persons at the same level of hierarchy).[51] However, while the appeal had focused on the same-person limb of the test, the Appeals Chamber in passing transformed the Pre-Trial Chambers' same-conduct limb. It concluded that the '"same person/same conduct" test applied by the Pre-Trial Chamber was the correct test',[52] but nonetheless itself defined the requirement for inadmissibility of the same case as that 'the national investigation must cover the same individual and *substantially* the same conduct as alleged in the proceedings before the Court'.[53] It did not elaborate on the implication of the qualification 'substantially'.

The Appeals Chamber's qualification may refer to the fact that a successful admissibility challenge requires domestic investigations into or prosecution of the same *conduct*, not necessarily the same *crime*.[54] In other words, a successful admissibility challenge does not require the same legal qualification of the underlying conduct in domestic proceedings as in the ICC's case. This is shown by article 20(3) of the Statute, which provides that, as a rule, the ICC may not try a person for '*conduct* also proscribed under article 6, 7, or 8' with respect to which the person has already been tried by another court. The use of

---

[51] *Admissibility Decision Ruto et al. (PTC)*:[56] and *Admissibility Decision Muthaura et al. (PTC)*:[52] ('a determination of the admissibility of a "case" must *at least* encompass the "same person"'), *Admissibility Judgment Ruto et al. (AC)*:[40]–[41] and *Admissibility Judgment Muthaura et al. (AC)*:[39]–[40]. It did so for challenges of admissibility pursuant to art. 19, leaving open the possibility of a less strict test when admissibility is assessed before opening an investigation (see this chapter, below: 'The complementarity assessment is case-specific').

[52] *Admissibility Judgment Ruto et al. (AC)*:[47] and *Admissibility Judgment Muthaura et al. (AC)*:[46].

[53] *Admissibility Judgment Ruto et al. (AC)*:[40] and *Admissibility Judgment Muthaura et al. (AC)*:[39] (emphasis added).

[54] For this interpretation of the qualification, see *Prosecution Response to Libyan Admissibility Challenge*:[25] ('The term "substantially" indicates that the national authorities are not necessarily required to charge the suspect under the exact same legal qualification. While the conduct itself must necessarily be the same, meaning the underlying acts and incidents concerned, the legal characterisation of such conduct may differ: it must be the same in substance, bearing in mind such factors as those described above.') and *Admissibility Challenge Libyan Government*:[86] ('It is significant that while earlier jurisprudence adopted the general term "conduct" the Judgment on Kenya Appeal referred specifically to "substantially the same conduct". The test therefore is whether the judicial action covers "substantially" the same conduct, indicating that the test to be applied is one of substance rather than form. Charging Mr Gaddafi and Mr Al-Senussi with "ordinary crimes" would not "deprive the alleged offence of its essential features".').

'conduct' in article 20(3) contrasts sharply with the use of 'crime' in article 20(2), which concerns the situation where a domestic court wishes to try a case after the ICC.[55] The reference to 'conduct' rather than 'crime' indicates that deference should be accorded to states' legal characterisation of the impugned behaviour. In other words, the fact that a state prosecutor characterises conduct as a different international crime than that the ICC Prosecutor would have charged or as an ordinary crime[56] should not render a case admissible before the Court.[57] Genuine domestic prosecution of the same conduct and incident as 500 counts of murder, rather than as an ICC crime

---

[55] See also ICTY, *Hadžihasanović Judgment*:[257] (concluding that 'the Statute of the International Criminal Court leaves the characterisation of the crimes open to national courts').

[56] UN Doc. A/49/10 (1994):58 describes trial of an 'ordinary crime' as one in which the act is tried as a common crime under domestic law instead of an international crime with the special characteristics of the international crimes as defined in the Statute. The distinction between ordinary crimes and crimes within the jurisdiction of the Court was deliberately omitted from the Rome Statute. See UN Doc. A/50/22 (1995):[43] and [179]. See also Politi 1997:145. In refutation, see Van den Wyngaert and Ongena 2002:725–7, Zahar and Sluiter 2008:489, Yang 2005b:288 and El Zeidy 2008b:286–98.

[57] Arguments to the effect that cases of ordinary crimes are nonetheless by definition admissible before the ICC because absence of domestic criminalisation of the crimes as defined in the Rome Statute is an indicator of *inability* genuinely to investigate or prosecute as defined in art. 17(3) (for such arguments, see e.g. Burke-White 2005:582, Doherty and McCormack 1999:149 and 152, Condorelli 2008:163–4, Greppi 2008:69, Hall 2003:17, Jensen 2006:167, Kleffner 2003:89, Lattanzi 2001:181, Schiff 2008:191, Turner 2005:8–9 and Zahar and Sluiter 2008:489), or that prosecution for ordinary crimes amounts to 'shielding the person concerned from criminal responsibility *for crimes within the jurisdiction of the Court referred to in article 5*' (emphasis added), as defined in arts. 17(2)(a) and 20(3)(a) (on which see this chapter, below), fail to persuade. Absence of international crimes in domestic law does not make a state 'unable to carry out its proceedings' – the state can carry out proceedings by charging ordinary crimes. Secondly, as Heller 2012:206 has argued, 'it would undermine Article 17(2)(a)'s intent requirement to automatically equate the intent to charge a perpetrator with a serious ordinary crime with the intent to shield the perpetrator from criminal responsibility for an international crime.' RS, art. 93(10)(a) also suggests that the Statute's interest is in seeing the conduct investigated and prosecuted, rather than investigated and prosecuted as one of the crimes within the jurisdiction of the ICC. The provision allows the Court to provide assistance to a state party 'conducting an investigation into or trial in respect of conduct which constitutes a crime within the jurisdiction of the Court *or which constitutes a serious crime under the national law of the requesting State*' (emphasis added).

eo nomine such as genocide by killing, should still make a case inadmissible before the ICC.[58]

Reasons to depart from the same-conduct test

There are, however, reasons to argue that the Appeals Chamber's qualification should be construed not just as an acknowledgment that admissibility is decided on the basis of proceedings for the same conduct – as opposed to the same crime – but as a departure from the same-conduct test in its strict interpretation as requiring the same person, conduct and incidents. If strictly interpreted, the test will leave complementarity, or primacy for that matter, with little role to play: since there will seldom be complete identity in person, conduct and incidents, there will seldom be complete concurrence of jurisdiction in the same 'case', and thus no need to apply a priority rule.

The same-conduct test originated in cases in which the ICC's role did not clash with the interests of the state: the DRC wished the ICC to prosecute Lubanga, Katanga and Ngudjolo. However, because it pertains to the general interpretation of the word 'case' in article 17, the test also applies if a state opposes the Court's involvement in a case. And the consequence of that test, if strictly applied, is that it is virtually impossible for a state to win an admissibility challenge if opposed by the ICC Prosecutor.

The consequence of strict application of the same-conduct test is that a state cannot be sure that the ICC will end its involvement in a case or refrain from opening a case unless the state selects not only the same person, but also the same factual conduct, incidents and perhaps even mode of liability that form, or could form, the subject of a case before the ICC.[59] Once the Prosecutor has brought a case before the

---

[58] The Rome Statute deviates in this respect from the respective statutes of the ICTY and ICTR, which explicitly allow the tribunals to retry a case if the conduct has been prosecuted domestically as an ordinary crime (see ICTY Statute, art. 10(2)(a) and ICTR Statute, art. 9(2)(a)). Indeed, the Appeals Chamber of the ICTY has justified the Court's primacy over domestic courts by reference to the risk that domestic courts might prosecute conduct constituting international crimes as ordinary crimes (ICTY, *Tadić Defence Motion Decision* (AC):[58]). For the ICTY, domestic characterisation of conduct within its jurisdiction as an ordinary crime is an explicit ground for claiming jurisdiction not only after but also during the domestic proceedings (ICTY RPE 1994, as updated, rule 9(i)). Rule 9 of the ICTR RPE 1996, as updated, no longer mentions this ground, but has been amended to the effect that the ICTR can practically always demand that states defer.

[59] See also Rastan 2011.

Court, the domestic justice system that wishes to render that case inadmissible must literally *copy* the ICC's case in terms of person, conduct, incidents and, possibly, mode of liability. It is even more difficult for the state that wishes to avoid ICC involvement and therefore begins investigations and prosecutions prior to the ICC Prosecutor's formulation of a case. That state must engage in the precarious exercise of *predicting* which person, conduct, incidents and possibly mode of liability the ICC Prosecutor would choose if he or she were to become involved.[60] If it turns out that the ICC Prosecutor focuses on different conduct, incidents and modes of liability, the ICC's case will be admissible on grounds of inaction of the state, no matter how much that state has investigated and prosecuted. As *Lubanga* illustrates, even if the domestic proceedings focus on conduct that constitutes the basis of charges of genocide or crimes against humanity, the ICC's case will be admissible as long as it involves only *one* type of conduct not covered by the domestic proceedings (in Lubanga's case, the charges of war crimes related to child soldiers), including where the ICC's charges are less serious.

A state can thus guarantee avoiding or ending ICC involvement only by investigating *all possible* persons, conduct, incidents and modes of liability, since, if the ICC Prosecutor wishes to pursue a case, he or she can always achieve it by intentionally selecting persons, conduct, incidents and modes of liability that have not been covered by domestic proceedings.[61] Once the Court's jurisdiction has been triggered, the state that wishes to avoid or end ICC involvement thus loses all prosecutorial discretion.[62] The ICC Prosecutor, by contrast, has in practice total discretion in his or her decision which person, conduct,

---

[60] See also Heller 2012:241 ('the same-conduct requirement expects states to be mind-readers').

[61] See also *Admissibility Challenge Katanga*:[39] ('The ICC Prosecutor could, in many instances, be in a position to put an end to serious investigations and prosecution at the national level, and for what reason? There would be no functional reason as it would merely substitute *bona fide* national proceedings for investigations which are just as selective – in some cases, even more selective. It is to be noted that in the present case the accused was investigated for a far wider range of alleged events.').

[62] See also *Government of Kenya Admissibility Reply Muthaura et al.*:[27] and *Government of Kenya Admissibility Reply Ruto et al.*:[27] (the same-person test 'could be seen as compelling State authorities to surrender independence on the "say-so" of the ICC Prosecutor whose mere identification of possible suspects could embarrass a State to "adjust" its own proper prosecution policy in order to avoid the State

incident and mode of liability to charge. This inequality in discretion is difficult to square with any idea of primacy of domestic justice systems.

But, as has been argued from the outset, complementarity as a legal principle – as opposed to as 'big idea' – exists only to the extent it is set forth in the Statute: if the erosion of any domestic prosecutorial discretion is a consequence of the way that complementarity is set forth in the Rome Statute, it is still a consequence of complementarity, even if difficult to reconcile with any *idea* one may have of complementarity being intended as primacy of domestic jurisdictions. The question is thus whether the Statute indeed requires the same-conduct test in its strict interpretation of requiring the same acts, same factual allegations and same modes of liability.

The Chambers have not explained why the same-conduct test was, in the Pre-Trial Chamber's words, a *sine qua non*;[63] after its *deus ex machina* appearance in *Lubanga*, the test was simply repeated by other Chambers. But OTP submissions and academic literature on the topic have put forward some cogent textual arguments.[64] First, the same-person-same-conduct requirement is explicit in the *ne bis in idem* scenario: article 20(3) requires trial of the same *person* for the same *conduct* for a case to be inadmissible.[65] Article 17(1)(c) refers to this article, and for reasons of consistency the term 'case' in article 17(1) (a), (b) and (d) should consist of the same two components: same person and same conduct.[66] It could be countered, however, that the

---

[63] *Decision Arrest Warrant Lubanga*:[31].

[64] See *OTP Response to Admissibility Challenge Katanga*, (OTP official) Rastan 2008, Rastan 2011 and Robinson 2012.

[65] *OTP Response to Admissibility Challenge Katanga*:[72] and Rastan 2008:437–8 and Rastan 2011:439–41.

[66] See Court of Venice, *Ministry of Defence* v. *Ergialli*:733 for the principle that identical terms used in different places in a treaty are presumed to have an identical meaning in each place. A counter-argument could be that art. 17 does not require consistency in the three inadmissibility scenarios, given that they are structured differently in other respects, too (for instance, inability is relevant for the scenarios in art. 17(1)(a) and (b), but not for (c)). However, in these other respects in which art. 17(1)(c) explicitly differs from art. 17(1)(a) and (b), it is *easier* to win an admissibility challenge after completed domestic trials; an inter-pretation according to which the strict same-conduct test applies only in the *ne bis in idem* scenario would lead to the paradoxical situation that it is easier to challenge

same person for the same conduct requirement referred to in the chapeau of article 20(3) does not apply in the application of article 17(1)(c), since the latter provision contains a different and broader criterion, namely, 'conduct which is the subject of the complaint'. It refers to article 20(3) only for the criteria that 'permit' retrial despite the prohibition in the chapeau of article 20(3), namely, the circumstances elaborated in article 20(3)(a) and (b).

The stronger argument is that the structure of article 90, an article in the part of the Statute on cooperation, suggests that admissibility can be challenged only if the case involves the same conduct.[67] In the context of competing extradition requests, subsections 1 to 6 discuss admissibility assessments in a 'case' (article 90(2)–(6)) involving 'the same person for the same conduct' as the ICC's request (article 90(1)). By contrast, article 90 does not refer to admissibility challenges in the scenario of competing requests for the extradition 'of the same person for conduct other than that which constitutes the crime for which the Court seeks the person's surrender' (article 90(7)), suggesting that in such a scenario there is no admissibility to challenge.[68] The same-conduct test thus finds some support in the Statute.

The Statute provides far fewer grounds for a 'same incident' or a 'same mode of liability' requirement as part of the same-conduct test. The only argument that has been put forward for the same-incident requirement is that for the purposes of *ne bis in idem* in domestic criminal law there usually is no *idem* if the suspect (A or B), conduct

---

admissibility while investigations are ongoing or after a decision not to prosecute than after a completed trial. See also Rastan 2011:440–1.

[67] *Ibid.*:444–5.

[68] *Ibid.*:443–4 and OTP *Response to Admissibility Challenge Katanga*:[77]–[82] have advanced as another argument that the Statute differentiates in Part IX between on the one hand cases in which there is 'an admissibility challenge under consideration by the Court' (art. 95) and on the other hand cases 'different from that to which the [Court's cooperation] request relates' (art. 94) or involving 'a crime different from that for which surrender to the Court is sought' (art. 89(4)). (As pointed out by Stahn 2012a:n. 109, 'crime' in art. 89(4) is a misnomer. It should refer to 'case', as art. 94 (the *lex generalis* with respect to the *lex specialis* in art. 89(4)) does.) However, what follows from this cooperation regime is that the Statute recognises that the ICC's proceedings may affect 'case[s] different from that to which the request relates' and in which there thus is no admissibility challenge. It does not follow, however, that admissibility can be challenged only if the case involves the *same conduct*.

(murder or rape), date (1 or 2 January), place (village C or village D) and victims (victim E or victim F) are not identical.[69]

This argument reveals the key reason why the same-conduct test, and particularly the same-incident test, makes it practically impossible for a state to win on grounds of complementarity when faced with an ICC Prosecutor determined to be or stay involved: the domestic analogy fails to recognise the different context in which international crimes are typically committed.[70] In the context in which domestic criminal law is ordinarily applied, namely, in situations in which crime is the exception, the same-conduct and same-incident test can be fulfilled relatively easily. The tests are, however, more difficult to fulfil in the context in which most international crimes take place, namely, in situations in which crimes come close to becoming the rule, or at least are so widespread that the literature refers to them as 'mass atrocity'.[71] In the ensuing 'universe of criminality',[72] it will in most circumstances be virtually impossible for any justice system, whether domestic or international, to investigate and prosecute all incidents of crime.

The fundamental question is whether the Statute recognises this different context, or, at least, whether it allows for this different context to be taken into account when interpreting the term 'case' for the purposes of complementarity. The textual arguments in favour of the same-conduct test, discussed above, suggest that the Statute does not make provision for the context of mass atrocity.[73] However, such textual arguments need not be treated as dispositive. As will be elaborated below, the Statute does not seem to allow the ICC

---

[69] The mode of liability, however, is likely to fall in the *idem* category (after having been convicted of murdering alone, one would not be retried for murdering with another person).

[70] As is acknowledged by Rastan 2008:438–40 and Rastan 2011:441–5, who concludes, however, that '[t]here is no reason that the ICC should compromise on the application of such a well-entrenched legal principle' as *ne bis in idem* (footnote omitted). He also acknowledges that the consequence of the strict application may negatively impact on the design of the complementarity scheme to encourage domestic proceedings, but considers these policy considerations to be addressed by the Assembly of States Parties, not by the Court. For the same view, see *OTP Response to Admissibility Challenge Katanga*:[4].

[71] See e.g. Aukerman 2002:43, Drumbl 2007:3 and Osiel 2009.

[72] Rastan 2008:439 and Rastan 2011:442.

[73] As has been pointed out above, there are fewer textual arguments for the same-incident test.

Prosecutor any prosecutorial discretion either, suggesting as it does that, in case of referrals, the Prosecutor 'shall' investigate and prosecute unless certain criteria are not fulfilled.[74] Yet in practice it is uncontested that the ICC Prosecutor must and does enjoy discretion given the universality of criminality that he or she faces.[75] Just as textual arguments are not decisive on the issue of the ICC Prosecutor's discretion, so too should they not be decisive for that of the domestic justice system.

Turning to the object and purpose of the complementarity principle, the early case law, public statements and literature explained complementarity as a principle balancing sovereignty and international criminal justice.[76] Given that the focus of the Statute as a whole is the promotion of international criminal justice, the object and purpose of complementarity specifically must be to protect sovereign interests in the wider context of the pursuit of international criminal justice. The principle thus recognises that states that join the anti-impunity struggle can have interests that do not entirely coincide with the pursuit of international criminal justice at the international level. For example, a state may have an interest in the assurance that if it genuinely investigates and prosecutes crimes within the Court's jurisdiction it does not risk ICC involvement. As the discussion on the Juba peace process in Chapter 3 will show, such assurance can be essential for the success of peace negotiations. A state trying to grapple with a past of mass atrocity may also need a moment of closure, a moment when it is accepted that the crimes of the past have been adequately dealt with.[77] In most scenarios of mass atrocity, the same-conduct test will prevent the state from achieving this certainty or closure on the basis of complementarity – given the massiveness of the crimes, there are always other incidents, conduct and modes of liability that the ICC Prosecutor could charge. The object and purpose of complementarity, a principle purposely inserted

---

[74] RS, art. 53. See further below on prosecutorial policy.   [75] *Ibid.*

[76] See Chapter 1, n. 17 for the literature.

[77] This argument also counters the otherwise compelling argument that domestic proceedings against the same person but for different conduct should be addressed exclusively by the cooperation regime and not by the admissibility regime, since the former leads to sequencing and the latter results in permanent inadmissibility of a case before the ICC (Robinson 2012:179). A state may have sovereign interests in guaranteeing suspects that the national proceedings will come instead of – and not be followed by – ICC proceedings. A state may also require closure of criminal proceedings in order to reach stability.

into the Statute to protect state sovereignty, thus requires an interpretation of 'case' that gives some deference to prosecutorial choices of the domestic justice system.

The Court's later case law, however, suggests that the Chambers perceive complementarity as a principle that subordinates the protection of state sovereignty to the goal of ending impunity.[78] In response to the Government of Kenya's argument that the Court when deciding on its admissibility challenge should take into account Kenya's sovereign interests,[79] the Pre-Trial Chamber responded, citing a consideration of the Appeals Chamber in *Katanga*:

> The Chamber is well aware that the concept of complementarity and the manner in which it operates goes to the heart of States' sovereign rights. It is also conscious of the fact that States not only have the right to exercise their criminal jurisdiction over those allegedly responsible for the commission of crimes that fall within the jurisdiction of the Court, they are also under an existing duty to do so as explicitly stated in the Statute's preambular paragraph 6. However, it should be borne in mind that a core rationale underlying the concept of complementarity aims at 'strik[ing] a balance between safeguarding the primacy of domestic proceedings *vis-à-vis* the [...] Court on the one hand, and the goal of the Rome Statute to "put an end to impunity" on the other hand. If States do not [...] investigate [...], the [...] Court must be able to step in.' Therefore, in the context of the Statute, the Court's legal framework, the exercise of national criminal jurisdiction by States is not without limitations. These limits are encapsulated in the provisions regulating the inadmissibility of a case, namely articles 17–20 of the Statute.[80]

The statement, including the quotation from the Appeals Chamber, is problematic. First, articles 17–20 do not contain any limitations on states; they are rules on the admissibility of cases *before the Court*. The Statute does not oblige states to stop domestic proceedings when a case is admissible before the ICC; states are merely obliged to cooperate with the Court.[81] Complementarity affects states' sovereignty not by depriving them of jurisdiction, but by allowing the ICC to exercise

---

[78] Ratan 2012.

[79] *Admissibility Challenge Government of Kenya*:[27]–[28].

[80] *Admissibility Decision Ruto et al. (PTC)*:[44] and *Admissibility Decision Muthaura et al. (PTC)*:[40], referring to *Admissibility Judgment Katanga (AC)*:[85].

[81] See below: 'A state's jurisdiction to adjudicate is unaffected by ICC intervention'.

concurrent jurisdiction under certain circumstances.[82] Secondly, the lofty aspirations expressed in the Statute's preamble are not the same as the Statute's object and purpose: as has been argued above, the object and purpose of the Rome Statute is not to 'end impunity' at any cost, but to create a permanent international criminal court, complementary to national criminal jurisdictions, and to regulate the conduct of the court and the obligations of states towards it.[83] Thirdly, the object and purpose of the Statute is not by definition also the object and purpose of each individual provision in the Rome Statute, in this case the provisions on complementarity. As has been argued above, given the Statute's overall focus on the interests of international criminal justice as pursued by the ICC, it can be argued that the specific object and purpose of complementarity is to protect sovereign interests in the pursuit of justice for crimes within the Court's jurisdiction. In the Appeals Chamber's approach, the purported object and purpose of the Statute as a whole – to 'end impunity' – swallows up the object and purpose of specific provisions. Finally, complementarity does not strike a balance between safeguarding the primacy of domestic proceedings *vis-à-vis* the Court on the one hand and something else; complementarity *is* the primacy of domestic proceedings, subject to the criterion of genuine proceedings.

If the Court's absolute anti-impunity approach persists and all other interests are subjected to the aim of eradicating impunity, the same-conduct test in its strictest interpretation may survive.[84] This test allows one to argue that if the ICC prosecutes a person who has been or is being investigated or prosecuted domestically for different conduct, or for the same conduct but different incidents, it does not compete with the national jurisdiction; all it does is to 'complement' the national jurisdiction to ensure that there is less impunity. This approach does not recognise, and does not want to recognise, that a state that has genuinely investigated or prosecuted that person for different conduct or for different incidents, possibly more serious ones,

---

[82] See also Ratan 2012:12.

[83] See RS, preamble, and RS, art. 1; see also above 'An obligation to investigate or prosecute pursuant to the Rome Statute?'.

[84] For which the OTP has argued in *OTP Response to Admissibility Challenge Katanga*: [82] ('[T]he "same conduct" test ensures comprehensive accountability for all relevant criminal conduct in a manner which is consistent with the object and purpose of the Statute.').

may have a legitimate interest in guaranteeing that he or she will not be tried before an international tribunal after a domestic trial.

The ICC is still to decide whether the same-conduct test also requires investigation and prosecution of the same incidents, and, indeed, whether the Appeals Chamber's qualification is an invitation to depart from the same-conduct test. In the latter case, there are alternative approaches that allow states to do their part in ending impunity without making their choices by definition inferior to the seemingly unfettered discretion of the ICC Prosecutor. The defence in *Katanga* has suggested a 'comparative gravity-test' and a 'comprehensive conduct-test'. The former would amount to

> comparing the gravity of the (intended) scope of investigations at the national level and the (intended) scope of investigations by the ICC Prosecutor. Only when the scope of investigations by the ICC Prosecutor would significantly exceed in gravity the scope of national investigations, would the admissibility threshold be met.[85]

The latter would involve comparing

> the factual scope of investigations. Only when the ICC Prosecutor's scope of investigation is significantly more comprehensive than the scope of national investigations, would there be a basis for admissibility.[86]

Each test would require difficult factual comparisons and possibly subjective assessments of 'gravity'. But they would allow more deference to the choices of a state that addresses impunity, particularly when the state investigates the same person and addresses a broader or graver range of facts. Such deference would also show some international humility – a recognition that selectivity is a feature of judicial responses to mass atrocity, whether domestic or international, and that the international selection is not by definition superior.[87]

The requirement of an 'investigation'
In addition to the question as to what amounts to the same 'case', the ICC's early case law on admissibility grappled with the question what

---

[85] *Admissibility Challenge Katanga*:[46].   [86] *Ibid.*:[47].

[87] For instance, selection to a large extent depends on the availability of evidence. A domestic prosecutor may have more evidence with respect to one incident; an international prosecutor may have more with respect to another incident. This does not make one incident inherently more serious than the other.

amounts to an 'investigation'. The Statute does not define what kinds of 'investigation' render cases inadmissible before the ICC. However, by referring to an investigation concluded by a decision 'not to prosecute', article 17(1)(b) suggests that investigations must have the potential to be followed by prosecution.[88] Moreover, article 1 provides that the ICC 'shall be complementary to national *criminal* jurisdictions'.[89] Read in this context, 'investigation' in article 17 probably does not cover investigations by commissions of inquiry that can only recommend that other bodies further investigate with a view to prosecution.[90]

What amounts to the opening of a criminal investigation varies from legal system to legal system; the ICC is still to pronounce on what suffices for the purposes of article 17. But, in terms of evidentiary standards, the Appeals Chamber has accepted the Pre-Trial Chamber's requirement that the state must show 'concrete investigative steps' and the Prosecutor's view that the 'Government must support its statement with tangible proof to demonstrate that it is actually carrying out relevant investigations'.[91]

It is on this ground that the ICC could and, it is suggested, should have found the cases of Lubanga and Katanga admissible. In those cases, the investigatory activities did not appear to have gone beyond the opening of a *dossier*.[92] Just as the Court found in the Kenya situation that asserting that investigations are ongoing does not suffice,[93] it could

---

[88] See also Robinson 2006:144.   [89] Emphasis added.

[90] Cf. *contra* Cárdenas 2005:58–9. Drumbl 2011:222–31 convincingly argues for an approach of 'qualified deference', which would create a rebuttable presumption in favour of local institutions even if these do not conform to the liberal criminal model. As an alternative to amending the Statute to include this standard, he proposes an interpretative canon. One guideline would be particularly relevant to the interpretation of 'investigation' in art. 17, namely, that of good faith, which 'would encourage a broader vision where transitional justice mechanisms that contemplate neither prosecution *per se* or investigation geared towards attributions of individual penal responsibility or stigma could pass muster in part owing to the good faith motivations behind their adoption' (Drumbl 2011:227–8 and 231–2). See also Drumbl 2007:187–94.

[91] *Admissibility Judgment Muthaura et al. (AC)*:[80] and [62] and *Admissibility Judgment Ruto et al. (AC)*:[82] and [63].

[92] *Transcripts Lubanga 2 February 2006*:39 line 8, *Observations DRC Admissibility Challenge Katanga*:3–4 and *Transcripts Admissibility Challenge Katanga*:77 line 16–78 line 19. See also Rastan 2011:446–8.

[93] *Admissibility Judgment Muthaura et al. (AC)*:[2] and [62] and *Admissibility Judgment Ruto et al. (AC)*:[2] and [63].

have held in *Lubanga* and *Katanga* that an 'empty file' is insufficient to prove ongoing investigations.[94] Had it done so, the cases would have been admissible on the ground of absence of actual investigations, instead of absence of investigations *in the same case*. Given the DRC's full cooperation with and support of the ICC proceedings, the Court may have tried to circumvent an assessment of the progress of the DRC's investigatory activities since such an assessment is more politically sensitive than the seemingly technical comparison of international and domestic charges. Nonetheless, by assessing whether there were actual investigations, the Court could have avoided developing the technical legal test that has come to dominate the Court's practice and that reduces the practical relevance of the rule of primacy of domestic justice systems almost to nil.

A decision not to prosecute
A case can be inadmissible not just when it is being investigated or prosecuted (article 17(1)(a)) or has been tried (articles 17(1)(c) and 20(3)), but also when it has been investigated but the state concerned 'decided not to prosecute' the person concerned, unless, again, 'the decision resulted from the unwillingness or inability of the State genuinely to prosecute' (article 17(1)(b)). In *Katanga*, DRC proceedings had been terminated because the suspect was transferred to the ICC. According to the Appeals Chamber, this decision did not, however, amount to a decision not to prosecute: 'The thrust of [the decision to transfer someone to the ICC is] not that the [person] should not be prosecuted, but that he *should* be prosecuted, albeit before the International Criminal Court.'[95] In the Chamber's view, there were thus neither ongoing domestic proceedings for the purposes of article 17(1)(a) nor a decision 'not to prosecute' for the purposes of article 17(1)(b), and the case was admissible. The judgment implies that, if a state has referred a situation and transfers a suspect, the case is by definition not

---

[94] OTP submission on the Congolese Lubanga proceedings: 'the file in respect of Thomas Lubanga Dyilo is empty – it is literally empty' (*Transcripts Lubanga 2 February 2006*:38 line 8).

[95] *Admissibility Judgment Katanga (AC)*:[82]. The reasoning was applied in *Decision Admissibility Challenge Bemba (TC)*:[83] ('a "decision not to prosecute" in terms of article 17(1)(b) of the Statute does not cover decisions of a State to close judicial proceedings against a suspect because of his or her surrender to the ICC') and confirmed in *Judgment Admissibility Challenge Bemba (AC)*:[74].

inadmissible on grounds of complementarity, unless the individual has already been tried in a manner which satisfies article 20(3).

Where domestic proceedings have been initiated: unwillingness and inability

Where a state has initiated relevant proceedings in the same case, the case is nonetheless admissible before the ICC if the state 'is unwilling or unable genuinely to carry out the investigation or prosecution' or its decision not to prosecute 'resulted from the unwillingness or inability of the State genuinely to prosecute'.[96] The emphasis of the test is not on being 'able and willing' – the state would seem to be so, given that proceedings are actually taking place or have taken place – but on the requirement that the proceedings be conducted 'genuinely'.[97] In this light, the attenuated reference in articles 17(2) and (3), respectively, to 'unwillingness' and 'inability' must be taken to be shorthand for 'unwillingness genuinely to investigate or prosecute' and 'inability genuinely to investigate or prosecute'.[98] 'Genuineness' is thus not a criterion independent of unwillingness and inability.[99] In the context of unwillingness, the meaning of 'genuinely' comes closest to 'in good faith' or 'not in a sham manner'. In combination with inability,

---

[96] RS, art. 17(1) and (2).

[97] See also Robinson 2006:141. One consideration of one Trial Chamber, some ICC officials and some scholars suggest that the adverb 'genuinely' is linked to the adjectives 'unwilling' and 'unable' rather than to the verb 'to carry out' (e.g. *Decision Admissibility Challenge Bemba (TC)*:[239] ('Under this provision, the case is inadmissible if the case has been investigated by a State which has jurisdiction over it and the State has decided not to prosecute, unless the latter is unwilling or genuinely unable to do so.'), ICC Registrar Arbia and Bassy 2011:56 ('discussion on what amounts to a genuine inability'), El Zeidy 2002:900 (but see differently: El Zeidy 2008b:165), Schabas 2004:87, Newton 2001:*passim* and Newton 2011:320). But recourse to the French text, the context provided by the unequivocal art. 17(1)(b), and the fact that the question of willingness and ability arises only in the case of ongoing or completed investigations or ongoing prosecutions contradict this. The word order 'to genuinely prosecute' must have been avoided on account of the grammatical protocol against split infinitives. See also Robinson 2010:87.

[98] Despite this, *Decision Arrest Warrant Lubanga*:[29] remarkably omitted the criterion of genuineness when setting out the admissibility test. A remark by the PTC in [32] suggests, however, that the Chamber can be taken to have intended to read the criterion of genuineness (art. 17(1)(a) and (b)) into its descriptions of unwillingness and inability (arts. 17(2) and (3) respectively).

[99] Cf. *contra* Newton 2011:317.

the meaning of 'genuinely' is close to 'effectively', the drafters' attempts to avoid that word notwithstanding.[100]

A determination of unwillingness genuinely to conduct proceedings involves an assessment of a state's intentions. States demanded 'objective' criteria for an assessment of inherently subjective intentions.[101] Article 17(2) provides:

> In order to determine unwillingness in a particular case, the court shall consider, having regard to the principles of due process recognized by international law, whether one or more of the following exist, as applicable:
> (a) The proceedings were or are being undertaken or the national decision was made for the purpose of shielding the person concerned from criminal responsibility for crimes within the jurisdiction of the Court referred to in article 5;
> (b) There has been an unjustified delay in the proceedings which in the circumstances is inconsistent with an intent to bring the person concerned to justice;
> (c) The proceedings were not or are not being conducted independently or impartially, and they were or are being conducted in a manner which, in the circumstances, is inconsistent with an intent to bring the person concerned to justice.

Shielding from criminal responsibility is the most subjective ground of unwillingness, necessitating an inquiry into the intent of a state. It is sufficient to establish that the purpose is to shield the person from being held criminally responsible, irrespective of whether there are defensible reasons for that shielding (for instance, an official decision not to prosecute, as in article 17(1)(b), in exchange for the person's participation in peace negotiations).[102] The last two grounds are more objective. The absence of the intent to bring to justice need not be positively proven, but can be inferred from an unjustified delay or lack of impartiality and independence seemingly inconsistent with such an intent.[103]

The three listed indicators of unwillingness confirm that what is at issue is unwillingness to conduct genuine proceedings. In all three circumstances, it is the lack of an 'intent to bring the person concerned to justice' that undermines the genuineness. This is implicit in

---

[100] See UN Doc. A/51/22 (1996):38, Holmes 2002:673–4 and Politi 1997:142–3.
[101] Holmes 1999:59.   [102] See also Kleffner 2008:137.
[103] See also Williams 1999:393–4.

the first circumstance, namely, proceedings 'made for the purpose of shielding the person concerned from criminal responsibility'. The second and third situations mention this lack of intent explicitly. The definition is not concerned with a general unwillingness to conduct proceedings: in most instances in which a state is unwilling to carry out proceedings, there will be no proceedings and the question of genuineness will therefore not arise. In this light, the decision of Trial Chamber I in *Katanga* – the only Chamber to find a case admissible on grounds of unwillingness so far – that in addition to the unwillingness provided for in article 17(2), a state should also be considered 'unwilling' if it transfers a person to the ICC,[104] is difficult to reconcile with the text of article 17.[105]

Article 17(3) provides criteria for the determination of inability genuinely to conduct proceedings:

> In order to determine inability in a particular case, the Court shall consider whether, due to a total or substantial collapse or unavailability of its national judicial system, the State is unable to obtain the accused or the necessary evidence and testimony or otherwise unable to carry out its proceedings.

Accordingly, the Court shall consider both the causes and the consequences of inability to investigate or prosecute.[106] As to causes, the provision mentions 'a total or substantial collapse or unavailability of its national system'. As regards the consequences thereof, the provision is more open-textured. The expression 'otherwise unable to carry out its proceedings' allows the Court to determine that a state is unable to investigate or prosecute in situations other than that of an inability to obtain the accused or the necessary evidence.[107]

---

[104] *Admissibility Decision Katanga (TC)*:[77]–[78].

[105] Not too much value should be attached to this decision, particularly since the Appeals Chamber did not adopt this reasoning. The reasoning was rejected in *Admissibility Decision Bemba (TC)*:[243]–[244].

[106] *Admissibility Decision Bemba (TC)*:[245]–[246], to date the only ICC decision in response to an admissibility challenge to engage with inability (albeit *obiter* since the case was found admissible on grounds of inaction), did not do a thorough ability assessment, probably because the Government of the CAR itself had argued it was 'unable' and the CAR's Cour de Cassation had found that 'there can be no doubt that the CAR judicial services are unable genuinely to investigate or prosecute [the charges]' (*ibid.*:[246]).

[107] See e.g. Holmes 2002:678.

The first two of the listed scenarios for inability to conduct genuine proceedings, namely, total or substantial collapse of the national judicial system, are the most obvious. In such situations, it is unlikely that any proceedings will have taken place, obviating the need for an assessment of their genuineness. However, if proceedings do take place, the state may not be able to conduct them genuinely, as evidenced by its being 'unable to obtain the accused or the necessary evidence and testimony or otherwise unable to carry out its proceedings'. Were these the only scenarios for inability to conduct genuine proceedings, states could be found unable to do so only in exceptional circumstances.[108]

However, the third scenario for such inability, namely, the unavailability of a national judicial system, expands the scope of the provision considerably and reveals the decisiveness of the factor of genuineness. Not only practical circumstances (for example, a lack of judicial personnel, an insecure environment or a lack of essential cooperation by other states) but also normative factors can render a system 'unavailable' genuinely to conduct proceedings.[109] Examples of such normative factors are the applicability of amnesty or immunity laws,[110] the lack of the necessary extradition treaties and the absence of jurisdiction under domestic law. In many of these situations, it would be far-fetched to argue that the domestic justice system as such is 'unavailable'. But in the particular case the system would be unavailable to conduct proceedings genuinely. Consequently, states with fully functioning criminal justice systems can be found 'unable', provided that, in the particular case, the system is unavailable genuinely to conduct proceedings.[111]

In the third situation of inadmissibility, namely, when the person investigated or prosecuted by the ICC has already been tried by another court,[112] the requirement of genuineness is implicit in the

---

[108] As is argued in Bassiouni 2005:138 and Olásolo 2005:154 and 166.

[109] In RS, art. 88, the term 'availability' is also used in the context of national legal procedures. Cf. contra Cárdenas 2005:126.

[110] ICC-OTP 2003c:15 and its Annex 4.

[111] In circumstances of normative unavailability the factors constituting the unavailability and flowing from the unavailability become hard to distinguish: legislation or absence thereof renders the national justice system 'unavailable' and at the same time makes the state 'unable to obtain the accused or the necessary evidence and testimony or otherwise unable to carry out its proceedings'.

[112] According to Decision Admissibility Challenge Bemba (TC):[248], being 'tried' requires a 'decision on the merits of the case' and must 'result in a final decision or acquittal of the accused'.

two exceptions to the prohibition of *ne bis in idem*. These exceptions are nearly identical to two of the circumstances that evince unwillingness genuinely to prosecute as defined in article 17(2).[113] Inability to conduct the proceedings genuinely, however, is no longer an exception to inadmissibility of a case before the ICC once a domestic trial has been concluded. This might be explained by the fact that, in many jurisdictions, the grounds for retrial, especially if they relate to blunders by the prosecution, are very limited. It would have been unacceptable to many states if the ICC had been granted extensive powers to retry. More generally, the states negotiating the Rome Statute wished to preclude the Court from acting in effect as an appellate court.[114] The result of the current arrangement, however, is that it is more attractive to states to wait until a domestic trial has ended before challenging admissibility.[115]

Low punishment or a pardon is not a ground for admissibility *per se*

As is apparent from the limited exceptions to the prohibition *ne bis in idem* embodied in article 20(3) of the Statute, a case which has resulted in an acquittal, insignificant punishment or an immediate pardon is not by definition admissible before the ICC.[116] It must be proved that the proceedings were vitiated from the outset by a lack of genuineness, or more precisely by the absence of an intent to bring to justice, which can be evinced by shielding (article 20(3)(a)) or a lack of independence and impartiality (article 20(3)(b)). It is not easy to prove after the trial the absence at the beginning of the proceedings of such an intent; but the requisite evidence could be provided by, for instance, an agreement that the accused will never be punished or will receive a mild sentence.

---

[113] Namely, where the proceedings were for the purpose of 'shielding the person concerned from criminal responsibility' or where the proceedings demonstrated 'a lack of independence and impartiality inconsistent with an intent to bring the person concerned to justice' (RS, art. 20(3)(a) and (b)).

[114] UN Doc. A/50/22 (1995):[43], UN Doc. A/CONF.183/C.1/SR.11 (1998):[19] and Holmes 2002:673.

[115] See also Chapter 3, 'Complementarity: the linchpin of the agreement'.

[116] Belgium's suggestion to this effect with respect to pardons (see UN Doc. A/CONF.183/C.1/SR.11 (1998):[28]) did not make it into the Statute.

The ICC is not a human rights court overseeing compliance with fair trial rights

Nor is the violation of the accused's right to a fair domestic trial an independent ground on which the ICC may or must find a case admissible.[117] Arguments to the opposite effect are founded on interpretations contrary to the text and context of article 17 of the Rome Statute. One argument occasionally made is that 'a national system should be considered "available" [for the purposes of an ability genuinely to investigate or prosecute] only when it incorporates the entire spectrum of substantive and procedural safeguards enshrined in the Statute and by which the ICC is to abide'.[118] However, the fact that the Statute requires the Court's own procedures to be in accordance with international human rights standards does not imply that the Court is entitled to apply the same standards as benchmarks for the genuineness of domestic proceedings.[119] Moreover, during the drafting of the Statute, a reference to fair trial rights was deliberately removed from the criteria for inability genuinely to conduct proceedings.[120]

A second argument sometimes heard is that the violation of fair trial rights to the detriment of the accused amounts instead to an unwillingness genuinely to conduct proceedings. However, the references in articles 17(2) and 20(3)(b) of the Statute and in rule 51 of the Rules of Procedure and Evidence (RPE) to due process principles permit recourse to these principles only by way of guidance in the interpretation of concepts such as an unjustified delay and lack of independence and impartiality. A domestic court's failure to abide by such principles is not an independent ground for finding cases admissible. Moreover, unjustified delay or a lack of independence and impartiality may be grounds for admissibility[121] only if the cumulative requirement that they be 'inconsistent with an intent to bring the person concerned to justice' is fulfilled.[122] A lack of independence and

---

[117] See also Heller 2006.

[118] Gioia 2006:1113 (footnotes omitted). See, in a similar vein, Ellis 2002:241, Yang 2005a:123 and, implicitly, UN Doc. S/2005/60 (2005):[586].

[119] This is argued in Gioia 2006:1111 and Ellis 2002:226.   [120] Holmes 1999:49.

[121] See RS, art. 17(2)(b) and (c) and art. 17(1)(c) in combination with art. 20(3)(b).

[122] The fact that this is not a ground for admissibility in its own right is apparent from the wording 'which ... is inconsistent with an intent' in art. 17(2)(b) and from the word 'and' in arts. 17(2)(c) and 20(3)(b). Contrast this with the wording in UN Doc. A/49/10 (1994):57 or e.g. the 2007 Statute of the Special Tribunal for

impartiality will be inconsistent with an intent to bring to justice only if it has worked to the benefit of the accused.[123]

It could perhaps be argued that the expression 'to bring to justice' in articles 17(2)(b) and (c) and 20(3)(c) means 'to bring to justice in a fair manner', with the result that the domestic violation of due process norms to the detriment of the accused would render a case admissible before the ICC.[124] This interpretation, however, goes against the ordinary meaning of 'to bring to justice', which is 'to catch ... and try [someone] in a court of law',[125] not to try someone in a fair manner. The expansive interpretation also renders redundant the first parts of articles 17(2)(b) and (c) and 20(3)(b),[126] namely, the references to unjustified delay and lack of independence and impartiality, since these are merely examples of inconsistency with an intent 'to bring to justice in a fair manner'. The context, too, militates against the expansive interpretation. Article 17 embodies admissibility criteria which render cases admissible before the ICC when there is a risk that, at the national level, a person will escape investigation and prosecution.

More generally, the ICC's mandate is to prosecute individuals under international criminal law, not to supervise states' compliance with their international human rights obligations. It is true that, according to the Statute, the 'application and interpretation of law ... must be consistent with internationally recognized human rights'.[127] However, this provision neither requires nor justifies an interpretation of 'to bring to justice' that not only turns the Court, whose *raison d'être* is to try individuals, into a court with jurisdiction to monitor domestic observance of fair trial rights but also goes against the ordinary meaning and context of the latter phrase.

A final argument raised in support of the claim that the Court may find a case admissible in the event of a domestic violation of the

---

Lebanon, art. 5(2), where the factors are alternative. See also Kleffner 2008:150. But cf. *contra* ICC-OTP 2003d:4.

[123] See also Carnero Rojo 2005 and Benzing 2003:612. Cf. *contra*, but on different grounds, Gioia 2006:1111–13.

[124] In this vein, see Gioia 2006:1101, Schabas 2004:84 and Van der Wilt 2011.

[125] *Cambridge International Dictionary of English* 1996:774.

[126] On the canon of construction according to which 'a legal text should be interpreted in such a way that a reason and a meaning can be attributed to every word in the text', see ICJ, *Anglo-Iranian Oil Co.*:105.

[127] RS, art. 21(3).

accused's right to a fair trial is that the wording 'shall consider whether' indicates that the enumeration of circumstances of unwillingness and inability in article 17(2) and (3) is merely illustrative.[128] However, there are compelling reasons to treat the provisions as exhaustive determinants of a state's unwillingness and inability genuinely to conduct proceedings.[129] There is no explicit indication that the circumstances cited therein are only illustrative.[130] Indeed, each provision directs the Court to consider whether 'one or more of the following exist', a formulation which rather suggests an exhaustive list of (not mutually exclusive) factors.[131] Moreover, as definitions of exceptions to the rule that cases are inadmissible when there are or have been domestic proceedings, articles 17(2) and (3) should be interpreted narrowly.[132] Lastly, the careful negotiations leading to the adoption of these provisions[133] do not support reading the factors cited therein as merely illustrative. In conclusion, violations at the domestic level of the accused's right to a fair trial do not constitute a ground on which the ICC, in contrast to the ICTY and ICTR,[134] may claim primacy over domestic proceedings.[135]

---

[128] For the argument that the list of circumstances is merely illustrative, see *OPCV Observations on Katanga Appeal on Admissibility*:[22]–[27], Hall 2003:15–16 and Robinson 2003:500.

[129] See also Cárdenas 2005:133 and Human Rights Watch 1998:70.

[130] By way of contrast, arts. 90(6) and 97 use 'inter alia' and 'including but not limited to'. See also Benzing 2003:606.

[131] Holmes 2002:675.   [132] Benzing 2003:606.

[133] Holmes 2002:675. See also L/2773 (1996).

[134] The ICTY can claim jurisdiction during or after, and the ICTR can claim jurisdiction after domestic proceedings on the ground that the domestic proceedings lack(ed) impartiality and independence, irrespective of whether this is to the benefit or detriment of the accused (ICTY Statute, arts. 9 and 10(2)(b), ICTY RPE, rule 9(ii) and ICTR Statute, art. 9(2)(b)). The ICTY and ICTR have also reviewed domestic fair trial standards when considering transferring cases to national courts under rule 11 *bis* of their respective RPE (see e.g. ICTY, *Stanković Referral Decision (AC)* and ICTR, *Bucyibaruta Referral Decision*).

[135] It could be that the ICC interprets and applies RS, art. 21(3) in such a way that it considers itself bound, following case law of the European Court of Human Rights and practice under the International Covenant on Civil and Political Rights, not to transfer an accused to a state on the ground that there is a risk that the person will be subjected to torture or other inhuman or degrading treatment or punishment, or will suffer a flagrant denial of a fair trial. However, this assessment is related to questions of cooperation with states; as set out above, it was intentionally not made part of the admissibility assessment. The fact that the Court cannot transfer a person to a certain state does not mean that it therefore must, indeed

The argument that, because (in some parts of the world) the death penalty violates international human rights law, a case originating from a country that applies the death penalty is admissible before the ICC founders on the same grounds. Moreover, the Statute explicitly provides that '[n]othing in [the part on penalties] affects the application by States of penalties prescribed by their national law'.[136]

In a nutshell, complementarity's substantive provisions give states that wish to render cases inadmissible before the ICC some guidelines (for instance, there must be genuine criminal investigations in the same case) but also considerable leeway (for example, states must charge the same conduct, but not necessarily the same crime, and the domestic proceedings need not resemble the ICC's in all respects, for instance in sentencing). By providing states with some sort of checklist for inadmissibility, the guidelines have the potential to shape complementarity's catalysing effect. The leeway, however, may limit complementarity's catalysing effect on the substance and procedure of domestic proceedings but may enhance its catalysing effect on domestic proceedings as such.

THE PROCEDURAL ASPECTS OF COMPLEMENTARITY

The procedural aspects of complementarity are as important for its potential catalysing effect as its substantive features. It will be argued that, first, complementarity contains a primary right for *all* states – states not parties to the Rome Statute can thus also invoke the principle to render cases before the ICC inadmissible, and for that reason begin domestic proceedings. Secondly, complementarity may or must be assessed by several actors and at several stages in the ICC proceedings. This is particularly relevant because states are not prohibited from conducting proceedings in parallel with the ICC. Depending on how the Court's jurisdiction is triggered, states can in some instances directly shape the scope of the ICC's investigations on grounds of complementarity. However, a state cannot force the

may, itself exercise jurisdiction over that person by changing the Statute's admissibility rules. See also the ICTR's *Ntuyahaga Referral Decision*, honouring the Prosecutor's request to withdraw the indictment but refusing to hand over the accused to Belgium in the absence of an express legal ground for such a transfer in the Tribunal's Statute or (pre-11 *bis* procedure) Rules.

[136] RS, art. 80.

Prosecutor to end an investigation. Complementarity's potential catalysing effect may also be limited by the fact that the ICC does not have a conditional deferral procedure like the ICTY and ICTR.

Complementarity contains a primary right for *all* states

The references in article 17(1) to 'a State', in contradistinction to 'state party', make it clear that genuine investigation or prosecution by any state, and not just by parties to the Statute, renders a case inadmissible. Accordingly, if Sudan, not a state party, conducts genuine domestic proceedings in the cases that the OTP has selected in the Darfur situation, the cases are inadmissible before the ICC.

The Prosecutor must assess complementarity prior to opening an investigation

The first moment in ICC proceedings when complementarity must be assessed is when the Prosecutor decides whether or not to open an investigation.[137] In cases of referral, article 53(1) provides that the Prosecutor shall initiate an investigation, unless he or she determines that there is no reasonable basis to proceed. For this determination, the Prosecutor must consider whether:

(a) The information available to the Prosecutor provides a reasonable basis to believe that a crime within the jurisdiction of the Court has been or is being committed;
(b) The case is or would be admissible under article 17; and
(c) Taking into account the gravity of the crime and the interests of victims, there are nonetheless substantial reasons to believe that an investigation would not serve the interests of justice.[138]

Being an aspect of admissibility under article 17, complementarity is thus, in accordance with article 53(1)(b), one of the factors that the Prosecutor must assess when deciding whether to open an investigation after a referral. Article 15(3) provides a special rule in respect of the Prosecutor's *proprio motu* investigations, but the test for opening an investigation ends up the same, since rule 48 of the RPE obliges the Prosecutor to consider the factors laid down in article 53(1) when

---

[137] See also Rastan 2008:441–2, Rastan 2011:454–8 and Olásolo-Alonso and Rojo 2011.
[138] RS, art. 53(1).

making the determination whether there is a 'reasonable basis to proceed', as required by article 15(3).[139]

The complementarity assessment is case-specific

The text of article 17 makes clear that complementarity must be assessed on a case-by-case basis. In other words, the question is whether 'the case' identified by the ICC is being or has been investigated, prosecuted or tried; the question is not whether the 'situation' that is or could be subject to the Prosecutor's investigation is or has been domestically investigated or prosecuted.[140]

The Statute provides no different assessment for the stage of the proceedings in which the Prosecutor decides whether or not to open an investigation. Even though the Prosecutor may not yet have identified concrete cases – indeed, the entire purpose of investigations seems to be to identify any such cases – article 53 confirms the case-specific character of the admissibility assessment. Accordingly, when the Prosecutor decides whether to open an investigation, he or she must consider whether '[t]he *case* is or would be admissible under article 17'.[141]

The Pre-Trial Chambers have, however, indicated that the word 'case' must be interpreted differently depending on the stage of the proceedings in which admissibility is assessed. In the view of one Pre-Trial Chamber, this

> reference to a 'case' in article 53(1)(b) of the Statute does not mean that the text is mistaken but rather that the Chamber is called upon to construe the term 'case' in the context in which it is applied. The Chamber considers, therefore, that since it is not possible to have a

---

[139] See also *Decision Authorizing Kenya Investigation*:[24] and *Authorisation Investigation Republic of Côte d'Ivoire*:[17].

[140] In *Decision VPRS 1–6 DRC*:[65], PTC I made the following distinction between situations and cases: 'Situations, which are generally defined in terms of temporal, territorial and in some cases personal parameters, such as the situation in the territory of the Democratic Republic of the Congo since 1 July 2002, entail the proceedings envisaged in the Statute to determine whether a particular situation should give rise to a criminal investigation as well as the investigation as such. Cases, which comprise specific incidents during which one or more crimes within the jurisdiction of the Court seem to have been committed by one or more identified suspects, entail proceedings that take place after the issuance of a warrant of arrest or a summons to appear' (footnotes omitted).

[141] RS, art. 53(1)(b) (emphasis added). Cf. *contra* Ambos 2010, analysing the admissibility of a situation.

concrete case involving an identified suspect for the purpose of pros-ecution, prior to the commencement of an investigation, the admissi-bility assessment at this stage actually refers to the admissibility of one or more *potential cases* within the context of a situation.[142]

The Pre-Trial Chambers have given some indications as to how to assess the admissibility of a case in a pre-investigation stage. According to one Pre-Trial Chamber, at the pre-investigation stage

> the admissibility assessment requires an examination as to whether the relevant State(s) is/are conducting or has/have conducted national proceedings in relation to the *groups of persons* and the *crimes* allegedly committed during those *incidents*, which together would likely form the object of the Court's investigations. If the answer is in the negative, the 'case would be admissible'.[143]

In other words, according to the Pre-Trial Chamber:

> The parameters of a potential case ... [comprise] two main elements: (i) the groups of persons involved that are likely to be the object of an investigation for the purpose of shaping the future case(s); and (ii) the crimes within the jurisdiction of the Court allegedly committed during the incidents that are likely to be the focus of an investigation for the purpose of shaping the future case(s).[144]

In situations in which crimes within the Court's jurisdiction have been committed on a massive scale, there will almost always be 'cases' that have not been investigated or prosecuted domestically[145] and

---

[142] *Decision Authorizing Kenya Investigation*:[48] (emphasis added). See also [182], where PTC II found that 'the admissibility assessment at [the situation] stage actually refers to the admissibility of one or more *potential* cases within the context of a "situation"'. The potential-cases approach was confirmed in *Authorisation Investigation Republic of Côte d'Ivoire*:[190]. See also ICC-OTP 2011c:[6].

[143] *Decision Authorizing Kenya Investigation*:[52] (emphases added). In *Admissibility Judgment Muthaura et al. (AC)*:[38] and *Admissibility Judgment Ruto et al. (AC)*: [39], the Appeals Chamber confirmed that '[t]he meaning of the words "case is being investigated" in article 17(1)(a) of the Statute must ... be understood in the context to which it is applied'. However, deciding on an appeal concerning admissibility at the prosecution stage, the Appeals Chamber refrained from defining the test at the pre-investigation phase other than acknowledging that 'the contours of the likely cases will often be relatively vague'.

[144] *Decision Authorizing Kenya Investigation*:[182]. See also *Authorisation Investigation Republic of Côte d'Ivoire*:[191].

[145] See e.g. *ibid.* [195]–[200].

thus 'sufficient information to believe that there are cases that would be admissible'.[146] When a state is investigating or prosecuting crimes within the Court's jurisdiction, the Prosecutor could, for reasons of prosecutorial strategy, refrain from opening an investigation with reference to the principle of complementarity. It is, however, unlikely that the Prosecutor will be *legally* prevented from opening an investigation. The consequence of the case-based assessment of complementarity, even in the pre-investigation phase, is thus that complementarity as such is unlikely to prevent a determined Prosecutor from opening an investigation.

For the ICC to grant a state more discretion as to which incidents and persons it investigates to address impunity in a situation of mass crime, it would probably be necessary to amend the Rome Statute and introduce a situation-based assessment of complementarity, at least in the pre-investigation phase. The test would then be whether the state concerned is conducting or has conducted genuine investigations into the situation as a whole. The selection of cases, including the choice of conduct charged, would then be left to the state, subject to the requirement of a genuine process.

Since in the Rome Statute as it stands the assessment of admissibility concerns a case, the assessment of willingness and ability to conduct genuine proceedings equally concerns the particular cases a state is investigating or prosecuting; complementarity does not require an assessment of the state's overall justice system.[147] The overall

---

[146] This is how the Prosecutor interpreted the admissibility question in the pre-investigation phase in *First Darfur report*:4.

[147] The Prosecutor has confirmed this in several documents and statements: see, *inter alia, First Darfur Report*:4, cited in Chapter 4, n. 93, and *Prosecutor's Libya Statement SC May 2012*:[7]. Other OTP documents (e.g. ICC-OTP 2003b and *Prosecutor's Application Arrest Warrants Libya*:[53]) sometimes nonetheless give the impression of an assessment of the ability of the overall justice sector. So did the Pre-Trial Chamber in *LRA Admissibility Decision (PTC)*:[50] where it observed: 'It remains a fact that the Agreement has not yet been signed and that neither the Agreement nor the Annexure has been submitted to the Parliament. It is not until both documents can be regarded as fully effective and binding upon the parties that a final determination can be made regarding the admissibility of the Case, since the Chamber will only be in a position *to assess the envisaged procedural and substantive laws in the context and for the purposes of article 17 of the Statute* after they are enacted and in force. In this respect, the contents of the envisaged legislation regarding the substantive and procedural laws to be applied by the Special Division, as well as the criteria presiding over the appointment of its members, will be critical.' (emphasis added).

justice system can influence the ability to investigate and prosecute in a particular case, but in its assessment of admissibility of a particular case the Court cannot find a state unable only on the basis of conclusions about the overall justice system. The reverse is also true: the fact that a state has adequate laws and courts does not prevent the ICC from finding a case admissible because the state is unwilling or unable genuinely to conduct proceedings in the particular case.

Complementarity must be assessed irrespective of the trigger mechanism

Complementarity must be assessed irrespective of whether the situation was referred to the Court by the Security Council or by a state party to the Rome Statute or whether the Prosecutor opened an investigation *proprio motu* with PTC permission.[148]

With respect to referrals of situations by states parties, the Statute does not provide for a different procedure in the event that a state refers a situation in its own territory.[149] Even in this case of a so-called 'self-referral', the Prosecutor must decide whether or not to open an investigation, considering, among other things, whether the referring state or any other is conducting genuine domestic proceedings. A state cannot waive the admissibility assessment:[150] article 17 provides that 'the Court shall determine that a case is inadmissible' if the criteria are fulfilled. Nor does the state referring a situation on its own territory implicitly waive the right to challenge admissibility. Here the difference between 'situation' and 'case' is again relevant: a state may refer a situation and nonetheless wish to challenge the admissibility of a particular case.

Equally, in the case of a Security Council referral, the Prosecutor must decide whether or not to open an investigation[151] and must

---

[148] On the ways in which situations can be brought within the Court's jurisdiction, see this chapter, below 'Other jurisdictional provisions: the triggers' and Chapter 1, 'The choice of a line-of-fire perspective'.

[149] On self-referrals, see also below 'Other jurisdictional provisions: the triggers'.

[150] Cf. *contra* Gaja 2008:50, El Zeidy 2006:749–50, El Zeidy 2008b:214 and former ICC Judge Politi 2011:147 (asserting that 'the admissibility of waiver of complementarity has . . . been upheld by the Appeals Chamber . . . in *Katanga*'. However, unlike the Trial Chamber and the parties to the proceedings, the Appeals Chamber in its reasoning did not refer to any 'waiver'.).

[151] This is confirmed by the Prosecutor's discussion of the admissibility of cases in the Darfur and Libya situations (see *First Darfur Report*:3–4 and *Prosecutor's*

consider the admissibility criteria,[152] even if the Council were to make a determination on admissibility in its resolution referring the situation.[153] The Court can act only as provided for in the Statute.[154] A situation referred by the Security Council is subject to different procedures only where the Statute so provides, which it does with respect to neither the Prosecutor's duty to determine whether to open an investigation nor the applicability of the admissibility rules.[155]

A state can directly influence the scope of the ICC's investigation on grounds of complementarity

One area in which the Rome Statute does provide for a different procedure depending on the mechanisms by which the Court's

Application Arrest Warrants Libya:[51]–[54]). But cf. *contra* Condorelli and Villalpando 2002:643 and Ntanda Nsereko 2008:margin 4.

[152] See also Cryer 2006:220. But cf. *contra* Triffterer 2008:margin 20, Bergsmo and Triffterer 2008:margin 22, Doherty and McCormack 1999:151–2, Bassiouni 2006:422, Ratner 2003:447, Sluiter 2008:879, Boot 2002:49–50, 61 and 72 and Yang 2005a:131.

[153] Cf. *contra* Arbour and Bergsmo 1999:19.

[154] According to RS, art. 21(1), the Court 'shall apply: (a) In the first place, [the] Statute, Elements of Crimes and its Rules of Procedure and Evidence, (b) In the second place, where appropriate, applicable treaties and the principles and rules of international law, including the established principles of the international law of armed conflict'. It is not evident that the UN Charter, pursuant to which a resolution would be adopted, is, in this context, an 'applicable treat[y]'; that application would be 'appropriate'; and that resort to art. 21(1)(b) would be necessary, since the sources mentioned in art. 21(1)(a) are straightforward. See also *Postponement Decision Gaddafi*:[28]–[29] and Cryer 2006:213.

[155] The Security Council could influence the Court's proceedings e.g. by obliging or prohibiting UN member states to conduct domestic proceedings, to allow the ICC to investigate, or to transfer a person to the Court. Pursuant to UN Charter, arts. 103 and 25, such a decision would prevail over states' obligations under the Rome Statute. The Council could also instruct the UN member states that are parties to the Rome Statute to take certain decisions in the Assembly of States Parties (see UN Charter, art. 48). If a Council decision prohibiting states from initiating or continuing proceedings were to be obeyed, the case would be admissible owing to the absence of domestic proceedings or, in the case of stayed proceedings, owing to the domestic justice system's being rendered 'unavailable' (see also Condorelli and Villalpando 2002:640). The Court, however, being neither a member – pursuant to art. 4 of the UN Charter only states can become UN members – nor a subsidiary organ of the UN, is not bound by decisions of the Security Council (see also Sarooshi 2001:40 and Cryer and White 2002:151; but cf. *contra* Lauwaars 1984:1605, 1606 and 1610). If a state has initiated genuine domestic proceedings in spite of the Council's decision, the Court shall declare the case inadmissible pursuant to art. 17(1) (but cf. *contra* Akhavan 2005:411).

jurisdiction is triggered is the extent to which a state can directly influence the scope of the Prosecutor's investigation on grounds of complementarity. Article 18 provides interested states with an opportunity to compel the Prosecutor to defer to their investigations. This procedure is available if the Prosecutor decides to open an investigation either *proprio motu* or after a referral of a situation by a state party, but not if the situation was referred by the Security Council.[156]

The core of the procedure, set out in article 18(2), is that a notified state has a month to 'inform the Court that it is investigating or has investigated its nationals or others within its jurisdiction with respect to criminal acts which may constitute crimes [within the Court's jurisdiction] and which relate to the information provided in the notification to States'.[157] If a state so requests, 'the Prosecutor shall defer to the State's investigation of those persons'.[158] If the Prosecutor nevertheless wishes to investigate, he or she must apply to the PTC for authorisation.[159]

Article 18(2) provides that the Prosecutor 'shall defer to the State's investigations of those persons' which the state claims to have investigated or to continue to investigate. The reference to 'those persons' may be taken to suggest that for a successful deferral request the state must have identified specific persons; but the state is obliged to inform the Prosecutor in its request only that it is investigating or has investigated 'criminal acts which may constitute crimes [within the Court's jurisdiction] and which relate to the information provided in the notification to States'.[160] At the same time, the Prosecutor's deferral does not concern the investigation into the situation as a whole. If, in the Prosecutor's view, there are potentially admissible cases not

---

[156] RS, art. 18(1) provides that, before commencing an investigation, the Prosecutor shall notify 'all States Parties and those States which, taking into account the information available, would normally exercise jurisdiction over the crimes concerned'. This obligation of notification does not apply to an investigation begun pursuant to a referral by the Security Council. Since according to RS, art. 18(2) the state's right to request that the Prosecutor defer to its investigation is available only '[w]ithin one month of receipt of *that* notification' (emphasis added), the entire procedure under art. 18 is not applicable to situations referred by the Security Council.

[157] RS, art. 18(2), and RPE, rule 53.   [158] RS, art. 18(2).

[159] *Ibid.* and RPE, rule 54.

[160] RS, art. 18(2). The periodic information that a state may be required to provide to the Prosecutor relates to the progress of 'its *investigations* and any subsequent prosecutions' (RS, art. 18(5), emphasis added).

subject to domestic proceedings, he or she may still investigate the situation with respect to those other cases.

The notification that the Prosecutor is obliged to give under article 18 must contain information about the acts that may constitute crimes within the jurisdiction of the Court,[161] but it need not inform states of which cases the Prosecutor intends to prosecute.[162] Indeed, the aim of the investigation to follow is to identify such cases. The procedure under article 18 is thus of little help to a state that wishes to prevent the ICC from investigating the situation as a whole but which itself has not yet identified all the cases that the ICC may wish to prosecute. So far, the procedure has never been used.

A state cannot force the Prosecutor to end an investigation

Once the Prosecutor has opened an investigation, states and other actors have no procedural avenue by which to end his or her investigation into a situation.[163] The Prosecutor can end an investigation, explicitly or implicitly, by deciding not to prosecute. Yet the Statute does not provide a deadline for the Prosecutor to take a decision whether or not to prosecute. The PTC, in turn, has explicit powers to review a decision, but not to compel the Prosecutor to take a decision.[164] Without such a decision, an ICC investigation could be open-ended.

A state's jurisdiction to adjudicate is unaffected by ICC intervention

At the same time, contrary to claims that the ICC deprives states of jurisdiction, there is no provision in the Rome Statute, unlike in the Statutes of the ICTY and ICTR, allowing the Court to request national courts to 'defer to its competence'.[165] The Statute obliges states parties merely to cooperate with the Court,[166] and prohibits them from prosecuting the same crimes only after the Court has convicted or acquitted the person.[167] Until an acquittal or conviction

---

[161] RPE, rule 52(1).

[162] The OTP's *Notification Investigation DRC*, *Notification Investigation Uganda*, and *Notification Investigation CAR* did not specify the OTP's focus in the respective situations.

[163] This is in contradistinction to the Prosecutor's prosecution of a case, as regards which see below.

[164] See OTP *Submission Status Conference Uganda*.

[165] ICTR Statute, art. 8(2). See also ICTY Statute, art. 9(2).

[166] RS, Part 9.   [167] *Ibid.*, art. 20(2).

by the ICC, states can, in theory, conduct national proceedings simultaneously with those of the Court.

A state may even initiate national proceedings after the ICC has become involved. The fact that the state has initiated its investigations only after the Prosecutor's notification pursuant to article 18 provides no grounds for the OTP to refuse a deferral when requested in accordance with that provision. The fact that a state has started proceedings merely to avoid the Court's doing so does not amount to shielding, as long as the state has the intent to bring the individual to justice.[168] In the absence of any article in the Statute to the contrary, states could initiate domestic proceedings even after the Court has issued arrest warrants in a specific case. If the state launching its domestic investigations were also requested by the Court to arrest and surrender the same person(s) to the ICC, the obligation to comply with the request[169] would be lifted pending the determination of any admissibility challenge.[170] In order to 'catch up' with ongoing proceedings before the ICC, the state must at least open an investigation, demonstrate that this investigation encompasses the same 'case' as the ICC's and, if challenged by the Prosecutor, show that it is willing and able to conduct proceedings genuinely.

The complementarity assessment is dynamic

The possibility for states to commence proceedings also after the ICC has opened its investigation or prosecution is relevant because of complementarity's dynamic configuration.[171] The fact that admissibility is assessed at several stages of the ICC proceedings and that findings can be reviewed gives states a chance to assert their primary right to exercise jurisdiction by conducting genuine domestic proceedings, even when these have been initiated after the ICC has become involved.[172]

After the Prosecutor has decided to open an investigation, a state, in the circumstances described above, can use the procedure in article 18 to pre-empt the Prosecutor's investigation in any given case. If the state does not avail itself of this procedure or is not successful under it, its domestic proceedings could still stay or put a stop to the ICC's involvement given that the Prosecutor may defer his or

---

[168] See also Sadat and Carden 2000:418.   [169] RS, arts. 89 and 86.
[170] Ibid., art. 95. See also Postponement Decision Gaddafi.   [171] Olásolo 2005:157.
[172] Cf. contra Mégret 2006:40 and Swart 2006:174.

her investigation[173] or may decide not to open a prosecution[174] in light of the domestic proceedings.

Once the Prosecutor has decided to prosecute – a decision which becomes apparent through a request for an arrest warrant or a summons to appear – article 19 entitles a range of actors to raise the admissibility of the specific case before the Court.[175] First, article 19(2)(a) grants the right to challenge admissibility to an accused[176] and to any person in respect of whom the ICC has issued a warrant of arrest or a summons to appear.[177] Secondly, article 19(2)(b) grants a right of challenge to 'a State which has jurisdiction over a case'.[178] Thirdly, article 19(2)(c) provides that 'a State from which acceptance of jurisdiction is required under article 12' may challenge admissibility.[179] Finally, pursuant to article 19(3), the Prosecutor may seek a ruling from the Court regarding a question of jurisdiction or admissibility. If the Court decides that a case is inadmissible, the Prosecutor may request the Court to review the decision if new facts regarding the admissibility of the case have arisen.[180]

A person for whom a warrant or summons has been issued, an accused person, or a state may challenge admissibility, but only once and 'prior to or at the commencement of the trial'.[181] A state,

---

[173] RS, art. 19(11).   [174] *Ibid.*, art. 53(2).

[175] At this stage, the assessment of the same case is more strict than before the opening of an investigation (see *Admissibility Decision Ruto et al. (PTC)*:[54], *Admissibility Decision Muthaura et al. (PTC)*:[50], *Admissibility Judgment Muthaura et al. (AC)*:[44] and *Admissibility Judgment Ruto et al. (AC)*:[45]).

[176] The Statute does not define when a person becomes 'the accused', and the ICC does not have an indictment procedure as the ICTY and ICTR, but a comparison of RS arts. 61 and 63 bears out that 'the person' becomes 'the accused' after the confirmation of charges. Cf. *contra* Hall 2008:margin 10.

[177] Such a challenge may be based on either complementarity or gravity, or both.

[178] The only ground of inadmissibility this state may invoke is that 'it is investigating or prosecuting the case or has investigated or prosecuted'.

[179] RS, art. 12(2) requires acceptance of jurisdiction from either the state where the crimes were committed or the state of which the accused is a national, but not if the Security Council has referred the situation. In the scenario of a referral by the Security Council, the state where, or by whose nationals, the crimes were allegedly committed can challenge admissibility only under art. 19(2)(b). For the state, the difference is that art. 19(2)(c), unlike art. 19(2)(b), allows challenges on all of the grounds of inadmissibility set out in art. 17, including insufficient gravity.

[180] RS, art. 19(10).

[181] *Ibid.*, art. 19(4). *Decision Darfur Jurisdiction and Admissibility Challenge* confirms that art. 19(2) cannot be invoked by the *ad hoc* defence lawyer in the period

moreover, must do so 'at the earliest opportunity'.[182] After the commencement of the trial, admissibility findings by the Court, whether *proprio motu* or as a response to a challenge or a request for a ruling, shall be considered *res judicata*, unless a later challenge is allowed in exceptional circumstances. Such allowance can be made only in the event that the person concerned has already been tried.[183]

The Court, for its part, 'may, on its own motion, determine the admissibility of a case in accordance with article 17'.[184] The same article provides that the Court 'shall satisfy itself that it has jurisdiction in any case brought before it'. The difference between 'shall' with respect to jurisdiction and 'may' with respect to the Court's *proprio motu* power to determine admissibility suggests that the Court is not obliged to consider admissibility in the event that neither the accused

---

before concrete cases have been identified. One Trial Chamber found that the commencement of the trial is not when the hearings begin, but when the Trial Chamber is constituted by the Presidency (*Admissibility Decision Katanga (TC)*: [49], on which see Jacobs 2010). In this Trial Chamber's view, admissibility challenges other than those based on arts. 17(1)(c) and 20(3), must be brought before the charges are confirmed. It may be argued in rebuttal that, until the charges are confirmed, it is difficult for parties to know whether the domestic case concerns the same persons, conduct and incidents as the ICC's and therefore on what grounds to challenge admissibility (see also the defence in *Admissibility Challenge Katanga*:[2] and [8]). In *Bemba*, another Trial Chamber explicitly departed from this interpretation of 'commencement of the trial' and held that 'the commencement of the trial occurs when the opening statements are made, immediately before the beginning of the evidence'. (*Decision Admissibility Challenge Bemba (TC)*:[210]). The Appeals Chamber has not ruled on the question when the 'trial' begins, but, in an appeal in *Katanga*, 'stress[ed] that the fact that [it refrained] from pronouncing itself on [this question] does not necessarily mean that the it [*sic*] agrees with the Trial Chamber's interpretation of the term "commencement of the trial" in article 19(4) of the Statute' (*Admissibility Judgment Katanga (AC)*:[38]).

[182] RS, art. 19(5).

[183] *Ibid.*, arts. 19(4) and 17(1)(c). A difficult situation could arise if a domestic court were to acquit or convict an accused *in absentia*. Pursuant to art. 19(4), *ne bis in idem* may be raised as a ground for inadmissibility after the commencement of the trial only in exceptional circumstances and with leave of the Court. A concluded domestic trial could constitute such an exceptional circumstance. The fact that the domestic verdict was rendered *in absentia* would not necessarily render the ICC's case admissible.

[184] 'The Court' in RS, art. 19, must be taken to refer only to the Court's adjudicatory organs (the Pre-Trial, Trial and Appeals Chambers) and not to 'the Court' as defined in RS, art. 34. This interpretation is supported by RS, art. 19(6), which refers to the adjudicatory organs. See also Kleffner 2008:181.

nor any state challenges it.[185] On the other hand, article 19(1) directs the Court to article 17, which provides, in paragraph 1, that the Court 'shall determine that a case is inadmissible' in the enumerated circumstances. This may oblige the Court to determine admissibility, even if it is not raised.[186]

The Appeals Chamber has found that the Court's *proprio motu* assessment of admissibility is discretionary[187] and that at the issuance of an arrest warrant a Chamber should 'exercise such discretion only when it is appropriate in the circumstances of the case, bearing in mind the interests of the suspect'.[188] Subsequent case law suggests that this instruction seems to have been directed to assessments of the gravity component of admissibility rather than of complementarity, and towards *ex parte* procedures behind closed doors rather than public ones.[189] Be that as it may, since the publication of the cautionary Appeals Chamber's Judgment, the Pre-Trial Chambers have refrained from *proprio motu* assessing admissibility when deciding on arrest warrants and summonses to appear.[190]

The Appeals Chamber's judgment and the subsequent practice reveal a particular vision of complementarity. The approach that discourages *sua sponte* review treats admissibility, and thus complementarity, more as an issue going to the rights of interested states and defendants than as a matter of public policy to be insisted on so as to avoid duplication of national and international proceedings and to encourage states to play their part in the prosecution of international crimes.

---

[185] See, in this vein, Hall 1999:408 and Kleffner 2008:181–2.

[186] See *Decision Arrest Warrant Lubanga*:[43]. Support for this view can also be found in UN Doc. A/50/22 (1995):[159], but this debate concerned an article that still combined the current arts. 17 and 19.

[187] *Judgment Arrest Warrant Ntaganda (AC)*:[48].

[188] *Ibid.*:[2]. See also *Decision Arrest Warrants Harun and Kushayb*:[18].

[189] *Judgment Proprio Motu Admissibility Assessment Uganda (AC)*:[85]. See also *Admissibility Judgment Katanga (AC)*:[85].

[190] See e.g. *Decision on Summons for Abu Garda*:[4], *Decision Arrest Warrant Bashir (PTC)*:[51], *Decision Summonses Banda and Jerbo*:[4], *Decision Arrest Warrant Muammar Gaddafi, Saif Gaddafi and Al-Senussi*:[12], *Decision Arrest Warrant Gbagbo*:[23]–[24], *Decision Arrest Warrant Mbarushimana*:[9], *Decision Arrest Warrant Hussein*:[10], *Decision Summonses Muthaura et al.*:[12], *Decision Summonses Ruto et al.*:[12], *Decision Arrest Warrant Mudacumura*:[18], *Decision Second Arrest Warrant Ntaganda (PTC)*:[13].

The procedures to challenge and review admissibility imply that the Court's findings on admissibility remain preliminary until the actors with a right to challenge admissibility are involved in the proceedings.[191] The Statute is less clear on whether the facts on the basis of which the Court decides on admissibility are also dynamic or whether they are frozen at the moment of the Court's first admissibility assessment. The Appeals Chamber has decided the former, namely, that 'the factual situation on the basis of which the admissibility of a case is established is not necessarily static, but ambulatory'.[192] Consequently, 'a case that was originally admissible may be rendered inadmissible by a change of circumstances in the concerned States and *vice versa*'.[193]

The ICC does not have a conditional deferral procedure like the ICTY and ICTR

Unlike the ICTY and ICTR, the ICC cannot conditionally defer otherwise admissible cases to domestic jurisdictions. As part of their completion strategies, the ICTY and ICTR have created a mechanism according to which the Tribunals can refer cases on their docket to domestic jurisdictions.[194] The ICTY and ICTR make the 'referrals' of

---

[191] See also *Arrest Warrant Kony*:[38] (representative of the approach in all LRA arrest warrants, referring to cases 'appear[ing]' to be admissible), *Decision Arrest Warrant Lubanga*:[20], *Decision Arrest Warrant Ntaganda (PTC)*:[20], *Decision Arrest Warrant Harun and Kushayb*:[25], *Arrest Warrant Harun*:2, *Arrest Warrant Kushayb*:2, *Decision Arrest Warrant Katanga*:[21], *Decision Arrest Warrant Chui*:[22] and *Decision Arrest Warrant Bemba*:[22].

[192] *Admissibility Judgment Katanga (AC)*:[56]. While the Statute permits this interpretation, the Appeals Chamber's reasoning does not serve to refute arguments of the Defence (*Admissibility Challenge Katanga*:[28]), and e.g. Bassiouni 2005:194, that the factual basis should be frozen at the moment of the arrest warrant. On the dynamic nature of the admissibility assessment, see also *LRA Admissibility Decision (PTC)*:[28].

[193] *Admissibility Judgment Katanga (AC)*:[56]. It could be argued, applying art. 18(7) *per analogiam*, that, once actors with a right to challenge admissibility have participated in proceedings which resulted in a finding of admissibility, they are thereafter estopped from challenging it unless they can show additional significant facts or a significant change of circumstances. But a significant additional fact or change of circumstances, which need not be unforeseen, could be that a state has started proceedings.

[194] The terms 'defer' and 'refer' are used in different contexts in the ICTY and ICTR Statutes on the one hand and the Rome Statute on the other, and sometimes within the Rome Statute. The ICTY and ICTR Statutes employ 'defer' for domestic jurisdictions' yielding to the tribunals' jurisdiction (ICTY Statute, art.

these cases conditional upon the receiving domestic jurisdiction's fulfilling certain criteria. The tribunals hand cases over only when they are satisfied that the accused will receive a fair trial and that the death penalty will not be imposed or carried out. The Tribunals' Prosecutors may send observers to monitor the domestic proceedings and can request the relevant Tribunal to revoke an order referring the case to the domestic courts.[195] After all, the case was admissible before the tribunal and this is unaffected by the referral.

With complementary jurisdiction, the ICC is in a different position. It *must* defer when a case is inadmissible before it and can therefore set no more conditions for a deferral than that the domestic jurisdiction continues to fulfil the criteria for rendering a case inadmissible before the ICC, namely, to conduct genuine investigations or prosecutions in the same case or to have done so.

The Rome Statute provides for two types of 'deferrals' by the ICC Prosecutor.[196] The first is the above-mentioned article 18 procedure, in which the ICC Prosecutor 'defers to' (in the sense of 'yields to') domestic proceedings.[197] The Prosecutor may review such a decision to defer and request the PTC to authorise his or her investigation despite a previous deferral. For the purpose of the review, the Prosecutor may request that the state concerned periodically inform the

---

9(2), and ICTR Statute, art. 8(2)) and 'refer' for transferring a case from the tribunal to a domestic jurisdiction (RPE, rule 11 *bis*). The Rome Statute uses 'defer' sometimes in the sense of to 'yield to' national jurisdictions (RS, art. 18(2) and (3) and the final sentence of art. 19(11)) and sometimes in the sense of 'to postpone' (RS, art. 16, by the Security Council, or the first sentence in art. 19(11) when the Prosecutor defers proceedings) and 'refer' for triggering the ICC's jurisdiction (RS, arts. 13 and 14). Neither 'refer' nor 'defer' denotes a 'transfer' of jurisdiction – cases may be transferred, but the jurisdiction stays where it is; it is just not exercised in the particular case (cf. *contra* Bekou 2009–2010:730).

[195] ICTY RPE and ICTR RPE, rule 11 *bis*.

[196] Robinson 2012:178 mentions two other ways in which the Court can defer (in the sense of postpone) its case: the consultation mechanism under the cooperation regime (in particular arts. 89(4) and 94(1)) and the interests of justice test pursuant to art. 53. However, the provisions in the cooperation regime allow the state to postpone execution of a request for cooperation; they do not affect the Court's jurisdiction, nor does it force the Court (temporarily) to stop investigating or prosecuting the case. The interests of justice can be a ground for not opening an investigation or a prosecution; it is not a ground for transferring a case.

[197] RS, art. 18(5), (6), (3) and (2).

Prosecutor of the progress of its investigations and any subsequent prosecutions. The standard for review must be the same as the admissibility assessment of article 17.[198]

The second deferral option is under the discretionary power granted to the Prosecutor in article 19(11). In this scenario, the Prosecutor 'defers' – in the sense of 'postpones' – his or her own investigations because it appears that the OTP's cases will be inadmissible under article 17.[199] The Prosecutor may ask for information from the investigating or prosecuting state.[200] The Prosecutor may thereafter decide to proceed with an investigation, but only on the ground that there are cases that would be admissible pursuant to article 17, in other words, that have not been genuinely investigated or prosecuted domestically.[201] Domestic fair trial standards and guarantees of no application

---

[198] See RS, art. 18(3) (with an unfortunate reference to the shorthand definition of complementarity: 'the State's unwillingness or inability genuinely to carry out the investigation'), art. 18(5) ('the Prosecutor may request that the State concerned inform the Prosecutor of the progress of its *investigations and any subsequent prosecutions*' (emphasis added)) and RPE, rule 55(2) ('[t]he Pre-Trial Chamber shall examine the Prosecutor's application and any observations submitted by a State that requested a deferral in accordance with article 18, paragraph 2, and shall consider the factors in *article 17* in deciding whether to authorize an investigation' (emphasis added)).

[199] The English text of art. 19, particularly the third sentence, could also support an interpretation of 'defer' in the sense of 'yields to'. The French text, however, suggests a different meaning of 'defer' in arts. 18(2) and 19(11), speaking of, in art. 18(2), 'le Procureur lui défère', and in art. 19(11), 'le Procureur sursoit à enquêter'.

[200] Pursuant to RS, art. 53(4), the Prosecutor may reconsider a decision not to investigate (or prosecute) 'at any time ... based on new facts or information', without needing to seek the PTC's authorisation. The Statute does not provide for an expiry date for the right to reconsider, but, since future situations cannot be referred, there must be a connection between the facts the Prosecutor wishes to investigate (or prosecute) and the time-period when the referral was made. Bergsmo and Kruger 2008:margin 40 suggest that the word 'whether' in art. 53(4) means that the Prosecutor could also reconsider a decision to open an investigation (or prosecution). However, the word 'initiate' suggests that the Prosecutor can reconsider only a decision not to investigate (or prosecute), since he or she cannot undo an initiation: having opened an investigation, he or she can decide only not to continue an investigation (or prosecution), which should be equated with the decision not to prosecute of art. 53(2). If Bergsmo and Kruger's analysis is correct, however, it stands to reason that for a reconsideration of a decision to investigate (or prosecute) the same criteria and review processes apply as for a decision not to investigate (or prosecute), as provided for in art. 53(1) (or art. 53(2)).

[201] RS, art. 19(10), *per analogiam*.

of the death penalty – conditions applied by the ICTY and ICTR in their rule 11 *bis* procedure – cannot be criteria for considering or ending a deferral pursuant to article 19(11) of the Rome Statute, since these are not grounds for admissibility in the first place. Nor does the Statute endow any ICC organs with powers to monitor domestic proceedings beyond, where provided, requesting information from the state to which the case has been deferred.[202]

In sum, with their (almost absolute) primacy of jurisdiction,[203] the ICTY and ICTR have been able to make referrals of cases to domestic justice systems conditional upon whatever criteria they wished to set; with its complementarity jurisdiction, the only conditions that the ICC can set are those that would render a case admissible before the ICC.

Taken together, the procedural aspects of complementarity thus in some ways increase its potential catalysing effect (for instance, complementarity must be assessed irrespective of the mechanism that triggered the Court's jurisdiction, states are not prohibited from conducting proceedings in parallel with the ICC and the assessment of admissibility is dynamic), while in other ways limiting it (for example, it is difficult for a state to prevent or end ICC investigations on grounds of complementarity and the complementarity assessment does not concern the entire justice system).

LOOKING FOR A CATALYSING EFFECT: THE POTENTIALLY CONFOUNDING AND INTERVENING VARIABLES

Factors other than complementarity also determine whether the Court exercises its jurisdiction and therefore have the potential to confound any inquiry into complementarity's putative catalysing effect. Chief among these factors are other jurisdictional provisions in the Rome Statute, the OTP's prosecutorial policy and the OTP's policy of 'positive complementarity'.

Other jurisdictional provisions: the triggers

The first additional factor determinative of when the Court may exercise its jurisdiction, a factor preliminary to the question of

---

[202] See also *OTP's Libya Trip Report*:[12] ('The Prosecutor reiterated that ... if Libya were authorized to proceed with the trial, the OTP would not monitor the fairness of the domestic proceedings, as this is not the role of the Prosecutor.').
[203] See Nouwen and Lewis 2013.

admissibility, is the trigger – or, more precisely, triggers – for the Court's jurisdiction specified in article 13. In accordance with this provision, a situation may be brought before the Court in one of only three ways, namely, referral by a state party, referral by the Security Council or the *proprio motu* initiation of an investigation by the Prosecutor with the approval of the PTC. In the event of referral by a state party or the Prosecutor's *proprio motu* initiation of an investigation, a precondition to the exercise by the Court of its jurisdiction is the acceptance of the Court's jurisdiction either by the state on the territory of which the impugned conduct is alleged to have taken place or the state of which the suspect is a national.[204]

Article 13(a) and (b) allow states parties and the Security Council to trigger the Court's jurisdiction by referring a 'situation in which one or more of such crimes appears to have been committed'. The phrase was inserted to exclude referrals of specific *cases*.[205] The Pre-Trial Chamber has explained that the phrase means that

> a referral cannot limit the Prosecutor to investigate only certain crimes, e.g. crimes committed by certain persons or crimes committed before or after a given date; as long as crimes are committed within the context of the situation of crisis that triggered the jurisdiction of the Court, investigations and prosecutions can be initiated.[206]

The Pre-Trial Chamber's elaboration was given in the context of a referral by a state party, but it may be assumed that it has the same meaning in the context of a referral by the Security Council since the relevant provision contains exactly the same phrase.[207]

The Statute does not specify the consequences in the event that the referring entity nonetheless tries to focus the Court's investigation on particular individuals by limiting the parameters of the Court's jurisdiction. According to an approach that emphasises the consent of the entity that refers, the referral would be null and void, unless the referring entity does not object when the Prosecutor informs it that

---

[204] RS, art. 12. States parties recognise the Court's jurisdiction by becoming party to the Statute. States not party to the Statute may accept the Court's jurisdiction in respect of a specific situation by way of a declaration lodged under art. 12(3).

[205] See more elaborately, Cryer 2006:212.

[206] *Decision on Jurisdiction Challenge Mbarushimana*:[27].

[207] Indeed, *ibid*.:n. 41 refers to the Court's response to a Security Council referral as an argument for its above-quoted consideration.

he or she will investigate the entire situation.[208] According to a more objective approach, the referral would trigger the Court's jurisdiction; any elements in the referral that try to set the parameters of the Court's jurisdiction would be severed.

The Court's practice to date is ambiguous. As Chapter 3 will elaborate, when the Government of Uganda referred the situation 'concerning the Lord's Resistance Army', the Prosecutor informed the government that he would investigate all sides to the conflict. Since the government did not object, it is not clear whether the information procedure was to seek the government's (implied) consent, confirming the consent approach, or merely to notify the government of the Prosecutor's subsequent actions, supporting the objective approach.[209] Any objection from the Ugandan Government would ultimately not be able to prevent the Prosecutor from opening an investigation as he could always have decided to use his *proprio motu* powers to trigger the Court's jurisdiction with respect to this state party, treating the referral merely as a communication of 'information on crimes within the jurisdiction of the Court' in the sense of article 15(1).

That is not an option, however, if the Security Council attempts to limit the parameters of the Court's jurisdiction in a situation concerning a non-state party that it refers – the Prosecutor has no *proprio motu* powers with respect to a non-state party. The fact that the Court's organs *have* acted upon the Council's resolutions referring the situations in Darfur and Libya – in both of which the Council decided to exclude certain foreign nationals from its jurisdiction[210] – could thus

---

[208] This approach is analogous to the one in the situation that a state lodges a declaration that it accepts the Court's jurisdiction only with respect to a specific crime. According to RPE rule 44, 'the Registrar shall inform the State concerned that the declaration under article 12, paragraph 3, has as a consequence the acceptance of jurisdiction with respect to the crimes referred to in article 5 *of relevance to the situation*' (emphasis added). But rule 44 does not specify the consequence of a state's objection to such information.

[209] *Decision on Jurisdiction Challenge Mbarushimana*:n. 41's reading of the Prosecutor's action with respect to Uganda appears to support the objective approach, stressing as it does that 'the Prosecutor disregarded the limitation and, consistently with the Principles of the Rome Statute, opened an investigation "into the situation concerning Northern Uganda", regardless of who had committed the crimes', without mentioning the Prosecutor's communication with Uganda to that effect.

[210] UN Doc. S/RES/1593 (2005):[6] and UN Doc. S/RES/1970 (2011):[6].

lend support to the objective approach[211] (unless the Court has in fact treated the exemption clause as valid).[212]

With respect to the trigger mechanism of referrals by states, the Statute does not forbid states to refer situations on their own territory to the Court. The fact that the literature had not anticipated these so-called self-referrals does not affect their legal validity.[213] Nor does it conflict with any duty to prosecute in the Statute.[214] The Appeals Chamber went a step further, reasoning that

> there may be merit in the argument that the sovereign decision of a State to relinquish its jurisdiction in favour of the Court may well be seen as complying with the 'duty to exercise [its] criminal jurisdiction', as envisaged in the sixth paragraph of the Preamble.[215]

More problematic than the finding of compliance with the duty is the Appeals Chamber's use of the concept of 'relinquish[ing] its jurisdiction'. A self-referral is a trigger mechanism; the referring state does not relinquish any jurisdiction. If the state wishes, it can continue exercising its jurisdiction, including over crimes within the Court's jurisdiction in the same situation, even in the same case, until the person has been tried for the same crimes by the ICC.[216]

---

[211] See also Cryer 2006:214.

[212] Whether it did is difficult to assess since no foreign national falling into the exempted category has publicly been the subject of ICC proceedings. Abdullah Al-Senussi, for whom an arrest warrant has been issued in the Libya situation, is likely to meet the criterion of the exemption clause that he is a foreign national of a non-state party (he was born in Sudan), but not the other criterion that his were 'acts or omissions arising out of or related to operations in the Libyan Arab Jamahiriya established or authorized by the Council'.

[213] See also Robinson 2011a.

[214] See also Nouwen and Werner 2010b, Kress 2004, Gaeta 2004, and, jubilant on self-referrals, Akhavan 2010a.

[215] *Katanga Admissibility Judgment (AC)*:[85] (with a reference to Kress 2004). The Trial Chamber considered in a similar vein, 'si un État juge plus opportun que la Cour mène les enquêtes et les poursuites, il n'en remplit pas moins ses obligations au regard du principe de complémentarité s'il assure le transfert du suspect dans les meilleurs délais et apporte à la Cour sa coopération pleine et entière conformément au chapitre IX du Statut' (*Admissibility Decision Katanga (TC)*:[79]). The reference to 'obligations au regard du principe de complémentarité' is inappropriate: as has been argued above, the complementarity principle as such is an admissibility rule for cases before the Court and does not contain 'obligations' for states.

[216] See above: 'A state's jurisdiction to adjudicate is unaffected by ICC intervention'.

Finally, a referral by a state or the Security Council triggers the Court's jurisdiction; it does not oblige the Prosecutor to open an investigation. He or she may refrain from doing so if there is 'no reasonable basis to proceed' pursuant to article 53. As discussed above, complementarity is part of the assessment, whether the referral was made by the Security Council or a state, and whether a state refers a situation on its own territory or elsewhere.[217]

Other jurisdictional provisions: a deferral requested by the Security Council

A second factor that may influence when the Court exercises its jurisdiction is the Court's obligation to accede to a request by the United Nations Security Council to defer its proceedings. Pursuant to article 16, '[n]o investigation or prosecution may be commenced or proceeded with under [the] Statute for a period of 12 months after the Security Council, in a resolution adopted under Chapter VII of the Charter of the United Nations, has requested the Court to that effect; that request may be renewed by the Council under the same conditions.' Other than that the resolution must be adopted under Chapter VII of the Charter, the Statute provides no criteria for such a decision – the Council's authority to make such a request derives not from article 16 but from the Charter. Article 39 of the Charter requires an act of aggression, breach of the peace or a threat to the peace before the Security Council may take a decision under Chapter VII and, as the ICTY Appeals Chamber held in *Tadić*, the Council has discretion in deciding whether something is a threat to the peace, what measures to take and whether these measures are necessary to maintain international peace and security.[218]

Other jurisdictional provisions: the admissibility criterion of gravity

The Court may not exercise its jurisdiction if '[t]he case is not of sufficient gravity to justify further action by the Court'.[219] According to articles 17 and 53, the assessment of gravity, like that of complementarity,[220] is at

---

[217] See above: 'Complementarity must be assessed irrespective of the trigger mechanism'.

[218] ICTY, *Tadić Defence Motion Decision (AC)*:[30]–[32] and [39].

[219] RS, art. 17(1)(d).

[220] See above: 'The complementarity assessment is case-specific'.

all stages of ICC proceedings case-specific rather than situation-based. In other words, even at the stage of deciding whether or not to open an investigation, the Prosecutor must assess whether there would be cases that meet the criterion of sufficient gravity, rather than assessing whether the situation as a whole meets the same criterion.

That said, so far the OTP has used the criterion of sufficient gravity to assess and compare situations,[221] in apparent disregard of the text of article 17(1)(d).[222] The PTC, too, has determined that 'at the stage of initiation of the investigation of a situation the relevant *situation* must meet [the] gravity threshold'.[223] Similarly, the OTP has used gravity as an instrument for comparing and selecting cases for prosecution rather than as a minimum standard for admissibility of an individual case. In the Uganda situation, in justifying why the OTP has issued arrest warrants only for members of the Lord's Resistance Army (LRA), the Prosecutor has argued that the crimes committed by the LRA 'were much more numerous' than the crimes allegedly committed by the government's forces.[224] Arguably, however, a state's involvement in the commission of crimes against civilians is an independent and sufficient indication of gravity, because of the high risk of impunity for such crimes.[225] The Uganda case study will show that the way in which the ICC Prosecutor has, with respect, wrongly applied the criterion of sufficient gravity has influenced complementarity's catalysing effect.[226]

No ICC proceedings because of the 'interests of justice'

When deciding whether to open an investigation or prosecution, the Prosecutor may decide to refrain from proceedings if he or she considers that these would not serve 'the interests of justice'.[227] Some

---

[221] See e.g. Moreno-Ocampo 2007b:4 (mentioning as one of the challenges '[h]ow to select the *gravest* situations to investigate' (emphasis added)), ICC-OTP 2006b:9, Moreno-Ocampo 2005b:11, Moreno-Ocampo 2006 and ICC-OTP 2006d:6–7.

[222] See also Seils 2011:992–5, pointing out (995): 'At best, the idea of situational gravity is a legitimate prioritizing rule, not an exclusionary rule.'

[223] *Decision Arrest Warrant Lubanga*:[44] (emphasis added). In *Decision Authorizing Kenya Investigation*:[189], PTC II followed the Prosecutor's practice of assessing the gravity of a situation.

[224] Moreno-Ocampo 2005a:2. See also Moreno-Ocampo 2005b:9 and Agirre Aranburu 2009:154. See further Chapter 3, 'Encouraging more trials, prosecutions and/or investigations'.

[225] See also Schabas 2008a:45–6 and Schabas 2008b:748.

[226] See Chapter 3.   [227] RS, art. 53(1)(c) and (2)(c).

have interpreted the term to allow the Prosecutor to factor in the impact of proceedings on, for instance, the conclusion or implementation of a peace agreement or to consider alternative accountability mechanisms within a state, such as amnesty in exchange for truthtelling.[228] The OTP, however, has argued against a broad interpretation of the 'interests of justice' that would encompass the interests of peace.[229]

Whilst both the interests of justice and complementarity are grounds on which ICC proceedings can be halted, the authority to invoke and decide on these grounds is allocated differently. Unlike complementarity, the interests of justice are not justiciable for the accused or states. In terms of decision-making, whether or not to investigate or prosecute in the interests of justice is left to the Prosecutor's discretion – the Pre-Trial Chamber can review his or her decision not to prosecute on this ground but it cannot oblige him or her actually to use this discretion or *proprio motu* apply the interests-of-justice criterion.

The OTP's prosecutorial policy

A well-known prosecutorial policy may alert states to the instances in which they need not fear the exercise of the Prosecutor's power, and may therefore influence states' recourse to domestic proceedings in order to render potential ICC cases inadmissible. Prosecutorial policy can exist only to the extent that the Rome Statute grants the Prosecutor a degree of discretion. It does so with respect to certain decisions.[230] Of particular relevance for complementarity's potential

---

[228] See e.g. Boot 2002:55, Razesberger 2006:108, 178–9 and Chapters 11 and 12, and Bourdon 2000:166–8. But cf. *contra* Amnesty International 2005.

[229] ICC-OTP 2007:1 emphasised '[f]irstly, that the exercise of the Prosecutor's discretion under Article 53(1)(c) and 53(2)(c) is exceptional in its nature and that there is a presumption in favour of investigation or prosecution wherever the criteria established in Article 53(1)(a) and (b) or Article 53(2)(a) and (b) have been met. Secondly, the criteria for its exercise will naturally be guided by the objects and purposes of the Statute – namely the prevention of serious crimes of concern to the international community through ending impunity. Thirdly, that there is a difference between the concepts of the interests of justice and the interests of peace and that the latter falls within the mandate of institutions other than the Office of the Prosecutor.' See also ICC-OTP 2011b:[8].

[230] These include whether to initiate an investigation; the personal, temporal and geographical parameters of the situation he or she investigates; whether or not to

catalysing effect are the OTP's policies with respect to opening an investigation, whom to charge and with which crimes to charge them.

According to article 53(1), the Prosecutor must open an investigation, unless certain exhaustively[231] listed conditions are not fulfilled.[232] However, in the Prosecutor's view, the OTP, 'in the light of its limited resources', has substantial discretion as to whether to open an investigation.[233] The OTP has declared itself willing to consider, '[i]n addition to ... the factors listed under Article 53',[234] the availability of evidence, the security of victims, witnesses and staff,[235] the feasibility of conducting an effective investigation in a particular territory[236] and whether 'the necessary assistance from the international community [will] be available, including on matters such as the arrest of suspects'.[237]

Whether or not in accordance with the Statute, a decision taken by the Prosecutor for reasons other than the ones listed in article 53(1) is

challenge a state's assertion of inadmissibility; whether there are 'reasonable grounds' to submit a request for the issuance of a warrant of arrest or summons to appear; whether to request a warrant of arrest or a summons to appear; whether to close a preliminary inquiry; whether to conclude an investigation; which persons to charge with which crimes; what evidence to bring; and during which phase of the proceedings to bring this evidence.

[231] See the discussion whether the word 'consider' in art. 17 indicates an exhaustive list of factors to be taken into account (this chapter, 'The ICC is not a human rights court overseeing compliance with fair trial rights'). See also McDonald and Haveman 2003:3–4.

[232] See this chapter: 'The Prosecutor must assess complementarity prior to opening an investigation'. See also the 2003 Draft Regulations of the Office of the Prosecutor:19, [12.2].

[233] ICC-OTP 2003a:1.

[234] ICC-OTP 2006e:8. It could be argued that the Prosecutor has more discretion when deciding whether or not to open an investigation by using his or her *proprio motu* power than after a referral. According to art. 15(1), the Prosecutor 'may' initiate an investigation, and according to art. 15(3) 'shall' submit a request for authorisation if he or she concludes that there is a reasonable basis to proceed (taking into account, pursuant to rule 48, the criteria of art. 53). After a referral, art. 53 determines that the Prosecutor 'shall' initiate an investigation, *unless* certain criteria are fulfilled.

[235] ICC-OTP 2006e:8.   [236] ICC-OTP 2003a:1.

[237] ICC-OTP 2003d:2. But cf. *contra* ICC-OTP 2006e:1–2 ('[T]he duty of independence goes beyond simply not seeking or acting on instructions. It also means that the selection process is not influenced by the presumed wishes of any external source, nor the importance of the cooperation of any particular party, nor the quality of cooperation provided. The selection process is independent of the cooperation-seeking process.').

likely to stand on account of the limited nature of the judicial review provided for in the Statute. The PTC's powers to review arise only when the Prosecutor requests authorisation for a *proprio motu* investigation or decides not to proceed after a referral or an investigation. In the case of potential *proprio motu* investigations, the PTC decides whether to authorise an investigation, but cannot review the Prosecutor's decision *not* to open an investigation.

In the event of referrals, the situation is the reverse: the PTC may review only the Prosecutor's decision not to open an investigation into a situation that has been referred to him or her. It may do so *proprio motu* only if the Prosecutor bases his or her decision solely on the 'interests of justice' ground.[238] Otherwise, it reviews only at the request of the entity (namely, the state party or the Security Council) that referred the situation to the Court.[239] Only in the case of *proprio motu* review does the Chamber have the power to reverse the Prosecutor's decision. If reviewing upon request, it can only request the Prosecutor to review his or her decision.[240] Neither the Statute nor the Rules sets the Prosecutor a time limit for deciding whether to open an investigation. Consequently, the Chamber has no power to review any absence of a decision, for instance when the Prosecutor refrains from deciding whether to open an investigation.[241]

In contrast to the relatively narrow discretion as to whether to open an investigation, the Statute grants the Prosecutor broad leeway as to whom to charge and with which crimes to charge them. Review of a decision not to prosecute is particularly limited. Article 53(2), applicable where a situation has been referred to the Court either by a state party or by the Security Council,[242] provides:

> If, upon investigation, the Prosecutor concludes that there is not a sufficient basis for a prosecution because:

---

[238] RS, art. 53(3)(b).   [239] RS, art. 53(3)(a).   [240] *Ibid.*

[241] But see *Decision Requesting Information on Preliminary Examination CAR:4* (in which the Pre-Trial Chamber put pressure on the Prosecutor to inform it about whether or not he was going to open an investigation into the CAR and considered: 'the preliminary examination of a situation pursuant to article 53(1) of the Statute and rule 104 of the Rules must be completed within a reasonable time from the reception of a referral by a State Party under articles 13(a) and 14 of the Statute, regardless of its complexity').

[242] The Statute does not provide for judicial review of a decision not to prosecute if the decision follows a *proprio motu* investigation.

(a) There is not a sufficient legal or factual basis to seek a warrant or summons under article 58;

(b) The case is inadmissible under article 17; or

(c) A prosecution is not in the interests of justice, taking into account all the circumstances, including the gravity of the crime, the interests of victims and the age or infirmity of the alleged perpetrator, and his or her role in the alleged crime; the Prosecutor shall inform the Pre-Trial Chamber and the State making a referral under article 14 or the Security Council in a case under article 13, paragraph (b), of his or her conclusion and the reasons for the conclusion.

It is unclear whether the phrase '[i]f, upon investigation, the Prosecutor concludes that there is not a sufficient basis for a prosecution' refers to a decision not to open any cases at all, or to a decision not to prosecute specific cases.[243] But, even if article 53(2) is taken to oblige the Prosecutor to notify the PTC of every case he or she decides not to prosecute, the Prosecutor has little incentive to comply. Notification of the Chamber and the entity (i.e. a state party or the Security Council) that referred the situation may result in review and interference by the PTC. If the Prosecutor does not notify the Chamber, the latter, lacking the information available to the former, cannot determine that he or she should have notified it and cannot force the Prosecutor to conclude that he or she has 'reasonable grounds to believe that the person has committed a crime within the jurisdiction of the Court'.[244] Consequently, regardless of what article 53(2) may or

---

[243] The ground sub (a) suggests that the Prosecutor must inform the Chamber only if he or she decides not to prosecute at all, since it is unlikely that he or she would have to report all instances that he or she decides not to prosecute for want of sufficient legal or factual basis – in other words, where there is no case. The grounds sub (b) and (c), however, are case-specific, and the Prosecutor could indeed be obliged to report that he or she has decided not to prosecute a particular case even though there is a sufficient legal and factual basis. The limited relevant case law implies that the PTC considers the provision to oblige the Prosecutor to report every case that he or she does not prosecute (see *Amicus Curiae Decision DRC (PTC)*:[5], *Decision Status Conference Uganda*, and, on the OTP's part, *OTP Submission Status Conference Uganda*).

[244] It could do so only if it infers from information that is available to it, for instance as a result of victims' participation, that the Prosecutor must have taken a decision not to prosecute. In doing so, the Chamber would usurp much of the Prosecutor's discretion. In *Amicus Curiae Decision DRC (PTC)*, the PTC implicitly declined a request to do so and suggested that a negative decision pursuant to art. 53(2) must be explicit.

may not say, in practice the Prosecutor enjoys substantial discretion as to which cases he or she prosecutes. The Prosecutor also enjoys discretion as to which crimes to charge or, more precisely, as to which crimes not to charge. Only the crimes charged are subject to review[245] – at the moment of the issuance of the arrest warrant or summons to appear,[246] at the confirmation of charges[247] and, ultimately, in the judgment.[248]

Enjoying as it does some discretion as to whether to open an investigation and substantial discretion as to whom to charge with which crimes, the OTP has stated or revealed parts of a policy as to how it intends to use its discretion. While policy is subject to change, some features of the stated and apparent policy could influence complementarity's catalysing effect. With respect to the opening of an investigation, the first Prosecutor stated that, while he was willing to use his *proprio motu* power to trigger an investigation, he preferred referrals, on account of the fact that they increase the chances of state cooperation.[249] With respect to prosecutions, he indicated that it was 'the policy of the OTP to bring only a few cases from each situation'.[250] The OTP announced a 'sequenced' approach to selection, 'investigating specific cases within a situation one after another rather than all at once'.[251] With respect to the substance, '[i]n principle, incidents will be selected to provide a sample that is reflective of the gravest incidents and the main types of victimization'.[252] Finally, the first Prosecutor announced that he would focus on 'those who bear the greatest responsibility'.[253] In his view, the Court 'was created to investigate and prosecute the worst perpetrators, responsible for the worst crimes, those bearing the greatest responsibility, the organizers, the planners, the commanders'.[254] This focus does not flow self-evidently from the Statute,[255] but the Prosecutor derived it from '[t]he global character of the ICC, its statutory provisions and

---

[245] Cf. *contra Amicus Curiae Request Women's Initiatives for Gender Justice DRC.*
[246] RS, art. 58(1)(a) and (7).   [247] *Ibid.*, art. 61(7).   [248] *Ibid.*, art. 74.
[249] ICC-OTP 2003a:5 and ICC-OTP 2006d:7.   [250] ICC-OTP 2006e:12.
[251] *Ibid.*:10.   [252] ICC-OTP 2006d:8.
[253] ICC-OTP 2003d:7. See also ICC-OTP 2003d:3, Moreno-Ocampo 2004b, ICC-OTP 2006e:10, ICC-OTP 2006d:23, and, adding a caveat, ICC-OTP 2003d:3 and ICC-OTP 2006e:13.
[254] Moreno-Ocampo 2007b:8.
[255] Unlike e.g. ICTY RPE, rule 28(A), and SCSL Statute, art. 1, the Rome Statute does not single out a particular group of perpetrators.

logistical constraints'.[256] These aspects of the Prosecutor's policy could influence complementarity's catalysing effect by indicating which cases the Prosecutor will focus on and hence with respect to which cases a state must proceed domestically if it wishes to avoid or end ICC proceedings.

The policy of positive complementarity

Soon after beginning its operations, the OTP launched the policy of 'positive complementarity', a policy presented as explicitly aiming to boost complementarity's catalysing effect.[257] Accordingly, the OTP 'will encourage national proceedings wherever possible'.[258] Some OTP or OTP-supported documents provided ideas for implementing the policy. Without going into detail, they mentioned the OTP's providing states with information received from public sources,[259] with evidence (gathered by the Court),[260] with advice regarding national proceedings[261] and with training and technical support;[262] acting as an intermediary between states, brokering assistance and facilitating situations where states may assist one another in carrying out national proceedings;[263] promoting national proceedings, traditional mechanisms or other tools;[264] and developing legal tools to facilitate cooperation and empower domestic criminal jurisdictions.[265]

The reference to 'complementarity' in the name of the policy is misleading. The rationale for the policy may be helping states to use their primary right to exercise jurisdiction over crimes within the Court's jurisdiction, as recognised by the complementarity principle. The effectuation of the policy, however, comes down to cooperation, albeit not the type of cooperation that dominates the Statute: rather than states assisting in the Court's proceedings, the policy requires the

---

[256] ICC-OTP 2003d:7. The statutory provisions referred to are recitals and articles on the substantive jurisdiction of the Court, on the requirement of sufficient gravity and on the interests-of-justice clause as a ground for refraining from proceedings.

[257] See, *inter plurima alia*, the OTP's Special Advisor on Crime Prevention Méndez 2011:50 ('Under its policy of positive complementarity, the Office of the Prosecutor can act as a catalyst for national action.').

[258] Moreno-Ocampo 2004c:1.

[259] Moreno-Ocampo 2003b, ICC-OTP 2003d:5, and, not referring to 'public', ICC-ASP/5/6 (2006):3.

[260] ICC-OTP 2006a.

[261] ICC-OTP 2003c:3–4. But cf. *contra* Moreno-Ocampo 2011:25.

[262] Moreno-Ocampo 2003b.   [263] ICC-OTP 2003c:6.

[264] ICC-OTP 2006c.   [265] ICC-OTP 2006d.

Court to facilitate domestic proceedings. But such a policy of assisting domestic jurisdictions is not inherent in complementarity – courts with primacy of jurisdiction could also have, indeed have had,[266] similar policies.[267]

Moreover, the Statute puts important limitations on the Court's, in particular the OTP's, capability to implement such policies. The organs of the Court enjoy only those powers that the Statute grants them, explicitly or impliedly.[268] Only for some of the suggested aspects of the policy of positive complementarity does the Statute explicitly provide the OTP with powers. For instance, the Prosecutor could use his power under article 15(2) and rule 104 to seek additional information from states when considering whether or not to open an investigation in order to alert states implicitly to the OTP's close monitoring of a situation. The notification procedure under article 18 also gives states a chance to claim their primary right to investigate and prosecute and allows the Prosecutor, if he or she defers, to request information on the domestic proceedings.[269] The most explicit power for action that could be classified as a form of positive complementarity is provided by article 93(10) of the Statute:[270]

> (a) The Court may, upon request, cooperate with and provide assistance to a State Party conducting an investigation into or trial in respect of conduct which constitutes a crime within the jurisdiction of the Court or which constitutes a serious crime under the national law of the requesting State.
> (b) (i) The assistance provided under subparagraph (a) shall include, *inter alia*:

---

[266] See e.g. Tolbert and Kontić 2011.

[267] Nonetheless, the ICC's use of the term 'complementarity' to describe its (potential) assistance to domestic jurisdictions seems to have been so successful that the ICTY Prosecutor describes the *ICTY's* cooperation with national jurisdictions as 'complementarity' (RC/11 Annex V(c) (2010):[14]: 'He recalled that, at the inception of the *ad hoc* tribunals, complementarity was a "side-product" while today it had become a main priority'). For similar usage of the term, see El Zeidy 2008a:406 and Stahn 2011a:2.

[268] Cf. *contra* Bassiouni 2005:194.

[269] See this chapter, 'A state can directly influence the scope of the ICC's investigation on grounds of complementarity', and RS, art. 18(5). If the Prosecutor defers to national proceedings pursuant to art. 18, he or she is not under an obligation to share information or evidence with the state requesting the deferral. See also Arsanjani 1999:71.

[270] See, on the discretionary nature of this power, UN Doc. A/51/22 (1996):72–3.

a. The transmission of statements, documents or other types of evidence obtained in the course of an investigation or a trial conducted by the Court; and

b. The questioning of any person detained by order of the Court;

(ii) In the case of assistance under subparagraph (b)(i)a:

a. If the documents or other types of evidence have been obtained with the assistance of a State, such transmission shall require the consent of that State;

b. If the statements, documents or other types of evidence have been provided by a witness or expert, such transmission shall be subject to the provisions of article 68 [relating to the protection of victims and witnesses].

(c) The Court may, under the conditions set out in this paragraph, grant a request for assistance under this paragraph from a State which is not a Party to this Statute.

While the forms of assistance listed in article 93(10)(b) are merely illustrative,[271] the text[272] and context[273] of article 93(10)(a) leave no doubt that the envisaged cooperation and assistance are limited to judicial assistance and do not extend to general or technical assistance. The text also makes clear that the state must take the initiative and request the specific assistance or cooperation with respect to that specific investigation or trial:[274] the article does not provide for the Court *proprio motu* to supply the state with information to encourage domestic proceedings. Moreover, the state concerned must have started some form of investigation with respect to specific conduct: the Court cannot just hand over all or part of its evidence regarding crimes committed in the entire situation. Apart from its powers to seek information from states and to provide judicial cooperation and assistance at a state's request in specific domestic proceedings, the OTP lacks explicit powers to encourage or facilitate domestic proceedings.[275]

---

[271] See also Moreno-Ocampo 2011:24 and Ciampi 2002:1742.

[272] The provision refers to a request by a state 'conducting an investigation into or trial in respect of conduct which . . .'.

[273] The other paragraphs of art. 93 also concern specific requests for cooperation, albeit requests from the Court to states.

[274] See also Kress and Prost 2008:margin 61. Note that national legislation may not allow the use of ICC evidence in national proceedings, on account of its not having been acquired in accordance with domestic rules of evidence.

[275] Burke-White 2008b:81–2, mentions art. 54(3)(d) as another legal basis for a power of the Prosecutor to encourage domestic prosecutions. However, art. 54,

Neither does the Statute provide a strong basis for the argument that powers to encourage or facilitate domestic proceedings may be implied. Implied powers are 'those powers which, though not expressly provided ... are conferred ... by necessary implication as being essential to the performance of [the ICC's/OTP's] duties'.[276] The Statute contains no duty that necessarily implies a power on the part of the Prosecutor to engage in discussions with states over national proceedings (beyond receiving information about such proceedings),[277] let alone a power to act as a state's advisor in national proceedings.[278] Nonetheless, if the OTP were to appropriate and exercise powers that it has not been explicitly or impliedly granted, its actions might in time become lawful if the ASP consistently acquiesces in them.[279]

Instead of implying powers to encourage and facilitate domestic proceedings, the mandate the Statute grants the OTP may actually limit the possibilities for implementing a policy of positive complementarity. The OTP must at all times be in a position impartially to

---

and in this context art. 54(3)(d), clearly concern cooperation by states to facilitate the Court's proceedings, not *vice versa*. Burke-White 2008a:68's response that this distinction 'is not legally significant' fails to explain why not. The argument that 'such strategic use of interactions is fully in keeping with the object and purpose of the Rome Statute' is too weak a straw in light of the analysis above ('An obligation to investigate or prosecute pursuant to the Rome Statute?') on the Statute's object and purpose. Burke-White 2008a:65 also argues that 'affirmative authority on the Prosecutor to engage in positive complementarity' can be conferred by a 'conception of the Rome System of Justice' according to which complementarity is 'a broader principle [than an admissibility rule] that allocates authority among concurrently empowered institutions at different levels of governance within an international justice system'. However, doctrinal conceptions are not a source of institutional powers.

[276] ICJ, *Reparation for Injuries*:182.

[277] Cf. *contra* Burke-White 2008b:80, referring for such a legal basis to art. 42 of the Statute (on the task of the OTP) and to the Statute's presumed object and purpose of ending impunity (see also Burke-White 2008a:69). However, art. 42 exclusively concerns proceedings before the Court and, even if the Court's object and purpose were to 'end impunity' (see above section, 'An obligation to investigate or prosecute pursuant to the Rome Statute?'), it is to end impunity by means of a court vested with the powers specified in the Statute. The preambular reference to this or any other aim does not allow an organ of the Court freely to arrogate powers to itself only because such powers would promote, in its opinion, the aims stated in the preamble.

[278] See also Bitti 2007.

[279] See PCIJ, *Serbian Loans*:38, ICJ, *South West Africa*:[22] and PCA, *Eritrea–Ethiopia Boundary Delimitation*:[3:8].

assess whether a state is genuinely conducting domestic proceedings. Some forms of assistance to states, for instance substantial involvement in domestic capacity-building, gathering evidence for domestic proceedings or providing advice on domestic legislation or prosecutorial policies, may threaten the Prosecutor's required impartiality, or appearance of impartiality, in making such an assessment, particularly if the assistance affects cases that the OTP considers prosecuting.[280]

Finally, even to the extent the Statute allows the Court to assist domestic justice systems, human and financial resource constraints limit its capacity actually to do so. Turning over evidence can be relatively cheap.[281] Equally, the budget may provide sufficient resources for the OTP's Jurisdiction, Complementarity and Cooperation Division (JCCD) to communicate to states the Prosecutor's potential involvement and to explain the relevant procedures.[282] However, sending staff as trainers, conducting investigations for the benefit of domestic proceedings or providing the physical infrastructure for domestic trials would be more difficult to bring within the budget.

To date, positive complementarity has not received endorsement from the ICC's Chambers. With respect to the only possible statutory basis for the policy, one Chamber refused to acknowledge any connection between article 93(10) and complementarity. In response to the Government of Kenya's argument that it could properly challenge admissibility only after the Court had decided on, and granted, a request for the OTP's sharing of evidence with the Kenyan authorities, the Chamber categorically separated article 93(10) as a provision on cooperation from complementarity as a rule of admissibility.[283]

---

[280] See also ICC-OTP 2003c:3 and 7 and Seils 2011:1011–13.

[281] Witness protection, which, pursuant to RS, art. 93(10)(b)(ii)(b), continues to be available if the ICC transmits evidence provided by a witness or expert to a state, could be expensive, but, according to RS, art. 100(1)(a) and (2), the state requesting the evidence would have to bear the costs of such protection.

[282] Arguing that 'the Office of the Prosecutor must have a strong capacity to conduct external relations activities as required by the complementarity regime of the Rome Statute [which] involves, *inter alia*, a complementarity dialogue with relevant states' (ICC-ASP/2/10 (2003):174), the Court has several times requested extra staff for the relevant section within the OTP. By and large, none or only a few of the requested extra positions have been granted. See, *inter alia*, ICC-ASP/3/25 (2004)-b:13, ICC-ASP/3/25 (2004)-c:193, ICC-ASP/4/32 (2005)-a:14 and ICC-ASP/4/32 (2005)-b:192–3.

[283] *Admissibility Decision Ruto et al. (PTC)*:[34] and *Admissibility Decision Muthaura et al. (PTC)*:[30] ('[T]he Cooperation Request ... is actually a request for

Nonetheless, the Chamber then denied the Government of Kenya's request on grounds remarkably similar to those used to reject the admissibility challenge, namely, lack of proof of domestic investigations:

> [T]he Government of Kenya has not satisfied the first requirement of the test [of article 93(10)], namely that there is or has been an ongoing investigation with respect to either 'conduct' constituting a crime set out in article 5 of the Statute, or in relation to 'a serious crime under the national law of the requesting State'. The Government submitted to the Chamber a two-page Cooperation Request, which lacked any documentary proof that there is or has been an investigation, as required pursuant to article 93(10)(a) of the Statute.[284]

Too strict an application of this evidentiary test[285] could result in a Kafkaesque situation. Confronted with ICC proceedings against persons with respect to whom a state has not opened a case because of a lack of evidence, a state may wish to ask the ICC for such evidence – but in order to obtain such evidence from the ICC it must first prove that it has investigated the person, for which it requires the evidence that it lacks. Even if conceptually and procedurally separated, the complementarity proceedings of articles 17 to 20 and the 'positive complementarity' proceeding of article 93(10) thus share in practice the characteristic that they make it difficult for a state confronted with a Court that is unwilling to let go of a case or of evidence.

---

assistance which falls within the pure ambit of part IX of the Statute regulating the cooperation between the Court and States or other intergovernmental organisations. As such, the request for assistance has no linkage with the issue of admissibility, which is regulated under part II of the Statute. Ergo, a determination on the inadmissibility of a case pursuant to article 17 of the Statute does not depend on granting or denying a request for assistance under article 93(10) of the Statute. This conclusion finds support in the fact that a State may exercise its national jurisdiction by way of investigating or prosecuting, irrespective of and independent from any investigative activities of the Prosecutor.'). See also, respectively, *ibid.*:[35] and [31].

[284] *Decision Cooperation Request Government of Kenya*:[34].

[285] Even more so if combined with the same-person test that the OTP proposed in its submissions (*OTP Submission Art. 93(10) Request in Ruto et al.*:[4]: 'Kenya has not established that there is an investigation ongoing in Kenya against *the same individuals* under investigation before the ICC. If there is no investigation, the request for assistance does not satisfy the statutory language in Article 93(10)(a).').

The Assembly of States Parties, for its part, has appropriated 'positive complementarity', thereby simultaneously endorsing the concept and divesting the Office of the Prosecutor of its monopoly on the policy. The preparatory report shaping the discussions at the Review Conference's 'stocktaking exercise' on complementarity limited the OTP's role in positive complementarity by definition:

> positive complementarity refers to all activities/actions whereby national jurisdictions are strengthened and enabled to conduct genuine national investigations and trials of crimes included in the Rome Statute, *without involving the Court* in capacity building, financial support and technical assistance, but instead leaving these actions and activities for States, to assist each other on a voluntary basis.[286]

It continued by stressing that it was 'important to note the Court's core mandate and function which is a judicial one and to emphasize that the Court is not a development agency'.[287] Instead, the report shifted positive complementarity to the action radius of states and their development agencies, international organisations and 'civil society'.[288] The concluding resolution, without using the term 'positive complementarity', embraced the ideas of the report, '[r]ecogni-[sing] the desirability for States to assist each other in strengthening domestic capacity to ensure that investigations and prosecutions of serious crimes of international concern can take place at the national level',[289] and '[e]ncourag[ing] the Court, States Parties and other stakeholders, including international organizations and civil society, to further explore ways in which to enhance the capacity of national jurisdictions to investigate and prosecute serious crimes of international concern as set out in the Report of the Bureau on complementarity, including its recommendations'.[290] In the Conference's 'Kampala Declaration', the states parties resolved 'to continue and strengthen effective domestic implementation of the Statute, to enhance the capacity of national jurisdictions to prosecute the perpetrators of the most serious crimes of international concern in

---

[286] ICC-ASP/8/Res.9 Annex 4 (2010):[16].

[287] *Ibid.*:[4]. Reiterated again in [42] ('The role of the organs of the Court is limited. It is not envisaged that the activities described here would entail additional resource for the Court, nor should the Court become a development organization or an implementing agency.') and [52] ('The aim is not to create new roles for the Court.').

[288] *Ibid.*:[17] and [42].   [289] RC/Res.1 (2010):[5].   [290] *Ibid.*:[8].

accordance with internationally recognized fair trial standards, pursuant to the principle of complementarity'.[291] Nonetheless, since Kampala, both the OTP and the Registry have continued to stress their roles in 'positive' or 'proactive' complementarity.[292]

In sum, whilst without a solid legal basis in the Rome Statute, the policy of positive complementarity, whether implemented by ICC organs or states, international organisations or non-governmental organisations, could be influential for complementarity's catalysing effect, as the policy's explicit aim is to catalyse developments at the domestic level.

CONCLUSION: COMPLEMENTARITY AND ITS POTENTIAL CATALYSING EFFECT

The principle of complementarity is, as a matter of law, not imbued with strong normativity *vis-à-vis* states; complementarity is embodied in an admissibility rule that binds the Court. Neither complementarity nor any other provision in the Statute obliges states parties to investigate or prosecute crimes within the Court's jurisdiction. Nor can the Court adjudicate upon or enforce any obligation under customary law to that effect. The Chambers have thus found no legal objection against states referring situations on their own territory to the Court. Nor does complementarity or any other provision in the Statute oblige states to proscribe genocide, crimes against humanity or war crimes as defined in the Statute.[293] In other words, the legal context in which the principle of complementarity operates does not require amendments to domestic criminal law.[294] Finally, the Statute does not prohibit states from using amnesties. These facts should reduce expectations of complementarity's catalysing effect on normative grounds.

If states do want to make use of their primary right to investigate and prosecute crimes within the Court's jurisdiction and displace the

---

[291] RC-4-ENG-04062010 (2010):[5]. The linkage of complementarity with general 'internationally recognized fair trial standards' is an example of complementarity as 'big idea' departing from complementarity as legal principle (see above: 'The ICC is not a human rights court overseeing compliance with fair trial rights').

[292] See e.g. Moreno-Ocampo 2011 and Arbia and Bassy 2011.

[293] The Statute obliges states parties to proscribe only crimes against the ICC's administration of justice: RS, art. 70(4).

[294] The Statute only requires states to ensure that domestic law facilitates cooperation with the Court: RS, art. 88.

Court on grounds of complementarity, some of the criteria set forth in articles 17 and 20(3) set clear standards for domestic proceedings to meet in order to render cases inadmissible before the ICC. For instance, the Statute suggests that only criminal investigations and prosecutions, and not alternative mechanisms, count as domestic proceedings. By providing states with a sort of checklist for inadmissibility, these criteria have the potential to shape such proceedings.

At the same time, these provisions give states considerable leeway. States must charge the same 'conduct', but not necessarily the same 'crime', as the ICC. Equally, they need conduct only a 'genuine' (in the sense of 'bona fide' and 'effective') domestic investigation or prosecution: they need not conduct their proceedings the same way as the ICC, so that, for instance, they need not apply the same fair trial rights or the same punishments. This may limit complementarity's catalysing effect on the substance and procedure of domestic proceedings but may at the same time enhance its catalysing effect on domestic proceedings as such by allowing states to join a global anti-impunity struggle by following their own procedures.

Some of complementarity's procedural aspects are also conducive to a catalysing effect. First, complementarity must be assessed irrespective of the mechanism by which the situation has come within the Court's jurisdiction. States have the primary right to investigate and prosecute even if the Security Council has referred a situation to the Court. Secondly, states are not prohibited from conducting proceedings in parallel with the ICC. Finally, the assessment of admissibility is dynamic. The Statute allows the Prosecutor and judges to review admissibility at several stages of the proceedings.[295] States can influence the factual basis on which admissibility is decided by beginning domestic proceedings in order to render ICC cases inadmissible, even after the ICC has begun proceedings.[296]

On the other hand, it is difficult for a state to prevent or end ICC investigations into a situation on grounds of complementarity. Since

---

[295] On the other hand, the Appeals Chamber's treatment of complementarity more as an issue going to the rights of interested states and defendants than as a matter of public policy to be insisted on so as to avoid duplication of national and international proceedings does not encourage states to play their part in the prosecution of international crimes.

[296] The case law that confirms this, *Admissibility Judgment Katanga* (AC), stems, however, from the opposite scenario, namely, one in which an ICC case becomes admissible because a state stays domestic proceedings.

the admissibility assessment is case-specific at all stages of ICC proceedings, the Prosecutor may decide to open an investigation when there are 'cases' that may be admissible, even if a state is investigating or prosecuting other cases emerging from the situation in question. Once the Prosecutor has opened an investigation into a situation, a state can render a specific case inadmissible before the ICC by conducting domestic proceedings, but has no way of obliging the Prosecutor to end his or her investigations into that situation.

The fact that the complementarity assessment is case-specific and not situation-specific may also limit the catalysing effect on a state's overall criminal justice system. In order to render a case inadmissible before the ICC, a state need prove not that its criminal justice system meets 'international standards' but merely that it is capable of conducting genuine proceedings in the particular case. At the same time, this could enhance a catalysing effect on proceedings as such: for a state the task of conducting such proceedings may be less daunting when it has to conduct genuine investigations and prosecutions only in the case at hand rather than overhaul its entire justice system.

In sum, as embodied in the Statute, complementarity does not give states concrete instructions, but allows states to displace the Court in a particular case (rather than a situation) by conducting genuine proceedings in that case. In terms of shaping domestic proceedings, complementarity's potential catalysing effect is thus limited, at least on the basis of the Statute. This may, however, at the same time encourage domestic investigations and prosecutions: various types of domestic criminal proceedings could be successful in rendering cases inadmissible before the Court. *Ex pluribus unum*, diverse domestic proceedings could all contribute to the same anti-impunity ideal symbolised by the Statute: in combating impunity, all roads lead to Rome.

However, the Court's case law on the definition of the same 'case' has significantly reduced this leeway should states wish to pre-empt future ICC proceedings or stymie ongoing proceedings before the Court. In finding all the cases before it to date admissible on grounds of complementarity, the Court has mostly relied on the ground that domestic proceedings did not cover the same 'case' as the one before the ICC. The Court has defined the term 'case' so narrowly that domestic proceedings are not considered to have taken place in the same 'case' unless they cover the same person, conduct, incidents and, possibly, mode of criminal responsibility as the case before the Court.

This case law was developed in scenarios in which the state with national and territorial jurisdiction perceived that it was in its interest that the ICC conducted the proceedings. A finding of inadmissibility before the ICC thus might well have resulted in impunity. But, instead of finding the case inadmissible on the basis of the real problem – a lack of actual investigations – the Chambers developed an interpretation of the word 'case' that makes it almost impossible for a state successfully to challenge admissibility on the basis of genuine domestic proceedings, also in scenarios where a state does not consider ICC intervention in its interest.

The case law is based on a vision in which there is no 'concurrence' in the sense of overlapping claims to jurisdiction, and therefore no reason to apply the priority rule of complementarity if the same person, conduct or incident has not been or is not being investigated or prosecuted domestically. In situations in which crimes within the Court's jurisdiction have been committed it usually is impossible for any prosecutor, domestic or international, to investigate and prosecute all suspects, criminal conduct and criminal incidents. Procedurally, it is also difficult for a state to 'catch up' with the ICC. On the one hand, the Statute requires the state to challenge admissibility 'at the earliest opportunity',[297] but the state can be sure of the contents of the ICC's case only after the confirmation of charges. As the Kenya decisions have borne out, for a successful admissibility challenge the state must show evidence of investigations into the same persons and (substantially) the same conduct. On the other hand, if a state investigated and prosecuted before the ICC opened a case it cannot be sure that it will keep the ICC at bay since the ICC Prosecutor can always choose different conduct or incidents. In practice, it is thus virtually impossible to render cases inadmissible before the ICC.

From an exclusive anti-impunity perspective, this is precisely why the Court was established: to eradicate every remnant of impunity. This vision counters the argument that there always is some subjectivity in the availability of evidence, whether to a domestic or international prosecutor, with the argument that this is even more a reason for domestic and international proceedings to complement each other (in the literal sense): more impunity will be combated.[298] This vision

---

[297] RS, art. 19(5).

[298] See *Admissibility Judgment Ruto et al.* (AC):[43]–[44] and *Admissibility Judgment Muthaura et al.* (AC):[42]–[43] ('Kenya [counters] that a national jurisdiction may

refuses to acknowledge that a state may have other interests (for instance, stability) that require some domestic discretion or avoidance of, or an end to, ICC involvement. In the Court's approach, complementarity thus protects sovereignty only to the extent that the state joins in a total war on impunity. Rather than encouraging domestic proceedings, this case law potentially dissuades states from trying to pursue cases in the ICC's stead. After all is said and done, the ICC prevails: all roads seem to lead to The Hague.[299]

Whilst this case law developed, ICC organs proclaimed outside the courtrooms a policy of positive complementarity with the explicit purpose of catalysing domestic proceedings. According to this policy, the OTP, and according to itself also the Registry, will do everything within their capabilities to ensure that states can and will investigate and prosecute international crimes. Given its purpose, this policy has an obvious potential to encourage complementarity's catalysing effect.

And yet, the fact that positive complementarity is based on policy rather than law makes its catalysing effect difficult to predict.

not always have the same evidence available as the Prosecutor and therefore may not be investigating the same suspects as the Court. This argument is not persuasive for two reasons. First, if a State does not investigate a given suspect because of lack of evidence, then there simply is no conflict of jurisdictions, and no reason why the case should be inadmissible before the Court. Second, what is relevant for the admissibility of a concrete case under articles 17(1)(a) and 19 of the Statute is not whether the same evidence in the Prosecutor's possession is available to a State, but whether the State is carrying out steps directed at ascertaining whether these suspects are responsible for substantially the same conduct as is the subject of the proceedings before the Court. Kenya also argues that there should be a "leeway in the exercise of discretion in the application of the principle of complementarity" to allow domestic proceedings to progress. This argument has no merit because, as explained above, the purpose of the admissibility proceedings under article 19 of the Statute is to determine whether the case brought by the Prosecutor is inadmissible because of a jurisdictional conflict. Unless there is such a conflict, the case is admissible. The suggestion that there should be a presumption in favour of domestic jurisdictions does not contradict this conclusion. Although article 17(1)(a) to (c) of the Statute does indeed favour national jurisdictions, it does so only to the extent that there actually are, or have been, investigations and/or prosecutions at the national level. If the suspect or conduct have not been investigated by the national jurisdiction, there is no legal basis for the Court to find the case inadmissible' (footnotes omitted)).

[299] The Court could head in a different direction by interpreting the Appeals Chamber's use of the phrase 'substantially the same conduct', instead of the Pre-Trial Chambers' requirement of the 'same conduct' in order to adopt a more general assessment of whether impunity has been sufficiently addressed.

Whether or not and if so how and when it is implemented is for the discretion of the Court's organs. States cannot rely on it. Indeed, as the Kenya cases show, the life of positive complementarity in public statements may be at odds with that in the courtroom. In public statements, 'positive complementarity' is a policy of cooperation with states inspired by states' primary right to investigate and prosecute. But, according to the Chambers, the only explicit legal basis for such a policy in the Statute, article 93(10), must be assessed separately from complementarity. And the Prosecutor, who first based the policy 'on the duty to cooperate established by art 93 10 and the principle of complementarity',[300] later submitted to the Court that it *disagreed* with the Government of Kenya that 'the Court is obligated to assist the Government of Kenya in order to promote complementarity and the State's effort to establish that the ICC prosecutions are inadmissible'.[301] The OTP continued by citing the Pre-Trial Chamber's dismissive statements in response to Kenya's invocation of the policy of positive complementarity, seemingly with approval, when arguing:

> This Chamber has previously held that 'the request for assistance has no linkage with the issue of admissibility'; 'a determination on the inadmissibility of a case pursuant to article 17 of the Statute does not depend on granting or denying a request for assistance under article 93(10) of the Statute'; 'a State may exercise its national jurisdiction by way of investigating or prosecuting, irrespective of and independent from any investigative activities of the Prosecutor'; '[t]hese domestic proceedings should be in principle carried out without the assistance of the Court'; and 'national investigative activities are conducted independently from this Court and based on the national laws of the Republic of Kenya'.[302]

Outside the courtroom, however, the OTP continues to express its commitment to its policy of positive complementarity.

---

[300] *Prosecution's Response Art. 93 Request Original Ruto et al.*:[13]. Note that the OTP seemed to backtrack on the obligatory character of its providing cooperation when amending this paragraph in *Corrigendum Prosecution's Response Art. 93 Request Original Ruto et al.*:[13] to read: 'Since 2003, the Prosecution has defined a policy of "positive complementarity" based on the provisions on cooperation established by article 93(10) and the preamble of Rome Statute.'

[301] *Prosecution's Response to Art. 93 Request in Kenya Situation*:[24] (footnotes omitted).

[302] *Ibid.* See also [6].

As the following chapters will illustrate, positive complementarity is only one illustration of the fact that complementarity's life as a legal principle in the Statute adjudicated upon in the courtroom has little to do with its life as 'big idea' in the wider world. And yet, it is particularly complementarity as 'big idea', and not as legal principle, that has spurred its catalysing effect. Undefined, devoid of judicial scrutiny and not legally binding as they are, big ideas are invoked, promoted and applied inconsistently and by various actors with various agendas. As a result, it is highly questionable that the effects catalysed by the 'big idea' of complementarity help in winning admissibility challenges adjudicated on the basis of the legal principle.

CHAPTER 3

UGANDA: COMPROMISING COMPLEMENTARITY

> *The Republic of Uganda has indicated that the ICC is the most appropriate and effective forum for the investigation and prosecution of those bearing the greatest responsibility for the crimes within the referred situation … Accordingly … the Ugandan authorities have not and do not intend to conduct national proceedings, preferring instead that the cases be dealt with by the ICC. With this in mind, I have determined … that the situation involves cases that would be admissible under article 17 of the Statute.*
>
> ICC Prosecutor Luis Moreno-Ocampo[1]

In December 2003, a Ugandan official flew to The Netherlands. In his briefcase was a twenty-seven-page letter containing the first ever referral to the ICC.[2]

Three months earlier and newly appointed, the Court's first Prosecutor had publicly stated his intention closely to follow the situation in the east of the Democratic Republic of the Congo (DRC) and had invited states to refer this situation to the Court.[3] The Ugandan official did not, however, carry a letter referring the situation in the DRC to the ICC. At the time, the International Court of Justice (ICJ) was adjudicating the DRC's claims that Uganda had violated international law in its involvement in eastern DRC.[4] The African Commission on Human and Peoples' Rights had already found for the DRC and against Uganda in relation to violations of human rights law and international humanitarian law.[5] Referral of the situation in the DRC

---

[1] *Notification Investigation Uganda*. Parts of this chapter also feature in Nouwen and Werner 2010a, Nouwen 2011, Nouwen 2012b and Nouwen 2014a, forthcoming.

[2] Interview with a Ugandan official involved in the referral, Kampala, October 2008.

[3] ICC-OTP 2003e:4.

[4] In *Armed Activities (DRC v. Uganda)*:[207] (see also [211] and [250]), the ICJ would later establish that the Ugandan armed forces had committed 'massive human rights violations and grave breaches of international humanitarian law' on the territory of the DRC.

[5] African Commission on Human and Peoples' Rights, *Democratic Republic of Congo v. Burundi, Rwanda and Uganda*.

to the ICC would trigger the jurisdiction of yet another international court that could establish the involvement of Ugandan state actors in war crimes in eastern DRC.[6] Rather than referring the situation in the DRC to the Court, Ugandan President Museveni wrote to the United Nations Secretary-General expressing his concern that an investigation into the conflict in the DRC would threaten the Congolese peace process.[7]

However, some of Uganda's foreign lawyers involved in the case before the ICJ, advised by colleagues working in international criminal justice, suggested to both the Government of Uganda (GoU) and the ICC's Office of the Prosecutor (OTP) that Uganda had a situation on *its own territory* that would be ideal for the ICC.[8] The OTP welcomed the idea.[9] So did the Ugandan Minister of Defence, Amama

---

[6] In its first judgment on the guilt of an accused, the ICC would mention in passing that Uganda had for some years supported defendant Thomas Lubanga in training child soldiers (*Judgment Lubanga* (TC) [1027]–[1037]).

[7] Letter from President Yoweri Katuga Museveni to H. E. Kofi Annan, Secretary-General of the UN, Re: Integration of Ituri Armed Groups, 3 July 2004, reported in: Human Rights Watch 2005a:117. See also, four years later, a letter from the Government of Uganda to the UN Sanctions Committee on the DRC, advising the Committee not to take any action upon the recommendation made by the Group of Experts to urge the DRC authorities to remove (ICC suspect) Bosco Ntaganda from his position of deputy commander of a specific operation of the national army. (UN Doc. S/AC.43/2009/COMM.64 (2009); thanks to Eric Witte for sharing this document).

[8] Interview with Minister of Internal Security (Minister of Defence at the time of the referral) Amama Mbabazi, Kampala, October 2008; interview with an international lawyer involved in the referral, The Hague, June 2008; phone interview with a former ICC official, June 2008 and email exchange with an international lawyer involved in the referral, July 2008. See also Schiff 2008:198. The idea of the ICC's investigating the situation in northern Uganda was not entirely new. Even before the entry into force of the Rome Statute, organisations such as UNICEF had suggested northern Uganda as a good case for the ICC (Allen 2006:82–3).

[9] Colleague Phil Clark goes further, arguing that 'for nearly a year before President Museveni referred the situation in Uganda to the ICC Prosecutor, there were substantial negotiations between The Hague and Kampala over the nature and ramifications of a state referral' and suggesting that 'Prosecutor Moreno-Ocampo approached President Museveni in 2003 and, despite the President's initial reluctance, persuaded him to refer the northern Uganda situation to the ICC' (Clark 2011:1198–9, referring to Clark 2008 and Clark 2009). Illustrating the difficulties of one type of empirical research, Clark cites interviews for his views, while the Ugandan officials and lawyers involved in the referral whom I interviewed explicitly denied that there was any such discussion between the ICC and Ugandan

Mbabazi,[10] one of President Museveni's closest advisors.[11] Subsequently, a foreign international lawyer drafted, the Ugandan Attorney-General signed and the Ugandan official, once arrived at the ICC in The Hague, submitted a letter referring the 'Situation concerning the Lord's Resistance Army' to the ICC.[12]

The referral was the wedding ring in an arranged marriage of convenience between Uganda and the ICC. Little catalysing effect was thus to be expected on the part of complementarity, a principle that allowed Uganda to obstruct the ICC's exercise of jurisdiction. Indeed, on the face of it, Uganda's history with the ICC shows the opposite of a catalysing effect on domestic proceedings. Rather than

officials prior to the referral. So did interviewed ICC officials. Whereas there may have been informal consultations between Ugandan and OTP officials, my data indicate that the initiative was not with the ICC Prosecutor but with Uganda's foreign lawyers. Moreover, it is questionable that the 'nature and ramifications' of the referral as such were discussed between Uganda and the OTP *prior to* the referral in December 2003. Only in 2008 did Prosecutor Ocampo begin to mention Uganda as an invited self-referral, whereas with respect to the DRC he had done so explicitly from the outset (Moreno-Ocampo 2008c). The correspondence between the ICC and Uganda that Clark cites in Clark 2011:1199 (reported in Izama 2008) dates from *after* the referral; it is uncontested that such discussions occurred after the referral. It can be argued that, precisely because the referral letter had been drafted by Uganda's foreign lawyers prior to substantive discussions on the 'nature and ramifications' of the referral, there was a lot to clarify in discussions between the GoU and the OTP after the referral, most importantly the fact that, despite Uganda's referral of the 'LRA', the OTP would be able to investigate all sides to the conflict in northern Uganda. Indeed, it is noteworthy that, in contrast to all other referral letters, the OTP has not made Uganda's letter public, perhaps because the letter clearly shows the GoU's intention that only the LRA would be prosecuted and because the GoU seems to deny in the letter that there is an armed conflict in northern Uganda. Possibly because of this experience, the OTP was in fact involved in the drafting of the letter by which the DRC referred the situation on its territory to the Court (interview with an ICC official involved in the drafting, The Hague, June 2008). With respect to the LRA referral, more evidence is needed to tell what was discussed prior to the referral.

10 Interview with Amama Mbabazi, Kampala, October 2008.
11 Amama Mbabazi is also referred to as the 'Super Minister' on account of the fact that he has held many important positions in the government (Minister of Defence, Minister of Security, Prime Minister, Attorney-General, sometimes at the same time) and positions in the National Resistance Movement (Chairman of the Delegates Caucus, Secretary-General).
12 Uganda 2003:[1]. Thanks to Adam Branch, who received the letter at a workshop on the ICC in Kampala in 2004 (see Branch 2011:276), for sharing this document.

trying to avoid ICC intervention through the conduct of domestic investigations and prosecutions, the GoU invited the ICC into Uganda by referring a situation on its territory to the Court. Rather than considering ICC intervention as costly to its sovereignty and reputation, the GoU expected, and obtained, dividends from the intervention.

And yet, complementarity did have a catalysing effect in Uganda, especially when the marriage began to show cracks.

THE CONTEXT FOR CATALYSIS

Before turning to the effects that complementarity catalysed in Uganda, we must understand the dynamics of the context in which they took place. One key dynamic is that of the relationship between the GoU and the ICC. As this section will elaborate, the referral launched a joint enterprise based on a convergence of ICC and GoU interests. Initially, neither party paid much attention to complementarity; scrutiny of admissibility could only threaten the partnership. However, the interests of the ICC and the GoU seemed to diverge at the start of the Juba peace process. Whilst itself still committed to ICC involvement, the GoU was under pressure to end this. It was then that complementarity became the linchpin of the talks and agreements. These agreements, in turn, provided the starting point for some important effects of complementarity. Some of these effects continued even when the GoU's and ICC's interests were visibly realigned.

The ICC in Uganda: a joint enterprise

The ICC Prosecutor and the Ugandan President announced the referral of the 'situation concerning the Lord's Resistance Army' at a joint press conference in London on 29 January 2004.[13] In the referral letter – not yet made public by the ICC – the Ugandan Government accused members of the Lord's Resistance Army (LRA) of crimes against humanity. The letter did not mention war crimes, presumably because the GoU believed that such allegations could be read as undermining its argument that 'the LRA does not qualify as a belligerent entitled to the lawful conduct of hostilities'.[14] The letter was equally silent on the possible commission of crimes by the Ugandan

[13] ICC 2004.   [14] Uganda 2003:[34].

114

People's Defence Forces (UPDF): the GoU referred to the Court the 'situation concerning the Lord's Resistance Army' – not the UPDF.

NGOs, however, were quick to advocate that the ICC should equally investigate the UPDF.[15] The Prosecutor thus informed the Ugandan authorities: 'we must interpret the scope of the referral consistently with the principles of the Rome Statute, and hence we are analyzing crimes within the situation of northern Uganda by whomever committed'.[16] The OTP changed the name of the situation from 'situation concerning the Lord's Resistance Army' into 'situation in northern Uganda'.[17]

Nonetheless, to date, the Prosecutor has opened an investigation and requested warrants of arrest only with respect to the LRA. On 8 July 2005, the Court issued warrants against Joseph Kony, Vincent Otti, Raska Lukwiya, Okot Odhiambo and Dominic Ongwen. The five LRA commanders are alleged to bear individual criminal responsibility for crimes against humanity and war crimes committed in a non-international armed conflict, including rape, murder, enslavement, sexual enslavement and forced enlistment of children.[18] At the time of writing, none of the five warrants has been executed. Two of the five persons are either dead[19] or presumed dead.[20] Concerning further cases against the LRA, the OTP has stated that it will further

---

[15] Amnesty International 2004b, Human Rights Watch 2004 and International Crisis Group 2004:20.

[16] *Letter from the Chief Prosecutor to the President of the Court Uganda*:4.

[17] The Presidency subsequently assigned to PTC II the situation 'in Uganda'. Geographical names of the situation are misleading with respect to the Court's jurisdiction, since many in the OTP acknowledge that the situation is defined by the scope of the conflict rather than on the basis of fixed geographical boundaries. In this view, the Prosecutor could, without prior PTC authorisation, investigate allegations of crimes committed by Ugandans in neighbouring countries as long as they relate to the conflict with the LRA (in this sense, it is still the 'situation concerning the LRA'). However, all public charges thus far relate to crimes committed in northern Uganda.

[18] *Arrest Warrant Kony, Arrest Warrant Otti, Arrest Warrant Ongwen, Arrest Warrant Odhiambo* and *Arrest Warrant Lukwiya*.

[19] The Chamber terminated proceedings against Raska Lukwiya, having established that he was killed on 12 August 2006 (*Decision to Terminate Proceedings against Lukwiya*) in a fight with the UPDF (*Submission Information Lukwiya*).

[20] The arrest warrant against deputy LRA leader Otti is still effective, even though Kony does not deny having had him executed (*Submission Information Otti* and Egadu and P'Lajur 2008).

investigate only crimes committed after the request for the arrest warrants for the LRA leadership.[21]

Officially, ICC analysis of information concerning UPDF crimes is ongoing,[22] and the OTP only 'started' with an investigation of LRA members because it believed their crimes were graver.[23] A more convincing legal reason could be that the majority of the UPDF crimes were committed prior to the beginning of the Court's temporal jurisdiction, namely, 1 July 2002.[24] Even with respect to crimes allegedly committed by state actors within the Court's jurisdiction *ratione temporis*, it has become unlikely that the OTP will open an investigation: the OTP has reassigned its investigative staff in Uganda to other situations. The more realist explanation for the ICC's starting with – in fact exclusive focus on – the LRA is that any investigation into UPDF crimes would fall outside the terms of the marriage of convenience between Uganda and the ICC.

Uganda and the ICC: a marriage of convenience

At the time of the referral, both the ICC and the Ugandan Government considered ICC intervention in Uganda in their respective interests.[25] The Ugandan Government perceived the referral of the LRA to the ICC as a new means to obtain international support in its long-standing conflict with the relentless Ugandan rebel movement.[26] After seventeen years of combat and aborted peace negotiations, the GoU had proven unable either to vanquish or come to a settlement with the LRA. Corruption scandals, the failing military operations,

---

[21] ICC Prosecutor on radio Mega FM, transcript in an email dated 8 December 2005.

[22] *OTP Submission Status Conference Uganda*, Moreno-Ocampo 2007a:4 and Musoke and Oluput 2010.

[23] See Chapter 2, 'Looking for a catalysing effect: the potentially confounding and intervening variables'.

[24] According to RS, art. 11(1), the ICC has jurisdiction only with respect to crimes committed after the entry into force of the Statute, 1 July 2002. Uganda, which ratified the Statute on 14 June 2002, extended the Court's temporal jurisdiction from 1 September 2002 back to 1 July 2002 by lodging a declaration pursuant to RS, arts. 11(2) and 12(3), accepting the Court's jurisdiction as of the Statute's date of entry into force. (The GoU's 'declaration on temporal jurisdiction', dated 27 February 2004, is referred to in *Arrest Warrant Kony*:[32].)

[25] Parts of this section also appear in Nouwen and Werner 2010a and Nouwen and Werner 2011, in which the developments are assessed through the theoretical prism of the politics of international criminal justice.

[26] See also Refugee Law Project 2004.

their disastrous humanitarian consequences and the UN's classification of northern Uganda as the 'world's biggest neglected crisis'[27] were beginning to tarnish the government's reputation. Riots in the streets of Kampala arising from prosecutions of the government's political opponents aggravated the image problem for what had been a donor-darling government. After several years of rewarding Uganda for being Africa's leading 'post-conflict' success story,[28] international donors, funding between 35 and 50 per cent of Uganda's budget,[29] added their voice to local leaders' criticism of the government's failure to resolve the conflict in the north and to calls to end the government's human rights violations in combating the LRA.[30] Pressure for a peaceful solution was building.

For the Ugandan Government, asking the ICC to investigate and prosecute the LRA was a way to counter that pressure. The referral had the potential to worsen the image of the LRA and to improve that of the GoU, to delegitimise any suggestion of peace talks and to rally international support for continuation and intensification of the executive's preferred military approach. Following the GoU's previous attempts to brand the LRA as irrational, religious fundamentalists or terrorists, the ICC could brand the LRA as internationally wanted 'criminals'. The ICC could transform the LRA from enemies of the Ugandan Government into enemies of the international community as a whole.[31] ICC supporters would then no longer treat the LRA and the government as equal warmongers, but would view President Museveni's administration as a legitimate government

---

[27] 'Northern Uganda "world's biggest neglected crisis"' 2004. See also Egeland 2008:201.

[28] See Hauser 1999:632–4, Perrot 2005:3 and Mwenda 2007.

[29] The figure depends on the way in which the budget is composed. See also Tripp 2010:186 and Perrot 2005:6.

[30] See, inter alia, Lomo 2004:3–4.

[31] See, for example, President Museveni's address on the state of the nation in June 2005: 'The International Criminal Court is a good ally because it makes Kony untouchable as long as it has got indictment; anybody who touches him will have problems with the International Criminal Court, therefore, that is the advantage ... Like for instance, if Kony goes in the part of Sudan which is far away from where we operate and there is an indictment, they will be under pressure to follow him, but if there is no pressure, then he will be free. They wouldn't be as pressurised as when there is an ICC indictment' (Uganda 2005b). See also Museveni 2010:1–2, equating the fight against impunity with the just war theory.

fighting a criminal movement. The referral would thus recharacterise the GoU, the first government to refer a situation to the ICC, as an ally of the ICC, a champion of international criminal justice and a friend of mankind.[32] Linking the arrest of the LRA leadership to the credibility of the ICC,[33] European governments – staunch ICC supporters – would replace their criticism of UPDF abuses and of the GoU's failure to ameliorate the humanitarian situation in the north with renewed support for the UPDF's operations against the LRA 'criminals'.[34] Finally, a referral of the situation concerning the LRA had the additional potential benefit that it would make the ICC's Prosecutor dependent on the cooperation of the Ugandan Government; and the OTP might hesitate to jeopardise such cooperation by charging UPDF officials with crimes committed in neighbouring DRC.

The referral also suited the OTP. The Rome Statute had obtained the sixty ratifications required for its entry into force in a surprisingly short period, and the Court's supporters expected the ICC to prove its right to exist. This was given added urgency by the open hostility of the US.[35] Fearing for the Court's survival, its newly appointed staff felt pressure to select for the first investigations situations that would, at the least, reassure doubting states that the Court was not driven by a prosecutor zealously using *proprio motu* powers and, ideally, convince them of the Court's usefulness.[36] 'For the ICC', according to one international lawyer advising the Ugandan Government, 'the voluntary referral of a compelling case by a state party represented both an early expression of confidence in the

---

[32] See e.g. the Minister of State for Defence, explaining to the Ugandan Parliament: 'When you are fighting and you are engaged in something, you should know who your allies are. The ICC is an ally to Uganda. Uganda approached them when we had a problem. The LRA were outside our jurisdiction so we could not handle them. We approached the ICC. They responded and indicted these leaders' (Uganda 2006c). See also President Museveni's reference to the ICC as his 'allies' in his address on the state of the nation (Uganda 2006a).

[33] See also Akhavan 2005:404.

[34] See also Branch 2007 and Branch 2004.

[35] Discussion with a former ICC staff member, The Hague, May 2008: 'The US had more money available to destroy the ICC than we had for the ICC's start-up budget.'

[36] On the need for a cautious approach if the Court wished to gain the confidence of states not parties to the Statute, see also Cryer 2009:121 *et seq.*

nascent institution's mandate and a welcome opportunity to demonstrate its viability.'[37]

For the OTP, a self-referral had at least three potential advantages.[38] First, fears of the ICC's trampling on state sovereignty could be calmed. As Uganda had referred the situation itself, neither the Ugandan Government nor any other state could reasonably argue that the Court disrespected state sovereignty. Secondly, a self-referral could ease the Court's greatest handicap, namely, its total dependence on state cooperation for acts ranging from issuing visas for its investigators to executing its warrants of arrest. In its letter referring the situation to the ICC, the GoU had pledged 'full cooperation', at least with respect to 'the investigation and prosecution of *LRA* crimes'.[39] Finally, in case of a referral, as opposed to when using his *proprio motu* powers, the Prosecutor need not ask the Pre-Trial Chamber (PTC) for authorisation to open an investigation.[40]

But it was not just the self-referral that made the situation in Uganda attractive for the OTP. In an OTP official's words, Uganda was 'a perfect case for [the OTP's] first ... investigation'.[41] First, the OTP expected an investigation in Uganda to be relatively easy. *Vis-à-vis* situations already under preliminary analysis, for instance the DRC and the Central African Republic (CAR), the situation in Uganda concerned fewer parties, involved a smaller territory and lacked the sensitivities of a transitional government.[42] Secondly, the LRA topped the list of internationally ostracised groups – few would come to the defence of an armed band whose leadership has for a long time been stereotyped as a self-styled prophet with his acolytes abducting children and committing other crimes in the name of the Ten Commandments. An investigation of the LRA might even warm the US, officially hostile to any ICC action, towards the Court. The US shared the revulsion towards the LRA, as evidenced by the LRA's appearance on the US international terrorist list, and it had already ensured that Uganda would not hand over any US national to the ICC by concluding a 'bilateral immunity agreement'. Finally, the OTP counted on international cooperation in the arrest of the LRA, even from Sudan. The reasoning was that, in the same way that Uganda had discouraged

---

[37] Akhavan 2005:404.   [38] See also Nouwen and Werner 2010a.
[39] Uganda 2003:4 (emphasis added).   [40] Cf. RS, arts. 13(a) with 15(3).
[41] Brubacher 2013, forthcoming:1.
[42] Interview with a former ICC staff member, Amsterdam, June 2009.

ICC proceedings against the UPDF in the DRC situation by extending cooperation in the LRA case, Sudan would cooperate in the LRA case in order to distract attention from the Sudanese Government's role in Darfur.[43]

There are suggestions, although nothing more than that, that there was another non-legal reason for the OTP to welcome a referral of the situation in Uganda in particular. Most situations under preliminary examination in 2003 were in francophone and civil-law African states. Their orientation rendered the Court particularly dependent on cooperation from France and Belgium. The UK, however, had been one of the staunchest supporters of the Court and, in particular, of the election of the first Prosecutor. The favour could be returned by enhancing the UK's potential influence by opening an investigation in an anglophone, common-law and Commonwealth-oriented state.[44] An investigation in an anglophone state would also go some way in justifying the predominance of English-speaking staff in the OTP, which was in sharp contrast to the Registry that was known as 'little France'. An investigation into a common-law state by anglophone staff could thus influence the outcome of the struggle for dominance between lawyers from a common-law and lawyers from a civil-law background.[45] The Fashoda Incident still reverberates, also in The Hague.

Compromised complementarity

Against this background, the Ugandan Government as well as the ICC (OTP and PTC alike) considered complementarity only as a potential obstacle to a mutually beneficial cooperation. Both explicitly argued that the principle did not block any ICC investigations of the LRA.

The Ugandan referral letter followed the shorthand description of complementarity, dominant in the academic literature at the time, as a test of the willingness and ability of the overall justice system of a state

[43] Prosecutor Moreno-Ocampo reportedly said 'Khartoum will help me because of Darfur' (interview, Kampala, 2008). On Sudan's willingness to cooperate with the ICC in the LRA case, see Allio 2004.

[44] This view was put forward in interviews with three ICC officials (two former, one present). One former official refuted it when asked about it. Another informant confirmed that French officials expressed dissatisfaction with the Ugandan referral since it 'stole the thunder from DRC'.

[45] More generally on this battle during the negotiations of the Rome Statute and of the RPE, see Bitti 2004:273–4.

with jurisdiction over the alleged acts; the referral letter was written before the case law that emphasises that article 17 first requires an assessment as to whether or not the state has conducted any domestic proceedings in the same case.[46] The GoU argued that, '[h]aving exhausted every other means of bringing an end to this terrible suffering', it 'now turn[ed] to the newly established ICC and its promise of global justice'.[47]It emphasised that the Ugandan judicial system was 'widely recognised as one of the most independent and impartial and competent on the African continent'. There was 'no doubt that Ugandan courts have the capacity to give captured LRA leaders a fair and impartial trial'.[48] Nonetheless, Uganda had referred the situation because

> without international cooperation and assistance, it cannot succeed in arresting the members of the LRA leadership and others most responsible for [crimes against humanity]. Furthermore, Uganda is of the view that the scale and gravity of LRA crimes are such that they are a matter of concern to the international community as a whole. It is thus befitting both from a practical and moral viewpoint to entrust the investigation and prosecution of these crimes to the Prosecutor of the ICC.[49]

With respect to factors relevant to the admissibility assessment, the GoU did not say that it had never conducted any proceedings (the relevant test); nor did it say that it was unwilling to conduct domestic proceedings genuinely. Rather, the GoU argued that it was unable to conduct proceedings (an argument only relevant where domestic proceedings are or have been on foot but have been impeded by other events). But the GoU immediately qualified its 'inability':

> Inability in this instance does not in any way imply the total or substantial collapse of the national judicial system within the purview of Article 17(3), but merely the 'unavailability' of the system, because Uganda is 'unable to obtain the accused' since those most responsible are either sheltered in the Sudan, or in remote regions of Uganda for limited time periods, making arrest and prosecution difficult without international assistance.[50]

In short, Uganda argued the admissibility of cases emerging from the situation concerning the LRA on two grounds: first, its own inability to arrest the LRA leadership; secondly, that the ICC would be the

---

[46] On the shorthand description and subsequent case law, see Chapter 2, 'The substance of complementarity: the criteria for inadmissibility'.
[47] Uganda 2003:[6].   [48] Ibid.:[24].   [49] Ibid.:[25].   [50] Ibid.:[30].

most appropriate forum. Only the inability-to-arrest argument is a ground for admissibility recognised in the Rome Statute[51] (even though the ICC, entirely reliant on state cooperation as it is, hardly has a comparative advantage when it comes to arresting suspects).

The OTP, for its part, also argued that complementarity was not an issue, despite its stated adoption of a policy of positive complementarity according to which the OTP would encourage domestic proceedings wherever possible.[52] As the citation opening this chapter illustrates, when notifying states parties of his decision to open an investigation into northern Uganda, the Prosecutor echoed the GoU's reasoning for the referral, stressing that the Ugandan authorities preferred ICC proceedings because of the appropriateness and effectiveness of the ICC.[53] No OTP document addressed the statutorily relevant question of admissibility, namely, whether Uganda had genuinely investigated or prosecuted crimes within the Court's jurisdiction. The OTP never mentioned existing Ugandan arrest warrants for Joseph Kony and other senior LRA members.[54] The sole ground for inability that Uganda had advanced, namely, inability to arrest, was not subject to critical reflection, the ICC's own inability on this front notwithstanding. No attention was paid to the irony that in many other ways, too, for instance with respect to the logistics of the investigations, military intelligence and forensic evidence, the OTP would rely heavily on the services of the 'unable' state. Instead, the OTP asked the Ugandan government for a letter explicitly confirming that it was not conducting domestic proceedings against the LRA, to serve as evidence in the event that one of the future accused were to challenge admissibility.

Some OTP officials recognised that in hindsight complementarity should have been reviewed more thoroughly. But at the time it was not an issue, they argued, because the GoU showed no interest in domestic proceedings.[55] The OTP seems to have reasoned that,

---

[51] See Chapter 2, 'The substance of complementarity: the criteria for inadmissibility'.
[52] Ibid., 'The policy of positive complementarity'.
[53] Notification Investigation Uganda.
[54] The present author found these in the archives of the Buganda Road Court in Kampala. See Warrants of Arrest for Otti Lagony, Kony Joseph and Matsanga David Nyekorach. See also Charge Sheet Otti Lagony, Kony Joseph and Matsanga David (Terrorism) and Otti Lagony, Kony Joseph and Matsanga David Nyekorach DPP Withdrawal Form.
[55] Interviews with a senior OTP official (The Hague, April 2008), another OTP official (The Hague, May 2008) and a former ICC official (The Hague, June 2008).

because the GoU considered the ICC 'the most appropriate and effective forum', it would abstain from conducting domestic proceedings and from challenging admissibility. The OTP presumed the GoU would not change its policy, glossing over the final sentence of Uganda's referral letter, in which 'in accordance with Articles 17 to 19 of the ICC Statute', it reserved 'the right to make relevant submissions and otherwise participate in the proceedings as to the admissibility or jurisdiction of the ICC'.[56]

When deciding on the issuance of the arrest warrants, the PTC for its part did not scrutinise the admissibility of the LRA cases either. PTC II merely stated with respect to complementarity that, 'based upon the application, the evidence and other information submitted by the Prosecutor, and without prejudice to subsequent determination, the case against [the LRA leaders] . . . appears to be admissible'.[57] In its arrest warrants, as seen from the following extracts, the Chamber repeatedly quoted from a letter which the OTP had requested from Uganda's Solicitor-General to bolster its admissibility arguments:

> 'the Government of Uganda has been unable to arrest . . . persons who may bear the greatest responsibility' for the crimes within the referred situation . . . 'the ICC is the most appropriate and effective forum for the investigation and prosecution of those bearing the greatest responsibility' for those crimes; and . . . the Government of Uganda 'has not conducted and does not intend to conduct national proceedings in relation to the persons most responsible'.[58]

The PTC did not engage with the GoU's argument that it was unable to conduct domestic proceedings only because of the LRA's absence from Ugandan territory. Nor did the PTC dismiss the (for admissibility irrelevant) assertions of the ICC's being 'the most appropriate and effective forum'. By highlighting Uganda's submissions that it neither had conducted nor intended to conduct domestic proceedings, PTC II seems to establish admissibility on grounds of domestic inaction. The cited sources suggest that the PTC, in arriving at this finding, relied only on the letters submitted by the Ugandan government. There is no indication of any investigation into past or existing Ugandan proceedings against the LRA. The PTC seems to have assumed that these were absent, and would remain absent.

---

[56] Uganda 2003:[44].   [57] *Decision Arrest Warrants LRA*:2.
[58] *Arrest Warrant Kony*:[37].

But then, in 2006, the possibility of Ugandan proceedings loomed, and the GoU's and ICC's interests began to diverge. At least, so it seemed. The ICC (the OTP and, even more so, the PTC) wished to maintain its case against the LRA. But the Ugandan government incurred domestic political costs when the ICC proved unable to do what the GoU had involved it for, namely, arrest or in any other way 'neutralise' the LRA leadership.[59] Northern Ugandans blamed the GoU for involving the Court and thereby obstructing a peaceful solution to the conflict. Local and regional demands to resolve one of Africa's longest civil wars by talks rather than trials increased.

The conflict in northern Uganda – and far beyond

In addition to the GoU–ICC relationship, the dynamics of the conflict in which the ICC intervened are key to understanding complementarity's catalysing effect in Uganda. At the surface, the conflict appears an armed struggle between the GoU and a rebel movement. However, mistrust and grievances *vis-à-vis* the GoU on the part of those who have suffered most from the LRA–GoU conflict constitute a deeper layer of conflict. Northern Ugandans are particularly suspicious of the failure of the national army (the UPDF) to protect them, and, against that background, of the absence of ICC proceedings against state officials.

Triggered by the seizure of power by Museveni's National Resistance Movement/Army (NRM/A) in 1986, but rooted in pre-existing tensions and grievances, the conflict between the GoU and northern Ugandan opponents had been ongoing seventeen years at the time of the referral.[60] Over time, dozens of groups resisted Museveni's rule, but most of them sooner or later were defeated, signed an agreement or were otherwise appeased.[61] Joseph Kony, however, continued with his

---

[59] See also Kakaire 2006: 'In a stinging attack on the United Nations, Museveni said he had been betrayed by the world body, which initiated the establishment of the ICC through the 1998 Treaty of Rome, because UN peacekeeping forces in the Democratic Republic of Congo, DRC – Uganda's eastern neighbour – had either failed or declined to arrest Kony. They had also denied permission to Ugandan forces to cross the border to kill or detain Kony and his followers.'

[60] See, more extensively on the conflict in northern Uganda, the sources mentioned in the references of this section and, *inter plurima alia*, Allen and Vlassenroot 2010b, Branch 2011, Dolan 2011, Finnström 2008, Behrend 1999 and Doom and Vlassenroot 1999.

[61] Lomo and Hovil 2004:4.

Lord's Resistance Army (as it was renamed in 1993), combining the military experience of remnants of the previous national armed forces with the spiritual drive of Alice Auma's defeated Holy Spirit Movement.[62] Kony claimed to be Alice's cousin and, like Alice, to be possessed by spirits that order him 'to kill evil', including the government and its supporters. Kony's own Acholi community has suffered the brunt of the conflict,[63] accused by the LRA of cooperating with Museveni's rule[64] and punished with indiscriminate killings, torture, mutilation, looting, arson, enslavement and forced recruitment.[65]

However, the conflict in northern Uganda is more complex than is suggested by the dominant caricature of an irrational movement whose only agenda is its own survival by the gun.[66] First, there are indications that the LRA does have a political agenda, albeit not communicated in conventional ways.[67] Secondly, even if not best represented by the LRA, the Acholi have political grievances that are shared by other northern groups. The origins of such discontent go back to pre-independence, when the British colonisers exploited tensions between northerners and southerners. Since its independence, Uganda has seen violent inter-ethnic struggle for power in the national government. A change in power was often followed by reprisals against the ethnic groups associated with the predecessor regime. It was in this light that many northerners interpreted harsh operations against possible rebels in northern Uganda by Museveni's National Resistance Army (in 1996 renamed UPDF), shortly after he

---

[62] On this movement, see Allen 1991.

[63] Areas other than the Acholi region have also been subjected to LRA violence, particularly (in Uganda) Lango and Teso, and (outside Uganda) in southern Sudan, eastern DRC and eastern CAR.

[64] On the LRA's distinction between an 'external' and 'internal' enemy, see Branch 2010:40–2.

[65] See OHCHR 2007:*passim* and Human Rights Watch 2005b:15–24.

[66] For an example of how Western media accounts use such stereotypes, see Farmar 2006. On the disgrace of that account, see Schomerus 2010a, Schomerus 2010b and Finnström 2010. See Titeca 2010:59 *et seq.* for a more general critical account of the 'often ethnocentric descriptions of religion and spirituality [that] give exoticizing and isolated reports which do not take into account the wider political, social and economic context, representing the LRA's activities as radically irrational and as such neglecting, for example, how a spiritual discourse [and acts of terrorism] can act as a medium through which other grievances can be framed'.

[67] For some LRA demands aimed at ending the economic and political marginalisation of the north, see Nyeko and Lucima 2002. See also Finnström 2008 and Finnström 2010.

had militarily defeated a president from the north. The fact that in those operations many civilians were robbed of their livelihoods confirmed their fear that southerners, who had suffered under previous northern presidents, were now after northerners.

The war between the government and the LRA subsequently exacerbated the northern population's resentment towards Museveni's administration.[68] If the risk of abduction by the LRA had not yet done so,[69] the GoU's encampment policy drove the Acholi off their land.[70] Anyone found outside the camps would be considered a rebel and killed, the Acholi were told.[71] At the conflict's peak, 1.84 million people[72] (90–95 per cent of the population in the three Acholi districts)[73] lived in camps for internally displaced persons in 'appalling' humanitarian circumstances.[74] More people died because of the encampment than from direct attacks by the belligerent parties.[75] The UPDF sometimes used the displaced as human shields, rendering the so-called 'protected camps' in fact 'pick-up centres' for LRA abduction raids.[76] Torture and killing became other risks of UPDF presence.[77]

Many northerners bitterly observe that the government has sent the UPDF on missions to promote peace throughout Africa, but did the opposite in northern Uganda.[78] They see the government's failure to address the situation as evidence of a policy to keep the north underdeveloped, steal land, ruin the local culture and socially disintegrate the Acholi.[79] In the words of one famous Acholi, ending with a

---

[68] Lomo and Hovil 2004:1 and 23 et seq. See also Dolan 2005.

[69] The numbers of abducted persons and the percentage of children are disputed. See Allen 2006:63–4. On the lives of (formerly) abducted persons, see Amone-P'Olak 2007.

[70] See OHCHR 2007:7, 12–17, 35 and 39. See also Human Rights Watch 2005b:4, 17 and 24–37. On the difficulties of reclaiming that land, see Okot et al. 2012.

[71] Branch 2008:154.   [72] UNHCR 2012.

[73] This figure does not include those who have taken flight in major urban centres such as Kampala, whose numbers remain uncounted. See Refugee Law Project 2007.

[74] Commission on Human Rights 2001:13.

[75] At one stage, about 1,000 people a week died on account of the conditions ('Uganda: 1,000 displaced die every week in war-torn north – report' 2005).

[76] See Nyakairu 2008a, Commission on Human Rights 2001:13 and Human Rights Watch 2005b:24 and 70.

[77] See, inter alia, Human Rights Committee 2004:[17] and Human Rights Watch 2003.

[78] See OHCHR 2007:24, see also 16 and 26.   [79] See e.g. Otunnu 2006a.

quotation from a Catholic missionary priest in the region: 'under the cover of the war against these outlaws [the LRA], an entire society, the Acholi people, has been moved to concentration camps and is being systematically destroyed – physically, culturally, and economically ... "Everything Acholi is dying."'[80]

Even if they did not intend to target the Acholi, political and military elites reaped such benefits from the conflict in northern Uganda that they had little incentive to secure a military victory.[81] First, the conflict secured an income for the bedrock of Museveni's rule: the army.[82] It provided a justification for a disproportionally high defence budget and an opportunity to supplement salaries with the fruits of plunder, commerce and creative administration. UPDF soldiers looted harvest and cattle. Others made money out of procurement and arms trade, including with the LRA. Commanders could multiply their salary by not reporting casualties of combat or HIV/ AIDS and collecting the income of those whose lives continued on the payroll only. At one stage, over half of the UPDF division operating in the north consisted of such 'ghost soldiers'.[83]

Secondly, the seemingly inexplicable cruelty meted out by Joseph Kony, even on his 'own' people, gave Museveni one of his core arguments for maintaining the support of his mostly southern constituency: any alternative party, particularly those with supporters in the north, would bring back the violence from the days of the 'northern' Idi Amin and Milton Obote.[84] Thirdly, the war offered an excuse for the use of repressive methods against opposition – political opponents, including a presidential runner-up, were imprisoned on charges of collaborating with LRA 'terrorists'. Last but not least, the presence of a local 'war on terror' provided a bonding experience with, and grounds for support from, the world's only superpower.

---

[80] Otunnu 2006b.

[81] See, *inter alia*, Tripp 2010:169–71, Dolan 2011:Chapter 4, Allen and Vlassenroot 2010a:12 and Mwenda 2010.

[82] See also Tripp 2010:52: 'From the outset of Museveni's government, the army was seen as the core of the state; the NRM was merely its political wing.'

[83] See Nyakairu 2008a.

[84] See a poster of Museveni's election campaign, reproduced and discussed in Atkinson 2010b:293–4, showing a field of skulls and bones and reading: 'Think. Don't forget the past: Over one million Ugandans, our brothers, sisters, family and friends lost their lives. Your Vote Could Bring it Back: in ten years under Museveni, peace and development has come to our country. Let's keep it. Vote Museveni.'

Against this background, it comes as no surprise that attempts over the years to end the conflict through negotiations have been equivocal. President Museveni has always favoured a military end to the LRA problem.[85] Refusing to recognise the LRA as a movement with political motives, he kept the conflict off Parliament's agenda for eleven years. However, showing goodwill to people from the north who criticised the failing military approach, he occasionally allowed others to pursue alternative tracks to peace.

For example, in 1994 Betty Bigombe, then Ugandan Minister for the Pacification of the North and herself from northern Uganda, managed to agree a ceasefire with the LRA.[86] But, when the LRA did not unconditionally surrender, Museveni laid down the ultimatum that, if the LRA did not abandon the armed struggle within seven days, his army would destroy them. The fighting resumed. The LRA moved its base to southern Sudan, where it received military support from the Government of Sudan (GoS) in exchange for joint operations against the Sudan's People Liberation Army, which for its part was backed by the GoU. Attacks on civilians in northern Uganda continued.

In December 1999, proponents of peace talks won an important battle when, after years of lobbying by religious leaders from northern Uganda,[87] Parliament adopted an Amnesty Act offering pardon to all Ugandans formerly or currently engaged in acts of rebellion against the Ugandan Government since 1986.[88] Parliament did not accept the President's proposal to exclude certain groups of people from the amnesty.[89] Kony, however, rejected the amnesty, since the offer of non-prosecution alone did not meet the LRA's demands and implied defeat.[90]

---

[85] 'Uganda: interview with President Yoweri Museveni' 2005 ('There are those who believe in the magic of the peace talks – which I do not believe in. However, I do not want to be obstructive to those who wish to pursue this avenue – if you believe that you can convince evil to stop being evil, go ahead. But in the meantime, I do not want to give up my option [the military option]. That is why we have a dual track.').

[86] Agreement between the Uganda Government and the Lord's Resistance Army 1994.

[87] See Khadiagala 2001:8, Otim 2009 and Apuuli 2011.

[88] See this chapter below, 'Discouraging amnesties'.

[89] See the extensive parliamentary debate on the Bill in Uganda 1999a and Uganda 1999b.

[90] See also Khadiagala 2001:15.

Meanwhile, a simultaneous improvement in GoU–GoS relations increased the hopes of hardliners in the GoU for a military solution. When in 2002 the GoS allowed the UPDF to fight the LRA in southern Sudan, the GoU launched 'Operation Iron Fist' to pursue this aim. However, the rebels moved back to northern Uganda 'like a swarm of bees'[91] and spread the conflict to the Ugandan regions of Lango and Teso.

It was in this context of failed attempts to defeat the LRA militarily or in peace talks that the Ugandan government referred the situation concerning the LRA to the ICC. But the Court's involvement did not herald the end of the military option.

Peace-making in the shadow of the ICC

The ICC's involvement initially gave an impetus to the military approach to addressing the conflict with the LRA. Immediately after the referral, the UPDF made a new attempt to defeat the LRA. It failed. The option of peace talks featured again when the GoU unilaterally declared a ceasefire and Betty Bigombe renewed mediation initiatives. At that point, in late 2004, the ICC had not yet issued arrest warrants, but the LRA leadership was apprehensive about the Court and insisted on guarantees for its security.[92] The ICC's involvement notwithstanding, President Museveni repeated the offer of amnesty to the LRA leaders.[93] He assumed that the Ugandan government, having itself referred the situation, could also 'withdraw' the referral of the situation to the ICC, 'like a plaintiff can withdraw the civil case he brought in court'.[94] Options were explored to find the LRA leadership asylum in a state not party to the Rome Statute.[95] But, in early 2005, when two high-level LRA commanders defected and the government resumed military operations, the talks collapsed.

But then, in July 2006, peace negotiations began in the city of Juba, the capital of the new semi-autonomous region of Southern Sudan, that were different from previous talks between the LRA and the GoU: for the first time, a representative of a foreign state conducted

---

[91] Interview with Rt Rev. Baker Ochola II, Kitgum, September 2008.

[92] Interview with a person involved in the mediation, Kampala, September 2008. For an account of the LRA's concerns about the ICC in 2005, see Schomerus 2010b:96.

[93] Interview with a person involved in the Bigombe mediation, February 2009.

[94] *Ibid.*   [95] *Ibid.*

the mediation, the GoU and the LRA agreed upon a broad substantive agenda, hostilities ceased and the parties concluded several agreements.[96] The talks have been widely considered the most promising chance for peace in northern Uganda.[97]

The beginning of the Juba peace talks not long after the publication of the ICC arrest warrants has often been cited as evidence for the claim that criminal justice can enhance peace negotiations.[98] However, there were more decisive reasons for the LRA to be interested in talks than the ICC arrest warrants.[99] The LRA had lost military support since the rapprochement between the GoU and the GoS. After the conclusion of the Comprehensive Peace Agreement (CPA) between the GoS and the Sudan People's Liberation Movement/Army (SPLM/A) it risked losing a core military asset: territorial sanctuary.[100] The CPA granted the newly formed Government of Southern Sudan (GoSS) considerable autonomy, including the right to have its own army (the SPLA), and obliged the Sudanese Armed Forces to withdraw from Southern Sudan. Faced with a few thousand LRA combatants and twice that number of UPDF soldiers on Southern Sudanese territory,[101] over and above the security risk created by southern militias allegedly supported by the Sudanese Armed Forces at the northern border, the GoSS gave the LRA three options:

---

[96] For captivating accounts of the Juba peace talks, see Atkinson 2010a and Atkinson 2010b:Afterword.

[97] See, *inter alia*, O'Brien 2007:2 and Atkinson 2010b:308.

[98] See e.g. *OTP Submission Information Status LRA Arrest Warrants*:6 (citing the GoU) and ICC official Brubacher 2010:277.

[99] Atkinson's correction of the dominant literature on the relationship between the peace talks and the arrest warrants is worthy of full citation: 'The role of the GoSS in getting the LRA/M into peace talks ... seems crucial, far more so than one of the most common alternative arguments: that the top rebel leaders feared [ICC] warrants issued against them in October 2005, and saw peace talks as a means to postpone or avoid arrest. This latter view has been put forth by the Court itself, and seems to have become part of accepted wisdom, repeated over and over again in the media, numerous reports, and public comments from a wider range of people in and outside Uganda. Although the ICC warrants surfaced as an issue for the LRA/M during the talks – and in the end became perhaps the main obstacle that derailed the talks – there is no evidence the warrants were a major factor in the rebels' decision to enter talks.' (Atkinson 2010b:308–9, footnote omitted). See also Atkinson 2010a:211–12 for a nuanced assessment of the LRA's interests in the talks. More elaborately on the ICC's impact on peace negotiations in Uganda and Sudan, see Nouwen 2012a and Nouwen 2012c.

[100] Mwenda 2010:57.   [101] See Atkinson 2010b:308.

leave Southern Sudan; negotiate; or be defeated by the SPLA. The LRA opted for negotiations.

The true accomplishment of the GoSS was to convince the GoU to commit to third-party-led negotiations. In the twenty years of conflict with the LRA, the GoU had always controlled the peace initiatives. Due to the GoU's unwillingness to recognise the LRA as a negotiating partner, such initiatives were in fact more opportunities for a submissive surrender, implying one side's victory and the other's defeat, than negotiations in which two parties would make concessions. Without any external actor monitoring the process, the GoU could set its ultimatums and go back to war at its sole discretion.

The involvement of the ICC had initially made the GoU less, rather than more, interested in the option of a negotiated settlement: with the community of ICC states parties and the war-on-terror coalition on its side, it had increased hopes of militarily defeating the LRA. But when it became apparent that the ICC arrest warrants as such did not increase the likelihood of arrest, when international pressure on the GoU to improve the humanitarian situation in northern Uganda increased, and when Salva Kiir, President of Southern Sudan and the leader of the SPLM, Museveni's long-standing ally against the GoS, personally visited Kampala and set out the GoSS's interest in the talks, President Museveni, despite contrary indications a few weeks earlier, consented to the first internationally mediated talks between the GoU and the LRA. For President Museveni, this concession was worthy of a justification in his 2006 address on the state of the nation:

> Although their ringleaders are indicted by the International Criminal Court, and our view is that these criminals should be hunted to the bitter end in order to provide a lesson for the people who may be inclined to behave in a similar way in [the] future[,] I agreed with His Excellency Salva Kiir's proposal for two reasons . . .
>
> First of all, it is clear that we have no reliable partners, as far as fighting terrorism is concerned, in the Democratic Republic of Congo Government and the United Nations who are now in charge of Eastern Congo; those two parties are not serious. The UN always excels in superficiality, their protestation to the contrary notwithstanding. If you want superficiality the best place to go is the United Nations.
>
> Secondly, the UPDF has defeated Kony in both Northern Uganda and Southern Sudan. Kony did not go to Garamba for tourism . . . we defeated Kony. Kony is now in the part of Congo that has no borders

with Uganda. We are making contingent plans to react vigorously in case Kony comes to the part of Congo that has got a border with Uganda . . .

As of now, however, where Kony is located is more a problem of Southern Sudan and Congo than ours. Our forces are in Southern Sudan just to help our brothers the SPLA but Kony as of now is not our problem . . . The remnants, which are still there, we are picking them. Even today we were hunting the group of Lasco Lukwiya near Juba–Tolit road, and I am sure we shall get that group, which was trying to join Kony in Congo.

Some people were asking . . . "Has Museveni become a softie? Why is it that he is willing to talk with Kony again?" Even my allies, the International Criminal Court, were doubting my credentials; they thought that I had become a softie. My answer is this . . . it is rational that since Kony now is not in Northern Uganda, he is not in the part of Southern Sudan where we were allowed to operate, he is in Congo, which is under the control of the United Nations and the Congo Government who are not allowing us to go there and he is in the part of Congo, which has no border with Uganda, it is rational that we follow the leadership of the government of Southern Sudan, they should be the ones to lead us. If they say we negotiate, we negotiate because it is their problem now, it is not ours.[102]

It was thus that a Ugandan delegation travelled to Juba to engage in talks with the LRA under the auspices of the GoSS.

The Juba peace talks produced an unparalleled number of substantive agreements between the delegations representing the LRA and the GoU. The first breakthrough came after a month of negotiations, when the Ugandan government and the LRA signed a Cessation of Hostilities Agreement[103] which immediately had a positive impact on security in southern Sudan. The signed agreement also served as the GoU's recognition of the LRA as a negotiating partner. The following one and a half years of on-and-off negotiations in Juba and lengthy stakeholder consultations in Uganda eventually generated agreements between the GoU and the LRA on the five adopted agenda items, as well as on implementation matters.

From the outset of the talks, it was obvious that the agenda item on 'accountability and reconciliation' would be one of the most

---

[102] Uganda 2006a.
[103] Agreement on Cessation of Hostilities between the Government of the Republic of Uganda and Lord's Resistance Army Movement 2006.

difficult.[104] The LRA's entry position was that '[n]o rebel w[ould] come out [of the war] unless the ICC revoke[d] the indictments'.[105] By then the GoU realised that it could not simply withdraw the referral[106] and that an amnesty could not undo the ICC's involvement. The closest thing the GoU could offer the LRA was to conduct domestic proceedings so that it would be possible for it or the ICC suspects successfully to challenge admissibility on the basis of articles 17, 19 and 20 of the Rome Statute.[107] Complementarity became the linchpin of the agreement on accountability and reconciliation.

Complementarity: the linchpin of the agreement

The Agreement on Accountability and Reconciliation (the A&R Agreement)[108] and its Annexure[109] (together: the A&R Accords) were never intended merely as the written reflection of a peace deal between two warring parties. They were also a message to all in the international-criminal-justice movement, ranging from the ICC Prosecutor to NGOs and states supportive of the ICC, that the pursuit of peace did not have to come at the expense of justice (understood holistically), and that the way the two parties had agreed to pursue peace and justice was entirely consistent with the Rome Statute. Indeed, the A&R Accords signalled that substituting the ICC with Ugandan alternatives was entirely in accordance with and in the spirit of the Rome Statute's cornerstone principle: complementarity.

It is thus that, in the preamble, the parties to the A&R Agreement, 'conscious of ... the need to honour the suffering of victims by

---

[104] Phone interview with a person involved in the negotiations, May 2008. The interviewee specified: 'It was blatantly obvious from the very first day of the talks that the ICC arrest warrants would be the biggest obstacle.'

[105] Wallis 2006. Pictures of the ICC's detention centre in Scheveningen, provided by the GoU, did not change this position. Interview with a Ugandan government minister, Kampala, October 2008.

[106] Cf. *contra* Bassiouni 2005:194.

[107] See also interview with a government minister, Kampala, October 2008: 'We moulded and developed ... domestic facilities [for domestic proceedings] in order for us to reach the peace agreement. This was a compromise, it was a sweetener to soften on our side, because the LRA team doesn't like the ICC. If we offered domestic proceedings, it would be more sellable to them.'

[108] Agreement on Accountability and Reconciliation between the Government of the Republic of Uganda and the Lord's Resistance Army/Movement 2007.

[109] Annexure to the Agreement on Accountability and Reconciliation 2008.

promoting lasting peace *with* justice',[110] express their commitment 'to preventing impunity and promoting redress in accordance with the Constitution and international obligations and recall ... in this connection, the requirements of the Rome Statute of the International Criminal Court (ICC) and in particular the principle of complementarity'.[111] The parties' first substantive commitment is to 'promote *national* legal arrangements ... for ensuring justice and reconciliation with respect to the conflict'.[112] For the purposes of the A&R Agreement, 'accountability mechanisms shall be implemented through the adapted legal framework *in Uganda*'.[113] The phrase 'in Uganda' refers to both the territory and the applicable law, thus ruling out, for the purpose of the A&R Agreement, use of extra-territorial justice mechanisms.[114] The same conclusion flows from the provision that the formal justice processes shall be handled by '[f]ormal courts provided for *under the Constitution*' or 'tribunals established *by law*'.[115] In the Annexure to the A&R Agreement, the parties recall 'their commitment to preventing impunity and promoting redress in accordance with the Constitution and international obligations, and ... the requirements of the Rome Statute of the International Criminal Court (ICC) and in particular the principle of complementarity'.[116] They also express their 'confiden[ce]' that the Principal Agreement embodies the necessary principles by which the conflict can be resolved with justice and reconciliation and consistent with national and international aspirations and standards'.[117]

It is in this spirit of complementarity that the A&R Accords set forth a framework based on exclusively national legal arrangements, existing or to be adapted or newly established. As regards 'formal measures', the Annexure provides for the establishment of a 'special division of the High Court of Uganda [(SDHC)] ... to try individuals who are alleged to have committed serious crimes during the conflict'[118] and 'a unit for carrying out investigations and prosecutions in support of trials and other formal proceedings'.[119] Recognising the transitional-justice context in which these formal measures are to operate, and that conflict

---

[110] Second recital (emphasis added).   [111] Third recital.
[112] A&R Agreement, clause 2.1 (emphasis added).
[113] *Ibid.*, clause 4.4 (emphasis added).   [114] Afako 2007:8.
[115] A&R Agreement, clauses 6.1 and 6.2, respectively (emphases added).
[116] Annexure, fifth recital.   [117] *Ibid.*, sixth recital.
[118] *Ibid.*, clause 7.   [119] *Ibid.*, clause 10.

resolution, truth discovery and reconciliation are difficult to square with the retributive penalties under the extant criminal law, the A&R Agreement also provides that '[l]egislation shall introduce a regime of alternative penalties and sanctions which shall apply and replace existing sanctions'.[120] The intention seems to have been to make trial by the SDHC more palatable a prospect than trial by the ICC.

The plan for dealing with the ICC is apparent in the A&R Agreement's obligations on the GoU,[121] which are specified in the Agreement on Implementation and Monitoring Mechanisms. The GoU shall 'take the necessary steps to establish national mechanisms of accountability and reconciliation', prioritising 'commencing criminal investigations and establishing the special division of the High Court'.[122] In order to allow Uganda to make such preparations without being at the same time under an obligation to execute the arrest warrants and transfer suspects to the ICC,[123] the GoU shall 'request the UN Security Council to adopt a resolution under Chapter VII of the Charter of the United Nations, requesting the International Criminal Court to defer all investigations and prosecutions against the leaders of the Lord's Resistance Army'.[124] The GoU shall also 'give to the ICC a comprehensive report on the Juba Peace Process, the Agreements between the Parties, and the progress on the implementation of the Agreement on Accountability and Reconciliation'.[125] The Agreement does not oblige the GoU to challenge admissibility, but the ICC suspects themselves could do so during or – with higher chances of success[126] – after having been subjected to domestic proceedings.

---

[120] A&R Agreement, clause 6.3.

[121] *Ibid.*, clauses 14.5 and 14.6. Note that clause 14.10 also obliges the LRA/M 'actively [to] promote the principles of [the] Agreement'. The Agreement encourages voluntary cooperation with accountability and reconciliation mechanisms (see e.g. clause 3.2).

[122] Agreement on Implementation and Monitoring Mechanisms 2008, clause 36.

[123] RS, art. 95, which allows a state to postpone the execution of a cooperation request pending an admissibility challenge, is by itself not enough to deal with the tension between an obligation to arrest and transfer a person to the ICC and the wish to investigate and prosecute the same person domestically. For the obligation to be postponed under art. 95, the admissibility challenge must be pending, whereas for this challenge to be successful sufficient progress in concrete investigations must be demonstrated, which requires time.

[124] Agreement on Implementation and Monitoring Mechanisms 2008, clause 37.

[125] *Ibid.*, clause 38.

[126] See Chapter 2, 'Where domestic proceedings have been initiated: unwillingness and inability'.

The transitional-justice structure agreed upon in the A&R Accords goes beyond formal criminal justice. As regards the 'complementary alternative justice mechanisms', the Annexure provides for a national truth-telling process[127] and gives instructions to the government for the creation of reparations schemes[128] and the identification of roles for traditional-justice mechanisms.[129]

In addition to accountability and reconciliation, the implementation mechanisms and the cessation of hostilities, the delegations of the GoU and LRA reached agreements on comprehensive solutions to the political, social and economic problems in eastern and northern Uganda; disarmament, demobilisation and reintegration; and a permanent ceasefire. Together these agreements constitute the Final Peace Agreement (FPA), to be signed by the leader of the GoU delegation and the leader of the LRA.

The ICC: sword of Damocles

But Joseph Kony refused to sign the FPA. He feared the consequences of compliance with the disarmament agreement for his personal security and did not trust that the GoU would save him from the ICC. According to some northern Ugandans, Kony had reason to be suspicious: there had been an incident in which UPDF soldiers killed a senior member of a movement with whom the GoU had just concluded peace.[130] Kony did not trust the international community either: he himself had read in the papers the news of the transfer of former Liberian President Charles Taylor to the Special Court for Sierra Leone despite a previous grant of asylum by Nigeria.[131] Already in 2006 he had addressed Acholi leaders and UN officials, saying:

> Take the example of Charles Taylor. He was accepting that the only way was to give up and call it quits, Taylor surrendered himself. But what happened to him? He was arraigned and put on trial. If this is the *modus operandi* of the international community you will not get any cooperation. The problem will only get worse.[132]

Similarly questioning the value of national promises in an international judicial market, the late Vincent Otti, at the time Kony's

---

[127] Annexure, clauses 4–6. [128] *Ibid.*, clauses 16–18. [129] *Ibid.*, clauses 19–22.
[130] See also Finnström 2010:79 and, on the death of Michael Kilama, Lamwaka 2002.
[131] Interview with a member of the Juba talks mediation team, Switzerland, July 2009. See also Schomerus 2010a:113.
[132] Joseph Kony, speech to UN and Acholi leaders in Ri-Kwangba, translation from Acholi, 12 December 2006, as reported in Schomerus forthcoming.

deputy, observed that Congolese ex-rebel 'Lubanga was arrested after a negotiated settlement but is now being tried in The Hague'.[133]

A catch-22 situation emerged. Kony would not sign 'if the ICC indictments were not dropped',[134] whereas the government was willing to make representations to the Security Council and ICC only once Kony had signed the FPA. If the arrest warrants had driven the LRA to the negotiating table, the ICC's sword thus proved double-edged, the sharpest side being an insurmountable obstacle to trust in the value of any agreement.

When Kony ignored the GoU's ultimatum demanding that he sign the FPA before 30 November 2008, the military approach to resolving the conflict regained the upper hand. The UPDF, nominally in cooperation with the armies of the DRC and the GoSS, launched 'Operation Lightning Thunder' in the DRC. LRA commanders were killed or captured,[135] but not the ones sought by the ICC.[136] The action came at a predictable price: consistent with its known war strategy, the LRA avenged against the soft targets that it sees as supportive of its enemy and killed a thousand or more civilians, abducted hundreds and caused the displacement of up to 200,000 people.[137]

Since Operation Lightning Thunder, the UPDF has continued military operations in the DRC, the CAR and Southern Sudan, sometimes with, sometimes without, the host government's consent, occasionally killing or capturing members of the LRA but also pushing the LRA into new areas. After the collapse of the Juba peace talks, the US openly provided military support to the UPDF's LRA hunt; the EU followed with financial support.[138]

Cracks in the marriage: the opening for complementarity's catalysing effect

During the Juba peace talks, the Ugandan Government publicly toyed with the idea of taking measures to facilitate ending the ICC's

---

[133] 'Uganda: IDPs unlikely to meet deadline to vacate camps' 2006. See also Otti's observations on Taylor, expressed to the Community of Sant'Egidio, an NGO with contacts with the LRA, as reported in Hume 2006b: 'Otti repeated several times that he does not want to share Charles Taylor's fate.'

[134] Nyakairu 2008b. See also Afako 2009, Iya 2010:181–2, Wasswa 2008, 'Uganda: US accuses LRA of abuses, calls for a quick peaceful solution' 2008 and Wheeler 2008.

[135] Baguma 2009.   [136] Eichstaedt 2008.   [137] See Atkinson 2010b:320.

[138] Matsiko 2011 and Muwonge 2011.

involvement. In order to show Ugandans that it still controlled the situation despite having referred it to the ICC, the GoU promised that it would take action domestically and internationally to displace the Court. By signing the Juba Agreement and its Annexure, the GoU committed to providing an alternative to the ICC.

But the GoU never took steps actually to end ICC involvement. It never requested the Security Council to defer the ICC's proceedings. When the PTC *proprio motu* assessed complementarity,[139] the GoU did not argue inadmissibility. Before, during and after the negotiations, it considered the ICC as a useful instrument of pressure on the LRA and did not want this removed until Kony actually signed the FPA and surrendered.[140]

ICC officials, by contrast, were fearful that the peace talks and the outcome could undermine the Court's first case. The Prosecutor, for his part, initially seemed to show an open mind about talks. Just after the referral, he was supportive of the Bigombe mediation and withheld his request for arrest warrants.[141] When the Juba talks started, the OTP emphasised that it was not a party to the negotiations and reminded actors of the obligation to execute the arrest warrants, but did not oppose the talks.[142] But when the parties ultimately agreed on national proceedings, the Prosecutor did not seem willing to give them a chance.[143] The OTP declared that it would 'fight any admissibility challenge in court',[144] apparently irrespective of the genuineness of eventual national proceedings.[145] In another comment that would not have increased Kony's willingness to sign the FPA, the head of the OTP's Jurisdiction, Complementarity and Cooperation Division stated in May 2008:

---

[139] See below, this section.

[140] Interview with a Ugandan official involved in the implementation of the Juba agreements, Kampala, October 2008: 'We have refused to request the ICC to lift the arrest warrants, as then there would no longer be pressure on the LRA.'

[141] Interview with a person involved in the Bigombe mediation, February 2009. See also 'Court rules out Kony immunity' 2005.

[142] See also UN Doc. S/PV.5525 (2006):4 (Mr Egeland). In *OTP Submission Information Status LRA Arrest Warrants*, the OTP defended Uganda's participation in peace talks instead of executing the arrest warrants before a less lenient PTC.

[143] See also Seils 2011:1001–3.

[144] OTP quoted in Glassborow 2008. See also ICC-OTP 2008b.

[145] See also interview with a Ugandan government minister, Kampala, October 2008: 'We've been in touch with the Prosecutor, but the Prosecutor insists that the case must be handled in The Hague. Our counter-argument is complementarity.'

> You cannot sign an agreement and tell a criminal that we're going to do [a trial] at a national level ... There is no way that anyone can guarantee to Kony that he will not be judged here.[146]

When northern Ugandan leaders, mediators and diplomats were trying to convince Kony to sign the FPA, the Prosecutor set his face against the Juba talks. He implicitly criticised those who had supported the Juba talks, stating that 'Kony [had been] allowed to use the time and the resources of the "Juba talks" to promote his criminal goals'.[147]

The Registrar has equally insisted that the LRA case should remain on the ICC's docket. Ironically, given that one of Uganda's stated reasons for referring the case to the ICC was its own inability to arrest the leadership of the LRA, the Registrar argued that Uganda's failure to execute the ICC warrants for the LRA leadership amounted to a lack of compliance with Uganda's obligation effectively to cooperate with the Court.[148] In her view, the establishment of the SDHC was a positive development if it was for future Ugandan cases, but not if it aimed at the withdrawal of the ICC arrest warrants.[149]

The ICC judges have guarded the Uganda case even more than the other organs of the Court. In a first-time move, the PTC on its own initiative requested the Ugandan government to provide the Chamber 'with detailed information on the implications of the Annexure [to the Agreement on Accountability and Reconciliation] on the execution of the Warrants'.[150] Uganda responded that it had yet to take steps to implement the agreements, but added that the SDHC was 'not meant to supplant the work of the International Criminal Court and accordingly, those individuals who [had been] indicted by the International Criminal Court [would] have to be brought before the special

---

[146] Ayugi and Eichstaedt 2008.

[147] Moreno-Ocampo 2008a:5–6. See also ICC official Brubacher 2010:275: 'The LRA needed space to finish its regrouping effort. After numerous failed attempts at contacting possible mediators to restart peace talks, the LRA found a willing party in the Government of Southern Sudan.'

[148] Participant observation, Assembly of States Parties, Sixth Resumed Session, New York, 2–6 June 2008, side event for African States. See also the head of the ICC's Jurisdiction, Complementarity and Cooperation Division (JCCD), cited by Ayugi and Eichstaedt 2008: 'When asked who had primary responsibility for Kony's capture, [the head of the JCCD] said, "Uganda has to do it and Uganda has to be leading all the efforts".'

[149] Interview with the ICC Registrar, The Hague, June 2008.

[150] *Request Information Execution Arrest Warrants Kony et al.*

139

division of the High Court for trial'.[151] Although potentially the ICC's first story of 'success' as defined in the Prosecutor's inaugural address,[152] the possibility of Ugandan proceedings for persons sought by the ICC did not appeal to the PTC. Not willing to wait until such time as Uganda or one of the accused might decide to lodge an admissibility challenge, the PTC decided on its own volition to initiate proceedings to assess complementarity.[153]

Unsurprisingly, considering the fact that the GoU did not conduct investigations as long as the FPA was still to be signed and the LRA leadership still outside Uganda's jurisdiction, the PTC found that the case remained admissible.[154] In doing so, the PTC pointed out that the GoU's statement on the envisaged role for the SDHC appeared contradictory: 'whilst it is said that the work of the Court, "will not be supplanted" by the establishment of the Special Division, it is also said, that the individuals sought by the Court in the Case "will have to be brought" before this Special Division'.[155] The PTC thus implicitly rejected the idea, promoted by the Prosecutor in speeches outside the Court, of a 'Rome System' based on complementarity in which domestic courts and the ICC together pursue the aim of ending impunity. Instead, it revealed what the admissibility rule in the Rome Statute boils down to: either a domestic court or the ICC may exercise jurisdiction. The decision also highlighted that Uganda's response had relied 'on a number of assumptions which [were] inconsistent both with the system enshrined in the Statute and principles of international law'.[156] Specifying only one such assumption, the PTC reminded Uganda that, 'once the jurisdiction of the Court [has been] triggered, it is for the latter and not for any national judicial authorities to interpret and apply the provisions governing the complementarity regime and to make a binding determination on the admissibility of a given case'.[157] Whilst staying within the boundaries of the law, the decision did more to discourage than to encourage domestic proceedings.

The apparent crisis in the marriage between the ICC and the GoU was resolved when the peace talks collapsed. The GoU resumed an exclusively military approach to the LRA and no longer seemed to seek an end to the ICC's involvement. The ICC had been more

---

[151] *Uganda Letter on Execution Arrest Warrants*:3.   [152] See Chapter 1, epigraph.
[153] *Decision Proprio Motu Admissibility Assessment LRA.*
[154] *LRA Admissibility Decision (PTC).*   [155] *Ibid.*:[45].   [156] *Ibid.*   [157] *Ibid.*

concerned than the GoU about losing its partner as a result of the peace talks. For the GoU, the ICC's concerns had been much ado about nothing, because it had never intended to challenge admissibility – at most, if Kony had signed, the peace agreement would have allowed the LRA to do so. In the GoU's view, ICC–GoU interests had barely diverged.

That said, the GoU's search for alternatives to the ICC, no matter how short and hypothetical, did allow complementarity to catalyse effects that, once set in motion, appeared untameable.

EFFECTS CATALYSED

Indeed, complementarity has catalysed at least seven effects: it led to the promotion of local alternatives to international criminal justice; it stimulated a debate on transitional justice; it broadened the approach towards the conflict in northern Uganda to include a legal dimension; it stirred the establishment of a Ugandan international crimes division; it increased the attention paid to 'international standards'; it had some influence on the Ugandan International Criminal Court Act; and, eventually, discouraged amnesties. Many of these effects have not been catalysed by complementarity directly, but have been encouraged by norm entrepreneurs.[158] As a result, the effects are often based more on the meaning of complementarity as mediated by these actors than on complementarity as set forth in article 17 of the Statute.

Promoting the study of local justice practices

For a moment, some people in northern Uganda were hopeful when news spread that the ICC would 'intervene': 'The ICC will come and arrest Joseph Kony!' But positions radically shifted when it was discovered that the ICC does not have its own enforcement powers. 'Does the ICC want to use *the UPDF* to arrest people? We are moving from the frying pan to the fire.'[159] People became even more critical of the ICC when it disclosed its arrest warrants for the LRA leadership. As one elder explained:

[158] See Chapter 1, n. 56 and accompanying text.
[159] Interview with an attendant of a workshop on the ICC in northern Uganda in 2004, Kampala, November 2011.

> If you want to issue arrest warrants, then make sure that Kony is within your reach. If you cannot arrest Kony, then it is the local people that will suffer. This is what [the government's] *Operation Iron Fist* has shown. Arms were cut off, because they had responded to the [government's] call to take up weapons against Kony. Ears were cut off because they had been used for picking up LRA messages for the government. Lips were cut off because they had been used for talking about the LRA to the government.[160]

The ICC's investigations in northern Uganda were also perceived as dangerous. According to one community leader:

> It was really bad. People who collaborated with the ICC could have lost their lives. The LRA tried to kill one camp commander who had cooperated with the ICC. Vincent Otti issued threats. People know who talk with the ICC. If you are a *mzungu* [foreigner[161]] and enter a camp, people know that, even if you keep, as the ICC claims to do, a 'low profile'.[162]

Thus, while longing for comprehensive justice probably more than anyone else, many northern Ugandans were alarmed by the price that they might have to pay for the ICC's intervention.

A second cause of concern was the possible effect of the ICC's intervention on people in LRA captivity – people who were often not just perpetrators of crimes committed against northern Ugandans but also northern Ugandans' abducted relatives.[163] Attempts to execute ICC arrest warrants were expected to be accompanied by military action, a type of action that many northern Ugandans had opposed because it was likely to harm first and foremost the abducted footsoldiers. Instead, they had supported an Amnesty Act, but the ICC arrest warrants undermined the Act and discouraged defections.

A third anxiety was that the arrest warrants painted the LRA leadership into a corner, limited the attractiveness to the LRA of any future peace agreement and thus perpetuated the conflict. As a result, chances of abducted people returning alive would decrease and 'free' northern Ugandans would continue to languish in camps.

---

160 Interview, Gulu, September 2008.
161 Literal meaning: 'someone who roams around aimlessly'. Footnote inserted.
162 Interview with a community leader, Kampala, November 2011.
163 See also Ogora 2007:290.

No prospect on peace meant no prospect on regaining control over land, livelihood and life.

Perceiving the ICC's intervention to undermine their advocacy for a more conciliatory approach towards the LRA, leaders of ethnic groups and clans ('traditional leaders'), religious leaders and community-based civil society organisations in northern Uganda became the voices of northern resistance against the ICC.[164] In addition to raising the above-mentioned primary concerns about the possible negative consequences on peace, these leaders challenged the ICC's notion of justice, employing a diverse set of arguments.

First, by failing to investigate the GoU's conduct in the conflict, the ICC provided 'partial' or 'selective' justice, an injustice in itself.[165] The ICC Prosecutor should equally have investigated crimes allegedly committed by state actors. The GoU's failure to protect civilians in northern Uganda was, in the view of many, as serious as the LRA's actions. There was little justice in a body of law that seemed to classify only Kony's acts as criminal and the GoU's acts as 'mere' human rights violations not involving criminal responsibility.[166]

Secondly, religious and traditional leaders contended that the ICC provided limited justice by focusing on a few top leaders and ignoring the larger group of offenders whom victims must confront in their communities.[167] Those offenders, too, should be subject to a form of justice.

Thirdly, the ICC failed to provide distributive justice. By portraying the conflict in northern Uganda as one between a legitimate government and a criminal organisation, the ICC ignored the political and economic grievances of the Acholi. In the view of the leaders, this

---

[164] See, inter plurima alia, Odongo 2004, Latigo 2006 and 'Uganda: peace groups and government officials worried about ICC probe into LRA' 2004.

[165] Inter plurima alia, a focus group on access to justice for conflict-related crimes, Gulu, 18 September 2008; participant observation of the Reflection Workshop on the Juba Peace Talks for Religious and Cultural Leaders, Gulu, 10–12 September 2008; Ochola II 2009:20–1 and Ogola 2010. See also Hovil and Quinn 2005:15. An ICC outreach officer confirmed in an interview in Kampala in November 2011 that '50% of the questions is: why does the ICC do one-sided justice?'

[166] Focus group on access to justice for conflict-related crimes, Gulu, 18 September 2008.

[167] Participant observation of the Reflection Workshop on the Juba Peace Talks for Religious and Cultural Leaders, Gulu, 10–12 September 2008.

required a political solution but 'political solutions have never been found in a court room'.[168]

Fourthly, community leaders argued that ICC-style justice failed to do justice in the restorative sense, in two ways. First, the ICC was not able to do the type of justice that northern Ugandans needed most urgently: socio-economic recovery. This need went far beyond any reparations that the ICC could hypothetically order a convicted person to pay to victims of the crimes charged. After decades of war, *all* northern Ugandans had a pressing need for return of their land and cattle and access to health care, schooling and infrastructure. Secondly, even in terms of symbolic justice, the ICC was unable to do what was most needed: to restore relationships. Instead of reconciling victim and offender, and their respective clans, criminal justice sets people apart. As a religious leader argued:

> The court system is justice through punishment. The offender and offended are put aside. This leads to polarisation which will lead to death.[169]

Moreover, ICC-style justice was unable to restore the existential relationships between an offender and the spirits of an offended person and between people and their land. As a result, *cen*, the vengeance of the spirit world (particularly of those who suffered from a wrongful death or were not buried correctly) would manifest itself in the form of nightmares, sickness or death and would haunt the entire clan of the wrongdoer, if not in this generation then in the next.[170] ICC-style justice did not redress these violations of the cosmological world. As one leader observed: 'There is a balance in the community that cannot be found in the briefcase of the white man.'[171]

Finally, leaders questioned whether the ICC was able to do what it was best known for: punitive justice. One elder stated:

> If [the LRA leaders] are taken to The Hague, they will be locked up with air conditioning and will live the lifestyle of Ugandan ministers. But they will have to come here and make up with the community. Let them live with the people whose ears they have chopped off. Let them

---

[168] *Ibid.*   [169] Interview with a religious leader, Kitgum, September 2008.
[170] See Liu Institute for Global Issues and Gulu District NGO Forum 2005:12, 72 and 124, Gulu District NGO Forum and Liu Institute for Global Issues 2007:7 and Ochola II 2009:36.
[171] The head of the Gulu-based Human Rights Focus, quoted in Allen 2006:87.

see for the rest of their lives what suffering they have caused. That is punishment. In our view, ICC punishment is very light. Let them morally come and confess.[172]

Resisting imposition of international norms and procedures,[173] cultural and religious leaders campaigned for local justice practices.[174] They emphasised that some of these practices focus, like formal criminal justice, on truth and accountability. However, arguing that local justice practices can do what the ICC cannot do, they also juxtaposed the former to the latter: local accountability practices tend to be collective (involving the clans of the perpetrator and victim), to be based on the voluntary participation of perpetrators, and to aim not for punishment of the individual perpetrator but for restoration of relations between the victim's and perpetrator's clans through truth, acknowledgment and compensation. One religious leader explained:

> The court system is justice through punishment after truth. We don't do it like that. Once the truth has been revealed we look for a healing process. We have restorative justice. *Mato oput* [an Acholi justice mechanism] is pro life and holistic.[175]

It was also argued that Acholi elders, unlike ICC judges, were close enough to the spiritual world to appease bad omens by conducting cleansing ceremonies.[176]

---

[172] Discussion with two Acholi elders, Gulu, September 2008.

[173] On 'imposed justice', see Dolan 2008.

[174] Local justice practices are sometimes also referred to as 'informal', 'alternative' or 'traditional' justice. All these terms are somewhat misleading. 'Informal' is incorrect in that these mechanisms often have formal procedures, albeit not always codified (see Quinn 2006). 'Alternative' suggests that another mechanism is the standard, whereas for many people it is not. Moreover, official and local justice mechanisms are often complementary and not alternative. 'Traditional' may raise the incorrect impression of a static mechanism, whereas local justice mechanisms are alive, contested like other cultural practices and hence dynamic (see also Baines 2007:96 and Harlacher 2006:9–10). Moreover, some scholars have contested that such practices ever 'traditionally' existed in the way that they are now propagated (see Branch 2011:Chapter 5 and Allen 2007). With these caveats, this chapter uses the term 'local justice practices' because it acknowledges their pluriformity, but at times the chapter also refers to 'traditional justice', since the A&R Accords and some Acholi leaders use this term.

[175] Interview with a religious leader, Kitgum, September 2008.

[176] See also Liu Institute for Global Issues and Gulu District NGO Forum 2007b:11.

Their range and divergence notwithstanding, the arguments against the ICC and in favour of local justice practices shared a central message. As Barney Afako has observed, for most Acholi praise for *mato oput* was simply shorthand for saying: 'Please leave us alone and let us address these problems ourselves.'[177]

The call by traditional leaders for local justice practices in opposition to the ICC must also be seen as part of an older struggle for authority with the Ugandan government and with competitors within Acholi society.[178] In the view of many traditional leaders, the powers of their institution as recognised in the 1995 Constitution fall far short of the political authority that such leaders enjoyed before Uganda's independence, let alone colonialism.[179] Some traditional leaders, and also religious leaders for that matter, expressed a concern that their position would be further undermined by the advance of formal court proceedings with the expansion of the government's authority in northern Uganda. As one leader explained:

> Since the situation has been more peaceful, since 2004, people go more to courts than to traditional justice mechanisms, because they want a quick fix. But they don't think about restoring relationships.[180]

Within Acholi society, traditional leaders have faced competition from other types of leaders that emerged during the conflict. Individuals with purchasing power became more influential than cultural leaders seemingly powerless to address the dire circumstances in the camps. The respect on which their leadership is based crumbled with the leaders' equally having to queue for food or resorting to corruption as a strategy for their own survival. Women became more assertive in

---

[177] Afako paraphrased in Waddell and Clark 2007:10. See also Allen in Waddell and Clark 2007:27.

[178] On the impetus provided by the ICC, see e.g. Liu Institute for Global Issues and Gulu District NGO Forum 2005:7 ('Following the announcement of the [ICC] Prosecutor ... that he would investigate crimes committed since July 2002, members in this loose coalition [Acholi community of traditional and religious leaders, human rights workers, the NGO community and the Liu Institute for Global Issues] recognized the urgency of documenting local traditional justice mechanisms and [analysing] the role cultural leaders were playing or could play in the promotion of justice in the region.').

[179] See Ugandan Constitution 1995, art. 246.

[180] Participant observation of the Reflection Workshop on the Juba Peace Talks for Religious and Cultural Leaders, Gulu, 10–12 September 2008.

the light of men's inability to cope with camp life,[181] thereby challenging the male monopoly on leadership. Generations of young Acholi grew up in camps where traditional leaders did not have the authority that their title would suggest. Irrespective of whether traditional leaders ever enjoyed the claimed 'traditional' authority and whether their practices are as 'traditional' as they are nowadays branded, attempts to reinvent or invent the practices are thus also attempts to reinvent or invent the position of those who perform them.[182]

An act of resistance against international norms, the rediscovery of the 'traditional' or 'local' has itself also been part of an international movement.[183] In response to the ICC's intervention, international researchers and NGOs working in northern Uganda offered their assistance to traditional and religious leaders in making their case for traditional justice. They documented proceedings on the basis of oral history, emphasised common features with international criminal justice and drew parallels with local justice practices used in other parts of Africa.[184] Formulating a forceful response to the 'globalisation of justice', international traditional-justice advocates have thus themselves been part of processes of what has been called 'glocalisation'.[185] In that process, the transnational traditional-justice movement may have romanticised traditional justice in a way similar to the international-criminal-justice movement's romanticisation of international criminal justice.[186] Traditional-justice

---

[181] See also Dolan 2003.

[182] See Allen 2006:154–5 and Branch 2011:Chapter 5. Notice in this light the suggestion made by the above-cited leader who worried about formal courts' lack of attention for the restoration of relationships: 'it would be good if traditional and religious leaders help implement court decisions'. Evidently, invention or restoration of authority of some will challenge that of others, in this case mostly women, youth, government officials and democratically elected leaders. See also Clarke 2009:131. For an illustration of youth resentment towards elders, see the excerpt from an interview with Jimmy Otim in Finnström 2006:211.

[183] See also Clarke 2009:xiv–xvi. This movement differs from the international-criminal-justice movement in that it promotes local or 'traditional' mechanisms as opposed to international courts. The movements share, however, a suspicion about the state's capacity to provide justice to communities.

[184] E.g. see the work of the Justice and Reconciliation Project at www.justiceandreconciliation.com.

[185] Tomlinson 1999:69 defines 'glocalisation' as the tendency for the promotion of the legal rights and cultural identities of indigenous peoples to be coordinated by political movements at a global level.

[186] On the 'dangers of eulogisation' of localised processes, see McGregor 2008:59–64.

advocates have been criticised for downplaying social transformations induced by sustained conflict and the risks of reintroducing a justice system that was the instrument of the colonial power's indirect rule,[187] and for overstating the actual practice of *mato oput* for conflict-related crimes and the forgiving nature of Acholi victims in general.[188] Valid or exaggerated, these criticisms do not deny that local justice practices are accessible and allow those directly affected by the conflict to play a role in the process of obtaining justice, including to dispute any romanticised version of 'traditional justice'.

Taking the promotion of Acholi forms of justice beyond local resistance against an international movement, some of its advocates packaged them as an export product. Rwanda's *gacaca* proceedings provided an inspiring example: these neo-traditional-justice practices had gained world-wide fame as an alternative to formal court proceedings for conflict-related crimes. Studies on Acholi justice practices were also, in the words of a prominent Ugandan bishop, 'a special gift' of the Acholi to 'humanity'.[189] In contrast to most of Uganda's legal profession, the then Principal Judge and chairman of the government's Transitional Justice Working Group, his Lordship James Ogoola, enthusiastically adopted the idea set forth in the A&R Agreement of allowing traditional justice to play a role in connection with the formal justice system:

---

[187] See Allen 2007:162, arguing that the 'accusation of "neo-colonialism" levelled at the ICC is actually more appropriately directed at those attempting to institutionalise local rituals'.

[188] Allen 2006:76, 132, 135 and 152 has described how traditional and religious leaders backed up by Christian organisations have emphasised the forgiving nature of the Acholi. Various population surveys bear out that many Acholi do want to see some form of accountability, but not if it threatens the prospects for peace or punishes their abducted children (see, *inter alia*, Hovil and Quinn 2005, International Center for Transitional Justice and Human Rights Center 2005, OHCHR 2007 and Human Rights Center and Payson Center for International Development and International Center for Transitional Justice 2007). See also International Crisis Group 2004:23, arguing that the wide diversity of opinions among the Acholi is not always represented by their spokespersons. If peace were achieved, forgiveness in the sense of amnesty would not suffice: the elements of acknowledgment and compensation in the *mato oput* procedure remained essential to those questioned.

[189] Interview with Rt Rev. Baker Ochola II, Kitgum, September 2008.

Let us not talk about the extremes, but let us bring Western justice and *mato oput* together. This is an opportunity for Africa to craft something for world jurisprudence.[190]

According to this view, northern Ugandan justice practices could be an internationally respected alternative or supplement to Western punitive justice.[191]

Proponents of local justice practices have had some successes. First, *mato oput* has become part of the national vocabulary. At first known only to Acholi and dismissed by many Ugandan lawyers as an inferior form of justice,[192] local justice practices were discussed in the national parliament, media and formal justice sector as a potential alternative or complement to criminal justice.[193] Leading international media gave attention to ceremonies such as the 'drinking of the bitter root' (*mato oput*) and 'stepping on the egg' (*nyono tong gweno*) as illustrations of ways of dealing with the past other than through courtrooms and prisons.[194]

Secondly, traditional justice attracted donor funding. Foreign development agencies paid for 'traditional' leaders to rediscover their 'traditions' and for the transport and animals required for the ceremonies. The promotion of reconciliation mechanisms had been part of the Amnesty Commission's mandate since its inception,[195] but it was only after the ICC's intervention that it obtained financial resources for doing so from donors.[196] While facilitating the conduct of such

---

[190] Participant observation of the Reflection Workshop on the Juba Peace Talks for Religious and Cultural Leaders, Gulu, 10–12 September 2008.

[191] See also Ogoola 2010:186: 'For the legal fraternity of the African Region, the issue is deeply fundamental. We are on the threshold of a new jurisprudence – an amalgam of the formal and the informal, the punitive and the reformative justice working in happy tandem – a crossbreed between Africa and Europe – truly, a poignant point where justice meets peace and where justice embraces healing.'

[192] In a similar vein, see Allen 2010:249, warning of the 'danger that the institutionalization of local justice will socially infantilize the whole of the war-affected North if it implies that the people of the region are at an earlier stage of development, and are not ready for modern forms of governance'.

[193] See e.g. Uganda 2006b, Uganda 2006c, Uganda 2007, 'Uganda: interview with President Yoweri Museveni' 2005. Also, explicitly, Principal Judge Ogoola at Reflection Workshop on the Juba Peace Talks for Religious and Cultural Leaders, Gulu, 10–12 September 2008: '*mato oput* is now part of the national vocabulary'.

[194] See e.g. Lacey 2005 and Afako 2006.   [195] Amnesty Act 2000, s. 8(c).

[196] Interview with a staff member of the Amnesty Commission, Kampala, September 2008.

processes and enhancing the purchasing power of those that perform them, the commercialisation of ceremonies also undermines their meaning and relevance.[197]

Thirdly, local justice practices received a prominent place in the transitional-justice framework of the A&R Accords. According to one person who met with the LRA leadership at the beginning of the Juba talks:

> Mato oput is an element that Kony and Otti talked to us about when we went to Garamba to meet them. They believe that it is the basis on which they can escape the International Criminal Court ... indictment and be reconciled with our people.[198]

For its part, the GoU had no objections to recognising practices that are by definition 'local' – it matches the government's depiction of the problem in northern Uganda as an *inter* and *intra* 'tribal' conflict. And thus, '[d]riven by the need for adopting appropriate justice mechanisms, including customary processes of accountability, that would resolve the conflict while promoting reconciliation',[199] the parties to the A&R Agreement agreed that, as a principle of general application:

> Traditional justice mechanisms, such as *Culo Kwor*, *Mato Oput*, *Kayo Cuk*, *Ailuc* and *Tonu ci Koka* and others as practiced in the communities affected by the conflict, shall be promoted, with necessary modifications, as a central part of the framework for accountability and reconciliation.[200]

The Annexure provides that '[t]raditional justice shall form a central part of the alternative justice and reconciliation framework'[201] and obliges the government to 'examine the practices of traditional justice mechanisms in affected areas, with a view to identifying the most appropriate roles for such mechanisms'.[202] Highlighting the envisaged integration of local justice practices in the larger transitional-justice framework, the Annexure suggests legislation to provide for '[t]he

---

[197] Interview with a civil society leader from northern Uganda, Kampala, November 2011. See also, critical of these developments, Branch 2010:43 and Branch 2011: Chapter 5 (on 'ethnojustice').

[198] Uganda 2006b.   [199] A&R Agreement, fourth recital.

[200] Clause 3.1.   [201] Clause 19.

[202] Clause 20. Clause 21 also lists *Okukaraba* in Ankole (which is surprising, since it is in the extreme southwest of the country) (see Quinn 2008:9) and 'communal dispute settlement institutions such as family and clan courts'.

recognition of traditional and community justice processes in proceedings' of the SDHC.[203] Whilst heeding the 'constitutional duty on the courts of Uganda to promote reconciliation between contesting parties',[204] such integration of local justice practices and formal state procedures would as such be new to the Ugandan legal system.

Gaining in recognition, local justice practices were also pushed to conform to international practices.[205] A first step in this direction was its documentation. As a prominent religious leader explained:

> Our problem is that these things have not been documented. We, Africans, see through the eyes of imagination, through telling stories. Western people see through the eyes of reading. We are now trying to document the *mato oput* justice system so that the world can see it ... We must show the ICC that we can do it on our own.[206]

According to one northern Ugandan author, 'work to codify the process in conformity with acceptable and feasible "Western" standards is already in an advanced stage'.[207]

Some northern Ugandan leaders have argued that traditional practices should not just be documented, but also be recognised by formal law.[208] According to the LRA delegation to the Juba peace talks, for instance, such provision had to be made, '[b]ecause of the apparent difficulty encountered in persuading the western countries to accept Traditional Justice system[s] as sufficient to meet the standards of international criminal justice'.[209] The Uganda Law Reform Commission has indeed been requested, as part of the preparation for the implementation of the Juba peace talks, to introduce legislation on

---

[203] Annexure, clause 9.

[204] A&R Agreement, fifth recital. See Constitution, art. 126(2): 'In adjudicating cases of both a civil and criminal nature, the courts shall, subject to the law, apply the following principles – ... (d) reconciliation between parties shall be promoted.'

[205] See also, more generally, Drumbl 2007:145.

[206] Interview with Rt Rev. Baker Ochola II, Kitgum, September 2008. A cultural leader argued in a similar vein during an interview in Gulu in September 2008 that harmonisation and documentation were necessary to explain traditional justice to people working for or researching the ICC.

[207] Latigo 2008:110.

[208] See e.g. Ochola II undated:3. Already in 2001 the Paramount Chief, with the advice and consent of Acholi chiefs and council of elders, 'enacted' a 'law to declare the Acholi customary law' (Ker Kwaro Acholi 2001). This law has never obtained the status of law promulgated by the state.

[209] LRA 2006:14.

traditional justice. If such legislation were to include codification, this would raise fundamental questions as to whether diverse and flexible local practices can be fitted into the rigid frameworks of formal law, and whether doing so would jeopardise their credibility with and usefulness for the populations from which they originate.

Secondly, as indicated by the term 'with necessary modifications' in the above-cited passage from the A&R Agreement, the implementation of the A&R Accords would continue, and possibly accelerate, the adjustment of traditional practices to external demands, whether of donors or changing circumstances. As one donor representative explained:

> For traditional leaders to be compliant with human rights standards, they have to modify their practices. That is what we want them to do.[210]

One example is the requirement in the Annexure to consider 'the role and impact of the processes on women and children'.[211]

Thirdly, the push of local justice practices towards international practices was apparent in the fact that ICC-style accountability became the point of reference for the debate over the merits of local practices. Proponents of international criminal justice had discarded local justice practices as an alternative to the ICC, arguing that they did not suffice for crimes within the ICC's jurisdiction. An ICC judge, indeed the Ugandan judge, publicly stated:

> Crimes against humanity, genocide, aggression against other states and war crimes are internationally condemned and cannot be tried by traditional courts but by the ICC ... You cannot expect someone who caused the death of 100 people to be tried in a traditional court if you are looking for justice to be done ... You must convince the international community that justice was done and that the punishment is proportionate with the crime.[212]

Similarly, international human rights NGOs argued that '[w]hile traditional justice processes may provide an important complement to prosecutions, they are not a substitute for them'.[213] In their view, traditional justice fails to meet 'international benchmarks',[214]

---

[210] Interview with a representative of a European development agency, Kampala, November 2011.

[211] Annexure, clause 20.   [212] Maseruka 2009.

[213] Human Rights Watch 2011:6–7.

[214] See also Ogora 2007:289, observing a 'tendency to downplay the significance of traditional justice, with the main argument that they do not conform to international benchmarks manifested in formal justice processes'.

comprising, 'consistent with the Rome Statute, other international standards, and international and domestic practice':

> impartial and independent investigation capable of leading to the identification of those responsible, and a determination of liability before an independent tribunal, during which an accused benefits from fair trial guarantees ... and, if convicted, [receives] appropriate punishment.[215]

Rather than rejecting the ICC framework as such, the proponents of local justice practices defended such practices from the same perspective, highlighting the similarities between local justice and formal court proceedings. For instance, the Justice and Reconciliation Project stated:

> *Mato Oput* encompasses the same principles of truth, accountability and compensation, and restoration of relationships as other justice processes. It is both an independent and transparent process, where elders act as neutral arbitrators of disputes.[216]

Similarly aware of the 'somewhat tragic reality that resistance must work, to some extent, within the parameters established by that which is being resisted',[217] the LRA delegation in Juba insisted that the A&R Accords describe traditional justice in terms used by proponents of international criminal justice. At the delegation's instigation, 'full accountability' was added to the definition of each and every practice listed in the A&R Agreement.[218] It is thus that the definition of *mato oput* reads: 'the traditional ritual performed by the Acholi *after full accountability* and reconciliation has been attained between parties formerly in conflict, *after full accountability*'.[219] The deliberate duplication suggests that in the LRA delegation's view it could not be stressed enough that local justice practices, like the ICC, pursue 'full accountability'.

---

[215] Human Rights Watch 2007.

[216] Liu Institute for Global Issues and Gulu District NGO Forum 2007a:3. For another example, see Ogora 2007.

[217] Rajagopal 2003:10. See also Wastell 2001:194.

[218] Interview with a member of the Juba mediation team, Kampala, September 2008.

[219] See A&R Agreement, clause 1 para. 9 (emphases added). See also clause 1 para. 8: '"Kayo Cuk" refers to the traditional accountability and reconciliation processes practiced by the Langi communities *after full accountability* and reconciliation has been attained between parties formerly in conflict, *after full accountability*' (emphases added).

The attempts to fit local justice practices into the ICC mould led to the downplaying of fundamental differences in the concepts of justice underlying the respective paradigms. The term 'justice' does not exist as an Acholi notion.[220] The term used by the Acholi to cover the English word 'justice' may be translated as 'correct judgment' or 'interpretation'.[221] More relevant to the Acholi experience of justice is *roco wat*, which means 'to restore relationships'.[222] An accountability mechanism such as *mato oput* aims to restore relationships between the clans of the perpetrator and the victim and includes truth-telling and compensation. Cleansing ceremonies, in turn, focus on restoring the wrong committed and can concern either the perpetrator or the victim. For some acts, for instance rape, there are cleansing ceremonies for the victim but no accountability mechanisms. Assessing Acholi traditional practices, international-criminal-justice experts commented that cleansing ceremonies did not suffice for accountability. They advised: 'If you want traditional justice to be credible, you'll have to adapt it so that it can deal with war crimes and crimes against humanity.'[223] In order to deal with international crimes, so it was argued, traditional justice had to shift from being communal to individual, to mete out punishment rather than provide compensation, to focus on the perpetrator instead of the victim, and to turn cleansing ceremonies for offences such as abduction and mutilation into accountability mechanisms.[224]

Attempts to show that traditional justice does ensure accountability resulted in a focus on the Acholi practice with the most aspects of accountability, namely, *mato oput*. While used only in cases involving death and where the perpetrator can identify the victim or the victim the perpetrator, *mato oput* became the umbrella term for all Acholi justice practices in national and international discussions of Acholi traditional justice. In 2008, the Ugandan Amnesty Commission advertised an event in which former LRA combatants would be

---

[220] Interview with an expert, Gulu, September 2008. On different understandings of the concept 'justice', see also Dolan, Tamale and Oloka-Onyango 2009:2.
[221] Interview with an expert, Gulu, September 2008.   [222] *Ibid.*
[223] *Ibid.*, citing international-criminal-justice experts commenting on whether traditional justice in northern Uganda meets ICC standards.
[224] *Ibid.* Ironically, this comes at a time when international-criminal-justice and criminal-justice systems in some Western countries are criticised for failing to provide sufficient rehabilitation and compensation for victims and are, in response to this criticism, becoming increasingly victim-oriented.

welcomed home as a *mato oput* ceremony.[225] In fact, what took place was *nyono tong gweno*, the stepping-on-the-egg ceremony, which is a cleansing ceremony to facilitate integration rather than an accountability mechanism.[226] But *mato oput* was used as a brand name for traditional justice, because that is the name that international donors know.[227]

Despite all the attention and study, there has thus far been hardly any catalysing effect on the actual practice of traditional accountability proceedings for conflict-related crimes.[228] People are still settling back into their communities and have considered it more important to carry out *moyo piny*, a ceremony to cleanse land blighted by unburied dead. Moreover, resources are scarce, especially for compensation. A more structural obstacle is that the practice of *mato oput* is based on the assumption that perpetrator and victim know each other.[229] One of the first attempts to apply *mato oput* to conflict-related crimes failed because the LRA commander who confessed his crimes could not identify his victims.[230] Reformist 'traditional' leaders argue that practices 'will be adjusted' to characteristics of conflict-related crimes.[231] When and how remain undetermined.

Even if the adjustment of the practices to the characteristics of conflict-related crimes were to continue, the study of, advocacy for, and practice of local justice practices have less and less to do with complementarity. In the first few years after the ICC's intervention, the link was stronger. Some religious and cultural leaders, members of the LRA delegation and government officials referred to *mato oput* as *the* Ugandan alternative to the ICC. The LRA stated in its position paper for the Juba talks:

> As these talks proceed, the Warrant of Arrest issued by the ICC hovers over the heads of the Chairman and the three surviving members of the

---

[225] 'Invitation for Mato-Oput Cleansing Ceremony in Gulu' 2008.

[226] *Nyono tong gweno* can be an element of a larger *mato oput* procedure (Ochola II 2009:23–4).

[227] The event was sponsored by the International Organisation for Migration, the United States Agency for International Development and the United Nations Development Programme. On 'donor-driven justice', see Oomen 2005:902–6.

[228] A religious leader in an interview in Kitgum in September 2008 reported one *mato oput* proceeding that had been set in motion for a conflict-related crime.

[229] See also Justice and Reconciliation Project 2011a:2.

[230] See 'Uganda: former LRA combatants struggle for forgiveness' 2010 and Negara 2011.

[231] Interview with elders, Kitgum, September 2008.

LRA High Command. This paper examines how the Traditional Justice system, which has for time immemorial been used by most of the
people in the affected areas, would be a perfect alternative, and would
be the preferred option to the formal prosecutory [sic] criminal justice
system of the ICC.[232]

The leader of the GoU delegation also presented traditional justice as
an alternative to the ICC, when explaining in Parliament:

> It is true that the ICC has taken steps to ensure that the indicted
> leaders of the LRA are tried for the crimes they have been indicted for.
> ICC's stand is that impunity should never be condoned and that those
> responsible for crimes committed must be brought to justice and pun-
> ished. The Uganda Government fully supports this stand … It is for
> this reason and in view of the fact that the indicted LRA leaders
> cannot easily be brought to book using the normal criminal justice
> system and the fact that the affected population is longing for peace
> and is willing to forgive so as to start new lives, that Government
> has proposed the use of the Acholi traditional system of justice called
> Mato put …
>
> Madam Speaker, it is not possible for the ICC to review the indict-
> ments before the question of impunity is adequately addressed. This is
> why Government has proposed the Acholi traditional alternative just-
> ice process of Mato put. The Government will formally engage the ICC
> only after a formal peace agreement has been reached or signed and
> after the LRA has gone through the process of Mato put. The Govern-
> ment has, however, maintained close contacts with the ICC and the
> UN on this very subject-matter …
>
> Government remains committed to a peaceful resolution to the
> conflict; Government sees the ICC as complementing the work of
> Uganda to see a peaceful end to this conflict.[233]

However, the more Ugandan delegations visited the ICC[234] and the
more lawyers were consulted, the more all involved in the talks
became convinced that local justice practices would probably not
amount to domestic proceedings in the sense of the ICC's complementarity principle, if only because traditional justice does not include
prosecution. As one religious leader recalled:

---

[232] LRA 2006:4.   [233] Uganda 2007.
[234] On the visits to the ICC, see ICC 2005, ICC-OTP 2005d, ICC-OTP 2005e, ICC
2008 and Glassborow and Eichstaedt 2008.

> When we [cultural and religious leaders from northern Uganda] were in
> The Hague, the ICC said that *mato oput* is lower than formal justice.
> They said their benchmarks were higher.[235]

Others suggested that, while 'traditional justice' on its own might not
be enough for a successful complementarity challenge, complementarity would be challenged on the basis of a package of mechanisms that,
taken together, could be an alternative to the ICC. The Minister of
State for Defence thus explained to Parliament:

> This is the package, which I am sure Government will present to the
> ICC, to convince them that we now have this process, the *Mato put*,
> and the legal base we will put on top of that. Maybe then the prosecu-
> tor will use the statute to say that on the issue of impunity, Uganda is
> going to handle and therefore the case falls by the way side.[236]

The idea reflects an understanding of complementarity as an assessment of how a state deals with impunity in a situation as a whole
rather than on a case-by-case basis.[237]

However, ever since the A&R Accords provided for the SDHC to
deal with serious crimes, the push for traditional justice as *the* alternative to the ICC diminished. As one religious leader explained:

> Uganda is now putting forward a complete system: formal and
> traditional ... if the ICC doubts the traditional justice system then it
> can trust the Special Division. The Special Division can do it alone.[238]

With the creation of the special division of the High Court as the
'complementarity court', it was this body alone, and not local justice
practices or any other transitional-justice mechanism, that was
expected to meet the ICC's complementarity standards. The debate
over whether local justice meets international standards, or more
specifically the ICC's complementarity requirements, thus went quiet.

[235] Interview with one of the members of the delegation, Kitgum, September 2008.
[236] Uganda 2006c. See also the Deputy Attorney-General, as reported in International Bar Association Human Rights Institute 2007:32 ('he had written to
the Uganda Law Reform Commission with the view to introducing legislation on
traditional justice. In this respect, he suggested that if peace talks were successfully
concluded, aspects of the traditional justice system such as *mato oput* instituted
and amnesty provided, this would reflect a "meaningful" process and would give
the GoU sufficient grounds to make an admissibility challenge before the ICC.').
[237] On the Statute's providing for a case-based assessment, see Chapter 2, 'The
complementarity assessment is case-specific'.
[238] Interview, Kitgum, September 2008.

The calls to 'codify' traditional justice were toned down, too. No longer under pressure to compete with the ICC, elders recognised the advantages of keeping local justice practices flexible:

> Codification is not useful since traditional justice evolves. There is also a risk that when you make it a legal document you take away the authority of the traditional leaders and shift it to the lawyers.[239]

More generally, advocacy for local justice practices faded with the weakening of resistance against the ICC. Disillusioned by Kony's refusal to sign the FPA even after their travelling to Garamba to implore him to sign, community leaders were tired of fighting for peace with the government, the ICC and the LRA. With the LRA out of Uganda and people returning home, disputes over land became more pressing than finding an alternative to the ICC. As one leader explained the change in positions:

> In the heat of the moment people express certain views, more or less because of the demands of the situation. [In the first few years after the ICC's intervention] there was high-level violence. There were a lot of leaders who were demanding traditional justice, mainly because of the pressure of IDP [internationally displaced persons] life, the level of violence and fear for reprisals. But when the Juba peace talks and the cessation hostilities forced the LRA out of northern Uganda, the demand for traditional justice decreased. Now people are home.[240]

Northern Uganda being more secure, many community leaders are less vehemently opposed to criminal justice, whether conducted by the ICC or Ugandan courts.[241] Local justice practices remain relevant, but in their own right; not as an alternative to the ICC.[242]

The catalysing effect on local justice practices began immediately when local leaders opposed the ICC's intervention in northern Uganda. Most other effects of complementarity in Uganda, however, were catalysed only when the Ugandan government searched for an

---

[239] Interview with an Acholi leader, Kampala, November 2011.
[240] Interview with an elder from northern Uganda, Kampala, November 2011.
[241] See also Allen 2010:261.
[242] According to some traditional leaders, the force of donor money driving 'traditional' practices has also diminished (interview with an elder from northern Uganda, Kampala, November 2011: 'traditional leaders are dependent on the support of international donors. That support has dried up. The focus has changed to issues of resettlement. No embassy now has interest in traditional justice.').

alternative to the ICC. It began to do so, at least seemingly, during the Juba peace talks.

Putting accountability and transitional justice on the peace-talks agenda

The ICC's sword of Damocles hanging over Juba resulted in the paradoxical situation that it was in the rebel movement's interests to insist on accountability instead of amnesty. In the dozens of earlier rounds of negotiations with movements fighting the GoU, accountability had not featured on the agenda. But in the Juba peace talks, the LRA stressed the importance of accountability. It was first and foremost driven by a desire to terminate the existence of the ICC arrest warrants against its leadership. But the LRA delegation did not merely require the lifting of the ICC arrest warrants 'in the interests of justice ... including ... the interests of victims'[243] – a reference to article 53 of the Rome Statute – and accept the government's proposal to use traditional justice. Rather, the LRA delegation insisted on all sides being held accountable, including for crimes committed before 1 July 2002, in order to cover the period when most of the alleged UPDF crimes were committed.[244] In doing so, the LRA informed its adversary: accountability could come to haunt you, too. It did the same by demanding, in line with long-held positions of some civil society organisations, a 'National Truth and Reconciliation Commission' and a 'Compensation Fund'.[245] Thus, as a result of the LRA's aggressive negotiation strategy on accountability and reconciliation, transitional-justice mechanisms other than criminal proceedings entered into the negotiations.

The GoU, in turn, offered in its initial position paper only amnesty and traditional justice.[246] It saw no need for reparations or for a truth commission, particularly not one that involved the nation as a whole.[247] Yet, over time it calculated that, in light of civil society's and international pressure for more comprehensive transitional-justice

---

[243] LRA 2006:5–6.   [244] *Ibid.*:1.   [245] *Ibid.*:11–12.   [246] Uganda 2006d.

[247] Interview with a government minister, Kampala, October 2008 and interview with an international advisor in the negotiations, The Hague, May 2008. The resistance to a national mechanism was in line with the GoU's propensity to describe the conflict as 'local' and an 'Acholi affair', to disregard the origins of the conflict and to underplay questions of political and economic tensions between the centre and periphery.

mechanisms, it was costly to be seen as obstructing an agreement on these points. It acceded to demands for a truth commission and reparations.[248]

But the parties realised that a truth commission, reparations and traditional justice, individually or together, were unlikely to be successful in rendering the ICC case inadmissible on grounds of complementarity. For cases of 'serious crimes', domestic criminal proceedings were agreed upon.[249] To the LRA leadership, both domestic and international trials were humiliating and off-putting. But an agreement on domestic proceedings could keep an untrustworthy and culturally remote international court at bay[250] whilst domestic proceedings could allow for more negotiations on charges and sentences. Seemingly aware of the complementarity principle, Kony argued that '[t]he ICC should leave Uganda to handle the issue of accountability since Uganda has a functional justice system with jails in Luzira, Lugore, etc.'.[251]

In order to make domestic accountability acceptable to the LRA, Ugandan sentences would have to be substantially reduced. Details could not be spelled out in any agreement, as this might have jeopardised any future assessment of the genuineness of the Ugandan proceedings by the ICC.[252] But the Agreement does provide for 'recognition of confessions or other forms of cooperation to be recognised for purposes of sentencing or sanctions'[253] and obliges the GoU to introduce alternative sanctions,[254] which are to 'reflect the gravity of the crimes or violations' and at the same time 'promote reconciliation between individuals and within communities; promote the rehabilitation of offenders; take into account an

---

[248] In order to overcome the GoU's resistance to an obligation to pay reparations and to allow fiscal questions to be addressed, Annexure, clause 4(j) pushed reparations down the time line of the transitional-justice programme by leaving it to the truth-finding body to make recommendations on a reparations regime.

[249] Annexure, clause 7.

[250] Expressing his distrust of international institutions, Kony referred to the 'poisoning of Milošević' (interview with someone involved in peace talks with Kony, February 2009).

[251] 'Uganda: IDPs unlikely to meet deadline to vacate camps' 2006.

[252] Interview with a member of the mediation team, Kampala, September 2008. See also Chapter 2, 'Low punishment or a pardon is not a ground for admissibility per se'.

[253] A&R Agreement, clause 3.6. See also the encouragement to cooperate with proceedings in clauses 3.2 and 3.5.

[254] Ibid., clause 6.3.

individual's admissions or other cooperation with proceedings; and, require perpetrators to make reparations to victims'.[255] Reflecting 'the very clear understanding by all parties that death penalties or long sentences would not have a role to play',[256] this provision implicitly excludes these sentences since they would not 'promote the rehabilitation of offenders'.

As the mediator, the GoSS took as a starting point that any agreement concerning the LRA would have to fit within the framework of the Rome Statute.[257] It did not do so out of a normative conviction:[258] a year before, the SPLM, the dominant party in the GoSS, had itself signed a 'comprehensive' peace agreement which has hundreds of provisions on wide-ranging issues but is silent on accountability.[259] However, the ICC's involvement had changed the context for the GoU–LRA negotiations. In the words of one of the Acholi traditional leaders advising the Mediator:

> The Uganda situation was negotiated against the backdrop of the ICC. Accountability had to be handled. You cannot remove the ICC unless you meet the complementarity standards.[260]

Commenting on the difference in context of the GoS–SPLM and GoU–LRA negotiations, chief mediator Riek Machar concluded, with a sigh: 'Accountability is a whole new thing in this world.'[261]

---

[255] *Ibid.*, clause 6.4.

[256] Email exchange with an advisor to the Chief Mediator in the Juba peace talks, 8 November 2009.

[257] Interview with Chief Mediator Riek Machar, Switzerland, July 2009. See also Afako 2010.

[258] In a discussion with Western diplomats, Chief Mediator Machar contrasted the ICC's approach to the conflict with his own initiative: 'I won't say the ICC was wrong, but it has no capacity to implement. The ICC is a European solution to an African problem, but what we're doing is an African solution to an African problem.' (Hume 2006a).

[259] See Chapter 4, 'Fostering interest in transitional justice'.

[260] Interview with an Acholi traditional leader, Kampala, September 2008. See also interview with Hon. Justice Benjamin J. Odoki, Chief Justice of Uganda, Kampala, 7 October 2008, comparing the negotiations with the LRA with the GoU's negotiations with other movements: 'This is different than other conflicts, because here the ICC has come in. "Accountability and Reconciliation" [the title of the agreement on agenda item 3] is camouflage for "ICC".'

[261] Interview with Chief Mediator Riek Machar, Switzerland, July 2009.

Whether ultimately considered beneficial or detrimental, with the ICC as 'bogeyman',[262] accountability in general and some type of formal criminal proceedings in particular had to be on the agenda of the peace talks as long as the LRA objected to the Court's involvement. The ICC investigations and, even more so, the ICC arrest warrants and the principle of complementarity thus helped to put the issue of accountability firmly on the Juba negotiating table – a first in the many negotiations between the GoU and rebel movements.

Stimulating a debate on transitional justice

The discussion has gone far beyond the parties at the negotiating table, far beyond Juba and far beyond accountability: civil society and government agencies throughout Uganda have taken up the concept of transitional justice. To some extent, this effect is one of ICC intervention as such – it started immediately after the referral. However, the transitional-justice debate really took off in the context of the search for alternatives to the ICC, in which complementarity, more as big idea than as legal principle, played a key role.

The referral of the situation in northern Uganda as such led to some civil society activity, ranging from organisations working in northern Uganda criticising the ICC's intervention,[263] to the creation of the Ugandan Coalition for the International Criminal Court (UCICC)[264] and the Advocates for Public International Law Uganda ('established to soften the perception of the Rome Statute').[265] During the Juba peace talks, both the GoU and the LRA conducted public consultations. The discussion expanded beyond the question whether the ICC obstructed peacemaking to questions as to how Uganda, not just

---

[262] A term used by Anton Baaré, consultant at the Juba negotiations, telephone conversation with the author, May 2008.

[263] See e.g. Refugee Law Project 2004 and responses from NGOs documented by Okumu-Alya 2006:44.

[264] Interview with a UCICC staff member, Kampala, September 2008. Initially funded by the Coalition for the International Criminal Court, the Ugandan Coalition *for* the International Criminal Court later changed its name in its publications and on its website into Ugandan Coalition *on* the International Criminal Court, to allow NGOs that were critical of the ICC to be part of the coalition.

[265] Interview with one of the founders of APILU, Kampala, November 2011. See also Adriko 2008:3.

northern Uganda, should deal with its past, characterised by the widespread commission of crimes of violence against civilians by state and non-state actors alike.

This is a revolutionary effect. Uganda – like many other states – has never developed a policy of dealing with the past other than moving on. Incoming governments lacked the legitimacy, stability or resources to prosecute the apparatus of the previous regime[266] where the latter had not fled into exile.[267] For the sake of national reconciliation, opponents were bought off with power, wealth and amnesty or informal guarantees of non-prosecution. To the extent that people were convicted, it was for treason.[268] Uganda had two government-sponsored truth commissions (the Commission of Inquiry into the Disappearance of People in Uganda established by President Idi Amin in 1974, and the Commission of Inquiry into Violations of Human Rights created by President Museveni in 1986),[269] but their findings were never widely disseminated, their recommendations not implemented, and their existence largely forgotten. Hardly any follow-up was given to the referral by Uganda's second truth commission of dozens of cases to the Director of Public Prosecutions or the Criminal

---

[266] Exceptionally, members of the previous regime were prosecuted for conflict-related crimes. See e.g. Ugandan courts, *Abdalla Nasur* (a lieutenant under Amin convicted of murdering a mayor), *Chris Rwakasisi* (Rwakasisi was a Minister of State under Obote's second administration and convicted of kidnapping with intent to murder) and *Haji Musa Sebirumbi* (a constituency chairman under the same administration convicted of murder of civilians who had been accused of supporting Museveni). After the fall of Idi Amin, a statute was drafted to establish a 'Human Rights Court for the Trial of Persons Accused of Offences Against Humanity and Others Specified Offences Committed During the Idi Amin Regime Up to the Date Of Total Liberation (3rd June, 1979) and to Make Provisions for Other Matters Connected Therewith or Incidental Thereto', with criminal jurisdiction over offences including genocide. The Statute was never enacted into law (Commission of Inquiry into Violations of Human Rights 1994:419–20 and Appendix 5; thanks to Joanna Quinn who had the 720 pages scanned and shared her copy).

[267] Former president Milton Obote fled to Dar es Salaam and later to Lusaka, General Tito Okello to eastern Sudan and Idi Amin to Saudi Arabia. See also Baker 2004:1493–5.

[268] This crime is not included in the concept of conflict-related crimes because it does not correspond with conduct also criminalised in the Rome Statute. One of the most famous treason cases related to the conflict with the LRA has been *Professor Isaac Newton Ojok*. Ojok was initially convicted and sentenced to death because of his support to Alice Lakwena's Holy Spirit Movement, but was finally acquitted.

[269] See Quinn 2010 and Hayner 2011:239–40 and 243.

Investigations Department.[270] Various reasons have been cited, including the high evidentiary standard in court (in contrast to that of a truth commission), the fear of witnesses of the possible consequences of cooperating with criminal investigations, the Criminal Investigations Department's lack of capacity, and unwillingness.[271] Only a handful of victims of conflict-related crimes have been successful in obtaining reparations by privately bringing cases before courts. A national debate on whether and how to come to terms with the past was never part of the aftermath of peace talks or violent changes of government.

In the final stages of the Juba peace process, when there were still hopes that Kony would sign the FPA, the GoU mandated its Justice Law and Order Sector (JLOS) to prepare the implementation of the legal aspects of the Juba Agreements.[272] JLOS, adopting concepts used by international advisors to the Juba talks, created its own 'Transitional Justice Working Group' with sub-committees on formal proceedings, traditional justice, truth-telling, integration of the different systems and budgetary issues.

JLOS 'donors', those states that traditionally provide financial support to JLOS programmes, including Austria, Denmark, Ireland, Norway and The Netherlands, were enthusiastic about the idea of JLOS doing its bit to implement the results of the Juba peace talks and promoting transitional justice in Uganda. JLOS's transitional-justice plans also attracted new donors such as Canada and the US. Donors offered to fund preparatory activities such as training courses, study tours, public consultations, needs assessments and courtroom improvement. They also paid for two transitional-justice advisors, one Ugandan, one foreign, to be embedded in the JLOS Secretariat, with a view to strengthening the JLOS Secretariat. An additional reason for funding two such persons was to have 'a contact person within

---

[270] Commission of Inquiry into Violations of Human Rights 1994:625–9 and Appendix 9.

[271] *Ibid.*:626, Hayner 2011:97–9 and interview with an official working for the Director of Public Prosecutions, Kampala, October 2008.

[272] JLOS is a coordinating forum bringing together senior officials in government agencies working in the areas of justice, law and order, including the Ministry of Justice and Constitutional Affairs, the Ministry of Internal Affairs, the judiciary, the Uganda Police Force, the Uganda Prison Service, the Directorate of Public Prosecutions, the Judicial Service Commission, the Uganda Law Reform Commission, the Uganda Human Rights Commission and the Uganda Law Society.

JLOS working on transitional justice', one donor explained, so that the transitional-justice agenda could be pushed.[273]

Donors' enthusiasm was matched by that of international NGOs. The ICC's intervention in Uganda, and especially the outcome – on paper at least – of the Juba talks, attracted a caravan of international NGOs with transitional-justice experience. One representative explained her NGO's 'anti-impunity programme' in Uganda as follows:

> We began that programme because we have expertise in international crimes. We had been involved in DRC since 2005. We try to use that expertise elsewhere ... With respect to international justice, our mandate is to fight against impunity. We also bring complaints from the country to the ICC. If the ICC opens up in a place, then [we] will open up an office.[274]

International NGOs' proposals to 'train', 'capacity-build', 'workshop' and 'advise' Ugandans were readily funded by donors. International NGOs for their part looked for 'local partners' with 'grassroots connections', thereby opening up a world of funding for Ugandan NGOs willing to adopt the international NGOs' anti-impunity agenda. The Ugandan economy, in which the NGO sector is the fastest growing employer after government,[275] readily supplied the international NGOs' demand.

The last piece of the puzzle was for NGOs and donors to find a Ugandan demand for the offered and funded international expertise. With project proposals with six-figure budgets annexed tucked under their arms, representatives of international NGOs queued up to meet with the chairman of the JLOS Transitional Justice Working Group and the registrar of the newly created International Crimes Division.[276] They would leave with an 'invitation' from the Ugandan government to implement their proposed programmes.[277] The efforts

---

[273] Interview with a donor representative, Kampala, November 2011.

[274] Interview, Kampala, November 2011.

[275] Mwenda 2007:34. As part of a larger explanation of the increasing authoritarianism in Uganda, he adds: 'The middle-class know-how and energy that might have gone into democratizing the state have instead been diverted into the work of NGOs that carry out "policy advocacy", "humanitarian relief" and bureaucratized human rights activism.' See also Dicklitsch and Lwanga 2003.

[276] See below, 'Stimulating the establishment of a Ugandan international crimes division'.

[277] When one Ugandan official was asked in an interview in Kampala in November 2011 whether an NGO had conducted a particular assessment at the request of

of international and domestic 'norm entrepreneurs' seem to have been successful: in Uganda, 'TJ' is in vogue.[278]

Nonetheless, it would be wrong to conclude that these processes evince 'norm infiltration'[279] or 'norm internalisation' as developed in theories on how international norms emerge, spread and become globally accepted.[280] First, 'transitional justice' owes its popularity in Uganda in large part to its nebulousness which allows everyone to embrace it, but at the same time caters for diverging (mis)understandings. For many of the norm entrepreneurs, transitional justice, defined by the UN Secretary-General as 'the full range of processes and mechanisms associated with a society's attempts to come to terms with a legacy of large-scale past abuses, in order to ensure accountability, serve justice and achieve reconciliation',[281] has at its core criminal accountability, possibly complemented by truth commissions and reparations. Operating in accordance with this understanding of transitional justice, the donor-funded JLOS transitional-justice advisors published on behalf of JLOS – but without any discussion within JLOS – a piece arguing against Uganda's amnesty law.[282] Many of the Ugandan government actors, by contrast, are interested in transitional justice precisely because it could be an *alternative to* ordinary criminal justice. The chairman of the JLOS Transitional Justice Working Group, for instance, understood transitional justice to refer to justice involving short punishments, which was best done through 'traditional justice'.[283] Transitional justice's universalist façade, to paraphrase Sally Engle Merry, thus obscures the fact that

---

the GoU, the official responded: 'We *kind of* requested it. They offered it, pushed for it, and then we accepted it.'

[278] For the concept of 'norm entrepreneurs', see Chapter 1, n. 56 and accompanying text.

[279] Norm infiltration is the process by which a norm becomes taken for granted as an internal (as opposed to imposed) norm. This process can take place with respect to national norms and individuals, but also with respect to international norms and domestic legal orders.

[280] See, *inter alia*, Finnemore and Sikkink 1998 and Risse, Ropp and Sikkink 1999.

[281] UN Doc. S/2004/616 (2004):[8].

[282] Transitional Justice Team of the JLOS Secretariat 2011.

[283] Interview with the chairman of the Transitional Justice Working Group, Kampala, September 2008. See also Justice Ogoola's comments at Refugee Law Project 2010: 'We were mandated to discuss three things from Juba: how to set up a court for punitive purposes, and then two other pillars: the transitional justice – the reformative justice side of the coin – and truth-telling.'

it is still understood in local ways.[284] In the norm entrepreneurs' view, Ugandan actors' interpretation of transitional justice comes closest to 'subversion' on Merry's continuum of 'vernacularization': 'The name and the transnational referent are retained but the content of the ideas ... is dramatically changed.'[285]

A second caveat is that, to date, the success of the transitional-justice norm entrepreneurs has been due less to the persuasiveness of the advocated norm than to the political economy of the entrepreneurship. In other words, government actors have allowed transitional-justice norm entrepreneurs to operate in Uganda because they have something to offer: training with 'sitting allowances',[286] study tours abroad[287] and needs assessments. Such offers are lubricants of the patronage system through which the state is administered.[288] Sitting allowances are welcome additions to officials' salaries; free study tours abroad are useful perks for the most loyal officials; and the outcomes of needs assessments constitute shopping lists for donors: this (buildings, computers, cars and petrol) is what we 'need' to do the transitional justice that you insist on.[289] Because it is donor-driven, transitional justice's popularity may decline with a decrease in donors' interest.[290]

Even with persisting donor interest, transitional justice has already lost some of its appeal to officials. JLOS, the GoU's leading actor on transitional justice, in 2011 omitted transitional justice from its draft

---

[284] Merry 2006b:43.   [285] *Ibid*.:44.

[286] Fees paid in exchange for a participant's attending an event.

[287] See also Clapham 1977:87 ('International relations offer the chance of an escape into the big time world of global politics, which must be justified rhetorically in terms of world peace or third world development, but in which the activity itself is to a large extent its own reward. This extends beyond the head of state to other members of the government.').

[288] See also International Crisis Group 2012 on the shift in Museveni's Uganda 'from a broad-based constitutional government to patronage-based personal rule'.

[289] See also Mwenda 2007:31: 'Civil servants who write projects typically set them up so that a project's main benefits go to its staffers in the form of salaries, allowances, official cars, and domestic or foreign trips complete with per-diems.'

[290] Indeed, this is what some Ugandan actors who have not been co-opted in the transitional-justice niche have warned. As one legal actor observed with respect to the creation of the SDHC: 'as usual, we are heavily relying on development partners ... We must think in terms not only of establishment but continuity. The sad story of the judiciary is that institutions are coming to a hold when development partners no longer fund.' (Participant observation, official meeting, Kampala, October 2008).

strategic investment plan for the next decade.[291] At donors' insistence,[292] transitional justice in the end received one page in the report, even though, according to the relevant JLOS actors, transitional justice is 'only transitional, and will thus not even be years', and therefore need not be incorporated in any long-term plans.[293] Three years after the creation of the Transitional Justice Working Group, JLOS had not yet developed a transitional-justice policy. Some officials cited a need for elaborate consultations. Others said there was a lack of political guidance, and thus interest, from the President and his cabinet.[294] The donor-funded transitional-justice advisors embedded within JLOS, expected to push the transitional-justice agenda, operate largely on their own. In the words of one donor representative: 'It seems that the JLOS Secretariat thinks "good, now TJ is covered by them."'[295] Many donors acknowledge that transitional justice has been donor-driven, but hope that in due course the GoU will consider transitional justice as unavoidable.[296]

However, transitional justice is not a priority of the Ugandan President, and thus, in a state characterised by head-of-state-driven politics, not of the Ugandan government.[297] Now that Kony has refused to sign the FPA, there is even less of an incentive for the GoU to develop a transitional-justice policy: there has been no transition.[298] Facing corruption scandals, protests against the NRM's twenty-five-plus years of rule and disputes over land, President Museveni and his cabinet have more pressing issues on their minds.

The GoU cabinet has not allowed implementation of transitional-justice instruments that it had conceded in the Juba peace talks. The cabinet had never been a great supporter of truth-telling, for instance, as the latter could expose the NRM's own past and result in

---

[291] Interviews with donors, Kampala, November 2011.

[292] Interview with a JLOS official, Kampala, November 2011: 'There is a lot of pushing from donors on transitional justice.'

[293] Interviews with donors, Kampala, November 2011, reporting the discussion with JLOS actors.

[294] Interview with government official, Kampala, May 2010.

[295] Interview with a JLOS donor, Kampala, November 2011.

[296] *Ibid.*

[297] Interview with a presidential advisor, Kampala, November 2011: 'Uganda is characterised by head-of-state driven politics ... The ministers prioritise what the head of state wants. That is not transitional justice.'

[298] According to a presidential advisor (*ibid.*), the cabinet had not devoted any time to transitional justice because 'the Final Peace Agreement has not been signed'.

recommendations for expensive reparations[299] (for example, for failure to protect the population).[300] The following excerpt from an interview with a Ugandan State Minister illustrates that extolling concepts of transitional justice does not imply commitment to taking any related measures. Asked about the GoU's plans to implement the Juba agreements as long as Kony refuses to sign the FPA, he replied:

> [W]ithin the government we are divided. The army is frustrated. We [in our Ministry] and [another Ministry] are more patient than in the Ministry of Defence. We say: 'We can implement agenda items 2 [comprehensive solutions] and 3 [accountability and reconciliation].'
>
> [INTERVIEWER:] *All elements of these agenda items? For instance, also a truth commission?*
>
> I am not so sure about it. We have debated against it. The idea of a TRC comes from civil society organisations, not from the government. People in the government are opposing it. How far back shall it go? Which conflict shall it cover?
>
> [INTERVIEWER:] *But Uganda has already had two truth commissions.* Has it?
>
> [INTERVIEWER:] *Yes, President Amin established one and President Museveni established the Oder commission.*
>
> [*Laughs*] People want a juicy-type of truth commission, like in South Africa, they want a juicy soap opera.[301]

Interviewed three years later, another government minister, asked about possible reform of the Amnesty Act, expressed similar scepticism about pursuing truth: 'A blanket amnesty is better than one in exchange for truth-telling: truth is dangerous.'[302] The coalescence of the interests of transitional-justice norm entrepreneurs and the GoU, which contributed to the sudden rise of the transitional-justice debate, is thus only partial and may be short-lived.

Some more home-grown transitional-justice initiatives, however, could continue. Transitional justice was an issue raised in campaigns

---

[299] Some claims have already emerged, the biggest case thus far being *Celestina Odong Adyera*, for damages for the unlawful acts of the NRA/UPDF committed in the cause and scope of its duties.

[300] A first case is *Albertina Opio*, in which the claimants request damages because the UPDF had been tipped off about an upcoming LRA attack but failed to intervene.

[301] Interview with a State Minister, Kampala, October 2008.

[302] Interview with a State Minister, Kampala, November 2011.

for the 2011 presidential election.[303] The ICC was referred to, mostly as an instrument to defame one's political opponent.[304] Demands for the truth have arisen in the elections also beyond northern Uganda, for example in the Luwero triangle where in the early 1980s the then government army took revenge against thousands of people for supporting Museveni's rebellion against Obote. The Beyond Juba Project of Makerere University's Refugee Law Project aims explicitly to move the debate on transitional justice beyond the Juba peace talks.[305] However, freedom of expression on matters of transitional justice may be limited the more the spotlight shifts to government accountability, as is suggested by incidents such as a raid on a Ugandan newspaper that had been reporting on UPDF scandals and detention of political opponents who accuse the GoU of international crimes.[306]

By making allowance for a national alternative to the ICC, the principle of complementarity fostered the emergence of a Ugandan transitional-justice debate. This effect is still a far cry from the conduct of domestic proceedings, the only action that can render ICC cases inadmissible on grounds of complementarity. Yet a debate may be a precursor to other effects and is, in itself, a break with the past.

---

[303] The northern Ugandan NGO Justice and Reconciliation Project campaigned to put transitional justice on the election agenda (see http://justiceandreconciliation.com/2011/01/campaign-to-put-tj-on-the-election-agenda).

[304] Independent presidential candidate Samuel Lubega 'promised to "take President Museveni to the International Criminal Court" if he refuses to hand over power peacefully or tampers with the electoral process' (Ninsiima 2010). The UPC's presidential candidate, Olara Otunnu, asked the ICC Prosecutor to investigate Museveni for 'crimes against humanity, war crimes, genocide, and aggression' committed in northern Uganda, the DRC and Kampala (Musoke and Oluput 2010). Ironically, given his uncritical response to the equally 'political' referral by the GoU of the situation concerning the LRA to the ICC (see Nouwen and Werner 2010a), the Prosecutor 'challenged Otunnu to produce concrete evidence, and not engage in "political debate"'. The GoU's response to these allegations demonstrated its limitations to any debate on transitional-justice issues: Otunnu was 'wanted by the Police for alleging that Museveni funded Kony's LRA rebels and masterminded the northern Uganda war for over 20 years' (Musoke and Oluput 2010).

[305] See www.beyondjuba.org and Refugee Law Project 2011a.

[306] See e.g. the facts of *Onynango-Obbo and Mwenda*, 'Uganda journalists held in raid' 2008 and Musoke and Oluput 2010. On developments in the freedom of the press in Uganda, see also Tabaire 2007.

Broadening the approach to the conflict to include a legal dimension

Covered in a legal cloak, the referral of the LRA to the ICC fitted neatly into the GoU's military strategy. The referral provided several opportunities. By referring the situation to the ICC, President Museveni could legitimise and intensify his military approach, and in doing so satisfy the demands of military elites. Meanwhile, ICC-supporting Western states would not criticise the military's counter-insurgency campaign when fought against internationally wanted 'war criminals'. The northern electorate, tired of conflict and demanding a peaceful approach, could be informed that the LRA was now an international problem, the resolution of which was no longer at the sole discretion of the Ugandan government, and that, as it happened, the ICC opposed conciliatory approaches to persons it sought. The referral thus offered an opportunity to placate two pillars of Museveni's regime – in order of importance: the military and Western international allies – while providing a seemingly legitimate though fallible argument to rebut criticism of the third and weakest pillar – the electorate.

The referral had other advantages for the military. The ICC Prosecutor would be cautioned against opening proceedings against the UPDF or other Ugandan officials in the DRC situation, needful as he was of the Ugandan government's cooperation in the LRA situation. Furthermore, the Sudanese government, wishing to be on the 'good' side in the 'war on terror' and under pressure on account of the conflict in Darfur, would try to avoid association with persons sought by the ICC and to that end discontinue its military support to the LRA. The referral could also reduce international criticism of Uganda's extraordinarily high defence budget – the UPDF now had to arrest 'war criminals' – and thus justify the securitisation of the Ugandan state.[307] Indeed, the GoU thought that the referral could rally international assistance for the Ugandan military. It was in this vein that the Minister of Defence answered a parliamentary question (conflating

---

[307] See, *inter alia*, Uganda 2006a, in which President Museveni promises in his address on the state of the nation: 'Security is a major pillar to our continued stability ... As I have stated at different fora in the recent past, I would like to reiterate that mistakes of the past, which tended to compromise the security of our country, will not be repeated. We shall never under-spend on defence. Never! It was a mistake, it will never be repeated. Consequently, although we may exchange experience with our development partners, we shall not accept a line we know will be fatal for our country.'

the ICC and ICTY and skipping over the fact that enforcement is the weakest chain in the ICC's operations):

> How does ICC operate?... They have the office of the prosecutor; they carry out investigations and actually the international community supports them. So, for this Serbian, for example, there is an international force, which is hunting for that person. So, should Kony be indicted, and should he be indicted before we capture him, who will look for him in order to compel him to appear before this committee? It is not Uganda; if they ask us we shall lend a hand, but actually it will be international forces.[308]

The ICC's legal and the Ugandan executive's military approaches thus shared the avowed aim of catching the LRA, the former with a view to legal proceedings, the latter in order to defeat the enemy. It was thus the Minister of *Defence* who introduced the idea of the referral to President Museveni. The Attorney-General's Chambers and the Ministries of Justice and Foreign Affairs became involved only 'when [the military] needed an official contact with the ICC' to submit the actual referral letter.[309] As another senior cabinet minister explained:

> [The Ministry of Foreign Affairs] was not involved in the ICC referral. It was a UPDF matter, so it was done by the Minister of Defence.[310]

Given the dominance of the military paradigm with which the GoU had always approached the conflict in northern Uganda, most Ugandan lawyers, whether working for the state or in private practice, did not consider the ICC's intervention as competition, a loss to Ugandan sovereignty or a stain on the reputation of the Ugandan legal sector. The Uganda Police Force, the Office of the Director of Public Prosecutions (DPP), the judiciary and the JLOS Secretariat simply did not consider the conflict as within their remit. The military would work on 'neutralising' the LRA, while religious leaders, civil society actors and politicians were at times permitted to negotiate. Law was involved only by means of the Amnesty Act 2000, which was to exclude legal accountability, and hence to curtail the role of the law and

---

[308] Uganda 2004. In 2004, neither Radovan Karadzic nor Ratko Mladic had been arrested.

[309] Interview with the (at the time of the referral) Minister of Defence, Kampala, October 2008.

[310] Interview with a Ugandan government minister, Kampala, October 2008.

of lawyers.[311] Because the situation in northern Uganda had been largely disregarded by domestic lawyers, the ICC did not usurp the role of any Ugandan legal player.

Once the ICC was involved, it bolstered the military paradigm. Internationally, it turned the LRA into an 'enemy of mankind' that should be defeated at any cost, and its opponent, the UPDF, into an international partner worthy of moral, political and military support in its war on the LRA, terror and impunity.

In the national context, the Court's involvement initially did not add a legal dimension to the conflict paradigm. For instance, asked about the UPDF's killing of Raska Lukwiya, one of the persons for whom the ICC had issued an arrest warrant, government officials did not see any inconsistency with the legal approach. In their view, the killing served the same purpose as the ICC's arrest warrant. They were strengthened in their view, they said, by the silence of the ICC in response to Lukwiya's death.[312]

The OTP, for its part, actively lobbied for a strong military approach. It fostered, so its officials suggest, an agreement between the DRC and Uganda to conduct joint military operations against the LRA in collaboration with MONUC, the UN peacekeeping mission in the DRC.[313] The agreement entitled the GoU to re-enter the DRC, two years after the ICJ had condemned it for its illegal activities in that country. The OTP called for the United States to provide military assistance to arrest Kony, thus legitimising a stronger US military presence in the region:

> In the case of Joseph Kony ... [w]e need ... the operational support of countries like the US, to the DRC, to Uganda, to the Central African Republic, to assist them in mounting an operation to arrest him. They have the will – so it's a totally legitimate operation, politically, legally – but they need this kind of assistance. And the US has to be the leader.[314]

The US boots-on-the-ground support was delivered. For the Ugandan government, it was one of the concrete and positive results of the ICC referral. A government minister explained:

> Uganda has been on the frontline in the fight against terrorism: Somalia, Great Lakes and anything that Uganda does in the fight

---

[311] When JLOS was constituted, the Amnesty Commission was not part of it. It was considered a commission concerned with military issues (namely, demobilisation), rather than legal matters.

[312] Interview with a senior government official, Kampala, October 2008.

[313] Brubacher 2010:276.

[314] Lerner 2010. See also, sharply, Al-Balushi and Branch 2010.

against crimes against humanity, terrorism and related crimes is part of this fight. This has improved our image internationally. The practical benefits come mainly from countries that are fighting wars against such crimes, particularly from the Americans. Recently America deployed 100 armed personnel to help the UPDF. That is a practical benefit from our focused measures, including the referral to the ICC.[315]

In addition to supporting the military approach, the ICC's involvement helped the GoU to discredit alternative approaches to the conflict. International calls for a negotiated settlement softened because many ICC supporters believed, and in some cases were made to believe by the OTP,[316] that, because the LRA leaders were internationally sought 'war criminals', they should not be negotiated with.[317] The above-mentioned GoU–DRC military agreement dealt a blow to the simultaneously ongoing peace talks in Juba. Domestically, the GoU referred to the ICC's powers to rebut calls for a peaceful resolution. When the Minister of Internal Affairs, the GoU's representative at the Juba peace talks, was asked in Parliament whether the ICC could not be substituted by *mato oput*, the Minister responded:

> Then the question of dropping ICC: ICC is an independent body set up by statute by more than 100 nations. Therefore, when we are talking about ICC here let us give no impression at all that ICC is a body there to be told by the Parliament of Uganda ... we should be talking about ICC with substantial amount of reverence.
>
> As Hon. Odonga Otto said, that what we are saying could be subjudice; could really affect what is happening in The Hague. So, I appeal to all of us and I agree with my younger brother that we should be [as] restrained as possible and we should not provoke the ICC to exercise its overwhelming authority over these matters. It has a lot of authority and definitely the Government of Uganda does not order ICC, we have no authority ... we can never attempt to undermine the independence and the authority of the ICC (Interruption)
>
> Mr John Odit: Honourable Minister seems to be threatening us. I want to understand from him. When the Government of Uganda took this case to the ICC, did you know that this power existed before and if so, why have you instituted this *mato put?*
>
> [Minister of Internal Affairs]: Madam Speaker, the Government of Uganda has always been fully aware of the authority and

---

[315] Interview with a Ugandan government minister, Kampala, November 2011.
[316] See Chapter 5.   [317] See also Schomerus and Acan Ogwaro 2010:12.

powers of the ICC. That is actually the very reason why we took the case to ICC because we tried to catch Kony and Otti and other leaders but we could not catch them. So, we said, who has the powers that can reach them and we found that ICC had these powers. So, we went to them very deliberately.

Secondly, we are going to them again now. Again very deliberately because we know they have powers but we also know that they have some limitations. If they had their own Police force and there was adequate international cooperation, they would have arrested, indicted people, but they have those limitations. So, we have gone to them because we think that this peace initiative, initiated by the Government of Southern Sudan and embraced by us in government and the country as a whole, is a viable route forward. So, government is consciously doing these matters dealing with ICC (Interruption)

MR KASSIANO WADRI: Honourable Minister, you have actually confused me the more. From the onset you do admit and accept that ICC has bigger powers than we as the government who went to report a criminal to them. Recognizing that ICC has bigger powers and knowing that it is a court of its own, we again went further to engage ourselves into a subjudice act by putting in place *mato put*. You have gone ahead to say you again went to ICC to say, 'Look, we do appreciate your weakness, you do not have an arresting institution of your own' – are you not trying to use the peace talks and *mato put* as a trap to lure Kony and his people into your custody and then thereafter say, 'ICC come they are in my possession you can now come'? Do you not think that will really not only undermine ICC but even the confidence that these people would have laid in these peace talks? Would you kindly clarify on that? . . .

[MINISTER OF INTERNAL AFFAIRS]: On the question of the terms of reference to the ICC, I think I have really made that point. The ICC is an independent body, it has its own constitution and it has its own methods of work. Uganda is just one of the more than 100 countries that are members to this body. If the Parliament of Uganda has got some good ideas, and I know we do, we can send those ideas for consideration by the ICC but we cannot tell them to do this or not to do that.[318]

The executive had thus found in the ICC a no-choice argument for its preferred military approach.

---

[318] Uganda 2007.

It was only at the negotiating table in Juba that the ICC's involvement in northern Uganda led the GoU to consider *judicial* mechanisms to deal with the conflict in northern Uganda. The Ugandan executive realised that it could be blamed for obstructing peace by having invited the ICC to northern Uganda. For it to be seen as still in control, the GoU had to show it was able to ward off international prosecutions, which was possible only by adopting an approach similar to that of the ICC. Whilst originally intended as an extension of GoU military policy, the ICC's involvement, and in particular the public search for a solution to the 'ICC problem', thus had the effect of adding a legal dimension to a military conflict paradigm.

This legal dimension of the Juba peace talks, in turn, awoke the Ugandan legal sector: Ugandan lawyers became relevant as alternative actors to the ICC. During the Juba talks, security people were dominant: thirteen out of the sixteen government delegates were officers, sometimes lawyers, in the different security forces.[319] However, in the A&R Accords the parties, including the executive, assigned Ugandan lawyers an important part in resolving the conflict with the LRA.

Keen to make such contribution, some Ugandan lawyers worked hard to implement elements of the Juba transitional-justice agenda. They saw the space opened up as an opportunity to strengthen the position of JLOS in the domestic political field, to advance their own institution within JLOS, to acquire prestige among national and international colleagues, to become part of (Western-dominated) transnational networks,[320] and possibly then to be co-opted into the priesthood of international lawyers.

Yet this effect of adding a legal dimension to the domestic approach to the conflict in the north and of awakening the Ugandan legal sector has to date been professionally limited. Professionally, this catalysing effect has been strong only on a few individuals participating in international-criminal-justice events; to most other Ugandan lawyers, not (yet) 'targeted' by NGO activities promoting the ICC or transitional justice, or not a member of the JLOS Transitional Justice Working Group, international criminal justice remains a hobby horse for the selected few. Those not targeted often fear that the investment in this special justice for conflict-related crimes will be at the expense

---

[319] Schomerus 2010b:231.
[320] For an enthusiastic welcome and promotion of such networks, see Slaughter 2005.

of the already backlogged ordinary justice system. Moreover, many officials in the Uganda Police Force and Directorate of Public Prosecutors continue to prefer staying outside these politically sensitive cases, relieved that 'the ICC now deals with the matter'.[321] Particularly those who have assisted the ICC in their investigations in Uganda argue that conflict-related crimes in northern Uganda now 'belong to' their 'colleagues' at the ICC. They look up to ICC staff as more advanced and are relieved that they do not have to enter the political minefield.[322] Their approach to the conflict in the north has thus expanded to encompass a legal dimension, according to which justice has a role to play, but in their view this role is to be played by the ICC rather than by domestic actors.

Geographically, the expansion of the paradigm also remains limited. Most law-enforcement officials outside Kampala still do not see any role for themselves in conflict-related criminal proceedings. They refer to the army,[323] the SDHC,[324] the ICC[325] or traditional leaders[326] as more relevant actors and to the applicability of the Amnesty Act[327] as an impediment to successful completion of proceedings.

The inclusion of a legal approach to the conflict may also be only temporary. The GoU's tolerance of norm entrepreneurs' promoting international criminal justice has to date primarily been based on a cost–benefit assessment, rather than on a belief that it is legally obliged or diplomatically compelled to prosecute international crimes domestically. When other options, such as militarily defeating the LRA, providing an amnesty[328] or handing over the LRA leadership

---

[321] Discussion with officials of the Criminal Investigations Department, Gulu, September 2008.

[322] Interview with a senior official of the Uganda Police Force, Kampala, October 2008 and interview with an official of the Criminal Investigations Department, Kampala, October 2008.

[323] Discussion with officials of the Criminal Investigations Department, Gulu, September 2008.

[324] Interview with an official in the Uganda Police Force, Kitgum, September 2008.

[325] Discussion with officials of the Criminal Investigations Department, Gulu, September 2008.

[326] Interview with a representative of the Uganda Police Force, Gulu, September 2008.

[327] Ibid.

[328] In response to rumours that two LRA commanders sought by the ICC were willing to surrender, Museveni repeated the offer of amnesty ('Odhiambo won't face

to the ICC[329] promise to be more convenient, the GoU is likely simply to discard its newfound commitment to domestic legal account-ability and leave lawyers without a role to play.[330]

Finally, the expansion of the role of lawyers and law-enforcement agents in the approach to the conflict in northern Uganda takes place against the background of a countervailing and probably stronger move towards the securitisation of the Ugandan state: the army and the illegal private security squads at the President's service assume responsibilities far beyond their constitutional roles to the detriment of organs such as the police and judiciary. In situations that matter to the President – rallies by the opposition, release of opposition candi-dates – security operatives take over. Thus, the army detained the President's political opponents after they had been released by the police on account of a lack of evidence;[331] and demonstrations were put down by organised armed groups in civilian clothes. In the words of one interlocutor, 'if the heat is hot, the police are no longer in charge of policing – the President and his men take over.'[332] Security agents were also part of the delegation that visited the ICC to discuss the referral and attend meetings of the UN Human Rights Council.[333] Securitisation of the state in the interest of its President has gone hand in hand with marginalisation of the police generally, and in particular organs such as the Criminal Investigations Department. It is thus not just conflict-related crimes, but crimes against civilians more generally that have received little investment from the state.

---

world court' 2009). See also interview with a representative of the Ugandan Government, The Hague, April 2008: 'We [in the GoU] have always said that *we* were willing to give amnesty.'

[329] When asked where Kony would go if he were arrested without having signed the FPA, a government minister replied, 'Why waste our time? We [the GoU] can send him to The Hague. This is the kind of punishment that he does not want' (interview, Kampala, October 2008).

[330] According to some lawyers, Operation Lightning Thunder already announced the end of the legal approach. Since then, 'the military approach has been dominant. The government allows lawyers to go ahead [with the International Crimes Division] but there is now less attention for the legal option. When [the President and his cabinet] engage the military, the legal thing is stuck. Harmonisation [of transitional-justice initiatives] will gather dust because the legal approach has failed to serve a political purpose' (interview with a senior government lawyer, Kampala, November 2011).

[331] Kobusingye 2010:65. [332] Interview, Kampala, November 2011.

[333] Interviews, Kampala, November 2011.

By providing that national legal proceedings can render an ICC case inadmissible, complementarity has thus expanded the Ugandan approach to dealing with the LRA to include a legal dimension. The search for an alternative to the ICC has also created a role for the Ugandan legal sector in an area that Ugandan lawyers and officials of law-enforcement agencies previously shunned. However, the legal dimension in the conflict paradigm remains limited, is far from secure and must be considered against the backdrop of the securitisation of the state.

Stimulating the establishment of a Ugandan international crimes division

Possibly the most visible effect indirectly catalysed by complementarity in Uganda is the creation of a Ugandan international crimes division. First envisaged in the A&R Accords as the 'Special Division of the High Court', then referred to by its creator as the 'War Crimes Court', then referred to as the 'War Crimes Division' and most recently renamed the 'International Crimes Division',[334] this special division of the Ugandan High Court has become the focus of donors' transitional-justice interest.

Recognising that a successful admissibility challenge on the ground of complementarity would require formal criminal justice proceedings at the domestic level, the A&R Accords provide for the SDHC 'to try individuals who are alleged to have committed serious crimes during the conflict'[335] and for 'a unit for carrying out investigations and prosecutions in support of trials and other formal proceedings'.[336] According to an LRA representative,

> in the Agreement on Accountability and Reconciliation, we came with the idea of forming the SDHC ... We did this as an indication to the ICC that we can also do these things amongst ourselves.[337]

---

[334] Annexure, clause 7, speaks of 'a special division of the High Court'; Administrative Circular No. 1 of 2008, clause 2, speaks of 'the War Crimes Court'; the International Crimes Bill Working Document 2009, Memorandum sub 2, speaks of 'the War Crimes Division of the High Court'; and the High Court (International Crimes Division) Practice Directions 2011 speaks of 'the International Crimes Division'. This chapter uses the terms interchangeably.

[335] Annexure, clause 7.   [336] Ibid., clause 10.

[337] Interview by Refugee Law Project researchers Alex Scheff and Justine Earl, Gulu, September 2008.

The envisaged division would be 'special' in that it, unlike the ordinary divisions of the High Court, would apply a regime of alternative sanctions and would take into account other transitional-justice mechanisms such as traditional justice, truth-telling and reparations. As envisaged by the A&R Accords, the establishment of the SDHC was thus one of many ingredients of a complex post-Juba transitional-justice recipe.

The A&R Accords left important issues for resolution to the executive, the legislature and, where necessary, the judiciary. For instance, it remained to be decided under which laws persons appearing before the SDHC would be tried, how possible issues of retroactivity would be addressed, which alternative sanctions would apply, how the Amnesty Act 2000 would be dealt with, how formal and traditional justice would relate to each other, and how individuals' cooperation with transitional-justice mechanisms would be rewarded.[338] In 2008, when Kony's signature to the FPA was still being pursued and in order to show its commitment to resolving these issues, the Ugandan cabinet instructed JLOS to prepare for the implementation of the A&R Accords. JLOS, for its part, established the Transitional Justice Working Group to develop a transitional-justice policy.

However, once the Transitional Justice Working Group was up and running, its preparations for a transitional-justice policy became more and more detached from the likelihood of Kony's signing the FPA. According to the Principal Judge, the chairman of the working group, whether or not Kony would sign was a 'political' question from which lawyers should stay clear of it.[339] Even if Kony never signed the FPA, he argued, the GoU should implement its parts of the agreement. 'The peace process has taken off' and 'Uganda has reached a point of no return.'[340]

---

[338] See A&R Agreement, clauses 3.6, 5.6, 6.3, 14.3 and 14.4, and Annexure, clauses 2 and especially 9 ('For the proper functioning of the special division of the court in accordance with the agreed principles of accountability and reconciliation, legislation may provide for: (a) The constitution of the court; (b) The substantive law to be applied; (c) Appeals against the decisions of the court; (d) Rules of procedure; (e) The recognition of traditional and community justice processes in proceedings.').

[339] When asked about the possible political impact of budgeted radio jingles announcing the establishment of a WCC, he responded: 'For political questions you are with the wrong people here' (meeting, Kampala, October 2008).

[340] The Principal Judge at the Religious and Cultural Leaders Reflection Workshop on the Juba Peace Talks, Gulu, 10–12 September 2008.

Leading by example, the chairman of the Transitional Justice Working Group did his bit to implement the A&R Accords. In his capacity as Principal Judge, he issued an administrative circular in which he announced plans to establish a new division of the High Court, called the War Crimes Court (WCC), and assigned judges and members of the registry to that court.[341] In hindsight he explained that '[t]he existence of the Uganda War Crimes Court … is derived from the Complementarity provision of the Rome Statute, Article 17'.[342]

In the Principal Judge's vision, the WCC would be a general 'court of complementarity' that would remain operational even after the LRA cases had been handled.[343] Recounting how Uganda in the past had 'exported' its judges to international courts such as the ICTR, the SCSL and even the ICC,[344] he described a Ugandan war crimes court that would be a role model for the region, just as the Ugandan Commercial Court had become.[345] A newspaper quoted a spokesperson for the judiciary expressing the same vision when the WCC was operational:

> 'Yes, [the ministers in Kenya accused by the ICC] can be tried here because this court now complements the Internal [sic] Criminal Court. We now have the equivalent of Geneva or Hague in Africa.' All African countries like Kenya, Libya and Sudan whose leaders were recently indicted by the ICC, he added, will be looking at the possibility of requesting for the referral of their cases to Uganda … [The spokesperson] said most international war crimes and crimes against humanity can now be tried in the Uganda International War Crimes Tribunal, the first of its kind in Africa.[346]

The establishment of the WCC was also enhanced by the expectation within JLOS that the special division would attract substantial international resources. Just as the JLOS donor group had been keen to support an Anti-Corruption Division, it would be equally if not more enthusiastic about a court covering conflict-related crimes, so it was rightly assumed.[347]

---

[341] Administrative Circular No. 1 of 2008, High Court Divisions and Circuits and Staff Deployment.

[342] Ogoola 2010:183.   [343] See also *ibid.*:184.

[344] Meeting, Kampala, September 2008.   [345] *Ibid.*   [346] Musoke 2011.

[347] Observation of a meeting between JLOS officials and JLOS donors, Kampala, September 2008.

In this sense, there was little 'special' about the creation of this special division of the High Court. In times of budget cuts as a result of structural adjustment programmes of the Bretton Woods Institutions, various 'special' commissions, agencies and courts have mushroomed in Uganda as alternative ways to maintain expensive patronage systems.[348] International donor money for such special bodies guarantees income outside the ordinary national budget. In the case of the SDHC, loyalty to the NRM could be rewarded by secondment to a body that promises training with sitting allowances, access to international networks and travel abroad as fringe benefits.[349]

So, while Parliament was still to decide on the law applicable in any domestic international-crimes proceedings, while the fate of the Amnesty Act was still to be determined, while the relationship between traditional and formal justice was still to be settled on, while the Chief Justice was yet to formalise the creation of the SDHC, while a transitional-justice policy was still to be developed, and, indeed, while the FPA was still to be signed, the judiciary presented to donors a preliminary budget for the start-up phase of the SDHC which envisaged a new building, radio jingles publicising the WCC and study tours for its staff to The Hague, Sierra Leone and 'Bosnia (Kosovo)'.[350]

The judiciary did this successfully, and donors and international NGOs embraced the WCC. The WCC provided foreign norm entrepreneurs the long-desired Ugandan focal point for their transitional-justice work in Uganda: with judges and a registrar with business cards

---

[348] See Mwenda 2007:30: 'According to an audit conducted by Uganda's Ministry of Finance, Planning, and Economic Development, as of 2003 the country had 95 semi-autonomous government agencies, mostly created with donor support. Almost four-fifths of these agencies revealed their budgets at the auditors' request, though nearly all refused to submit figures on the numbers of people that they employ. The audit found that the total budget allocated to these bodies had been growing by 30 percent every year, and that as of 2003 it was US$280 million. This is a huge sum in Uganda, whose entire Gross Domestic Product (GDP) for 2006 is estimated to amount to only slightly more than $8.5 billion.' See also Green 2010, demonstrating that new sub-national political units (districts) proliferated in Uganda also as an alternative source of patronage.

[349] See also Quinn 2010:69, suggesting that President Museveni created the 1986 truth commission not to deal with the past but to reward the commissioners for their loyalty to the NRM during its rebellion against the then incumbent Ugandan government.

[350] JLOS 2008 and observation of a meeting between JLOS donors and JLOS officials, Kampala, September 2008.

saying 'War Crimes Court', there was 'real' transitional-justice work that could be done, even though Kony moved further and further away from Uganda and the FPA. Of all the transitional-justice components in the A&R Accords, formal criminal proceedings were also best aligned with the normative agendas of most international actors.

Consequently, ever since the creation of the Transitional Justice Working Group, and in particular of the WCC, the Principal Judge, the judges and registrar of the court have had an almost full-time job in receiving visiting diplomatic delegations, international NGOs and foreign scholars (present author included), offering 'capacity building', 'study tours' and asking questions about the Ugandan experience with trying international crimes. The WCC staff have also toured the world to participate in seminars on transitional justice, visit international courts and observe truth commissions. Donors and international NGOs, for their part, have funded or conducted these study tours, the refurbishment of a building for the WCC, several needs and risks assessments, training for court interpreters and brainstorm sessions on outreach strategies.[351] Ugandan actors have observed the international enthusiasm with some amazement. As one of the judges observed after serving on the WCC for three years:

> [International NGOs] are all seeking to assist. They all come and offer training. But we are trained enough now. Now they want to come and sit with us during our work. We never reject it, out of diplomacy, but usually say 'perhaps in the future'. Meanwhile, they duplicate their work ... are competing and ... all have their personal interests. On their websites they claim to have done more than they have, because they have received money from a government to do something. We have never seen that money.[352]

And yet, international norm entrepreneurs have been influential in shaping the WCC. On the basis of discussions with foreign human

---

[351] When the first case came before the WCC, donors were reluctant to provide any form of support to the defence: 'As donors we cannot be seen supporting the defence. We always talk about the victims; then we cannot say that we pay for the defence. Instead, we trained court interpreters.' Interview with a donor representative, Kampala, November 2011. Another donor representative observed that JLOS and its donors 'do not want to prioritise the offenders of international crimes, while other offenders have bad state-brief lawyers, too'. Interview with a donor representative, Kampala, November 2011.

[352] Interview with a WCC judge, Kampala, November 2011.

rights activists who explained complementarity, and in order to tally with a perceived wish-list on the part of international donors, the Principal Judge modelled the WCC on international criminal tribunals. In his words:

> Complementarity means: 'We do something close to the real thing here.' We have a fair procedure, a just procedure and we give the accused a proper defence, representation and due process. There is no *in absentia* trial. All the standards we have are similar to the international ones. What we don't have is a prosecution unit that is part of the court. In Uganda these are separate. But because of the international practice we are going to explore a unit of the prosecution and a unit of the defence all as part of the court. The War Crimes Court will be a holistic court.[353]

So the Principal Judge's administrative circular envisaged a WCC that would 'comprise a bench of at least three judges and a Registry; to which [would] be attached an OTP, and an Office of the Defence Counsel'.[354] Nothing in the Rome Statute suggests that, in order to benefit from the principle of complementarity, domestic proceedings must be conducted in a specific war crimes court that integrates judges, prosecutors, defence lawyers and a registry. In the domestic context, many Ugandans consider this integration into one court a threat to the separation of powers and the independence of the judiciary. However, by reference to the ICC, the ICTR and the SCSL, senior officials in JLOS argued that judges, prosecution, defence and registry must at least be 'under one roof'[355] in order to meet the complementarity criteria.[356] Similarly, the Ugandan practice of a single high court judge adjudicating most serious crimes was substituted by the use of a bench:

---

[353] Interview with the then Principal Judge, Kampala, September 2008. See also Ogoola 2010:184: 'The Court's standards and procedures – including a trial bench of three Judges, Prosecution, Investigation and Defence Office, and in-house translation service – all mirror those of the modern international criminal courts such as the Hague, Arusha, Bosnia, Yugoslavia, Sierra Leone, etcetera.'

[354] Administrative Circular No. 1 of 2008, clause 2.

[355] Interview with a prosecutor involved, Kampala, October 2008: 'We will have to work under one roof as in Sierra Leone'; and in Kampala, June 2010: 'The Court is supposed to be The Hague kind of style: all under one roof.'

[356] Interview with the then Principal Judge, Kampala, September 2008.

[T]he way that [these international] courts work is to have a bench of three. But the nature of these cases is such that they take forever: a year, or two, just to hear one case. In the course of the year also, the three judges that started may not all still be around. So I am told what the practice is in international courts, is to have a fourth judge, for instance in case one of three exits or gets sick or something.[357]

A fourth judge was appointed to the WCC.

The ICC, a court which has taken pains to mirror diverse domestic legal systems, was thus itself mirrored – not only in substance but also in form – in the domestic sphere. One of the officials appointed to the WCC explained this mimicry as follows:[358] 'If you are driving, you need a driving mirror; the War Crimes Court mirrors the ICC-van.'[359] The mirroring goes so far that those explaining the proposed WCC budget argued that it must be a long-term budget since the cases against the LRA will take a very long time, given the duration of the cases before the ICTR.[360]

The ICC, rather than the Juba A&R Accords, became the template for the SDHC.[361] With the retirement of Principal Judge Ogoola, the judiciary lost interest in developing a framework that integrates formal and traditional justice. The chair of the SDHC was said to have no intention of taking into account local justice practices in the absence of the legal framework envisaged in the Juba Agreements.[362]

Less intentionally, the WCC also mirrored the first years of practice of the ICC Chambers: no trials, even no cases before it. In its

---

[357] The Principal Judge cited in Refugee Law Project 2010:9. See also Ogola 2010: 'Justice Akiiki Kiiza, who presides over the division, says that war crimes trials held in the country will function in a similar fashion to those in The Hague, with three judges officiating each case. The court currently has four judges capable of overseeing war crimes trials, and is searching for a fifth, which Kiiza hopes could come from the international community, in order to bring some outside expertise.'

[358] The term 'mimicry' in the legal context is derived from Drumbl 2007:Chapter 5.

[359] Interview, Kampala, September 2008.

[360] Meeting between JLOS officials and JLOS donors, September 2008.

[361] Note how Judiciary of the Republic of Uganda (undated) distinguishes between the court envisaged in the peace agreements and the 'court of complementarity': 'While originally meant to be part of a comprehensive peace agreement with the LRA, the international crimes division has now come to be viewed as a court of "complementarity" with respect to the international criminal court, thus fulfilling the principle of complementarity stipulated in the preamble and Article 1 of the Rome Statute.'

[362] Interview, Kampala, November 2011.

enthusiasm in setting up the WCC, the judiciary had left the Uganda Police Force, specifically the Criminal Investigations Department, and the Directorate of Public Prosecutions behind. Enjoying less independence than their judicial counterparts, investigators and prosecutors waited for a political imprimatur for criminal proceedings for conflict-related crimes. Entering into politically sensitive areas such as the implementation of a peace agreement[363] could be costly to their careers.[364] So they argued that the Court's jurisdiction and applicable law should first be determined and that it would be a waste of time and resources to start building cases against persons who may never be arrested.[365]

When on the eve of the Review Conference of the Rome Statute in Kampala there was still not a single case before the WCC, the Ugandan Chief Justice expanded the Court's jurisdiction and rebranded it as the 'International Crimes Division' (ICD). According to paragraph 6(1) of the High Court (International Crimes Division) Practice Direction, the Division shall try any offence relating, not just to genocide, crimes against humanity and war crimes, but also to 'terrorism, human trafficking, piracy and any other international crime as may be provided for under the Penal Code Act, Cap 120, the Geneva Conventions Act, Cap 363, the International Criminal Court Act, No. 11 of 2010 or under any other penal enactment'. With its jurisdiction expanded to include terrorism, a crime for which many were (and still are) lingering in prisons, the ICD soon had its first case.

Offered to the LRA as a carrot to match the stick of The Hague, the SDHC was an effect catalysed by complementarity. But, as a court meant to facilitate a transition, it failed before it was created: the idea could not offset the LRA's fear of the ICC. Nonetheless, international norm entrepreneurs and Ugandan donor spotters hand-picked the special division out of the A&R Accords and freed it from its

---

[363] Paradoxically, implementation of some parts of the signed agreements could jeopardise the signing of the FPA. For instance, it is questionable whether the radio jingles that were initially budgeted to publicise the WCC would encourage Kony to sign.

[364] These views emerged in interviews with senior police officers and prosecutors in Kampala and northern Uganda in September and October 2008, in June 2010 and in November 2011.

[365] *Ibid.*

transitional-justice context.[366] Without institutional links to other transitional-justice instruments such as amnesties, reparations and truth-telling mechanisms, it could pursue criminal justice without concessions. Not tied up in a transitional-justice deal, it did not have to sacrifice some retributive justice for the benefit of, for instance, truth, peace, democracy or restorative justice. Rather than an instrument of transitional justice that was meant to contribute to a complex balance of peace, restorative justice, accountability and democracy, the SDHC became an aim in itself. Without these inherently political aims to pursue, the SDHC also seemed a technical rather than a political enterprise, which made it easier for donors and domestic lawyers to run with it.

But there was a price to pay for the transformation from a court embedded in a transitional-justice framework to a stand-alone ICC-style court, from an instrument to an aim in itself and from a component of an inherently political endeavour to a technical development project. First, in mimicking the justice model of the ICC, the SDHC does no better than the ICC in pursuing a concept of justice that resonates with the people directly affected by the conflict with the LRA. Secondly, no transition without politics: without a political deal, the SDHC as such does nothing to facilitate a transition, in this case, an end to the conflict in northern Uganda. The result is a 'court of complementarity' that mimics the ICC not just in design and rhetoric but also in its effectiveness in addressing the LRA and bringing justice to northern Uganda.

Increasing the attention paid to 'international standards'

As the section on the WCC began to reveal, the preparation for domestic proceedings went hand in hand with a belief that domestic proceedings must be like proceedings in the ICC or must at least meet so-called 'international standards'. Asked about the rationale for the SDHC, Uganda's Chief Justice, for instance, explained:

> To meet international standards ... it must meet ICC standards. A special division is necessary to convince the ICC.[367]

---

[366] See also the legal draftsman of the A&R Accords, Afako 2010: 'Whilst laudable, these unilateral moves on the question of justice might, without the benefit of the oversight mechanisms envisaged by the agreement, risk losing the nuances that were designed to make the agreements palatable to the LRA and to affected communities.'

[367] Interview with Chief Justice Benjamin Odoki, Kampala, October 2008.

And one senior JLOS official elaborated on these standards:

> If [the A&R Accords are] going to be implemented, complementarity
> means that there will be two units: one in The Hague and one
> municipal. These two must not divorce each other. It must be comple-
> mentary. [The domestic Court] must look like the real thing in The
> Hague: the benchmarks, the procedure, substantive definitions, what is
> a war crime, what are massacres, violations of human rights. The Rome
> Statute has these, ours cannot be different ... We have to be comple-
> mentary to the ICC, even with sentences, otherwise we have to justify
> why we differ. If the ICC says 10 years, we cannot say 100 years or 10
> days ... Complementary means let us do something they [the ICC] can
> live with. That is why we are trying to live up to their norms.[368]

The belief that complementarity requires a mirroring of ICC proceedings led to proposals to adjust several features of Ugandan criminal law
and practice in case of international-crimes proceedings. One example
is the role of victims. As it is, Ugandan law of criminal proceedings
does not provide for victim participation with a view to reparations. In
order to make up for their absence in the negotiations, the A&R
Accords anticipated an increased role for victims in transitional-
justice proceedings. However, in JLOS's preparations for the SDHC,
complementarity rather than the A&R Accords became the dominant
rationale for considering increasing victims' participation. Although
there is nothing in articles 17 and 20 of the Rome Statute that
supports the argument that cases are admissible before the ICC if
victims cannot participate or obtain reparations in domestic criminal
proceedings,[369] many JLOS actors believed that proceedings in the
WCC would have to include victim participation and reparations in
order to meet the complementarity standard. They found support in
statements from international actors. For instance, when submitting
its observations on the admissibility of the LRA case, the ICC Office
of the Public Counsel for Victims concluded:

---

[368] Interview, Kampala, September 2008.

[369] Cf. *contra* the (in this context inapplicable) ICTY case law on rule 11 *bis* referrals
(see Chapter 2) in particular ICTY, *Ademi and Norac Referral Decision*:[53]: 'In the
present context, the explicit requirement under Rule 11bis for a fair trial of the
Accused is properly complemented by a concern for fairness towards other
interested parties, such as victims and the international community, and has a
relevance as a policy consideration for the referral Bench when it considers
whether or not to refer a case.'

[C]onsidering that the Ugandan legal framework derives from the common law system where victims' participation is not recognised as such, the victims ... are of the view that the exercising of its jurisdiction by the Special division of the High Court would deprive them of their rights as granted in the Rome Statute, unless the Ugandan Authorities carefully implement the said rights with regard to the establishment of the Special division of the High Court, for the participation of victims to be meaningful.[370]

With respect to witness protection too, it was argued that international regimes should be copied. In a conference organised by the United Nations High Commissioner for Human Rights, Ugandan judges argued that there was a need to relocate high-risk witnesses from their villages. According to a newspaper report, Uganda's judge on the Special Court for Sierra Leone added: 'It's advisable for the sake of protecting our witnesses that they should be driven in cars with tinted glasses from where they are kept to the court rooms.' Local actors thought this was unnecessary. Revealing a different perception of justice, the Gulu district chairman argued that 'all the people need is restoration of human dignity and maintaining social relationship with other community members'.[371]

JLOS actors also held up a mirror to the ICC for inspiration for detention facilities. In 2008, when there was still some hope that Kony would sign the FPA, the Chief Justice mentioned that the Prisons Department had

asked for good holding facilities, commensurate with international standards. Kony is different – he should not be kept with ordinary criminals.[372]

And, indeed, the Commissioner General of Prisons said he was readying detention facilities that met 'international standards' for the persons sought by the ICC.[373] Asked about such standards, one

---

[370] *Observations on behalf of Victims Kony et al.*:[32]. The conclusion was based on responses to *Questionnaire Ugandan Victims on Admissibility*, containing questions such as 'Do you think a Ugandan criminal procedure will take into account your concerns?', 'What should a Ugandan court do to respect your needs?' and 'Do you want the LRA trial to be in Uganda or at the ICC?' It is of note that the responses were given by victims who have applied for participation in ICC proceedings and hence have an interest in the continuation of these proceedings.

[371] Eriku and Livingstone 2011.   [372] Interview, Kampala, October 2008.

[373] Interview with a senior official in the Ministry of Internal Affairs in Kampala, October 2008.

government minister suggested that the gym and DVD players in the ICC's detention centre were representative.[374] Another official proposed to build 'hotels' in Luzira, Kampala's run-down maximum-security prison.[375] Motivating his support for the Ugandan ICC Bill (see next section), one parliamentarian expressed his enthusiasm for the Rome Statute, citing the detention facilities of the ICC (or ICTY/ ICTR for that matter):

> The ICC, particularly the Rome Statute, has done great work to resolve the dispute in Yugoslavia and Rwanda. I visited the UN facility, the ICC detention facility in Arusha and I recommend that honourable members, especially Cabinet members, visit this detention facility to acquaint themselves with what happens there, particularly considering the sort of crimes the inmates committed.[376]

'Outreach' is another oft-invoked 'international standard'. During study tours in The Hague, Sierra Leone and Sarajevo, JLOS members were bombarded with the importance of courts' doing 'outreach'.[377] Donors, too, have been keen on outreach,[378] and funded NGOs to do outreach for JLOS – a striking resemblance to donors' funding of NGOs to do outreach for the ICC.[379] The concept of outreach has inspired the JLOS sector beyond the field of transitional justice. While judges have remained reluctant to tour the country to talk about their cases, the sector as such has been considering doing more to inform the public about its work.[380]

Only a few senior Ugandan judicial officials have explored developing alternatives to the ICC with a view to a possible admissibility challenge on grounds of complementarity that do not follow all the Court's and other 'international standards'. The same senior JLOS

---

[374] Interview with a Ugandan government minister, Kampala, October 2008.

[375] Participant observation at an official meeting, Kampala, October 2008. The intended special facilities for special criminals present a clear risk of a Rwanda scenario, where initially those suspected of being most responsible in the genocide received imprisonment sentences and the best detention facilities, while the much larger number of less important actors faced the possibility of a death sentence, languishing in overcrowded jails.

[376] Uganda 2010a:[3.37].

[377] Interview with a participant of a study tour, Kampala, November 2011.

[378] Interview with a JLOS donor, Kampala, November 2011: 'We insisted: outreach, outreach.'

[379] Interview with a JLOS donor, Kampala, November 2011.

[380] Interview with a JLOS advisor, Kampala, November 2011.

official who stated that '[i]f the ICC says 10 years, we cannot say 100 years or 10 days' expressed support in a later discussion for the use of traditional justice at sentencing. He was inspired by the Colombian Peace and Justice Act, which provides for investigations and prosecutions of crimes in the Statute, but contains sentences milder than in ordinary Colombian law.[381]

The obsession with 'international standards' stems in part from a lack of study of the actual provisions in the Rome Statute. Primarily regulating proceedings before the ICC, the Rome Statute is, as has been explained in Chapter 2, relatively silent on domestic proceedings. It provides only that, in order to render an ICC case inadmissible, domestic proceedings in that case must be genuine. The manifestations of inability and unwillingness which would demonstrate this lack of genuineness are narrowly described.[382] Victim participation, reparations for victims, outreach, and the quality of detention centres are, no matter how important, not part of the definition of inability or unwillingness. Because its jurisdiction is conditional upon the statutory requirements of complementarity being fulfilled, the ICC does not have the same freedom in setting conditions for referrals of cases to domestic jurisdictions as the ICTY and ICTR enjoy on the basis of their primacy of jurisdiction.[383]

For many influential actors in the international-criminal-justice movement, this is precisely the problem with complementarity. Their argument is that the ICC should not just serve as a back-up court to avoid impunity but also oversee domestic compliance with various human rights and other 'international standards' when adjudicating international crimes. As part of their promotion of a laudable human rights agenda far beyond the Rome Statute, they explain complementarity as how it, in their view, should have been regulated.[384]

---

[381] Peace and Justice Act 2005, arts. 3 and 30, providing for an alternative punishment of between five and eight years' imprisonment.

[382] RS, arts. 17 and 20(3). See Chapter 2, 'Where domestic proceedings have been initiated: unwillingness and inability'.

[383] See Chapter 2, 'The ICC does not have a conditional deferral procedure like the ICTY and ICTR'.

[384] NGO representatives who fly in and out, or write from afar, are often most uncompromising in demanding compliance with so-called 'international standards'. Local staff and international staff who live in Uganda for a substantial amount of time are more oriented towards marrying international norms with the contextual reality, intuitively aware of Merry's 'paradox of making human rights

Thus, when the Juba A&R Accords provided for domestic proceedings as an alternative to the ICC, many international NGOs expressed strong views on whether this was desirable and on the 'benchmarks' that such proceedings should meet.[385] They were aided by diplomats with instructions from European capitals who argued that 'international standards' must be met for domestic proceedings to be 'ICC-proof' and left it to the international-criminal-justice movement to specify what these standards were.[386] The practice of the ICC is still fairly limited, so, when drawing up these standards and benchmarks, experts relied on experience of other international criminal tribunals, in particular the ICTY's and ICTR's case law on rule 11 *bis* referrals.[387] It was considered self-evident that a statute of an international court requires national proceedings to meet international standards, whether for trials, for prisons or for court design.[388] The promoted norms are laudable from a human rights perspective, but do not fit complementarity.

Uganda proved an easy target for such norm hijacking. When the option of domestic proceedings began to feature, few government ministers, JLOS actors and judges appointed to the WCC had ever read the Rome Statute.[389] But, accustomed to donors offering 'technical experts'[390] to accompany financial support for development programmes, JLOS welcomed their project proposals for 'transitional justice

in the vernacular', which is that '[t]o be accepted, they have to be tailored to the local context and resonant with the local cultural framework. However, to be part of the human rights system, they must emphasize individualism, autonomy, choice, bodily integrity, and equality – ideas embedded in the legal documents that constitute human rights law' (Merry 2006b:49).

[385] E.g. see Amnesty International 2007, Human Rights Watch 2007 and Human Rights Watch 2008. See also Keppler 2013, forthcoming:*passim*.

[386] Interview with a European diplomat, Kampala, August 2008.

[387] See e.g. Burke-White and Kaplan 2009:273.   [388] See e.g. Nakandha 2011.

[389] See also, rather explicitly, President Museveni in his opening speech for the Review Conference: 'I belong to a political organization that has been fighting impunity for the last 45 years ... [O]ur contribution to this debate is to reintroduce words which I do not hear so much in the international jargon. I have not read the Rome Statute, but I do not know whether those words are there. We, in our political tradition, we make a distinction between just and unjust wars. This war you are fighting; what war is it? Is it a just war, or is it a war of aggression? I do not know whether the Statute sorts that one out.' (Museveni 2010:1–2).

[390] Baylis 2008:385 aptly queries the qualification required for the title 'expert' ('people with no real expertise in areas that matter, like international criminal law ... have been deemed experts merely because they are foreigners with expertise in some area of the law').

workshops', 'study tours' and 'legislative drafting assistance'. In exchange, they listened to the advice of international experts. Consequently, some of the principal defenders of the WCC, who said in interviews that they had never read the Rome Statute, *were* reading Human Rights Watch's 'Benchmarks for Justice for Serious Crimes in Northern Uganda'.[391] Similarly, one government minister, who confessed never to have seen the Rome Statute prior to the Juba talks, pointed on his desk to a 122-page 'Manual for the Ratification and Implementation of the Rome Statute', written by Canadian NGOs, when he said:

> We really realised the role of the ICC only when the Juba peace process started; now there is a Rome Statute on my desk.[392]

Nonetheless, perceived requirements of complementarity for a successful admissibility challenge were not the decisive factor in catalysing Ugandan expressions of devotion to international standards. At least as important were donors' checklists. From experience Ugandan JLOS actors knew that donors are keen to subsidise their own export products. References to 'international standards' could thus be construed as funding for training abroad and infrastructure (buildings and cars). Interest in international standards thus also quickly evaporated where donors were reluctant to pay, for instance, for reparations, defence counsel or prisons. When, three years after the first interview, the Commissioner General of Prisons was asked about the progress he had made with readying cells for the LRA, he answered:

> We did not prepare anything. There was no money. We keep the cells just like the ordinary cells. We have only [one accused of the LRA] in jail, who will soon be released. We had wanted to convert some cells, to have a library, flushing toilets and very humane treatment in accordance with international standards.
>
> [INTERVIEWER:] *Do the prisons now meet these standards?*
>
> Luzira does not meet these standards.
>
> [INTERVIEWER:] *Could donors not provide assistance?*
>
> Donors funding prisons?! [*Laughs*][393]

---

[391] Human Rights Watch 2007. The report was distributed during a JLOS meeting. The UCICC, funded by foreign organisations, has been equally influential. Mistaking the UCICC for a satellite of the ICC, many officials e.g. one of the judges appointed to the WCC, consider the Coalition's information as authoritative (interview, Kampala, September 2008).

[392] Interview with a government minister, Kampala, October 2008.

[393] Phone interview, November 2011.

Finally, and paradoxically, part of the explanation of the popularity of references to 'international standards' is that 'international standards' appeared to offer discretion, an escape route from the constraints of Ugandan law. Many Ugandan lawyers for instance believed – with reason – that the evidentiary requirements of international criminal law were lower than those of Ugandan law.[394] When drafting the practice directions for their court, the judges of the ICD thus provided that the applicable rules of procedure and evidence would be not just those applicable to criminal trials in Uganda, but also 'international practices and rules'.[395] Protecting the rule of law against the rule of lawyers, the practice directions eventually adopted by the Chief Justice reined the judges back in,[396] foregrounding the Ugandan legal order of which the ICD, no matter how special, remains part.

Shaping the International Criminal Court Act?

When Uganda ratified the Rome Statute in 2002, the prospects of the GoU's adopting legislation to give effect to its obligations under the treaty were bleak. Uganda had joined the Rome Statute because it was internationally fashionable and improved the GoU's image in the eyes of European donors (the US being placated by a 'bilateral immunity agreement').[397] It had paid hardly any attention to the obligations

---

[394] See e.g. interview with the Director of Public Prosecutions, Kampala, November 2011: 'It is easier to prove an international crime than a domestic crime because of the jurisprudence that has developed with respect to war situations.' And a judge on the International Crimes Division, asked about the applicable law of evidence: 'Perhaps we will use that of international criminal procedure, because it is more flexible' (Kampala, November 2011).

[395] Interview with a judge, Kampala, November 2011.

[396] For remains of the provision as initially drafted, see a speech written for the Deputy Attorney-General to be delivered at a 'Policy Dialogue on Complementarity and Transitional Justice' organised by the United Nations Development Programme in New York, where it says: 'Procedurally, the ICD will adopt rules of procedures and evidence applicable to criminal trials in Uganda *as well as international practices and rules, including those by the ICC or other international criminal tribunals*', footnoting a 'High Court (International Crimes Division) Order, 2011' (Ruhindi 2011:2, emphasis added).

[397] Interviews with officials, Kampala, September and October 2008. Asked why the GoU signed a treaty that departed from Uganda's practice of transitions without justice, while it refused to follow the Western fashion with respect to, for instance, the rights of homosexuals, one Ugandan lawyer working for the government explained: 'The type of [international] pressure for gay rights is nothing in comparison to war crimes. Those shock the conscience of mankind. You've got

actually incurred when it ratified the Statute, not unlike when it became party to other 'human rights' treaties.[398] Uganda had ratified the Genocide Convention,[399] the 1977 First Additional Protocol to the Geneva Conventions[400] and the Convention against Torture[401] without giving them any follow-up in domestic legislation.[402] Some international NGOs and one Ugandan MP, part of a transnational network of parliamentarians supporting the ICC, pushed for Ugandan legislation to give effect to obligations in the Rome Statute,[403] but such legislation was not a priority for either the executive or the legislature.[404] So, contrary to the widespread expectation in academic literature, in Uganda domestic legislation criminalising the offences in the Rome Statute was not an effect catalysed by the principle of complementarity *per se*.[405]

The referral, however, catalysed sudden Ugandan attention on ICC legislation. The OTP stressed to Ugandan officials the need for legislation to facilitate the ICC's investigations in Uganda. For the

---

to belong to the community of nations. In the past there was a lack of will and not so much pressure of the international community ... The world was not so much talking about prosecution, prosecution. They were more concerned about remedying it' (interview, Kampala, October 2008).

[398] Not unlike elsewhere, in Uganda the term 'human rights treaties' is frequently used to cover everything with a 'humanitarian dimension', ranging from human rights law proper to international criminal law and international humanitarian law. The Rome Statute is thus frequently considered a 'human rights treaty' (for a clear distinction between the loose and proper concepts of 'human rights law', see O'Keefe 2011:1003–4).

[399] Entry into force on 12 January 1951, Uganda acceded on 14 November 1995.

[400] Entry into force on 7 December 1978, Uganda acceded on 13 March 1991.

[401] Entry into force on 26 June 1987, Uganda acceded on 3 November 1986.

[402] Since its ratification of the Rome Statute, Uganda has also ratified the Protocol for the Prevention and the Punishment of the Crime of Genocide, War Crimes and Crimes against Humanity and All Forms of Discrimination 2006, which obliges Uganda (art. 9) to criminalise genocide, crimes against humanity and war crimes. For other treaties that Uganda has ratified, but failed to implement, see ICRC 2008. Uganda gave domestic effect to the Convention against Torture 1984, to which it had acceded in 1986, through a private member's bill in April 2012 (see Mugerwa 2012).

[403] See also Clarke 2009:133–5.

[404] Interview with the parliamentarian concerned, Kampala, September 2008.

[405] As argued in Chapter 2, 'An obligation to criminalise in domestic law?', the Statute requires states to adopt legislation only to facilitate cooperation, but many states have also criminalised the Rome Statute offences by way of national legislation for the purpose of domestic investigations and prosecutions.

purposes of cooperation, it would have sufficed to adopt legislation on cooperation only – indeed, the OTP feared that comprehensive legislation including Rome Statute crimes would slow down the adoption of cooperation provisions[406] – but international NGOs successfully lobbied for legislation also domesticating the crimes within the ICC's jurisdiction. With influential assistance from the Commonwealth Secretariat, the Ministry of Justice drafted a Ugandan ICC Bill on the basis of the Canadian, South African and New Zealand ICC legislation,[407] which then was hastily gazetted in May 2004.[408] The rationale for the legislation was thus to smooth the progress of the ICC's proceedings, rather than to use it for challenging the ICC's jurisdiction on grounds of complementarity.

But, after its hasty introduction, the Ugandan ICC Bill lingered in Parliament. First, in 2004/5, it was considered that discussing the Bill could jeopardise the progress that Betty Bigombe was making in her talks with the LRA.[409] Next, a petition was filed in the Constitutional Court challenging the constitutionality of the government's ratification of the Rome Statute. The petition contended that Parliament rather than cabinet should have ratified the Statute, as ratification necessitated constitutional amendments.[410] This petition was ultimately dismissed, officially for want of prosecution,[411] but in the

---

[406] Interview with a former OTP official, The Hague, June 2008.

[407] Email exchange with an official in the Ministry of Justice and Constitutional Affairs, December 2008 and Hurinet-U 2005.

[408] International Criminal Court Bill 2004 (ICC Bill 2004).

[409] See also Uganda 2005a:[12.03]: the 'debate [on the ICC Bill 2004] could not move on because government said there were processes that are going on for negotiation with the LRA and they did not think it would be appropriate to begin discussing the ICC Bill at that time.'

[410] The Constitutional Court of Uganda at Kampala, *John Magezi, Judy Obitre-Gama, Henry Onoria v. Attorney General.* The petitioners mentioned four aspects of the Rome Statute that required constitutional amendment. First, the non-applicability of immunities before the Court undermined the President's constitutional immunities. Secondly, the ICC could retry persons who had been convicted or acquitted in Uganda. Thirdly, the ICC does not respect national pardons, whereas the Ugandan Constitution protects them. Finally, Uganda's cooperation with the ICC could violate the right to protection against self-incrimination if Uganda were to hand over information obtained from persons seeking or benefiting from an amnesty in accordance with the Amnesty Act 2000.

[411] In reality due to government obstruction. Interview with one of the lawyers involved, Kampala, October 2008.

meantime the Bill was not discussed on second reading.[412] In addition, preparations for the first multiparty elections in 2006 occupied much of Parliament's attention and created a backlog in parliamentary activity.[413] As it happened, cooperation with the ICC proved possible even without domestic ICC legislation.[414]

As the 2004 Bill lapsed with the prorogation of that Parliament, a new but substantially similar ICC Bill was tabled before the next Parliament on 5 December 2006.[415] In international fora, the Ugandan Minister of Justice promised that the Bill would be enacted before the end of 2008, in view of Uganda's bid to host the Rome Statute Review Conference in 2010 and, more remotely, for Uganda to be elected to the UN Security Council.[416] Back in Uganda, however, Parliament was instructed 'to go slow' with the Bill[417] as its passage was thought to send the wrong message in relation to the ongoing Juba talks.[418] Members of the international-criminal-justice movement organised, with international funding, seminars for parliamentarians

---

[412] Email discussion with a parliamentarian involved, October 2008.

[413] See also Afako 2008:94 and 99.

[414] Instead, a Memorandum of Understanding between the Government of Uganda and the Registry of the Court was concluded on 20 August 2004 (see ICC-ASP/6/ WGRC/INF.1 (2008):6).

[415] International Criminal Court Bill 2006 (ICC Bill 2006).

[416] Makubuya 2008. See also ICC-ASP/6/WGRC/INF.1 (2008):5: 'The Ugandan authorities expressed their full commitment to expedite the approval of the implementing legislation for the Rome Statute, which would most likely occur within 2008.' Similarly, a government minister, asked about the status of the ICC Bill, replied in an interview in Kampala on October 2008: 'We have urged [the legal and parliamentary affairs committee to consider the Bill] as soon as possible.' [Interviewer:] 'Why?' 'Because we are bidding for the 2010 ICC Review Conference. One of the conditions is that we have passed this Bill. Even though we should not be put under pressure to pass our own national legislation.'

[417] Interview with a senior government official, Kampala, October 2008: 'When there was a prospect for peace [Parliament] was instructed to go slow' with the Bill.

[418] See also the Minister of State for Justice and Constitutional Affairs' explanation to Parliament for the long time it had taken for the Act to be adopted: '[T]he long time taken on deliberating on this matter was not by accident. Interestingly, we are not even recalling that the first one was a 2004 Bill which lapsed with the Seventh Parliament. Then we came out with the 2006 Bill and at one point, you may recall that we were in very serious negotiations with the Kony group and everyone of us was actually quite reluctant to disturb that process by coming on the Floor of the House and at the end of the day derailing the process. But as we speak, that has gone bad and there is nothing to stop us from going ahead with the enactment of this law in full swing' (Uganda 2010a).

and lawyers to keep the legislation on the parliamentary agenda (not always effectively – one of the more active MPs on the ICC legislation file was on an ICC event abroad when the Bill was eventually discussed in Parliament).[419] But the executive prioritised commercial laws for debate in the overburdened Parliament.[420] As it happened, Uganda was elected a member of the Security Council and chosen to host the Review Conference without domestic ICC legislation.

It was only the imminent arrival of thousands of delegates for the Rome Statute Review Conference in Kampala in May 2010 that provided the decisive push for Parliament's adoption of the ICC Bill. The JLOS Transitional Justice Working Group, judges of the Ugandan WCC and the Ugandan judge on the ICC pressed the importance of an ICC Act on parliamentarians.[421] As the JLOS Secretariat reviewed the Act's adoption:

> As a result the Government of Uganda was able to successfully host the ICC review conference. This could not have been possible since one of the conditions that was set by the ICC to allow the country to host the conference was domestication of the Rome statute.[422]

So, on 10 March 2010, six years after the first introduction of the Bill and less than three months before the beginning of the Review Conference, Parliament adopted the ICC Act 2010.[423]

The debate of 10 March 2010 and the preceding discussions reveal a notable confusion between the concepts of, on the one hand, ratification, and on the other, adoption of domestic legislation to comply with obligations under the Rome Statute, and between on the one hand giving effect to the obligations imposed on states parties by the Rome Statute and on the other embodying the entire Rome Statute in domestic law.[424] For instance, it was argued that article 11 of the

---

[419] Interview with a parliamentarian, Kampala, May 2010.

[420] Interview with a parliamentarian, Kampala, October 2008.

[421] See Judiciary of the Republic of Uganda (undated) and Uganda 2010a.

[422] JLOS 2010:65. See also Uganda's ambassador to the Assembly of States Parties: 'It was important to have the bill signed before the review conference took place ... [The Assembly of States Parties] wouldn't have cancelled the review conference if it hadn't been, but it was an understanding that we would' (cited in Oketch 2010).

[423] Uganda 2010a.

[424] See *ibid.* (e.g.: The Speaker: 'This Bill is giving the force of law in Uganda [to] the Statute of International – there is already a statute, the Rome Statute ... I think it is not intended to amend the statute but to give force to this. The statute which

Rome Statute prohibited domestic trials for crimes committed before 2002, whereas as a matter of Ugandan law it was more relevant that the Ugandan Constitution prohibited domestic proceedings under a Ugandan ICC Act for crimes committed before its enactment.[425] The ICC contributed to this lack of clarity by stating in outreach activities that 'States Parties are obliged to implement *all* the provisions of the Rome Statute'.[426]

The Bill that was passed in 2010 was almost the same as the one introduced in 2006; Parliament made only a few amendments.[427] The resulting ICC Act 2010 proscribes war crimes, crimes against humanity and genocide in Ugandan law – almost all of these for the first time in Ugandan history[428] – by reference to the Rome Statute's definitions. It also declares applicable the Statute's 'general principles of criminal law' in Ugandan proceedings for these crimes,[429] including

you see ... you may not actually go beyond what it says ... But as to whether we can amend the Rome Statute, I do not know.').

[425] Participant observation, symposium on 'The Domestication of the Rome Statute in Africa: Challenges and Prospects', Entebbe, 5–6 September 2008. See also Ogoola 2010:183–4.

[426] Email exchange with ICC outreach office, May 2008. For a similar confusing statement in the Kenyan context, see Moreno-Ocampo 2009a:2 ('Kenya is a state party to the Rome Statute. The ICC is therefore a part – an independent part – of the legal and judicial system of Kenya, in the same way it is part of the legal system of the other 109 States Parties of the Rome Statute.').

[427] See Uganda 2010a. The amendments concerned mostly procedural roles (consent for prosecution required from the DPP instead of the Attorney-General and jurisdiction of the High Court instead of the Magistrates Court). The only substantive amendment was to change the punishments from those under the Penal Code (which includes the death penalty) to those under the Rome Statute. The amendment ensured that persons prosecuted in Uganda under the ICC Act would not by definition get a harsher punishment than those tried under the Rome Statute by the ICC (Uganda 2010a:[3.02]), but created a discrepancy in the Ugandan courts, namely, that a person prosecuted under the Penal Code Act can receive a harsher punishment than a person prosecuted under the ICC Act. A proposal to delete the provision according to which someone's official capacity is no ground to refuse complying with a cooperation request from the ICC was rejected (ultimately with the unconvincing argument that the irrelevance of official capacity is provided in the Rome Statute and the Statute prohibits reservations).

[428] Grave breaches of the Geneva Conventions of 1949 had already been criminalised in the Geneva Conventions Act 1964. When the ICC Act was adopted in March 2010, the Geneva Conventions Act had never been applied in court.

[429] ICC Act 2010, s. 19. It adds the Rome Statute's article on *ne bis in idem*, which in the Statute falls under 'jurisdiction, admissibility and applicable law', to the part with 'general principles of criminal law'.

the modes of responsibility.[430] Another novelty for the Ugandan legal order is the establishment of extraterritorial jurisdiction on grounds other than nationality, namely, employment by the state of Uganda, passive personality and universality on the condition of the offender's subsequent presence in Uganda.[431]

Still, for some NGOs, donors and international consultants the 2010 Act came as a disappointment. USAID-funded American lawyers had produced for JLOS, in the words of one of the American lawyers involved, 'a state-of-the-art ICC Act, better than in many western countries'.[432] This unofficial draft International Crimes Bill included even more references and similarities to the Rome Statute than the 2006 Bill.[433] For instance, it provided that '[g]rounds for the excusal or disqualification of a judge shall be consistent with Article 41 of the Statute'[434] and listed Article 68 of the Statute (on witness and victim protection) as one of the provisions applicable as part of 'general principles of criminal law'.[435] The International Crimes Bill also explicitly provided for the jurisdiction of a 'War Crimes Division',[436] which would be remarkably open to international elements. For instance, the War Crimes Division could seek the services of foreign advisors to provide assistance to the judges, prosecution and defence counsel, similar to the practice of the Iraqi Special Tribunal.[437] Moreover, as amended by the American advisors, the draft Bill provided that the War Crimes Division would adopt its own rules of

---

[430] Not included are those principles that are already part of Ugandan domestic law (most of the *nullum crimen* and *nulla poena sine lege* guarantees) and the principles on the irrelevance of official capacity.

[431] Cf. ICC Act 2006, s. 18 with the Penal Code Act 1950, ss. 4 and 5. The Geneva Conventions Act 1964, s. 2(1) and (2), already recognised such broad extraterritorial jurisdiction (even without requiring any link to Uganda) for the grave breaches of the four Geneva Conventions of 1949. Note that the ICC Act 2010 establishes this broad jurisdiction not merely for war crimes, crimes against humanity and genocide but also for offences against the administration of justice. It is questionable whether international law permits the exercise of such broad jurisdiction over offences against the administration of justice. RS, art. 70(4)(a) requires jurisdiction on the basis of territoriality and nationality only. See also Commonwealth Expert Group 2004:[35].

[432] Discussion, Amsterdam, June 2009. Amnesty International, too, had lobbied Uganda to adopt an International Court Act that would be more progressive than the Rome Statute itself (see Amnesty International 2004c).

[433] International Crimes Bill Working Document 2009.   [434] *Ibid.*, clause 20(2).

[435] *Ibid.*, clause 19(a)(xi).   [436] *Ibid.*, clauses 18 and 18 *bis*.

[437] *Ibid.*, clause 20(3).

procedure and evidence, apparently in deviation from existing rules for Ugandan courts. The provision continued that 'the judges may adopt modifications [to the existing rules for the Ugandan High Court] modeled after the best practices of international tribunals'.[438] Equally unprecedented in the Ugandan context would be that 'representatives of victim's [sic] groups may present perspectives on matters related to sentencing',[439] and that the 'ICC may send a designated observer ... to attend public proceedings before the [War Crimes Division] to provide first-hand information to the ICC for the purposes of its findings related to Article 17'.[440] In the end, demonstrating the influence of international-norm entrepreneurship when push comes to shove in Uganda, this draft International Crimes Bill was never formally introduced in Parliament.

While the text of the ICC Act 2010 does not differ much from the 2004 Bill, the rationale for its adoption changed. In 2004, the focus was on cooperation with the ICC;[441] in 2010, the immediate reason for adoption was the Review Conference, but the dominant rationale was complementarity.[442] The focus had shifted from facilitating ICC proceedings to conducting domestic trials. Implicitly recognising thorny questions of retroactivity, the A&R Accords had not referred to any still-to-be-adopted ICC Act; as set out above, the A&R Accords had explicitly left the determination of the law to be applied in such proceedings to the legislature.[443] As an instruction for prosecutorial policy – not necessarily for applicable law[444] – the Annexure provided that '[p]rosecutions shall focus on individuals alleged to have

---

[438] *Ibid.*, clause 20(4).   [439] *Ibid.*, clause 20(6).   [440] *Ibid.*, clause 20(7).

[441] The Committee on Legal and Parliamentary Affairs, however, did not share the focus of the executive. For the first and only time that the 2004 Bill would be discussed in Parliament the committee produced a report that recommended adding provisions on alternative criminal justice proceedings, alternative sanctions and the role of the Amnesty Commission (see Committee on Legal and Parliamentary Affairs 2004 and Oulanyah 2004). The Ministry of Justice wrote a negative reply, but sent it to the ICC rather than the committee (interview with a parliamentarian involved, Kampala, September 2008).

[442] See e.g. one parliamentarian arguing in the debate on the adoption of the ICC Act: 'My support to the passing of this Bill into law is based on three fundamental grounds: One is that this Bill, when passed into law, will empower the local courts to carry out trials rather than having to appeal to The Hague.' (Uganda 2010a: [3.09]).

[443] Annexure, clause 9(b).

[444] Interview with a member of the mediation team, Kampala, September 2008.

planned or carried out widespread, systematic, or serious attacks directed against civilians or who are alleged to have committed grave breaches of the Geneva Conventions'.[445] From the perspective of a future admissibility challenge on the ground of complementarity, this focus on conduct rather than applicable law was sufficient. As discussed in Chapter 2, domestic proceedings can render ICC cases inadmissible as long as the same conduct is charged. The Ugandan Penal Code Act covers almost all the conduct stated in the ICC arrest warrants.[446] Nonetheless, after several workshops and discussions with international advisors, many parliamentarians as well as JLOS officials believed that, if Uganda were not to charge the conduct in terms corresponding to the crimes provided for in the Rome Statute, the gravity of the offences would not be accurately reflected and the complementarity criteria not met.[447]

A key obstacle to applying the ICC Act 2010 to crimes allegedly committed by the LRA before 2010, for instance for the crimes of which LRA leaders have been accused by the ICC, is the prohibition against retroactivity. In this case, international human rights law is not the biggest impediment, as it makes an explicit exception to the prohibition in case of acts or omissions that were crimes under international law at the time they were committed.[448] So, as long as the offences in the Rome Statute were crimes pursuant to international law at the time they were committed, which is doubtful with respect to some of the Statute's crimes before 1998, Uganda would not violate international law by applying the ICC Act retroactively. The

---

[445] Annexure, clause 14.

[446] With the exception of the enlistment of children. The UPDF Act 2005, s. 52(2) (c) (arguably applicable to the LRA because it applies, according to s. 119(1)(h), to every person found in unlawful possession of arms) prohibits, but does not criminalise, enrolment of persons under eighteen. See also Wrange 2008a:1.

[447] Participant observation of discussions among parliamentarians (among which 'The Domestication of the Rome Statute in Africa: Challenges and Prospects', organised by the UCICC, Entebbe, 5 and 6 September 2008), participant observation JLOS meeting, Kampala, October 2008 and discussions at the Uganda Law Reform Commission, Kampala, October 2008. See also Glassborow 2008: '[A representative] of Parliamentarians for Global Action, a network of members of parliament from around the world promoting democracy and peace, said that if Uganda could apply the definition of crimes as laid out in the ICC statute in its investigations, prosecutions and adjudications, it could successfully challenge the jurisdiction of the international court.'

[448] International Covenant on Civil and Political Rights 1966, art. 15.

Ugandan Constitution, however, contains a stricter prohibition: 'No person shall be charged with or convicted of a criminal offence which is founded on an act or omission that did not at the time it took place constitute a criminal offence.'[449] It has been argued that this does not prevent application of the proposed ICC Act, since

> [t]he Constitution does not say 'constitute a criminal offence under Ugandan law', but leaves it open whether it is restricted to domestic legislation or not. These acts did constitute criminal offences under international law, which is a law binding also on Uganda. Hence, under this reading, there is no obstacle to introducing new legislation which criminalises acts under domestic law that have already been criminalised under international law.[450]

In this light, JLOS's American international law consultants suggested adding the following provision to the Bill:

> In accordance with Article 15 of the International Covenant on Civil and Political Rights, to which Uganda is a Party, the legislature recognises that Genocide, Crimes Against Humanity, and War Crimes, as defined in this law and Articles 5–8 of the Statute, constitute crimes under customary international law and as such Uganda may prosecute these crimes domestically even where their commission occurred before Uganda enacted provisions expressly criminalising such offenses in its domestic law.[451]

However, article 15(2) of the International Covenant on Civil and Political Rights (ICCPR) does not fulfil the constitutional requirement of a pre-existing criminal offence. In a state with a dualist approach to the international order, the term 'a criminal offence' in the constitutional provision must be read as 'a criminal offence under Ugandan law' (and not foreign or international law), unless the Constitution had made an explicit exception for crimes pursuant to international law, in accordance with article 15(2) of the ICCPR, which it does not.

---

[449] Constitution of the Republic of Uganda 1995, art. 28(7).

[450] Wrange 2008b:61 (footnote omitted).

[451] International Crimes Bill, Working Document, 2009, clause 18 bis(2). Cf. a government official's report of what he had learnt during the study tour to The Hague, Sierra Leone and Sarajevo: 'There the argument was that you can try these suspects because customary international law has been in existence. The argument is strengthened by the existence of the Geneva Conventions and the ICCPR' (interview, Kampala, November 2011).

A way to reconcile the constitutional prohibition against retro-activity with the application of the ICC Act to crimes committed prior to its entry into force is to distinguish between 'act' and 'offence'. Wrange has convincingly argued that

> the Constitution provides that '[n]o person shall be charged with or convicted of a criminal offence which is founded *on an act or omission* that did not at the time it took place constitute a criminal offence' (emphasis added). Hence, it is not prohibited to introduce new crimes with retroactive application, as long as the acts or omissions in question were criminal at the time of commission. Otherwise the Constitution would have said, '[n]o person shall be charged with or convicted of a criminal offence, which is founded on an act or omission that did not at the time it took place constitute *that* criminal offence'.[452]

Whether or not Ugandan law supports this interpretation remains for decision by the Constitutional Court if the ICC Act ever were to be retroactively used and this were challenged.

Alternatively, it was suggested that problems of retroactivity could be avoided by using the 1964 Geneva Conventions Act for the LRA crimes.[453] That Act, however, does not cover crimes against humanity or war crimes committed in a non-international armed conflict.[454] Faced with all this legislation, none of which neatly covered the conflict between the GoU and the LRA, Principal Judge Ogoola playfully proposed his own solution – 'supplementarity':

---

[452] Wrange 2008b:62. See for a similar reasoning in a different jurisdiction, High Court of Australia, *Polyukhovich v. Commonwealth*.

[453] See also below, on the case against Thomas Kwoyelo, who was charged under the Geneva Conventions Act 1964.

[454] The Geneva Conventions Act 1964 criminalises 'grave breaches' of the four Geneva Conventions of 1949, which concern war crimes committed in inter-national armed conflicts only. It is questionable whether the GoS ever had the 'overall control' (see *Tadić Judgment*:[122]) over the LRA required to render the conflict an international armed conflict. Nonetheless, if it wished to use this Act as part of the implementation of the Juba Agreements, Parliament could have made a legislative determination that, for the purposes of the implementation of the FPA, the conflict in northern Uganda must be considered an international armed conflict. Alternatively, if the question whether the conflict amounted to an international armed conflict were to arise in proceedings, the Minister, pursu-ant to s. 2(4) of the Geneva Conventions Act 1964, could determine this and issue a binding certificate accordingly.

What about we leave the doctrine of complementarity and we use the Ogoola doctrine of supplementarity? We will use all three: the ICC Bill, the Penal Code and the Geneva Conventions Act.[455]

Part of the explanation for the attempts closely to mimic ICC charges and procedures could be that in the absence of clear precedents of challenging complementarity the safer route is to follow the ICC as closely as possible, particularly in light of the ICC's narrow definition of what constitutes the same 'case', as discussed in Chapter 2. The Principal Judge, for instance, explained the readiness to copy the ICC model by saying that '[t]he ICC wants us to do everything the way they did it: we must use the same Statute and the same standards'.[456]

But the mirroring of the international norms and practices is also explained by international advice according to which international crimes must be prosecuted as international crimes and as in international proceedings.[457] An example often cited to the Ugandan JLOS actors was the ICTR's refusal to hand over Michel Bagaragaza for trial in Norway because the Norwegian criminal code did not contain the crime of genocide with which the ICTR had indicted him.[458] Only a few advisors explained that this decision was made under the ICTR's regime of primacy, and would be difficult to square with the ICC's arrangement of complementary jurisdiction.[459] Most presented this simply as reflective of 'international law'.[460]

And yet again, when push came to shove and the first LRA member was to be tried before the ICD, the lobbying of the international norm entrepreneurs who wished to see the LRA charged with crimes under the ICC Act proved insufficiently persuasive. The DPP brought charges

---

[455] Discussion, Kampala, October 2008. See also Ogoola 2010:184.

[456] Principal Judge at the Reflection Workshop on the Juba Peace Talks for Religious and Cultural Leaders, Gulu, 10–12 September 2008.

[457] For this view, see e.g., *Amicus Curiae Brief Uganda Victims' Foundation and Redress Trust*:[40]: 'The use of ordinary offences in lieu of international crimes itself fails to capture the gravity and aggravated nature of the international crimes.' See also Human Rights Watch 2012:27, recommending Uganda to 'pursue prosecutions of crimes against humanity and war crimes as defined by the ICC Act for crimes committed prior to 2010'. See also Human Rights Watch 2011:6.

[458] ICTR, *Bagaragaza Referral Decision (AC)*.

[459] See Wrange 2008b:55.

[460] See also Drumbl 2011:202–3, predicting that the ICC is likely to be inspired by ICTR rule 11 *bis* case law, even though it operates under another jurisdictional regime.

against Thomas Kwoyelo (on whom more below), first on the basis of the Penal Code Act, then exclusively under the Geneva Conventions Act,[461] and then on the basis of the Geneva Conventions Act with alternative charges under the Penal Code Act;[462] the DPP did not charge Kwoyelo under the ICC Act. To the Ugandan lawyers involved, the prohibition on retroactivity was too strong an impediment.

Discouraging amnesties

Without considering any possible inconsistency in obligations, Uganda passed the Amnesty Act 2000 within a year of signing the Rome Statute. Also, after Uganda's ratification of the Rome Statute and adoption of legislation giving domestic effect to the Statute, the Amnesty Act remained in force.[463] Uganda thus belied the widespread assumption that states would consider joining the Rome Statute incompatible with the use of amnesties.[464]

Unique in comparison to amnesties across the globe, the Amnesty Act 2000 had been lobbied for by representatives of *victims* of the conflict, not by its would-be direct beneficiaries.[465] Religious leaders from northern Uganda hoped that an amnesty would entice the LRA leadership to give up their armed struggle. Addressing possible fear of prosecution, an amnesty could also encourage abductees to defect. In return for the government's amnesty, the Acholi communities would welcome members of the LRA back as their prodigal children.[466]

Amnesty was not new to Uganda. It had been used before to ensure impunity for crimes committed by state agents as well as to persuade

---

[461] *Uganda v. Kwoyelo Thomas* (Indictment 2010). See also *Charge Sheet Kwoyelo* September 2010.

[462] *Uganda v. Kwoyelo Thomas* (Indictment 2011).

[463] Uganda did not issue a declaration as Colombia did upon ratification, according to which '[n]one of the provisions of the Rome Statute concerning the exercise of jurisdiction by the International Criminal Court prevent[s] the Colombian State from granting amnesties, reprieves or judicial pardons for political crimes, provided that they are granted in conformity with the Constitution and with the principles and norms of international law accepted by Colombia.' (United Nations Secretary-General 2002).

[464] See Chapter 2, 'A prohibition on amnesties?'

[465] See also Wierda and Otim 2011:1160.

[466] In this vein, Mr Jacob Oulanyah, MP from northern Uganda, at the event 'Dialogue: The Crossroads of Amnesty and Justice', Kampala, 11 November 2011. On Acholi feeling a sense of responsibility for the LRA as originating from the Acholi community, see Finnström 2006.

armed opposition groups to lay down their weapons. Sometimes the promise of non-prosecution was given in a legal instrument,[467] other times it was an implicit component of a package including government jobs, money and other benefits.

The Amnesty Act 2000 contains an amnesty that does not require any consent of the President in individual cases. It 'declares' an amnesty[468]

> in respect of any Ugandan who has at any time since the 26th day of January, 1986, engaged in or is engaging in war or armed rebellion against the government of the Republic of Uganda by—
> (a) actual participation in combat;
> (b) collaborating with the perpetrators of the war or armed rebellion;
> (c) committing any other crime in the furtherance of the war or armed rebellion; or
> (d) assisting or aiding the conduct or prosecution of the war or armed rebellion.[469]

President Museveni and army officials had wished to exclude 'heinous crimes',[470] in much the same way that the 1987 Amnesty Statute had explicitly ruled out genocide, murder, kidnapping and rape.[471] But leaders from northern Uganda considered any exclusion of combatants an obstacle to a peaceful resolution of the conflict and insisted on a general amnesty.[472] Nor does the Act exclude crimes committed after its entry into force. The only crimes that are not within the scope of the amnesty are those not committed 'in the furtherance' or 'in the cause' of the war or armed rebellion.

---

[467] See e.g. Decree No. 8, promulgated by Idi Amin on 8 May 1972, according to which '[n]otwithstanding any written or other law, no court shall make any decision, order or grant any remedy or relief against the Government or any person acting under the authority of the Government in respect of anything done or omitted to be done for the purpose of maintaining public order or public security in any part of Uganda, or for the defence of Uganda or for the enforcement of discipline or law and order in respect of or anything relating to, consequent upon or incidental to any those purposes during the period between 24.1.1971 and such date as the President shall determine'. See also the 1987 Amnesty Statute. On amnesty in Uganda, see also Afako 2002, Apuuli 2005, Mallinder 2009 and Tripp 2010.

[468] Amnesty Act 2000, s. 1(a) defines 'amnesty' as 'a pardon, forgiveness, exemption or discharge from criminal prosecution or any other form of punishment by the State'.

[469] Ibid., s. 2(1).   [470] Amnesty Bill 1998.   [471] Amnesty Statute 1987, s. 2.

[472] Acholi Religious Leaders 1999. See also Afako 2002 and Allen 2006:74.

A 'reporter', which is 'a person seeking to be granted amnesty under this Act',[473] shall be taken to be granted the amnesty only if he or she:

(a) reports to the nearest army or police unit, a chief, a member of the executive committee of a local government unit, a magistrate or a religious leader within the locality;

(b) renounces and abandons involvement in the war or armed rebellion;

(c) surrenders at any such place or to any such authority or person any weapons in his or her possession; and

(d) is issued with a certificate of amnesty as shall be prescribed in regulations to be made by the Minister.[474]

If the person has already been charged or lawfully detained, he or she is still deemed to be granted the amnesty if he or she:

(a) declares to a prison officer or to a judge or magistrate before whom he or she is being tried that he or she has renounced the activity referred to in section 2;[475] and

(b) declares his or her intention to apply for the amnesty under this Act.[476]

In that case, the reporter

shall not be released from custody until the Director of Public Prosecutions has certified that he or she is satisfied that—

(a) the person falls within the provisions of section 2; and

(b) he or she is not charged or detained to be prosecuted for any offence not falling under section 2.[477]

The Amnesty Act thus does not make the enjoyment of amnesty conditional upon a confession, truth-telling or an apology.

It is ambiguous whether the amnesty certificate, mentioned in section 3(1)(d), is a criterion for enjoyment of the amnesty or merely a piece of paper evincing qualification for the benefits of the Act.

---

[473] Amnesty Act 2000, s. 1(e).   [474] *Ibid.*, s. 3(1).

[475] The Amnesty Act as incorporated into the Laws of Uganda refers here to s. 3 instead of s. 2. When the Amnesty Act was incorporated into the Laws of Uganda, all sections moved up by one but not all cross-references were adjusted. The fact that the correct reference is to s. 2 is confirmed by *Kwoyelo* (Constitutional Court Ruling), p. 11. The same applies to the references to s. 2 in s. 3(3)(a) and (b).

[476] *Ibid.*, s. 3(2). The word 'apply' in subsection (b) is misleading in that the Act does not provide for an 'application' process; '[a] reporter shall be taken to be granted the amnesty declared' if he or she completes the required steps.

[477] *Ibid.*, s. 3(3).

While the text of section 3(1)(d) suggests the former, its context suggests the latter: the Act 'declares' an amnesty, a reporter 'shall be taken to be granted the amnesty [that has already been] declared' and section 3(6) provides that a reporter who fulfils the conditions of the Act shall be granted an amnesty certificate.[478] It would be illogical to make the grant of an amnesty certificate conditional upon the issuance of an amnesty certificate.

The consequence of the amnesty is that the reporter

> shall not be prosecuted or subjected to any form of punishment for the participation in the war or rebellion for any crime committed in the cause of the war or armed rebellion.[479]

The Act does not protect against civil suits.[480] In 2002, the Act was amended to exclude persons who rejoined the LRA.[481]

The Amnesty Act also establishes an Amnesty Commission

    (a) to monitor programmes of—
        (i) demobilisation;
        (ii) reintegration; and
        (iii) resettlement of reporters;
    (b) to coordinate a programme of sensitisation of the general public on the amnesty law;
    (c) to consider and promote appropriate reconciliation mechanisms in the affected areas;
    (d) to promote dialogue and reconciliation within the spirit of this Act;
    (e) to perform any other function that is associated or connected with the execution of the functions stipulated in this Act.

Originally valid for six months,[482] the Amnesty Act had its twelfth anniversary in 2012. In May of that year, 26,288 people had benefited from it.[483] Forty-nine per cent of these people were members of the LRA.[484] The questionnaire that each reporter was requested to fill in did not ask whether he or she had committed

---

[478] The provision is ambiguous in that it makes obtaining the certificate conditional upon compliance with any of the provisions of subsections (1), (2), (3), (4) and (5), but a reporter cannot comply with subsections (3) and (4) as they contain obligations on the Director of Public Prosecutions.

[479] Amnesty Act 2000, s. 2.   [480] See also *ibid.*, s. 1(a) *a contrario.*

[481] Amnesty (Amendment) Act 2002.   [482] Amnesty Act 2000, s. 16.

[483] Amnesty Commission 2012.

[484] The other reporters were part of one of twenty-seven other rebel groups.

any crimes.[485] Nobody was denied an amnesty certificate on the ground that his or her acts, for instance rape in the base camps, were not committed 'in the furtherance' or 'in the cause' of the war.[486]

The practical relevance of the Amnesty Act has extended beyond its legal consequences. A resettlement package consisting of seeds, saucepans, a mattress, blanket and cash payment of 263,000 USH (approximately US$100) handed out by the Amnesty Commission to each reporter was for many at least as attractive as the promise of non-prosecution.[487] The UPDF made people who reported while in its captivity debrief and then join the army to fight the LRA.[488] State agents at times also abused the Amnesty Act by making release after arbitrary detention conditional upon confession of links with 'terrorist organisations' in exchange for amnesty.[489]

Neither the Ugandan executive nor the Ugandan legislature considered the application of the Amnesty Act to be incompatible with the ratification of the Rome Statute; one was an instrument of domestic peacemaking, the other foreign policy. Rather than, as many legal writers seemed to expect, seeing the principle of complementarity as an incentive to end the application of the Amnesty Act, Ugandan government officials initially argued that the Amnesty Act was fully consistent with complementarity. As the Minister of State for Justice

[485] Amnesty Commission 2008a.

[486] Interview with a Commissioner of the Amnesty Commission, Kampala, September 2008. Amnesty was denied, however, to persons who first committed crimes outside the context of the conflict, then joined the rebellion and asked for an amnesty (interview with a staff member of the Amnesty Commission, Kampala, September 2008) or to those who feigned to have been a rebel in order to obtain amnesty, and particularly, a reintegration package (Mallinder 2009:26). Paradoxically, the argument that rape is not a crime committed 'in the cause of' the conflict and hence cannot be covered by amnesty is undermined by the emerging case law of international criminal courts, recognising rape as an instrument of war, albeit an illegal one.

[487] For a critique of these packages, see Lomo and Hovil 2005:14.

[488] Dolan 2011:100. In the absence of any vetting procedure, senior LRA commanders have been incorporated into the UPDF. One example is Charles Arop, accused by the Ugandan army of leading one of the LRA's attacks on civilians in DRC towns during Christmas 2008, leaving hundreds dead. See Human Rights Watch 2009c:34.

[489] See e.g. Kobusingye's account of how her brother in prison had received visits of state officials to try and persuade him to apply for amnesty (Kobusingye 2010:131). See also Human Rights Watch 2009a:Chapter VIII.

and Constitutional Affairs and Deputy Attorney-General explained to the Ugandan Parliament:

> Hon. Alaso also talked about amnesty – do we throw it overboard; what happens to our amnesty law? No. You need to understand the concept of enforcing this process under the international criminal justice system. Do you understand the principle of complementarity, for instance? As Hon. Kyanjo has put it, there is where the state is unwilling or is unable, but where it is willing and able, that is where the matter should be tried first. In other words, that is the principle of complementarity . . .
>
> International criminal justice does not throw away our own initiatives to try some of these renegades. In other words, we can still have our amnesty law. However, you cannot invoke amnesty when a person is indicted to go to the ICC, because it will not be applicable. You cannot say, We have already granted amnesty to Kony or whoever. You cannot invoke amnesty when these persons or suspects are being indicted at the international level. However, you can actually have amnesty internally or domestically under the complementarity principle.[490]

Nevertheless, the practical effect of the executive's referral of the situation concerning the LRA to the ICC was to undermine the legislature's amnesty law by triggering the jurisdiction of a forum not bound by Ugandan law. The executive also tried to amend the Act without revealing its motive. In December 2003, when due to its confidentiality the referral was not yet known to the Ugandan Parliament, the executive gazetted an Amendment Bill to exclude 'leaders of rebellion' as beneficiaries of the amnesty.[491] The link between the gazetted amendment to the Amnesty Act and the referral to the ICC was disclosed only when the ICC issued a press statement announcing the referral which noted:

> In a bid to encourage members of the LRA to return to normal life, the Ugandan authorities have enacted an amnesty law. President Museveni has indicated to the Prosecutor his intention to amend this amnesty so as to exclude the leadership of the LRA, ensuring that those bearing the greatest responsibility for the crimes against humanity committed in Northern Uganda are brought to justice.[492]

---

[490] Uganda 2010a:[4.12].   [491] Amnesty (Amendment) Bill 2003.
[492] ICC 2004.

Parliament opposed the hastily drafted Amendment Bill on account of its possible consequences for any peace process.[493] An amended version was ultimately passed in 2006, empowering the Minister of Internal Affairs to draw up a list of specified individuals ineligible for amnesty, a list that Parliament must approve for it to take effect.[494]

As such, the amendment to the Bill should not be considered an effect catalysed by complementarity. As explained by the parliamentary Defence and Internal Affairs Committee:

> Uganda has asked the International Court of Justice [sic] (ICC) to indict the LRA leaders, a position that has in principle been agreed to. The ICC is in custody of adequate information to indict the LRA leaders. However, the current position in the Amnesty Act puts the government's cooperation with the ICC in jeopardy, by providing for amnesty to the LRA leadership as provided for in the current Amnesty Act.
>
> The passage of this Bill will therefore ...
> - Enable the ICC [to] indict the LRA leaders and other similar groups ... without any impediments,
> - Explicitly express [the] government's position on the fact that rebel leaders who are regarded as international terrorists, and are operating within our country, are not protected by our domestic legislation against trial in the International Court of Justice [sic],
> - Provide a basis for [the] government to collaborate with international institutions in the fight against terrorism.
> - Harmonise the amnesty Law and the ICC Law, which was passed by this House [sic: the ICC Bill would be passed four years *after* this statement].[495]

While enhancing the possibility of domestic proceedings against the LRA leadership, the amendment was thus primarily introduced to facilitate ICC proceedings.[496]

The Juba A&R Accords for their part did not undermine the amnesty process either. The A&R Agreement explicitly stated that '[t]he parties consider that ... the Uganda Amnesty Commission [is] capable of implementing relevant aspects of this Agreement'.[497] It also

---

[493] Interview with a parliamentarian involved, Kampala, September 2008.
[494] Amnesty (Amendment) Act 2006.
[495] Seventh Parliament of Uganda Defence and Internal Affairs Committee 2006.
[496] Interview with a Cabinet Minister involved in the referral of the situation concerning the LRA to the ICC, Kampala, October 2008.
[497] A&R Agreement, clause 5.5.

ensured legal certainty by providing that '[w]here a person has already been subjected to proceedings or exempted from liability for any crime or civil acts or omissions, or has been subjected to accountability or reconciliation proceedings for any conduct in the course of the conflict, that person shall not be subjected to any other proceedings with respect to that conduct'.[498] Only with a view to possible future proceedings did the A&R Agreement instruct the government to '[i]ntroduce any amendments to the Amnesty Act' to bring it into conformity with the agreement.[499]

The ICC, for its part, has not discouraged Uganda's amnesty process as such.[500] According to a member of Uganda's Amnesty Commission, the OTP told the Commission: 'We are only interested in a few people; we will not affect existing amnesties and we will not undermine the amnesty process.'[501] True to its word, the OTP has not charged any high-level LRA commander who has received amnesty, not even those who renounced the rebellion only after the ICC had opened its investigation and against whom substantial evidence existed, for instance Kenneth Banya, Sam Kolo or Charles Arop.[502] The Prosecutor explicitly encouraged LRA members to defect, promising on Ugandan radio that he would not issue new warrants unless commanders committed new crimes.[503] He stated in an interview:

---

[498] *Ibid.*, clause 3.10. Even if not covered by this clause, the amnesty is protected by art. 28(10) of the Constitution ('No person shall be tried for a criminal offence if the person shows that he or she has been pardoned in respect of that offence').

[499] A&R Agreement, clause 14.4. See also clause 5.6: 'The Government will introduce any necessary legislation, policies and procedures to establish the framework for addressing accountability and reconciliation and shall introduce amendments to any existing law in order to promote the principles in this Agreement.'

[500] The decrease in the number of reporters after the issuance of the ICC arrest warrants (Amnesty Commission 2008b) should probably not be attributed to potential defectors' concern over ICC prosecutions, but rather to a decrease in direct combat with the LRA. If the ICC warrants have had any influence on the decrease in the number of applications, it has been to cause the LRA leadership to tighten its control, reducing opportunities for defections (interview with a humanitarian aid worker, Gulu, September 2008).

[501] Interview with a Commissioner of the Amnesty Commission, Kampala, September 2008.

[502] Banya received amnesty on 12 August 2004, Kolo surrendered on 16 February 2005 and Arop in November 2009 and received amnesty shortly afterwards.

[503] Transcript of a public radio announcement of the ICC Prosecutor, Mega FM, December 2005: '[I]f new commanders of the LRA commit new crimes, I may

> We want just the five top leaders. They can do whatever with the others; they can invite them to come out . . .[504]

suggesting that only persons sought by the ICC cannot benefit from amnesty.

The OTP's statements and practice are difficult to reconcile with the Court's stated aims of ending impunity and contributing to deterrence. They are not, however, inconsistent with the letter of the Statute, which, as Chapter 2 has noted, is silent on amnesties. Moreover, the statements and practice reflect the Court's institutional interest insofar as widespread defections from the LRA increase the chances of arrest of those against whom the ICC has issued warrants. In contrast, ICC proceedings against persons whom the Ugandan Government has already granted an amnesty certificate could jeopardise the GoU's willingness to cooperate with the Court.

The anti-amnesty campaign came, however, from other actors outside Uganda. To the surprise of its Ugandan proponents, international human rights organisations turned against the Amnesty Act, especially after the ICC's intervention. For instance, one international human rights organisation asked a local human rights group: 'How can you as a human rights organisation lobby for amnesty?'[505] For the local human rights organisation, the answer was clear: the Amnesty Act could be a means for the realisation of the most basic human rights such as security, land, family life and dignity. But international human rights organisations focused on the 'fight against impunity'. One parliamentarian from northern Uganda observed:

> Amnesty International is dead against amnesty. I do not know why they called themselves Amnesty. They work day and night to kill amnesty.[506]

With a view to the upcoming ICC Review Conference a year later, Ugandan JLOS actors used the arrest of Thomas Kwoyelo in March 2009 to prepare a first case for the Ugandan ICD. But, for a long time, the question remained: on what legal ground could he be denied amnesty?

---

request new arrest warrants against them . . . All other members of the LRA can come out and return home. I will not prosecute them.'

[504] 'Uganda: Kony will eventually face trial, says ICC prosecutor' 2006.

[505] Statement by a human rights activist at 'Dialogue: The Crossroads of Amnesty and Justice', Kampala, 11 November 2011.

[506] Statement by Mr Jacob Oulanyah, MP from northern Uganda, at 'Dialogue: The Crossroads of Amnesty and Justice', Kampala, 11 November 2011.

Thomas Kwoyelo was captured by the UPDF during Operation Lightning Thunder in the DRC, twenty-two years after the LRA had abducted him at the age of thirteen.[507] In June 2009, Kwoyelo was charged with crimes allegedly committed as a member of the LRA. On 12 January 2010, after a visit in prison from the Principal Legal Officer of the Amnesty Commission, Kwoyelo signed a form renouncing the rebellion.[508] According to the Amnesty Act, once amnesty was taken to be granted, Kwoyelo's release further depended on the DPP's certifying that Kwoyelo was not charged with, or detained in order to be prosecuted for, an offence unrelated to the rebellion. The Amnesty Commission interpreted the Amnesty Act to make the issuance of an amnesty certificate conditional upon the DPP's consent. It wrote to the DPP, saying that in its view Kwoyelo qualified to benefit from the amnesty process, and asked for the DPP's views.[509] The DPP did not respond, and so Kwoyelo remained in prison.

Just over a month before the opening of the ICC Review Conference, the Ministry of Internal Affairs requested Parliament to approve the exclusion of four persons from eligibility for amnesty: Joseph Kony, Dominic Ongwen, Okot Odhiambo and Thomas Kwoyelo.[510] The first three were the ICC suspects who were still alive; Kwoyelo was the only senior LRA commander in Ugandan custody. But Parliament refused to approve the Ministry's proposed statutory instrument on account of procedural irregularities and a lack of information on the reasons for the proposal. Members resented that the executive had not bothered to report that the peace talks had come to an end.[511] The Minister of State said he would come back with a renewed proposal, but never did. Kwoyelo was still not granted amnesty and remained in prison. One prosecutor explained: 'The ICC Review Conference put Uganda in the spotlight; then it is not good to grant an amnesty.'[512] A few months later, Kwoyelo was the first person to be committed to the ICD to face trial for conflict-related crimes.[513]

---

[507] *Uganda v. Thomas Kwoyelo (Proceedings Kasule)*:3.

[508] Kwoyelo 2010. Nonetheless, three months later, the Minister of State for Internal Affairs informed the Ugandan Parliament that Kwoyelo had 'never taken advantage of the [amnesty] law' (Uganda 2010b:[3.26]).

[509] Amnesty Commission 2010.   [510] Uganda 2010b.   [511] *Ibid.*

[512] Interview with a prosecutor involved in the Kwoyelo case, Kampala, June 2010.

[513] Anyoli 2010.

The different application – indeed, the *non*-application – of the Amnesty Act in Kwoyelo's case did not reflect a change in policy: there was no policy. The lack of policy is illustrated by the diversity in legal reasons advanced by officials for why Kwoyelo could not benefit from the Amnesty Act. The Ugandan Deputy Attorney-General explained in 2009 that the Amnesty Act did not apply to Kwoyelo because he had been captured.[514] This argument fails to convince: the Amnesty Act provides for application for amnesty by detained persons,[515] and in practice many persons who had been captured have been released under the Amnesty Act.

A prosecutor involved in the Kwoyelo case argued in the same year that the Amnesty Act did not apply because Kwoyelo had been charged with crimes other than 'crimes against the state'.[516] Considering the text of the Amnesty Act, this could constitute an explanation only if it meant that Kwoyelo's crimes, comprising kidnapping with an intent to murder, were not committed 'in the cause of' the conflict. The weakness of this argument is that kidnapping has been one of the main tactics of the LRA rebellion. The argument does indicate, however, a revolutionary reinterpretation of the Amnesty Act; in no other case has the DPP argued that crimes committed by an LRA member while part of the rebellion were not covered by the Amnesty Act. One year earlier, the DPP had explained the fact that proceedings against members of the LRA were seldom initiated by arguing the exact opposite, namely, that LRA members could *always* invoke the Amnesty Act.[517]

In 2010, a prosecutor in the team responsible for cases before the ICD was the first to make a link between the denial of amnesty to Kwoyelo and the ICC. He explained that Kwoyelo could not be granted amnesty now the ICC Act had been adopted. The ICC Act is silent on amnesties, and is, like any other penal act, not by definition incompatible with an amnesty act. But his argument went as follows:

> The Amnesty Act and the ICC Act are in apparent conflict. Implicit is that when two acts of law are in conflict, the latter should prevail. The

---

[514] Discussion with the Deputy Attorney-General, The Hague, September 2009.
[515] Amnesty Act 2000, s. 3(2).
[516] Phone interview with a prosecutor involved in the Kwoyelo case, September 2009.
[517] Interview with the Director of Public Prosecutions, Kampala, October 2008.

argument now used goes that amnesty was in respect of penal code crimes, but not international crimes. They may thus have to amend the charges [against Kwoyelo] into international crimes.

[INTERVIEWER:] *But the Amnesty Act does not say it is only for Penal Code Act crimes.*

Amnesty has in mind the crimes under the penal code. When [the Amnesty Act] was drafted one did not have the ICC on the back of their minds. The ICC Act frowns upon immunity. Even constitutional guarantees of immunity may not apply. The framers of the Amnesty Act did not have the ICC Act in mind.[518]

The interviewed prosecutor argued that the Amnesty Act must be reinterpreted as not to apply to international crimes, not just international crimes in the ICC Act, but also in the much older Geneva Conventions Act. Unlike the ICC Act, the Geneva Conventions Act could be applied in the Kwoyelo case without problems of retroactivity (although raising the separate question whether the armed conflict was international in the sense of the 1949 Geneva Conventions).[519] It was this argument, that the Amnesty Act does not cover international crimes, that the Director of Public Prosecutions maintained when asked why he had not given the Amnesty Commission the green light to issue an amnesty certificate:

Kwoyelo was the first to be charged under the Geneva Conventions. If he had been charged under the laws of Uganda alone, he would have qualified for amnesty. We maintain the position that amnesty is inapplicable to international crimes.[520]

The weakness of the argument is that Kwoyelo has not been charged under the Geneva Conventions, but under the Geneva Conventions Act. This latter act, like the Penal Code Act, is a domestic act. Crimes under domestic law are excluded from the scope of the Amnesty Act only if there is an act explicitly stating so. There is none that does.

---

[518] Interview with a prosecutor involved in the SDHC, Kampala, June 2010.

[519] See above, nn. 453 and 454. Initially, Kwoyelo's defence lawyers challenged the applicability of this Act. They dropped that challenge, however, possibly because the maximum punishment under the Geneva Conventions Act is lower than under the ordinary Penal Code Act, a pattern consistent with the fact that in many instances penalties for international crimes are lower than those for ordinary crimes (see Heller 2012).

[520] Interview, Kampala, November 2011.

The most revolutionary argument against the Amnesty Act was brought by a representative of the Attorney-General's Chambers before the Ugandan Constitutional Court in August 2011. During preliminary proceedings before the ICD in July 2011, Kwoyelo had successfully applied for a reference to the Constitutional Court complaining, among other things, that the DPP and the Amnesty Commission had not accorded him equal treatment under the Amnesty Act and had thus discriminated against him in contravention of the Constitution.[521] The response of the Attorney-General's representative, who acted on behalf of the DPP, came as a surprise to many, including the DPP[522] and, as later appeared, the Attorney-General and his Deputy.[523]

The representative argued that Kwoyelo could not derive any legal right to amnesty under the Amnesty Act because the Amnesty Act was unconstitutional.[524] She admitted that it was 'rather unusual for the Attorney General to contend that a law is unconstitutional because he is involved in its enactment'.[525] Nonetheless, she continued, 'whereas the [Attorney-General] has the power to amend or appeal laws when their illegality comes to his attention, where the issue arises in a suit and there is no time for amendment/repeal, it is his duty as an officer of Court to guide the Court on the same'.[526] She claimed the Amnesty Act infringed on the constitutional independence of the DPP, the constitutional independence of the judiciary, Article 287 of the Constitution and Uganda's obligations under international law.[527] On the first point, she elaborated that 'the Act in granting a blanket amnesty without provision for the DPP's consent, denies him the opportunity to consider the facts/circumstances of

---

[521] *Uganda v. Thomas Kwoyelo (Proceedings)*:23–4 and *Uganda v. Thomas Kwoyelo (Reference to the Constitutional Court)*:2.

[522] The DPP commented in an interview in Kampala, November 2011: 'Unconstitutionality was never our argument. It was never our position before the Court. Someone in the Attorney-General's Chambers developed this, on the basis of the *Susan Kigula* case. [Laughs] The argument came suddenly when we were in court.' (In the *Susan Kigula* case, the Supreme Court held that a mandatory death sentence was unconstitutional.)

[523] See below, text preceding footnote flag 552.

[524] *Uganda v. Thomas Kwoyelo (Constitutional Directions Proceedings)*:3; *Uganda v. Thomas Kwoyelo (Proceedings Kasule)*:7; and *Uganda v. Thomas Kwoyelo (Attorney-General's Legal Arguments)*.

[525] *Uganda v. Thomas Kwoyelo (Attorney-General's Legal Arguments)*:1.

[526] *Ibid.*   [527] *Ibid.*

individual cases, available evidence and then take the specified issues into consideration and make an independent decision to prosecute or not to prosecute'.[528] Among the factors that the DPP should be able to consider were, according to the Attorney-General's representative:

- Whether the offences constitute violations of international humanitarian law and whether the suspect was individually responsible for such violations?
- Does Uganda have any international obligation to prosecute the offences? Is there universal jurisdiction by other states on international tribunals e.g. ICC over these offences?
- Uganda's *foreign policy* supporting the prosecution of international crimes as illustrated by its enactment of the ICC Statute and establishment of an International Criminal [sic] Division of the High Court.[529]

The inconsistency with Article 287 was argued on the basis that this article 'recognizes the validity of ratified treaties under Ugandan law', including the Geneva Conventions. However, Article 287 does not specify the status of international treaties in the domestic legal order – it is merely a transitional provision according to which the new Constitution does not affect Uganda's obligations under pre-existing treaties.

So in addition, but without providing an explanation of how this would lead to a *constitutional* violation, the Attorney-General's representative argued that the Amnesty Act compelled Uganda to violate its 'international legal obligation to punish grave breaches of the Geneva Conventions on war crimes'.[530] Reference was made to the principle of *pacta sunt servanda*, the unavailability of the excuse of municipal law to justify a violation of international law, the finding of the Inter-American Court of Human Rights in *Barrios Altos* v. *Peru* that the Peruvian amnesty laws lacked effect, the decision of the Special Court for Sierra Leone in *Prosecutor* v. *Morris Kallon and Brima Bazzy Kamara* denying validity to an amnesty for serious war crimes, and the ICTY's (*obiter*) finding in *Furundžija* that a state cannot take national measures absolving its perpetrators of torture through an amnesty law.[531] The Attorney-General's representative explained the adoption of the Amnesty Act as 'a justifiable case of human error': the existence of the Geneva Conventions Act had 'escaped the attention of the [Attorney-General] and Parliament'.[532]

---

[528] *Ibid.*:2.   [529] *Ibid.*:3 (emphasis added).   [530] *Ibid.*:4.
[531] *Ibid.*:5–6.   [532] *Ibid.*:6.

Kwoyelo's lawyers in turn referred to the constitutional protection of a pardon and the decision of the South African Constitutional Court to uphold South Africa's amnesty act in *AZAPO*. They also distinguished between amnesties granted for the benefits of rulers and, as in Uganda, abducted children.[533]

The Constitutional Court dismissed the Attorney-General's argument that the Amnesty Act was unconstitutional, found that Kwoyelo had been given unequal treatment and directed the ICD to cease his trial forthwith.[534] In upholding the Act's constitutionality, the Constitutional Court argued that pardon was a constitutionally protected right, that the use of amnesty to bring a rebellion to an end was within the framework of the Constitution, and that the Ugandan Amnesty Act, unlike the South African, benefited only rebels. It stressed that the DPP could still prosecute people, namely, those who refused to renounce rebellion, those who were declared ineligible for amnesty by the Minister of Internal Affairs (with Parliament's approval) and government agents. The Constitutional Court explicitly rejected the idea that Uganda had an obligation under the Rome Statute not to grant amnesties:

> There is evidence on record contained in the affidavit of the applicant to the effect that top commanders of the LRA were indicted by the International Criminal Court under the Rome Statute. *Their indictment clearly shows that Uganda is aware of its international obligations, while at the same time it can use the law of amnesty to solve a domestic problem.* We have not come across any uniform international standards or practices which prohibit states from granting amnesty.[535]

In the same way that the Deputy Minister of Justice argued before Parliament, the Constitutional Court thus separates compliance with the Rome Statute from issuing amnesties.

Following the Constitutional Court's ruling, the ICD directed the Amnesty Commission and the DPP 'to comply with the provisions of the Amnesty Act',[536] leaving room for interpretation as to whether this required the Amnesty Commission to issue Kwoyelo with an amnesty certificate or whether certification by the DPP was still

---

[533] Summarised in *Uganda v. Thomas Kwoyelo (Proceedings Kasule)* and *Kwoyelo (Constitutional Court Ruling)*:18–19.
[534] *Kwoyelo (Constitutional Court Ruling).*　　[535] *Ibid.*:24 (emphasis added).
[536] *Uganda v. Kwoyelo Thomas (ICD Order)*:2.

required. Believing the latter to be the case, the Amnesty Commission again asked for the DPP's permission to issue a certificate, but in vain.

When Kwoyelo sought an order of *mandamus* to compel the Chairman of the Amnesty Commission and the DPP to grant him an amnesty certificate, the Attorney-General's representative argued that Kwoyelo did not qualify for amnesty as he also faced charges for offences other than kidnap with an intent to murder, including grave breaches of the Geneva Conventions for which no amnesty could be granted.[537] In an interview, the DPP elaborated:

> Neither the Constitutional Court nor the High Court gave me an instruction to release Kwoyelo. They just said: do your job, act. Now our position is that amnesty does not apply to international crimes. That is why Kwoyelo is still in prison.[538]

In January 2012, the High Court judge deciding on the request for an order of *mandamus* rejected the DPP's arguments, finding that the alleged offences were committed by the applicant during the period in which he was a participant in the rebellion and that this brought him within the operation of the Amnesty Act.[539] It was clear to the judge that the Constitutional Court found that violations of the Geneva Conventions Act also fell within the scope of the Amnesty Act, and he issued the order of *mandamus* compelling the Chairman of the Amnesty Commission and the DPP to process and grant an amnesty certificate to the applicant for his immediate release.[540]

And yet, the DPP continued to refuse to certify the grant of an amnesty certificate and to release Kwoyelo,[541] stating: 'This office maintains the position that under the principles of international law, no amnesty can be granted to persons accused of committing war crimes under the Geneva Convention.'[542]

The prosecution of Kwoyelo was prompted by opportunism rather than law or policy. Kwoyelo is considered of little use by the ruling party.[543]

---

[537] *Thomas Kwoyelo v. Attorney General (Order of Mandamus)*:7 and 18.

[538] Interview, Kampala, November 2011.

[539] *Thomas Kwoyelo v. Attorney General (Order of Mandamus)*:18.

[540] *Ibid.*:19 and 20.

[541] Kwoyelo is not the first not to be released despite qualification for amnesty. See also the story of Ismail Ssenfuka (see Okanya and Akampa 2010 and the comments by parliamentarian Kamya in Uganda 2009:[3.47]).

[542] Anyoli 2012.

[543] See also Chapter 5, 'High cost of action: obstacles to domestic proceedings' on political trials and political impunity.

Rather, Kwoyelo, as a Ugandan 'Tadić', could satisfy the ICD's institutional craving for a first case, and during the ICC Review Conference in Kampala the preparations for his case served to demonstrate the host country's commitment to international justice at home. As a prosecutor interviewed in Kampala explained during the ICC Review Conference:

> The DPP has little room to manoeuvre. Legally, Kwoyelo would qualify for amnesty. Politically, as a country that has committed to the ICC, we must give an example. We don't have a single case before the War Crimes Court. If he gets amnesty it pulls the carpet under our feet and we shall have nobody.[544]

With the Review Conference successfully concluded, the pressure diminished. In the words of the interviewed prosecutor: 'Now that we are done with the ICC review conference',[545] law could prevail over opportunism.

The Kwoyelo case was thus pursued at all costs, obvious legal obstacles notwithstanding. The Attorney-General's Chambers' argument that the Amnesty Act was unconstitutional put at risk the legal certainty of more than 26,000 beneficiaries of the Amnesty Act in order to prosecute one man before the ICD.[546] In the words of one Ugandan lawyer, musing on this 'trial by ambush': 'They fell every man to get their man; we the people are bleeding.'[547]

Donors, for their part, also changed their position on the amnesty. Welcoming the Act in 2000 as a peaceful conflict-resolution mechanism and afterwards putting pressure on President Museveni to extend its application,[548] they expressed shock when the Act appeared to obstruct the work of the ICD and echoed international

---

[544] Interview with a prosecutor involved in the Kwoyelo case, Kampala, June 2010.

[545] *Ibid.*

[546] Possibly in an attempt to convince the judges that a finding of unconstitutionality would not have such far-reaching consequences, the Attorney-General's representative argued before the Constitutional Court that any such finding would not have retrospective effect (*Uganda v. Thomas Kwoyelo (Proceedings Kasule)*:9). However, according to the Ugandan Constitution, a law inconsistent with the Constitution is void to the extent of the inconsistency (Constitution, art. 2(2)), making it impossible for an unconstitutional act to have any legal effect.

[547] Phone discussion with a Ugandan lawyer, November 2011.

[548] See Dolan 2011:99.

human rights organisations in arguing that international crimes should be excluded from its scope.[549]

If the Kwoyelo case reveals any policy, it is the absence thereof. Individuals in JLOS, backed by donors and international NGOs, were given a free hand to pick and develop one component of the Juba transitional-justice package, namely, criminal justice for the LRA. Once created, the Division needed cases to justify its existence.[550] The Juba A&R Accords had foreseen the need to reconcile criminal accountability with the existing amnesty and with other transitional-justice aims and had therefore instructed the government to develop a comprehensive transitional-justice policy, including amendments to the Amnesty Act.[551] But, in the absence of a signed Final Peace Agreement, a transitional-justice policy never became a priority for the cabinet. In interviews in 2011, it appeared that neither the Attorney-General nor the Deputy Attorney-General were even aware, let alone supportive, of their representative's argument that the Amnesty Act was unconstitutional. The Attorney-General explained

---

[549] Interviews with donors, Kampala, November 2011.

[550] Actors working for or supporting the International Crimes Division, including donors, international NGOs, and the donor-funded transitional-justice experts seconded to JLOS, thus condemned the Constitutional Court's decision upholding the constitutionality of the Amnesty Act for frustrating the work of the ICD. (Interview with the DPP, Kampala, November 2011: 'We were shocked when we heard that Kwoyelo could walk free ... We need the Supreme Court Decision. People will say: if you cannot try Kwoyelo, then you cannot try anybody.'; Interview with an ICD judge, Kampala, November 2011: 'If the Supreme Court upholds the decision of the Appeals Court [in Kwoyelo], nobody will be tried. That would be ridiculous.'; Discussion with a JLOS donor, November 2011: 'This Amnesty Act is unacceptable and in violation of international standards. It is to be hoped that the Supreme Court will overrule the Constitutional Court on the amnesty issue so that Kwoyelo can be tried.'; Interview with a JLOS official, Kampala, November 2011: 'It was a shock: everybody was ready, and then, now this trial is not going to take place.'). For more general criticism of the decision, see Transitional Justice Team of the JLOS Secretariat 2011:3 ('This decision has created serious concern with regard to its implications on the pursuit of justice and accountability in Uganda. In particular, the decision has implications for Uganda's national and international human rights obligations and its duty to ensure justice for victims of these violations.' See also *ibid.*:8: 'The sector is concerned about the serious implications created by the ruling of the Constitutional Court especially with regard to our own commitments at the Juba Peace process, our international obligations, and our obligations to the victims of crimes.') and Amnesty International 2011.

[551] A&R Agreement, clauses 5.6, 14.3 and 14.4.

that he had not been involved in the case at all.[552] The Deputy
Attorney-General, for his part, said:

> I believe the Act is constitutional. I know that it offends international
> norms. But the ICC also recognises complementarity; it has ceded
> much of its mandate to try to partner states. Then it is up to partner
> states to do their best to handle these offenders, including through
> amnesty.
>
> [INTERVIEWER:] *But this is not what the Attorney-General's represen-*
> *tative argued in Court.*
>
> In Court it is all a different matter. We should not have argued
> unconstitutionality. Sometimes our staff are short of instructions what
> to do.[553]

Nonetheless, even if itself not guided by any policy, the Kwoyelo case
itself did bring about a general, and radical, departure from the
practice of the twelve-year-old Amnesty Act. The events in the case
provided reasons for international organisations, most of which were
against amnesties for crimes under international law, to host events on
the future, or the 'expiration', of the Amnesty Act.[554] Representatives
from northern Uganda, Ugandan NGOs and JLOS actors including
the Amnesty Commission met to discuss whether the Amnesty Act
should be extended (as had happened in previous years), be amended
to set more conditions for amnesty or be abolished altogether. Many
representatives from northern Uganda argued for continuing to renew
the Amnesty Act for as long as the conflict persisted.[555] While they
have opposed the ICC to a lesser degree ever since the LRA migrated
out of northern Uganda, and resent the fact that the Amnesty
Commission gave packages to former rebels and not to victims, they
continued to see the Amnesty Act as a useful mechanism as long as
members of their own communities were held captive by the

---

[552] Interview, Kampala, November 2011.

[553] Interview, Kampala, November 2011.

[554] UNHCHR and UN Women changed the title proposed by the Ugandan NGO,
the Refugee Law Project, from 'Reconciling Amnesty and Accountability: Mission Impossible?' to 'Dialogue: The Crossroads of Amnesty and Justice –
A Reflection on the *Expiration* of the Amnesty Act in May 2012' (emphasis
added).

[555] See e.g. interventions by representatives from northern Uganda at 'Dialogue: The
Crossroads', Kampala, 11 November 2011. See also Justice and Reconciliation
Project 2011b.

movement,[556] communities in neighbouring countries were terrorised by the LRA or there was a real threat of the LRA returning.[557] Some civil society organisations argued that the Amnesty Act should be amended to make it part of a broader transitional-justice arrangement that includes, for instance, truth-telling.[558]

JLOS, however, adopted the anti-amnesty arguments provided by its donor-funded transitional-justice advisors. These arguments were primarily based on international law, including purported 'complementarity obligations':

> The Amnesty Act presents challenges to Uganda's ability to *comply* with the principle of complementarity under the Rome Statute. Under this principle, the ICC can only intervene when a national government is *'unwilling or unable'* to investigate. The complementarity principle would *require* those responsible for serious human rights violations to be excluded from the amnesty process, and instead, be investigated by the national courts. However, without any declaration from the Government thus far that certain individuals are ineligible for amnesty, the ability of the ICD to hear cases against those alleged to have committed serious crimes during the conflict is unclear. Uganda's amnesty law raises important issues for the ICD's operation, Uganda's ability to *comply* with the principle of complementarity, and the effectiveness of current and future accountability mechanisms for holding perpetrators to account.[559]

---

[556] That number is declining. Since 2006, the LRA has operated outside Uganda, and its new abductees are Congolese, South Sudanese and Central African. To them, the Ugandan Amnesty Act is of little relevance.

[557] For instance, one northern Ugandan representative responded to the Office of the UN High Commissioner for Human Rights' line that 'there can be no amnesty for war crimes, genocide, crimes against humanity and gross violations including gender-based violence' with the question: 'Are international doctrines saving the mothers and children being killed there?' (Discussion, 'Dialogue: The Crossroads', Kampala, 11 November 2011).

[558] Interventions at *ibid.*

[559] JLOS 2012a:3 (footnotes omitted; emphases added). See also JLOS 2012b:11: 'The Rome Statute of the ICC *establishes* the *duty* to prosecute serious violations of international law, first in its Preamble and then in Article 17 of the Statute, whereby national courts have not only the first opportunity to prosecute international crimes, but an *obligation* to prosecute them, thereby placing on the State the *primary responsibility* of bringing perpetrators of crimes within the jurisdiction of the ICC to justice. Uganda domestication of both the Geneva Conventions and the Rome Statute signify that these instruments have become part of national law and therefore, the obligations are directly enforceable in Uganda' (emphases

As the italicised words illustrate, JLOS thus invoked complementarity as 'big idea' rather than the admissibility rule in the Rome Statute (which, as Chapter 2 has pointed out, does not contain obligations on states and is silent on amnesties).

On the basis of these arguments, the Minister of Internal Affairs adopted in May 2012 a remarkable statutory instrument, declaring that 'the operation of Part II of the Amnesty Act' – containing the actual declaration of the amnesty and the procedure for benefiting from it – had 'lapsed'.[560] At the same time, he adopted a statutory instrument extending the 'expiry period of Part I, III and IV of the Amnesty Act' – on the Act's interpretation, the Amnesty Commission and general issues – for another twelve months.[561] If this move is treated as valid, the consequence is that the (donor-funded) Commission survives but the amnesty for which it was created does not. (The Minister's statutory instruments seem *ultra vires*: section 16 of the Amnesty Act allows the Minister to extend the expiry period of the Act; it does not allow him to pick and choose provisions for extension and expiration.)

Four features of these developments are particularly noteworthy. First, complementarity's effect on Uganda's Amnesty Act has been largely indirect. Kwoyelo himself was never accused by the ICC – in his case there was no complementarity to invoke to render an ICC case inadmissible. However, entering the country in the wake of the ICC's intervention, international human rights activists, backed by donors, extended the ICC's anti-impunity spirit to advocate against amnesty. Indeed, they argued that not just the Statute, but specifically complementarity prohibited amnesties, a position for which neither the Statute nor complementarity as set forth in article 17 of the

---

added). See also Kastner 2011:84 ('Although the Ugandan Amnesty Act is inconsistent with the requirements of the Rome Statute ... '). See also interview with a prosecutor involved in the Kwoyelo case, Kampala, November 2011: 'The Amnesty Act is in violation of the ICC Act, article 17 [what the prosecutor probably meant was the Rome Statute; art. 17 of the ICC Act concerns the requirement of consent for domestic proceedings], which does not agree with amnesty; it frowns at amnesty ... Now when we insist on justice, we use the Hague approach, which is a departure of amnesty. The Ocampos would say that amnesty is impunity.'

[560] Amnesty Act 2012 (Declaration of Lapse of the Operation of Part II) Instrument, s. 2.

[561] Amnesty Act 2012 (Extension of Expiry Period) (No. 2) Instrument, s. 2.

Statute gives much support. Secondly, whilst the advocacy against the amnesty has to a large extent been done in the name of victims' rights, those few people from northern Uganda who were 'consulted' had in fact not criticised the amnesty *per se* – indeed, many argued for its extension – but held that it did not do *enough*, particularly in terms of reparations to victims.[562] As a result of anti-amnesty advocacy, however, the victims' baby – recall how the Act had been lobbied for by people from northern Uganda – has been thrown out with the bath water: the amnesty has expired without the implementation of the other mechanisms for which northern Ugandans lobbied. Thirdly, the objective of excluding people from the amnesty could have been achieved in accordance with the law, since the Act allowed for exclusion of individuals with parliamentary approval. Instead, Parliament was bypassed.

This leads to the fourth remarkable feature: whilst increased chances for accountability may seem beneficial for the enhancement of the rule of law in Uganda, the process and the outcome of the anti-amnesty campaign suggest the opposite. First, the pick-and-choose way to end the amnesty – itself probably an *ultra vires* act – was chosen by JLOS while the question of the Act's constitutionality was still before the Supreme Court.[563] Secondly, cabinet ministers accepted this JLOS proposal on the assumption that the President could still give amnesties on a case-by-case basis (even though, constitutionally, the President may grant only pardons). If the pre-Amnesty-Act practice of the President's promising impunity in individual cases resumes, the grant of amnesty will have shifted from the will of Parliament, lobbied for by people from northern Uganda, to the discretion of the President. This development would fit neatly into a trend that Andrew Mwenda has called the 'personali[sation] of power' in Uganda.[564] Favouritism, rather than the rule of law, has been promoted.

---

[562] See e.g. JLOS 2012b.

[563] *Kwoyelo Thomas* v. *Uganda (Notice of Appeal)*. The grounds for appeal are summarised in *Uganda* v. *Thomas Kwoyelo (Affidavit in Support of Application)*.

[564] Mwenda 2007. Just before this book went to print, on 24 May 2013, the Minister of Internal Affairs adopted, at Parliament's instigation, two statutory instruments to bring the amnesty back into operation: Amnesty Act (Revocation of Statutory Instrument No. 34 of 2012) Instrument 2013 revoked the statutory instrument by which the Minister had declared the lapse of Part II of the Amnesty Act, and Amnesty Act (Extension of Expiry Period) Instrument 2013, extended the application of the Amnesty Act until 25 May 2015.

EFFECTS EXPECTED BUT NOT CATALYSED

No matter how unexpected or revolutionary complementarity's effects on local justice practices, transitional-justice debates, court institutions and amnesties, for the purpose of rendering a case inadmissible on grounds of complementarity the only relevant effect is that on actual investigations, prosecutions and trials.

Encouraging more trials, prosecutions and/or investigations?

Shortly after the referral to the ICC, there were indications that the strongest potential for a catalysing effect on domestic proceedings would be with respect to crimes committed by state actors. The GoU had been willing to outsource jurisdiction over the LRA, but it was protective of its 'own' people.[565] The referral of the 'situation concerning the Lord's Resistance Army' was meant to focus the ICC's proceedings exclusively on the LRA. Informed by the OTP that the referral was interpreted as a referral of the entire situation, all parties included, the GoU made a clear distinction between the LRA and state actors, as is illustrated by the statement that the Minister of Defence made in Parliament to announce the Prosecutor's decision to open an investigation:

> [A]llow me to brief this august House and the general public on the progress so far made in the preparatory process that will eventually culminate in the international criminal prosecution of the leaders of Lord's Resistance Army (LRA) terrorists by the International Criminal Court ...
>
> The office of the prosecutor has, during the last several months, been undertaking independent, preliminary investigations with a view to determining whether there is sufficient basis to proceed with formal investigations that will eventually lead to the international criminal prosecution of the LRA terrorists in the ICC.
>
> Yesterday, the Prosecutor of the International Criminal Court issued letters of notification to all states parties to the Rome Statute of the ICC and other concerned states, in which he announced his decision to formally initiate an investigation in relation to the situation concerning atrocities committed by LRA terrorists against the people of Northern Uganda ...

---

[565] For a discussion of 'self' in the context of 'self-referrals', see Nouwen and Werner 2010b.

> Lastly, the Government of Uganda wishes to profoundly thank the prosecutor for his very important decision, and takes the opportunity to renew the assurance of its commitment to providing all assistance that may be required by the prosecutor to advance the realization of justice and peace in the Northern part of Uganda. Should the International Criminal Court come across any information or evidence implicating any Ugandan Government official in the commission of any of the crimes complained of, Uganda shall immediately prosecute such officials. (*Applause*)[566]

In sum, in the GoU's vision the LRA would be tried by the ICC, and government officials by Uganda '[s]hould the International Criminal Court come across any information or evidence implicating any Ugandan Government official'.

But most Ugandan officials are convinced that the ICC will not investigate state actors. They argue that state actors seldom commit crimes, and, if they do, the crimes are always immediately investigated, prosecuted, tried and punished, with even the death penalty being handed down by field courts-martial and carried out summarily.[567] In addition, they are convinced that the ICC's proceedings concern the 'situation concerning [only] the Lord's Resistance Army', despite the OTP's use of the name 'situation in northern Uganda' or 'situation in Uganda'.

Apart from changing the name of the situation, the ICC has not given the GoU any reason to believe that state actors may be subject to its proceedings. First, it has not opened an investigation into crimes allegedly committed by state actors. When asked about the absence of Ugandan proceedings against senior UPDF officers for crimes committed on a widespread or systematic scale, army officials express a sense of vindication by the absence of ICC proceedings and argue that 'even the ICC has not found anything'.[568] Ugandan officials refer to

---

[566] Uganda 2004. See also 'Museveni pledges to cooperate with ICC to probe Uganda war crimes' 2004 and 'Uganda: interview with President Yoweri Museveni' 2005.

[567] *Inter plurima alia*: Interview with senior UPDF official, Kampala, October 2008; interview with a military intelligence officer, Kampala, October 2008 and interview with a military lawyer, Kampala, October 2008. See also 'Uganda: interview with President Yoweri Museveni' 2005. The GoU has used the same reason to argue that the UPDF need not be subjected to local justice practices. See the statement by the Minister of Internal Affairs in Uganda 2007.

[568] Interview with a military intelligence officer, Kampala, October 2008. See also Ogola 2010 ('Army spokesman Lieutenant-Colonel Felix Kulayigye ... maintains

headlines in a national newspaper, which announced that the ICC had 'cleared' the UPDF.[569] The article quotes an ICC outreach official to the effect that 'the Prosecutor said there was evidence against Kony and not against the UPDF commanders'.[570] Theoretically, the OTP could still open an investigation into Ugandan state actors, for instance when the case against the LRA reaches its conclusion. However, it has not been lost on Ugandan officials that the ICC's investigation team has been reassigned to other situation countries.

Moreover, the OTP's actions from the announcement of the referral onwards have left Ugandan officials with an indelible impression that the ICC acts at the behest of the Ugandan President. Prosecutor Ocampo and President Museveni announced the referral in a joint news conference.[571] The accompanying ICC press release mentioned 'locating and arresting the LRA leadership' as a key issue,[572] even though the Prosecutor still had to conduct an official investigation. Subsequently, a Uganda–ICC team spirit emerged, at least on the Ugandan side. This was nourished, at the practical level, by joint conduct of investigations between ICC staff and Ugandan military intelligence, police and army in Uganda, and at the diplomatic level of most senior OTP officials on the one hand and the Minister of Defence and Attorney-General on the other by joint leisure activities such as a boat trip along the Dutch canals.[573]

In the context of allegations against state actors, and in sharp contrast to the investigation into the LRA, ICC officials emphasised the importance of complementarity. When Olara Otunnu, a political leader of a Ugandan opposition party (and formerly the UN Secretary-General's Representative for Children in Armed Conflict) requested ICC officials to begin an investigation into crimes allegedly committed by the UPDF, Prosecutor Ocampo 'advised Ugandans to only involve the ICC in cases which they feel the national legal system is inadequate to handle', according to the reporters at the press

---

that during its investigation into events in northern Uganda, the international court probed the army and came up with little. "The ICC has investigated the UPDF, but only found isolated cases that do not measure up to the atrocities that the LRA committed in the country," he said. "I find that these allegations [against the army] are nothing more than politicking.'"); and Lt. Col. Kulayigye 2009.

[569] Focus group, Gulu, September 2008.

[570] Mugisa and Nsambu 2008. The newspaper's correction of this article ('Corrections Column' 2008) seems to have gone largely unnoticed.

[571] ICC 2004.   [572] *Ibid.*   [573] See below, Chapter 5, n. 233.

conference.[574] In a similar vein, ICC President Song 'pointed out ...
that the ICC was supposed to be a court of last resort and that it should
be up to national courts to try lower-level perpetrators'. He was quoted
as adding:

> I realise others, too, have committed crimes and all who commit crimes
> should be held responsible ... But the ICC is only one piece of the
> puzzle. It is an important part, but by no means a full answer to your
> search for peace and justice.[575]

As long as there are no ICC proceedings against state officials, a
catalysing effect on domestic proceedings against state officials is
unlikely. Neither the army nor the police nor the DPP has an incentive to enter into this political arena, and risk their job,[576] without
external pressure or 'cover'. Consequently, allegations that UPDF
crimes were the rule rather than the exception and that the government's policy of forced displacement[577] or indiscriminate air attacks
killing civilians[578] could amount to crimes have, to date, not been
investigated at an official level, either domestically or by the ICC.
Rather than catalysing procedures to increase the accountability of
state actors, the ICC, by demonstrating an apparent lack of interest in
state actors, may have entrenched their impunity.

With respect to crimes committed by non-state actors, specifically the
LRA, the Kwoyelo case is so far the only case indirectly catalysed by the
ICC's complementarity principle. Prosecutors attached to the ICD say
they are investigating other cases, but it is unclear how far these investigations have progressed. After the signing of the A&R Accords, some
within the Ugandan political leadership were convinced that Uganda
was 'ready' for domestic trials. In the words of one government minister:
'We are ready, we have overwhelming evidence ... I laugh at them who
say we are not ready.'[579] Underlining this, the Minister and his colleagues
emphasised that the ICC's case was based on Ugandan evidence and was

---

[574] Musoke and Oluput 2010.   [575] Ogola 2010.

[576] As one JLOS actor confided to researcher Tessa Wright: 'There would be fear
by ... people in the DPP that they might be putting themselves out of a job' if
they were to investigate state actors (Wright 2011:141).

[577] See RS, art. 8(2)(e)(viii). Additional Protocol II to the Geneva Conventions, art.
17, is more specific, but does not criminalise conduct. See also Seils 2009:60.

[578] See RS., art. 8(2)(e)(i).

[579] Interview with a cabinet minister, Kampala, October 2008.

investigated with the support of the Ugandan military, the Ugandan Criminal Investigations Department and Ugandan forensic experts.[580]

However, technocrats in the police and the Directorate of Public Prosecutions expressed doubts as to whether their institutions were ready.[581] To the extent that the ICC's case was built on Ugandan material, it was largely on military intelligence. The ICC had used this material as a springboard for the collection of evidence for criminal proceedings; the Criminal Investigations Department was yet to do this. Police had reports of incidents, but, apart from the investigations conducted with or for the ICC, most reports had not been investigated further owing to insecurity in the north. Even after the conflict in northern Uganda began to subside, they were still not investigated. Revealing a possible opposite of a catalysing effect on domestic proceedings, namely, burden-shifting to the ICC, some police explained that they no longer needed to investigate the LRA since the ICC was now involved.[582] Other Ugandan officials explained the absence of investigations by referring to the impossibility of arresting suspects and the continued applicability of the Amnesty Act – there are few incentives to investigate a person who can be assured of amnesty.[583] While Kwoyelo's test-case was ongoing, investigations in other cases were put on hold.[584]

Whether Kwoyelo was just the first or also the last to be brought before the ICD for conflict-related crimes remains to be seen. The ferocity with which his case was pursued, legal obstacles notwithstanding, can to some extent be explained by the circumstances at the time. The ICC Review Conference put Uganda in the spotlight. JLOS took pride in Uganda's being

---

[580] Interview with a senior government official, assisting the cited cabinet minister, Kampala, October 2008 ('The ICC case is based on our evidence. Otherwise they couldn't know. How do you think that the white man otherwise does investigations here?').

[581] Interviews, senior officials in the Directorate of Public Prosecutions and the Criminal Investigations Department, Kampala, September and October 2008, June 2010 and November 2011.

[582] Discussion with officials in the Criminal Investigations Department, Gulu, September 2008, interview with an official in the Criminal Investigations Department, Gulu, September 2008 and interview with a senior official in the Criminal Investigations Department, Kampala, October 2008.

[583] Interview with a police spokesperson, Gulu, September 2008.

[584] Interview with a prosecutor involved, Kampala, November 2011.

the first African country to try nationally those alleged to have committed war crimes and crimes against humanity, all crimes of international concern and the first country complementing the works of the International Criminal Court.[585]

The problem for this 'frontline country in applying the complementarity principle' was, in the words of a government minister, that, 'since establishing the War Crimes Division, no one had been tried; luckily enough we had Kwoyelo'.[586] A prosecutor attached to the ICD felt the same pressure: 'After two years of existence [of the ICD], we had to make an example of Kwoyelo to show that something was being done.'[587] In addition to satisfying an institutional hunger, Kwoyelo's case made, in the prosecutor's words, 'good PR on the international plane: we were the first state to refer a situation; doing a case makes us look like the good guys'.[588]

While both the institutional hunger for cases and a desire to be seen internationally as 'the good guys' will continue to exist, when the memory of the Review Conference has faded they may be satisfied by cases other than those involving crimes within the ICC's jurisdiction, particularly now the ICD's jurisdiction has been expanded to include terrorism. In the context of a regional scramble for US support, a judicial war on terror is one way to demonstrate commitment to the primary agenda item of the world's most desired international ally. Moreover, there is no shortage of detained terrorism suspects. Even the case against Kwoyelo, although not charged on that count, fitted into the terrorism paradigm. The military parade at the opening of his trial before the ICD, and the army's presence as a 'stakeholder' during the trial, signalled internationally that Uganda was an active ally in the war on terror.[589] If terrorism becomes its bread and butter, the ICD can do its part in clearing a notorious backlog of cases. It will also mean that, despite its origins in the complementarity principle, the ICD will bring Uganda not much that is new: a focus on crimes against the state, as opposed to crimes against civilians.

---

[585] See JLOS 2011. See also interview with an ICD judge, November 2011: 'We are the only African court that is complementary to the ICC. Kenya had been given the opportunity but did not take it.'

[586] Interview with a government minister, Kampala, November 2011.

[587] Interview, Kampala, November 2011.   [588] *Ibid.*

[589] View the scene in the documentary Refugee Law Project 2011b.

CONCLUSION: COMPLEMENTARITY'S CATALYSING EFFECT IN UGANDA

On the face of it, Uganda's history with the ICC shows the opposite of the widely anticipated catalysing effect on domestic proceedings. Rather than trying to avoid ICC intervention by conducting domestic investigations and prosecutions, the GoU invited the ICC into Uganda, introduced the International Criminal Court Bill and Amnesty Amendment Bill to facilitate ICC proceedings and conducted domestic investigations into conflict-related crimes primarily to support ICC prosecutions. These effects were catalysed by the ICC's existence in general and by the ICC's intervention in particular, not by complementarity.

It was only when Ugandan actors began to search for alternatives to the ICC that complementarity spurred domestic developments. Cultural and religious leaders in northern Uganda, considering the ICC's involvement an endorsement of the military approach to the conflict with the LRA and an obstacle to peace, did so from the outset of the ICC's intervention. Their response was to promote local justice practices as an alternative to the ICC (albeit largely within the parameters of ICC-style justice).

The Ugandan Government for its part began to explore alternatives to the Court only once its interests seemed to diverge from those of the Court. It was thus during the Juba peace talks that the seeds for most of complementarity's catalysing effects were sown. When Joseph Kony refused to sign the FPA and the GoU reverted to its preferred exclusive military approach, the ICC's and GoU's strategies and interests in ICC involvement were realigned. Nonetheless, the GoU did allow others to run with projects based on the complementarity arrangements in the A&R Accords.

Complementarity thus catalysed several processes in Uganda. It spurred the study of local justice practices as an alternative to the ICC; put accountability firmly on the agenda of the Juba peace talks; triggered a national debate on transitional justice; broadened the national approach to the conflict in northern Uganda to include a legal dimension; set in motion preparations for a Ugandan WCC; and focused attention on compliance with so-called 'international standards'. However, with the exception of one case pursued for opportunistic reasons, domestic investigations and prosecutions of conflict-related crimes, the only action that could render ICC cases inadmissible, seem not to have increased.

Analysis of how these effects were catalysed reveals that normative processes and cost–benefit analyses, the factors that underpin the expectations of complementarity's catalysing effect,[590] have been instrumental in bringing about both this effect and discouraging effects on domestic proceedings. The GoU's initial cost–benefit analysis resulted in the opposite of a catalysing effect on domestic proceedings, namely, the outsourcing of proceedings to the ICC. Rather than considering ICC intervention as costly to its sovereignty and reputation, the GoU expected, and obtained, dividends from the intervention. The GoU recognised that providing the ICC with its first situation could be good for its international reputation and serve its military interests. It introduced ICC legislation because this seemed necessary for the ICC to be able to do its work and in order to win the bid for the Review Conference. In Juba, however, the GoU's analysis changed. The ICC had been unable to 'neutralise' the LRA and was publicly regarded as the major obstacle to the successful conclusion of the talks. The GoU felt obliged to be seen domestically to take initiatives that could end the ICC's involvement. The only way to end the ICC's involvement in the long term was on the basis of complementarity. The focus shifted, at least on paper, to the possibility of domestic proceedings. In order to gain international credit by showing its commitment to the peace process (in stark contrast to the LRA), the GoU co-opted norm entrepreneurs' emphasis on transitional justice and allowed the Principal Judge of the High Court to establish a WCC. Acting on the basis of their own cost–benefit analysis, members of the Ugandan judiciary pushed for the WCC so as to enhance the position of their professional group, domestically and internationally.

The GoU's actions in the first ten years after the Rome Statute's entry into force have not been inspired by any infiltration of a putative expectation on states to investigate and prosecute crimes within the Court's jurisdiction. For the Ugandan executive, signing and ratifying the Rome Statute appears not to imply such a (non-legal) responsibility. For instance, for almost a decade it applied the Amnesty Act without considering this at odds with its ratification of the Statute. The judiciary, in turn, never considered the executive's referral as an outsourcing of its responsibility to an international body.

---

[590] See Chapter 1, 'Assumptions underlying the expectation of a catalysing effect'.

However, the ICC's involvement triggered the attention of, and created space for, organisations with normative agendas. The questions that the ICC's involvement raised created an opportunity for local organisations to push for transitional justice in Uganda. The ICC's involvement led international NGOs to seek and build alliances with Ugandan institutions and organisations, which they supported financially in exchange for promotion of their agenda on transitional justice or, more specifically, international criminal justice.

The catalysing effect was strongest when branches of government co-opted, on the basis of their cost–benefit analysis, the agendas of the norm entrepreneurs.[591] Examples are the executive's referral of the situation to the ICC; the Amnesty Commission's funding of traditional-justice practices; JLOS's creation of a Transitional Justice Working Group; and the judiciary's preparations for the WCC. The actors had institutional and financial incentives, primarily offered by foreign donors, to adopt these agendas:[592] international donors became less critical of the GoU's human rights violations in northern Uganda; provided the Amnesty Commission with funds to encourage traditional justice; funded JLOS study tours all over the world; and gave the judiciary financial support for the WCC. In addition to the financial and personal freedom that went with adoption of the transitional-justice discourse, international law seemed to offer legal discretion in that it appeared, and probably is, less strict than Ugandan law with respect to issues such as retroactivity, evidence and procedure.

---

[591] This is not to say that norm entrepreneurs did not act rationally and according to their own cost–benefit analyses. (On the political economy of morality-driven NGOs, see Clarke 2009:Chapter 1.) Equally, the above observations as to the GoU's rational cost–benefit analysis do not mean that the GoU paid no attention to norms. Norm entrepreneurs operate rationally and governments' rational strategies encompass norms. The difference is mainly in the reason for invocation of the norm, namely, whether it is because of a belief in the value of the norm itself or because the norm serves interests external to it. On combining constructivist and rational choice approaches, see Finnemore and Sikkink 1998:888 and 909–15, pointing out that the two schools are divided over the role that choice plays in norm-based behaviour, about what motivates choice and about the role persuasion plays in normative processes, rather than about whether or not states act rationally. See, on the relevance of the combination of normative and material explanations in the context of the ICC specifically, Wippman 2004:155–6 and Schiff 2008. See also Burke-White 2008c:n. 78 and Mégret 2006:14.

[592] On bureaucrats as rational economic actors seeking to maximise power, see Mueller 2003:Chapter 16.

The dynamics of the creation of the WCC illustrate this coalescence of norm, institutional and personal entrepreneurship on the part of rational actors in a space that the government has (temporarily) supplied. The government's agreement to conduct domestic proceedings provided the Ugandan judiciary with an opportunity to strengthen its institutional position by way of a new, specialised division that could attract international attention and funding. International norm entrepreneurs equally entered this space and adopted into their transnational networks the Ugandan transitional-justice proponents.[593] The latter, in turn, promoted a domestic war crimes court resembling an international court. The government allowed this for its international-reputation benefits and patronage potential.

The GoU's role in these developments followed the logic of governance practices in Uganda generally: based on expediency rather than law or policy and used for the benefit of those who are loyal to those in power and against those whose loyalty has been lost. It thus never developed the transitional-justice policy envisaged in the A&R Accords but gave coalitions of norm and patronage entrepreneurs *carte blanche* to pick, choose and develop their preferred parts of the Agreements, on the implicit but well-understood condition that they would target only the government's enemies. Elements of the agreement that involved burdens on the state and were unlikely to be funded by donors, for instance reparations, were ignored. The transitional-justice deal upon which the Juba A&R Accords were founded was thus undone and the delicate balance of transitional-justice aims that the Accords encapsulated unsettled. Given Kony's unwillingness to accept the agreement in the first place, it may seem that little was lost. But the use of transitional-justice instruments in the absence of a transition is bound to be one-sided and aimed at strengthening the position of the side that 'does' transitional justice.

Many of the effects were thus catalysed by complementarity but subsequently took on a dynamic of their own. Complementarity triggered the effects by acknowledging a domestic alternative to the ICC. But the processes that followed the debate over whether and how to use the primary right to investigate and prosecute became increasingly detached from the possibility of actually using this right in order to challenge admissibility. The Statute's requirements for a successful admissibility

---

[593] See Khagram, Riker and Sikkink 2002:17 on how international norms can create political opportunities, providing resources for leverage and spaces for access.

challenge were soon given less attention than the 'international stand-ards' that must be met, at least rhetorically, to please international observers whose satisfaction is relevant to goodwill and funding.

Analysis of complementarity's catalysing effect also shows that the ICC, rather than bringing about an immediate catalysing effect, pro-vided through its intervention an occasion for other organisations with more horizontal relations *vis-à-vis* Ugandan actors to boost a catalysing effect indirectly.[594] Through transnational interactions, international norm entrepreneurs adopted into their networks Ugan-dan legal professionals, who, in turn, promoted activities initially catalysed by complementarity, such as the discussions in the JLOS Working Group on transitional justice and preparations for the WCC. Through their direct interactions with government officials, legal practitioners and grassroots NGOs, these organisations were in a better position to promote familiarisation with concepts such as accountability and transitional justice than were ICC officials in The Hague, who kept a professional and physical distance.

Indeed, despite the OTP's espoused policy of positive complemen-tarity,[595] the Court in many ways did the very opposite of encouraging a catalysing effect on Ugandan proceedings. First, the OTP's diplo-matic efforts to obtain self-referrals encouraged Uganda to outsource to the ICC rather than to conduct domestic proceedings. Secondly, neither the Prosecutor nor the judges took the opportunity publicly to consider admissibility at stages where the Prosecutor was obliged, or the judges were allowed, to do so.[596] They ignored the fact that the GoU once issued an arrest warrant for Joseph Kony and that the GoU explicitly reserved, in the final sentence of the referral letter, the right to challenge admissibility. Instead of encouraging domestic proceed-ings, the OTP requested the GoU to confirm in a letter that it had 'not conducted and [did] not intend to conduct national proceedings in relation to the persons most responsible'.[597] Thirdly, the Court uncrit-ically echoed Uganda's extra-statutory arguments about the ICC being

---

[594] With respect to such developments in the DRC, see Baylis 2009.

[595] See Chapters 1 and 2 ('The policy of positive complementarity').

[596] In accordance with theories stressing the importance of communication about the meaning of rules to promote compliance (e.g. Chayes and Chayes 1993), the mere paying of attention could foster complementarity as a norm in the sense of a political expectation on states to conduct domestic proceedings.

[597] Cited in *Arrest Warrant Kony*:[37]. The latter part of the statement is irrelevant to complementarity. If Uganda conducted genuine domestic proceedings, these

the 'most appropriate and effective forum for the investigation and prosecution of those bearing the greatest responsibility'.[598] Fourthly, the Court demonstrated a prickly protectiveness over the cases on its docket. The OTP stated that it would 'fight any admissibility challenge [ensuing from the A&R Accords] in court',[599] apparently irrespective of the genuineness of eventual national proceedings. The Prosecutor also incorrectly suggested that national proceedings could be useful only for 'those who did not bear the greatest responsibility'.[600] The judges, faced with the prospect of the case becoming inadmissible in view of the A&R Accords, initiated a review of admissibility, which concluded on the discouraging note that, despite the GoU's preparations, the situation in Uganda had remained 'one of total inaction on the part of the relevant national authorities'.[601] A fifth way in which the Court refrained from encouraging domestic proceedings in Uganda was by fostering a team spirit with Ugandan officials that strengthened the latter's perception of OTP staff as their 'brothers' from whom they had nothing to fear.[602] Domestic proceedings against state officials so as to avoid ICC proceedings have thus not been considered necessary. In all these ways, the Court did the opposite of encouraging Ugandan proceedings.

The OTP began to implement aspects of the policy of positive complementarity that envisage concrete support for domestic proceedings[603] only when officials of the ICD emphasised that they would be 'complementary' to the ICC in that they would prosecute persons *other* than those sought by the ICC. In the words of one judge at the ICD:

> Ocampo thought we were going to get his cases. But why should we fight him? The ICC can have the top leaders. As far as we are

---

could render cases before the ICC inadmissible, irrespective of the GoU's earlier statements of intent.

[598] *Arrest Warrant Kony*:[37]. See also *LRA Admissibility Decision (PTC)*:[37] and this chapter, 'Compromised complementarity'.

[599] OTP quoted in Glassborow 2008.   [600] Moreno-Ocampo 2008a:4.

[601] *LRA Admissibility Decision (PTC)*:[52].

[602] Interview with a military intelligence officer, Kampala, October 2008. See further Chapter 5, n. 233 and accompanying text.

[603] See Chapter 2, 'The policy of positive complementarity'. The OTP provided mobile phones, airtime and a taxi budget to Ugandan police officials, but these were meant to improve their ability to protect ICC witnesses, not to facilitate domestic investigations (interview with an official of the Criminal Investigations Department, October 2008).

concerned, a court is a court. Since we said that, Ocampo agreed to assist us. The DPP got some evidence against Kwoyelo. This is because we are not competing [with the ICC]: we are complementary to them.[604] That is the principle of complementarity.[605]

While the OTP facilitated Ugandan proceedings by handing over some material that the ICD prosecution could use against Kwoyelo,[606] it also complicated domestic investigations by having instructed ICC-protected witnesses not to cooperate with other courts. Moreover, Uganda was not offered access to the Case Matrix of the Court's Legal Tools Project,[607] since, in the words of one person working for the Court's Legal Tools Project, Uganda's officials 'could use it as an excuse for not cooperating with the Court, arguing that with the Case Matrix they themselves could prosecute'.[608] All in all, the OTP's causal claim in the following statement seems exaggerated:

> We have worked with the Ugandan authorities, sharing our experiences and information with them and showing them at least how to handle cases of this magnitude. And this has resulted in the war crimes

---

[604] On this use of the term 'complementarity', see Chapter 5 'Complementarity as primary right: confusion, ambiguity and misrepresentation'. Footnote inserted.

[605] Interview, Kampala, November 2011. See also Coalition for the International Criminal Court 2011:31 reporting a statement by one of the ICD's judges as follows: 'Justice Akiiki Kiiza talked of the Ugandan government's initiatives in addressing the impunity gap. This involved the creation of a reconciliation commission and the War Crimes Division of the High Court which Justice Kiiza emphasized worked in partnership and not in competition with the ICC. In this regard, Justice Kiiza pointed to the fact that the War Crimes Division was trying the remaining bulk of criminals and not those pursued by the ICC.' See also Van de Wiel 2011, reporting on the 'stakeholders meeting' prior to the opening of the Kwoyelo trial before the International Crimes Division: '[T]he ICD judges publicly stated that the ICD "[is] not after the ICC cases" but that it is able to try them were they [to] be brought before the Division. It was stated that the ICD seeks to "complement" the ICC proceedings.'

[606] ICC-OTP 2010c:1 mentioned as possible assistance to the Ugandan ICD: logbooks and radio intercepts (originally provided by the Ugandan authorities), transcripts in English and Acholi and searchable records of these intercepts and of handwritten logbooks and maps and graphs. See also ICC-OTP 2011a.

[607] While most of the Legal Tools Project's resources on international criminal law are available to all Internet users, its Case Matrix is available only to those institutions working in the field of international criminal prosecutions which have concluded an agreement with the Court. The Case Matrix is a data management system that provides a template for recording, categorising and cross-referencing evidence to link it to elements of crimes. See www.icc-cpi.int/legal_tools.html.

[608] Discussion, November 2007.

tribunal in Uganda being able to investigate and prosecute one of the criminals in Uganda.[609]

Norm entrepreneurs did boost complementarity's catalysing effect, but their work led not just to norm promotion but also to norm distortion. Many members of the international-criminal-justice movement interpreted the Statute on the basis more of their functional biases than of the international rules of interpretation as codified in the Vienna Convention on the Law of Treaties.[610] The biases of international experts stem from their background in international fora and favour the international:[611] an international court, international crimes and international standards. Often having never worked at the domestic level, let alone in the Ugandan justice system, their frame of reference and language is that of the international. On the basis of their rich international experience, they often give more attention to the practice of other international tribunals such as the ICTY, ICTR and SCSL than to the text of the Rome Statute, even though the Statute's complementarity is a different jurisdictional arrangement from the other tribunals' primacy. Having hardly studied the Rome Statute themselves, Ugandan officials have received these 'international norms' with open arms, at least rhetorically. Experience had taught that echoing 'international standards' could serve the state as a shield against international criticism.[612]

One example of norm distortion is the suggestion that, in order for a state to be able successfully to challenge admissibility on the ground of complementarity, it needs a special international-criminal-justice infrastructure, consisting of special legislation and special courts, at the domestic level. Illustrative is the consideration of PTC II when it assessed the admissibility of the LRA case:

> It remains a fact that the Agreement has not yet been signed and that neither the Agreement nor the Annexure has been submitted to the

---

[609] The head of the JCCD quoted in International Center for Transitional Justice 2012.

[610] On such biases, see Koskenniemi 2005:600–15.

[611] More generally, see also Drumbl 2007:125.

[612] Cf. Mwenda 2007:32 on the effects of international donor support for the GoU generally: 'Amongst the most important consequences of Museveni's relationship with donors was that once he gave them nearly the free rein over the policy- and budget-making processes, the donors left him a free hand (and sometimes even gave him a helping hand) with his military plans.'

Parliament. It is not until both documents can be regarded as fully effective and binding upon the parties that a final determination can be made regarding the admissibility of the Case, since the Chamber will only be in a position to assess the envisaged procedural and substantive laws in the context and for the purposes of article 17 of the Statute after they are enacted and in force. In this respect, the contents of the envisaged legislation regarding the substantive and procedural laws to be applied by the Special Division, as well as the criteria presiding over the appointment of its members, will be critical.[613]

This emphasis on legislation stems from legal and factual misunderstandings. First, the quoted consideration of the PTC suggests that the PTC could determine admissibility once Ugandan legislation was in place. But the test is, as Chapter 2 has set out, whether the state conducts genuine proceedings in a specific case, not whether the state's overall justice system is 'willing and able' and, in this context, has the appropriate legislation. Secondly, as also discussed in Chapter 2, an admissibility challenge based on complementarity in a specific case requires prosecution of the same conduct, not necessarily the same crime. A charge of the ordinary crime of murder could cover the same conduct as a charge of murder as a crime against humanity. Specific legislation is not necessarily required. Finally, and most importantly, the emphasis on legislation and courts gives the wrong impression that the absence of legislation and the courts are the key impediments to conducting domestic proceedings. It distracts attention from some of the real obstacles, which will be discussed in Chapter 5.

The sustainability of the effects that complementarity has catalysed is doubtful. The A&R Accords may have been signed, and theoretically do not require Kony's signature on the FPA, but without his signature and subjection to Uganda's jurisdiction implementation remains to a large extent theoretical. Faced with diminishing chances of a successful conclusion to the Juba peace talks, the GoU seems to have discarded its newfound commitment to domestic legal accountability in favour of other options. Based on *ad hoc* expediency rather than long-term policies, the GoU's interest in transitional justice is over as soon as it flips the hour-glass.

---

[613] *LRA Admissibility Decision (PTC)*:[49]. *Decision Authorizing Kenya Investigation*: [183] equally suggests that a special tribunal is needed for domestic prosecution of crimes within the ICC's jurisdiction.

The fact that some of the activities catalysed by complementarity have taken on a dynamic of their own suggests that they could continue irrespective of any implementation of the FPA. Their sustainability may be limited, however, since they have been driven more by short-term cost–benefit assessments than by a normative commitment. References by Ugandan officials to 'international standards', for instance, do not imply that these standards have infiltrated. So experienced at drafting proposals that at one stage 50 per cent of the national budget was externally funded, the GoU knows what jargon to use to please international donors. Once the money has been collected, however, many programmes have not been implemented in accordance with their purpose.[614] Activities catalysed by complementarity but sustained by other external incentives, for instance debates on transitional justice and the establishment of the WCC, may wither on the vine.

Nonetheless, it is possible that the continuation of these processes, even if inspired by external incentives, may lead to infiltration of a norm, in the form of an expectation on states to address issues of transitional justice or, more specifically, to investigate and prosecute conflict-related crimes. Only then will the phenomena catalysed by the ICC's principle of complementarity have truly taken on a life of their own.

---

[614] See e.g. Omach 2009a on how Uganda received British financial support for programmes to reduce its military, but in fact used the programmes to expand militarisation and to 'shed-off' soldiers who had been integrated into the UPDF from rival armed groups.

CHAPTER 4

SUDAN: COMPLEMENTARITY IN A STATE OF DENIAL

All perfumes of Arabia will not clean this dirt ...
For us the ICC doesn't exist ... and we are in no way
going to cooperate with it.
Sudan's Ambassador to the United Nations[1]

Upon landing in Khartoum in 2008, the visitor was given a literal illustration of Sudan's official response to the ICC. Along the avenue from the airport into town, one was greeted by rows of enormous billboards showing the President, with accompanying texts like 'Ocampo's plot: A malicious move in the siege', 'Protect the International Law from Ocampo's illusions' and 'No for the oppression of peoples under the name of international law!'

The Government of Sudan's official response to the ICC's proceedings in relation to Darfur has been one of rejection and denial. It has rejected the Security Council's referral, the Prosecutor's opening of an investigation and, most vociferously, the Prosecutor's application for an arrest warrant for President Bashir. It has denied the applicability of the Rome Statute and the relevance of the principle of complementarity. As explained by the (at the time of the interview) Minister of State for Humanitarian Affairs – and ICC suspect – Ahmad Harun:

> Theoretically, complementarity is recognised by the Rome Statute ... [W]e have our own legal position: we completely reject the ICC. So complementarity is not applicable.[2]

With the Sudanese Government's officially approaching complementarity as inapplicable, it seemed unlikely that the principle would catalyse many effects. It was particularly unlikely that complementarity would catalyse effects that require government action.

But it did and, as in Uganda, it did so indirectly.

---

[1] 'Sudan's UN envoy invokes Macbeth to condemn ICC' 2009.
[2] Interview with Ahmad Harun, Khartoum, December 2008.

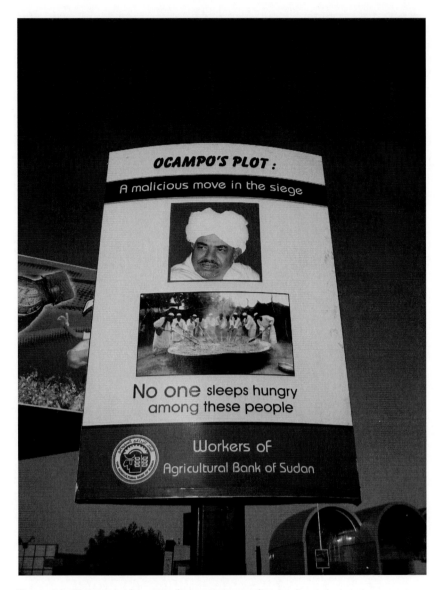

Figure 4.1 'Ocampo's plot: A malicious move in the siege'

THE CONTEXT FOR CATALYSIS

Context matters for complementarity's catalysing effect. In Sudan, of particular relevance is the ICC–Government of Sudan relationship. This relationship rapidly deteriorated after the Office of the Prosecutor

Figure 4.2 'Protect the International Law from Ocampo's illusions'

(OTP) brought its first case with respect to the situation in Darfur. The Government of Sudan's response was primarily political. To the extent that it was legal, it focused on the Court's jurisdiction with respect to Sudan, not on the admissibility of its cases. And yet, international actors, including the International Commission of Inquiry into Darfur and the International Criminal Court, gave complementarity more attention in the situation of Darfur than in that of northern Uganda.

Sudan and the ICC: souring relations

Sudan has not always rejected the ICC. Before the establishment of the ICC, Sudan welcomed the idea of an international court that respected sovereignty[3] and was based on complementarity.[4] With a divided delegation in Rome, it ultimately abstained on account of disagreement with various provisions, such as the subject-matter jurisdiction over crimes committed during non-international armed conflict, the power of the Security Council to refer situations to the Prosecutor of the Court and the prohibition on reservations.[5] Yet, during a closed symposium in Khartoum in 1999, Sudanese scholars and legal counsel of government ministries unanimously recommended joining the Court, as this would do credit to the Government of Sudan (GoS).[6] Some Sudanese lawyers advised the government to become party to the Statute even if it was not convinced of the ICC's worth. 'Accede to escape',[7] they argued, pointing to provisions in the Statute that benefit only states parties,[8] for instance the possibility to exclude war crimes from the Court's jurisdiction for a period of eight years.[9]

---

[3] Yassin 1998.

[4] During the negotiations of the Statute, the Sudanese representative stressed the importance of complementarity, which he interpreted to mean that '[t]he role of the court should be to exercise its jurisdiction when the concerned State no longer existed or when its judicial system became ineffective' (UN Doc. A/C.6/52/SR.11 (1997):[65]). The principle of 'complementarity' initially caused some concern among Arab states, Sudan included, as it was inappropriately translated by the Arabic word for 'integration', suggesting processes as in the European Union. This word is at times still being used to translate 'complementarity' (see e.g. Sudan Bar Association 2008e:3 and El-Gizouli 2009:270).

[5] Interview with a former Minister of Justice, Khartoum, December 2008; UN Doc. A/CONF.183/C.1/SR.4 (1998):[76] (Mr Fadl) and L/ROM/22 (1998). See also Roach 2005:151.

[6] Interviews with a senior legal advisor in the Ministry of Justice, November 2008, and with a representative of a humanitarian organisation, Khartoum, December 2008.

[7] See also Sudan Bar Association 2008d:5.

[8] Discussion with a senior legal advisor in the Sudanese Ministry of Justice, UK, January 2007.

[9] Rome Statute, art. 124. This provision does not exclude war crimes from the Court's jurisdiction in the event of a referral by the Security Council, since it is an exception to art. 12(1) and (2), which does not apply in case of a referral by the Security Council pursuant to art. 13(b).

Guided by a diplomat rather than the Minister of the Interior, who strongly opposed becoming a party, President Bashir signed the Rome Statute during the 2000 Millennium Summit Treaty Event.[10] Subsequently, the Ministry of Justice pushed for ratification, yet the Ministry of Foreign Affairs, wishing to follow other Arab states that advised against becoming parties to the Statute, won the battle.[11] The calculation was that ratification of the Statute would not change Sudan's status as an international pariah, while it would increase the risk of hostile Western states using the instrument against the GoS.

And so they did, in the ruling party's perspective. In January 2005, the International Commission of Inquiry on Darfur (ICID), which the Security Council had established to investigate the reports of gross violations of international humanitarian and human rights law,[12] argued that it would 'be consistent for the Security Council, the highest body of the international community responsible for maintaining peace and security, to refer the situation of Darfur and the crimes perpetrated there, to the highest criminal judicial institution of the world community'.[13] Two months later, on 31 March 2005, the Security Council adopted resolution 1593 under Chapter VII of the UN Charter, referring 'the situation in Darfur since 1 July 2002' to the ICC.[14] The ICC Prosecutor also received the list of fifty-one individuals that the ICID had named as suspects in relation to crimes allegedly committed in Darfur.[15]

For the Court, the referral was in itself a legal milestone and a political victory. For the first time, its jurisdiction was extended to a state not party to the Statute. Moreover, adopted by eleven in favour to none against, the resolution was an international vote of confidence in the ICC. The US, which had been campaigning against the ICC since its creation precisely because of the Court's potential jurisdiction over nationals of states not parties to its Statute, had initially lobbied the other Security Council members to refer the situation in Darfur to

---

[10] Signed on 8 September 2000; see www.un.org/millennium/law/sept800.htm.

[11] Interview with a former Minister of Justice, Khartoum, December 2008.

[12] UN Doc. S/RES/1564 (2004):[12].   [13] UN Doc. S/2005/60 (2005):[589].

[14] UN Doc. S/RES/1593 (2005):[1].

[15] Of these, there were ten high-ranking central government officials, seventeen government officials operating in Darfur, fourteen militia members, seven members of rebel movements and three members of foreign armies (UN Doc. S/2005/60 (2005):[531]). The Prosecutor emphasised that the list did not bind him (ICC-OTP 2005a).

another jurisdiction, for instance a joint African Union/United Nations Special Court for Darfur. But ultimately the US and even China, Sudan's largest trading partner, did not veto the Council's first referral to the ICC.[16]

But the US's acquiescence in the resolution came at a price. First, explicitly recognising that states not parties to the Rome Statute had no obligations under it, the Council required only the GoS and other parties to the conflict in Darfur to cooperate with the Court. Other states and international organisations were merely urged to cooperate fully.[17] Secondly, the Council decided that 'nationals, current or former officials or personnel from a contributing State outside Sudan which is not a party to the Rome Statute of the International Criminal Court shall be subject to the exclusive jurisdiction of that contributing State for all alleged acts or omissions arising out of or related to operations in Sudan established or authorized by the Council or the African Union, unless such exclusive jurisdiction has been expressly waived by that contributing State'.[18] For Sudan, these provisions were and would remain evidence of the Council's 'double standards'.[19]

Publicly, Sudan rejected the Security Council's referral and the Prosecutor's opening of an investigation into the situation in Darfur.[20] President Bashir swore 'thrice in the name of Almighty God ... never [to] hand any Sudanese national to a foreign court'.[21] But, outside the view of the Sudanese gallery, the GoS extended some cooperation to the Court. On 2 October 2005, it signed an agreement with the ICC to cooperate with the Court in its case against the LRA.[22] With respect to the Darfur situation, the GoS allowed five diplomatic ICC missions to visit Khartoum to assess questions of admissibility. It made some attempts to convince the OTP that Sudan has a functioning justice system – at one stage, Sudanese postgraduate theses were collected 'to show that Sudan has able

---

[16] For the US considerations, see Kaufman 2006.

[17] UN Doc. S/RES/1593 (2005):[2].   [18] *Ibid.*:[6].

[19] UN Doc. S/PV.5158 (2005):12 (Mr Erwa). Not just for Sudan: for Brazil they were a reason to abstain instead of vote in favour: 'the referral should not be approved at any cost' (*ibid.*:11, the President, speaking in his capacity as representative of Brazil).

[20] *First Darfur Report*:5. See also ICC-OTP 2005b.

[21] Hoge 2005. See also Baldo 2007:3.

[22] *Request for a Finding of Non-cooperation in Harun and Kushayb*:[45].

judges, who are academically qualified'.[23] Sudan never officially denied ICC criminal investigators access to Darfur, simply because the ICC Prosecutor, arguing that it would be too dangerous for ICC staff and for witnesses cooperating with the Court,[24] in fact never sent them.[25]

All cooperation came to an abrupt end, however, when, nearly two years after the referral, the ICC Prosecutor applied for summonses to appear, or in the alternative warrants of arrest, for Ahmad Muhammad Harun and Ali Muhammed Abd-al-Rahman, also known as Ali Kushayb.[26] The then Minister of State for Humanitarian Affairs and the militia leader, respectively, were alleged to bear criminal responsibility in relation to fifty-one counts of crimes against humanity and war crimes. According to the Prosecutor, Harun, as Minister of State for the Interior and head of the 'Darfur Security Desk' at the time, recruited, funded, armed and incited militias, knowing that they would commit crimes such as murder, rape, torture, pillaging and forcible transfer of civilian populations.[27] He was alleged to have committed these crimes together with Kushayb, the 'colonel of colonels' of the militias in West Darfur.[28]

In response to the OTP's charges against Harun and Kushayb, Sudan broke off all communication with the ICC. The Sudanese Embassy in The Hague literally refused to open the door to accept the arrest warrants.[29] No more ICC delegations were welcome in Sudan. In 2010, when three years after their issuance the Court's warrants for Harun and Kushayb remained unexecuted, the ICC Pre-Trial Chamber (PTC) informed the Security Council of Sudan's lack of cooperation.[30]

---

[23] Interview with a senior legal advisor in the Ministry of Justice, Khartoum, November 2008.

[24] See, *inter alia*, *First Darfur Report*:4, *Third Darfur Report*:1, and *Fourth Darfur Report*:3.

[25] According to an ICC official in a phone discussion in June 2009, there has been one interview of potential relevance to criminal investigations, which took place with a senior army officer during a visit by the OTP's Jurisdiction, Complementarity and Cooperation Division (JCCD) to Khartoum.

[26] *OTP Application Harun and Kushayb.*   [27] *Ibid.*:4–5.   [28] *Ibid.*:5–6.

[29] *Decision Arrest Warrant Bashir PTC*:[229].

[30] *Decision Non-cooperation Sudan in Harun and Kushayb.* The decision lacks an operative paragraph actually finding non-cooperation by Sudan. On the poor drafting of the decision, see Sluiter 2010.

But the nadir in Sudan–ICC relations was reached when, on 14 July 2008, the Prosecutor requested an arrest warrant against the Sudanese President. The Prosecutor's allegations that Omar Hassan Ahmad al-Bashir had committed, through the state apparatus, crimes against humanity, war crimes and genocide,[31] turned the Court, and particularly Prosecutor Ocampo, into the arch-enemy of the Sudanese state.[32] The Sudanese National Assembly resolved that the signing of the Rome Statute by the GoS was 'considered not to have taken place'[33] and Sudan 'unsigned' the Rome Statute,[34] ironically following the precedent set by Sudan's ultimate political foes, the US and Israel.

Sudan's 'unsigning' did not prevent the ICC judges from issuing in 2009, for the first time in the Court's history, a warrant for an incumbent head of state, on counts of war crimes and crimes against humanity.[35] After instructions from the Appeals Chamber to use a different standard of proof,[36] the PTC in 2010 also issued, equally for the first time in the Court's history, a warrant of arrest in respect of the crime of genocide.[37] Arrest warrants notwithstanding, President Bashir won the 2010 presidential elections and travelled to various countries, including states parties to the Rome Statute, without being apprehended.

In 2008, while the judges were considering the Prosecutor's request for an arrest warrant against the Sudanese head of state, the Prosecutor also brought a case against three members of armed movements fighting the Sudanese Government. He accused them of war crimes committed during an attack on the African Union Mission in Sudan in the Darfurian village of Haskanita.[38] In the opinion of a

---

[31] *Application Arrest Warrant Bashir* and ICC-OTP 2008a.

[32] Sudanese authorities have described the ICC Prosecutor as, among other things, 'the mercenary of death and destruction' ('Sudanese ambassador to UN lashes at Ocampo' 2009), 'a fugitive of Sudanese justice' and someone practising 'criminal tourism' ('Sudan says ICC prosecutor "messenger of destruction"' 2009).

[33] Decision No. 2 of the Emergency Session of the National Assembly to Refuse to Ratify the Rome Statute of the International Criminal Court 2008. See also Decision No. 1 of the Emergency Session of the National Assembly: Rejection of the Accusations of the Prosecutor of the ICC against Leading Officials of the State headed by the President of the Republic 2008.

[34] It did so by a notification to the UN Secretary-General of 27 August 2008 (see http://treaties.un.org/Pages/ViewDetails.aspx?src=TREATY&mtdsg_no=XVIII-10&chapter=18&lang=en).

[35] *Decision Arrest Warrant Bashir (PTC).*   [36] *Judgment Arrest Warrant Bashir (AC).*

[37] *Second Decision Arrest Warrant Bashir (PTC).*

[38] *Summary Prosecutor's Application Haskanita.*

government legal advisor, the Prosecutor brought this case only because he 'wanted to convince the world that he is neutral'.[39] But he did not convince the GoS. Indeed, the facts that all three suspects voluntarily cooperated with the Prosecutor and obeyed summonses to appear, that the judges declined to confirm the charges against one of them on grounds of insufficient evidence linking him to the alleged crimes,[40] and that the other two suspects reached agreements with the prosecution on undisputed facts,[41] only increased the Sudanese Government's suspicion that the case against its opponents was a put-up job.

In 2011, the ICC Prosecutor's request for an arrest warrant for the then Minister of Defence, Abdel Raheem Muhammed Hussein, on the ground that, in his previous position as Minister of the Interior and the President's Special Representative in Darfur, he had made 'essential contributions to the Common Plan' that led to the crimes of which Ahmed Harun and Ali Kushayb had been accused[42] did not elicit any strong response from the Sudanese government. Nor did the PTC's issuance of the requested warrant in March 2012.[43] ICC accusations against its officials had become business as usual.

Complementarity: less than a secondary response

Sudan's total rejection of the Court has been accompanied by a total rejection of its Statute, including the principle of complementarity. In the eyes of the GoS, the ICC is just another international political instrument that Western powers in the Security Council use selectively to topple governments of which they do not approve[44] – an

---

[39] Interview with an NCP lawyer, Khartoum, July 2011. Another political consideration could have been the need to convince the African Union, which had been very critical of the Prosecutor's request for an arrest warrant against President Bashir, that the Court also prosecutes crimes committed against AU personnel.

[40] *Decision Confirmation of Charges Abu Garda.* The Prosecutor's request for leave to appeal this decision has been declined (*Leave to Appeal Decision Confirmation Abu Garda*).

[41] *Joint Submission Confirmation Banda and Jerbo* and *Joint Submission Trial Banda and Jerbo.*

[42] *Summary Prosecutor's Application Hussein.*   [43] *Decision Arrest Warrant Hussein.*

[44] See e.g. Sudan Bar Association 2008e:2 ('[T]here are two states who are permanent members of the Council who adopt negative policies against the Sudanese government and who consider such government as being unworthy to exist.') and an interview with a senior legal advisor to the NCP, Khartoum, July 2011 ('Why does the West want to diminish us? This is a clash of civilisations. Since the collapse of the Soviet Union there is Islamophobia.').

instrument which engages in regime change by arrest warrant.[45] Its political character became impossible to deny, in the GoS's view, when the Prosecutor brought charges against the Sudanese head of state. Confronted with this political measure, Sudan had to address its 'ICC crisis' politically, so the Sudanese government and its legal advisors reasoned.[46] According to an Arabic saying quoted by one National Congress Party lawyer, Sudan must stab the elephant (the political move by the Security Council) rather than the shadow (the legal niceties of the ICC framework).[47] In other words, instead of pursuing inadmissibility of the Prosecutor's cases on grounds of complementarity in the ICC, the GoS pursued political decisions in the Security Council. It wanted the Security Council to 'withdraw' the referral, suspend the ICC proceedings 'indefinitely' or 'cancel' the arrest warrants, powers for which the Statute does not provide.[48] As a second best, it aimed for a deferral of ICC proceedings by the Security Council pursuant to article 16 of the Statute and Chapter VII of the UN Charter, although it preferred not to state this publicly, as reference to article 16 could be taken to suggest recognition of the applicability of the Rome Statute.[49]

It was the desire to obtain goodwill in the Security Council, more than complementarity, that catalysed all kinds of GoS action. However, while the Rome Statute is relatively clear on what a state should do to render a case inadmissible before the ICC, the Western permanent members of the Security Council did not indicate specific measures that Sudan must take for them not to veto a potential resolution deferring the ICC proceedings. At most, they specified that Sudan would have to make 'meaningful steps',[50] take 'bold, concrete action

---

[45] At the same time, GoS officials argue, the Security Council refuses to do justice in Iraq, Afghanistan and Israel and exempts the US and peacekeepers from the Court's jurisdiction (interview with a former Minister of Foreign Affairs, Khartoum, November 2008, interview with a former Chief Justice, Khartoum, December 2008, interview with a former Minister of Justice, December 2008 and Sabderat 2008:[11]; see also El-Gizouli 2009:261 and Tisdall 2011).

[46] See e.g. Sudan Bar Association 2008d:4.

[47] Interview with an NCP lawyer, Khartoum, November 2008.

[48] See e.g. Mirghani 2009 ('Al-Bashir ... call[ed] for the revoking of his indictment and warrant for arrest, and not just its suspension, "otherwise it is up to them to cancel it and drink its water" [an Arab insult]' (second insertion in original).

[49] Interview with an NCP legal advisor, Khartoum, November 2008.

[50] Van Oudenaren 2008, citing the US Special Envoy for Sudan.

for peace in Darfur, reflected in real change on the ground'[51] and implement a 'radical and immediate change'[52] in its policies. In response, the GoS agreed to set up a human rights forum with the UN; announced a new policy for internally displaced persons; committed extra money to the Darfur compensation fund; stated its willingness to re-open the Darfur Peace Agreement; declared a unilateral ceasefire (but violated it within a few days); improved its facilitation of deployment of UN peacekeepers in Darfur; launched the 'Sudanese People's Initiative', a meeting for Sudanese of all political colours to brainstorm solutions to the Darfur conflict; expressed support for a Qatari peace initiative; appointed a long-overdue civilian administration for the contested area of Abyei; and extended the moratorium on restrictions on humanitarian aid two months before it expired (while in previous years this was done only at the last moment).[53] All these measures, announced soon after the Prosecutor had requested an arrest warrant for the Sudanese President, were political responses to what the GoS considered political demands, and aimed at obtaining international political credit.

To the limited extent that Sudanese officials did respond in legal terms to the ICC's involvement, the main argument has been that the Court lacks jurisdiction. The following legal reasoning can be sifted from the writings of the Sudanese Bar Association, which does not hide the fact that it writes on behalf of the GoS,[54] as well as from official statements and interviews with government officials.[55]

The first prong of the GoS's objections focuses on the Rome Statute. The argument is that, as a treaty, the Rome Statute cannot bind states that are not parties to it.[56] For support, the GoS points to Security Council resolution 1422 (2002),[57] because it implicitly

---

[51] Response of the UK Secretary of State for Foreign and Commonwealth Affairs, Seventh Report from the Foreign Affairs Committee Session 2008–09, Annual Report on Human Rights 2008, Cm 7723, cited in UKMIL 2010:872.

[52] Bouwknecht 2008, quoting French President Sarkozy.

[53] See also Polgreen and Gettlemen 2008.

[54] Sudan Bar Association 2008c and interview with an NCP lawyer, Khartoum, November 2008.

[55] Not discussed here is the other (obviously unsuccessful) argument that the Prosecutor could not charge the President with genocide since the ICID had found that no genocide had been committed (Sudan Bar Association 2008e:1).

[56] Sabderat 2008:[9] and Sudan Bar Association 2008b:11, referring to the Vienna Convention on the Law of Treaties, art. 34.

[57] Sudan Bar Association 2008e:3 and Sabderat 2008:[10].

provides, in the context of international peacekeeping, that only states parties have accepted the Court's jurisdiction.[58] The Rome Statute, GoS lawyers submit, must be interpreted in accordance with the fundamental – according to some Sudanese lawyers even peremptory[59] – rule of customary international law that a treaty cannot bind states not parties to it. Hence, so the argument goes, article 13(b) of the Rome Statute, which provides for Security Council referral of a situation to the Court, must be read to mean that the Security Council can refer situations involving states parties only.[60] This is confirmed, so the argument continues, by article 4(2), which stipulates that the Court 'may exercise its functions and powers ... on the territory of any State Party and, by special agreement, on the territory of any other State',[61] and by article 87(5), which regulates such special agreements.[62] Moreover, the Sudanese lawyers argue,[63] operative paragraph 2 of resolution 1593 is internally contradictory and violates the basic principle that there should be no discrimination in the application of a single legal rule: the clause obliging Sudan to cooperate with the Court at the same time recognises the fundamental rule that 'States not party to the Rome Statute have no obligation under the Statute'. Such 'intellectual dishonesty', which by these

---

[58] UN Doc. S/RES/1422 (2002): 'The Security Council ... Noting that not all States are parties to the Rome Statute, Noting that States Parties to the Rome Statute have chosen to accept its jurisdiction in accordance with the Statute and in particular the principle of complementarity, Noting that States not Party to the Rome Statute will continue to fulfil their responsibilities in their national jurisdictions in relation to international crimes ... Acting under Chapter VII of the Charter of the United Nations, 1. Requests, consistent with the provisions of Article 16 of the Rome Statute, that the ICC, if a case arises involving current or former officials or personnel from a contributing State not a Party to the Rome Statute over acts or omissions relating to a United Nations established or authorized operation, shall for a twelve-month period starting 1 July 2002 not commence or proceed with investigation or prosecution of any such case, unless the Security Council decides otherwise.' On resolution 1422 (2002), see also Weller 2002.

[59] Sudan Bar Association 2008d:8, 14, 15 and 17, argues that, since this is a dispute about a peremptory rule, it can be submitted to the International Court of Justice pursuant to VCLT, art. 66(a). However, there is little evidence to prove that the *pacta tertiis nec necent nec prosunt* rule of art. 34 is *jus cogens*.

[60] Sudan Bar Association 2008e:2, Sudan Bar Association 2008b:6 and Sudan Bar Association 2008d:3.

[61] Sudan Bar Association 2008b:3 and interview with a former Minister of Foreign Affairs, Khartoum, November 2008.

[62] Interview with an NCP lawyer, Khartoum, November 2008.

[63] Sudan Bar Association 2008e:3.

accounts demonstrates that only Sudan is targeted, is also said to be on display in paragraph 6, cited above, which excludes certain foreign persons in Sudan from the Court's jurisdiction.[64]

Most of these arguments are not convincing, most evidently because article 13(b) read with article 12(2) of the Statute clearly provides that the Security Council can refer a situation in a state not party to the Statute. Articles 4(2) and 87(5) concern the exercise and not the existence of jurisdiction. Sudan's strongest ground for objection is probably operative paragraph 6. It could argue that, by trying to exclude a category of persons from the Court's jurisdiction, the Security Council did not refer a 'situation' as such and that, since the Rome Statute allows the Council to refer only a 'situation',[65] the Court's jurisdiction has not been triggered.[66]

The second prong of the GoS's objections concentrates on the UN Charter. The argument is that, even if the Statute were to allow a referral of a situation in a state not party to the Statute, the Security Council does not have the competence under the UN Charter to make a referral to the ICC.[67] According to the Sudanese lawyers advising the GoS, the Security Council cannot refer a matter to an organisation that is not part of the UN[68] or make a state a party to a treaty. Additionally, they maintain that the situation in Darfur should be considered a matter of internal affairs. Indeed, for this reason, the world had never opened investigations into crimes committed in Southern Sudan, so the Sudanese lawyers argue.[69]

These arguments do not hold much water. The Security Council has not made Sudan a party to a treaty,[70] but has referred a situation to

---

[64] Interview with an NCP lawyer, Khartoum, November 2008. Others, such as a senior legal advisor in the Ministry of Justice interviewed in Khartoum in November 2008, argued that resolution 1593 as a whole is internally inconsistent, calling as it does for peace, justice and national reconciliation at the same time. They argued that it would be difficult for the government to implement all clauses simultaneously.

[65] See Chapter 2, 'Other jurisdictional provisions: the triggers'.   [66] *Ibid.*

[67] Sudan Bar Association 2008e:5, Sudan Bar Association 2008d:2, 6 and Sabderat 2008:[15].

[68] Sudan Bar Association 2008e:2.

[69] Interview with an NCP lawyer, Khartoum, November 2008; Sudan Bar Association 2008e:2 and interview with a long-serving member of parliament, Khartoum, November 2008 ('Nobody intervened in the South. Nobody said that international law had to be applied.').

[70] On the consequent lack of clarity as to the legal regime applicable to Sudan, see Sluiter 2010.

an existing Court. Just as the Council has been considered to have the competence to establish international tribunals by resolution,[71] so it has the power to refer matters to existing courts.[72] As regards the determination of whether a situation constitutes a threat to international peace and security,[73] the Security Council has always had substantial discretion.[74]

Its rejection of the Rome Statute notwithstanding, Sudan *has* alluded, albeit in a subsidiary fashion, to the principle of complementarity. Ever since the Security Council's referral, many official statements disputing the Court's jurisdiction, while opening with the fact that Sudan is not a state party, have continued immediately with a comment about the 'ability and willingness' of the Sudanese legal system.[75] For instance, the Minister of Justice told an ICC delegation in early 2007: 'We as a government are willing and able to try all perpetrators of offences in Darfur, and for this reason the ICC has absolutely no right to assume any jurisdiction.'[76] A year later, just after the request for the Bashir arrest warrant, the new Minister of Justice told the African Union Peace and Security Council:

> The Sudan does not condone impunity and would prosecute crimes of all sorts. Sudan is not governed by the law of the jungle. It is a responsible State with an independent judicial system. The principle of complementarity constitutes the core premise of the Court and gives primacy to national jurisdictions.[77]

However, the more entrenched Sudan became in its rejection of the Court, the more careful officials became about making references to complementarity. They began to argue that a rejection of the applicability of the Statute means a rejection of the entire framework,

---

[71] ICTY, *Tadić Defence Motion Decision (AC)*:[26]–[48].

[72] In UN Doc. S/RES/1192 (1998), although it did not 'refer' a case to an existing court, the Security Council did oblige Libya to cooperate with a Scottish court trying Libyan defendants on Dutch territory.

[73] In various earlier resolutions, e.g. in UN Doc. S/RES/1556 (2004) and UN Doc. S/RES/1564 (2004), the Council had already determined that the situation in Darfur constituted a threat to international peace and security.

[74] ICTY, *Tadić Defence Motion Decision (AC)*:[28]–[30].

[75] UN Doc. S/PV.5158 (2005):12, 'Sudan reiterates opposition to try Darfur suspects before ICC' 2005 and 'Sudan on collision course with UN over Darfur trials' 2005. See also Sudan Bar Association 2008a:3–4 and Sabderat 2008:[16], [17] and [19].

[76] De Montesquiou 2007.   [77] Sabderat 2008:[16].

complementarity included.[78] 'Arguing complementarity', a senior Sudanese legal official warned, 'might be a trap', as by challenging admissibility on this ground Sudan would recognise the Court's jurisdiction.[79] Sudan has hired Western lawyers and has instructed them to find avenues for challenging the Court's jurisdiction without recognising the Court.[80]

Complementarity: the views of the ICID and the ICC

Complementarity was already assessed before any specific Darfur case was brought before the Court. The International Commission of Inquiry on Darfur (ICID) considered factors relevant to complementarity when it recommended that the Security Council refer the situation in Darfur to the ICC. It contended:

> The Sudanese justice system is unable and unwilling to address the situation in Darfur. This system has been significantly weakened during the last decade. Restrictive laws that grant broad powers to the executive particularly undermined the effectiveness of the judiciary. In fact, many of the laws in force in Sudan today contravene basic human rights standards. The Sudanese criminal laws do not adequately proscribe war crimes and crimes against humanity such as those carried out in Darfur and the Criminal Procedure Code contains provisions that prevent the effective prosecution of these acts. In addition, many victims informed the Commission that they had little confidence in the impartiality of the Sudanese justice system and its ability to bring to justice the perpetrators of the serious crimes committed

---

[78] See e.g. Sudan Bar Association 2008e:3, Sudan Bar Association 2008b:3 and interview with an NCP member of the Legal and Parliamentary Affairs Committee of the National Assembly, Khartoum, November 2008 ('We do not need complementarity; we have our own jurisdiction.').

[79] Interview with a member of the office of the Special Prosecutor for Darfur, December 2008. Similarly, interview with an NCP lawyer, Khartoum, November 2008.

[80] 'Sudan hires UK law firm to handle ICC indictment of Bashir' 2008. One of the ideas has been to have the UN General Assembly request an advisory opinion from the ICJ on the competence of the Security Council to refer a situation to the ICC (interview with a law professor, Khartoum, November 2008). Sudanese 'trade' organisations and a 'non-governmental' committee of Sudanese citizens, established out of concern about the negative effects that ICC arrest warrants could have on the peace process in Sudan and on ordinary Sudanese, have also hired European lawyers, who produced an application for *amicus curiae* status in which they warned of the political consequences of an arrest warrant for the President. See *Application Citizens' Organisations of the Sudan*.

in Darfur. In any event, many feared reprisals if they resorted to the national justice system.[81]

It added:

> The measures taken so far by the Government to address the crisis have been both grossly inadequate and ineffective ... The reality is that, despite the magnitude of the crisis and its immense impact on civilians in Darfur, the Government informed the Commission of very few cases of individuals who have been prosecuted or even simply disciplined in the context of the current crisis.[82]

Elsewhere in the report, the Commission explained that its 'recommendation for a Security Council referral to the ICC [was] based on the correct assumption that Sudanese courts are unwilling and unable to prosecute the numerous international crimes perpetrated in Darfur since 2003'.[83] In other words: 'The Sudanese justice system has demonstrated its inability and unwillingness to investigate and prosecute the perpetrators of these crimes.'[84]

The fact that the Commission considered complementarity is of note. All the Rome Statute requires for a referral by the Security Council is that the Council acts under Chapter VII of the UN Charter,[85] which for its part does not require any consideration other than whether there exists a threat to the peace, breach of the peace, or act of aggression.[86] In other words, an assessment of admissibility, including complementarity, is not a legal requirement for a Security Council referral. But the ICID had good reasons to consider complementarity as a factor relevant to the Security Council's decision-making on a referral. Pragmatically, a referral would be rather ineffective if subsequently the Prosecutor or judges would find all cases inadmissible on grounds of complementarity. Politically, the ICID may have considered that normative considerations may add legitimacy to what remains a political decision by the Council.

However, while borrowing the principle of complementarity from the Rome Statute, the ICID put its own spin on the application of the admissibility rule. First, as laid down in the Rome Statute, complementarity requires an assessment of a state's willingness and ability genuinely to conduct proceedings only if there is an affirmative answer

---

[81] UN Doc. S/2005/60 (2005):[586]. [82] Ibid.:[587]. [83] Ibid.:[609].
[84] Ibid.:[647]. [85] RS, art. 13(b). [86] UN Charter, art. 39.

to the question whether there are or have been such domestic proceedings.[87] The ICID, however, began with and focused on an assessment of willingness and ability.[88] Secondly, while according to the Statute the decisive factor as to whether a case is admissible is whether there are or have been proceedings in that case conducted by a state willing and able to conduct those particular proceedings genuinely,[89] the ICID assessed Sudan's overall justice system, separate from any concrete proceedings.[90]

The ICC Prosecutor, for his part, began to discuss complementarity almost immediately after the referral. Upon receipt of the ICID document archive, the Prosecutor announced to the press his next steps. He did not just have to assess the crimes, he said:

> I have an additional duty: to assess national proceedings. The Sudanese authorities report they have begun investigations. This could be very important. I will carefully and independently assess these proceedings.[91]

He opened an investigation having established, with respect to admissibility, 'the existence of sufficient information to believe that there are cases that would be admissible in relation to the Darfur situation'.[92] However, contrary to the ICID, which had concluded that the Sudanese justice system as a whole was 'unable and unwilling', the Prosecutor emphasised that his decision on admissibility did 'not represent a determination on the Sudanese legal system as such, but [was] essentially a result of the absence of criminal proceedings relating to the cases on which the OTP is likely to focus'.[93]

When the OTP brought its first case in the Darfur situation, that against Ali Kushayb and Ahmad Harun, it elaborated on the admissibility of the case. The Under-Secretary of the Sudanese Ministry of Justice had informed the Prosecutor that Sudan had collected information on, among others, Kushayb. The OTP observed, however, that there was no reason to believe that the case against Harun and

---

[87] See Chapter 2, 'The substance of complementarity: the criteria for inadmissibility'.

[88] See the order of the discussion in UN Doc. S/2005/60 (2005):[586] and [587], cited above, nn. 81 and 82. See also the discussion of complementarity in [606] as 'the principle whereby the Court only steps in when the competent national courts prove to be unable or unwilling genuinely to try persons accused of serious international crimes falling under the Court's jurisdiction'.

[89] See Chapter 2, 'The substance of complementarity: the criteria for inadmissibility'.

[90] See n. 81.   [91] ICC-OTP 2005c.   [92] First Darfur Report:4.   [93] Ibid.

Kushayb would be inadmissible. It noted that the Sudanese investigations concerned neither the same person, in the case of Harun, nor the same conduct, in the case of Kushayb.[94] The PTC reiterated the same-person–same-conduct test and also found that the case against Harun and Kushayb appeared admissible.[95]

Absent any hint of Sudanese investigations into the Sudanese President, no such elaboration on complementarity was needed in any of the ICC proceedings related to President Bashir.[96] In the Haskanita village case, too, the PTC simply adopted the Prosecutor's information, not contested by any party to the proceedings, that no state with jurisdiction over the case had investigated or prosecuted the case.[97]

In none of these cases did the GoS challenge admissibility. Denying the Court's jurisdiction, it dismissed any relevance of the Rome Statute, including the principle of complementarity. And yet, complementarity did catalyse some effects in Sudan. The fact that some of these are legal in character does not change the fact that they were part of a political response, primarily aimed at the Security Council. Before discussing these effects, however, it is necessary to provide some basic background to a complex conflict.

The Darfur conflict

The once independent state of Darfur became a periphery to the powerful capital and markets of Khartoum early in the twentieth century. Since Sudan's independence in 1956, ecological and economic stress aggravated by the political misuse of ethnicity all fostered long-term instability in the region. In 2003, recurring violence turned into a full-scale rebellion when armed movements mobilising around ethnicity and using discourses of marginalisation[98] directly attacked government positions in Darfur.[99] The Sudanese Government

---

[94] OTP Application Harun and Kushayb:[267]. See also Chapter 2, 'The "same case" requirement: same person, same conduct, same incidents?'

[95] Decision Arrest Warrants Harun and Kushayb:[24]–[25].

[96] See Application Arrest Warrant Bashir:[3], Decision Arrest Warrant Bashir (PTC): [46]–[51] and Second Decision Arrest Warrant Bashir (PTC):[44].

[97] Decision Confirmation of Charges Abu Garda:[29] and Confirmation of Charges Banda and Jerbo:[28].

[98] See, inter alia, Seekers of Truth and Justice 2000 and SLM/SLA 2003.

[99] More extensively on the conflict, see the sources mentioned in the references of this section and, inter alia, AU Doc. PSC/AHG/2(CCVII) 2009, Flint and De Waal 2008, Prunier 2005, Hassan and Ray 2009a, Tanner 2004, Tubiana 2009 and Tubiana 2010.

responded with a forceful counter-insurgency campaign, bombing entire villages that it considered militarily or politically supportive of the rebels. On the ground, it mobilised tribal militias, whose tactics gained for them worldwide notoriety as the *Janjaweed*, in exchange for arms, money and positions in state organs such as the Popular Defence Forces, the Central Reserve Police and the Border Guards. Most of these pro-government militias hailed from Darfurian and Chadian camel-herding tribes who felt marginalised by comparison to other Darfurian groups owing to their weak titles to land. Their opponents, the members of the rebel movements, mostly belonged to the more sedentary tribes with stronger land rights. With the former emphasising Arab lineage[100] and the latter African descent,[101] the conflict centrifuged identities that used to overlap.[102] For instance, people that used to describe themselves as Muslim/Sudanese/Fur with some Rizeigat ties began to refer to themselves as 'African' to show their position in a conflict that was internationally described as 'Arab versus African'.

The scale and character of the violence and its consequences have been heavily contested. The estimated figure of conflict-related deaths ranges between 10,000 (GoS statistics) and 400,000 (Save Darfur Coalition).[103] The United Nations have reported that at least 2.7 million people have been displaced.[104] International opinion has been divided as to whether the crimes committed in Darfur amount to genocide.[105] But killing of civilians, torture, enforced disappearances, destruction of villages, sexual violence, pillaging and forced displacement committed by the militias and government forces, and to a lesser

---

[100] Note that Arab tribes with stronger land rights, mostly cattle-herding tribes, have for the most part refrained from joining the government's counter-insurgency campaign. See also Tanner 2005:22, Babiker 2002:8–10 and De Waal and Young 2005:[38].

[101] Note, however, that there are also 'Arab' farmers and 'African' nomads (Tubiana 2006:112) and that many nomads have adopted a transhumant lifestyle (Willemse 2009:217).

[102] See also AU Doc. PSC/AHG/2(CCVII) 2009:11, Mamdani 2009:107 *et seq.*, Hassan and Ray 2009b:17–19 and De Waal 2004b.

[103] On the politics of Darfur death-rate statistics, see Dealy 2007, Hagan and Rymond-Richmond 2009:Chapter 4, Mamdani 2009:25–39 and Degomme and Guha-Sapir 2010.

[104] 'At five-year mark, Darfur crisis is only worsening – UN aid chief' 2008.

[105] Cf. *contra* UN Doc. S/2005/60 (2005), arguing that the crimes committed in Darfur do not amount to genocide, with US Secretary of State Powell (as described in Crook 2005) stating that they do. See also Cayley 2008.

extent by the movements, have been widely reported, particularly for the first three years of the war.[106]

Since 2005, the systematic attacks against villages inhabited by groups perceived as ethnic constituencies of rebel movements, characteristic of the early years of the conflict, have decreased. By 2008, the conflict could be considered 'low-intensity'.[107] Rebel groups, some more resembling criminal gangs than political movements, have splintered, changed allegiances, reunited and splintered again. Militias, not seeing their services to the government rewarded, have gone solo or joined the rebel movements.[108] Some militias have been fighting each other over the land of displaced persons. With arms widely circulating in the region, the government lacking control over large parts of the territory and peacekeepers having neither the mandate nor the ability to enforce law and order, the lawlessness that first fostered the conflict has become entrenched. An armed conflict between rebel movements and a government has turned into a situation of permanent insecurity in which the government, various movements, their splinter factions, and militias fight each other and among themselves, depending on the alliance of the day. The insecurity has ripped the region's social fabric and divided the population along ethnic lines, increasing the prospects for persistent inter-communal war.[109]

An analysis of the conflict in Darfur defies reduction to a single and stable 'root cause'. While it originates from local experiences of a threatened existence owing to contested land rights in the context of desertification, the Darfur conflict is inseparable from national and regional politics.[110] Like the conflicts in southern and eastern Sudan,[111] the Darfurian rebellion has to a large extent been about marginalisation of the periphery by the few riverine tribes that have run

---

[106] See e.g. Hagan and Rymond-Richmond 2009 and UN Doc. S/2005/60 (2005).

[107] Charbonneau 2009.   [108] See also Flint 2009.

[109] On the consequences of the conflict turning into causes, see Suliman 1997.

[110] On the interrelationships between various conflicts in Sudan, see Johnson 2007, in particular Chapter IX. On the link with world politics, see Mamdani 2009.

[111] See the Comprehensive Peace Agreement 2005 and the Eastern Sudan Peace Agreement 2006. An important difference between the conflict in Darfur and the conflict in what used to be Southern Sudan and now is the independent Republic of South Sudan, is that, whereas the Southern Sudanese claimed the right to external self-determination, the Darfurians consider themselves as quintessential Sudanese, entitled to more of a say at the centre. Since 2010, however, some of the Darfurian armed movements have also made secessionist claims (sometimes invoking the ICJ's Advisory Opinion in *Kosovo*).

the country since the British–Egyptian condominium ended in 1956.[112] While overt and covert coups and occasional elections have reconfigured the ruling groups at the centre, this centre has always consisted of an elite, disproportionally wealthy in economic, political and social terms, from a relatively small area in and around Khartoum.[113] The continuous power struggles within this elite have reverberated throughout the country. Elites have tried to shift the balance of power to their advantage in the centre by changing it in the periphery; provincial elites have used their allies in Khartoum for the advancement of their local causes.[114]

Accordingly, the conflict in Darfur has been inextricably linked to a rift within the National Islamic Front in Khartoum between President Bashir and his former mentor Hassan al-Turabi.[115] After the falling-out, Bashir remained in power as leader of the National Congress Party (NCP) while Turabi formed his own Popular Congress Party (PCP). Like other parties, the PCP was left out of the NCP's peace negotiations with the Sudan People's Liberation Movement (SPLM). Equally, Darfurian elites felt excluded from the process that would result in the Comprehensive Peace Agreement (CPA), containing power- and wealth-sharing deals that affected the entire country and ushered in South Sudan's independence. Turabi's 'marginalised' elite in Khartoum encouraged ideologically related elites in Darfur, mostly associated with the Justice and Equality Movement (JEM), to rise up against the marginalisation of the Darfurians. The Sudanese Liberation Movement/Army (SLM/A), in turn, was politically and militarily incited by the SPLM, the rebel movement originating in southern Sudan that had set the example of successfully fighting Khartoum's elites with a view to a more inclusive Sudan. With Darfur awash with weapons supplied by the governments of Chad and Libya to their proxies, the rebellion was easily armed.

Several states and international organisations have attempted to bring peace to Darfur by negotiating between the movements and the government.[116] Chad mediated two ceasefires.[117]

---

[112] See, *inter plurima alia*, Khalid 2009:35 and Yongo-Bure 2009:68.
[113] De Waal 2007:4–8.   [114] *Ibid.*:21.
[115] See also De Waal 2004a and Daly 2007:Chapter 12.
[116] See also Flint 2010. More generally on Sudan's divided and divisive peace processes, see Nouwen 2006.
[117] Ceasefire Agreement 2003 and Agreement on Humanitarian Ceasefire 2004.

The N'Djamena humanitarian ceasefire coincided with a drop in fatalities in Darfur and an improvement in humanitarian access,[118] but did not end the conflict. The African Union (AU) took over and started the Inter-Sudanese Peace Talks on Darfur, most of which took place in the Nigerian city of Abuja. Seven rounds of talks resulted in 2006 in the Darfur Peace Agreement (DPA). However, while the GoS, along with one faction of one of the armed movements (SLM/Mini Minawi) and a host of international observers embraced the DPA, the politically and militarily strongest movements (SLM/Abdul Wahid and JEM) refused to sign.[119] Two Special Envoys from the UN and AU then tried to unite the fissiparous movements, but, when the peace talks reconvened in the Libyan town of Sirte in November 2007, the dominant armed movements were again conspicuous by their absence. Between 2008 and 2011, peace talks took place under the leadership of the AU–UN Joint Chief Mediator in the city of Doha, at the invitation of the Emir of Qatar. The resulting Doha Document for Peace in Darfur (DDPD) was adopted with much fanfare in 2011, but was signed only by the GoS and the Liberation and Justice Movement (LJM), itself more a product of the peace process than a movement with military and political clout on the ground – and therefore described, by one of its competitors, as a 'civil society group armed with water pistols'.[120] SLA/Abdul Wahid did not participate in Doha; JEM did at times, but its ceasefire agreement with the GoS[121] was honoured mostly in the breach and it refused to sign the DDPD. Meanwhile, the African Union Mission in Sudan, initially deployed as a small force to protect the military observers monitoring the implementation of the N'Djamena ceasefire, was transformed into a peacekeeping operation with a mandate that included the protection of civilians and was replaced, in December 2007, by the 'hybrid' AU–UN peacekeeping mission UNAMID.

---

[118] AU Doc. PSC/AHG/2(CCVII) 2009:[161].

[119] For the reasons to refuse signing, see Abuelbashar 2009:345.

[120] JEM leader Khalil Ibrahim, cited in Murphy and Tubiana 2010:8.

[121] Framework Agreement to Resolve the Conflict in Darfur between the Government of Sudan (GoS) and the Justice and Equality Movement 2010.

EFFECTS CATALYSED

Despite the fact that the GoS mostly used political rather than legal arguments, and that when it did use legal arguments it focused on issues of jurisdiction rather than admissibility, complementarity did catalyse some noticeable effects in Sudan. The ICC's involvement generally and complementarity more specifically fostered an interest in transitional justice; triggered the establishment of domestic accountability mechanisms; motivated the adoption of laws on international crimes; put accountability (back) on the agenda of peace negotiations; and, to some extent, provided a boost for traditional justice.

Fostering interest in transitional justice

'In Sudan, we always forgive the past', stated an interlocutor from the Ministry of Justice when explaining why the concept of transitional justice was new to Sudan.[122] The conflict-related crimes of the past have never been much discussed officially,[123] even though many such crimes were committed in the various conflicts that the country has fought with itself since independence.[124] The general rule for dealing with conflict-related human rights abuses or acts of treason by pacified rebels has been to let bygones be bygones. So, in 1964, General Abboud and his ministers were pardoned for human rights violations committed during their reign;[125] his successors signed an act to restrict legal proceedings for their own acts 'in the public interest';[126] the first civil war for autonomy of Southern Sudan was concluded by an agreement in which the only transitional-justice-related provision was an amnesty clause;[127] and a failed coup attempt in 1976 was followed by a National Reconciliation Agreement and yet another Indemnity Act.[128] In the few instances in which former officials were prosecuted for crimes, it was on charges of treason, corruption or, on one occasion, the smuggling of Jews from Ethiopia to Israel via

---

[122] Discussion with a representative of the Ministry of Justice, Khartoum, July 2011.
[123] Perhaps with the one exception of the crimes of abduction and enslavement, for which Sudan established a body that had the power to prosecute and to provide restitution. See Thomas 2011.
[124] See, more elaborately, Ajawin 2001.   [125] Ibid.:119.
[126] Indemnity Act 1966.
[127] Addis Ababa Agreement 1972, Protocols on Interim Arrangements, Chapter III.
[128] Indemnity Act 1977.

Sudan.[129] Only exceptionally have officials been prosecuted for human rights abuses. In those instances, victims and their families, rather than the state, pursued the cases.[130]

The 2005 Comprehensive Peace Agreement (CPA), concluding what had been at that time Africa's longest civil war, did not contain an amnesty clause since it had been struck out at the insistence of international observers at the peace talks.[131] Instead, a provision calling for a process of national reconciliation was inserted.[132] During the subsequent six-and-a-half-year implementation period, no action was taken upon it. According to many Sudanese officials, the provision has been fully implemented even so: still referring to it as 'the amnesty clause',[133] they consider 'national reconciliation' to be synonymous with forgetting the past.[134]

The CPA illustrates how the various transitional-justice aims of peace, justice and reconciliation have hitherto been ranked in Sudan. The CPA did not set forth a transitional-justice policy, but, to the extent that it nonetheless pursued aims of transitional justice, it was first and foremost peace, secondly distributive justice[135] and to a limited extent legal justice.[136] From a transitional-justice perspective, this exclusive focus on predominantly future-oriented aims missed the component of rectificatory justice, namely, looking back and addressing the direct consequences suffered by individuals due to human rights abuses[137] through retributive and restorative justice. The CPA provided for neither criminal accountability nor reparations (wealth-

---

[129] See Karadawi 1991.   [130] Ajawin 2001:121.

[131] Crawford-Browne, Basha and Alexander 2006:141.

[132] CPA 2005, Chapter II, section 1.7, incorporated in Interim National Constitution 2005 (INC), art. 21.

[133] Interview with members of parliament, Khartoum, November 2008.

[134] Interview with an official of the Ministry of Foreign Affairs, Khartoum, November 2008.

[135] Mani 2002:6 describes distributive justice as 'addressing structural and systematic injustices such as political and economic discrimination and inequalities of distribution that are frequently underlying causes of conflict'. The CPA's provisions on power-sharing, wealth-sharing and self-determination aimed to address political and economic discrimination and inequalities of distribution.

[136] Mani 2002:5 describes legal justice as addressing 'the breakdown or corruption of the rule of law and absence of legal redress, that is a common symptom preceding and during most conflicts'. The CPA's Bill of Rights and the provisions on reform of the judicial system could be classified as promoting legal justice.

[137] See Mani 2002:5.

sharing between north and south was deemed sufficient). To the extent that reconciliation was aimed for, it was pursued through amnesia. To date, there has been no official truth-finding and no accountability for any of the human rights abuses committed during fifty years of conflict between north and south Sudan.[138] The same holds with respect to the human rights violations committed by several of Sudan's authoritarian regimes outside the context of armed conflict.

The practice fits within the Sudanese legal paradigm, in which crimes committed against civilians, unlike crimes committed against the state (treason) or public morality (adultery and fornication), are considered to be private affairs. It is therefore up to the victim or his or her relatives to initiate prosecution. Police and prosecutors rarely initiate a case in the absence of a complaint and do not follow up if the affected party does not insist. If the affected party persists in pursuing a case involving death or physical injury, it can also decide to settle the case at any time, even after the judge has rendered a decision, by accepting blood money. Also, in *judiya*, a centuries-old mechanism in Darfur that combines mediation and arbitration by respected persons, settlement through compensation is prioritised over truth-telling; the payment of compensation is considered an implicit acknowledgment of wrongdoing. This is also how many Sudanese interlocutors understand the NCP's signature of the CPA, with its concessions to Southern Sudan in terms of power-sharing, wealth-sharing and the right to self-determination. Similarly, some interviewees in Darfur argued that a peace agreement providing for compensation and wealth-sharing would amount to government acknowledgment of crimes.[139]

In Sudan, the ICC's intervention, and to a lesser extent the Rome Statute's principle of complementarity, have led to an unprecedented interest in transitional justice as a field dealing with past human rights abuses and conflict-related crimes. First, the ICC's intervention raised awareness among the Sudanese of the conflict in Darfur, a part of the country that many Sudanese refer to as the 'wild west'. Acknowledgment of the existence of a serious conflict in Darfur is a prerequisite for

---

[138] In post-independence South Sudan there have been moves at least to acknowledge that crimes were committed, also by southern forces, in the context of the war with Khartoum. See e.g. 'South Sudan's Machar confirms Bor "apology", calls for wider reconciliation' 2011.

[139] Interviews with community leaders, El-Fasher, May 2010.

any policy of transitional justice for the region. While around the world 'Darfur' has become a household name for massive suffering, the majority of the Sudanese population long seemed unaware of the seriousness of the situation. Censorship, travel restrictions and lack of interest, but also unwillingness and inability to comprehend, fostered ignorance and denial.[140] The May 2008 JEM attack on Omdurman, a twin city of Khartoum, brought the war only a little closer to the nation's consciousness. The ICC's involvement, in particular the arrest warrant against the Sudanese President, raised general awareness that the 'Darfur troubles' are considerable, if only because the conflict looms large in the eyes of dominant foreign powers. Acknowledgment of the scale of the crimes committed remains, however, exceptional. For instance, not only the GoS[141] but also some human rights defenders in Khartoum[142] portray the reports of rape as fabricated. Explaining these reports, a Sudanese doctor argued that these incidents did not involve true 'rape', stating that '[t]he West' – by which he meant Darfur – 'is promiscuous. Western [Sudanese] women are whores.'[143]

Secondly, the ICC's intervention, and again particularly the ICC Prosecutor's accusations against the President, triggered attention on the topic of transitional justice in the Sudanese media, albeit rather one-sidedly: the ICC's involvement in Sudan also led the GoS to limit the space for views diverging from its own. After the request for the arrest warrants against Harun and Kushayb, the media[144] was prohibited from reporting on domestic trials related to Darfur.[145] After the request for the arrest warrant against Bashir, newspapers were censored by the National Intelligence and Security Services (NISS).[146] Knowing that independent articles on the ICC would be

---

[140] See also Arbour 2006:2 and Assal 2009:289.

[141] 'Sudan president says only DNA test can prove rape in Darfur' 2008.

[142] Interviews with a human rights lawyer, outskirts of Khartoum, November 2008.

[143] Reported by a friend of the doctor, El-Fasher, December 2008. A similar view was expressed by a human rights lawyer in an interview on the outskirts of Khartoum in November 2008. See also Fricke and Khair 2009:278.

[144] Almost all radio and television is under state control; the few private stations have difficulties in obtaining licences or their broadcasts are disrupted.

[145] Ali 2007 and 'Sudan official report to UNSC in September shows no arrest of Kushayb' 2008.

[146] Interview with a Sudanese journalist, Khartoum, November 2008, 'Sudanese police arrest 70 journalists over protest for press freedom' 2008, and an interview with three human rights activists, Khartoum, December 2008. Pre-publication

cut,[147] some journalists tried to cloak them under discussions of transitional or international justice, but most stopped writing them altogether.[148] The 'debate' on transitional justice in the media was therefore for most of the time a monologue against 'international injustice'.

Nonetheless, owing to the government's own domestic propaganda against the ICC, the public became aware of the government's 'ICC problem'.[149] The posters that decorated the city and the corridors of ministries, banks and the National Assembly, featuring the head of state in the context of the ICC or Darfur, reminded the Sudanese that the President had good reason to worry about his image. One prominent opposition member observed:

> When Ocampo first presented his request, it was so shocking to everybody that they considered it appalling. There was an overwhelming rage and anger. The NCP conducted a nagging mobilisation campaign at the popular level, in the mosques, in the community, among students, working people, in the media. Yet as a result, they have been speaking about the ICC at an hourly, not even a daily, basis. As a result, they [the NCP] have familiarised the idea that the President is a criminal.[150]

censorship was lifted in September 2009, but the announcement was immediately followed by a warning to editors-in-chief that they should 'avoid what leads to exceeding the red lines and avoid mixing what is patriotic and what is destructive to the nation, sovereignty, security, values and its morality' ('UN hails lift of censorship on Sudanese press' 2009). A deputy editor-in-chief immediately commented, 'There is no way [the security services] are going to tolerate anything about security [or] about the International Criminal Court' ('Sudan president lifts press censorship but warns from "exceeding red line"' 2009). The (pro-government) Press Council had already agreed with the security service on a 'journalistic honour code' according to which journalists exercise 'self-censorship' by avoiding reporting on topics that would be censored under normal circumstances.

[147] In one week, more than twenty articles related to the ICC were taken out of the newspapers *Al-Midan* and *Ajras Alhurria* (African Centre for Justice and Peace Studies 2009:5).

[148] Interview with a Sudanese journalist, Khartoum, November 2008.

[149] Interview with a leading figure in the Democratic Unionist Party, Khartoum, December 2008.

[150] Interview with a leader of the Umma Party, Khartoum, December 2008.

Figure 4.3 'No to surrendering any Sudanese citizen to an unjust international court'

While newspapers could not provide the counter-arguments to the government's campaign, the campaign itself kept the issues of international criminal justice and Darfur on the agenda. During the second part of 2008 and much of 2009, the arrest warrant against the President made the ICC the talk of the town.

271

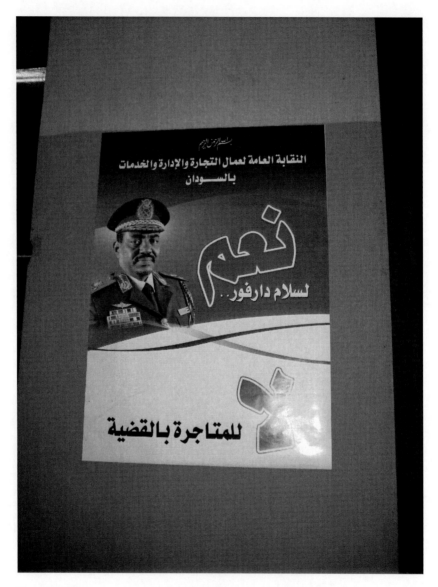

Figure 4.4 'Yes to peace in Darfur; No to commercializing the cause'

Posters of a defiant Omar al-Bashir stayed in the streets and on the windows of taxi mini-vans, but the context of the battle in the 'international court of injustice' gradually changed into that of the 2010 presidential elections. According to insiders, Bashir, tired after twenty-one years of being in charge, had considered handing over to a protégé in the NCP. However, facing an arrest warrant from the ICC, Bashir reckoned that he could not risk losing the protection provided by the Republican Palace. By the time he emerged victorious in the elections, public attention on the ICC had subsided: the ICC had proved to be another international actor too weak to defeat the NCP.

The opposition parties continued to have some interest in the ICC and transitional justice. While never publicly debating the topic – the National Assembly rejected the ICC Prosecutor's charges against the President without discussion – the parties internally deliberated on how to position themselves *vis-à-vis* the ICC. Some political elites reflected on broader questions of transitional justice, for instance, whether lessons could be learnt from experiences in South Africa and Morocco.[151]

Political parties' interest was not so much in justice *per se*, but in the potential costs and benefits of ICC intervention for their position in the political arena. Most of Sudan's northern opposition parties dismissed the NCP's policy of denial and spoke in favour of legal engagement with the Court,[152] but opposed the Prosecutor's request for an arrest warrant for the President, fearing his arrest would result in a 'Somalisation' of Sudan, and cautious not to be seen as unpatriotic by expressing support for an international court that criminalised the head of the Sudanese state. Only parties with a stated agenda of regime change publicly hailed Prosecutor Ocampo's move against the Sudanese President. In addition to the Darfurian armed movements, the ousted ideological mastermind of Bashir's regime, Hassan al-Turabi, advocated Bashir's being tried in The Hague[153] – and was immediately jailed (again).[154]

The political considerations are best illustrated by those of the SPLM, the long-term military opponent of the NCP and its

---

[151] See e.g. El-Gizouli 2009:271–2.

[152] Interview with members of the National Democratic Alliance, Democratic Unionist Party and SPLM, Khartoum, November 2008, interview with a member of the Democratic Unionist Party, December 2008, Polgreen and Gettlemen 2008 and Secretariat-General of the Sudan Communist Party 2008.

[153] Interview with Hassan al-Turabi, leader of the Popular Congress Party, Khartoum, November 2008 and 'Turabi calls on Sudan's Bashir to face ICC charges' 2009.

[154] 'Sudan's Turabi jailed over Bashir remarks; family says no regrets' 2009.

predecessors until the CPA's power-sharing agreement transformed it into the major government coalition partner between 2005 and 2010. When the Prosecutor requested an arrest warrant for the President, the SPLM advocated engagement with the Court, but rejected the charges against the President.[155] Privately admitting that the party would not mind seeing Bashir prosecuted one day, SPLM representatives dreaded that Bashir might be successful in portraying Ocampo's move as an attack on the nation, thereby increasing the NCP's chances in the 2010 elections.[156] The SPLM was also soon confronted with the financial costs of the ICC–Sudan row: Southern Sudan missed out on highly valuable EU development funding owing to the NCP's refusal to ratify the amended Cotonou agreement according to which '[t]he Parties shall seek to take steps towards ratifying and implementing the Rome Statute'.[157] Southern Sudan would equally have to pay if the Security Council were to impose sanctions for Sudan's lack of cooperation with the Court.[158] The SPLM's greatest fear was that the NCP would use the ICC's intervention to declare a national state of emergency, which had been lifted only after the signing of the CPA in 2005, and cancel the 2010 elections and the referendum on an independent Southern Sudan that was planned for 2011.[159] SPLM politicians also wished to avoid the scenario in which the ICC would cause Bashir's downfall and hardliners within the NCP would take over and unilaterally scrap the right of external self-determination that the CPA granted to the South Sudanese. For the SPLM, the costs of siding with the ICC were too high.

But the SPLM's position *vis-à-vis* the ICC began to change once it had secured South Sudan's independence in July 2011 and its army, ousted from the contested area of Abyei, resumed the war in Sudan's

---

[155] Such engagement could entail challenging jurisdiction, admissibility and evidence, or handing over Harun and Kushayb (SPLM 2008, interview with an SPLM member of parliament, Khartoum, November 2008 and 'Interview: Deng Alor [Minister of Foreign Affairs], "There are two outlooks inside the ICC Crisis Management Committee"' 2008).

[156] Interview with a prominent member of the SPLM, Khartoum, November 2008 and Polgreen and Gettlemen 2008.

[157] Agreement amending the Partnership Agreement between the Members of the African, Caribbean and Pacific Group of States and the European Community and its Member States 2005, in particular art. 11(6)(a).

[158] Interview with a prominent member of the SPLM, Khartoum, November 2008.

[159] 'Sudan first VP pleads case against ICC arrest warrant for Bashir' 2009.

'new South', namely, the states of South Kordofan and Blue Nile. No longer recognised as political party, and publicly resuming calls for regime change, the SPLM lobbied for ICC investigations beyond Darfur.[160]

For organisations and people with a specific interest in transitional justice, organising events in Sudan became increasingly difficult after the ICC's intervention. In 2005, a few months after the referral, international and local NGOs could still organise a public seminar on the ICC in which even government officials participated.[161] After the arrest warrants for Harun and Kushayb, and particularly since the request for an arrest warrant for the President, the environment became more hostile. For the first time since the initial years after the 1989 coup, the NISS resumed the practice of torturing human rights defenders, now on allegations of cooperating with the ICC.[162] In court, people were convicted for such cooperation.[163] International humanitarian NGOs were expelled and national human rights NGOs were closed on the same allegations fifteen minutes after the ICC's decision on an arrest warrant against Bashir came out.[164] Fearing the same fate, international actors such as UNAMID adjusted their human rights work, avoiding at all costs being associated with the politically sensitive topic of international justice.[165] Human rights activists left the country and many stayed away even after the threat subsided. Students who organised an event in support of the arrest warrant against the President were shot at by government militias.[166] Lecturers in law were hesitant to raise issues related to the ICC and Sudan, afraid that their opinion would be passed on to the NCP leadership.[167]

---

[160] Garang 2011.   [161] Participant observation, Khartoum, October 2005.

[162] Unlike in the old days, it sent home its victims without insisting on their prior recovery in detention. Their wounds had to serve as a warning against supporting the ICC. See Fernandez 2008b.

[163] 'Three human rights activists arrested in Sudan' 2008 and 'Sudanese gets 17 years for "spying" for war crimes court' 2009.

[164] See, inter alia, UN Doc. S/2009/201 (2009):[26] and African Centre for Justice and Peace Studies 2009:5.

[165] When they seemed not to do so, their activities were interrupted, as an official of an international programme conducting training sessions on the rule of law recounted in an interview in El-Geneina in May 2010: 'After the ICC arrest warrant [for President Bashir] national security closed three of our trainings. We had fifteen minutes to get out.'

[166] 'Sudanese students wounded in clashes with government militia over ICC' 2009.

[167] Interview with a lecturer in law. University of Khartoum, November 2008.

The ICC's intervention thus drew attention to accountability and transitional justice, but at the same time led the GoS to restrict the space for dissenting voices. The GoS interpreted any interest in the ICC, or ICC-related issues such as criminal accountability, as support for yet another Western instrument aiming to achieve regime change in Sudan.

It was the African Union's engagement with transitional justice in Sudan that opened up the space for discussion and triggered even the GoS's interest in the topic. 'Concern[ed] with the misuse of indictments against African leaders',[168] the AU established an African Union High-Level Panel on Darfur (AUPD) and mandated it to submit recommendations on 'how best the issues of accountability and combating impunity, on the one hand, and reconciliation and healing, on the other, could be effectively and comprehensively addressed, including through the establishment of truth and/or reconciliation Commissions'.[169] Since the Panel had been created in response to the ICC Prosecutor's request for an arrest warrant for the Sudanese President and the AU in the same resolution 'request[ed] the United Nations Security Council, in accordance with the provisions of Article 16 of the Rome Statute of the ICC, to defer the process initiated by the ICC',[170] the Panel was widely expected to focus on how to end the ICC's proceedings against an African head of state.[171] However, in its 2009 report the AUPD focused on resolving the conflict in Darfur, and treated the ICC as a side-issue.[172] It merely stressed that 'the ICC is a "court of last resort"' and that the Rome Statute recognises the duty of states to exercise jurisdiction over international crimes.[173] It identified complementarity as a way of addressing ICC involvement, but with the following caveat:

> The Panel does not believe that the motivation, or the rationale, for taking national steps to address justice issues should derive solely, or predominantly, from the perceived need to deal with the ICC issue. Whilst the ICC action might be a catalyst for acts of accountability in

---

[168] AU Doc. PSC/MIN/Comm CXLII Rev.1 2008, clause 3.
[169] Ibid., clause 11(ii).   [170] Ibid., clause 11(i).
[171] See e.g. 'Mbeki "outraged" over his panelist remark on Darfur mission' 2009 ('The timing [of the establishment of the AUPD] fueled speculation that the AU is seeking to circumvent the ICC indictment of Bashir particularly in light of the pan-African body position opposing the warrant.').
[172] AU Doc. PSC/AHG/2(CCVII) 2009.   [173] Ibid.:[244]–[245].

Sudan, Darfurians deserve attention not because of the threat of international action, but principally because they have a right to justice, in their own country, on account of what they have suffered.[174]

Without spending many more words on the ICC, the Panel proposed an 'Integrated Justice and Reconciliation Response', based on the broad understanding of 'justice' that Darfurians had conveyed to the Panel, encompassing 'processes of achieving equality, obtaining compensation and restitution, establishing the rule of law, as well as criminal justice'.[175] The proposed response included national trials, a hybrid court, reconciliation and truth-telling mechanisms, compensation programmes, witness protection programmes and measures for strengthening the justice sector in Darfur.

By focusing on the need for justice *and* peace *and* reconciliation, and adopting the broad understanding of justice that is prevalent in Darfurian society, the Panel broke the ICC's monopoly on the definition of justice and made transitional justice discussable in Sudan. Transitional justice became attractive to the Sudanese authorities precisely because it encompassed more than, and could perhaps be distinguished from,[176] criminal justice, recognising that sometimes a balance must be struck with other worthwhile aims such as peace and reconciliation. A senior official in the Ministry of Justice, for instance, explained his request for training for his staff in transitional justice by arguing that 'transitional justice is very important for Sudan; traditional justice [by which he meant the formal justice system] is not well-suited to war.'[177]

While international attention focused on the GoS's rejection of the idea of hybrid courts, the GoS did not dismiss the AUPD report as a

---

[174] *Ibid.*:[245].   [175] *Ibid.*:[317].

[176] The Heidelberg Darfur Dialogue Outcome Document containing Draft Proposals for Consideration in a Future Darfur Peace Agreement, drafted by Sudanese civil society representatives, does something similar where, in art. 283, it provides that their proposed 'hybrid court' or 'extraordinary chambers' shall refer all files outside their subject-matter jurisdiction to 'the competent institution providing for transitional justice' (Max Planck Institute for Comparative Public Law and International Law and Peace Research Institute 2010:79 and 81).

[177] Discussion with a senior official in the Ministry of Justice, Khartoum, July 2011. See also 'Sudan fires Darfur war crimes prosecutor amid talk of "transitional justice"' 2010, citing the Minister of Justice as saying: '[I]f we cannot present [any] cases to the courts, we can resort to the axis of the reconciliations and transitional justice.'

whole.[178] The report thus provided development agencies with openings to discuss transitional justice with the Sudanese authorities, to spread brochures on the ABC of transitional justice among Sudanese judicial and law-enforcement agencies and to conduct training in transitional justice for officials from the police, Ministry of Justice and NISS. The Joint Special Representative of UNAMID created his own Advisory Board on Justice, Accountability, Truth and Reconciliation, to advance the topic through UNAMID's work.

Transitional justice, for a while taboo because of its association with the ICC, thus became fashionable as an *alternative* to the ICC. As in Uganda, it was thus the search for an alternative to the ICC that had the greatest catalysing effect on national interest in transitional justice. Also as in Uganda, this effect was not directly catalysed by the ICC's involvement, but mediated by others, in the case of Sudan by the AU, following in the wake of the ICC's intervention.

It would be an exaggeration to suggest that the GoS has embraced all elements of transitional justice: its 'new Darfur strategy', presented in 2010, proposed 'to peacefully resolve the situation through efforts focused on five main elements: security, development, resettlement, reconciliation, and negotiations' – the ten-page report contains only one sentence on accountability.[179] But discussion of transitional justice, as opposed to international criminal justice, became possible, even with the government.

Only exceptionally has the increased national attention on questions of transitional justice been directly catalysed by the principle of complementarity. The pro-Bashir propaganda campaign, for instance, was evidently not catalysed by the Rome Statute's principle of complementarity (the billboards did not read 'Let us try Bashir domestically'), but was a response to the ICC's intervention in Sudan, specifically the

---

[178] 'Sudan reiterates rejection of Darfur hybrid courts' 2009 ('[T]he Sudanese presidential adviser Mustafa Osman Ismail said that Khartoum accepts the AU report "in its generalities" and the "African solution for the Darfur crisis" ... Ismail said Sudan wants further dialogue with the AU on the judiciary mechanism for Darfur for the purpose of "securing the independence of the Sudanese judiciary and at the same time the necessary transparency to achieve justice on its most noble levels and punishing the perpetrators who committed crimes in Darfur".').

[179] Office of the Presidential Advisor 2010:7 ('The government recognizes the psychological and practical importance of justice and, as such, remains committed to supporting the work of Sudan's appointed special prosecutor for Darfur and related national tribunals to carry out their mandates.').

Prosecutor's request for an arrest warrant against the President. None-theless, some of the interest in transitional justice can be linked more directly to complementarity. Some political parties, particularly those with the rule of law on their agenda, blamed the government for having allowed the ICC situation to escalate by not conducting domestic proceedings. Prior to the AUPD report, the Umma Party had already proposed a 'hybrid court' of Sudanese and other Arab and African judges to implement the Rome Statute and prosecute at least the cases selected by the ICC.[180] The Democratic Unionist Party proposed independent domestic proceedings, because '[f]ailure to do so forthwith paves the way for international prosecution before [the] ICC'.[181]

Triggering the establishment of domestic accountability mechanisms
An effect of ICC involvement which is more directly related to complementarity has been the creation of domestic mechanisms to address conflict-related crimes. The Sudanese authorities responded to the ICC's movements as if playing a game of ping-pong. So many new courts, prosecution offices, investigative bodies and committees have been established that not only the ICC[182] but even the Sudanese authorities that created them have difficulties distinguishing them.[183]

Before the ICC's involvement, Sudan had already established vari-ous bodies with a view to addressing impunity. In May 2004, before the Security Council established the ICID, President Bashir created a national Commission of Inquiry to investigate alleged human rights violations committed by armed groups in Darfur.[184] The commission

---

[180] 'A middle way for justice in Sudan' 2008 and interview with a prominent member of the Umma Party, Omdurman, December 2008. Still advocating for a hybrid court in 2010, the President of the Umma Party explained the proposal for the hybrid court not by focusing on the need to mix Sudanese and foreign judges but as 'an attempt to reconcile retributive justice with restorative justice ... Abiding by the letter of the ICC indictment will upset restorative justice. Ignoring it will upset retributive justice.' (Al-Mahdi 2010:2).

[181] Hassanein 2008:5. See also interviews with leaders in the Democratic Unionist Party, Khartoum, November and December 2008.

[182] See e.g. the errors in *Third Darfur Report*:4–6 with respect to which authority established the judicial investigation and special prosecution committees.

[183] Interview with a senior official in the Ministry of Justice, Khartoum, December 2008.

[184] Presidential Decision No. 97 Establishing a Commission to Investigate Alleged Human Rights Violations Committed by Armed Groups in the Darfur States 2004.

concluded that 'grave violations of human rights had occurred involving the three Darfur states in which all parties to the conflict had participated in varying degrees and these had inflicted human suffering on the people of Darfur'.[185] It observed violations of common article 3 of the 1949 Geneva Conventions and killing amounting to crimes against humanity, but also noted that it had not found evidence of genocide and that international claims about mortality rates and systematic rape had been exaggerated.[186]

As a partial follow-up to the recommendations of the report, three commissions were established: a commission to determine appropriate compensation, a commission to establish tracks for herdsmen and a Judicial Investigation Commission (JIC). The JIC, established by a State Minister of Justice who himself was presumed to be on the ICID's 'list of fifty-one' criminal suspects, was mandated to investigate further some of the incidents mentioned in the Commission of Inquiry report, now with a view to judicial proceedings.[187] Meanwhile, various other committees mushroomed, for instance committees against rape, along with a Unit for Combating Crimes against Women.[188]

Yet it was the ICC's involvement and the Prosecutor's moves that spurred most of the institutional proliferation in the Sudanese legal system. Immediately after the referral, the GoS sent a delegation to Cairo for legal advice. If Sudan seriously investigated and prosecuted these crimes, the ICC would not intervene, so Egyptian officials and lawyers counselled.[189] Hence, the GoS established committees to implement the various clauses of resolution 1593. But the OTP moved faster than Sudan. On 6 June, the Prosecutor announced that he was opening an investigation into the Darfur situation. The next day, Sudan's Chief Justice issued a decree establishing a Special Criminal

---

[185] UN Doc. S/2005/80 (2005):[19.1].

[186] *Ibid.*:[19]. The report mentioned Ali Kushayb as involved in killings. The Commission had interviewed Ahmad Harun.

[187] The Commission of Inquiry was a fact-finding commission pursuant to the 1954 Commissions of Inquiry Act. In accordance with art. 12, '[n]o statement made in the course of any inquiry under this Act shall be admissible as evidence in any Court of law, whether civil or criminal'. The JIC was established by Minister of Justice, Decision No. 3/2005 2005.

[188] See Hashim 2009:237–38.

[189] Interview with a senior legal advisor in the Ministry of Justice, Khartoum, November 2008.

Court on the Events in Darfur (SCCED).[190] Its jurisdiction encompassed acts constituting crimes 'in accordance with the Sudanese Penal Code and other penal codes', as well as any charges submitted to it by the JIC and 'any charges pursuant to any other law, as determined by the Chief Justice'.[191] In November of the same year, the Chief Justice expanded the substantive jurisdiction of the SCCED to include acts constituting crimes under 'international humanitarian law'.[192] A few days later he issued decrees pursuant to which the then-roving SCCED would stay in North Darfur, and established two additional special courts for South and West Darfur.[193]

The Minister of Justice, for his part, appointed a Committee of Prosecution for Special Criminal Cases in Darfur, with a mandate to prosecute all criminal cases referred to it by the JIC.[194] He also set up a Specialised Attorney Agency for Crimes against Humanity, to 'perform the authorities stated in … International Humanitarian Law, international agreements to which the Sudan is party, and any other related law in any crime against humanity or any other crime stated in any other law that touches on the security and safety of humanity'.[195]

---

[190] Chief Justice, Decree Establishing the Special Criminal Court on the Events in Darfur 2005 (SCCED Decree). Chief Justice, Resolution No. 702 2005 appointed three judges to the Court. The Chief Justice also appointed members of the Appeals Court to adjudicate cases before the Special Court (Chief Justice, Resolution No. 981 2005). The Chief Justice's power to establish a special court is based on the Judiciary Act 1986, s. 10(e), and the Criminal Procedure Act 1991, ss. 6(h) and 14. Officials stress that 'special', in this context, means 'specialised', rather than 'extraordinary'. Established for a specific situation, the Court is part of the normal justice system. 'Special' and 'specialised' courts had been established in Darfur in 2001 and 2003 respectively, pursuant to the Emergency and Public Safety Protection Act 1997, s. 6(2). For the argument that international human rights law permits special courts as long as they guarantee a fair trial, see ICTY, *Tadić Defence Motion Decision* AC:[45].

[191] SCCED Decree, art. 5.

[192] Chief Justice, Amendment of the Order of Establishment of Criminal Court for Darfur's Incidents 2005. This decree also made provision for observers to trials in the Special Court.

[193] Chief Justice, Order of the Establishment of Criminal Court for Darfur's Incident (Geneina) 2005. The members of the courts were appointed by Chief Justice, Resolution No. 1128 2005, and Chief Justice, Resolution No. 1129 2005.

[194] Minister of Justice, Decision No. 9/2005 Establishing a Committee of Prosecution for Special Criminal Cases in Darfur 2005. Following the creation of the two additional special courts, he divided the prosecution team also into three teams.

[195] Minister of Justice, Decree on the Establishment of a Specialized Prosecution for Crimes against Humanity 2005, s. 3.

The geographical jurisdiction of the Agency extended to all of Sudan.[196] Then, within days of the ICC Prosecutor's request for an arrest warrant against Bashir, the Minister of Justice appointed a Special Prosecutor for crimes in Darfur.[197] The appointment was made with much fanfare, even though the person appointed was the same as the chairman of the previous Committee of Prosecution for Special Criminal Cases in Darfur. His responsibility was merely extended to include investigations.[198]

In October 2010, a new Minister of Justice replaced this Special Prosecutor with the Under-Secretary of the Ministry of Justice. The ICC Prosecutor implied that the Special Prosecutor was punished for opening an investigation into an attack on Tabra market in 2010,[199] in which at least thirty-seven people were killed. But the story told by persons close to the Special Prosecutor and the Minister of Justice is slightly different. One month after the attack, the Minister of Justice, himself from Darfur, had been criticised for the slow process of the inquiry.[200] The Special Prosecutor refused to investigate in Tabra, located in an area of frequent clashes, without security and special transport such as helicopters being made available. The Minister of Justice then entrusted the Darfur investigations to the most senior civil servant in the Ministry.[201]

Within six months of his appointment, this Special Prosecutor resigned, both as Under-Secretary and as Prosecutor. Some newspapers and foreign officials insinuated he had been frustrated by obstruction of his investigations by other government agencies.[202] Officially and privately, he cited personal reasons for his resignation; close colleagues explained that he and the Minister disagreed on the management of the Ministry. In September 2011, the new Under-Secretary of the Ministry was the third person in three years to become the Special Prosecutor for

---

[196] *Ibid.*, s. 4.
[197] Decision of the Minister of Justice, Appointment of Special Prosecutor for Crimes in Darfur 2008.
[198] Interview with a senior official in the Ministry of Justice, Khartoum, December 2008.
[199] See *Prosecutor's Darfur Statement SC December 2010*:[12]–[13] and *Twelfth Darfur Report*:[74]–[76].
[200] 'Sudan minister criticized for slowness of Darfur massacre inquiry' 2010.
[201] 'Sudan fires Darfur war crimes prosecutor amid talk of "transitional justice"' 2010. Discussions with close colleagues and friends of the Special Prosecutor and Minister of Justice, Khartoum, October 2011.
[202] 'Sudan's former spy chief slams slow pace of Darfur crimes probe' 2011.

Darfur.[203] Within four months, the Minister of Justice appointed a new Special Prosecutor for crimes committed in Darfur since 2003, this time as part of the implementation of the Doha Document for Peace in Darfur.[204] Usefully, the Minister's decree authorised the new Special Prosecutor to create a coordination mechanism between the Prosecutor's office and other agencies that deal with related issues.[205]

Unlike in Uganda, the special mechanisms have not (yet) created their own dynamic. Judges and prosecutors have no incentive to operationalise institutions that the Minister of Justice and Chief Justice created for international spectators only. In private, judges of the Special Court were cynical about the *raison d'être* of their Court. One judge, when asked about the reason for the creation of a court without cases, replied that it was 'to fool us, and the Americans'.[206] International donors and organisations, in turn, have stayed away from supporting any domestic courts that they feared the GoS may put forward as (sham) alternatives to the ICC.[207]

While the committees of inquiry and on gender-based violence may have been established in response to criticism of impunity more generally,[208] the Special Courts and prosecution bodies have been presented from the outset as an alternative to the ICC, in line with the complementarity principle.[209] Publicly, officials have usually denied that the creation of these bodies is a response to any international pressure, let alone linked to the complementarity

---

[203] 'Sudan appoints new Darfur prosecutor' 2011.

[204] On the DDPD, see this chapter, below, 'Putting accountability on the agenda of peace negotiations'.

[205] 'Sudan to establish special court for Darfur crimes and appoints new special prosecutor' 2012.

[206] Interview with a Sudanese judge, October 2007.

[207] Interview with Western donor representatives, Khartoum, November and December 2008.

[208] See e.g. interview with a senior official in the Ministry of Justice, Khartoum, December 2008 ('There were allegations from organisations like MSF [Médecins Sans Frontières] that 5,000 women had been raped. For that reason we established a specialised bureau.').

[209] See e.g. UN Doc. S/2005/403 (2005), 'Sudan reiterates opposition to try Darfur suspects before ICC' 2005, 'Sudan: National court to try suspects of Darfur crimes' 2005 and diplomatic letter, June 2005 ('Both the Ministers of Justice and Foreign Affairs of the Sudan ... emphasized the fact that this step is in conformity with International Law, and with the Rome Statute of the ICC which gives priority to states to try their nationals within [sic] the principle of complementarity, whether party or non party to the Statute'). See also *Third Darfur Report*:5.

principle. Officially, all measures are taken for domestic reasons. But in one-on-one interviews almost all officials responded that the establishment of many of these bodies was in response to the ICC or, more particularly, to take advantage of the principle of complementarity.[210]

However, while created in the light of the complementarity principle, the mechanisms were never established with a view to challenging admissibility before the ICC. Rather, the GoS expected or hoped that the mere creation of these bodies would convince the international community, and more specifically the Security Council, that Sudan had its own Special Courts, specialised prosecution bodies and other committees addressing accountability and that therefore the ICC's role in Sudan was redundant.[211]

Motivating the adoption of laws on international crimes

The adoption of Sudanese laws on international crimes has been another effect catalysed by complementarity. For the first time in Sudanese history, the December 2007 amendment to the Armed Forces Act 1986 incorporated genocide and crimes against humanity into Sudanese law. The amendment also reintroduced war crimes as crimes under Sudanese law[212] and expanded the list of war crimes that had been in the People's Armed Forces Act 1983. The 2007 amendment does not mention the terms 'genocide', 'crimes against humanity' and 'war crimes' explicitly, let alone refer to their international legal sources such as the Genocide Convention and Geneva Conventions. But the structure of the chapter incorporating these crimes reveals that it is based on the 'Arab Model Law on crimes within the ICC jurisdiction'. Demonstrating that complementarity can have a catalysing effect in states not party to the Statute, the Arab Justice Ministers Council adopted this Model Law by way of guidance to the member

---

[210] E.g. interviews with a senior legal advisor and an advisor in the Ministry of Justice, November 2008.

[211] See e.g. 'Sudan says ICC prosecutor "messenger of destruction"' 2009 ('The Sudanese official called on the UNSC to put an end to Ocampo's mandate saying that his government appointed a special prosecutor to look into Darfur crimes.').

[212] On the introduction and removal of war crimes in Sudanese law by President Nimeiri and the subsequent civilian administration, respectively, see Babiker 2010:84–5 and Babiker 2011:162–3.

states of the Arab League, the majority of which did not intend to become party to the Rome Statute.[213]

The Arab Model Law roughly follows the Rome Statute's definition of crimes,[214] but the amended Sudanese Armed Forces Act[215] contains an interesting selection, and in some instances modification, of the crimes and principles as laid down in the Model Law and Rome Statute.[216] For instance, as regards crimes against humanity, the list of *actus rei* omits murder, extermination, illegal imprisonment, enforced disappearance, apartheid and 'other inhumane acts' and adds adultery and fornication.[217] Adultery – all sexual intercourse outside marriage (possibly) except rape[218] – can thus amount to a crime against humanity when committed 'within the framework of a methodical direct and widespread attack, directed against civilians'.[219] The

---

[213] AL Doc. 598-21d-29/11/2005 (2005). Of the members of the Arab League, only Comoros, Djibouti, Jordan and, after its revolution in 2011, Tunisia have ratified the Statute.

[214] Exceptions are the categorisation of war crimes per subject-matter instead of per legal source and the integration of the Rome Statute's definitions of technical terms into the definitions of the offences.

[215] The references in the present chapter are to an English version of the Act, provided by the Ministry of Justice. The section numbers of that version at times diverge from those of the Arabic text.

[216] Comparison of the Draft Sudanese Armed Forces Act 2007 with the Armed Forces Act 2007 reveals that the earlier draft of the amendment was in several respects closer to the international definition of the crimes, but did not survive deliberations in the Council of Ministers.

[217] Armed Forces Act 2007, s. 153(2). Another difference is that, whereas the Rome Statute requires a 'widespread or systematic' attack for a crime against humanity, the Armed Forces Act refers to a 'direct and widespread attack'. With respect to the crime of genocide, Armed Forces Act s. 153(1) suggests that murder is required for all the *actus rei* of genocide. Some of the differences in the definition of crimes between the English version of the Armed Forces Act, on the one hand, and the English versions of the Arab Model Law and Rome Statute, on the other, may be a result of the retranslation of the Sudanese Act from Arabic into English.

[218] This is controversial. Section 145(1) of the Criminal Act 1991 defines adultery by the absence of a lawful bond between the man and the woman, irrespective of consent. Section 149(1) defines rape as 'sexual intercourse, *by way of adultery, or sodomy*' with any person without his consent' (emphasis added). The reasonable and dominant interpretation is that, since rape is adultery or sodomy without consent, adultery requires consent (which is also suggested by the definition of adultery in s. 145(1)(b) as committed by a woman who 'permits' a man to have sexual intercourse with her). Some Sudanese lawyers, however, are of the view that rape is a *specialis* of adultery and that a case of rape therefore also amounts to adultery.

[219] Armed Forces Act 2007, s. 153(2)(d).

list of war crimes, by contrast, omits those involving sexual violence. In another contrast to international criminal law, some war crimes definitions suggest that ignorance of the law can exculpate a perpetrator by requiring that the person 'knowingly and voluntarily violates the laws'.[220] In addition, by on the one hand maintaining the defence of superior orders and on the other hand omitting the modes of responsibility of ordering, indirect perpetration and command responsibility, the amended Armed Forces Act seeks to ensure the dismissal of any prosecutions brought against soldiers who comply with orders and the commanders who give them.[221]

Since the Armed Forces Act is believed to apply only to persons related to the armed forces,[222] the Criminal Act 1991 was expanded 'to complete the picture'.[223] According to the explanatory note, a chapter with 'the crimes of genocide, war crimes and crimes against humanity' was added because 'the Arab Ministers of Justice determined [these] to be included as part of the criminal laws in order to cover any acts associated with these crimes in the future'.[224] Equally based on the Arab Model Law, the new chapter to the Criminal Act incorporates the Rome Statute's crimes more comprehensively than the Armed Forces Act. In some ways, the crimes as incorporated in the amended Criminal Act are more in accordance with customary international law than the Rome Statute. For instance, the Criminal Act does not require for a crime against humanity that an attack is 'pursuant to or in furtherance of a State or organizational policy to

---

[220] *Ibid.*, s. 155.   [221] *Ibid.*, s. 34.

[222] While in all other respects only persons related to the military are subject to the Act, s. 4(h) covers 'any' person accused of committing the defined international crimes if committed by or against a Sudanese national, on Sudanese territory or if the accused is in Sudan. According to a member of the Special Prosecutor for Darfur's team, interviewed in Khartoum in December 2008, this must have been 'a mistake', as civilians cannot be tried by military courts (cf. *contra* International Commission of Jurists 2007:11, citing a Constitutional Court decision according to which Sudanese military courts may try civilians). A military lawyer confirmed in a discussion in Khartoum in September 2011 that the government was working on an amendment to correct this 'error'.

[223] Interview with a senior legal advisor of the Ministry of Justice, Khartoum, November 2008.

[224] Explanatory note to the Criminal Act Bill (Amendment) 2008. According to UNMIS Rule of Law 2009:1, the National Assembly adopted the Bill on 25 May 2009; the President signed the resulting Act into law on 28 June 2009. As with the Armed Forces Act 2007, the numbering of sections in the English and Arabic versions appears incongruent.

commit such an attack'.[225] Going beyond positive international law, with respect to war crimes the amended Act criminalises offences irrespective of whether the conflict in which they took place was international or non-international in character.[226] Still, in some ways the Criminal Act also falls behind international law. As in the 2007 Armed Forces Act, the definition of genocide in this Act suggests that genocide always requires killing as part of the *actus reus*.[227] The amended Criminal Act also omits the Rome Statute's modes of liability[228] and does not exclude a defence of superior orders.

The Criminal Procedure Act 1991 was amended to provide that 'no criminal procedures ... may be taken against any Sudanese national accused of any act or omission that constitutes violation of the provisions of the International Humanitarian Law including crimes against humanity, genocide and war crimes save before the effect that it grants the Sudan police, General Prosecution and Judiciary'.[229] In other words, it aims to prohibit non-Sudanese actors from taking criminal proceedings against Sudanese nationals. More likely to have an effect is the paragraph in the same article that prohibits 'assistance or support to any entity to hand over any Sudanese national in order to be prosecuted overseas for committing any crime that constitutes violation of the International Humanitarian Law including crimes against humanity, genocide and war crimes'.

The fact that there have been various other incentives for incorporating international crimes in Sudanese law may suggest that it is difficult to attribute these legal reforms to the ICC in general and to complementarity in particular. Sudan was already legally obliged – by,

---

[225] Cf. s. 186 of the Criminal Act 1991 (as amended in 2009) with RS, art. 7(2)(a).

[226] Cf. s. 188 of the Criminal Act 1991 (as amended in 2009) with RS, art. 8.

[227] Criminal Act 1991 (as amended in 2009), s. 187.

[228] E.g. superior responsibility and concepts such as joint perpetration as codified in RS, arts. 28 and 25(3)(a), respectively. The Criminal Act 1991 does provide in s. 21 for 'joint acts in execution of criminal conspiracy' but the conspiracy must be proven and according to most judges interviewed *all* persons involved must be prosecuted for *any* conspirator to be successfully prosecuted. Section 23 criminalises ordering an offence or compelling someone to commit an offence, but only if the person who commits the crime is 'immature' or 'of good faith'. Section 25 criminalises abetment, defined as the inducement of one person by another to commit an offence, or the ordering of any person under his control to commit it. But 'ordering' is different from perpetration through another person as per RS, art. 25(3)(a).

[229] Criminal Procedures Act (Amendment) 2009, s. 2.

variously, the Geneva Conventions and their first Additional Protocol, the Genocide Convention and the Protocol for the Prevention and the Punishment of the Crime of Genocide, War Crimes and Crimes against Humanity and All Forms of Discrimination – to criminalise some of the crimes incorporated in the Rome Statute. Moreover, implementation of the CPA set in motion an overhaul of all legislation to make it compatible with the Interim National Constitution,[230] including the 'human rights' treaties that are declared part of the Bill of Rights. Finally, organisations other than the ICC, for instance national human rights organisations, the influential Group of [Human Rights] Experts sent by the Human Rights Council and, for decades, the International Committee of the Red Cross, had been lobbying for the incorporation of international crimes into domestic law.[231]

Yet none of these various extraneous incentives had been sufficient to convince the GoS to criminalise international offences under domestic law. Sudan has been under an obligation of domestic criminalisation pursuant to the Geneva Conventions since 1957, but in 1986 deleted the few provisions that criminalised international war crimes in Sudanese law[232] and did not reincorporate them until the ICC became involved. Of the sixty-one laws slated for amendment in light of the CPA, only very few were actually changed. In fact, if the discussed amendment to the criminal code had been part of the CPA reform package, the SPLM would have insisted on a review of all sharia-inspired provisions.[233] Some Sudanese international lawyers,

---

[230] See also Sherif and Ibrahim 2006:42.

[231] Human Rights Council 2007a and National Commission on International Humanitarian Law (undated). See also International Commission of Jurists 2007:41.

[232] See Babiker 2010:85 and Babiker 2011:162–3.

[233] Fearing that the process may get bogged down by broader reform demands, the Ministry of Justice stressed that the introduction of international crimes constituted not an 'amendment' of but an 'addition' to the Criminal Act 1991. Whereas a September 2008 draft still included the crime of female circumcision and a provision on state compensation for crimes committed by the police and army, the December 2008 version contained only the Rome Statute crimes. All that mattered to the GoS was that these crimes were seen to have been incorporated into domestic law as soon as possible. It was considered so urgent that the normal procedure whereby other ministries participated in the drafting process was not followed (interview with an official in the legislative drafting department in the Ministry of Justice, Khartoum, December 2008).

politicians and officials in the Ministry of Justice had lobbied in the past for the incorporation of these crimes even in the event that Sudan did not ratify the Rome Statute.[234] Unofficial drafts had circulated since 2002, but a politically powerful group of government legal advisors successfully blocked this move.[235]

Only the ICC's intervention, in particular the 2008 'Ocampo campaign' against the President, made it important enough for the GoS to push legislation incorporating the crimes in the Rome Statute into Sudanese law.[236] Both the ICID and the ICC President had given the impression that domestic criminalisation of ICC offences could limit ICC involvement. The ICID based its advice to the Security Council to refer Darfur to the ICC on the conclusion that Sudan was unable to conduct proceedings because, *inter alia*, it lacked domestic criminalisation of the Rome Statute offences.[237] Sudanese officials had also heard that ICC President Philippe Kirsch had briefed diplomats from a wide range of states to '[g]o and do your homework and don't worry: change your laws, establish courts, and the ICC will not intervene'.[238] On the basis of such considerations, the legislative department of the Ministry of Justice was instructed to crank out a bill in July 2008, immediately after the OTP's request for a warrant for Bashir's arrest.[239] As the then Under-Secretary of the Ministry of Foreign Affairs explained, '[n]ow we have made the process of changing the law so as not to give any excuse to the Prosecutor that we do not have the laws.'[240] The rationale for the amendment of the Armed Forces Act was similar. Asked why the Armed Forces Act had been amended, an influential member of the Council of States noted:

---

[234] Interview with a member of the Legal and Parliamentary Affairs Committee of the National Assembly, Khartoum, November 2008, interview with a former Minister of Justice, Khartoum, December 2008 and interview with a senior legal advisor in the Ministry of Justice, Khartoum, November 2008.

[235] Interview with a former Minister of Justice, Khartoum, December 2008.

[236] Interview with two staff members of the legislative department in the Ministry of Justice, Khartoum, December 2008.

[237] UN Doc. S/2005/60 (2005):[451] and [586].

[238] Interview with a senior legal advisor in the Ministry of Justice, Khartoum, November 2008.

[239] Interview with two staff members of the legislative department in the Ministry of Justice, Khartoum, December 2008.

[240] Interview with Mutrif Siddiq, Under-Secretary of the Ministry of Foreign Affairs, Khartoum, December 2008.

> Now courts start looking into crimes committed in the West
> [Darfur] ... you have to have sections [in the law] that cater for that.
> Crimes are committed in conflict areas.
> [INTERVIEWER:] *But crimes have been committed in the conflict in the*
> *South since the fifties and were never prosecuted.*
> Now they are, because of a lot of factors: there now is the ICC. You
> have to cater for that.[241]

That said, while in essence a legal reform, the amendment of the laws
was first and foremost a 'change-of-policy show' designed to curry
favour in the Security Council. Like the establishment of the various
special bodies, the special legislation making international crimes
domestic offences was introduced neither on normative grounds nor
in order to facilitate a formal legal challenge to the ICC's jurisdiction
on the basis of complementarity. Instead, it was intended to show
Western busybodies peering into Sudan's windows that the GoS had
its legal house in order.[242]

The concession was a politically inexpensive one. First, the absence
of domestic criminalisation of international offences had in reality
never been the main obstacle to Sudanese proceedings for conflict-
related crimes.[243] Secondly, the laws are unlikely to be used against
those in government. According to a former Minister of Justice, 'laws
are not dangerous' for politicians.[244] Even from a legal perspective,
politicians do not have to fear that the amended laws will be applied
to crimes committed during the height of the Darfur conflict in 2003–5.
Most Sudanese lawyers interviewed, including members of the Special
Prosecutor's Office, were of the view that the amended laws could not
be applied retroactively.[245] When asked why the laws were amended

---

[241] Interview with an influential member in the Council of States, Khartoum,
November 2008.

[242] Interview with an NCP parliamentarian, Khartoum, November 2008, suggesting
the Armed Forces Act was amended to 'appease donors'. Also: interview with an
SPLM parliamentarian, Khartoum, November 2008.

[243] See Chapter 5.   [244] Interview, Khartoum, December 2008.

[245] Some held a different view: an international lawyer in the Ministry of Justice
argued during an interview in November 2008: 'international humanitarian law
has always been applied retroactively'; a senior legal advisor in the same Ministry
observed: 'Sharia law is highly unprocedural. You do not allow procedure to defeat
justice. Justice is timeless' and a member of the Special Prosecutor's team argued
in July 2011 that the amended Criminal Act would be applied if this was
beneficial to the accused. Which law will be considered beneficial to the accused
is difficult to predict. In the case of murder, for instance, the punishment is death

with a view to the Darfur conflict even though they could not be applied to this conflict, one legal advisor in the Ministry of Justice responded: 'Maybe it is done because it looks good on the books.'[246] In 2011, two years after its adoption, the amendment to the Criminal Act was unknown to most interviewed Sudanese lawyers, including those assigned to prosecute crimes in Darfur. The amendments had not yet been applied.[247] Just like the ratification of multilateral norm-setting treaties,[248] Sudan's amendment of its laws has mostly been an exercise of paying lip-service to 'the religion of Europe: human rights'.[249]

Putting accountability on the agenda of peace negotiations

Initially, the ICC had the opposite of a catalysing effect on the inclusion of accountability as agenda item in Sudanese peace negotiations. In the first round of the Inter-Sudanese Peace Talks on the

---

by retribution or, if the victim opts for blood money, imprisonment of up to ten years (Criminal Act 1991, s. 130(1)). The punishment for the crime of genocide is death or life imprisonment or a lesser penalty (Criminal Act 1991, s. 187). Much therefore depends on the decision of the victim and the judge's use of his or her discretion. One interviewee, a member of the Democratic Unionist Party, interviewed in November 2008, referred to art. 15(2) ICCPR, which is part of Sudanese law pursuant to INC 2005, art. 27(3), as an argument to justify retroactivity. AU Doc. PSC/AHG/2(CCVII) 2009:[231] adopts this last argument against the prohibition on retroactive application. There are, however, two problems with this reasoning. First, art. 15(2) ICCPR provides that '[n]othing in *this article*' (emphasis added) prejudices proceedings against a person accused of an act that was criminal according to international law: this does not render the further protection afforded by the Sudanese Criminal Procedure Act, s. 4(b), and Criminal Act, s. 4, ineffective. (On the national prohibition against retroactivity being stricter than the international, see also Gallant 2009:277–8 and 370.) Secondly, as the AUPD recognises, INC 2005, art. 27(3), making the ICCPR part of the Sudanese Bill of Rights, came into force only on 9 July 2009. The Sudanese High Court has suggested in *Abdel Rahman Nugdallah* that, before 2005, the ICCPR was not part of Sudanese law. Whether this is an obstacle to retroactive application depends on whether one adopts a substantive or procedural interpretation of the prohibition on non-retroactivity. A substantive interpretation never allows retroactivity; a procedural interpretation allows amendments to the prohibition to have retroactive effect.

[246] Interview with a legal advisor in the Ministry of Justice, Khartoum, November 2008.
[247] Interview with a humanitarian law specialist in the Ministry of Justice, Khartoum, July 2011.
[248] See Chapter 5, 'A domestic context inhospitable to a responsibility to conduct proceedings'.
[249] Interview with a former Minister of Justice, Khartoum, December 2008.

conflict in Darfur, in July 2004, the rebel movements, putting justice forward as one of their purported causes,[250] had insisted on the launching of an international inquiry to investigate the charges of genocide and bring the perpetrators to justice as a precondition to comprehensive political dialogue.[251] But before the fifth round of the Abuja talks, just four months after the Security Council's referral of the situation in Darfur to the ICC, the AU mediating team took accountability off the table.[252] The mediation team dropped this divisive item – in the words of one advisor to the Chief Mediator, 'the peace negotiations would have collapsed' had accountability been pursued[253] – by arguing that the Security Council had delegated the issue to the ICC. The rebel movements, expecting the ICC to strengthen their position, did not object. The Declaration of Principles that was subsequently adopted in Abuja in July 2005 stresses the parties' commitment to respect international humanitarian law and to promote and protect human rights, and provides that steps shall be taken to compensate the people of Darfur, to promote reconciliation and to restore traditional peaceful coexistence among the communities of Darfur,[254] but makes no mention of criminal accountability for conflict-related crimes. Based on this Declaration, the Darfur Peace Agreement provides for compensation and reconciliatory dialogue, but equally omits any reference to accountability for crimes committed during the conflict.[255]

After the miscarriage of the DPA, rebel movements that had refused to sign it called for a review of several elements of the Agreement, but did not push for a revisiting of the issue of accountability. Acting on the mistaken assumptions that the complementarity assessment is situation-specific rather than case-specific and can no longer be influenced once the Security Council has referred a

---

[250] Seekers of Truth and Justice 2000.   [251] Toga 2007:220.

[252] De Waal 2008:33. See also Daly 2007:315. In the final hours of the DPA negotiations the ICC was referred to, not in the context of complementarity, but to pressure the parties to agree. The US Deputy Secretary of State tried to address the movements' concerns over the draft DPA by pressuring the government to accept amendments to this end. 'If you don't agree, I'll see you in The Hague', he stated, in order 'to convey a sense of the stakes involved and the consequences' (interview with Robert Zoellick, former US Deputy Secretary of State, Washington, February 2009, as clarified in author's email exchange with his office, August 2009).

[253] Interview, Khartoum, November 2008.   [254] Declaration of Principles 2005.

[255] DPA 2006, arts. 199–213 and Chapter 4.

situation,[256] some spokespersons reasoned that, since the ICID had found Sudan 'unable and unwilling' and the Security Council had subsequently referred the situation to the ICC, conflict-related crimes were now within the Court's exclusive jurisdiction.[257] They, like the Ugandan government initially, invoked the further argument that the ICC was the more convenient forum, even though this is not part of the admissibility test.[258]

While the ICC's involvement provided a reason for taking accountability off the Abuja agenda, it is an exaggeration to consider the rebel movements' preference for ICC proceedings over domestic proceedings an effect of 'reverse catalysis', in other words, an effect of the ICC's intervention leading to less rather than more domestic proceedings. It is not evident that the movements would have pursued accountability anyway.[259] Familiar with a criminal justice system which countenances blood money as an alternative to punishment, they might well have dropped the issue of accountability if the amount of compensation offered had been satisfactory.[260] Yet for the mediation team the ICC's involvement was a reason to check off the agenda item, AU agreements calling for accountability notwithstanding.[261] And for Western observers, by and large intoning the 'no peace without justice' mantra, the ICC's involvement was a reason no longer to insist on domestic accountability. The issue was being taken care of, and, for most of them, by their preferred court.

---

[256] In fact, according to the Statute, the test is whether Sudan is investigating or prosecuting the specific cases before the ICC, and, if so, whether it is willing and able genuinely to investigate or prosecute these cases. In other words, what matters is the willingness and ability of the Sudanese justice system in those particular cases; a finding about the general state of the Sudanese justice system is not decisive. Moreover, a state can influence the outcome of an admissibility assessment by opening investigations and prosecutions, even if it does so only after the Security Council has referred a situation. See Chapter 2.

[257] Discussions with representatives of JEM and SLA/AW, Germany, October 2007.

[258] See 'Darfur rebel group says world must not turn its back on the ICC' 2007.

[259] It is clearer that the ICC's actions have had a dampening effect on the willingness of rebel movements to negotiate. For further elaboration of the ICC's impact on peace negotiations, see Nouwen 2012c.

[260] This is not to say that the movements' leaders supported ICC proceedings because of an expectation of compensation. Indeed, in their view the key contribution of the ICC to justice would be in bringing about regime change. For an elaboration of this argument, see Nouwen and Werner 2010a.

[261] E.g. see the Constitutive Act of the African Union 2000, art. 4(o).

However, the ICC Prosecutor's application for an arrest warrant against the Sudanese President indirectly put the issue of justice back on the agenda of the Darfur peace talks. Convinced 'that the search for justice should be pursued in a way that does not impede or jeopardize efforts aimed at promoting lasting peace', and concerned 'with the misuse of indictments against African leaders', the Peace and Security Council (PSC) of the African Union adopted a communiqué in which it established the African Union High-Level Panel on Darfur (AUPD); requested the UN Security Council to defer the ICC proceedings against the Sudanese President; and 'encourage[d] the Sudanese parties, with the support of the Joint Chief Mediator, to ensure that issues of impunity, accountability and reconciliation and healing are appropriately addressed during the negotiations aimed at reaching a comprehensive peace agreement'.[262] Whereas the AU mediation team had taken justice off the agenda in Abuja, the PSC reinserted it into the Doha talks. The AUPD endorsed this reinsertion by observing in its report that dropping accountability from the Abuja talks had been 'an error'[263] and contending that 'external interventions will not, and cannot, of themselves, provide the answers to the range of difficult questions that Sudan faces'.[264] In this light, the AUPD, as discussed above,[265] stressed that 'the ICC is a "court of last resort"', that the Rome Statute recognises the duty of states to exercise jurisdiction over international crimes and that cases before the ICC could be rendered inadmissible on grounds of complementarity.[266]

A month after the publication of the AUPD report, a group of representatives of Darfurian 'civil society' flew to Doha to present civil society's views on various issues on the agenda of the peace talks, including justice and reconciliation. The mediation team conceived of 'civil society' as a group other than the two sides of the negotiations, namely, the Government of Sudan on the one hand and armed movements on the other. As such it identified 'traditional leaders', 'civil society organisations', 'internally displaced persons', 'women', 'youth' and 'nomads'. As was to be expected, the representatives of 'civil society' groups were not without their own, often diverging, opinions on politically contested issues. Their joint declaration

---

[262] AU Doc. PSC/MIN/Comm CXLII Rev.1 2008, clause 11(iii).
[263] AU Doc. PSC/AHG/2(CCVII) 2009:[173]. See also [238].
[264] Ibid.:[245].   [265] See this chapter, nn. 172–4.
[266] AU Doc. PSC/AHG/2(CCVII) 2009:[244]–[245] and [254]–[255].

therefore remained silent on the ICC. They could, however, agree upon the looser notion of 'transitional justice'. Adopting many of the proposals of the AUPD, they recommended: truth and reconciliation commissions; reparation and compensation; reconciliation; accountability for perpetrators of war crimes, crimes against humanity and 'serious crimes such as rape'; 'access to transitional justice at all levels, whether national or regional or international'; reform of the judicial system 'to ensure the realization of transitional justice'; 'reform of criminal legislation in line with international conventions to ensure inclusion of international crimes not provided for in Sudanese law'; reform of legislation regarding immunities; and to 'erect a monument commemorating the Darfur crisis to be a history preserved for future generations and the invigoration of their memories and to commemorate the victims of war'.[267]

Fearing further complications in already complicated talks, the joint AU/UN mediation team in Doha only reluctantly reintroduced the 'justice and reconciliation' item onto the agenda. The 2009 'Agreement of Good Will and Confidence Building for the Settlement of the Problem in Darfur' and the 2010 'Framework Agreement to Resolve the Conflict in Darfur', both between the GoS and JEM, still did not provide for criminal accountability. Indeed, the parties agreed on the release of persons detained in relation to the conflict and a general amnesty, respectively.[268] The 2010 'Framework Agreement to Resolve the Conflict in Darfur' between the GoS and LJM also contained an amnesty, but at the same time agreed upon 'justice, the rule of law and reconciliation' as an issue of negotiation.[269] So, when in July 2010 the negotiations on a 'final agreement' between LJM and the GoS commenced, the mediation team also set up a cluster to negotiate justice and reconciliation.[270]

---

[267] Darfurian Civil Society 2009:[2.4]. See also for a few additional recommendations, particularly related to victims of rape, Darfurian Civil Society 2010:[2.4].

[268] 2009 Agreement of Good Will and Confidence Building for the Settlement of the Problem of Darfur, measure 3(c), and 2010 Framework Agreement to Resolve the Conflict in Darfur between the Government of Sudan (GoS) and the Justice and Equality Movement (JEM), art. 2.

[269] Framework Agreement to Resolve the Conflict in Darfur between the Government of Sudan (GoS) and the Liberation and Justice Movement (LJM) 2010, arts. 3 and 4(9).

[270] Interview with a member of the mediation team, Addis Ababa, July 2011.

Once on the agenda, criminal accountability was pushed by the mediation team and the movements. The movements demanded provisions on cooperation with the ICC. For the GoS this was a 'no-go area'.[271] When the LJM kept demanding a provision obliging the GoS to cooperate with the Court,[272] the GoS delegation left Doha in protest and returned to the talks only after the Mediator's supplications in Khartoum. Ultimately the mediation team and the GoS convinced the LJM that there was no need to have any provisions on the ICC: the ICC could not be negotiated away; it would do its work irrespective of this agreement.

The rest of the transitional-justice package remained subject to negotiation. Both parties cited from the AUPD report, and many of its recommendations found their way into the final document. The Doha Document for Peace in Darfur sets an ambitious transitional-justice agenda in terms of aims, principles and scope. It provides for strengthening of the justice sector;[273] compensation;[274] reconciliation[275] including apologies;[276] truth-telling;[277] accountability;[278] amnesty;[279] and vetting.[280] Among the mechanisms are a Truth, Justice and Reconciliation Commission, composed of a Justice Committee and a Truth and Reconciliation Committee.[281] The former is responsible for 'receiving, examining and assessing claims, and determining the nature of compensation/*Jabr al Darar* as well as the amount to be paid to the victims as appropriate'.[282] The latter 'shall assess the root causes of the conflict in Darfur, investigate violations, crimes and human rights abuses including violations of economic, social and cultural rights committed from February 2003, address issues of impunity and build a culture of confidence, peace and reconciliation'.[283]

The DDPD also provides for yet another Special Court for Darfur, 'which shall have jurisdiction over gross violations of human rights and serious violations of international humanitarian law committed in Darfur, since February 2003',[284] and 'shall apply the Sudanese criminal law, international criminal law and international humanitarian and

---

[271] *Ibid.*

[272] 'Darfur mediators hand compromise proposals to Sudanese parties' 2011.

[273] DDPD 2011, art. 56.   [274] *Ibid.*, art. 57.   [275] *Ibid.*, art. 58.

[276] *Ibid.*, s. 307(vi).   [277] *Ibid.*, ss. 316 and 319.   [278] *Ibid.*, art. 59.

[279] *Ibid.*, art. 60.   [280] *Ibid.*, art. 61.   [281] *Ibid.*, s. 311.

[282] *Ibid.*, s. 312.   [283] *Ibid.*, s. 316.   [284] *Ibid.*, s. 322.

human rights law'.[285] 'The GoS shall appoint the Prosecutor of the Special Court, and shall enable him/her to assume his/her role in bringing perpetrators to justice.'[286] The mediation team had adopted the AUPD's proposal of a hybrid court, composed of Sudanese and non-Sudanese judges and senior legal support staff, but this was rejected by the GoS[287] on the basis of the (unconvincing) argument that such a court would be unconstitutional.[288] It also argued that the Sudanese authorities were competent to investigate and prosecute conflict-related crimes. As evidence it referred to the appointment of the Under-Secretary of the Ministry of Justice as the new Special Prosecutor for Darfur and his instructions to update the Minister monthly on his progress.[289]

The missing keystone in the DDPD's panoply of transitional-justice mechanisms is a political deal on transitional justice. Agreeing that people will give apologies, denounce violence, 'adopt ... justice, reconciliation and forgiveness as principles leading to peace' and 'share their experiences, establish a common understanding of the past, facilitate genuine healing within and among communities and promote reconciliation and prevention in the future' is one thing. It is quite another to ensure that people will actually do so. The latter requires incentives, for instance truth and apologies in exchange for amnesty. The DDPD, however, already determines that there shall be an unconditional amnesty for ordinary crimes and none at all for international crimes.[290] The agreement thus does not provide perpetrators with incentives to come forward to tell the truth; either one already benefits from an amnesty or one risks prosecution by disclosing. And, while justice and reconciliation shall be based on the principle that 'all perpetrators of violations of human rights and international humanitarian law are held accountable',[291] the DDPD does not oblige the Prosecutor of the Special Court, or anybody else for that matter, to uphold this principle.[292] Without an arrangement

---

[285] Ibid., s. 324.   [286] Ibid., s. 323.

[287] See also 'Sudan reiterates rejection of AU plan for Darfur hybrid courts' 2011.

[288] 'Darfur mediators hand compromise proposals to Sudanese parties' 2011. The INC does not prescribe the nationality of judges; section 23(a) of the 1986 Judiciary Act does, but that does not make the proposed arrangement unconstitutional and could be amended more easily than the Constitution.

[289] Interview with a person involved in the mediation, Khartoum, September 2011.

[290] DDPD 2011, art. 60.   [291] Ibid., s. 283.

[292] In the early morning of the day of the signing ceremony, UN Headquarters proposed language to strengthen the commitment to prosecute, but the GoS did not accept it.

on how the system fits together, a system with many transitional-justice mechanisms may lead to the implementation of none.

Unlike in the Final Peace Agreement concerning the LRA, complementarity was not the lynchpin of the Doha negotiations on justice and reconciliation in Darfur. The key difference was that the LRA needed a guarantee of domestic proceedings for the cases against it to be rendered inadmissible before the ICC;[293] the GoS did not need such a guarantee in a peace agreement – if it ever wished to conduct domestic proceedings to render the ICC's cases inadmissible, it could initiate domestic proceedings, with or without a peace agreement.

Nonetheless, indirectly the ICC and to a limited extent complementarity did spur the negotiations on transitional justice. Having first taken accountability off the agenda on account of the ICC's involvement, the AU put it back in light of the controversy around the arrest warrant for the Sudanese President. The AU's reconsideration of a decision to leave questions of justice to an international court and the identification of the principle of complementarity as a way to undo the ICC's involvement resemble the above-discussed developments in the Ugandan situation.[294] But, whereas the Juba Agreements envisaged domestic proceedings that could render cases inadmissible under article 17 of the Rome Statute, the AUPD did not explicitly recommend Sudanese proceedings in the same cases as those before the ICC, probably realising that this would be asking the impossible of the GoS. It remained silent on what for the GoS was a rather discouraging interpretation by the ICC of the requirement of the same case. Instead, it encouraged the Sudanese authorities to take charge of accountability irrespective

---

[293] On the question whether proceedings conducted by non-state actors can render ICC proceedings inadmissible, see Kleffner 2011. More generally on courts of armed opposition groups, see Sivakumaran 2009.

[294] There are, of course, differences. In Uganda, the ICC's involvement became an obstacle when the LRA refused to sign any peace agreement until the ICC had dropped its case against the LRA; in Sudan, the ICC's involvement emboldened the rebels, leading them to refuse to negotiate with 'war criminals' (see Nouwen and Werner 2010a:956–8). In Uganda, it was in the interests of the rebel movement to insist on domestic proceedings, and the GoU backtracked on outsourcing justice to the ICC; in Sudan, the rebel movements preferred ICC proceedings and the mediating regional organisation tried to address the consequences of the ICC's involvement in the Darfur conflict.

of whether this would render the ICC's cases inadmissible on grounds of complementarity.[295]

Providing a boost for traditional justice

In response to the ICC's intervention, the GoS frequently praised what can collectively be called 'traditional justice' mechanisms. The Sudanese President "'call[ed] on all the children of Sudan to respond to the call of historical national reconciliation", adding that this "would be inspired by the heritage of Africa and our traditions in the reconciliation councils and mediations led by elders'".[296] The Minister of Justice has stated that the Darfur–Darfur Dialogue[297] would trigger the use of traditional mechanisms.[298] The Sudanese Bar Association promoted such mechanisms, proclaiming that they, unlike judicial procedures, promote peace and security.[299] In government-organised rallies, government-appointed traditional leaders demonstrated against the ICC, maintaining that they are perfectly capable of addressing Darfur's problems. The Sudanese People's Initiative[300] recommended using traditional mechanisms, establishing a national fund for the payment of blood money and rehabilitating the native administration.[301] The Heidelberg Darfur Dialogue Outcome Document containing Draft Proposals for

---

[295] The AUPD did so by stressing that the Darfurians deserve justice irrespective of the ICC's intervention (see above n. 174 and accompanying text), and by emphasising that the Court is 'of limited practical capacity'. See AU Doc. PSC/AHG/2(CCVII) 2009:[244], [245] and [254].

[296] International Center for Transitional Justice 2007:21 citing 'President of the Republic Calls in his Independence and Peace Day speech for National Reconciliation', Akhbar al-Youm, 8 January 2007.

[297] DPA 2006, art. 448 defines the 'Darfur–Darfur Dialogue and Consultation' (DDDC) as 'a conference in which representatives of all Darfurian stakeholders can meet to discuss the challenges of restoring peace to their land, overcoming the divisions between communities, and resolving the existing problems to build a common future'. While most parts of the DPA have never been implemented, the AU and UNAMID have conducted DDDC activities at grassroots levels. See www.dddc.org/about.shtml.

[298] Sabderat 2008:[20].   [299] Sudan Bar Association 2008e:5.

[300] See this chapter, above text preceding n. 53.

[301] Sudan 2008. 'Native administration' is a form of governance by which the central government decentralises authority to the leadership of ethnic or tribal kinship groups. The colonial government used the term to distinguish this form of governance from administration by expatriates. See Abdul Jalil, Mohammed and Yousuf 2007:39.

Consideration in a Future Darfur Peace Agreement suggested that '[t]he *Ajaweed*, a traditional procedure for the resolution of conflicts, shall be institutionalized and assume the function of a truth and reconciliation mechanism'.[302] New laws on the native administration were drafted.[303]

However, to the extent that the GoS put forward traditional mechanisms as an alternative to the ICC,[304] this was, again, more an attempt to influence the Security Council than the ICC. The rhetorical references to such mechanisms are part of Sudan's broader argument before the Security Council that it has its house in order and is making genuine steps to address the situation in Darfur. Whereas the GoS has often ruled by division, it has been interested, particularly since the application for the arrest warrant against the President, in being seen to settle 'local conflicts' through traditional mechanisms.[305] It is in this context of conflict resolution that the Sudanese government put forward traditional mechanisms. It did not advance them as providing a basis for invoking article 17 of the Rome Statute.

Insofar as the Sudanese authorities ever wished to invoke traditional mechanisms in the context of an admissibility challenge on

---

[302] Max-Planck-Institute for Comparative Public Law and International Law and Peace Research Institute, 'Heidelberg Darfur Dialogue Outcome Document Containing Draft Proposals for Consideration in a Future Darfur Peace Agreement', art. 291.

[303] 'New native administration law for Darfur submits for presidency of the republic' 2009.

[304] Note that the government has had additional reasons for promoting traditional mechanisms. First, the presentation of tribal mechanisms as a solution to the conflict fits the government's presentation of the conflict as 'tribal'. Secondly, traditional mechanisms result in reconciliation rather than in punishment, which the government prefers in cases against state officials (according to UN officials reporting in March 2006, people have been forced to settle with state officials in order to end domestic criminal proceedings against the latter). Finally, it is widely believed that reconciliation and compensation better meet the immediate demands of the displaced than does the punishment of perpetrators. Even the prosecutor appointed to investigate conflict-related crimes in Darfur argued that 'the court may hand down the death sentence, but in the end, tribes will sit together and nobody will be hanged. The death penalty will not solve tribal fights. Darfur is not the US or Europe.' (interview with the then Special Prosecutor, Khartoum, December 2008).

[305] Interview with a person supporting traditional dispute resolution in Darfur, El-Geneina, May 2010.

the ground of complementarity, the OTP has already rejected the option, arguing that 'traditional reconciliation mechanisms ... are not criminal proceedings as such for purposes of assessing the admissibility of cases before the ICC'.[306]

Darfurian traditional justice mechanisms, like northern Ugandan, have also received recognition in a peace agreement concluded in the wake of ICC involvement. Unlike the DPA, the DDPD contains provisions on traditional justice as part of a comprehensive transitional-justice package.[307] As one of the principles for justice and reconciliation it adopts 'recognition of the role that independent and impartial traditional mechanisms can play in complementing processes of justice and reconciliation and the importance of making full use of their potential while maintaining international human rights standards'.[308] It also embraces as a principle '[t]he importance of drawing upon African and international experiences and best practices with respect to accountability, reconciliation and truth seeking in addressing what occurred in Darfur and the use of the mechanisms of justice, compensation and reconciliation for the settlement of the conflict'.[309] The DDPD may be indicative of a transitional-justice trend, set by Rwanda, in which, as reflected in the above-cited principle, 'traditional mechanisms' 'complement' formal justice mechanisms.[310] More specifically, the trend suggests that traditional justice is meant for 'low-level' perpetrators while court proceedings take care of 'high-level' perpetrators.[311] The DDPD also reflects a general international concern about the compatibility of 'traditional justice' and human rights, stipulating that traditional mechanisms can play a role only if they are 'independent and impartial' and 'maintain ... international human rights standards'.[312]

---

[306] *Third Darfur Report*:6.
[307] 'Traditional mechanisms' are also given a role in settling disputes arising from the return process. See DDPD 2011, s. 267.
[308] *Ibid.*, s. 287.   [309] *Ibid.*, s. 288.
[310] The Sudanese Government, too, has showed interest in the Rwandan model, in particular in the fact that Rwanda used an 'indigenous' process as an alternative to Western formal justice. Senior officials in the Sudanese Presidency instructed a Sudanese international lawyer to reflect upon a Sudanese traditional-justice law like the Rwandan act on *gacaca*.
[311] Indeed, this is the meaning that the ICC's OTP has at times given to 'complementarity'. See Chapter 5, 'Complementarity as primary right: confusion, ambiguity and misrepresentation'.
[312] See DDPD 2011, s. 287.

The DDPD pays little attention to what traditional justice in Darfur actually entails.[313] 'Traditional justice' could refer to two conceptually distinct processes in Darfur. One such process is *judiya*, which is conflict resolution through a mix of mediation and arbitration by respected persons (*ajaweed*). The other is the administration of justice by 'traditional' or 'native' courts, so-called rural and town courts, which are headed by traditional leaders and constitute at the same time the lowest tier of the formal justice system. In practice, there is overlap between the two processes, if only because many of the traditional leaders who head 'traditional' courts are also involved in *judiya*. The DDPD formalises this conflation by assigning reconciliation to 'the *Ajaweed* Council' and 'the Native Administration'[314] while defining '*Ajaweed* Council' as 'a Mediation Council which consists of the Native Administration and community leaders'.[315] Since there is no permanent 'Ajaweed Council' – *judiya* is an *ad hoc* mechanism – it will be difficult to determine who is part of this envisaged Council. Similarly, it is not clear who constitutes 'the Native Administration' since it was officially abolished in the 1970s,[316] and, while the practice of special administrative roles for the leaders of tribes has continued to exist, it has been contested who qualifies as such. The government has recognised only those leaders who are loyal to it, thereby depriving other traditional leaders of the necessary resources to govern.[317]

Judiya as a process could advance many of the aims of transitional justice, but, as a truth-telling mechanism or an alternative to a formal accountability mechanism, it would have to be considerably adjusted, not unlike what happened to Rwandan *gacaca*. When compared to the formal justice system, *judiya*'s advantage is considered to lie in promoting reconciliation: 'a judge must decide either/or; *judiya* can reach a compromise conclusion'.[318] Or, according to another Darfurian

---

[313] More elaborately on traditional justice in Darfur, Nouwen 2010b.

[314] DDPD 2011, ss. 288 and 307.   [315] *Ibid.*:5.

[316] Interview with traditional leaders of the Fur, Nyala, December 2008 and UN Doc. S/2005/80 (2005):5, 22 and 23. See also Mohamed 2002:6–7, Babiker 2002:11 and Mahmoud 2004:5.

[317] Interview with a traditional leader of the Birgid, Nyala, December 2008 and interview with a prominent member of the Umma Party, Omdurman, December 2008. See also Mohamed 2002:7 and UNDP and Ministry of Higher Education 2002:34.

[318] Interview with a traditional leader of the Massalit, El-Geneina, May 2010.

interlocutor: 'A judgment can give you your right; an *ajaweed* decision can give you your right *and* heal.'[319] *Judiya* is also strong from a restorative-justice perspective in that it usually results in compensation and blood money (*dia*) and helps to restore relationships. *Judiya* is weaker in terms of finding the truth or encouraging apologies: truth is secondary to a settlement, consent to pay compensation considered a sufficient implicit acknowledgment of wrongdoing, and an apology not required, indeed, seldom made. While truth-telling had never been the primary focus of *judiya*, it has been observed that, during the height of the debate about the ICC's involvement, from mid-2008 to mid-2009, local peacemakers intentionally avoided talking about the past: some said 'we do not talk about the past, because the ICC will do that', whereas others reasoned 'we do not talk about the past, because otherwise people will be sent to the ICC'.[320]

Judiya is not focused on protecting legal entitlements either. As one interlocutor distinguished *judiya* from the formal system: 'A judge does justice; *judiya* is a compromise for co-existence.'[321] Others elaborated on this, explaining that *judiya* is 'a *compromise* between justice and reconciliation' and 'a *sacrifice* of a person entitled to justice who forgives for the sake of his/her community'.[322] Originating in and tailored to a tribal society, *judiya*'s strength is restoring communal relations;[323] it is weak in terms of enforcing individual obligations and protecting individual rights. Individual perpetrators are not held accountable; it is the perpetrator's group that takes the burden of being held accountable and paying for the consequences. At the same time, the victim's group represents the victim.

As included in the DDPD, traditional justice is not presented as an alternative to the ICC. There is therefore no need to adjust any traditional-justice processes for these to meet the requirements for rendering ICC cases inadmissible on grounds of complementarity.

---

[319] Interview with a Darfurian lawyer, El-Fasher, May 2010.
[320] Discussion with Jérôme Tubiana, researcher with expertise in *judiya*, Khartoum, September 2011. See also Tubiana 2011.
[321] Focus group with *ajaweed*, El-Fasher, May 2010.   [322] *Ibid.*
[323] It is because of this comparative advantage that *ajaweed* ask a prosecutor or a judge to defer a case to them if they consider it better for the communal relations that the issue is settled outside the court-room. Similarly, the judge will recommend that the case be settled outside the courtroom if he or she deems that application of the law would not benefit future coexistence in the community (more elaborately, Nouwen 2010b).

But this does not deny that the increased attention on traditional justice in the peace agreement and in political debates has indirectly been catalysed by the ICC's intervention generally, and to a more limited extent by complementarity. The ICC's intervention, and in particular the Prosecutor's application for an arrest warrant for the President, led to the creation of the AUPD and the search for a more integrated approach towards peace and justice in Darfur. This in turn triggered Sudan's interest in transitional justice, including mechanisms of traditional justice. Although never suggesting the use of complementarity as a principle to render the ICC's cases inadmissible, the AUPD report did stress that the ICC alone would not achieve justice in Darfur and in that sense would always have to be 'complemented' by other mechanisms. It is in this broader, non-legal, meaning that complementarity has had a catalysing effect on the consideration of Darfurian traditional-justice mechanisms.

Unlike in Uganda, Darfurian traditional leaders themselves have seldom advocated traditional justice as an alternative to the ICC. Local leaders opposed to the government have lacked any incentives to help the government with its 'ICC problem' by offering an alternative to the Court.[324] Indeed, the most vocal of them, namely, the representatives of the displaced in the camps, initially pinned their hopes on the ICC, envisaging that the Court, an external actor pursuing the President on behalf of the international community, would incapacitate the government by executing its arrest warrants, if necessary through military intervention.[325] Parroting rebel leaders, who operated from Paris, London and Kampala, and, for their part, echoed slogans of Western lobby groups such as the 'Save Darfur Coalition', the leaders in camps proclaimed 'No peace without justice' and 'We need justice, not reconciliation'.[326]

More fundamentally, and again unlike in Uganda, local leaders did not perceive traditional mechanisms as alternatives to the ICC. Indeed, the ICC was seen as having 'nothing to do with the *ajaweed* system'.[327] It is of note that the distinction pointed to is not, as one might expect, that traditional mechanisms' focus is on peace through

---

[324] See also Ibrahim 2005–2006.

[325] Interview with a person working on traditional justice in Darfur, Nyala, December 2008.

[326] *Ibid.*

[327] Interview with a traditional leader of the Birgid, Nyala, December 2008.

compensation and the ICC's on retributive justice. Rather, the ICC is seen as a global political power that may secure peace through regime change, after which the *ajaweed* can secure justice.[328]

As in Uganda, the *practice* of traditional justice with respect to conflict-related crime has hardly increased.[329] At the beginning of the conflict some traditional leaders tried to use the developed practice of government-sponsored *judiya*.[330] They meticulously recorded the incidence of attacks, the persons involved and the losses incurred, reported these to the President and Minister of Justice and petitioned for an end to the violence and for compensation.[331] But no reply, besides further attacks, was forthcoming.

There are substantial obstacles to applying *judiya* to the events that have taken place since 2003. First, the conflict has challenged the authority of traditional leaders by demonstrating that the power of the gun trumps the power of tradition.[332] Secondly, the government has forfeited its role as impartial facilitator in government-sponsored inter-tribal *judiya*, by arming some groups to fight others.[333] Thirdly, being either pro- or anti-government, *ajaweed* themselves are sometimes too politicised to function as mediators in disputes related to the conflict with the government.[334] Fourthly, despite the government's attempts to depict it as such, the conflict is not purely tribal and may therefore be difficult to resolve through procedures for tribal reconciliation. Fifthly, *ajaweed* work on the basis of precedent, but there is no precedent for the numbers of victims and perpetrators of this conflict, for its regional dimensions and for some of the crimes it has involved. For instance, traditional mechanisms have previously been used for murder and looting, but never for systematic rape.[335] Finally, and most obviously, a climate in which there is no end to the conflict in sight, in which millions of people languish in camps, in which

---

[328] As is illustrated by part of an interview cited in Nouwen 2012a:330.

[329] Traditional mechanisms have, however, been used in two other contexts. In camps for displaced persons, where traditional leaders have solved conflicts by negotiating compensation, such mechanisms have been almost the only form of justice available. Traditional mechanisms have also been employed to nip in the bud emerging tribal conflicts over land vacated by displaced persons.

[330] See also UNDP and Ministry of Higher Education 2002:49.

[331] International Center for Transitional Justice 2007:30.

[332] See also Mohamed 2002:9.   [333] See also *ibid.* and Babiker 2002:31.

[334] Interview with a traditional leader of the Meidob, El-Fasher, December 2008.

[335] Interview with an expert on traditional justice in Darfur, Nyala, December 2008.

alliances are constantly changing, in which parties are awash with arms, in which 'people who rode camels now drive landcruisers'[336] and in which traditional mechanisms are insufficiently backed by enforcement agencies is hardly conducive to reconciliation conferences.

And yet, some obstacles may also turn into reasons for increased practice of *judiya*. Absence of precedence may be a reason to develop it, as in any other legal system. Moreover, after seven years of international involvement in the Darfur conflict, it is more and more evident, in particular to Darfurians, that outsiders cannot resolve the conflict. As a lean and lenient home-grown method, *judiya* may become more attractive as a coping mechanism.

EFFECTS EXPECTED BUT NOT CATALYSED

While complementarity catalysed some effects, other effects observed in Uganda could not be found in Sudan, in particular the broadening of the approach from the military and political to the legal and the discouragement of amnesties. As in Uganda, the only effect directly relevant to an admissibility challenge on the ground of complementarity, namely, more trials, prosecutions and/or investigations, did not take place.

Broadening the approach from the military and political to the legal?

Many of the interviewed lawyers in Sudan see no role for their profession in addressing the conflict in Darfur. A senior magistrate in North Darfur explained why, in his view, criminal proceedings were not useful in the context of the Darfur conflict:

> In Darfur, conflicts are not criminally investigated. It is solved through the *ajaweed* system. That is the only way to solve this problem. If we follow international people, it will take a long time. Look at Rwanda: they have done very few people. Time will lapse. *Ajaweed* is the system here, already since the days of the English. If there is a political solution, all tribal leaders will solve the problem together. We have no major role in these cases. Only if they fail to pay money, we may enforce, but such cases are rare. The government may even help them to pay. Nobody is punished. An accused person will be released.[337]

---

[336] Interview with a traditional leader of the Birgid, Nyala, December 2008.
[337] Interview with a senior magistrate, El-Fasher, December 2008.

A judge of one of the SCCEDs, the courts created officially to adjudicate crimes committed during the war in Darfur, in turn, argued that the conflict should be ended by offering the rebels money, government positions and amnesty.[338] One of the Special Prosecutors for Darfur agreed: 'courts will not provide the solution to the Darfur problem.'[339]

With respect to crimes committed by state actors, many Sudanese legal professionals consider it unfair to hold the government to account for a conflict 'solicited by the aggression of rebels', while the rebels have mostly stayed beyond the reach of law.[340] Asked about the legality of aerial attacks by the Sudanese Armed Forces on villages where there had been no indication of rebel presence, a Sudanese lecturer in criminal law replied: 'If there is a war, villages are attacked; a government has the right to defend itself.'[341] On this view, civilians die as collateral damage or because they are 'oxygen' for the rebels.[342] The applicability of international law is rebutted with the argument that international law is part of Western foreign policy, not Sudanese law.[343] To demonstrate the arbitrariness of the international community, Sudanese lawyers referred to the decades-long war between the government and the SPLM; in that context, international criminal law was never enforced.[344] Unlike in Uganda, the paradigm through which most Sudanese lawyers and politicians perceive the conflict has not (yet) been broadened to include a legal dimension. *Silent enim leges inter arma*[345] has remained the dominant view, even among lawyers.

The main reason that the Sudanese paradigm of the conflict in Darfur has not expanded to include a legal dimension is that the GoS

---

[338] Interview with a Sudanese judge, Khartoum, March 2007.

[339] Interview with a former Special Prosecutor for Darfur, Khartoum, July 2011.

[340] One government lawyer explained during an interview in Khartoum in December 2008: 'If we are not able to punish the rebel movements, why should we punish our own people?' This view was also expressed by lawyers critical of the government.

[341] Interview with a lecturer in criminal law, Khartoum, November 2008.

[342] Interview with a Sudanese human rights lawyer, Khartoum, November 2008.

[343] Interview with a member of the directorate of legal affairs in the Ministry of Foreign Affairs, Khartoum, March 2007. In a similar vein, a chief magistrate in Darfur, interviewed in El-Fasher in December 2008 ('International law is a big question now any politician in the West uses it for political ends. We are deceived by Western politicians. Until a few days ago, President Nixon [*sic*] was still bashing on Sudan.').

[344] See also this chapter, above, 'Fostering interest in transitional justice'.

[345] Cicero 52 BC:5 ('For among [times of] arms, the laws fall mute.').

has resisted the legal approach. It has perceived the ICC as simply another patch of turf for political battle.[346] So has the Ugandan Government, but, whereas the GoU opted to enter this battlefield, the GoS has been forced into the legal domain against its will. For the GoS, the ICC is just another international political instrument that Western powers in the Security Council use selectively to topple regimes of which they do not approve. The referral is therefore, in its view, just as political a measure as the international condemnations, the arms embargo, the obligation to disarm the *Janjaweed* and the imposition of UN peacekeepers in Darfur.[347]

Government officials argued that this was evinced by the sequence of events leading to the referral by the Security Council. The referral was made in the same week that the Council imposed sanctions.[348] It came only two months after the GoS had made, in its view, far-reaching concessions to Southern Sudan and the international community, namely, signing an agreement granting the south the right to self-determination, committing itself to share substantial parts of its wealth and power and consenting to the presence of 10,000 UN peacekeepers to monitor implementation of the peace agreement. In the words of the Sudanese representative to the Security Council, Sudan was 'rewarded for putting an end to the longest conflict in Africa with further sanctions and procedures'.[349] The Sudanese authorities believe their view of a US-led ICC to be confirmed by statements made by the US representative to the Council[350] and by the manner in which the Prosecutor requested a warrant for the President's arrest: the US announced the request for Bashir's arrest warrant before Ocampo.[351] Finally, the Sudanese authorities see the Prosecutor's case against the President as the former's revenge for the latter's refusal to hand over Ahmad Harun

---

[346] More elaborately on the International Criminal Court as a political battlefield, see Nouwen and Werner 2010a and Nouwen and Werner 2011.

[347] See also De Waal 2008:34.   [348] UN Doc. S/RES/1591 (2005).

[349] UN Doc. S/PV.5158 (2005):12 (Mr Erwa).

[350] *Ibid.*:3 (Mrs Patterson: '[W]e expect that, by having the Security Council refer the situation on Darfur to the ICC, firm political oversight of the process will be exercised. We expect that the Council will continue to exercise such oversight as investigations and prosecutions pursuant to the referral proceed.').

[351] Sabderat 2008:[6.8] and interview with a former Minister of Foreign Affairs, Khartoum, November 2008.

and Ali Kushayb, the objects of the Prosecutor's first case in relation to the situation in Darfur.[352]

Against this background, the GoS considers the formulation of a legal response, and hence the expansion of the domestic approach to the conflict to encompass a legal dimension, as engaging in a political debate on the opponent's terms. Instead, the GoS has to date adopted what is primarily a strategy of 'rupture',[353] refusing to acknowledge, at least officially, any legal dimension to the conflict.[354] An awakening of the domestic legal sector as a result of the government's recognition of a legal dimension to the conflict, an effect catalysed by complementarity in Uganda, has therefore remained absent in Sudan.

Sudanese lawyers, for their part, have not used the ICC's intervention to emphasise the legal dimension to the conflict and to expand their own role, as happened in Uganda. One factor obstructing such action is that, in Sudanese legal practice, law frequently yields to the executive.[355] The Constitutional Court has been reluctant to find the state's actions unconstitutional: for instance, the Court upheld President Bashir's decision to declare a state of emergency and dissolve the Parliament when parliamentary speaker and political rival Hassan al-Turabi attempted to have the assembly limit the President's powers;[356] the Court refused a petition complaining of police harassment and advised informal settlement instead;[357] the Court upheld immunity of officials and prescription in case of torture allegations;[358] the Court dismissed a case challenging the Bar Association elections on the ground that there was no legal dispute; the Court ruled that decisions by the Minister of Justice are not subject to judicial review; and the Court rejected a challenge of pre-censorship on the ground that

---

[352] The Prosecutor links the case against Harun to the case against Bashir in *Prosecutor's Darfur Statement SC December 2007*:10 ('Maintaining Harun in his position is clear indicia [sic] of collusion with other officials. Who is taking responsibility for supporting him? This is the new case I will bring to the judges.').

[353] A defence strategy of 'rupture' attacks the system rather than the facts presented by the Prosecutor within that system. See Koskenniemi 2002a:26.

[354] The steps that the GoS has made, such as the establishment of Special Courts and amendments of laws, are legal in appearance but political in substance, aimed as they are at convincing international political rather than legal actors. See this chapter, above, 'Complementarity: less than a secondary response'.

[355] See more elaborately El-Gaili 2002.

[356] 'Constitutional Court rejects petition against Bashir' 2000.

[357] El-Gaili 2002:16.

[358] *Farouq Mohamed Ibrahim Al Nour v. (1) Government of Sudan; (2) Legislative Body.*

freedom of expression was secondary to national security needs.[359]
Illustrative of the tendency to bend to the executive is a decision of
the Constitutional Court in which it concluded, after finding that the
special procedural rules for the Special Terrorism Courts[360] violated
principles protected by the Constitution, as follows:

> [T]his Court is not a political body, however, it is also not an isolated
> island from what was happening in the country ... [T]his Court, in
> considering the contested constitutionality of the rules cannot manage,
> except to coexist with some derogation from the normal standards, and
> this is not unprecedented. As in Nuremberg, the heavy losses in the life
> and property and the cruelty and brutality with which the whole was
> conducted, compelled those in charge to neglect one of the renowned
> established legal rules to the non-retroactivity of laws ... I reject the
> judgment of the non-constitutionality ... notwithstanding that ... no
> doubt, this is contradictory with the accepted principle of gradation
> [read: 'hierarchy'] in constitutional jurisprudence and justice, as the
> constitutional provisions in their force and supremacy comes at the top
> of the pyramid followed by the legislative power ... [T]his required me
> to decide the non-constitutionality and nullity of the provision of
> Article 25 of the rules, had it not been for the exceptional circum-
> stances which required the issuance of the rules.[361]

With the executive being able in times of 'exceptional circumstances'
to overrule the Constitution, the Constitution's impressive catalogue
of human rights has thus far remained more of a letter of assurance for
foreign observers than the state's legal foundation embodying enforceable individual entitlements.

This in turn reveals a further reason why the Sudanese legal profession has not, of its own accord, used the ICC's intervention to
emphasise the potential role of law and lawyers in the conflict,
namely, the lack of independence of the legal profession.[362] The
Constitution of 2005 guarantees the judiciary's independence from
the executive,[363] but this independence is in practice limited by several
institutional and historical factors. As regards the institutional factors,

---

[359] Information from experts on Sudan's Constitutional Court, 2010.

[360] These courts were established to prosecute the rebels involved in the May 2008
attack on Omdurman.

[361] Cited in Mekki Medani 2008. No state of emergency was declared in Khartoum
during or after the attack.

[362] See more extensively El-Gaili 2002.

[363] INC 2005, arts. 123(2) and 128. See also Constitution of the Sudan 1998, art. 101.

the Chief Justice is the chairman of the body responsible for appointing judges, the National Judicial Service Commission.[364] He has the power not only to assign specific judges to specific cases and to transfer cases but also to establish special courts, to set their special procedures and to appoint special judges with temporary contracts.[365] Secondly, cases that the National Intelligence and Security Service considers in its interest are assigned to 'judges' who are on the NISS payroll.[366] Thirdly, in some cases the judge acts simultaneously as both magistrate and prosecutor. As for the historical factors for the lack of independence, purges in the judiciary after various changes in government, particularly after the 1989 coup by Bashir, have instilled an executive-mindedness in the judiciary. Judges who were not supportive of the new ideology were considered against it, and more than 500 judges, from the Supreme Court down, received a three-line letter that they were dismissed 'in the public interest'.[367] The remaining and newly recruited judges are on their guard against stepping out of line. They refrain from referring to international law out of fear that such a reference would be considered 'anti-government'.[368]

As in many legal systems, the question of the independence of the prosecution is even more vexed an issue. The Constitution guarantees that prosecutors, as state legal advisors, shall perform their duties impartially,[369] but their chief, the Minister of Justice, is a political actor.[370] In theory, a prosecutor must prosecute if there is a *prima facie* case and the Minister cannot give instructions in individual cases of serious crimes.[371] In practice, in politically sensitive cases prosecutors refrain from prosecuting or ask the Minister for permission or the latter intervenes.[372] The police equally try to avoid such cases. By way of example, when Chadian opposition groups attacked villages in West

---

[364] National Judicial Service Commission Act 2005, art. 4(a).

[365] Judiciary Act 1986, s. 10(e), and Criminal Procedure Act 1991, ss. 31(2) and 212.

[366] Interview with parliamentarians, Khartoum, November 2008, interview with an opposition leader who had often been tried, Khartoum, December 2008 and interview with another opposition leader, Khartoum, December 2008.

[367] Letter shown by a Sudanese human rights lawyer, Khartoum, November 2008.

[368] Phone interview with a judge, October 2007.

[369] INC 2005, art. 133(3).   [370] *Ibid.*, art. 133(2).

[371] Criminal Procedure Act 1991, s. 58(2), discussion with Sudanese judges and prosecutors, October 2007.

[372] If permission is denied, prosecutors simply explain publicly that there is not enough evidence for a *prima facie* case (discussion with Sudanese judges and prosecutors, October 2007).

Darfur, a local police officer explained that the police were unable to investigate the incidents on account of the fact that the Chadian rebels had been 'invited by the higher authorities'.[373]

Internal divisions within the Sudanese legal profession provide a third explanation as to why it has not used the ICC's intervention as an opportunity to expand the national conflict paradigm with a legal dimension. Human rights activists have long tried to do so,[374] but they have been too marginalised to bring about a paradigm shift in the profession as a whole. Instead of giving their work an impetus, the ICC's involvement complicated it, at least within Sudan. After the torture of human rights activists on allegations of 'fabrication of evidence for the ICC', many human rights lawyers fled abroad or ceased to practise.[375] Disillusioned by the national legal system, this group of lawyers does not advocate domestic proceedings but has focused its hope on the ICC.

The lawyers at the other end of the spectrum, pro-NCP lawyers such as the Chief Justice and the leadership of the Sudanese Bar Association, have not advocated domestic proceedings either. Instead of *la bouche de la loi*,[376] they are *la bouche du chef politique*, who has already determined his position on the ICC.[377] By way of illustration, Figure 4.5 shows a banner that decorated the club of the Sudanese Bar Association after Ocampo requested the arrest warrant for Bashir.

In between the two extremes of human rights activists and pro-NCP lawyers is a broad range of technocrats, formally supportive of the government, but mostly silently trying to stay within the limited

---

[373] As reported by human rights lawyers, August 2006.

[374] Lawyers in the rebel movements also speak out against the GoS, but they operate separately from their professional colleagues.

[375] *Inter plurima alia*, interview with three Darfurian human rights lawyers, Khartoum, December 2008, interview with a Darfurian human rights lawyer in El-Fasher, May 2010 ('Many of the lawyers formerly of [the dissolved NGO] Amel [Centre] have left Fasher. This was after the arrest warrant. They feared something was coming up.'), interview with a Darfurian human rights lawyer in Nyala in December 2008 ('If Bashir is touched, they will kill every human rights defender everywhere in Sudan. This is what [Presidential Assistant] Nafi ali Nafi has said in the press.') and in August 2011 ('I no longer do human rights cases. I do not want to get my family in trouble . . . I am now alone here. [My former colleagues] are in Sweden, the UK, and Kampala.') and author's email exchange with a human rights lawyer who used to be in Khartoum and moved abroad, December 2009. See also Fernandez 2008b.

[376] Montesquieu 1862.　　[377] See e.g. Sudan Bar Association 2008c.

Figure 4.5 'Taking Sudan to Ocampo's court is a political decision with a legal cover'

'politically neutral' terrain on which they can exercise their profession. Remarkably, quite a few senior government positions concerning human rights and humanitarian law are held by Darfurians. Yet, as one such senior lawyer explains:

> I am in this position only to justify the Government's conduct. These posts have their red lines. I know mine.[378]

By definition political, the conflict in Darfur is beyond the red lines for technocratic lawyers. Wishing to avoid getting their fingers, and careers, burnt on politically sensitive cases, they do not pursue them. As a legal advisor in the Ministry of Justice said: 'Here, in the Ministry, we do the non-political cases ... Political cases are done by the lawyer-politicians, like the Chairman of the Bar Association.'[379] Even a former cabinet minister did not dare to push for domestic trials, as he explained:

---

[378] Interview, Khartoum, February 2011.
[379] Interview with a senior legal advisor in the Ministry of Justice, Khartoum, December 2008.

> I would spoil ... my [entire] programme if I were to go in the direction
> of domestic accountability. I focused on the goals I could focus on ...
> I did not intend to be nosy in other things, as this would stop my
> programme. The people [in the cabinet] would not allow me. Account-
> ability for the military would create madness.[380]

During a study tour abroad, Sudanese judges and prosecutors skilfully
applied the statutes of international criminal tribunals to hypothetical
case studies ('this is genocide'), but refused to discuss the situation in
Darfur as a case study, arguing that this was a political rather than
legal issue. Part of the explanation is that participants close to the
Chief Justice would subsequently brief him on who had said what.[381]
But the other part of the explanation is that many lawyers share the
government's perception of the ICC as an instrument of aggressive
Western foreign policy. 'Why did the Cassese report lead to a referral
of the situation in Darfur to the ICC, but the Goldstone report not to
a referral of the situation in Gaza?', asked a senior official in the
Ministry of Justice with reference to the ICC's involvement in his
country.[382] Just as Sudanese doctors in Darfur are reluctant to allege
rape, many judges and prosecutors refrain from bringing conflict-
related cases before domestic courts, fearing that such cases would
only confirm foreign allegations of widespread crime, thereby further
worsening the country's image abroad.

The space within which international and foreign organisations can
promote transitional justice through transnational judicial processes –
a factor contributing to the paradigm shift in Uganda – has been
limited in Sudan. After the Prosecutor's request for an arrest warrant
for the President, a decree was issued denying visas to persons working
in the field of 'human rights'.[383] For organisations already present in
Sudan, the ICC's involvement spurred some developments for which
they had lobbied for decades, for instance domesticating international
humanitarian law, but overall it complicated their work. The political

---

[380] Interview with a former Minister of Justice, Khartoum, December 2008.
[381] Discussion with participants.
[382] Interview, Khartoum, July 2011.
[383] Interview with a lawyer in a Sudanese human rights organisation seeking visas
(the organisation would later, after the issuance of the arrest warrant for the
President, be closed down), Khartoum, November 2008. In Sudan, as in Uganda
(see Chapter 3, n. 398), 'human rights law' and 'international humanitarian law'
are often considered one and the same.

sensitivities surrounding the ICC affected everything that could in the slightest bit be related to the Court, such as human rights or humanitarian law. A representative of a humanitarian organisation observed:

> Now with the ICC, it is over. The request for the arrest warrant against Bashir was a turning point, for Sudan, and for African states more generally. They now say: 'We cannot commit ourselves to any new convention, agreement, related to international humanitarian law.' These fields have been politicised and this will backlash on our work.[384]

Since the GoS perceives the referral as part of an international conspiracy against it, international and foreign organisations are easily branded as accomplices of the Court. Realistically fearing expulsion after the Prosecutor's application for an arrest warrant against the President,[385] they began to avoid topics related to international law. UNAMID, for instance, took care not to raise the topic of justice, afraid that this would suggest even more of a link between the UN and the ICC, and lead the government to impede their peacekeeping activities further.[386] Only after the AUPD report did they take up issues of international justice again, through the backdoor of the concept of 'transitional justice'.

Finally, transnational professional contacts between Sudanese lawyers and foreign colleagues have been complicated too. For instance, the Chief Justice must give permission for judges' professional interactions with foreigners and has the final word on the lists of participants and the contents of workshops and study tours. To the extent that they have had international exposure, Sudanese officials have been trained by international lawyers but, unlike their Ugandan colleagues, have not become part of international professional networks. Only the human rights activists who have fled abroad have been incorporated into international networks of human rights activists and pro-ICC advocacy groups, but by moving abroad they have lost most of their influence on the Sudanese legal profession.

---

[384] Interview with a senior representative of a humanitarian organisation, Khartoum, October 2008.

[385] 'Defiant Sudan expels aid agencies after Beshir warrant' 2009.

[386] Discussion with a representative of an international organisation, El-Fasher, December 2008.

Nonetheless, some steps taken since the OTP's request for the arrest warrant for the President suggest that technocratic lawyers, while normally shying away and kept from politically sensitive cases, may suddenly be called upon once these cases become urgent.[387] If the costs of denial become too high, the GoS may ultimately decide to engage with the Court through the legal avenues prescribed in the Statute. This could open up some space for lawyers and for a legal dimension to an overwhelmingly political and military conflict paradigm.

Discouraging immunities and amnesties?

Immunity is a big thing in Sudan. It is one of the attractions of holding a government job. In the years since independence, the entire spectrum of state officials, from the President,[388] ministers[389] and members of the national legislature[390] to the rank and file of the armed forces,[391] police[392] and National Intelligence and Security Services,[393] have come to be protected by some form of immunity, sometimes substantive, sometimes only procedural. Soldiers, police and security officers, for instance, cannot be prosecuted without the permission of the suspect's superiors.[394] The process of obtaining such permission

---

[387] For instance, the GoS mandated the University of Khartoum to 'prepare a memo to assist concerned competent authorities to refute the decision' of the ICC Prosecutor. The University's legal committee in fact recommended the GoS to invoke complementarity. Arguing that the admissibility assessment is continuous, it proposed taking a 'real preemptive step as to initiate independent procedures commensurate with the Rome Statute; the international standards of human rights; the international humanitarian law; and the post-CPA/DPA democratic laws.' (University of Khartoum 2008:8–9). But the Vice-President, himself a lawyer, rejected the University's finding that the Court had jurisdiction (interview with a member of the University of Khartoum, Khartoum, November 2008).

[388] INC 2005, art. 60(1) and Constitution of the Sudan 1998, art. 45(1).

[389] Privileges and Immunities Appropriation Constitutional Officeholders, Executive and Legislative Act 2001, s. 21 (as reported in Pichon 2008:221).

[390] INC 2005, art. 92 and Constitution of the Sudan 1998, art. 74.

[391] Armed Forces Act 2007, s. 34, People's Armed Forces Act 1986, s. 8, as amended by the People's Armed Forces Act (Amendment) 1999, s. 6. Pursuant to the Judiciary Headquarters, Criminal Decree No. 3/95, 1995, the Chief Justice takes the final decision on whether or not immunity is lifted.

[392] Police Forces Act 1999, s. 46.

[393] National Security Act 2010, s. 52(1). National Security Forces Act 1999, s. 33(b).

[394] See also UN Doc. CCPR/C/SDN/CO/3/CRP.1 (2007):[9].

has been arbitrary and non-transparent, and has usually resulted in no or a negative reply, particularly if the relevant crime is alleged to have been committed in the context of state operations.[395]

The ICC's involvement has done nothing to limit the scope or increase the lifting of immunities. Indeed, within two weeks of the Security Council's referral of the situation in Darfur to the ICC, the Sudanese President decreed the expansion of the immunity available under the Armed Forces Act. A substantive defence was introduced and from then on immunity could be lifted only by the President or a person authorised by him.[396] The Police Forces Act was amended without affecting the immunities for the police.[397] In 2008, the Constitutional Court found that 'procedural immunity for the security and police services is routine ... and one cannot argue that it is unconstitutional'.[398] The DDPD provides that 'immunities enjoyed by persons of the official status or functions shall not obstruct the speedy dispensation of justice nor shall they prevent the combating of impunity' but does not declare immunities irrelevant.[399] The number of beneficiaries of immunities has only increased over the years since the ICC's involvement, as a result of the integration of pro-government militias and former rebels into the Popular Defence Forces, the Central Reserve Police, the Border Guards and other state-affiliated institutions. Indeed, according to one member of the opposition, the entire 'list of fifty-one', the confidential list of suspects identified by the ICID, has been given positions that come with immunity.[400] The practice of the lifting of immunities has remained non-transparent.[401]

---

[395] Interview with Sudanese human rights lawyers, El-Fasher and Nyala, December 2008.

[396] Sudan Armed Forces Act (Amendment) 2005. When this decree lapsed, the President passed a new one, containing only the immunity. The latter decree lapsed when the National Assembly, by way of exception, refused to pass the expiring decree into law. But the immunity provisions of the former were incorporated into the amended Armed Forces Act 2007, s. 34.

[397] National Police Forces Act 2008, art. 45(1).

[398] Judge Altayeb Abass al-Ga'ali in *Farouq Mohamed Ibrahim Al Nour* v. (*1*) *Government of Sudan;(2) Legislative Body.*

[399] DDPD 2011, s. 295.

[400] Interview with a member of the opposition, Khartoum, March 2011.

[401] Human rights lawyers in Nyala, first interviewed in November 2005, reported in interviews in December 2008 an improvement in the lifting of immunity in rape cases in Nyala, which they attributed to particular superiors in the army. Cases of torture, however, were kept beyond judicial scrutiny.

Nor has the ICC's involvement ended the practice of amnesties. Soon after the conclusion of the 2006 Darfur Peace Agreement, an amnesty was declared, the Prosecutor's opening of an investigation into Darfur notwithstanding. Decree 114 provided a general amnesty for those belonging to armed movements that had signed or adhered to the DPA and to parties that participated in officially endorsed tribal reconciliation procedures.[402] Whether the decree applies only to those who took up arms against the government or also to those who fought on the government's behalf remains controversial: no policy document on its application or overview of its beneficiaries has been made available.[403] Anecdotal evidence suggests that it has been given a wide interpretation and applied in instances in which the government wished to amnesty certain persons.[404]

In the subsequent Darfur peace negotiations in Doha, aimed at the armed movements that had refused to sign the DPA, amnesty featured again. Despite JEM's and LJM's espoused commitment to accountability, both movements signed framework agreements with the GoS containing an article providing for the '[i]ssuance of a general amnesty for ... members of [JEM and LJM, respectively], and the release of the war prisoners and convicted persons from both sides, after the final signing of this Agreement'.[405] Armed groups that had fought for the *government* subsequently sought association with one of the rebel movements, LJM, if only to benefit from the amnesty.[406] Only the Joint Chief Mediator had to pay a price for this provision in the Framework Agreement: he was reprimanded by UN Headquarters for signing an agreement

---

[402] Decree No. 114, 2006.

[403] Interviewed senior officials in the Ministry of Justice working for the Special Prosecutor's Office thought the decree to apply to all sides of the conflict (interviews in Khartoum, July 2011).

[404] A senior magistrate in North Darfur justified in an interview in El-Fasher in December 2008 the release of two convicted military intelligence officers (see next section) by arguing that a private blood-money settlement was in line with the 'tribal reconciliation' referred to in the amnesty decree, even though the case had not involved a dispute between tribes.

[405] Framework Agreement to Resolve the Conflict in Darfur between the Government of Sudan (GoS) and the Justice and Equality Movement 2010, art. 2; Framework Agreement to Resolve the Conflict in Darfur between the Government of Sudan (GoS) and the Liberation and Justice Movement (LJM) 2010, art. 3.

[406] Interview with a prosecutor, El-Fasher, August 2011.

that contained a blanket amnesty without appending a rider that would exclude the UN's list of amnesty-unworthy crimes from the scope of the amnesty.[407]

The Mediator learnt his lesson: the final outcome document of the Doha negotiations, the DDPD, again includes an amnesty provision,[408] but, for the first time in the history of Sudanese peace agreements, makes an exception for 'war crimes, crimes against humanity, crimes of genocide, crimes of sexual violence, and gross violations of human rights and humanitarian law'. The GoS had proposed an alternative exception clause, namely:

> The Parties agree that the individual rights in relation to the crimes and violations which have taken place in Darfur during the conflict, including war crimes, crimes against humanity, crimes of genocide, crimes of sexual violence, and gross violations of human rights and humanitarian law shall not be included in the scope of application of the amnesty.[409]

The GoS's proposal was not accepted. For the protection of individual rights the amendment was not necessary; the text reflects Islamic law as applied in Sudan, according to which amnesties, as laws promulgated by the state, can never deprive an individual of his or her Quranic entitlement to *qisas* (retribution) or *dia* (blood money). This law will continue to apply with or without provision in the DDPD. The consequence of the GoS's proposal's not having made it into the DDPD is thus only that the text it was meant to substitute, namely, the exclusion of a category of special crimes from the scope of the amnesty, still stands. The practical relevance of this exception to the amnesty is of course questionable, since the state that proposed to replace it can easily secure a *de facto* amnesty by refraining from prosecutions in practice.

It is unlikely that the new immunity and amnesty provisions reflect a 'reverse catalysis' on the part of the ICC. They are more a continuation of past practice than a response to the Court. The fact remains, however, that the ICC's intervention has not discernibly spurred the

---

[407] Interview with persons close to the mediation team, Khartoum, May 2010.

[408] DDPD 2011, s. 329: 'In order to create a conducive environment for peace and reconciliation, the GoS shall grant a general amnesty in accordance with the Sudanese Constitution and Laws, to civil and military members, to prisoners of war and those sentenced from the Parties, and on this basis, release the prisoners of war.'

[409] Sudan 2011.

GoS to decrease the use of immunities or amnesties, even though both may obstruct attempts to render ICC cases inadmissible on grounds of complementarity.

Encouraging more trials, prosecutions and/or investigations?

Special courts, new laws and transitional-justice talk notwithstanding, the only product of a catalysing effect on the part of complementarity that could render ICC cases inadmissible, namely, genuine domestic investigations and prosecutions, has remained largely absent in Sudan. This is not to say that there have been no proceedings related to the conflict. There have been several trials of members of the armed movements, most notably of people accused of being supporters of JEM in the attack on Khartoum's twin city, Omdurman.[410] More indirectly related to the conflict, people have been investigated and prosecuted for having links to the ICC. However, the offences prosecuted, mostly treason and terrorism, are different in character from those in the Rome Statute.

With respect to the persons sought by the ICC, the GoS has sometimes appeared to initiate domestic proceedings.[411] A week after the Prosecutor had requested the Court to issue summonses for the appearances of Ali Kushayb and Ahmad Harun, Kushayb was reportedly sent for trial by the Special Court in West Darfur. The Sudanese Prosecutor-General attempted to open an investigation into Harun. However, Kushayb was released for lack of evidence and the Sudanese President aborted the investigation into Harun.[412] Immediately after the ICC Prosecutor's application for an arrest warrant for the President, newspapers reported that Kushayb was in custody again[413] (but several interviewees said they had spotted him walking as a free man

---

[410] At least 103 persons have been sentenced to death in tribunals especially created to deal with this attack (UN Doc. S/2009/352 (2009):[4]).

[411] Other officials have seemed to test the waters by suggesting that Sudan might hand Harun and Kushayb over to the Court 'as a protection from further indictments' (Ali 2008a).

[412] 'UK, France agree to Chinese proposal on Darfur trials: report' 2008 and El-Gizouli 2009:261. Harun remained the State Minister responsible for humanitarian affairs including in the Darfur region until he was appointed governor of the state of South Kordofan in 2009.

[413] On Kushayb's transitions in and out of prison, see 'Sudan official report to UNSC in September shows no arrest of Kushayb' 2008, 'Sudan detains militia leader wanted by ICC in preparation for trial' 2008, and 'Darfur war crimes suspect transferred to Khartoum' 2009.

in north Khartoum and in West Darfur)[414] and some officials suggested publicly that even Harun might be prosecuted domestically, if the ICC provided the evidence.[415] But, in a private interview, a prosecutor responsible for the investigation claimed to have found evidence only against Kushayb, not against Harun.[416] He said he had not looked for evidence against the President, since the latter could be prosecuted only if three quarters of the National Legislature decided to charge him before the Constitutional Court.[417]

The special bodies set up to investigate, prosecute and try persons for crimes committed in the context of the Darfur conflict largely failed to fulfil their (purported) mandates. Alternatively, their recommendations were not implemented.[418] The government has given more attention to their establishment than to their functioning. For instance, after its establishment, the Specialised Attorney Agency for Crimes against Humanity, mandated to prosecute crimes against humanity throughout the country, was not mentioned again in any government records. In 2008, the highest officials in the Ministry of Justice did not seem to know of the existence of this agency that was created in 2005.[419] The JIC, mandated to investigate certain incidents that had been highlighted by the national Commission of Inquiry with

---

[414] Two years later, he was officially still in 'police custody' – Kushayb had been integrated into the 'Central Reserve Police' and the normal practice is for suspects belonging to the army or police to be detained by their employer during the course of the investigation. But in August 2011 he could be spotted drinking tea in the streets of Nyala, without any indication of detention.

[415] Ali 2008b and Tisdall 2008.

[416] Interview with a member of the office of the Special Prosecutor for Darfur, Khartoum, December 2008. In fact, even when no longer a state minister, Harun continued to enjoy immunity as a governor. Kushayb, integrated into the Central Reserve Police, may be protected by immunity, which applies even though the alleged crimes were committed before he joined the police.

[417] INC 2005, art. 60.

[418] For instance, when a Commission on Reparations, the establishment of which coincided with the release of the ICID report, recommended the payment of billions of Sudanese pounds to Darfurian victims (Abu Al Gasim 2005 speaks of approximately US$2 billion and of 200 billion in Sudanese pounds), the Vice-President refused to receive the report. Payment of the suggested amounts to the identified Darfurian victims, he said, could open a Pandora's box in Southern Sudan (interview with a member of the Commission on Reparations, Khartoum, November 2008).

[419] Interview with a senior official in the Ministry of Justice, Khartoum, December 2008.

a view to prosecution, never completed its work. Consequently, the Special Prosecution Commissions, which were supposed to prosecute cases investigated by the JIC, did not have any cases. Initially, they took some investigated cases from ordinary prosecutors to the Special Courts.[420] But, after a few months, the Special Court in El-Fasher received no more cases. The Special Courts in El-Geneina and Nyala decided their last cases in 2006. While the Special Courts officially still exist, the judges have long since taken up other positions, some of them abroad.[421]

It is difficult to appraise the number and contents of Sudanese proceedings for conflict-related crimes,[422] but it is clear that the SCCEDs have not, with one exception, tried cases inherently connected with the conflict.[423] The dozen cases that they have considered have involved charges of (though not always convictions for) armed robbery, receipt of stolen goods, possession of firearms without a licence, intentional wounding, murder and rape. The majority of the acts have been committed by civilians[424] or low-ranking armed forces, and have been only tangentially related to the armed conflict.[425] In the two cases against low- and middle-ranking military intelligence officers on the grounds of their interrogation causing the death of persons suspected of rebel activities (a thirteen-year-old boy and

---

[420] Interview with three prosecutors from North Darfur, El-Fasher, December 2008.

[421] Repeat interviews with one of the judges, 2007, 2008 and 2011.

[422] A complicating factor is that there is no rule determining which cases are brought before the Special Courts or other courts. General courts, the Specialised Courts of 2003 and military courts have continued to adjudicate similar cases.

[423] This paragraph is based on an analysis of Sudan 2008, *Third Darfur Report*:5 and incident reporting in newspapers. Over-reporting has been sought to be avoided through careful comparison of descriptions of the reported cases, among others the charges and sentences. If many cases have not been reported, the analysis may suffer from under-reporting. For a description of many of the cases taken into account in this paragraph, see Human Rights Watch 2006 and International Commission of Jurists 2007. See also Barends 2007.

[424] See e.g. Special Court, Nyala, 6271/2004, 25 July 2005 (four civilians convicted of armed robbery of a vehicle) and Special Court, Nyala, 462/2005, 28 August 2005 (a civilian acquitted of armed robbery and intentionally wounding a staff member of the United States Agency for International Development during an attack against a humanitarian convoy, sentenced to nine months' imprisonment for possessing an unlicensed weapon).

[425] See e.g. Special Court, El-Fasher (no case number or date available), convicting three low-level members of the Sudanese army of armed robbery (stealing sheep) and a civilian (a butcher) of receiving stolen property.

sixty-year-old man), the accused were sentenced to death. In one of the two cases, the family of the deceased granted full pardon in return for *dia* (blood money). Using its discretion in exercising the 'public right',[426] the Court sentenced the men to two years' imprisonment. Shortly thereafter, however, they were pardoned.[427] Of the two rape cases, one resulted in an acquittal due to a lack of evidence.[428] The other case was successful, as the accused had been caught red-handed and confessed.[429] No high-level official has been convicted and no case has involved an allegation of a widespread or systematic attack on civilians. The jurisdiction of the SCCEDs may have been expanded to include 'actions which constitute crimes pursuant to ... the international humanitarian law',[430] yet all the charges, with one noteworthy exception, have involved only Sudanese law.

The one noteworthy exception is a case brought in Nyala. Four days after militias had assaulted the villages of Tama and Kashkur, leaving forty-one persons dead, the accused were found looting and were arrested. Silent on the legal effect of international law in Sudanese law in general, the decision shows a willingness directly to apply international humanitarian law as embodied in the Geneva Conventions and Rome Statute. As the only available Sudanese case concerning the Darfur conflict in which international criminal law is referred to and even applied, it is worth quoting the Court's considerations *in extenso*:[431]

> The case we are deliberating herein constitutes an illustration of war and tribal violence. Conforming to section 5-a [of the amended decree

---

[426] According to the Criminal Procedure Act 1991, s. 36(1), '[a]n injured, or interested party ... may relinquish his private right in the criminal suit, by pardon or conciliation [i.e. payment of *dia*] at any time before passing a final judgment therein, without prejudice to the public right'. The 'public right' is the right of the state to punish the perpetrator despite the private settlement. A judge may exercise this right at his or her discretion, but the sentence may be only minimal in comparison to what the sentence had been in the absence of a private settlement.

[427] See this chapter, above n. 404.

[428] Special Court, Nyala (no case number available), 27 August 2005 (eight members of the Popular Defence Forces and two military personnel were acquitted of rape of a sixteen-year-old girl during an attack on two public buses).

[429] SOAT/Amel Centre 2006.

[430] Chief Justice, Amendment of the Order of Establishment of Criminal Court for Darfur's Incidents 2005.

[431] The following citations related to this case come from *Adam Abras Adam* (no paragraphs or page numbers).

> establishing the Special Court], the mandate ... of this tribunal includes the incidents considered as crime according to the Sudanese criminal act, other penal acts and the International Humanitarian Law. Therefore, this tribunal enjoys a legal style [similar?] to [the] International Criminal Court.
>
> One of the significant principles agreed on in Rome's Statute is reaffirmation of inter-community ties that constitute ... a common heritage. It is a concern that this strong fabric might be torn off any time. Hence, the judicial provisions maintained by this tribunal aim at controlling the jeopardy of crimes worrying the international community – see section 4-1 [sic] [of] the Statute of Rome for [an] ICC,[432] section 4 of [the] Criminal Procedure Act 1991.[433]

The Court then discussed the charges of robbery and criminal misappropriation in accordance with the Sudanese Criminal Act and 'sections 8\16 of humanitarian criminal act'. With respect to 'section 8 of international human criminal act – Statute of Rome', the Court cited article 8(1) and (2)(a)(i)–(iv) of the Statute, but not the crime charged, namely, that under article 8(2)(b)(xvi) ('pillaging a town or place, even when taken by assault'). Remarkably, both the crimes cited and the crime charged represent provisions applicable in *international* armed conflict. The Court went on to quote the beginning of common article 3 of the 1949 Geneva Conventions, applicable to non-international armed conflict, and considered:

> The international community has faced various difficulties to have [...] access to a specific law tackling the aftermath of current armed conflict. As a consequence of the growing complexity of modern armed conflict, the law of war is also becoming more and more complicated. And this law from the strategic level downward, application of the law of war becomes increasingly a matter of internal order and discipline.

The Court concluded that the prosecution failed to prove a link between the looting and the military action, hence the 'law of war or humanitarian criminal law' did not apply, so that 'section 16\8 of humanitarian criminal law – Statute of Rome [was] inapplicable'. In

---

[432] The relevance of art. 4(1) of the Rome Statute in this context is questionable, reading as it does: 'The Court shall have international legal personality. It shall also have such legal capacity as may be necessary for the exercise of its functions and the fulfilment of its purposes.'

[433] The Criminal Procedure Act 1991, s. 4 contains 'principles to be regarded', the first principle being that 'prevention of offences is a duty of all'.

the event, the accused were convicted of theft pursuant to the Sudanese Criminal Act. The heaviest sentence imposed was three years' imprisonment.

This case of direct application of international criminal law has not set a trend. The case was decided at a time when the GoS grudgingly and quietly extended some cooperation to the ICC, still hoping that by cooperating in the Court's assessment of admissibility it would avoid ICC cases. Some Sudanese officials even considered asking the ICC for support in domestic trials. After the arrest warrants for Harun and Kushayb, however, the GoS ended all cooperation, became more explicit in its rejection of the Rome Statute and made fewer references to complementarity. No more instances of direct application of international criminal law followed, possibly because it could suggest an implicit recognition of the Statute. The Special Prosecutor's team claimed to focus on 'cases that affect many people', such as group attacks on villages, but one of the team members stated in an interview that he had no intention of applying international law directly. He said he had not heard of the case decided in Nyala, and added that he did 'not know the Rome Statute', even though he had participated in a course on international criminal law in The Hague a year earlier. Other sources of international law, such as the Geneva Conventions, could, in his view, not be applied as they failed to specify punishments. The amended Armed Forces Act and Criminal Act could not be applied retroactively. When asked 'what, then, is the applicable law?', he answered 'we will see when investigations are completed'.[434]

The appointment of a Special Prosecutor for Darfur and the subsequent shuffles in the position occasionally stirred up investigative activities. In 2010, the office of the Special Prosecutor for Darfur brought its first cases since the creation of the position in 2008 (which led one of the members of the Office of the Special Prosecutor to ask the interviewer: 'Are you going to put me in the Guinness Book of Records?').[435] The cases were judged by new special courts, established for the occasion, and governed by rules of evidence and procedure as determined by the Chief Justice for these special courts specifically; the Special Courts created in 2005 were not revived to try the Special Prosecutor's first cases.

---

[434] Interview with a member of the Special Prosecutor for Darfur's office, Khartoum, December 2008.
[435] Interview, August 2011.

One of the cases brought by the Special Prosecutor concerned an attack by JEM members on a GoS convoy in Sanyi Afandu (South Darfur) in May 2010, in which more than fifty government soldiers were killed. Five of the defendants claimed to be under the age of eighteen, but the medical authorities accepted only one of these claims as valid. The other four, together with five undisputedly adult defendants, were convicted and sentenced to capital punishment by hanging.[436] The Supreme Court quashed the decision on grounds of procedural errors. After a retrial, seven persons, including two who were minors at the time of the offence, were sentenced to death and three to imprisonment.[437]

Two other cases concerned bank robberies, one in Nyala and one in Kabkabiya. The Nyala bank robbery case led to the conviction of the accused, Mattar Kharalla Isgak, on counts of armed robbery and, after the quashing of the first judgment, also terrorism. His initial sentence to cross-amputation (right hand and left foot) was changed into imprisonment.[438] The Kabkabiya case led to convictions for armed robbery and killing. The other cases involved the abduction of UN-contracted pilots and the hijacking of a car of an international non-governmental organisation. In the former, one minor was sentenced to six years of reform school; the other suspects are still at large. In the latter, two suspects were convicted and sentenced to ten years' imprisonment.[439]

In the Tabra case, the slowness of which had been the purported reason for the replacement of one Special Prosecutor, arrest warrants have been issued, including for members of the Popular Defence Forces, and sent to the police and security authorities;[440] most remain to be executed.

In terms of crimes prosecuted, with the exception of the Tabra case, none of these cases involved widespread or systematic attacks on civilian populations or war crimes characteristic of the first years of the conflict. A member of the office of the Special Prosecutor explained that they started with 'recent crime', and that this was

---

[436] Interviews with lawyers involved, Nyala and Khartoum, August 2011.
[437] See African Centre for Justice and Peace Studies 2011.
[438] Case 30870.
[439] Interviews with lawyers involved, Nyala, August 2011. See also 'Carjackers in World Vision case convicted in Darfur' 2011.
[440] 'Darfur crime prosecutor admits impact of politics on legal cases' 2010.

intended to 'stop the signal of lawlessness'. In due course, they would work backwards, he said.[441]

While there are several factors confounding any assessment of causation,[442] the timing of the few (supposed) domestic proceedings and officials' references to actions by the ICC suggest sufficient correlation between complementarity and the proceedings to consider them Sudanese responses to the ICC's complementarity principle. A prosecutor tasked with conflict-related crimes in Darfur, for instance, stated in an interview shortly after the ICC Prosecutor requested the arrest warrant for President Bashir that he 'read everything they [the OTP] have, all the charges in the applications'.[443] One of the most senior officials in the Ministry of Justice explained:

> We are now focusing on domestic proceedings, in accordance with the complementarity principle. The ICC has no jurisdiction. But even if it had jurisdiction: there would be complementarity.[444]

However, again, as with the amendments to laws and the establishment of courts, the catalysing effect on (purported) developments in Sudanese proceedings is more an indirect effect of complementarity stemming from attempts to satisfy the international community, in particular the Security Council, than an effort to render the ICC's

---

[441] Discussion with a former member of the Special Prosecutor's team, Khartoum, July 2011.

[442] Investigating and prosecuting crimes is a core responsibility of governments and need not be an effect catalysed by complementarity. Indeed, Sudan Bar Association 2008e:4 underlined that Sudan is conducting proceedings for conflict-related crimes 'according to its own conviction'. A prosecutor appointed to investigate conflict-related crimes in Darfur stressed that he has 'nothing to do with the ICC' (interview, Khartoum, December 2008). The fact that bodies other than the ICC have pressured Sudanese authorities to conduct more domestic proceedings constitutes another confounding factor (see e.g. Human Rights Council 2007b:Annex 1, in particular recommendation 3.1). The increase in prosecuted rape cases observed in the town of Nyala (see McDoom 2008), for instance, was not catalysed by complementarity. These prosecutions are not an attempt to render cases inadmissible before the ICC but an answer to successfully targeted pressure on certain enforcement agencies by international organisations with a presence in the area and local human rights lawyers (interviews with human rights lawyers in Nyala, Nyala, December 2008).

[443] Interview with a member of the office of the Special Prosecutor for Darfur, Khartoum, December 2008.

[444] Interview with a senior official in the Ministry of Justice, Khartoum, December 2008.

327

cases inadmissible on grounds of article 17. Whereas the Rome Statute and the Court's first case law would require genuine domestic proceedings against the same person for the same conduct and same incidents as covered by the OTP's case for the latter to be inadmissible on grounds of complementarity, the GoS expected the Security Council to be satisfied when Sudan addressed impunity in respect of the overall situation in Darfur. As a former Minister of Foreign Affairs recounted:

> We were trying to satisfy the UN. The UN has obliged us to cooperate [with the ICC]. We wanted to convince the Security Council that we were able and willing. We set up courts.[445]

Sudan believed that apparent action to counter impunity was required to convince the Council to vote in favour of a deferral pursuant to article 16, and, more generally, to persuade individual states, in particular the US, to lift their punitive measures against the GoS. These states had emphasised that Sudan had to 'move' on the accountability front in Darfur, without setting requirements as strict as in article 17 of the Statute and the Court's case law on complementarity.

CONCLUSION: COMPLEMENTARITY'S CATALYSING EFFECT IN SUDAN

The GoS's denial of the ICC's intervention notwithstanding, complementarity catalysed several processes in Sudan. Various domestic accountability mechanisms were created, laws were amended and transitional and traditional justice received more attention in peace negotiations and other fora. Nonetheless, unlike in Uganda, the domestic conflict paradigm has not (yet) been expanded to include a legal dimension. Immunities have continued to block domestic proceedings. As in Uganda, the only effect that could render ICC cases inadmissible, namely, genuine domestic proceedings for conflict-related crimes, was difficult to discern.

Overall, the ICC's intervention sometimes seems to have had the opposite to a catalysing effect. The topic of accountability was taken off the agenda of the Abuja peace talks because mediators, rebel movements and observers considered it to be dealt with by the ICC. The space for debate on issues related to justice for conflict-related

---

[445] Interview with a former Minister of Foreign Affairs, Khartoum, November 2008.

crimes was restricted after the ICC's intervention, in particular after the ICC Prosecutor's application for a warrant of arrest for the Sudanese head of state. While it is difficult to assess what would have happened had the ICC not intervened, one can observe that the ICC's intervention has had a retarding rather than catalysing effect in these areas.

The absence in Sudan of some of the effects catalysed by complementarity in Uganda, most notably the expansion of the conflict paradigm with a legal dimension, can be explained by the fact that in Sudan there has been far less space for normative processes than in Uganda. In Sudan, unlike in Uganda, there has been no coalescence of a cost–benefit analysis on the government's part and the interests of norm entrepreneurs in promoting accountability. Perceiving itself as under attack by yet another instrument of Western states, the GoS, or more specifically the NCP, shut down the already limited public debate on sensitive issues such as international criminal justice.[446] As a result, the opportunities for NGOs and human rights activists became even narrower than they were before. Rather than opening a window for the promotion of international norms, which it did in Uganda, the ICC's intervention in Sudan made horizontal transnational normative processes more difficult.[447] It was only when the African Union High-Level Panel on Darfur presented transitional justice as an alternative to criminal justice alone that transitional justice was inserted as an item on the agenda of the Doha negotiations and that it became a topic for discussion with the GoS. To some extent it was the character of the messenger that made the message

---

[446] Freedom of expression is generally more limited in Sudan than in Uganda, and even more so since the ICC's intervention. (On the freedom of the press, see e.g. Freedom House 2011, where Uganda is considered 'partly free' with a shared 112th rank and Sudan 'not free' with a shared 168th position (out of 196)).

[447] The GoS has not been able to prevent all transnational processes. Leaders of displaced persons in camps in Darfur are in touch with Hollywood celebrities (e.g. Jolie 2007), and echo the 'Save Darfur Coalition' in stating that they are victims of 'genocide'. Babies born in camps have been named Okampo ('Darfur refugees named their children Okampo – Farrow' 2009). Children in a camp for displaced persons in Darfur who had put a rope around a hedgehog's neck commented: 'This is Bashir and we are taking him to the International Criminal Court' (interview with a representative of an international organisation, El-Fasher, December 2008). Ideas about the conflict's causes and solutions have been influenced by international concepts and actors (see also De Waal 2004b). But these are not effects specifically of complementarity.

swallowable for the GoS; a senior Sudanese legal advisor observed that the Sudanese 'prefer an African solution to that of the international community'.[448] But it was also due to the contents: transitional justice allows for a balancing of pursued aims (peace, justice, reconciliation) that international criminal justice does not.

The OTP, for its part, initially paid more attention to complementarity with respect to Darfur, and by doing so encouraged domestic proceedings, than it had done with respect to Uganda. Attempting to reach an *entente* with the GoS,[449] the OTP stressed that the GoS still had a chance to end the ICC's involvement on grounds of complementarity.[450] Only once the GoS's response to the first arrest warrants dashed the Prosecutor's hopes for cooperation from Sudan did he change his cautious approach into one of full confrontation.[451]

Most of the processes that were catalysed by complementarity stemmed from cost–benefit analyses on the part of the government. Perceiving the ICC's intervention to be against its interests, the GoS tried to end it by showcasing efforts to improve the situation in Darfur. Opting for pronouncement over actual proceedings and form over substance, the government took measures it considered

---

[448] Interview, Khartoum, February 2011.

[449] The OTP tried to avoid confrontation with the GoS in several ways. In its first reports to the Security Council, the OTP highlighted the instances in which Sudan granted cooperation, while making no mention of any refusal to cooperate, only of some outstanding requests (*Third Darfur Report*:9 and *Fourth Darfur Report*:9 and 10). In the discussion of domestic efforts to conduct proceedings, the OTP circumvented offending the GoS by focusing on the practical obstacles instead of the GoS's willingness (*Second Darfur Report*:6). The Prosecutor abstained from publicly making cooperation requests that the GoS was likely to turn down. For instance, Ocampo never publicly requested Sudan to allow ICC investigators to work in Darfur, arguing that the ICC's presence would be too dangerous for witnesses who cooperate with the Court (*Second Darfur Report*:4, *Third Darfur Report*:1 and *Fourth Darfur Report*:3 and 4). The OTP requested summonses to appear rather than warrants of arrest for Ahmad Harun and Ali Kushayb since summonses would not oblige Sudan to transfer them to the Court. The OTP hoped that the GoS would sacrifice these relatively less powerful figures to the ICC in the expectation that it would end its ICC problem. Ocampo reportedly made an informal statement to a high-level African Union official to the effect that 'if Sudan had handed over these two guys, it would not have had the problem of the President' (interview with AU advisors, Khartoum, December 2008). See also, Nouwen and Werner 2010a.

[450] ICC-OTP 2005c.   [451] See also Cryer 2011.

relatively inexpensive such as amendment of laws and establishment of special mechanisms.

The fact that complementarity has had a catalysing effect in Sudan, a state that is not a party to the Rome Statute and that is careful to reject the applicability of the entire Statute, reveals the principle's normative power.[452] For Sudan, complementarity is acceptable for two main reasons. First, it reflects state sovereignty, a fundamental tenet of international law. Secondly, it grants states considerable leeway as to how to conduct domestic proceedings for crimes within the jurisdiction of the Court. However, to the extent that Sudan embraces the principle of complementarity, it accepts a primary right to address impunity in general, including the right to decide which cases to investigate and prosecute, rather than a responsibility to investigate and prosecute the same cases as the ICC. The fact that even states not party to the Statute consider the principle to be legitimate may have enhanced its 'compliance pull',[453] but 'compliance' is of little relevance to complementarity when complementarity is considered a right rather than an obligation.

Remarkably, the effects were catalysed by complementarity only indirectly. The GoS hardly considered domestic proceedings with a view to challenging admissibility under article 17, if only because challenging admissibility could imply acceptance of the applicability of the Rome Statute. The GoS sought to tackle the problem where it originated, namely, in the Security Council. It aimed for the withdrawal of the referral (which would not bind the Court, as it is not

---

[452] For Sudanese officials expressing support for the principle of complementarity, see e.g. 'Dr Ghazi Salah El Din Attabani: "We have to pay an expensive political tax for resolving the Darfur crisis!"' 2008 ('Even if we are members, there is a section 17, which provides in the first paragraph that national criminal courts take the matter unless a country is not willing or not able. We are willing, we are able.'), 'Sudanese Justice Minister on Darfur crisis, efforts to achieve peace, AU force' 2006 ('We are fully convinced that the ICC must not have any jurisdiction in the matter of Darfur as long as we are serious in, have the desire to, and are capable of trying the crimes that are committed in Darfur. That is stated in the charter of the ICC itself.'), Sabderat 2008:[7] ('The ICC Prosecutor General had actually compromised the very obvious principles of international law, including the principle of complementarity enshrined in the Rome Statute 1998 itself, to the vicious pressures pounded on him by certain Western governments and pressure groups.') and interview with a long-standing member of parliament, Khartoum, November 2008 ('It is also the strongest logic in the Rome Statute itself that places an independent national judiciary above the ICC.').

[453] See, generally, Franck 1990.

provided for in the Statute) or a deferral pursuant to article 16. While the Statute does not stipulate any conditions for the Council to take into account when deciding whether or not to request a deferral,[454] Sudanese officials came to believe that complementarity plays a role in Security Council decision-making,[455] as is illustrated by the answer of a Sudanese judge to a question about plans for domestic proceedings:

> Now, [the GoS is] going to investigate and try Kushayb. He will be sacrificed. This would influence any article 16 decision in the Security Council. That is what Sarkozy has said.[456]

A prominent opposition leader similarly argued that the 'hybrid court' that he had proposed 'must be part of a package acceptable to the Security Council'.[457] The belief that the Security Council takes into account complementarity is also illustrated by a legal opinion provided by the University of Khartoum:[458]

> [F]or the requirements of justice, the [Security Council] would link the issue of achievement of peace to the issue of impunity. This would be done through inducement of the Sudan to introduce alternative means of justice to substitute for international criminal prosecution through the adoption of either of the following models:
> a. internal/international courts or mixed courts, in accordance with a UNSC resolution and upon an agreement with the UN along the model adopted with Sierra Leon[e] and other countries.
> b. establishment of real internal justice mechanisms, using mechanisms provided for in the CPA, to lead to national fair trials under international supervision. This provides a model for internal fair prosecution that substitutes for international criminal prosecution while striking at the same time a positive formula to achieve peace and justice and be satisfactory to all parties.[459]

---

[454] See Chapter 2, 'Other jurisdictional provisions: a deferral requested by the Security Council'.

[455] This has been encouraged by reports such as International Crisis Group 2009:ii, which recommends that partners in the Sudan peace process 'deliver a firm message in Khartoum that they will only consider a Security Council resolution suspending execution (via the procedure for one-year renewable deferral provided in Article 16 of the Rome Statute . . .) if the NCP first takes a series of specific and irreversible steps, including but not limited to acceptance of judicial reforms and transitional justice mechanisms as key elements of a Darfur settlement'.

[456] Interview with a Sudanese judge, Khartoum, November 2008.

[457] Al-Mahdi 2010:2.   [458] See also this chapter, above, n. 387.

[459] University of Khartoum 2008:11.

Hence, in addition to all the policy changes that it announced, and putting forward the argument that the ICC would jeopardise peace in Sudan and therefore was not in the 'interests of justice',[460] the GoS considered it necessary to demonstrate some action on domestic accountability for conflict-related crimes in order to garner the required international support for its diplomatic offensive against the ICC.[461]

Various international actors nourished Sudanese officials' belief that complementarity features in Security Council decision-making. For instance, by assessing complementarity as part of its consideration of whether or not the Council should refer the Darfur situation to the Court, the ICID suggested that complementarity is a relevant factor for the Security Council.[462] According to international newspapers, the UN Secretary-General, for his part, 'said [that] the Sudanese government should start its own "reasonable and credible" judicial process before seeking to defer al-Bashir's prosecution by the ICC'. The reporter continued: 'If Sudan launched judicial proceedings, Ban said it would then be up to the UN Security Council and the International Criminal Court to determine whether the measures taken by the Sudanese government would meet "the expectations and requirements of relevant provisions" of the council's resolution and the court's statute.'[463] The AUPD, too, suggested that the Security Council considers in its decision-making the extent to which Sudan addresses accountability.[464]

The fact that the Security Council is not legally required to consider admissibility when deciding whether or not to refer or defer a situation does not mean it makes no sense for it to do so. First, pragmatically, its referral would not have a long lifespan if all the ICC's cases were subsequently found to be inadmissible on grounds of complementarity. Secondly, consideration of provisions other than the relevant article, article 13(b) in case of a referral and article 16

---

[460] See Chapter 2, 'No ICC proceedings because of the "interests of justice"'.

[461] See Tisdall 2008. The Council itself had already demanded that the GoS address impunity e.g. in resolutions UN Doc. S/RES/1556 (2004):[6], and UN Doc. S/RES/1564 (2004):[7]. But, since the ICC's involvement, addressing impunity has come to be seen as a precondition for a deferral of ICC proceedings, which has given the demand a stronger compliance pull.

[462] See this chapter, above, 'Complementarity: the views of the ICID and the ICC'.

[463] 'UN chief: Sudan president could avoid prosecution' 2009 (emphasis added).

[464] See e.g. AU Doc. PSC/AHG/2(CCVII) 2009:[245], [249] and [339].

in case of a deferral, could imbue a discretionary decision with legal principle and hence constitute a defence against accusations of arbitrariness.

Whether the Security Council does so in practice or not, the fact that some states believe that the Council considers complementarity encourages complementarity's catalysing effect. Conducting domestic proceedings then becomes necessary not only for states that plan to challenge admissibility on grounds of article 17 but also for states that wish to avoid a Security Council referral pursuant to article 13(b), to obtain a Security Council deferral under article 16 or to influence any other Court-related, or even more generally, any related decision by the Security Council.[465] The Court's legal principle has become, or at least is believed to have become, one of the Council's political criteria.[466] This contributes to a political expectation on states to conduct proceedings for conflict-related crimes.

However, the Security Council's political criterion does not coincide with complementarity as a legal rule in the Statute. Whereas article 17 requires a state to address the same cases as the ICC if it wishes to obviate proceedings in the ICC, complementarity as a

---

[465] The expectation that the Security Council will take into account domestic accountability efforts is also visible in the Ugandan context. As is evident from the following clauses, the Agreement on Implementation and Monitoring Mechanisms 2008 envisages the Security Council's taking into account Ugandan preparations for domestic proceedings when deciding whether or not to grant Uganda's request to defer ICC proceedings: '[36] During the Transitional Period, the Government shall urgently take the necessary steps to establish national mechanisms of accountability and reconciliation as are provided for in the Agreement on Accountability and Reconciliation. In this regard, the Government shall give priority to commencing criminal investigations and establishing the special division of the High Court. [37] *On the basis of the steps taken under clause 36 of this Agreement*, the Government shall request the UN Security Council to adopt a resolution under Chapter VII of the Charter of the United Nations, requesting the International Criminal Court to defer all investigations and prosecutions against the leaders of the Lord's Resistance Army.' (emphasis added).

[466] In the Ugandan context, too, diplomats have suggested that domestic proceedings feature in Security Council decision-making on deferrals (interview with a diplomat from a European state, Kampala, October 2008: 'There is no official position on a Security Council deferral [but] our legal experts at headquarters are sceptical about Uganda's capacity to take this [domestic LRA] case far.'; and interview with another diplomat of a European state, Kampala, October 2008: 'When the talks progressed, [our headquarters] were ready to support a deferral as long as they would consider the national proceedings adequate.').

political criterion in Security Council decision-making is believed to require the state to address impunity in general. Sudan initially believed that this meant demonstrating that its system was 'willing' and 'able'. Hence Sudanese officials pointed to fair trial guarantees in Sudanese law and the Sudanese judiciary's being a role model for the Arab world. In addition, they established extra courts and adopted new laws to demonstrate Sudan's efforts to end impunity.[467] When GoS officials realised that Security Council members required actual proceedings, they still did not deem it necessary for these proceedings to involve the same persons as the ICC's cases.[468] This explains why, for instance, Ahmad Harun argued that the Security Council may defer the ICC proceedings in the case against the President if Sudan were to try him and Ali Kushayb:

> The Americans ... are talking about a certain process that should take place. [The ICC's case against the Sudanese President] could be ended if Harun and Kushayb are presented before local courts.[469]

A proposal by the Arab League was based on the same belief that the Security Council would request a deferral of the proceedings against Bashir if Sudan addressed impunity in Darfur generally.[470] According to a legal advisor in the Ministry of Foreign Affairs, the French for their part had proposed to the Sudanese, in the margins of the Doha negotiations, that, if Kushayb were tried domestically and Harun stripped of all official responsibilities, Bashir could benefit from a deferral of his case by the Security Council in accordance with article 16 of the Statute.[471]

---

[467] Similarly, Uganda included traditional justice in the transitional-justice package of the Juba agreements to show its comprehensive approach towards accountability, even though traditional justice would probably not render ICC cases inadmissible.

[468] The UN Secretary-General has been ambiguous on this point. See 'UN chief: Sudan president could avoid prosecution' 2009 ('The secretary-general was then asked whether he was suggesting that the Sudanese courts launch their own prosecution against their president. He did not answer the question but told reporters that he had urged al-Bashir "to take, first of all domestic judiciary measures – very credible (ones)" which could then be considered by the Security Council and the ICC.').

[469] Interview with Ahmad Harun, Khartoum, December 2008. See also Polgreen and Gettlemen 2008.

[470] 'Egypt warns Sudan that Bashir not immune from ICC prosecution' 2008.

[471] Discussion with a legal advisor in the Ministry of Foreign Affairs, Khartoum, June 2011. Whether the French actually said this in these terms is of little relevance – what matters more is that the GoS *believes* the Security Council to consider complementarity.

The fact that many of the phenomena catalysed by complementarity in Sudan have so far been cosmetic in character does not prevent them from facilitating domestic proceedings in the future. Courts established and laws enacted may one day be used, depending on the extent to which the (next) government allows this.

CHAPTER 5

PARADOXES UNRAVELLED: EXPLANATIONS FOR COMPLEMENTARITY'S WEAK CATALYSING EFFECT ON DOMESTIC PROCEEDINGS

> States not only have the right to exercise their criminal
> jurisdiction over those allegedly responsible for the commis-
> sion of crimes that fall within the jurisdiction of the Court,
> they are also under an existing duty to do so as explicitly
> stated in the Statute's preambular paragraph 6. However, it
> should be borne in mind that a core rationale underlying the
> concept of complementarity aims at 'strik[ing] a balance
> between safeguarding the primacy of domestic proceedings
> vis-à-vis the [. . .] Court on the one hand, and the goal of
> the Rome Statute to "put an end to impunity" on the other
> hand . . .'.
>
> ICC Pre-Trial Chamber II[1]

For all the effects it has catalysed, the complementarity principle has to date not led to a substantial increase in Ugandan and Sudanese proceedings in respect of cases within the ICC's purview. This is remarkable in that only genuine domestic proceedings can render the ICC's cases inadmissible on grounds of complementarity. Part of the explanation may simply be time – investigations and prosecutions require preparation, and the ICC began its work, and its catalysing role, only a decade ago. However, some developments in Uganda and Sudan, or the lack thereof, challenge the very assumptions underpinning the widespread expectation of a catalysing effect on domestic proceedings – assumptions with respect to the normative character of complementarity and with respect to the cost–benefit analyses engaged in by states.[2]

---

[1] *Admissibility Decision Ruto et al. (PTC)*:[44] and *Admissibility Decision Muthaura et al. (PTC)*:[40].

[2] See Chapter 1, 'Assumptions underlying the expectation of a catalysing effect'.

COMPLEMENTARITY'S NORMATIVE CHARACTER

A number of factors contribute to an explanation of the weakness of complementarity as an expectation on states to investigate and prosecute conflict-related crimes. The underlying factor is that, as has been argued in Chapter 2, there is no legal obligation to conduct domestic proceedings under the Statute. To the extent that complementarity as big idea contains a non-legal political expectation, its catalysing effect has been thwarted by three other factors.

First, there has been considerable confusion, ambiguity and even misrepresentation with respect to the content of complementarity as the principle that grants states the primary right to investigate and prosecute crimes within the Court's jurisdiction. The clearest example of norm misrepresentation is the gradual replacement of the explanation of complementarity as a state's primary right to investigate and prosecute by a seemingly similar but essentially different understanding according to which the international and domestic jurisdiction 'complement' each other, the former being responsible for the big cases and the latter for the smaller ones.

Secondly, even more than with complementarity as admissibility rule granting states a primary right, there is ambiguity with respect to complementarity as big idea entailing the responsibility or duty of states to investigate and prosecute. To some extent this ambiguity reflects the discrepancy between on the one hand the big-idea discourse on complementarity as a reminder to states of their responsibility to investigate and prosecute, and on the other the Rome Statute that creates a court on the very assumption that states do not always fulfil that responsibility. The Court's interpretation of the Statute, and particularly the OTP's policy of inviting self-referrals, has intensified this normative paradox of complementarity. By prioritising the fight against impunity over the responsibility of the state and by providing too ready a back-up, the Court diminishes the expectation on states to investigate and prosecute and thus the potential catalysing effect of complementarity on domestic proceedings. The expectation has been further countered by the emergence of a *pro-ICC ideology*, which, on various grounds, prefers ICC proceedings to domestic ones.

Finally, at the domestic level, the context in Uganda and Sudan has not been hospitable to the infiltration of a norm according to which the state has a responsibility to investigate and prosecute conflict-related crimes. In part, this context is specific to Uganda and Sudan;

in part it is related to the character of conflict-related crimes and thus also potentially confronts other states dealing with such crimes.

Complementarity as primary right: confusion, ambiguity and misrepresentation

A first reason why complementarity's catalysing effect on domestic proceedings has remained limited is confusion, ambiguity and misrepresentation with respect to its content. As Chayes and Chayes have demonstrated, norm compliance is enhanced by norm clarity and norm-clarifying procedures.[3] Since, as Chapter 2 has argued, complementarity is an admissibility rule that binds the Court – not states – there is little for states to 'comply' with. Nonetheless, clarity about the fact that this admissibility rule accords states the primary right to investigate and prosecute crimes within the Court's jurisdiction could enhance complementarity's catalysing effect by reminding states of that right and encouraging them to take advantage of it. In fact, however, there has been considerable confusion, ambiguity and even misrepresentation of complementarity as a primary right.

One example of confusion is the widespread idea among national as well as international officials in Uganda and Sudan that willingness and ability are assessed on a situation-wide, rather than case-by-case, basis.[4] In Sudan, the assessment by the International Commission of Inquiry on Darfur (ICID) of the legal system as a whole has contributed to this idea.[5] In the Uganda situation, the PTC judges have fostered the same idea by suggesting that they can make a final determination regarding admissibility once the laws to be applied by the Ugandan War Crimes Court have been determined.[6] This confusion potentially limits complementarity's catalysing effect by suggesting that an overhaul of the entire domestic justice system is required, as opposed to genuine proceedings in the particular case.

Another example of norm confusion is the pervasive idea that a determination of admissibility is permanent. When interviewed in 2008, many Ugandan and Sudanese officials and officials from international organisations believed that, once a case had been held admissible, the facts relevant to admissibility were frozen, whether this was at the stage of the ICID report, at the moment of the referral

---

[3] Chayes and Chayes 1993 and Chayes and Chayes 1995.
[4] See Chapter 2, 'The complementarity assessment is case-specific'.
[5] See Chapter 4, nn. 81 and 90 and accompanying text.   [6] See Chapter 3, n. 613.

or when the Court issued arrest warrants. Subsequent domestic proceedings would not be able to render ICC cases inadmissible. Such a view obviously forestalls any catalysing effect, because after an admissibility assessment domestic proceedings would be futile.[7] The OTP has at times contributed to this view:

> [The efforts of the ICC and regional organisations] complement each other ... In accordance with the Rome Statute, the ICC is a Court of last resort, complementary to the national judiciary. We have six cases. Should Regional organizations succeed in promoting national accountability mechanisms for the victims of other crimes, and stop new abuses, we would not need to further intervene.[8]

The statement suggests that national accountability mechanisms are relevant only to cases that the ICC has not yet opened.

The clearest example of norm misrepresentation or norm hijacking has been the use of the term 'complementarity' in its literal rather than legal meaning.[9] Whereas complementarity in the legal sense is a rule of priority that determines a competition for jurisdiction, complementarity in the literal sense is used to describe a collaborative effort to end impunity in which the ICC's proceedings and domestic efforts 'complement' each other.[10] The OTP has often referred to complementarity in this literal sense, for instance in the following statement:

> [C]omplementarity ... may play a part in preventing impunity. If the ICC has successfully prosecuted the leaders of a State or organisation, the situation in the country concerned might then be such as to inspire confidence in the national jurisdiction. The reinvigorated national authorities might now be able to deal with the other cases. In other instances, the international community might be ready to combine

---

[7] For instance, a Sudanese political observer explained as follows the lull in domestic investigations and prosecutions between the issuance of the arrest warrants for Harun and Kushayb and the request for Bashir's warrant: 'After the Prosecutor requested the summonses to appear the show ended, the show had failed and we had all been indicted' (interview, Khartoum, September 2007).

[8] *Prosecutor's Darfur Statement SC June 2009*:8. In his first reports to the Security Council on Sudan, the Prosecutor, however, correctly explained that the complementarity assessment was a continuous process. See Chapter 4, n. 93.

[9] See also Schabas 2004:85, arguing that the term 'complementarity' is 'a misnomer' for a rule of precedence, in which ultimately one jurisdiction has priority in a specific case. 'Subsidiarity' would have been more telling, but according to Crawford 2003:138–9 this term was not chosen because the EU had already 'taken' it.

[10] Some academic literature has also used the term in this way, see e.g. Bos 1998:253.

national and international efforts to ensure that perpetrators of serious international crimes are brought to justice.[11]

In this context, the OTP uses 'complementarity' to describe a 'division of labour' in which the ICC focuses on alleged perpetrators bearing the greatest responsibility, while the state, possibly with international assistance, handles the remaining cases, whether through formal court proceedings or 'alternative means'.[12]

Probably because both are based on an idea of 'positive' and 'cooperative'[13] – in fact what is meant is 'uncompetitive' – relations between the ICC and domestic jurisdictions, it is mostly in the context of the policy of positive complementarity that the term complementarity has been used to describe a division of labour between the ICC and domestic jurisdictions.[14] Indeed, some authors claim that such a division of labour is a 'tactic' of positive complementarity.[15]

However, this argument, and the use of complementarity in its literal sense more generally, is misleading because it ignores the fact that the admissibility rules giving effect to the principle of complementarity apply to *all* cases before the ICC, including those pertaining to persons bearing the greatest responsibility. Thus, if a state genuinely investigates or prosecutes a case involving those bearing the greatest responsibility for conduct within the Court's jurisdiction, complementarity grants that state primacy over the ICC, even if this does not reflect or result in 'positive' relations with the ICC. Any policy of

---

[11] ICC-OTP 2003d:7. For other examples of the OTP using complementarity in its literal rather than legal meaning, see: ICC-OTP 2006d:8, Moreno-Ocampo 2007b:8, ICC-OTP 2006e:10 and Moreno-Ocampo 2011:22 ('the Court should handle a limited number of cases. My Office ... will select for prosecution those most responsible for the most serious crimes, based on the evidence. The strength of the system lies therefore in the possibility for shared responsibility and complementary action between the Court and the domestic judiciary.').

[12] For the suggestion of alternative means, see ICC-OTP 2003d:3. For similar suggestions for such a division of labour, see e.g. ICC-OTP 2003c:4, Moreno-Ocampo 2004c:1–2 and 4, Moreno-Ocampo 2008a:5, Schabas 2003:3, El Zeidy 2002:967, and also 874 and 876 and Totten and Tyler 2008:1070–1 and 1099–1100. Cf. *contra* Bitti 2007.

[13] Or, in the words of one OTP official cited by Verrijn Stuart 2005, the policy of positive complementarity would make it possible 'to establish a warm and fuzzy partnership within [situation] countries with all parties to a conflict'.

[14] See e.g. Moreno-Ocampo 2011:26, ICC-ASP/8/Res.9 Annex 4 (2010):[15] and [24]–[25] and ICC Registrar Arbia and Bassy 2011:62.

[15] Burke-White 2008b:59–63. Similarly, El Zeidy 2008a:405, El Zeidy 2008b:305 and Stahn 2008:109–10.

positive complementarity aimed at establishing cooperative relations cannot overrule the law of complementarity which grants states the primary right to investigate and prosecute crimes within the Court's jurisdiction.

And yet, some of the ICC judges appear to share the OTP's preferred reading of complementarity as a division-of-labour rule. One former ICC judge, for instance, writes:

> What then is the ultimate purpose of complementarity? There is no doubt that one important goal is to establish a division of labour between national jurisdictions and the ICC, under which the Court should essentially concentrate on those who have the major responsibility for the crimes involved.[16]

The fact that this interpretation of complementarity is without judicial endorsement has not precluded it from influencing how complementarity is understood: the public's understanding of the principle is based more on the OTP's public statements than on considerations in judicial decisions. The public understanding, in turn, influences complementarity's catalysing effect.

In Sudan, for example, international officials have replicated the misleading use of the term and thereby discouraged Sudanese proceedings. When the Sudanese Minister of Justice was quoted as stating that the Special Criminal Court on the Events in Darfur was 'considered a substitute to the International Criminal Court', an ICC public information advisor responded:

> Before the prosecutor decided to take on the Darfur case, he first analysed the admissibility of the case, which included ICC complementarity with what the Sudanese legal system was doing ... Given that the prosecutor would focus his investigations on individuals who bear the greatest criminal responsibility for crimes committed in Darfur, the analysis concluded that an ICC investigation would complement [the work of] the Sudanese judiciary.[17]

The Minister of Justice, quite rightly, retorted with an invocation of article 17 of the Statute. The Special Representative of the UN Secretary-General in Sudan, however, argued that the Sudanese SCCED could 'not be a substitute for the International Criminal Court' and suggested that the two courts operate side by side, referring to the ICTR's operating alongside Rwandan national courts.[18]

[16] Politi 2011:145.
[17] 'Sudan: judiciary challenges ICC over Darfur cases' 2005.   [18] *Ibid.*

Even where international actors did not copy the division-of-labour reading of complementarity, the OTP has summarised their work by stating that they did. Thus, whilst the African Union High-Level Panel on Darfur discussed complementarity in its legal sense, in other words as applicable to all cases including those involving persons bearing the greatest responsibility, the Prosecutor summarised the AUPD's report as proposing 'additional solutions including the creation of a hybrid court to complement the action of the ICC, to address those cases that the ICC will not deal with'.[19]

In Uganda, as Chapter 3 has begun to reveal,[20] the distorted understanding of complementarity as assigning the big cases to the ICC and the smaller ones to domestic mechanisms is even more prevalent. In Uganda, unlike in Sudan, the ICC has an office to conduct its 'outreach', in other words to explain the ICC and the Rome Statute to Ugandans and others present in Uganda. Asked how the office dealt with the public's confusion between the ICD (the Ugandan International Crimes Division) and the ICC, one ICC outreach officer responded:

> We tell them: 'this is complementarity at play. Those who cannot be tried by ICC will be done at the national level: it is a complementary court.'[21]

Against this background it is not surprising that Ugandan reporters write in their articles: 'Recently, Kampala tasked a division of the High Court to try alleged war criminals that the ICC is unlikely to deal with',[22] or:

> Since the ICC does not have the resources to try all suspected war criminals, its mandate is to prosecute only those deemed most

---

[19] Moreno-Ocampo 2009b:9. See also *Tenth Darfur Report*:[103], *Prosecutor's Darfur Statement SC December 2009*:[18] ('[During a meeting between the AUPD and the OTP] [i]t was ... clarified that the cases against President Bashir, Ahmad Harun and Ali Kushayb as well as Abu Garda and two other rebel commanders will be decided by the judges of the International Criminal Court. Additionally we had exchanges on the complementary role that other courts can play to investigate *other* perpetrators.') and the Prosecutor's Special Advisor Méndez 2011:46.

[20] See the explanation of complementarity given by a judge on the Ugandan International Crimes Division, cited in Chapter 3, n. 605.

[21] Interview with two officers of the ICC outreach office, Kampala, November 2011.

[22] Ogola 2010.

responsible for atrocities, with the remainder being tried by national courts, provided that the local judiciary is capable of doing this.[23]

As one lawyer's explanation of the ICD's workload illustrates, the division-of-labour reading of complementarity has been so successfully promoted that the international jargon of 'the big fish' for the international courts and 'the small fry' for national mechanisms is literally being vernacularised: 'In the ICD . . . we try the tilapia, not the nile perch.'[24]

This distorted explanation of complementarity goes against the stated aim of positive complementarity, namely, of encouraging domestic proceedings. The transformation of complementarity into a division-of-labour rule promotes the notion that the ICC is always responsible for those bearing the greatest responsibility and that the state may handle (only) the remaining cases.[25]

Complementarity as big idea: a responsibility to investigate and prosecute?

Even more than over the content of complementarity as admissibility rule, there is ambiguity over the content of complementarity as big idea entailing the 'responsibility' of states to investigate and prosecute. The term 'responsibility' means all things to all people. The Rome Statute, positing complementarity merely as a norm relevant to when the Court may exercise jurisdiction, provides no guidance. Nonetheless, support from states for, and the ICC's insistence on, such a responsibility could crystallise such a norm. For example, the Security Council's consideration of complementarity as a political criterion[26] and the Prosecutor's espoused policy of positive complementarity[27]

---

[23] Oketch 2010.   [24] Interview, Kampala, November 2011.

[25] There are signs of this notion's spreading in other countries, too. For instance, the Principal Public Prosecutor Office of the Central African Republic requested the Court of Appeal of Bangui hold that 'the offences affecting persons, referred to as "blood crimes" (crimes de sang), should be tried by the ICC and that the economic crimes should be tried by the Cour Criminelle' (see *Judgment Admissibility Challenge Bemba (AC)*:[40b]; in the end, the Central African Republic referred the situation on its territory to the ICC). Similarly, in Côte d'Ivoire, President Ouattara wrote to the ICC Prosecutor arguing that the Ivorian justice system was dealing with minor infractions, but that those bearing the greatest responsibility should be addressed by the Court (see 'Letter President Ouattara to the Office of the Prosecutor' 2011).

[26] See Chapter 4, 'Encouraging more trials, prosecutions and/or investigations?' and 'Conclusion: complementarity's catalysing effect in Sudan'.

[27] See Chapter 1 and Chapter 2, 'The policy of positive complementarity'.

suggest that international organisations, the member states of these organisations and the OTP foster a non-legal expectation that domestic proceedings be pursued. Clarification of any such expectation by the ICC or political actors could enhance its normativity and thus its catalysing effect.

However, two ICC-related developments have in fact weakened this expectation. First, the *normative paradox of complementarity* is that the creation of the 'Rome System', and particularly the way it has so far been implemented, may, by projecting the Court as an institution to take over from states the responsibility to investigate and prosecute conflict-related crimes, actually undermine the expectation on states to discharge that responsibility. Secondly, this expectation has been further undercut by the emergence of a *pro-ICC ideology* that counteracts complementarity both as a primary right and as a responsibility to investigate and prosecute.

The normative paradox of complementarity

The roots of the normative paradox of complementarity are in the Rome Statute. On the one hand, the preamble recalls every state's duty to exercise its criminal jurisdiction over those responsible for international crimes. It is with reference to this recital that many authors have argued that complementarity reflects states' responsibility or duty to investigate and prosecute the crimes within the Court's jurisdiction.

On the other hand, as argued in Chapter 2, neither this preambular recital nor any other provision in the Statute *creates* an obligation for a state to investigate or prosecute.[28] What the Statute does create is a court that is based on the very assumption that states do not always investigate and prosecute. The Statute even allows states to refer situations on their own territory to the Court. The Japanese representative may have observed during the negotiations of the Statute that the Court 'should not be used as a "garbage can" into which national court systems could dump criminals that they should be punishing at the national level',[29] but no sooner had the Court been created than

---

[28] Akhavan 2010b therefore proposes an Optional Protocol to the Rome Statute containing an express and enforceable obligation to exercise national jurisdiction.

[29] L/2773 (1996).

Uganda,[30] the DRC[31] and the CAR,[32] and later also Mali,[33] effectively outsourced their responsibility to investigate and prosecute to the ICC.[34] The Statute has thus created not just a court of last resort, but also a court of convenience.

The Rome System lacks not only a norm obliging states to investigate and prosecute but also any infrastructure for the enforcement of such a norm.[35] Admissibility proceedings do assess whether or not

---

[30] See Chapter 3.

[31] 'Letter of the President of the Democratic Republic of the Congo, Joseph Kabila, to the Prosecutor of the International Criminal Court' 2004, stating: 'En raison de la situation particulière que connaît mon pays, les autorités compétentes ne sont maulheureusement pas en mesure de mener des enquêtes sur les crimes mentionnés ci-dessus ni d'engager les poursuites nécessaires sans la participation de la Cour Pénale Internationale.'

[32] As reported by the ICC Appeals Chamber in *Judgment Admissibility Challenge Bemba (AC)*:[45], the Central African 'Court of Cassation held that "there can be no doubt that the Central African judicial services are unable genuinely to investigate or prosecute" in the proceedings against Mr Patassé, Mr Bemba and others ... The Court of Cassation therefore held that "recourse to international cooperation remains in this case the sole means of averting such impunity" and as such, in its view, the Senior Investigating Judge erred *in not availing himself of this option*' (footnotes omitted, emphasis added).

[33] 'Letter from Malick Coulibali, Minister of Justice of the Republic of Mali, to the Prosecutor of the ICC, "Renvoi de la situation au Mali"' 2012:1 ('l'Etat du Mali ... a l'honneur de déférer devant vous les crimes les plus graves commis depuis le mois de Janvier 2012 sur son territoire dans la mesure où les juridictions maliennes sont dans l'impossibilité de poursuivre ou juger les auteurs').

[34] Not a state party to the Statute, Côte d'Ivoire could not refer the situation on its own territory, but it has used the possibility of RS, art. 12(3) to accept the Court's jurisdiction on an *ad hoc* basis. It explained its decision to do so also with reference to the fact that the Court was better suited to investigate and prosecute the crimes within its jurisdiction. See 'Letter President Ouattara to the Office of the Prosecutor' 2011:2 ('Dans ce contexte, et après consultation avec le parquet général et les autorités judiciaires, il apparaît ... que la justice ivoirienne n'est, à ce jour, pas la mieux placée pour connaître des crimes les plus graves commis au cours des derniers mois et toute tentative d'en traduire en justice les plus hauts responsables risquerait de se heurter à des difficultés de tous ordres. Par la présente, j'entends confirmer mon souhait que votre Bureau mène en Côte d'Ivoire des enquêtes indépendantes et impartiales sur les crimes les plus graves commis depuis le 28 novembre 2010 sur l'ensemble du territoire ivoirien, et fasse en sorte que les personnes portant la responsabilité pénale la plus lourde pour ces crimes soient identifiées, poursuivies et traduites devant la Cour pénale internationale.').

[35] See also *Admissibility Judgment Katanga AC*:[86]. On the importance of an enforcement framework for norm compliance, see Finnemore and Sikkink 1998, Chayes and Chayes 1993 and Chayes and Chayes 1995.

genuine domestic proceedings have taken place, but they result only in a finding on admissibility; the Court does not pronounce upon state responsibility. The Statute does not provide for other monitoring mechanisms either, for instance reporting procedures by which states must inform the Assembly of States Parties (ASP) of domestic implementation of any obligations arising from the Statute. The procedure in the Statute that seems to come closest to sanctioning states for not investigating and prosecuting domestically is a finding of inability and unwillingness genuinely to investigate or prosecute, which could be an implicit 'naming and shaming' instrument. However, as Chapter 2 has argued,[36] an assessment of willingness and ability is necessary only in the event of domestic proceedings in the same case as the ICC's. Moreover, as the section on cost–benefit assessments will show, states have not necessarily considered such a finding to be a sanction; indeed, they themselves have at times argued that they are 'unable'.[37]

The Court has implicitly recognised the normative paradox of complementarity. PTC II presented complementarity as a principle '*reconciling* the States' persisting duty to exercise jurisdiction over international crimes with the establishment of a permanent international criminal court having competence over the same crimes'.[38] In another case, Trial Chamber II went a step further, conceptualising a self-referral and transfer of a suspect to the Court as a fulfilment of the duty to exercise its jurisdiction and implicitly referring to the idea of the ICC as a court of convenience:

> [L]a Chambre rappelle que, comme le prévoit le sixième alinéa du préambule du Statut 'il est du devoir de chaque État de soumettre à sa juridiction criminelle les responsables de crimes internationaux'. Cependant *si un État juge plus opportun* que la Cour mène les enquêtes et les poursuites, il n'en remplit pas moins ses obligations au regard du principe de complémentarité s'il assure le transfert du suspect dans les meilleurs délais et apporte à la Cour sa coopération pleine et entière conformément au chapitre IX du Statut.[39]

On appeal, the defendant argued that this reasoning 'violates paragraph 6 of the Preamble, as well as the fundamental values underlying

---

[36] 'The substance of complementarity: the criteria for inadmissibility'.
[37] See e.g. n. 32 above.
[38] *LRA Admissibility Decision (PTC)*:[34] (emphasis added).
[39] *Admissibility Decision Katanga (TC)*:[79] (emphasis added). See Chapter 2, n. 215, on the unfortunate use of 'obligations au regard du principe de complémentarité'.

the complementarity principle as inherent in the Preamble, Articles 1 and 17 of the Rome Statute', and continued: 'Indeed, if States are granted an unconditional right not to prosecute, this would seriously jeopardize any encouragement for States to prosecute domestically and thereby endanger the correct application of the principle of complementarity.'[40] Explicitly mentioning a catalysing effect as one of complementarity's purposes and reminding the Prosecutor of his inaugural statement, the defendant argued:

> One of the objectives of the establishment of the ICC was to encourage States to investigate and prosecute international crimes and to reinforce their legal capacity to do so. The drafters of the Rome Statute envisaged the ICC as a Court of last resort to come into action in the most exceptional circumstances only, when a State is genuinely unable or unwilling to take action within its own jurisdiction. A successful ICC has no or very few cases, the majority of cases being investigated and prosecuted domestically.[41]

The Appeals Chamber disagreed and followed the PTC's image of complementarity as a principle balancing a state's duty and the creation of the Court. However, in the Appeals Chamber's view the principle balances the duty to exercise jurisdiction not with the creation of the ICC, but with the fight against impunity:

> The Appeals Chamber is not persuaded by the argument of the Appellant that it would be to negate the obligation of States to prosecute crimes if they were allowed to relinquish domestic jurisdiction in favour of the International Criminal Court. The Appeals Chamber acknowledges that States have a duty to exercise their criminal jurisdiction over international crimes. The Chamber must *nevertheless* stress that the complementarity principle, as enshrined in the Statute, strikes a balance between safeguarding the primacy of domestic proceedings *vis-à-vis* the International Criminal Court on the one hand, and the goal of the Rome Statute to 'put an end to impunity' on the other hand. If States do not or cannot investigate and, where necessary, prosecute, the International Criminal Court must be able to step in.[42]

---

[40] *Defence Appeal Admissibility Katanga*:[64].   [41] *Ibid.*:[67].

[42] *Admissibility Judgment Katanga (AC)*:[85] (footnotes omitted, emphasis added). The concept of a balance was quoted and used by the PTC in *Admissibility Decision Ruto et al. (PTC)*:[44] and *Admissibility Decision Muthaura et al. (PTC)*:[40] but in that case a state's primary right, not duty, was at issue.

Whilst the complementarity principle could be understood as a principle that enhances the fight against impunity by granting states a primary right (and possibly responsibility or even duty) to investigate and prosecute – after all, the combined capacity of domestic jurisdictions far exceeds that of the ICC – the Appeals Chamber presents it as a principle that subordinates the primacy of domestic jurisdictions to the fight against impunity (as defined by the ICC). By prioritising the fight against impunity over the primary responsibility of the state and by then providing too ready a backup, the Court diminishes the notion of the responsibility of the state.

The Appeals Chamber not only implicitly recognised the normative paradox of complementarity, it explicitly diminished the responsibility of the state by – admittedly rather speculatively – conceptualising the duty recalled in the preamble as an obligation *aut dedere aut judicare*, rather than an obligation to investigate or prosecute domestically:

> [T]here may be merit in the argument that the sovereign decision of a State to relinquish its jurisdiction in favour of the Court may well be seen as complying with the 'duty to exercise [its] criminal jurisdiction', as envisaged in the sixth paragraph of the Preamble.[43]

Whilst keeping the option open not to act upon a state's self-referral,[44] the Chamber concluded that 'the general prohibition of a relinquishment of jurisdiction in favour of the Court is not a suitable tool for fostering compliance by States with the duty to exercise criminal jurisdiction'.[45] More critical with respect to self-referrals, Pre-Trial Chamber I held that for the Court to have jurisdiction there must be a link between a referral and crimes committed afterwards,

> precisely with a view to avoiding that referrals become instruments 'permitting a State to abdicate its responsibility for exercising jurisdiction over atrocity crimes for eternity', which – as the Defence correctly points out – 'would be wholly antithetical to the concept of complementarity'. The Statute cannot be interpreted as permitting a State to permanently abdicate its responsibilities by referring a wholesale of present and future criminal activities comprising the whole of its territory, without any limitation whether in context or duration. Such an interpretation would be inconsistent with the proper functioning of the principle of complementarity.[46]

---

[43] *Admissibility Judgment Katanga (AC)*:[85].   [44] *Ibid.*

[45] *Ibid.*:[86]. See Chapter 2, 'Other jurisdictional provisions: the triggers', on the problematic use of 'relinquishment' in this context.

[46] *Decision on Jurisdiction Challenge Mbarushimana*:[16] (footnote omitted).

Implicitly endorsing the normative paradox of complementarity, the Chamber does not seem to consider *temporal* abdication of this responsibility as inconsistent with the principle of complementarity.

The Office of the Prosecutor has for its part diminished the expectation on states to investigate and prosecute domestically by actively encouraging states to refer situations to the Court. It is one thing for the Rome Statute not to prohibit a self-referral; it is quite another for the OTP to make it an explicit policy to invite states to refer to the Court situations concerning their own territory and nationals, stating that '[t]here may be cases where inaction by States is the appropriate course of action' and arguing that the Court may have 'superior evidence and expertise relating to that situation, making the Court the more effective forum'.[47]

This policy of inviting self-referrals has often been associated with or even considered part of the policy of positive complementarity, possibly because they are both based on an idea of cooperative relations between the ICC and a state.[48] However, the effect of the policy of inviting self-referrals is the opposite of the stated aim of positive complementarity: domestic proceedings are outsourced rather than encouraged. Where the policy of positive complementarity focuses on the ICC's cooperating with a state to help the state conduct proceedings, the policy of encouraging self-referrals aims at states' assigning situations to the ICC.[49] Where the policy of positive complementarity could enhance the expectation on states to investigate

---

[47] ICC-OTP 2003d:5.

[48] For examples of the OTP's amalgamating policies that share the characteristic of cooperative relations between a state and the ICC as part of one overarching policy, see Moreno-Ocampo 2004a:2, ICC-OTP 2006c:5 and ICC-OTP 2006d:22–3. See also, in the literature, Cryer 2011:1105, Stahn 2008:94 and 112, and Takemura 2007.

[49] The only way to reconcile the two policies is the Prosecutor's idea of a division of labour, challenged in this chapter, above, 'Complementarity as primary right: confusion, ambiguity and misrepresentation'. One can also counter that the two policies are not inconsistent because they apply at different moments. More recent policy documents on positive complementarity suggest that the policy is considered particularly prior to the OTP's decision whether or not to open an investigation, whereas the policy of inviting self-referral becomes relevant once the OTP has decided to open an investigation (see ICC-OTP 2011c:[14]–[15]). However, this reduced relevance of the policy of positive complementarity equally reduces the extent to which the policy contributes to an expectation on states to investigate and prosecute. Moreover, the policy of inviting self-referrals continues to do the opposite of encouraging domestic proceedings.

and prosecute domestically, the policy of inviting self-referrals suggests states are better international actors if they refer situations to the Court.

Despite lip-service to the policy of positive complementarity, the OTP in its first years prioritised the policy of inviting self-referrals. To an OTP that needed to prove its worth,[50] self-referrals seemed ideal as they were thought to imply a state's willingness to cooperate with the Court[51] – thus covering the Court's Achilles' heel.

Whilst the seeds for the normative paradox of complementarity are in the Rome Statute, the Court's organs have thus further diminished the idea of a domestic responsibility to investigate and prosecute by arguing that in some instances the ICC is the better forum for the prosecution of international crimes, that self-referrals are consistent with the anti-impunity ideal of the Rome Statute and that a state that refers a situation and transfers a suspect has not taken a decision not to prosecute in the meaning of article 17(1)(b).[52] Moreover, by defining narrowly the concept of same case, the Prosecutor and the PTCs have avoided findings of inability or unwillingness and thus, to the extent that there is any,[53] the naming-and-shaming effect of the ICC's involvement.

From the Court's perspective, all these developments are consistent with the aim of ending impunity. Regardless of the virtue of this argument, it does not negate the existence of the normative paradox of complementarity: the creation of the 'Rome System', and particularly the way it has been implemented so far, may, by projecting the Court as an institution to take over from states the responsibility to investigate and prosecute conflict-related crimes, actually undermine the expectation on states to discharge that responsibility. In other words, the Rome Statute and the ICC have fostered a norm according to which crimes may not go unpunished, but weakened the idea that states have the responsibility to this effect. The latter idea has been further weakened by the emergence of a *pro-ICC ideology*.

---

[50] See also the Prosecutor in the documentary Yates, de Onis and Kinoy 2009, MacMillan 2007:210, Clark 2009:263 and 265 and Greenawalt 2009:160.

[51] ICC-OTP 2003a:5, ICC-OTP 2006d:7 and Moreno-Ocampo 2008c. See also Gallavin 2006:50.

[52] See Chapter 2, 'A decision not to prosecute'.

[53] See this chapter, 'Low costs of inaction'.

*Pro-ICC ideology countering a political expectation on states
to conduct proceedings*
Complementarity as a principle that grants states the primary right to
investigate and prosecute, and *a fortiori* as a norm according to which
states are politically expected to do so, has been undermined by *pro-
ICC ideology*. This ideology is based on three sometimes interrelated
beliefs, namely, that (1) international courts mete out better justice
than domestic systems;[54] (2) international crimes, particularly those
committed by those bearing the greatest responsibility, must be prosecuted as international crimes and, ideally, in international courts,
because such crimes have been committed 'against humanity';[55] and
(3) at a minimum, once the ICC is involved it should not be publicly
criticised or rendered less relevant because as a fledgling court it must
be seen to succeed.[56] By favouring ICC proceedings, pro-ICC ideology
has countered the political expectation on states to conduct domestic
proceedings for conflict-related crimes and thus complementarity's
catalysing effect.

At the international level, this ideology is backed by the
international-criminal-justice movement,[57] some Western governments and, unsurprisingly, the ICC itself.[58] Having spent decades
lobbying for the creation of the ICC,[59] the international-criminal-
justice movement is one of the best exemplars of pro-ICC ideology.
Members of the Coalition for the International Criminal Court
(CICC), for instance, have joined an alliance whose aim is not just
fighting impunity, but supporting the ICC as the institution chosen to
fight this battle.[60] As Chapter 3 in particular has illustrated, the CICC
and other members of the international-criminal-justice movement

---

[54] For case law and literature supporting this view, see, *inter alia*, ICTY, *Tadić Defence
Motion Decision (AC)*:[62] and Goldstone 1997:238.

[55] See e.g. ICTY, *Tadić Defence Motion Decision (AC)*:[57] and UN Doc. S/PV.3453
(1994):13 (Mr Bakuramutsa). For an example of this view in the literature, see
Pellet 2004:438–9.

[56] See the Swiss Ambassador's considerations reported in Hume 2006c, cited below,
n. 72. For additional arguments for preferring international to domestic trials, see
Arendt 1977:270, Mégret 2005 and Burke-White 2002:93.

[57] See Chapter 1, text above n. 58.

[58] For supporters of this ideology at the domestic level, see this chapter, 'A domestic
context inhospitable to a responsibility to conduct proceedings'.

[59] See Glasius 2006, Schiff 2008:Chapter 5 and Treves, di Rattalma, Tanzi, Fodella,
Pitea and Ragni 2005:Part II.

[60] See www.coalitionfortheicc.org.

have had significant influence on complementarity's catalysing effect. The Court's opening of its respective investigations saw a parade of international NGOs marching into Uganda or standing ready to organise events for Sudanese abroad. Whether providing information about the Court, assisting victims in applying for participant status in ICC proceedings or setting in motion transnational processes in which activists in situation countries interact with foreign members of the international-criminal-justice movement, these organisations have done much by way of outreach for the Court.[61]

However, when these organisations promote the Court and its Statute, they do not just provide all the information; they interpret and select information strategically.[62] They do not pay much attention to complementarity, a principle that could end the ICC's involvement in situations with respect to which they have lobbied for the ICC's exercise of jurisdiction. When these organisations do discuss complementarity, they elaborate on the high 'international standards' that domestic proceedings must meet and argue that offences must be charged in accordance with the definitions of the Rome Statute because charges of ordinary crimes do not reflect the seriousness of the crimes,[63] thus going beyond the requirements of the Statute.

---

[61] Locally, these NGOs are often seen as mouthpieces of the ICC. In part, this is due to the fact that they fail to distinguish themselves from the ICC. Indeed, the ICC Outreach Office has explained its joint outreach trips with the Ugandan Coalition on the ICC on the ground that they 'have the same message' (interview ICC outreach officers, Kampala, November 2011) and the UCICC has used the ICC's template for PowerPoint presentations (participant observation, UCICC session on the ICC at Kampala International University, Kampala, 16 October 2008). But such identification is also encouraged by the fact that the ICC outreach office is less visible than these NGOs, purportedly for reasons of security. In Uganda, the location of the ICC 'outreach' office in Kampala is not disclosed to the public, and the ICC is almost the only international agency driving in Gulu without its logo on its landcruisers.

[62] See Keck and Sikkink 1998:30, arguing that transnational advocacy networks rely, like epistemic communities, on information, but that for transnational advocacy networks it is the interpretation and strategic use of information that is most important.

[63] Interview with a CICC representative, New York, June 2008 ('The complementarity package in the Juba Agreement is irrelevant unless Uganda enacts implementing legislation ... The Special Division of the High Court cannot really function because the Rome Statute crimes are not part of Ugandan law ... Ordinary crimes are not the same as Rome Statute crimes.'); interview with a representative of a human rights organisation in Kampala, October 2008 ('The law here is inadequate to deal with the crimes. There is no proscription of international

The movement's propagation of pro-ICC ideology has both practical and normative underpinnings. Practically, many international-
criminal-justice experts are considered as such on the basis of their
experience with other international tribunals, none of which has
thus far had a jurisdictional arrangement based on complementarity.
Many experts are thus accustomed to the primacy of an international
court. Moreover, the 'organizational platform'[64] from which the
international-criminal-justice movement promotes its norms – an
international network – is more naturally suited to one overarching
institution such as the ICC than a principle, such as complementarity,
which allows for diversity among justice systems. The normative
underpinning of pro-ICC ideology is that many members of the
international-criminal-justice movement consider complementarity
an uncomfortable concession to state sovereignty.[65] Their ideal
remains primacy.[66] For proponents of this view, the battle for primacy
was lost on the road to Rome,[67] but can be reopened in the courtrooms of The Hague.[68]

crimes. Ordinary crimes are not going to reflect the magnitude of the crimes.'). See
also Human Rights Watch 2001:16 n. 46, International Commission of Jurists
2007:27, and Ellis 2002:224–5. For a compelling critique of this stance, see Mégret
2011.

[64] Finnemore and Sikkink 1998:899.

[65] For this view in the literature, see e.g. Brown 1998:386. In a discussion, one
international lawyer described complementarity as an 'evil invention of the
Americans' (Cambridge, October 2009). On NGOs' view of complementarity as
a 'regrettable necessity', see also Becker 2004:481. On the remaining preference for
primacy, see also Ratner 2003:453.

[66] For this view in the *travaux*, see UN Doc. A/50/22 (1995):6–7. See also Stigen
2008:70, arguing that during the negotiations on the Statute a majority of the
NGOs seemed to favour primacy, inspired by a speech by former ICTY Prosecutor
Arbour. Her preference for primacy is clearly expressed in Llewellyn and Raponi
1999:96–7 ('the most serious flaw is the primacy of national courts ... I think this
is an extremely bad provision ... I think the complementarity issue is an absolute
recipe for disaster. The simple solution is to put primacy in the ICC.').

[67] See e.g. ICC Judge Fernández de Gurmendi 2011:xix, writing extra-judicially:
'[M]any left Rome with the feeling that the complementarity provisions, which
failed to recognize primacy to the international jurisdiction, were a necessary but
regrettable concession to national sovereignty that could weaken the future institution to some extent'.

[68] See former ICTY President Cassese 2003:355 ('[I]nternational courts are by definition better suited to pronounce upon large scale and very grave crimes allegedly
perpetrated by political or military leaders. For such cases the rule of complementarity ... may appear to be questionable. However, since the draftsmen of the

Equally taken with this pro-ICC ideology, many Western governments have promoted ICC proceedings more than they have encouraged domestic investigations and prosecutions. Officials in such Western governments, the US being the most striking exception, have strong ties with or even consider themselves part of the international-criminal-justice movement.[69] They participated in the creation of the Court, defended it against American antagonism and are determined to see it succeed. This commitment has made European governments, and some sections within the UN, cautious of any move that could be seen as undermining the ICC.[70]

This pro-ICC ideology of Western governments explains their initial reluctance to support the Juba peace talks.[71] Particularly headquarters, legal advisors and human rights activists argued that a state's ratification of the Rome Statute or support for the ICC implied that it could not endorse negotiations concerning persons sought by the Court.[72] More concerned with the implications of the outcome of the negotiations for the ICC than for Uganda and the region, these actors backed the absent though decisive party at the talks: the ICC. In the words of one official of a Western government, the fear was that

Statute have opted for that model, one can only hope that the Court will interpret and apply the relevant rules of the Statute in such a way as to assert the Court's jurisdiction whenever cases in that category are brought before the Court.').

[69] See also Simpson 2007:35, Glasius 2006:129 and Tallgren 1999.

[70] See, however, Aoun 2012, arguing on the basis of interviews with ICC officials that the EU does not sufficiently live up to its normative preference for the ICC.

[71] See also Lomo 2006. Those few European states that did support the talks from the outset were told by other European states that they should not be seen as 'relaxing' their support for the ICC (interview with a European diplomat, Kampala, October 2008).

[72] See e.g. speaking notes of a European minister for a phone call with the mediator of the Juba peace talks, August 2006 ('I am not in a position to provide support – in whatever form – to the peace talks, due to our obligations towards the ICC.'). See also a US code cable (Hume 2006c), reporting on a meeting with Swiss Ambassador Bieler, who described 'the paradox of the Swiss position' as that the Swiss 'want to support the talks without undermining the authority or legitimacy of the nascent ICC'. The cable concluded: 'The Swiss Ambassador does not believe there will be an acceptable legal solution to this conundrum, so he would like the international community to find a political one. While difficult, Bieler thinks this is essential for the continued viability of the ICC. He requested US support in finding this solution.' See also 'Interview: Julian Hottinger – Perspectives of a Mediator' 2010.

'if the ICC did not come out [of the talks] smelling like a rose, the whole international justice project would collapse'.[73]

The Juba peace agreements, particularly the Juba Accountability and Reconciliation Agreement and its Annexure, were therefore at least as much directed to an international pro-ICC audience as to the parties whose conflict it aimed to resolve. The Agreements had to break the prevailing pro-ICC ideology in order to buy Ugandan actors space to assume responsibility for justice. To some extent, they were successful: when a cessation of hostilities was reached and the security dividends became tangible,[74] the voice of the field offices, political advisors and aid workers gained the upper hand over the headquarters, legal advisors and human rights activists.[75] Gradually and grudgingly,[76] the UN and some 'schizo[ph]renic donors',[77] torn between supporting the peace talks or the ICC, provided financial and logistical support,[78] arguing that the ICC's success could take the form of the spurring of domestic proceedings. That said, some states parties to the Rome Statute remained disinclined to support Ugandan trials. For example, asked for his views on the exceptional Canadian offer of assistance to the Ugandan Special Division of the High Court, one European diplomat responded, somewhat surprised, that the Canadians '[were] interested, despite their strong ICC credentials'.[79]

The same countries' and international organisations' desire to protect the ICC has been even stronger in the context of Darfur. Back in 2005, when the Security Council negotiated the referral of the situation there, the Chairman of the African Union launched the option of an alternative *Panel africain pour la Justice criminelle et la Réconciliation*.[80] The panel, to consist of African (including Sudanese) judges,

---

[73] Interview, Kampala, October 2008.

[74] See also Simonse, Verkoren and Junne 2010:232.

[75] Interview with officials and advisors involved in the talks, May and June 2008. See also International Refugee Rights Initiative 2011:5 on headquarters' being more pro-ICC than field offices, and Simonse, Verkoren and Junne 2010:240 on the different views between diplomats and lawyers. See also Perrot 2010:194 on the different views between foreign and locally based actors.

[76] See also Schomerus 2010b:100 and Simonse, Verkoren and Junne 2010:238.

[77] A term used by a UN official cited in Perrot 2010:199 to refer to donors 'caught in a dilemma between supporting the promising Juba peace process or supporting the ICC implementation of the arrest warrants'.

[78] See also Afako 2010:21.

[79] Interview with a European diplomat, Kampala, October 2008.

[80] See also Elgak 2008:3.

would punish 'those who committed crimes against humanity and grave violations of human rights and international humanitarian law in Darfur and in the future in other situations'. The panel, 'unlike international justice', would do justice 'the African way' by acknowledging the need for reconciliation and taking into account the sensitive political situation and the specifics of the African context.[81] The argument was that ICC involvement in Sudan would no longer be necessary,[82] even if not on grounds of complementarity in a legal sense. But European countries feared that this proposal would 'weaken' the Court and never seriously considered it.[83]

After the hard-won Security Council referral of the situation in Darfur, states supporting the Court did not want to be seen to be undermining the Court's position, especially as the Court faced immediate resistance from the Sudanese government, and needed to be bolstered. Supporting a deferral by the Security Council under article 16 or assisting Sudan to conduct domestic proceedings have both been construed as undermining or 'politicising' the Court.[84] Field representatives of these Western states and of international organisations frequently resent the pro-ICC ideology of their own institutions. 'At headquarters', they say, 'ICC politics are ruling over Darfur politics.'[85]

The reluctance of donor agencies of Western states to support domestic trials as an alternative to the ICC also stems from a belief that international courts deliver better justice than domestic systems. Donors do not want to be seen supporting, directly or indirectly, proceedings that may violate fair trial rights and result in penalties such as flogging or death. Backing a state-of-the-art international criminal court is considered less risky and easier to sell to domestic constituencies than funding politically sensitive

---

[81] EU diplomatic correspondence, 16 March 2005.
[82] EU diplomatic correspondence, undated.
[83] EU diplomatic correspondence, 15 March 2005.
[84] Goldstone 2008:5, Human Rights Watch 2009b, Human Rights Watch official Keppler 2013, forthcoming:n. 14 and a diplomat quoted in International Crisis Group 2009:17. See also Oette 2010:354. The argument of 'politicisation' does not seem to take into account, first, that the Statute provides for the possibility of a deferral by the Security Council as much as it provides for the possibility of a referral by the Council, and secondly, that in the event of Sudanese proceedings ultimately ICC judges will decide whether Sudan has conducted genuine proceedings.
[85] Interview with a European diplomat, Khartoum, December 2008.

national proceedings.[86] It is assumed that proceedings in international courts are exemplary.[87]

To the extent that donors have supported the idea of domestic proceedings, this support has been mostly limited to cases not addressed by the ICC. Misinterpreting the concept of complementarity in the way discussed above,[88] the EU, for instance, has declared itself 'committed to supporting the strengthening of domestic judicial capacity in countries where the ICC has commenced investigations to ensure that local jurisdictions can, according to the principle of complementarity, deal themselves with the crimes which will *not be addressed by the ICC*'.[89]

A final component of the pro-ICC ideology of Western states is that many of their officials at headquarters, like members of the international-criminal-justice movement, consider complementarity to be a concession by international criminal justice (deemed inherently virtuous) to state sovereignty (deemed vicious, at least when seen to protect 'bad' governments).[90] With a commitment to international criminal justice as part of their state's self-image, European ministers find expressions of support for the ICC politically beneficial, as long as it is not their state that is under investigation. Equating structures with outcome, Western politicians and their constituencies often consider promoting the ICC more gratifying than the task of undertaking less visible and more complex attempts to address the causes of the conflicts in which the crimes were committed.[91]

---

[86] Rule-of-law programmes supporting foreign justice systems have often been politically sensitive in the donor state. Western ministers responsible for development cooperation have been in difficult positions when repressive police operations in the receiving state appeared to have been equipped as part of the donor's rule-of-law programme.

[87] For instance, whereas the GoS would not get financial assistance to address crimes in Darfur, Denmark and Canada established two separate trust funds to assist the OTP in its investigations, after the situation in Darfur had been referred to the Court but not yet budgeted. See ICC-ASP/5/32 (2006)-b:312.

[88] See this chapter, 'Complementarity as primary right: confusion, ambiguity and misrepresentation'.

[89] European Commission 2008:3 (emphasis added, highlighting omitted).

[90] Interview with a European diplomat, Kampala, October 2008 ('[W]e believe that these are international crimes, hence best tried at the international level ... [W]e consider complementarity as a sacrifice to sovereignty, not as a preference.'). See also former Netherlands legal advisor Bos 1998:259 and Toscano and Pocar in Politi and Gioia 2008b:136–7.

[91] For a similar argument with respect to the human rights movement, see Kennedy 2004:23 and 116.

The Court itself is the fiercest proponent of the pro-ICC ideology. The structural bias of many of the Court's international criminal lawyers is not so much towards law or international law but towards international criminal justice. While criminal law places a strong emphasis on the procedural rights of the defendant and international law posits state sovereignty as a fundamental tenet of the international system, international criminal justice has become increasingly victim-oriented.[92] State sovereignty is viewed as an unfortunate extra-legal vestige of politics.[93] Echoing the sentiments of the international-criminal-justice movement, influential ICC officials consider complementarity to be the price paid by global justice to state sovereignty in order to secure the establishment of the Court.[94] While some make rhetorical references to concepts such as the 'Rome System', many consider that the ICC should have been granted primacy, just like the ICTY, the ICTR and the SCSL.

The pro-ICC ideology is apparent in the Court's early decisions. As a result of the case law on what constitutes the same 'case', national authorities can render ICC cases inadmissible only if they investigate substantially the same conduct, the same persons and the same incidents as the ICC.[95] It is thus the ICC's OTP, and not domestic prosecutorial policy, that determines which impunity is intolerable and which, given the limited resources to address a universe of criminality, must be accepted. Moreover, the Appeals Chamber has increased the likelihood that cases remain admissible before the Court by characterising complementarity as a right of the parties rather than as a matter of public policy that the judges must consider.[96] Finally, the Chambers seem to have conceptualised the principle of complementarity not as a principle balancing state sovereignty and international criminal justice but rather as a principle that protects sovereignty only to the extent that a state joins in what they consider

---

[92] See also Robinson 2008:930 *et seq.* On the 'disembodied victim' as the moral platform of international criminal justice, see Clarke 2009:94 and 143–6.

[93] E.g. see Cassese 1998:section 7. On the ICC 'as the triumph of international civil society in favor of the judicialization of that last fortress of sovereignty, criminal law', see Alvarez 2003:407.

[94] See e.g. ICC Judge Kaul 2001:69 and ICC Judge Politi 1997:147.

[95] See Chapter 2, 'The "same case" requirement: same person, same conduct, same incidents?'.

[96] See Chapter 2, 'The complementarity assessment is dynamic'.

the ICC's object and purpose: the fight against impunity. All other interests of the state are subordinated to this putative goal of the ICC.

Other organs of the Court have also promoted a pro-ICC ideology. The first Prosecutor may well have claimed, as he had before, that 'the absence of trials led by this court as a consequence of the regular functioning of national institutions, would be its major success'; but in the very same speech he stated that, on account of their character, international crimes belong in the International Criminal Court.[97] Deploying the latter argument, the OTP and PTC have uncritically echoed the GoU's argument that the ICC is the most appropriate forum for crimes of the nature committed by the LRA.[98] For its part, the Registry's outreach activities have hardly ever raised complementarity[99] and, when they have, 'we say', according to one outreach officer, 'we are here to do A, B and C, leaving it to the government to do the rest',[100] thus explaining complementarity in the misleading division-of-labour reading discussed above. These respective characterisations may reflect a professional chauvinism summed up in one ICC official's response to a question about complementarity: 'I believe more in the Court than in complementarity.'[101] Taken together, these characterisations of the principle of complementarity tend to assert the *de facto* primacy of the Court's jurisdiction.

The pro-ICC ideology is also present among certain professional groups at the national level. Many of the Ugandan officials who have cooperated with the Court, whether it is in the Ministry of Justice, the police or the army, consider their ICC counterparts as better equipped to deal with conflict-related crimes.[102] The same holds true for many Ugandan and Sudanese human rights lawyers who have been exposed to transnational professional processes concerning the ICC.[103] The

---

[97] Moreno-Ocampo 2003b.

[98] See Chapter 3, 'Conclusion: complementarity's catalysing effect in Uganda'.

[99] Interview with an ICC outreach officer, Kampala, October 2008.

[100] *Ibid.* ICC in-house training instructs ICC staff that complementarity means that 'the ICC will only investigate or prosecute if a state is unwilling or unable to prosecute' (participant observation ICC induction programme, The Hague, April 2008). This, too, is a problematic summary of article 17, as has been argued in Chapter 2, 'The inadequacy of the shorthand description'.

[101] Discussion with an ICC official, The Hague, April 2008.

[102] Interview with an official in the Ministry of Justice, Kampala, September 2008 and with a Ugandan lawyer involved in ICC–Uganda cooperation in the investigations, Kampala, October 2008.

[103] Interview with Ugandan lawyers trained by the American Bar Association, Kampala, September and October 2008.

following excerpt from a discussion with a member of the Ugandan Human Rights Commission is illustrative of the mélange of arguments put forward by officials who favour the ICC over domestic proceedings, ranging from the leadership position of the accused and the nature of the crimes to local capacity:

> [INTERVIEWER:] *Does the Uganda Human Rights Commission have a preference for ICC or domestic proceedings?*
>
> High-profile people like Kony and the leaders of the LRA should go to the ICC.
>
> [INTERVIEWER:] *Why?*
>
> Because of judicial precedent: Taylor, Lubanga, Milosevic, [Kony] ranks in that, or even outranks that category. It is also to remove local sentiments. We would need witness protection. These are crimes against *humanity*. Here people want to barter peace for justice. But they are very very local people and they will not understand the complexities of the crime ... If we are going to set a precedent, we'd better do it right. We'd better take these people to the ICC.[104]

This view, revealing the belief that international crimes are better prosecuted in an international court because of the quality of justice and the character of the crimes, counteracts infiltration of the idea that states have a responsibility to conduct domestic proceedings for conflict-related crimes. The domestic context makes it even more difficult for such an idea to infiltrate.

A domestic context inhospitable to a responsibility to conduct proceedings

Legal anthropologists have argued that the likelihood of successful norm promotion increases the more the frame within which a norm is promoted resonates with cultural traditions and narratives of the local context (while acknowledging that the greater the resonance, the smaller the transformative impact).[105] In the Ugandan and Sudanese context, there is little that resonates with a norm according to which the state has the duty to investigate and prosecute conflict-related crimes, thus impeding the reception of such a norm and its catalysing effect.

---

[104] Interview, Kampala, October 2008.

[105] See Merry 2006b:41, applying insights from legal anthropology to human rights promotion. See also Merry 2006a:5.

One reason is the dominant conflict paradigm. As Chapters 3 and 4 have argued, the Ugandan and Sudanese governments have perceived the conflicts with the LRA and in Darfur as predominantly political and military issues, not legal ones. This is not unique to these states – from Northern Ireland to Mozambique and from the United States to Indonesia, states have addressed their own conflict-related crimes as acts requiring a political solution rather than a criminal response, particularly in the context of negotiated settlements[106] and particularly when the crimes are ongoing or have only just ceased.

It has also been shown, however, that in Uganda, unlike in Sudan, the ICC's intervention has led to a broadening of the national approach towards the conflict to encompass a legal dimension, as a result of which the environment has become more open to infiltration by the idea of a domestic responsibility to conduct proceedings for conflict-related crimes. An influential factor in whether or not the conflict paradigm has taken on a legal dimension has appeared to be whether national legal professionals have used the ICC's intervention to act as norm entrepreneurs[107] and to assert their own role in any response to the conflict.[108] In Uganda, the search for national alternatives to the ICC has created an opportunity for national lawyers to do so. In Sudan, the ICC's intervention has resulted in the converse, as one senior legal advisor observed:

> I have stopped following the ICC. The government does not listen to you. As a result of our positive attitude towards the ICC in the beginning, [members of the government] now dislike us even more. They feel we support the ICC.[109]

In neither Uganda nor Sudan does the legal profession speak with one voice as to whether law has to play a role in war and, if so, whether the state has a responsibility to investigate and prosecute. In Sudan, some interviewed officials preferred traditional-justice mechanisms.[110] In Uganda, where most interviewed legal officials preferred formal justice,[111]

---

[106] See, *inter plurima alia*, Huntington 1995.

[107] See Chapter 1, 'The story of complementarity's catalysing effect in Uganda and Sudan'.

[108] See, more generally, Finnemore and Sikkink 1998:899 and 905 and Widner 2001:73.

[109] Interview with a senior lawyer in the Ministry of Justice, Khartoum, December 2008.

[110] See Chapter 4, 'Providing a boost for traditional justice'.

[111] A human rights lawyer in Kampala, for instance, argued against *mato oput* as an alternative to the ICC, stating: '*Mato oput* would not solve accountability. It is

relevant actors were divided as to which court should exercise jurisdiction over conflict-related crimes. Government lawyers who had been involved in the referral and had cooperated with the Court were more in favour of proceedings in the ICC than domestic proceedings. The same held true for many private lawyers who had been trained by the International Bar Association. Many lawyers involved in the JLOS Transitional Justice Group were in favour of specialised domestic alternatives to the ICC. Those working in the ordinary justice system, however, feared that such special courts would undermine the capacity of the ordinary criminal justice system and were in favour of mainstreaming conflict-related crimes.[112] Human rights activists, both in Uganda and in Sudan, usually preferred the ICC to the national domestic justice systems, as they were fully aware of the drawbacks of the latter and were members of international coalitions promoting the ICC. The various preferences expressed were thus heavily dependent on personal positions and the biases of the transnational processes in which the speakers participated.[113] In sum, lawyers may have become convinced of the legal dimension to internal armed conflicts, but this has not automatically resulted in the acceptance of a norm that the state has a responsibility to conduct domestic proceedings.

Infiltration of an idea that it is the state's primary responsibility to investigate and prosecute conflict-related crimes has also been impeded by the fact that in both states, but in Sudan even more than in Uganda, criminal proceedings depend heavily on victims' initiating them and following them through. In Sudan,[114] the Criminal Procedure Act authorises the police to investigate crimes such as murder and rape on its own initiative,[115] but the practice is, in the words of a police officer in El-Fasher, that of 'without a complaint, no

---

just a ritual. It does not provide for redress and reparation. It has never been tested. It is something we abandoned ages ago.' (interview, Kampala, September 2008). During a participatory action focus group, conducted in Gulu in September 2008, it was remarkable how, in the group consisting of representatives of the formal justice sector, those who came from the north had to introduce those from other areas of the country to Acholi traditional-justice practices, even though all worked and lived in northern Uganda.

[112] Interviews with judges and prosecutors in Kitgum, Gulu and Kampala, September and October 2008.

[113] On structural biases, see Koskenniemi 2005:600–15.

[114] For a lively account of a victim's pursuit of criminal justice for a conflict-related crime in Uganda, see Rice 2009.

[115] Criminal Procedure Act 1991, s. 35(a)(i) and Schedule II.

investigation'.[116] After the registration of the complaint, the victim or the victim's family must continue pursuing the criminal case, usually through a private lawyer.[117] Lack of representation of the victim at the trial can lead to dismissal of the case.[118] If the injured party and accused agree on the amount of compensation, the Prosecutor does not pursue the case,[119] even in respect of crimes where the law does not grant the right of private relinquishment, for instance rape and murder.[120] In the event of *qisas* (retribution) crimes,[121] such as murder and intentionally causing wounds, victims can opt for *dia* (blood money) instead of retribution, up until the point when the sentence is carried out. The judge may then impose only a minimal sentence.[122] Judges usually try to promote private settlements, instead of imposing public sentences.

In comparison with ICC proceedings, Sudanese proceedings are thus radically more victim-driven, not only in the reparations phase, but also in the determination of the sentence. Indeed, as regards crimes considered a 'private' issue, such as murder, rape and looting,[123] the existence and pursuit of the case depends on the victim's actions. But in conflict situations, many victims do not pursue cases because they lack access to or trust in government institutions. Even if victims do pursue justice, Sudanese police and prosecutors do not follow up on

---

[116] Discussion, December 2008.

[117] Public prosecutors spend much time on duties other than prosecuting, such as serving on the state security committees.

[118] Special Court, Nyala, 462/2005, 28 August 2005. (On account of the fact that the victim did not appear at the proceedings, the accused was acquitted of armed robbery and intentionally wounding a USAID staff member during an attack against a humanitarian convoy.)

[119] Interview with a prosecutor in El-Fasher, Khartoum, December 2008. In a case in which a 'Janjaweed' killed a man in the market of El-Fasher, the army agreed to pay blood money and the case was closed.

[120] Criminal Procedure Act 1991, s. 36(2) and Schedule I.

[121] *Qisas* crimes are those crimes for which the Quran grants victims the right to choose between retaliation and compensation.

[122] Criminal Act 1991, s. 38 and Criminal Procedure Act 1991, ss. 36(1) and 195(1). See also Chapter 4, n. 426.

[123] Interview with a criminal law professor, Khartoum, November 2008. Theoretically, crime is by definition a public concern; but in Sudan officials take *proprio motu* action usually only in cases of crimes that lack obvious direct victims, such as crimes against the state and against public morality (see also Schacht 1964:177). Crimes against the state are usually suppressed by security agencies, instead of by the ordinary justice system.

politically sensitive cases, for instance against state officials or state-supported militias, without backing from political superiors. If proceedings are allowed, they involve only the direct perpetrator implied in the victim's report, and not indirect perpetrators or persons bearing command or other superior responsibility. A responsibility to investigate and prosecute conflict-related crimes does not sit well with this professional culture.

None of the above is altered by the fact that both Uganda and Sudan have ratified 'human rights treaties'[124] that contain a formal legal obligation to investigate and prosecute certain international crimes.[125] Uganda has been a serial but also sleepwalking ratifier of such treaties. Sudan has been more cautious, fearing that such treaties may be used against it. But for both states, ratification of human rights treaties has been first and foremost a display of foreign policy. Foreign policy, in turn, is primarily used to enhance the ruling party's authority at home by demonstrating its acceptability to international actors.[126] Ratification of human rights treaties, like participation in photo shoots at diplomatic conferences, sends the message that the state and its statesmen[127] are part of the 'international community', which benefits the reputation of both the state and the statesmen.[128] As one of the longest-serving members of the Sudanese Parliament explained when asked why the GoS had ratified the Genocide Convention in the year that the Darfur conflict was at its peak:

> [We ratify] because we are part of the international community. We cannot say, 'we do not sign this because of our situation back home'.[129]

---

[124] On the broad lay understanding of this term, see Chapter 3, n. 398 and Chapter 4, n. 383.

[125] See Chapter 2, n. 12.   [126] Clapham 1977:84.

[127] Finnemore and Sikkink 1998:903–4.

[128] See also the question by parliamentarian Beti Kamya in Uganda 2009:[3.47] ('Would the Minister not think, as I think, that some of these treaties are more of PR exercises, to look good but not to be applied at home?').

[129] Interview, Khartoum, November 2008. Similar explanations were given by a Sudanese professor (interview, Khartoum, November 2008) ('This is an issue of foreign policy ... You want to be part of the society of states. Signing up to an agreement alters very little.') and a representative of a humanitarian organisation (interview, Khartoum, December 2008) ('Conventions are used to clear the face of the government, they are good for the image.'). On the relationship between ratifying human rights treaties and complying with human rights more generally, see Hathaway 2002.

Thus, when the Ugandan or Sudanese governments ratified human rights treaties, their focus has usually not been on any ensuing obliga-tions that could limit sovereignty, but on the mere fact that the ratification consolidates the government's representation of that sov-ereignty – a valuable benefit in states where sovereignty and its representation are in practice heavily dependent on external recognition.

Additionally, financial benefits from donor countries are some-times conditional upon ratifying 'human rights treaties'. For instance, states can benefit from development cooperation with the EU under the amended Cotonou Agreement only if they 'seek to take steps towards ratifying and implementing the Rome Statute and related instruments'.[130] Put less legalistically by a Ugandan lawyer: 'Sign up the ICC, and you get more donor money, and thus a couple of more jets.'[131] After ratification,[132]

---

[130] See Chapter 4, n. 157.

[131] Interview with a Ugandan lawyer, Kampala, November 2011.

[132] In Uganda, the President signs treaties and the Cabinet ratifies them (Consti-tution of Uganda 1995, art. 123, and Ratification of Treaties Act 1998, s. 2). Treaties have domestic effect only if they have been transformed by acts of parliament into municipal law (Uganda 1996:[40]–[41]). In Sudan, the President ratifies treaties with the approval of the National Legislature (INC 2005, art. 58 (1)(k)). In official reports, the GoS has argued that 'Sudan has adopted a common law system, like the United Kingdom, under which the provisions of any treaty to which Sudan is a party become part of domestic law and acquire the same force as national legislation. Also, the Sudan has ratified the Vienna Convention on the Law of Treaties which makes obligations arising from international agreements prevail over other obligations arising from national laws.' (Committee on the Elimination of Racial Discrimination 2000:[197]). However, the system described is not the system of the United Kingdom, and the VCLT does not regulate the status of international treaties in domestic law (VCLT, art. 27 providing only that, on the international plane, a state cannot invoke domestic legislation as an excuse not to comply with international law). Sudanese international lawyers explain that in theory all international instruments that have been ratified are part of the law of the land and are superior to national laws (interviews with Sudanese international lawyers working for the Sudanese government, Khartoum, March and September 2007). Whether one can successfully invoke these instru-ments in court depends on whether the treaty is considered self-executing. A treaty is self-executing if it is suitable for direct application or where a rule of reference in a domestic act stipulates direct applicability of treaties. Where this is not the case, the treaty must be incorporated into national law to have domestic effect. For a rare example of such direct effect, see *Syrian Arab Airways Corporation v. Khadeeja Mohammed El Shaekh*. In almost all instances, however, it is assumed

little attention is paid to giving the treaty effect in the domestic legal order.[133]

Whilst inhospitable to infiltration of a norm according to which the state has a responsibility to investigate or prosecute, this context begins to reveal the cost–benefit assessments on the basis of which decisions about domestic proceedings are also made.

COMPLEMENTARITY AND THE STATE'S COST–BENEFIT ANALYSIS

The developments in Uganda and Sudan also call for a review of the assumptions concerning states' analyses of the costs and benefits of domestic and ICC proceedings. The expectation of a catalysing effect is based on the assumption that complementarity spurs domestic proceedings because it allows states to avoid the costs of an ICC intervention. Thus, according to William Burke-White:

> Often the most potent means available to the Court to motivate an unwilling State to exercise jurisdiction is to make clear to that State should it continue to abstain from investigating or prosecuting particular crimes, that intervention by the OTP is likely, or even inevitable. Such a possibility of international prosecution is likely to make the alternative of domestic prosecutions appear far less costly and preferable to the high sovereignty costs imposed by ICC intervention.[134]

It is thus assumed that states consider intervention by the ICC in their state as a sovereignty cost.[135] It has also been suggested that the ICC's

---

that international treaties require implementing legislation, particularly in the areas of international humanitarian law, international criminal law and international human rights law (even though INC 2005, art. 27(3) explicitly provides that international human rights treaties that Sudan has ratified are part of the Bill of Rights). The practice has led Babiker 2007:238 to conclude that, 'as a matter of general practice, the Sudan follows the dualist tradition ... Thus, any obligations incurred by the Sudan or accorded to its citizens under international law only become national law after being incorporated through a legislative act'. This is also the position adopted in *Abdel Rahman Nugdallah*.

[133] Nonetheless, as the International Criminal Court Act 2010 and the Prevention and Prohibition of Torture Act 2012 have illustrated in Uganda, in states with a relatively well developed civil society, ratification does give domestic activists a starting point for lobbying for implementing legislation.

[134] Burke-White 2008a:71.

[135] Sovereignty costs have been defined as 'the symbolic and material costs of diminished national autonomy' (see Abbott 1999:375). In the event of the ICC's opening an investigation, these sovereignty costs will be mostly symbolic: no

involvement in a state results in reputational costs,[136] on the ground that 'the accusation shifts from the individual accused of having committed an international crime to the State accused of having tolerated it by not trying him effectively'.[137] As a result of these costs, undertaking domestic proceedings was expected to acquire greater priority, since only national investigations and prosecutions can avoid or end the ICC's involvement on grounds of complementarity.

The Ugandan and Sudanese experiences show a more nuanced story: rather than considering ICC intervention costly, Uganda considered (targeted) ICC intervention as beneficial to its sovereignty and reputation. Moreover, even though Sudan does consider ICC intervention very costly to its sovereignty and reputation,[138] it has refrained from conducting genuine domestic proceedings in the ICC's stead.

Assuming that a catalysing effect will occur if the ICC's intervention decreases the costs of domestic proceedings or increases the costs of refraining from them, two types of costs must be revisited: the costs of domestic proceedings and the costs of ICC intervention.[139] On that basis, the rest of this chapter will argue that complementarity's

actual sovereignty is 'lost'. While a state may be under an obligation to cooperate with the Court, including to execute arrest warrants, no provision in the Statute obliges states to defer to the Court's jurisdiction. In other words, states are not prohibited from initiating or continuing domestic proceedings, even *in absentia*. See Chapter 2, 'A state's jurisdiction to adjudicate is unaffected by ICC intervention'. For a critical discussion of the relationship between sovereignty and international criminal justice more generally, see Cryer 2005a.

[136] Mercer 1996 points out that reputation is not in a state's possession, but is formed by other states. Reputational costs in this context consist of the damage a state perceives to be done to its reputation.

[137] Mégret 2006:11. For others who consider ICC intervention as damaging to a state's sovereignty or reputation, see Chapter 1, nn. 17 and 68.

[138] See e.g. 'Beshir brands ICC warrant "infringement" on Sudan' 2009, citing statements by the Sudanese President on international attempts to prosecute him for war crimes: 'Such a move ushers a new era of domination and infringement upon the independence and sovereignty of Sudan.' A Sudanese human rights activist has reported that Sudan's head of the National Intelligence and Security Services characterised the ICC's role in Sudan as 'the most serious challenge this country has faced since we came to power' (see Fernandez 2008b). The Prosecutor's charges, while based on the notion of individual criminal responsibility, essentially do accuse the entire Sudanese state by arguing that the Sudanese President committed crimes 'by using the state apparatus' (*Application Arrest Warrant Bashir* (*passim*, but in particular [62] and [250]–[343]).

[139] Benefits are discussed only as negative costs. For instance, if ICC intervention is considered to bring benefits, this reduces the costs of ICC intervention.

catalysing effect on domestic proceedings in Uganda and Sudan has been limited because, first, the costs of domestic proceedings, particularly the political costs, have been prohibitive. Neither the ICC nor donor countries have reduced these costs, the ICC's policy of positive complementarity notwithstanding. Secondly, the costs of ICC proceedings have either not been high enough to encourage domestic proceedings or were able to be avoided by means other than the invocation of complementarity.

High cost of action: obstacles to domestic proceedings

A key reason for the absence of a strong catalysing effect on domestic proceedings for crimes within the Court's jurisdiction is the high cost of domestic action. This cost consists of the sacrifices that must be made either to remove practical and political obstacles to domestic proceedings for conflict-related crimes or to conduct such proceedings.

Some of the obstacles are the same as those discussed as factors impeding infiltration of the idea of a state's responsibility to conduct domestic proceedings for conflict-related crimes,[140] namely, the absence of a legal dimension to the approach to armed conflict, the limited independence of the legal profession and an expectation that civilians will pursue justice themselves. In addition, Chapters 3 and 4 have shown how police and prosecutors have lacked incentives to launch on their own initiative investigations into and prosecutions of politically sensitive conflict-related crimes. Theoretically, the government, if it wished, could remove these obstacles relatively easily, for instance by recognising the legal dimension to the conflict, by giving instructions to investigate and prosecute to law-enforcement agencies, and by lifting the immunity of militia members.

But the conflict has placed further obstacles in the path of criminal proceedings.[141] Large parts of Darfur have at several times during the conflict been beyond government control, and even government-held areas have been dangerous for police, prosecutors and magistrates.[142]

---

[140] See this chapter, 'A domestic context inhospitable to a responsibility to conduct proceedings'.

[141] Many of these have also prevented the ICC from even requesting the GoS to allow it into Sudan to conduct investigations in Darfur.

[142] According to prosecutors in Darfur, a colleague in South Darfur was killed, another in West Darfur was injured and prosecutors' cars were hijacked (interview, El-Fasher, December 2008).

Outweighed in manpower and weaponry by the rebel movements, militias and some tribal leaders, police have been unable to trace perpetrators or gather forensic evidence outside the cities.[143] Complaints and witness statements in relation to conflict-related crimes have been difficult to obtain on account of displacement. Accusations against 'some masked armed men on horseback' are difficult to follow-up on: which men and where, in an area the size of France with few roads and a long porous border with Chad and Libya, did they go to?[144] As for Uganda, when the LRA was still present in the north of the country, the GoU faced, *mutatis mutandis*, similar obstacles to the conduct of investigations into conflict-related crimes.[145]

Moreover, no matter how technically presented by lawyers, investigations and prosecutions of conflict-related crimes are in themselves dangerous acts of war that civilians shy away from, particularly when the conflict is ongoing. In Uganda, witnesses have been reluctant to cooperate with government investigators out of fear of reprisals by the LRA or out of a lack of trust in a government that they suspect of aiming to destroy Acholi culture.[146] In Sudan, too, witnesses have refused to assist, lacking trust in authorities accused of backing the militias responsible for the crimes in the first place, or fearing revenge, or having been instructed by rebel movements not to cooperate with the government.[147]

---

[143] Interviews with lawyers in Darfur, some of whom worked for the government, others being human rights activists, El-Fasher and Nyala, December 2008.

[144] Interview with a prosecutor in El-Fasher, Khartoum, December 2008 and a Sudanese lawyer in Nyala, December 2008.

[145] Since the LRA left for southern Sudan and the eastern DRC, civilian rule has begun to return to northern Uganda, but the recently arrived police and prosecutors focus on current crimes, not on crimes committed by the LRA or UPDF (interviews with police officers and prosecutors in Gulu and Kitgum, September and October 2008). Conflict-related crimes are the domain of headquarters in Kampala, but officials there argue that it would be a waste to spend scarce resources on criminal proceedings against persons that may either never be arrested or benefit from the existing amnesty law (interview with a senior official in the DPP, Kampala, October 2008).

[146] Interview with a senior official in the Uganda Police Force, Gulu, September 2008.

[147] Interviews with Sudanese lawyers working in Darfur, as prosecutors and as private lawyers, El-Fasher and Nyala, December 2008. See also interview with private lawyers in Nyala in August 2011 ('People fear to bring cases because if you file a complaint while the government was involved in the crime, you file against the government and receive many indirect threats.').

However, even where their identities and locations are known and witnesses keen to testify, key suspects have enjoyed impunity on account of a defining feature of the state in Uganda and Sudan: state institutions are often subordinate to patronage networks.[148] As Christopher Clapham has argued, '[i]n the absence of a genuine national feeling or common ideological identity ... clientelism provides the only means short of brute force for binding together the disparate power centres within the state, and creating at least the appearance of legitimacy and effectiveness, the twin requirements for making tolerable the enormous powers which the modern state presumes to exercise'.[149] As a result, in both Uganda and Sudan the government's rule is heavily dependent on the loyalty of powerful groups, both within the constitutional order such as the army, and outside it, for example an abundance of security forces and persons enjoying authority independent of the state. In exchange for loyalty, the patron (the ruling party or a person who himself or herself is a client of the ruling patron) provides a share of the scarce resources to which the state has unique access: government positions, arms, money and security. Security includes impunity.

Thus in Sudan, where Khartoum's control over Darfur has always been limited,[150] successive Sudanese governments have kept Darfur continuously under emergency law[151] and, unable to win wars against resistance on their own, offered militias money, weapons, titles to land, administrative positions and a *carte blanche* to fight the rebellion.[152] Having fostered a climate of impunity, the government cannot easily introduce the rule of law, even if it wished.

Times of competition, whether through elections or armed conflict, render the patronage market more volatile and drive up the price of loyalty,[153] as is illustrated by the story of Musa Hilal, considered the leader of the *Janjaweed*. Thus, when Hilal was in detention for leading an armed robbery of the central bank in the capital of South Darfur,

---

[148] See, *inter alia*, Clapham 1982a, Clapham 1982b, Mwenda 2007, Omach 2009b, De Waal 2009 and De Waal 2010b.

[149] Clapham 1982b:76.

[150] See also Ibrahim 2005–2006:13 and De Waal and Young 2005:[17].

[151] Emergency and Public Safety Protection Act 1997. Article 5 provides the competent authorities with powers, *inter alia*, to ban gatherings, arrest individuals, expropriate property and 'any other powers which the President of the Republic may deem necessary'.

[152] See also De Waal 2007:33.   [153] De Waal 2009 and De Waal 2010b.

Sudan's First Vice President secured his release in 2002 in order for him to fight the rebellion in Darfur. In a discussion with a US diplomat, Hilal explains:

> I was let out of prison and was angry at the world. My tribe had been attacked. Khartoum armed me . . . We don't feel we had a choice as our tribal enemies were with the rebels.[154]

In January 2008, Khartoum appointed Hilal as an Advisor to the Ministry of Federal Rule. As the diplomat comments, this was 'a move widely criticized in the West but one seemingly intended to keep him on a short leash after he flirted with joining the SPLM in Juba in late 2007'. Despite Khartoum's insistence on the value of its protection, Hilal sought, according to the leaked US code cable, a better-paying patron:

> Hilal described Darfur's Arab militias as 'disloyal to Khartoum . . . '. Hilal added that the Arab tribes of Darfur were constantly told by Khartoum officials that the Americans were 'out to get them'. There is a rumor that you are taking Zaghawa tribesmen for training in Afghanistan (the fierce Zaghawa make up the bulk of Darfur's rebels and are bitter enemies of the camel herding Arabs) but we know that is not true. 'If we had a choice, we would be with America against the NCP.' . . . Hilal asked for understanding: 'we want a place in the American agenda for Darfur.' We want to see your policy goals succeed there. He said that he wanted to find 'whatever way I can to be helpful to the Americans'. Hilal added that he wanted nothing for himself except the opportunity to travel freely (evidently Hilal feels that he may well be arrested if he travels too far afield). Hilal added that 'we don't understand what is your goal in Darfur, we want to understand and be helpful'. He repeatedly emphasized that the loyalty of Darfur's Arab tribes, and presumably his own, is up for grabs, if the West is interested.[155]

As the diplomat rightly concludes his comment, '[i]f anything, this meeting . . . underscores the shallow, mercurial nature of Khartoum's relationship with their most trusted allies in the field in Darfur'. Similarly, a lawyer in Darfur explained in an interview:

> If one wants to make real money in Darfur, law is not the right business. One has to fight the government. Then the government will buy you to their side. Many of my relatives now have a rank.[156]

---

[154] Fernandez 2008a.   [155] *Ibid.*   [156] Interview, Nyala, August 2011.

This patronage market encompasses virtually the entirety of political life, including that of state institutions. Thus, as Chapter 3 argued with respect to Uganda, donor-funded bodies such as an International Crimes Division and study trips abroad are used to trade loyalty for positions or tickets abroad. In Sudan, as compellingly explained by Alex de Waal, one armed movement refused to sign the Darfur Peace Agreement not because of the substance of the agreement, but because the loyalty fee offered was too low: '[W]hat mattered was the amount of money in the compensation fund, which would be under his personal control (and thus available for patronage purposes) ... He also demanded a personal pay-off, reportedly of $5 million, as a signing fee.'[157]

The patronage bazaar also determines the chances for accountability: impunity is one of the currencies in which loyalty transactions are paid. Whether or not someone is prosecuted depends on the value of the suspect's loyalty to the patron and on the prospect of obtaining or maintaining such loyalty. The former is determined by the individual's political or military might and ties to others with such might; the latter depends on the price of the loyalty.

Where the value is high, but the price is prohibitive, for instance in the case of outspoken senior members of the opposition, a prosecution is one way for the ruling party to defeat this (potential) threat factor, if need be without criminal evidence, resulting in the notorious 'political trial'.[158] Thus, in Uganda, opposition leader Kiiza Besigye faced at several times charges of treason, terrorism and rape.[159] Even if he was always acquitted,[160] the proceedings and his detention were successful in inhibiting his electoral campaigns.[161] In Sudan,

---

[157] De Waal 2010b.

[158] See, *inter alia*, Shklar 1986, Kirchheimer 1961 and Nouwen and Werner 2010a.

[159] See Kobusingye 2010:Chapter 8: 'We Have Culprits, Now Let's Find the Crime'.

[160] With respect to the rape charges, the Ugandan judiciary directed strong words to the prosecution. Justice Katutsi commented: 'The evidence before this court is inadequate even to prove a debt, impotent to deprive a man of his civil rights, ridiculous for convicting of the pettiest offence, scandalous if brought forward to support a charge of any character, monstrous if to ruin the honour of a man who offered himself as a candidate for the highest office in the country. I find that prosecution has dismally failed to prove its case against the accused', adding that the manner in which the investigations were conducted and carried out was 'crude and amateurish and betray[ed] the intentions behind this case' (*ibid.*:107).

[161] *Ibid.* and International Crisis Group 2012:30.

hundreds of persons have been prosecuted on allegations of support for the armed movements.[162]

Trials are possible but less imperative in cases where the price and the value of loyalty are low. This explains why it was possible for the National Resistance Movement (NRM) to select Thomas Kwoyelo – in contrast to LRA commanders whose loyalty seemed more useful – to serve as the first case for the Ugandan International Crimes Division.

In cases in which both the value and the prospect of obtaining or maintaining loyalty are high, a loyalty transaction results in the reverse of a political trial, namely, in what can be called 'political impunity'. In Uganda, reports of parliamentary and judicial investigations committees implicating senior UPDF officials in looting minerals in the DRC and key NRM figures in diverting foreign loans and government funds to election campaigns have rarely been followed by prosecutions.[163] In Sudan, as Chapter 4 has elaborated, members of the police and army by definition enjoy immunity, which in practice is hardly ever lifted. For militias fighting for the government, immunity is implied. Prosecutors see clear red lines, as the following fragment from an interview with a prosecutor in Darfur illustrates. Asked why the Special Prosecutor for Darfur did not prosecute the so-called border guards (armed men incorporated into a government paramilitary group), he responded:

> We also wonder why the ... border guards were not arrested. When the conflict started the government established the border guards to fight the rebels. They are illiterate people. They consider themselves government when they support the government. That is why the Prosecutor is afraid to address them.
>
> [INTERVIEWER:] *But prosecutors, you included, are part of the government that they support.*

---

[162] For instance, alleged JEM members after the attack on Omdurman (see Chapter 4, 'Fostering interest in transitional justice') and an SLA/AW member accused of attempted murder of a person that the GoS wanted to participate in the Doha peace talks.

[163] See Tangri and Mwenda 2003, Tripp 2010:67–8 and International Crisis Group 2012. The charges against Major-General James Kazini for his role in the ghost soldier scandal are a notable exception, but can be explained by his falling out with the President. He was killed by his mistress before a military firing squad could implement the court-martial verdict (see Mwenda 2009).

> We wrote to the government to arrest [them]. But nothing has been done. The problem is now stuck at the level of the Ministry of Justice and the Military ... We have no information on what is going on. It is directly between the ministers.[164]

The Minister of Justice, for his part, also knows the red lines. As one of his advisors explains:

> [The Minister] has been given the green light by the government to move on the justice aspect in Darfur. But he must be careful. First, because he is from Darfur he himself cannot be seen to go after the Arabs; he would be accused of bias. He therefore lets the prosecutors from Khartoum – all Arabs – do that ... Secondly, there are red lines that he cannot cross. He focuses on present crimes, but will try to go back. He cannot go after the regime, national security, military intelligence or militias of the Arab tribes. He cannot raise the issue of the Darfurians detained without charge by national security. I advise [the Minister] ... not to touch the red lines. It is better to maintain his job than to lose it.[165]

Whether a prosecutor can take the risk of prosecuting someone depends to a large extent on whether the suspect will receive backing from a powerful constituency. In many instances of conflict-related crimes, individuals can rely on the support of their tribes.[166] Musa Hilal's men, for instance, have not been arrested despite the warrants of arrest issued against them in private prosecutions.[167] One of the most senior officials in the Ministry of Justice justified the lack of arrests by arguing:

> Europeans think it is easy to trace suspects. We have tribes. They take every possible step to protect their members. It is not like Europe, where people are well educated and will not protect criminals. In places like Darfur tribes dominate everything. It is not easy to govern.[168]

In a follow-up interview three years later, he elaborated:

> It is difficult to arrest members of powerful tribes. This is not Paris or London. If the government goes after the tribes that are friendly to the

---

[164] Interview, El-Fasher, August 2011.   [165] Interview, Khartoum, February 2011.

[166] E.g. in 2008, a judge and prosecutor withdrew from the town of Kabkabiya having been threatened by members of tribes of convicted militias (discussion with a prosecutor in North Darfur, El-Fasher, December 2008).

[167] Interview with a lawyer bringing these cases, Nyala, August 2011.

[168] Interview, Khartoum, December 2008.

government, the tribes may become less friendly towards the government. They have more arms than the government. Tribes are very important in Darfur, more than in northern Sudan: they provide most of the security.[169]

Prosecution is less politically risky if suspects are also considered criminals by their own communities. Thus, some kidnappers were prosecuted because, in the advisor's words:

these criminals [were] not supported in their crimes by their tribes; they acted as individuals. Moreover, the *wali* [the governor of the state] supports the prosecution. [The Special Prosecutor] will focus on these kinds of crimes; he cannot look into massive attacks on civilians. He cannot do anything that is against the government.[170]

The assessment of the extent of tribal support remains risky. In 2011, the Special Prosecutor brought a case against someone who had first fought for the government, then, feeling neglected by the government when he ended up wounded in hospital, joined a rebel movement, and, then again, feeling discriminated against as a member of the Rizeigat tribe by the rebels from the Fur tribe, accepted the government's offer to return to its side. He helped the government in its efforts to clear the Jebel Marra from rebellion and was given a house in Nyala. While still negotiating his security arrangements, in other words, a position in which he would be part of one of the many security forces and therefore enjoy immunity, he robbed a bank. He was convicted, in response to which his family and troops threatened the government:

Yes, he committed a bad crime, but he did everything for the government; this is not justice. We are going to join the rebels in their fight against the government.[171]

Thus, even if internationally dismissed as not amounting to the conflict-related crimes included in the Rome Statute, the cases that the Special Prosecutor initiated were related to the conflict in that they could have a huge bearing on political alliances. Illustrative is the following excerpt from a discussion with a Prosecutor in Darfur, who is asked, in the context of a discussion about war crimes, crimes against

---

[169] Interview, Khartoum, July 2011. [170] Interview, Khartoum, February 2011.
[171] Account of the defence lawyer, interview, Nyala, August 2011.

humanity and genocide, about the bank robbery case that the Special Prosecutor brought:

> But that case has nothing to do with the conflict in Darfur!
> [INTERVIEWER:] *Why is it then prosecuted by the 'Special Prosecutor for conflict-related crimes in Darfur'?*
> Because it is politically sensitive. [The suspect] is a Rizeigat who fought for the government. His people can now turn against the government. They are strong.

It was precisely because of their political character that the cases brought by the Special Prosecutor were dealt with by him as opposed to ordinary prosecutors: he has more access to political figures whose consent is required for enforcement of arrest warrants and sentences. But, even where prosecutions were brought and successfully pursued, defendants have subsequently been released, for instance by the Central Reserve Police, another group of pro-government militias integrated into a semi-state institution.

For this reason, the Special Prosecutor did not go beyond investigating ICC suspect Ali Kushayb, a member of the powerful Ta'aisha tribe and incorporated into the same Central Reserve Police. Ahmad Harun, a state minister, has been even more untouchable. Almost every ruling party will consider the political costs of investigating and prosecuting its own members to be too high, especially when individuals will implicate others. When rumours circulated in Khartoum that President Bashir might sacrifice Kushayb and Harun to the ICC to avoid further ICC arrest warrants against government officials, the latter was quick to state publicly that he was merely implementing government policy, thereby signalling the risk of exposure of other government members in the crimes[172] and giving them a good reason to protect him.[173]

---

[172] *Application Arrest Warrant Bashir:*[47] illustrates the risk for some members of a government of the trial of other members of the government. The Prosecutor claims that 'Ahmad Harun said that [President Bashir] had given him the power to kill whoever in Darfur'.

[173] See also a former (South Sudanese) state minister for justice in the GoS: 'The [special] prosecutor [for Darfur] may find some difficulties taking procedures against them [Harun and Kushayb] because they are being protected by the government' ('Darfur's special prosecutor asks government to accept resignation' 2011).

Against this background, it is evident that, no matter how high the sovereignty and reputational costs of ICC proceedings may be, the costs of domestic proceedings may remain prohibitive and thus prevent any catalysing effect on the part of complementarity on genuine domestic investigations and prosecutions.

ICC involvement has not reduced the costs of domestic action

In Uganda and Sudan, the costs of domestic proceedings, set out in the previous section, have not been diminished by the ICC's intervention. Reduction of these costs could have been a consequence of implementation of the policy of positive complementarity, designed as it was to help states to overcome obstacles to domestic proceedings, and could thus have contributed to a catalysing effect. However, the policy has been too underdeveloped and erratically implemented to have such a catalysing effect in Uganda or Sudan.

First, the contents of the policy have oscillated between expansive and narrow interpretations, the former including the OTP's assisting states in conducting domestic proceedings and building capacity, the latter limited to the OTP's merely encouraging states to investigate and prosecute. In practice, the implementation of the policy has not gone beyond handing over information to domestic justice systems in a few isolated cases. In interviews, senior OTP officials admit that 'positive complementarity was not well conceptualised when it was launched',[174] and have justified reduced attention on its implementation by arguing that the policy was developed when 'we [did] not [have] much to do ... [but now] the ICC machine has started and we have to focus our time and resources on these tasks'.[175]

Secondly, the importance attached to the policy of positive complementarity as part of complementarity as big idea, expressed in diplomatic, academic and NGO circles, is not reflected in the OTP's and the PTCs' legal positions. In his first statement to the Assembly of States Parties, the Prosecutor stated:

> The principle of complementarity ... compels the prosecutor's office to collaborate with national jurisdictions in order to help them improve their efficiency. That is the first task of the prosecutor's office: make its best effort to help national jurisdictions fulfil their mission.[176]

---

[174] Interview with a senior ICC official, The Hague, April 2008.
[175] *Ibid.* See also Moreno-Ocampo paraphrased in Waddell and Clark 2007:13.
[176] Moreno-Ocampo 2003b.

But, six years later, in its response to the first admissibility challenge before the Court, the OTP countered a defence submission that the OTP should have encouraged domestic proceedings rather than having expropriated the case as follows:

> There is no duty on the Prosecutor to assist states in their investigations ... [T]he Prosecutor is not obliged to consult and assist States in their investigations and prosecutions, and it bears no burden 'to convince the Pre-Trial Chamber [...] that it has taken all steps that could be reasonably expected to assist the state in its national investigation/ prosecution' ... There are ... substantial reasons based on the object and purpose of the Statute for why such a burden, even if remotely conceivable under the statutory language, should be avoided. The ICC was not created to be an international investigative bureau with resources to support national authorities. It is instead a judicial body with jurisdiction over the most serious crimes of international concern and established to be complementary to national criminal jurisdictions ... Furthermore, Article 93(10), which addresses requests for cooperation from states to the Court, does not impose an obligation on the ICC to render assistance to States. Compliance with a request is discretionary.[177]

Similarly, the Pre-Trial Chamber has, with approval from the Appeals Chamber, confirmed that legally there is no connection between the principle of complementarity as admissibility rule and article 93(10) of the Statute, which the OTP has invoked as the basis of the Prosecutor's policy of positive complementarity.[178] Positive complementarity is thus not a policy that states are entitled to or can rely on – whether and how it is implemented is entirely within the discretion of the Court's organs.

Consequently, the Court's organs are free to apply the policy more with respect to some states than to others, even where both states are, for instance, situation countries. In Uganda and Sudan, this initially led to the paradoxical situation that, while the chances for genuine domestic proceedings were greater in Uganda than in Sudan, the OTP paid more attention to complementarity with respect to Sudan, and by doing so encouraged domestic proceedings there, than it did with respect to Uganda.[179] Uganda had referred the situation, seemed

---

[177] *OTP Response to Admissibility Challenge Katanga*:[98]–[101] (footnotes omitted).

[178] See also *Admissibility Decision Ruto et al. (PTC)*:[34]–[35] and *Admissibility Decision Muthaura et al. (PTC)*:[30]–[31].

[179] Cf. Chapter 3 ('Compromised complementarity') with Chapter 4 ('Complementarity: the views of the ICID and the ICC').

willing to cooperate and thus provided the OTP with a situation where it had a good chance of success. Wishing to keep the LRA case on its docket, the Court in many instances did the very opposite of fostering an expectation on the GoU to conduct proceedings for conflict-related crimes.[180] In contrast, the prospects of cooperation, and thus success, in the Darfur situation were gloomy from the start.[181] The Security Council had obliged only Sudanese parties to cooperate with the Court, the situation had been referred against the will of the Sudanese government, and, in view of the experiences of the *ad hoc* tribunals, the chances were slim that the Security Council would enforce the obligation to cooperate.[182] The OTP therefore initially stressed that the GoS still had a chance to end the ICC's involvement on grounds of complementarity.[183] This changed only when it was clear that Uganda was not likely to challenge the admissibility of its cases before the ICC, and Sudan was not going to cooperate under any circumstances.

This paradox can be explained by the fact that the extent to which the OTP, or any other organ of the Court for that matter, pays attention to the policy of positive complementarity in a particular situation is determined more by its institutional interests than by the policy's possible success in catalysing domestic proceedings. As bureaucracies, international organisations are known not only to expand their own mandates, resulting in so-called 'mission -creep', but also to refuse new missions if these could 'take them into politicised areas that might compromise their authority (and thus a source of their autonomy)'.[184] Specifically with respect to international courts, Yuval Shany has argued that international courts' decisions on jurisdiction and admissibility are influenced by strategic considerations as to how the case would affect the court's legitimacy and effectiveness.[185] If this is the case for decisions on jurisdiction and admissibility, which are to a large extent prescribed by law, it is even more so for an entirely discretionary policy such as positive complementarity.

In its first years of practice, the OTP has focused on two institutional interests: (1) to insure its enforcement handicap by nourishing good relations with relevant states in specific situations and with those great powers whose assistance is essential to the Court's effectiveness (such as the permanent members of the Security Council);

---

[180] See Chapter 3.   [181] See Chapter 4.   [182] See also Peskin 2009.
[183] ICC-OTP 2005c.   [184] Barnett and Finnemore 2004:159.   [185] Shany 2012.

(2) to keep cases in which it has invested substantial amounts of resources on its docket. Thus, in practice, the OTP has stressed the importance of the policy most when it has not yet invested resources in cases, particularly in the phase of preliminary examinations,[186] and particularly with respect to those states (Afghanistan, Colombia, Russia, Georgia) from which cooperation is not likely to be forthcoming or in which intervention would go against the interest of a permanent Security Council member whose cooperation in other situations is essential (US, UK, France and, to a lesser extent, Russia and China).[187]

Once the Court has spent resources on specific cases, it considers it against its interests to risk losing those cases by encouraging domestic proceedings. This is illustrated by an ICC judge who, having taken hundreds of procedural decisions in the three years that the Uganda situation had been before the Court, sighed when referring to the recently concluded A&R Accords of the Juba peace process, remarking: 'Let's hope that they are not going to raise complementarity now.'[188] The fact that the OTP, too, considers losing situations and cases on grounds of complementarity to be against its interests appears from the 'indicators of achievement' of the Office of the Director of the JCCD, one of which is 'a minimal number of challenges to OTP determinations on jurisdiction and admissibility, and upholding of OTP decisions by the Court'.[189] This 'indicator of achievement' does not encourage the JCCD to implement the policy of positive complementarity in situation countries. Consequently, in the context of situation countries the OTP has mentioned the policy of positive complementarity mostly with reference to the division-of-labour reading of complementarity, namely, that states are encouraged to investigate and prosecute domestically cases other than the ICC's.[190] Against this

---

[186] A good example is the OTP's negotiations with Kenya, prior to the OTP's *proprio motu* investigation. See ICC-OTP 2009. See also Moreno-Ocampo 2011:25: 'Recent years have shown that the preliminary examination phase offers the most promising, or at a minimum the first opportunity, for the OTP to serve as a catalyst for the initiation of national proceedings.'

[187] For instance, Afghanistan, Colombia, Georgia and Russia. See e.g. ICC-OTP 2010a and ICC-OTP 2011c:[30] and [85].

[188] Informal discussion, The Hague, April 2008. [189] ICC-ASP/3/25 (2004)-a:75.

[190] See e.g. ICC-OTP 2011b:[19] ('Consistent with positive complementarity, the Office supports national investigations of alleged crimes that do not meet the criteria for ICC prosecution.').

background, it has handed over evidence to the German authorities with respect to suspects in the DRC that it did not intend to prosecute.[191]

Another paradox is that the ICC with complementary jurisdiction has fewer institutional incentives to implement a policy of positive complementarity than the *ad hoc* tribunals with their primacy of jurisdiction. A first reason is the ICC's permanence. The *ad hoc* tribunals became concerned with leaving a legacy only when, under pressure from the Security Council, they adopted completion strategies. The ICC is unlikely to be forced to encourage domestic justice systems to take over its work on account of its prospective demise. In the possibly analogous situation in which the Court is about to end its proceedings in a situation this incentive may arise. However, the Statute does not oblige the OTP to decide that it has ended its investigations – theoretically, once an investigation has been opened, the Court can remain seised of it forever – and, since article 53(4) of the Statute allows the Prosecutor to reconsider a decision not to investigate or prosecute,[192] the question of admissibility may arise again before the Court. In this light, and given the need for the OTP to appear independent when assessing complementarity,[193] ICC officials have been reluctant to engage with legal officials in situation countries with a view to discussing and encouraging national proceedings.[194] For instance, while the Prosecutor identified providing training and technical support as one of the elements of a policy of positive complementarity,[195] the OTP, with an eye to possible future admissibility proceedings, declined to address Sudanese judges and prosecutors present in The Hague on an international law course. A representative of the OTP explained: 'We have to stay at an arm's length [in case] we have to litigate admissibility with them.'[196]

The second component of this paradox is that the complementary character of the ICC's jurisdiction makes it difficult for the Court to

---

[191] Moreno-Ocampo 2011:27. [192] See Chapter 2, n. 200.

[193] See also ICC-OTP 2003c:3.

[194] Even when the OTP has concluded its own proceedings in a particular situation, there are obstacles to implementing the policy of positive complementarity. For instance, concerns over witness protection and the confidentiality of information have made the OTP hesitant to share evidence with the authorities of situation states. However, these concerns are not related to the permanent or complementary character of the ICC – the ICTY and ICTR had similar concerns.

[195] Moreno-Ocampo 2003b. [196] Interview, The Hague, April 2008.

implement a policy of positive complementarity by referring cases from the ICC to domestic courts, this being a way by which the ICTY, and to a lesser extent the ICTR, have encouraged national proceedings. Endowed with primary jurisdiction, the *ad hoc* tribunals have been able to set the standards that a domestic justice system in general and the proceedings in a specific case would have to meet for the latter to receive a case from the former. If domestic justice systems and proceedings did not meet these standards, the tribunals could refuse to refer or could reclaim jurisdiction over the case they had referred. With complementary jurisdiction, the only standard the ICC can set is that domestic proceedings are genuine in accordance with the relatively general criteria set out in article 17.[197] Lacking the mandate to supervise domestic proceedings in a manner as stringent as the *ad hoc* tribunals, the ICC may be reluctant to pass on its files to domestic justice systems.

An increasingly important component of the idea of positive complementarity has been that actors other than the Court, for instance states parties to the Rome Statute, would implement the OTP's policy of positive complementarity. It has been argued that the ICC's involvement in a state flags the need for international support and that donors will respond with assistance.[198] If donors do not come in automatically, the OTP could broker such assistance, or at least so it has been suggested.[199] But in the first years of ICC practice, the OTP has not brokered,[200] and donors have not provided, financial or technical assistance to encourage Uganda or Sudan to conduct proceedings for crimes within the Court's jurisdiction with a view to helping these states to fulfil their responsibility.[201] In part this is due

---

[197] See Chapter 2, 'The ICC does not have a conditional deferral procedure like the ICTY and ICTR'.

[198] Kleffner 2006:96.   [199] ICC-OTP 2003c:6.

[200] According to Moreno-Ocampo 2007a, the OTP has brokered assistance, but senior OTP officials confirmed in interviews in The Hague in April and May 2008 that this was done only in the DRC, and consisted of not much more than commenting on a needs assessment conducted by the European Union.

[201] Donors' interest in the Ugandan International Crimes Division seems an exception, but their initial support was not linked to positive complementarity. Rather, they saw such support as a part of their broader rule-of-law programme in Uganda. Other donors interested in supporting the SDHC consider such support as their contribution to the peace process. They are motivated by complementarity in that domestic proceedings could be the key to the peace negotiations by convincing Joseph Kony to sign the FPA (interview with a European diplomat, Kampala,

to the lack of coherence between donors' diplomatic action and their development programmes.[202] Thus, the units in Western ministries of foreign affairs covering the ICC's involvement in Sudan and Uganda have not associated ICC intervention with a need for support for rule-of-law programmes in those states.[203] The ministries' rule-of-law development specialists, in turn, usually try to stay away from ICC issues.[204] They concentrate instead on long-term projects, wish to address 'technical' issues and need to engage with the receiving governments. The short-term, politically loaded and sometimes anti-government ICC intervention does not fit with this approach, and even threatens it. One representative of a large donor agency from a state not party to the Rome Statute explained this as follows with respect to the creation of the Ugandan International Crimes Division as an alternative to the ICC:

> Our concern is that this will affect a very limited group of people and not on the long term. From an international law perspective it is important to get the ICC away [to allow the peace talks to succeed],

October 2008). But this is different from supporting the SDHC because of a belief that domestic justice systems must be enabled to fulfil their primary responsibility in the prosecution of crimes within the ICC's jurisdiction.

[202] See, similarly, Hauser 1999:624, pointing out the inconsistency between donors' political and foreign policy on the one hand and their development programmes on the other in the context of promoting democracy abroad.

[203] One official responsible for ICC affairs in a European Ministry of Foreign Affairs explained this disconnect as follows: 'Rule of law has more to do with good governance and ending corruption, while the ICC is a matter of peace and security.' (interview, May 2008). Similarly, an official of the UN Development Programme responded to a question as to whether ICC intervention was a cue for more support to a domestic justice system: 'the ICC affects political issues; not justice' (interview, El-Fasher, May 2010). The offer from the Canadian government to assist in drafting implementing legislation to be applied by the SDHC does stem from a policy related to the ICC, yet it is no exception to the institutional disconnect between rule-of-law and ICC affairs: it is a special programme within the Canadian Ministry of Foreign Affairs to support the universality of the ICC rather than part of the agenda of the Canadian International Development Agency. On this disconnect, see also Open Society Justice Initiative 2010:4 and 9.

[204] Similar divisions exist within international organisations such as the EU and UN. While the Office of Legal Affairs and the UNHCHR (who is now and was most recently an ex-official of the ICC and ICTR and of the ICTY, respectively) are generally keen to support the ICC's role, the Department of Peacekeeping Operations and the Department of Political Affairs wish not to be associated with the ICC's work as it complicates the fulfilment of their mandates.

but it is not important from a widespread community level, with which we prefer to work ... Why this Special Division [of the High Court] if access to justice in general is so poor in Uganda? ... It would be a sacrifice of standard justice for special justice.[205]

By contrast, in departments in which development programmes and ICC policy in fact were coordinated, the pro-ICC ideology often prevented implementation of the policy of positive complementarity.[206]

Finally, the key strategies that the Assembly of States Parties has been developing for the implementation of the policy of positive complementarity appear of little relevance since they are based on incorrect assumptions about the obstacles to domestic proceedings. 'Legislative assistance', 'technical assistance and capacity building' and 'assistance with the construction of physical infrastructure'[207] have been identified as the strategies to overcome the '[t]hree main challenges facing the application of complementarity in practice'.[208] However, the effects observed in Uganda and Sudan show that, if desired, legislation is easily drafted, introduced and passed and courts can be established overnight and that even infinite capacity building does not result in systematic investigations and prosecutions into conflict-related crimes. As the previous section has argued, the real obstacles to domestic proceedings are more ingrained.[209]

Low costs of inaction

A strong catalysing effect on domestic proceedings has been absent not merely because the costs of domestic action are high (and have not been reduced by ICC intervention) but also because in some

---

[205] Interview, Kampala, October 2008. In Sudan, the concerns of development workers about the possibly disruptive effect of ICC intervention on their programmes were confirmed after the issuance of an arrest warrant against the President. The GoS suspended several international humanitarian programmes on accusations of cooperation with the ICC (see Chapter 4, n. 164), the security situation became too hostile for the implementation of programmes and Western governments reconsidered their development work, contemplating to what extent they wished to support a state whose president had been charged by the ICC.

[206] See also US diplomat Kaye 2004, commenting on the 'potential for Ocampo's "positive complementarity" to work too successfully, from the perspective of committed ICC-backers', by serving 'to undermine the justification for the ICC's substantial growth'.

[207] ICC-ASP/8/Res.9 Annex 4 (2010):[17] (emphases omitted). See also ICC President Song 2010:4, emphasising the importance of legislative assistance.

[208] Bergsmo, Bekou and Jones 2010:801.   [209] See also Moreno-Ocampo 2011:28.

situations, for instance in Uganda, the costs of inaction have been considered low. Contrary to assumption, states do not necessarily consider the involvement of the ICC to be costly. Accordingly, they do not necessarily conduct domestic proceedings in order to avoid or end ICC involvement. Quite the reverse: as the Ugandan self-referral illustrates, a state can deem the ICC's involvement beneficial to its interests, including its perceived sovereignty and reputation.

With respect to sovereignty, the GoU calculated that it would incur sovereignty benefits, not costs, from ICC involvement. Indeed, the ICC's proceedings against the LRA have given the GoU leverage to convince the DRC and the CAR to allow the UPDF onto their respective territories, (temporarily) dissuaded Sudan from supporting the LRA, and have cautioned the ICC Prosecutor against opening proceedings against the UPDF in the DRC situation. ICC inter-vention thus came as support, externally strengthening Uganda's sovereignty *vis-à-vis* other states and internally that of the GoU *vis-à-vis* the LRA.

The sovereignty costs of the ICC's intervention, on the other hand, have been limited. Such costs would be high if the ICC were to prosecute state officials, as the statements by President Museveni and Minister Mbabazi guaranteeing domestic proceedings against such persons confirm.[210] But the GoU has not considered the ICC's exer-cise of jurisdiction over the LRA to be costly in sovereignty terms. This difference in the sense of ownership over crimes committed by state officials and over those committed by the LRA is partly related to whether or not the crimes implicate the government.[211] But it also reflects the weakness of the Ugandan national identity.[212] The GoU may have considered the outsourcing of cases against northern Acholi to an international forum less of an encroachment on sovereignty than if the cases had concerned members of Ugandan ethnic groups more closely associated with power.[213]

---

[210] See Chapter 3, n. 566.

[211] Although now renamed the Uganda People's Defence Forces (UPDF), the former National Resistance Army is still inextricably intertwined with Museveni's governing National Resistance Movement (NRM). On how the NRM does not make a distinc-tion between the state of Uganda and the NRM regime, see Omach 2009a.

[212] On the lack of post-independence nation-building, see also Commission of Inquiry into Violations of Human Rights 1994:[2.2 vi] and Mutua 2007:26.

[213] On the phenomenon of '[c]osmopolitan law [being] for other people', see also Simpson 2007:44. See also McCormack 2006.

Equally, the GoU calculated that it could incur benefits from the ICC's intervention with respect to its reputation.[214] The GoU could portray itself as a champion of international criminal justice by providing the ICC with its first situation. In addition, the ICC's accusations against the LRA granted legitimacy to the GoU's military counter-insurgency by branding the LRA an enemy of mankind and changing the GoU's image from that of warmonger to that of defender of humanity. Conversely, any costs to the GoU's reputation were minimised. In the referral letter, the GoU went out of its way to stress the reputation of Uganda's legal sector.[215] It emphasised that its only limitation was its inability to arrest the suspects,[216] which, if it was a confession of weakness, was one with which most states and the ICC were likely to sympathise. Moreover, the referral had the potential to shift responsibility for this shortcoming onto the ICC and show the GoU in a positive light: either the ICC would arrest the GoU's opponents, for which the GoU would also take credit, or the ICC would fail and legitimise Uganda's inability to arrest the suspects.

The Court's actions have confirmed that intervention by the ICC need not adversely affect a state's reputation. Accepting at face value the GoU's claim that it had not conducted and was not conducting domestic proceedings against the LRA, the ICC avoided the question that had the potential negatively to impact on Uganda's reputation, namely, that of its ability and willingness genuinely to investigate or prosecute. Instead, the OTP and PTC implicitly praised Uganda for its referral of the situation by repeating the non-statutory consideration that the ICC was 'the most appropriate and effective forum'.[217] Accordingly, the GoU, rather than being shamed by the referral as an indicator of its unwillingness or inability genuinely to investigate or prosecute the crimes in question, has been able to portray the referral as an illustration of its commitment to international criminal justice.[218] One government minister reasoned:

> Don't you agree that [the fact that Uganda was the state to give the Court its first situation] is the reason why the Review Conference should be here? We deserve it.[219]

---

[214] See, more elaborately, Chapter 3.

[215] See Chapter 3, 'Compromised complementarity'.   [216] *Ibid.*

[217] See *Notification Investigation Uganda, Arrest Warrant Kony*:[37] and *LRA Admissibility Decision (PTC)*:[37]. See Chapter 3, opening quotation and 'Compromised complementarity'.

[218] Interview, Kampala, September 2008.   [219] Interview, Kampala, October 2008.

With respect to sovereignty and reputational costs at the sub-state level, lawyers did not consider the ICC's actions to be intervention by a professional competitor claiming cases within their jurisdiction or undermining their reputation. They never considered conflict-related crimes part of their domain in the first place.

All this said, the cost–benefit analysis changed somewhat in Uganda when the ICC's involvement came to be seen as the most significant obstacle to the successful conclusion of the Juba peace talks. For the Ugandan government, the hoped-for benefit of the ICC's securing the arrest of the LRA had not materialised, while the inability to conclude a peace agreement as long as the ICC remained involved emerged as a sovereignty cost. This situation also undermined the government's domestic reputation, as the GoU was blamed for having referred the situation to the Court in the first place. This change in cost–benefit analysis catalysed several moves by the GoU, including, as a concession to the LRA, an undertaking to conduct domestic proceedings.

The Juba talks also altered the calculations of the Ugandan legal sector. As Chapter 3 has demonstrated,[220] the search for domestic alternatives to the ICC led to a broadening of the approach to the conflict in the north to encompass a legal dimension. Since then, some lawyers in the Ugandan JLOS have realised that the need for domestic lawyers provides them with an opportunity to strengthen the position of their profession within the national government and to boost the reputation of Uganda's legal sector within the region. The International Crimes Division attracted international financial support and has been given its first case because the division can enhance Uganda's reputation, problems of legitimacy with the prosecution of that first case notwithstanding. Similarly, the amnesty was abolished, because international opinion had turned against it, despite the Constitutional Court's finding of constitutionality.

The *status quo* may suit the GoU best. It has shown its commitment to both justice and peace, but it has not had to deliver on either. Neither has it needed to backtrack on its cooperation with the ICC[221] nor has it been confronted with unwelcome exposure of UPDF actions

---

[220] 'Broadening the approach towards the conflict to include a legal dimension'.

[221] Indeed, when PTC II assessed *proprio motu* the admissibility of the LRA case, the GoU's submissions consisted of a mere two pages to the effect that the case was still admissible because the Juba agreements remained without legal force as long

that is likely to be part of any trial of the LRA. Kony's refusal to sign a peace agreement after two years of internationally funded peace talks has convinced Western states that Museveni's preferred military solution is the only viable option left.[222] Meanwhile, the war against the LRA continues to be used as an excuse for the securitisation of society, covers up patronage scandals and provides a reason for an alliance with the US, which in turn is a lease of life to the NRM. With the abolition of the Amnesty Act, the grant of amnesty has again become a matter of personal discretion for the President. Those whose loyalty is of little value or is unlikely to be maintained or obtained can be brought before the International Crimes Division. The justice talk cannot disguise that in essence much of the practice has remained unchanged in Uganda.[223]

Costs of inaction can be avoided by means other than the invocation of complementarity

Even if the costs of ICC intervention are high, there might still be no catalysing effect on genuine domestic proceedings given the possibility that ICC involvement can be avoided, ended or obstructed by means other than the invocation of complementarity. There are several such confounding and intervening variables, including restrictions on the Court's jurisdiction, the admissibility criterion of sufficient gravity, limitations on the Court's resources, the OTP's prosecutorial policy and the Court's dependence on cooperation, particularly of the state (s) where the crimes are alleged to have been committed and where the suspects reside.[224] In short, the ICC's other in-built limitations have the potential to dilute complementarity's catalysing effect.

These ICC-endogenous confounding and intervening variables go a long way to explaining the absence of a catalysing effect on genuine domestic proceedings for alleged UPDF crimes in Uganda. While Ugandan officials have suggested that the GoU would conduct

as Kony did not sign the FPA (*Observations GoU on Proprio Motu Admissibility Assessment LRA*).

[222] In UN Doc. S/PRST/2008/48 (2008), the UN Security Council 'welcome[d] the joint efforts ... made [by states in the region] to address the security threat posed by LRA'.

[223] See also Merry 2006b:43 discussing work by Richard Rottenburg ('The universalist facade obscures the fact that things are still being done in local ways.').

[224] See Chapter 2, 'Looking for a catalysing effect: the potentially confounding and intervening variables'.

domestic proceedings were the ICC to investigate Ugandan state actors,[225] the GoU has had no reason to follow up on these statements, since the ICC has not opened investigations into crimes committed by individuals associated with the government – and this for reasons other than complementarity.

First, many of the GoU's acts in northern Uganda clearly amount to human rights violations, but less obviously so to international crimes incorporated in the ICC Statute. Whilst for victims a legal finesse without justification, this distinction diminishes the risk of ICC proceedings against those who committed the violations and thus the need for domestic proceedings. Secondly, as most of the alleged UPDF crimes were committed before the start of the Court's temporal jurisdiction in 2002, they cannot be investigated by the Court, so that there is again no need for the GoU to pre-empt ICC proceedings by conducting domestic proceedings. Thirdly, the OTP has invoked the standard of gravity as a reason for prioritising proceedings against the LRA over investigations of Ugandan state actors, thereby depriving the GoU of an incentive to conduct proceedings against the latter.[226] Fourthly, the finitude of the Court's resources has compelled it to assign the investigators working on the Uganda file to another situation,[227] with the result that the chances are now slim that the OTP will ever open an investigation into crimes committed in northern Uganda on the government side.[228] The need for the GoU to conduct proceedings in order to block potential ICC cases against state officials is accordingly greatly reduced. Fifthly, as it is the Prosecutor's policy to prosecute only those bearing the greatest responsibility, domestic proceedings aimed at rendering ICC cases inadmissible would be necessary only for this circumscribed group.[229]

Finally, 'endowed with no more powers than any tourist in a foreign State',[230] the Prosecutor is reluctant to jeopardise existing cooperation with the Ugandan government in the LRA case by going

---

[225] See Chapter 3, n. 566.

[226] See Chapter 2, 'Other jurisdictional provisions: the admissibility criterion of gravity', and Chapter 3, 'The ICC in Uganda: a joint enterprise' and 'Encouraging more trials, prosecutions and/or investigations?'.

[227] ICC-ASP/5/32 (2006)-a:[60].

[228] However, see also ICC-ASP/8/10 (2009):[14].

[229] As is confirmed by statements such as in *Fifth Darfur Report*:6.

[230] Swart and Sluiter 1999:115, commenting on RS, art. 99(4). But see also art. 57(3)(d).

after state actors.[231] The GoU, for its part, knows that the OTP relies on it to a large extent to execute arrest warrants, to protect witnesses and to provide evidence. Indeed, many in the GoU believe that the 'situation concerning the LRA' is a joint project of the GoU and OTP. They consider the OTP's case their own, given their substantial cooperation with the Prosecutor.[232] These officials do not believe that their ICC 'friends' will go after those who first helped the OTP so generously.[233] Moreover, the GoU enjoys protection from the US, which has been supportive of the OTP's case against the LRA but has pressured it not to deal with UPDF activity.[234] The OTP has reasons to take heed, given its attempts to secure US cooperation in various situations.[235] In short, the OTP's dependence on cooperation has given the GoU the impression that the OTP will not proceed against state actors. Without actual or likely ICC cases against state officials to be rendered inadmissible, there has been no catalysing effect on Ugandan proceedings against state actors.

The Sudanese government's investigative and prosecutorial apathy could initially be ascribed in part to its having pinned its hopes on Security Council deferral under article 16 of the Rome Statute. The GoS insisted that the Security Council, as the cause of its problem, overrule the ICC by 'withdrawing' its referral or suspending indefinitely the ICC proceedings in respect of Darfur.[236] But more and more the GoS has relied on the Court's dependence on it for enforcement. The GoS knows that without its cooperation the arrest warrants are unlikely to be executed, particularly if the individuals who have been charged by the Court do not leave the country and the NCP holds on

---

[231] A Ugandan lawyer quoted the ICC's Deputy Prosecutor as saying that cases against the UPDF would be opened only after the LRA leaders were in the dock at the ICC (discussion, Gulu, September 2008).

[232] Interview with a cabinet minister, Kampala, October 2008.

[233] Interview with a Ugandan official who had closely cooperated with the ICC, Kampala, October 2008. To underline his partnership with the ICC, this official privately showed pictures in which the Ugandan Defence Minister Mbabazi and his lawyers sit side-by-side with officials of the JCCD on a boat in Dutch canals, with the Prosecutor himself, dressed in leisure wear, at the helm. The JCCD, unofficially known as the OTP's Foreign Office, may organise such diplomatic courtesy outings to encourage cooperation, but the ensuing team spirit makes it more difficult for all to believe that one part of the team will later prosecute the other.

[234] See Perrot 2010:199.   [235] See e.g. Lerner 2010.

[236] See Chapter 4, 'Complementarity: less than a secondary response'.

to power. This defiance may come at the cost of more international isolation and sanctions; but, as one NCP stalwart put it, 'What's new?'[237] The NCP, or at least the President, may estimate these costs to be lower than the costs of either surrendering to the ICC or conducting genuine domestic proceedings in the same cases as the Court. The Court's dependence on cooperation thus tempers complementarity's potential catalysing effect. States can rely on their ability to impede the Court's proceedings by refusing cooperation, instead of by conducting genuine domestic proceedings. Complementarity is clearly not the only escape route from the consequences of ICC involvement.

Paradoxes of complementarity: cost–benefit analyses combined

Several scholars have observed that the combination of the complementary character of the Court's jurisdiction and its heavy dependence on the cooperation of other actors gives rise to the 'complementarity paradox', that is, that the 'unwilling and unable[238] fora are required to cooperate with the ICC in order to achieve effective prosecution and trial'.[239] With respect to inability, the paradox is illustrated by the requirement that Uganda arrest the LRA suspects. Uganda, having referred the situation to the ICC on account of its inability to arrest the LRA leaders, was subsequently accused by the ICC Registrar of violating its obligation to cooperate with the Court by failing to execute the ICC warrants for the LRA leadership.[240] With respect to unwillingness, the paradox is illustrated by the Sudan situation. Perceiving the cost of ICC prosecutions to be higher than the reputational cost of non-cooperation, the GoS has simply

---

[237] Interview, Khartoum, November 2008.

[238] In the context of this statement, inability and unwillingness are not the terms of art as defined in art. 17, which indicate the circumstances in which domestic proceedings lack genuineness; rather, the words are used in their lay sense, and can refer to societal circumstances that may equally explain the absence, rather than the lack of genuineness, of domestic proceedings.

[239] Bekou and Cryer 2007:63, who refer to Benvenuti 1999:50, who identifies the problem without calling it the 'complementarity paradox'. For similar observations, see Aptel Williamson 2006:26, Bekou and Cryer 2004:xix, Bergsmo 2000:98, Cameron 2004:92, Cryer 2005b:157, Cryer 2011:1097 and 1103, Eckert 2009:218 *et seq.*, Kaul and Kress 1999:160–1, Swart and Sluiter 1999:92, Yang 2003:606 and Yang 2005b:288. On this paradox in international law more generally, see Simpson 2007:46 and Smith 2009:324.

[240] See Chapter 3, n. 148.

refused all cooperation. Without guaranteed means by which to enforce obligations of cooperation,[241] the ICC can see its proceedings thwarted by an unwilling state's refusal to cooperate with it.

The Ugandan story reveals, however, the need to qualify this complementarity paradox. Willingness and ability, in the context of this paradox used in sociological rather than legal terms, are relative concepts. On one side of the ability-and-willingness spectrum is the state that is willing and able to investigate and prosecute domestically, opposes international involvement and is thus unlikely to cooperate with the Court. Post-Qaddhafi Libya could fit into this scenario. On the other side of the spectrum are situations of almost absolute unwillingness and inability: the state from which cooperation is required is neither willing nor able to conduct domestic proceedings nor supportive of international proceedings, and, by refusing cooperation, also leaves the Court relatively unable. In other words, in these situations the unwillingness and inability concern proceedings at both the domestic and the international levels and there is little the ICC or other external actors can do to offset this. Examples are the Sudan situation, Ugandan proceedings against state actors and Ugandan and international attempts to arrest the LRA. In the middle of the ability-and-willingness spectrum is the scenario of partial unwillingness or ability, in which the unwillingness or inability concern domestic

---

[241] When states parties refuse to cooperate, the Court may notify the Assembly of States Parties (ASP) (RS, art. 87(7)). In the event of a referral by the Security Council, the Court may notify the Security Council. (RS, art. 87(5)(b) makes provision for the situation where a state not party to the Statute that has entered into an *ad hoc* cooperation agreement with the Court fails to comply with such an agreement. The Statute is silent on the situation where a state not party to the Statute that has not entered into such an agreement fails to comply with a Security Council resolution obliging it to cooperate. But the Prosecutor could report such a failure to the Council should he report to it periodically pursuant to the resolution by which the situation was referred to the Court.) The Statute does not specify the measures that the ASP, on receipt of such notification, can take. On the basis of the general international law of retorsion and counter-measures (see Articles on Responsibility of States for Internationally Wrongful Acts, art. 22, Chapter 2 and commentaries, 180–3 and 324–55), states parties, or some of them, could agree on conditionality of membership of other international organisations or economic sanctions. Such reactions, however, depend on consensus in the specific situation. The Security Council, for its part, could take binding measures, but it does not necessarily prioritise justice by international courts over the other interests it is mandated to safeguard. Moreover, even the ASP and the Security Council rely ultimately on states to enforce their resolutions.

proceedings only, for which the ICC, and other external actors, can compensate. In other words, the ICC can do what the state concerned will not (or cannot) do. The ICC's case against the LRA, in aspects other than arrest, is an example.

In the first scenario, there is no paradox of complementarity: the state investigates or prosecutes and there is no need for the ICC to intervene. In the second scenario the complementarity paradox is a real contradiction. For instance, a contradiction exists to the extent that Uganda is expected to arrest the LRA leadership, even though Uganda referred the situation to the Court in the first place on account of its inability to arrest the same people. This is a scenario of almost absolute inability since Uganda is unable to arrest while the ICC, and other external actors, prove equally unable and cannot remedy Uganda's inability. In the third scenario, the complementarity paradox is only an apparent contradiction. For instance, Uganda, although itself at the time not preparing domestic proceedings against the LRA leadership, did refer the situation to the Court and cooperate extensively with it. Domestic unwillingness and inability could be compensated by external actors such as the ICC. As regards unwilling-ness, the ICC provided an opportunity for the GoU to externalise the political costs that impeded domestic proceedings against the LRA. As regards ability, the ICC had at its disposal investigation techniques and resources for witness protection that the GoU did not.

The potential for complementarity to have a catalysing effect on the basis of influencing a cost–benefit assessment differs per scenario. In the first scenario, that of domestic ability and willingness, the catalysing effect is likely to be limited. Domestic proceedings may well occur, but it is unlikely that complementarity is the catalysing factor: the state may well have investigated and prosecuted irrespect-ive of the ICC's complementary jurisdiction. To the extent that complementarity does have a catalysing effect it is likely to be mostly in shaping domestic proceedings on the model of the ICC's (potential) cases in terms of suspects, conduct, crimes and incidents.

In the second scenario, that of (almost) absolute unwillingness or absolute inability, the opportunities for a catalysing effect on genuine domestic proceedings are limited, too. In this scenario, the effect is limited because it is unlikely that there will be any domestic proceed-ings: the state's unwillingness or inability concerns both domestic and international proceedings and the ICC and other actors cannot remedy the causes of the inability or unwillingness. Take the Bashir administration in Sudan, which can be considered absolutely unwilling on account of the fact that it could never externalise the political costs of proceedings, whether domestic or international, where those proceedings target the core of the administration.[242] In these circumstances, the opportunities for a catalysing effect on genuine domestic proceedings are low, since no matter how much Sudan opposes ICC intervention, it is equally unwilling to conduct genuine domestic proceedings in respect of the suspects. Equally, Uganda's almost absolute inability to arrest the LRA leadership is not easily remedied, since the ICC and its supporters are, so far, as unable as the GoU to arrest Kony *et al.*

Partial unwillingness or inability presents most opportunities for a catalysing effect on genuine domestic proceedings. The causes of such relative unwillingness and inability can be remedied by outside assistance. For example, were the LRA leaders to surrender to Ugandan jurisdiction and in doing so cure Uganda's inability to arrest them, international teams could assist the GoU with evidence-gathering and witness protection, addressing one of the causes of Uganda's relative inability and transforming it from 'relatively unable' into 'able'. The possibility of shifting the political costs of LRA proceedings onto the ICC could transform Uganda from 'relatively unwilling' to 'willing'. For example, during the Juba talks, the GoU was in a position to externalise the political costs of possible domestic proceedings against the LRA leadership in that it could have argued that domestic proceedings were necessary since, without them, the admissibility of the OTP's case could not be successfully challenged and the ICC arrest warrants for the LRA leadership would stand.[243]

The OTP's policy of positive complementarity is, in theory, ideal for helping a relatively unable state to become able. The OTP's practice with respect to Uganda, however, has revealed the 'paradox of positive complementarity', by which is meant that the policy is easiest to implement in a state that is willing to cooperate with the Court but

---

[242] The same scenario of absolute unwillingness exists in Uganda with respect to investigations and prosecutions of senior state officials.

[243] But the LRA's refusal to sign the FPA may have changed the GoU's calculation of the political costs once again. If domestic opposition to trying the LRA leadership were to jeopardise the government's position, the latter may well be unable to externalise these costs and may, as a result, move towards absolute unwillingness, refusing both to hand over the LRA and to conduct domestic proceedings.

that, given this willingness to cooperate, it is not in the OTP's interest to implement the policy in that state, at least for as long as the OTP needs successful cases.[244] The flipside of the paradox is that a policy of positive complementarity is most difficult to implement in states that refuse to cooperate with the Court, but – by reason of the state's unwillingness to cooperate, which promises little chance of success, especially if the state is backed by powerful allies – the OTP prefers addressing impunity in that state by encouraging domestic proceedings.

The overarching paradox, which includes the paradox of positive complementarity, might be called the 'catalysing effect paradox': that is, defining as it does its own success by pointing to completed cases before the Court, the ICC is most reluctant to give up jurisdiction in those states where it has the best chance of having a catalysing effect on domestic proceedings. The ICC has the best chance of having a catalysing effect in partially unable or partially unwilling states, but in such scenarios it is least likely to relinquish jurisdiction, as it can count on effective cooperation. In its first years of operation, the ICC has wanted to play host to potential success stories, rather than assist in domestic proceedings. Northern Uganda reveals how the ICC has striven to obtain the situation and retain cases arising from it, even after the prospect of possible domestic proceedings emerged.

By the same token, in states in which the ICC is least likely to have a catalysing effect on domestic proceedings, for instance Sudan, it was initially reluctant to exercise jurisdiction, as the chances of successful proceedings were slight. From the perspective of countering impunity, ICC proceedings seem most necessary in just such situations of almost absolute unwillingness or absolute inability, because here the chances of a catalysing effect on genuine domestic proceedings are very limited. But it is precisely here that the ICC is least keen on exercising jurisdiction, since its own chances of success are slim, given its dependence on the cooperation of the absolutely unwilling or unable state.

CONCLUSION: UNRAVELLING THE PARADOXES

Great expectations of a catalysing effect on domestic proceedings attended the creation of the International Criminal Court. These

---

[244] See for the same paradox with respect to the OTP's focus in DRC, Clark 2011:1192–4.

expectations were primarily based on assumptions about complementarity's normative character and about states' analysis of the costs and benefits of domestic proceedings in comparison to those of ICC intervention. Whilst normativity and cost–benefit analyses played some role in catalysing effects in Uganda and Sudan, they were not enough to bring about systematic investigations or prosecutions of conflict-related crimes (see Chapters 3 and 4). The assumptions must thus be reviewed and adjusted.

The catalysing effect of complementarity on normative grounds on domestic proceedings in Uganda and Sudan has been marginal since the principle has not been translated into an expectation on states to investigate and prosecute domestically the crimes listed in the Rome Statute. Legally, the explanation is evident: complementarity as provided in the Statute recognises states' primary right to conduct proceedings for conflict-related crimes but does not oblige them to do this. Nonetheless, the preamble to the Rome Statute, the OTP's policy of positive complementarity and the idea of a 'Rome System' could have given complementarity a normative flavour by fostering a non-legal expectation that states will conduct proceedings.

However, the development of such a political expectation on states has been countered by three other factors. First, there has been considerable confusion, ambiguity and even misrepresentation with respect to the content of complementarity as the principle that grants states the primary right to investigate and prosecute crimes within the Court's jurisdiction. The clearest example of misrepresentation is that of complementarity as a division of labour between the ICC and national jurisdictions, the former being responsible for the big cases and the latter for the less serious ones.

Secondly, there has been even more ambiguity with respect to complementarity as big idea entailing the responsibility or duty of states to investigate and prosecute. To some extent this ambiguity reflects the discrepancy between on the one hand the big-idea discourse on complementarity as a reminder to states of their responsibility to investigate and prosecute, and on the other the Rome Statute that creates a court on the very assumption that states do not always fulfil that responsibility. But the Court's interpretation of the Statute and particularly the OTP's policy of inviting self-referrals have further weakened this expectation, giving rise to the normative paradox of complementarity: instead of complementarity's contributing to an expectation on states to investigate and prosecute, the creation of the 'Rome System', and particularly its implementation so far, may, by projecting the Court as an institution to take over from states the responsibility to investigate and prosecute conflict-related crimes, actually undermine the expectation on states to discharge that responsibility. By prioritising the fight against impunity over the primary responsibility of the state and by providing too ready a back-up, the Court diminishes the notion of the responsibility of the state.

In addition to the normative paradox of complementarity, the emergence of 'pro-ICC ideology' has caused ambiguity with respect to complementarity as big idea entailing the responsibility or duty of states to investigate and prosecute. Pro-ICC ideology counters any idea of the responsibility of the state because it entails the view that the ICC is the better forum for the adjudication of international crimes.

Finally, a third factor opposing the development of a political expectation on states to investigate and prosecute conflict-related crimes domestically has been a context in Uganda and Sudan that is inhospitable to the infiltration of any such norm.

With respect to expectations of a catalysing effect based on assumptions about complementarity and the cost–benefit analysis engaged in by states, the costs of both domestic action and ICC intervention must be reconsidered. On the one hand, the practical and political costs of investigations and prosecutions in Uganda and Sudan have been so insuperable that the sovereignty and reputational costs incurred by ICC interference have not swayed the outcome of the state's comparative assessment of the costs of domestic inaction. Nor has the policy of positive complementarity reduced the costs of domestic action. On the other hand, the costs of inaction, which were expected to spur domestic proceedings, have not necessarily been high. On the contrary, the GoU calculated that it could gain political favour internationally by referring the situation to the Court and thus by remaining inactive domestically. Even where, as in Sudan, the costs of ICC involvement have been high, this has not automatically resulted in the state's recourse to domestic proceedings. ICC proceedings have also been impeded by Court-endogenous characteristics that function as confounding and intervening variables. Limitations on the Court's jurisdiction, the application of the criterion of gravity in the selection of cases, the Court's prosecutorial policy of focusing on those bearing the greatest responsibility, restraints on the Court's operational capacity, the possibility of the Security Council's requesting the deferral of the Court's proceedings and, most of all, the Court's dependence on the cooperation of other actors have all played their part in diluting complementarity's potential catalysing effect.[245]

The ICC itself has been double-faced with respect to encouraging domestic proceedings.[246] Whereas both faces have been presented as parts of, or consistent with, the policy of positive complementarity, in fact only one of them results in the encouragement of domestic proceedings. The other, whilst possibly reflecting or resulting in positive, in the sense of cooperative, relations with states, and thus potentially beneficial for the fight against impunity as defined by the Court, in fact discourages domestic investigations and prosecutions.

One face is that which promotes complementarity as big idea entailing states' responsibility or even duty to investigate and prosecute conflict-related crimes domestically. It was this face that the first Prosecutor put on when he defined in his inaugural address a successful ICC as one with no cases thanks to the complementarity of its jurisdiction.[247] This face was also shown immediately after the situation in Darfur had been referred, when prospects for cooperation were grim and the OTP had not yet invested resources in cases. This face has been most visible in situations which the OTP has had under preliminary analysis but in which it has not yet opened investigations (Afghanistan, Colombia, Georgia, Russia and more recently Guinea).

The other face, however, is that which discourages domestic proceedings through the OTP's policy of inviting self-referrals, the promotion of a pro-ICC ideology, transformation of complementarity into a division-of-labour rule and subordinating complementarity to the fight against impunity as defined by the ICC's organs.

The explanation for this face-changing can be found in the Court's, and in particular the OTP's, perception of its institutional interests. In its first years of operations the Court had to prove its supporters right by showing its effectiveness. At the same time, the OTP felt it

---

[245] Theoretically, the interpretation of the 'interests of justice' (see Chapter 2, 'No ICC proceedings because of the "interests of justice"') could be another such factor, but, while both the LRA and the GoS have referred to the provision, it does not appear to have played a role in the GoS and GoU's respective calculations.

[246] More international institutions appear to have two faces. See e.g. Verdirame and Harrell-Bond 2005 with respect to the Office of the UN High Commissioner for Refugees.

[247] See Chapter 1, opening quotation.

had to persuade the world's great powers of the Court's usefulness, or at the least not intensify their suspicion or open hostility towards it, in order to enhance the Court's legitimacy (which, in turn, could enhance its effectiveness). Self-referrals were thus ideal because they not only provided the Court with its first work but also enhanced its legitimacy (states were seen to agree with ICC intervention) and its effectiveness (states promised cooperation). On the other hand, domestic proceedings have been encouraged in those states where cooperation has been unlikely to be forthcoming and intervention would give rise to some great power's objections (Colombia, Russia, Georgia, Afghanistan and possibly post-Qaddhafi Libya). The OTP has thus preferred to exercise its jurisdiction in situations of relative unwillingness or relative inability, namely, where states are unwilling or unable to conduct domestic proceedings but are not opposed to international investigations and prosecutions. Ironically, these are the very situations in which the ICC and its foundational principle of complementarity could have had the strongest catalysing effect on domestic proceedings, in that the states in question could have been propelled from unwillingness and inability to willingness and ability. This illustrates the 'catalysing effect paradox', which is that the ICC is most keen to exercise its jurisdiction in precisely those cases where complementarity has the greatest chances of catalysing genuine domestic proceedings, whether through the implementation of a policy of positive complementarity or by providing an institution to which the political costs of domestic proceedings could be transferred.

The more the ICC has established itself as an institution, and provided the Court is seised of sufficient situations, the more it may be in the OTP's institutional interest to encourage domestic proceedings even in states with respect to which great powers have no objections to intervention: having more situations than it can deal with could undermine its effectiveness.[248] At that stage, the influence of pro-ICC ideology may also diminish and, as the next phase in the

---

[248] Indeed, the OTP waited almost four years to open an investigation into the third situation that was referred to the Court, that in the Central African Republic, which the OTP had not invited. With respect to Guinea, a state under preliminary analysis, the OTP stated to the press that it 'insisted that Guinea could become a model for Africa and for the world of a State Party that does not require the ICC to fulfil its Rome Statute obligations to investigate and prosecute the most responsible perpetrators of the most serious crimes' (ICC-OTP 2012:1).

development of the 'Rome System', the Court, the ASP and the international-criminal-justice movement may shift their attention to promoting a norm in accordance with which states have a responsibility to investigate and prosecute conflict-related crimes at the domestic level. The Review Conference suggests this shift may have begun,[249] albeit with a focus on domestic legislation, infrastructure and capacity – issues that, as this chapter has shown, are not the key obstacles to domestic proceedings. Moreover, positive complementarity still seems subject to a division-of-labour reading of complementarity, according to which the ICC prosecutes those bearing the greatest responsibility, while national authorities investigate or prosecute the rest, or hold them accountable by other means; a reading which has nothing to do with complementarity as set forth in the Rome Statute.

The ICC may also become more supportive of the idea of implementing a policy of positive complementarity once it has completed its cases in a particular situation or sub-situation. In shifting its attention to another situation or sub-situation, the OTP may hand over to domestic justice systems files on other suspects.[250] There are some indications of such a development.[251] However, the question remains whether any policy of positive complementarity will ever be able to address the real obstacles to domestic proceedings. No technical assistance can overcome unwillingness and even in situations of inability the question arises whether the ICC is the most appropriate institution for the facilitation of domestic proceedings and whether the Court should be involved in such matters in the first place. In situations of absolute inability, the ICC cannot remedy the essential obstacles to domestic proceedings. For instance, Uganda is not able to arrest the LRA suspects, but the ICC is even less able to do so. The ICC may be able to rely on more international support, but it is unclear why such assistance should not be provided directly

---

[249] See Chapter 2, n. 286 and surrounding text.

[250] See Burke-White 2008c:328–35. Nonetheless, as has been explained in this chapter ('ICC involvement has not reduced the costs of domestic action') the fact that the Court is permanent and may therefore exercise its jurisdiction in the same situation in the future may reduce its willingness and ability to become involved in supporting domestic justice systems.

[251] The OTP has indicated plans to hand over evidence from its third investigation in the DRC situation to the DRC authorities (Bensouda 2009:5).

to a state that is willing to conduct genuine proceedings but unable to arrest the suspects.

One paradox, however, is likely to persist. As the analysis of obstacles to domestic proceedings has shown, one of the key causes of impunity, and thus reasons for ICC intervention, is the cycle of impunity that results from patronage networks: ruling parties do not amputate the hands that vote in their favour, whether in elections or by demonstrating other forms of loyalty. Similarly, the ICC is unlikely to amputate the arm that it needs for enforcement. The ICC, judicially independent but practically dependent on cooperation, is thus itself embedded in a *de facto* patronage network in which it accepts impunity with respect to the powers on whose cooperation it depends in order to achieve accountability for others. Just as for the Special Prosecutor for Darfur it is dangerous to prosecute certain individuals if this entails turning their tribes against the GoS, it is dangerous for the OTP to go after the allies of the world's great powers.[252]

This paradox, like the 'catalysing effect paradox' that it produces, stems from the literal double standards involved in complementarity. With respect to states, the principle adopts a realist perspective: it is based on the acknowledgment that states may be unable or unwilling, in the lay sense of the terms, to investigate and prosecute, resulting in the absence of genuine domestic proceedings. This realist perspective is justified: as a guardian against impunity the ICC must take reality as its starting point. However, the ICC does not merely guard; it also intervenes and, effectively, then assumes responsibility for

---

[252] This may partly explain the OTP's different attitude towards Uganda during and after the Juba peace talks and post-Qaddhafi Libya. In Uganda, it discouraged domestic proceedings; in post-Qaddhafi Libya, it has been positive towards them. In the latter situation, Western powers have made clear diplomatically that 'Libyans should try their former leaders at home' (see Simons 2011). Similarly, the OTP has had a different attitude with respect to different parties within one situation, based on considerations of cooperation and the position of the world's great powers. The OTP did not pay much attention to complementarity when deciding whether to open an investigation into the LRA, whereas it made public statements encouraging Uganda to conduct domestic proceedings for state officials. As it happens, this coincides with US policy according to which the ICC should go after the LRA but take no action with respect to the UPDF. Similarly, in the DRC, the OTP did not open an investigation into persons close to President Kabila, under pressure from foreign donors not to cause political instability (see Clark 2011:1190).

accountability. But then, with respect to the Court, complementarity's perspective is idealist: it assumes that, but does not assess whether, the Court is willing and able, even though in reality the Court has sometimes proved to be as unwilling or unable as the state, or even more so.

In a case of ICC unwillingness, and thus an absence of an investigation into a situation or a particular case, the ensuing impunity is obviously not caused by the ICC – it would also have existed without it. One can thus defend this situation with the same argument with which the ICC's selective justice is often justified: even though the ICC does not investigate and prosecute all, it contributes some more accountability and this is better than none. Partial justice does come at a price, though: the gains the Court makes in ending the impunity of some could be offset by its seeming legitimation of the impunity of those on whom it depends.[253]

A case of apparent inability on the part of the ICC is even more problematic from an accountability perspective, since it raises the question whether accountability is actually better served at the international than at the domestic level. When the benefits of ICC intervention do not seem to outweigh those of domestic justice, the solution to the problem may be elsewhere than in substituting the ICC for domestic jurisdictions. For instance, the solution to the problem of the inability to arrest the LRA leadership may be better sought in improving traditional state-to-state cooperation than replacing the Ugandan justice system by an international and, in this respect, equally unable forum.

The solution to this mismatch between standards of evaluation is not to find a super-guardian to guard the guardian,[254] or, more tailored to the context of the ICC, a 'court of final resort' to back up the 'court of last resort'. Any such guardian or court will not be able to escape the political reality of patronage either. Instead, the Court should take the political reality as its explicit starting point,[255] both for the definition of its own success and for its evaluation of admissibility.

---

[253] See e.g. Chapter 3. See also Al-Balushi and Branch 2010, citing Lerner 2010.

[254] See also Verdirame 2011, addressing the difficulty of ensuring accountability of the United Nations for its human rights violations.

[255] For a powerful call for 'Real Politics' as the starting point for political action and political philosophy, see Geuss 2008. The obvious counter-argument is that the Court does not practise politics or political philosophy, but law, and that law must

With respect to the Court's definition of its own success, taking the political reality as the starting point requires the Court to acknowledge and accept its greatest handicap: in Antonio Cassese's metaphor, the fact that the giant lacks arms and legs and needs artificial limbs to walk and work.[256] At times, ICC officials have rightly argued in this vein that the Court is not to blame if it cannot complete proceedings through the failure of others to cooperate.[257] They have equally argued that the Court can be deemed successful if it is deprived of all cases by genuine domestic proceedings. Yet the amount of attention that ICC officials in practice pay to enforcement indicates that their perception of success still depends on the extent to which proceedings in the ICC can be completed. Inspired by this definition of success, they have tried to cover up the handicap by relying on others as artificial limbs in exchange for *de facto* impunity: one part of the body is unlikely to hurt its newly acquired limbs. The Court could go some way to liberating itself from this self-constructed patronage system by following Martti Koskenniemi in accepting that '[e]ffectiveness, implementation and compliance . . . are not the lawyer's problem – unless the lawyer has internalized the self-image of the political decision-maker's little helper'.[258] For true independence, the Court must internalise another self-image, namely, that of its own statements as to the standard by which the Court's success is to be measured.

With respect to the evaluation of admissibility, political reality as starting point entails that the Court, aware of its own limited willingness and ability, shows some humility – not subordination – towards states struggling with ensuring accountability for a universe of criminality. Recognition of the fact that, for instance, selectiveness is a necessary evil not just for domestic justice systems but also for an

---

by definition be based on ideals and principles, not on a messy reality. However, whilst this may be (somewhat) true for the Chambers' application of the Statute to defendants, it is not so for the OTP's decisions regarding situation and case selection, in which the legal principle of complementarity, and the OTP's policy of positive complementarity, play key roles. In this regard, as Chapter 2 has shown, the OTP has in practice substantial discretion, which it uses to pursue certain goals (which, as this chapter has shown, are primarily its own legitimacy and effectiveness). Since the use of discretion for the attainment of certain goals is inherently political, a theory that takes the political reality as a starting point is well suited. On other ways in which the Court's work is *inherently* political, see Nouwen and Werner 2010a.

[256] Cassese 1998:13.   [257] E.g. see Moreno-Ocampo 2007c:5.
[258] Koskenniemi 2002b:495.

international court could lead to greater deference for a state's prosecutorial choices than that paid by the Court's same-person–same-
conduct requirement for a successful admissibility challenge.[259] This
humility would suit an international court, an 'international community' and, indeed, in Michel Quint's words, a 'humanité ... qui veut
enfermer l'univers dans son poing fermé et ne peut y tenir un
papillon'.[260]

---

[259] For a suggestion as to what such 'qualified deference' might look like, see Drumbl
2007:187–94.

[260] See the epigraph to this book, taken from Quint 2004:89–90.

CHAPTER 6

COMPLEMENTARITY IN THE LINE OF FIRE

> *[I]n the context of the Statute, the Court's legal framework,*
> *the exercise of national criminal jurisdiction by States is not*
> *without limitations. These limits are encapsulated in the*
> *provisions regulating the inadmissibility of a case, namely,*
> *articles 17–20 of the Statute.*
>
> ICC Pre-Trial Chamber II[1]

Fulfilling some of the great expectations that have attended the creation of the world's first permanent International Criminal Court, the principle of complementarity has catalysed several effects in Uganda and Sudan. Few of these effects can be traced directly to complementarity the admissibility rule as set forth in article 17 of the Rome Statute. Instead, demonstrating that the power of ideas, the political pressure of the Security Council and the economy of donor intervention can be stronger than legal rules, these effects have been spurred by the explanations that the ICC's OTP, international NGOs, Security Council members and donors have given to complementarity.

Effects were strongest when pressure exerted by these actors coalesced with the outcome of a government's cost–benefit analysis. At the same time, these effects were usually politically inexpensive for the government concerned. Measures such as the adoption of domestic laws incorporating the crimes within the ICC's jurisdiction or the establishment of special courts – both the focus of international advocacy – do not address the real obstacles to domestic proceedings.

Indeed, a strong catalysing effect on such proceedings – the only effect directly relevant to an admissibility challenge on the ground of complementarity before the Court – is yet to occur. To a large extent this is because of the real obstacles to domestic proceedings, key among which are the weakness of law-enforcement agencies in

---

[1] *Admissibility Decision Ruto et al. (PTC):*[44] and *Admissibility Decision Muthaura et al. (PTC):*[40], referring to *Admissibility Judgment Katanga (AC):*[85].

conflict areas and the pervasive reach of patronage systems. The ICC, despite its policy of positive complementarity, has not helped to overcome such obstacles. On the other hand, ICC intervention proved not costly enough – indeed, in some instances, beneficial – or its enforcement threat too weak, to provide an incentive to investigate and prosecute ICC suspects domestically.

In fact, the ICC and its supporters have in some instances *discouraged* domestic proceedings. Seemingly in contradiction to the big-idea version of complementarity according to which the principle reflects a state's 'responsibility', 'duty' or even 'obligation' to investigate and prosecute, this result is to some extent inherent in the Statute. The Statute merely refers to a state's duty to exercise criminal jurisdiction over international crimes in a preambular recital while it establishes at the same time a court on the very assumption that states fail to investigate and prosecute. Moreover, the Statute does not contain the legal machinery to assign responsibility for failure to investigate or prosecute domestically and does not prohibit states from outsourcing situations to the Court. The ICC is thus not merely a court of last resort; it is also a court of convenience.

But the ICC and its supporters have further diminished the notion of a responsibility to investigate and prosecute domestically. First, the OTP made it a policy to invite states to refer situations on their own territory to the Court. Secondly, the OTP has at times explained complementarity in its literal rather than legal meaning in order to advocate a division of labour according to which the ICC deals with the cases involving those bearing the greatest responsibility while domestic justice systems handle only the less serious cases. This reading fails to acknowledge that complementarity accords states the primary right with respect to *all* cases. Thirdly, the Chambers, too, have suggested that a state may fulfil its duty to exercise its jurisdiction by referring situations and transferring suspects to the Court. Finally, the ICC and its supporters have promoted a *pro-ICC ideology* that effectively counters the idea of states' primary responsibility by propagating one or several of the following three beliefs, namely, that (1) international courts mete out better justice than domestic systems; (2) international crimes, particularly those committed by those bearing the greatest responsibility, must be prosecuted as international crimes, ideally in international courts, because such crimes have been committed 'against humanity'; and (3) at a minimum, once the ICC is involved the fledgling Court must be seen to succeed. The Rome

Statute and the ICC have thus fostered a norm according to which crimes may not go unpunished, but weakened the idea that states have a responsibility to this effect domestically. The *normative paradox of complementarity* is thus that the creation of the Court, and particularly the way the Statute has been implemented so far, may, by projecting the Court as an institution to take over from states the responsibility to investigate and prosecute conflict-related crimes, actually erode the pressure on states to discharge that responsibility.

When the ICC, and in particular the OTP, have encouraged and when they have discouraged domestic proceedings has depended on their assessment of their institutional interests, especially the Court's effectiveness. Thus, the OTP has encouraged domestic proceedings – and stressed complementarity – in those situations and cases in which cooperation is unlikely to be forthcoming, in which intervention would upset an international great power and in which it has not yet invested many resources. But it has discouraged domestic proceedings – and marginalised complementarity – in situations and cases where it could count on essential cooperation, which have not encountered objections from the world's great powers and in which it has invested its resources. This gives rise to the *catalysing effect paradox*, which is that the ICC is most keen to exercise its jurisdiction in precisely those cases where complementarity has the greatest chances of catalysing genuine domestic proceedings.

The explanation for the paradox is that not just state institutions but also international institutions such as the ICC are subordinated to patronage networks. In its perception, the Court's effectiveness depends on cooperation, for which it is entirely dependent on states and international organisations. Consequently, when a situation or case could undermine the Court's (perceived) effectiveness because of a lack of, or a threat to, cooperation, the OTP may in practice prove 'unwilling' or 'unable' (in the lay sense of the terms) to investigate and prosecute.

Whereas the OTP's choice as to when to emphasise states' primary *responsibility* to investigate and prosecute is thus inspired by the *reality* of its own limited capacity, the Court's case law on complementarity as states' primary *right* to investigate and prosecute has developed on the basis of an *ideal* model. This ideal model is that of zero tolerance towards impunity, as defined by the ICC. Pursuant to the Court's definition of the same case, a state can render a case inadmissible only by investigating the same person, (substantially) the same conduct and, possibly, the same incidents as those prosecuted before the ICC. When faced with the universe of criminality that often characterises the situations before the Court, it is virtually impossible for any domestic court – and for the ICC for that matter – to investigate and prosecute all persons, conduct and incidents, thus always leaving instances of impunity that, according to the ICC's reading of the same-case requirement, justify ICC intervention.

From the Court's radical anti-impunity perspective this is precisely the point of the ICC: to eradicate as much impunity as possible. This perspective gives no reason to apply the rule that accords states the primary right if the domestic case and the case before the ICC cover different persons, or the same persons but different conduct and incidents. There is no need to apply the priority rule because nothing prevents the state from investigating and prosecuting, if it wishes, other persons, conduct and incidents. Indeed, in such a scenario the ICC and national courts 'complement' each other in the literal sense, in a joint effort to combat impunity. It is this vision of a united effort towards the eradication of impunity that underpins the Court's conceptualisation of complementarity not as a principle balancing state sovereignty and international criminal justice but as a principle that protects state sovereignty only to the extent that a state joins in the fight against impunity. Indeed, as the above-cited passage illustrates, in the Court's view, complementarity does not protect state sovereignty, but *limits* it: complementarity respects sovereignty only to the extent that this sovereignty is used for the anti-impunity struggle of the ICC. States are free to pursue other objectives, but, if they clash with the ICC's anti-impunity programme, the latter prevails.

In reality, however, states – and the ICC – pursue other interests (survival, cohesion, legitimacy, stability, effectiveness, development, security) that at times *clash* with the absolutist anti-impunity approach. Whereas the ICC cannot but accept this reality for its own conduct, it does not with respect to states: the ICC neither assesses nor needs to assess its own lack of action, willingness or ability, but it does critically assess whether states investigate and prosecute genuinely. The discourse of the ICC and domestic courts – or justice and peace initiatives for that matter – 'complementing' each other fails to recognise that, in reality, issues are not resolved by 'complementing' *in aeternam*, but require prioritisation. Indeed, complementarity as an admissibility rule was designed to resolve such competition.

In the first decade of the Court's practice, complementarity has not merely operated in the line of fire; it has also come under fire. As 'primary responsibility', to the extent that it has been presented as such, it is under fire only in those states in which the OTP wishes to intervene or keep cases. As 'primary right' it is under fire because of a conception of complementarity that subordinates sovereignty to the anti-impunity struggle, as defined by the ICC, and particularly the OTP. Both as a responsibility and as a right it is under the attack of a pro-ICC ideology, particularly once the ICC has intervened in a state.

For complementarity to survive this line of fire, the reality in which the Court operates must be recognised. For the Court, this means that precisely because it is dependent on state cooperation, it should not consider a lack of cooperation as *its* failure. Instead it should truly accept the Prosecutor's definition of a successful court as one without cases on account of complementarity. For the admissibility assessment, a more realistic approach recognises that a state can genuinely address impunity *and* have a legitimate interest in the absence of or an end to ICC intervention, without pursuing a total war on impunity.

EPILOGUE: BEYOND COMPLEMENTARITY IN THE LINE OF FIRE

> *... parce que les parenthèses n'existent pas dans l'Histoire,*
> *que l'humanité profonde, la dignité, la conformité au bien*
> *moral échappent au droit, à la légalité!*
>
> Michel Quint[1]

Six years since our first encounter, I go to see the Advocate General. I drive to his home instead of his office; he has retired. The heat has not relented. Seated on one of the beds in his living room, surrounded by his beautiful daughters and pictures from life at an American university, we joke that I look pretty happy even though I still do not take sugar in my coffee and am not yet married. But we also discuss the latest change in Special Prosecutors for Darfur and the possibilities of and obstacles to Sudanese people obtaining security, food, freedom, jobs, democracy, visas, accountability and opportunities; goods and values closely related to concepts of peace and justice. My final question is whether I may open this book by telling the story of our first discussion on complementarity. His is: 'What are your conclusions?'

In Darfur a few months earlier, traditional leaders welcome me back into their midst. Years ago, they expressed the hope that the ICC would come and end the conflict. Now, while violence continues, changes in methods, intensity and parties notwithstanding, the leaders mention the ICC as one in a series of organisations that promised peace but failed to bring it. 'What do *you* think?', they ask at the end of hours of conversation.

A few months later, in Uganda, I catch up with an Acholi leader. People in northern Uganda have left the camps. When I ask his view about the Attorney-General's argument before the Constitutional Court that the Amnesty Act is unconstitutional, he is shocked. First, about the substance – the Amnesty Act that he and other Acholi had advocated more than a decade ago is under attack. But possibly even

---

[1] Quint 2000:62. Translation: '... because parentheses do not exist in History, because deep-rooted humanity, dignity, conformity to the moral good elude the law, and legality!'

411

more shocking to him is that he had not even been *aware* of the argument: 'Why is it that we need to learn from a *muzungu* what is happening to our own legislation?' Since the LRA moved out of northern Uganda and the petering out of the Juba peace process, Acholi leaders have shifted their attention from resolving the LRA conflict, including advocacy for the Amnesty Act, to the conflicts emerging from 'peace', primarily land disputes. The chief and I meet every day to share documents and arguments. When I bid him farewell, he asks: 'What do you make of all this?'

Elsewhere in the world, I run into the ICC official who once said 'I believe more in the Court than in complementarity'. He has left the Court, finding more satisfaction in work *in situ*. Over a lemonade at a filthy airport where he is about to take off for his next situation, he, too, confronts me: 'So, Nouwen, what do you conclude?'

I could tell, and indeed have tried to tell, them and you, the story of complementarity's catalysing effect in the line of fire. The story of Thomas Kwoyelo who found himself on trial because of anti-amnesty advocacy in the name of international law and, more specifically, complementarity; the story of numerous Special Prosecutors for Darfur, all trying to investigate but constrained by political barbed wire; the story of acts adopted under international pressure; the story of a domestic war crimes court mimicking an international court in terms of procedures, jargon, effectiveness and selectiveness; a story of an international court that sometimes ignores complementarity and sometimes stresses it, depending on whether it wants or does not want to intervene; and a story of people, all invoking and shaping complementarity for an agenda that they deem worthwhile, whether it is obtaining donor funding, promoting 'international standards' or advancing 'traditional' practices.

But this does not *conclude* the story. First, the ICC will refine and reinterpret its case law, complementarity will continue to catalyse, and effects will develop further or die out. Secondly, the story is bigger than that of effects catalysed. Setting out to identify effects catalysed by complementarity bears the risk of supersizing change in a landscape of continuity. The LRA has left northern Uganda, but continues to make people its victims in other parts of East Africa. Judges sit on new courts, but investigators and prosecutors hardly go beyond existing political boundaries. Presidents have stressed the importance of accountability, but state actors and protégées continue to enjoy impunity. Another peace agreement for Darfur has been signed, but rebel movements continue to fight the government, and *vice versa*. Domestic lawyers have discovered the transitional-justice niche, whilst violations of fundamental tenets of the rule of law go largely unchallenged. The ICC has ushered in an 'age of accountability',[2] but, dependent as it is on the great powers, further entrenches their impunity.

Finally, and essentially, seeking to answer my original questions about complementarity's catalysing effect while living in the worlds in which complementarity is considered, invoked and contested, I was confronted with a more disquieting question: What do all these effects have to do with this fundamental value in the name of which it all takes place: *justice*?

Surely, more criminal accountability for international crimes must contribute to justice. But could it be that, in the mirroring of one particular type of justice, its biases and silences are copied too? That, in mimicking the international focus on ending impunity through 'special' justice for those bearing the 'greatest responsibility' for war crimes, crimes against humanity and genocide, domestic justice systems – like the international[3] – turn a blind eye to wider problems that explain pervasive impunity, also for 'ordinary' crimes? Could it be that international criminal law creates the comforting illusion that 'passing sentence' equates to 'doing justice',[4] and that, by buying into this focus on punitive justice, domestic actors neglect elements of justice that are possibly more meaningful to many people's immediate needs? That the energy invested in the advocacy, and in responding to that advocacy, for justice *à la* ICC for a few individuals has usurped the

---

[2] Ban 2010.

[3] Citing preambular recitals, the OTP argued in *OTP Submission Information Status LRA Arrest Warrants*:4 that 'lasting peace requires that there be no impunity for crimes of concern to the international community as a whole', suggesting, *a contrario*, that impunity for crimes with which the international community is not concerned does not affect 'lasting peace'. For a similar suggestion, see *Decision Authorizing Kenya Investigation, Dissenting Opinion Judge Kaul*:[8] ('As a Judge of the International Criminal Court . . . I would like to ask all in the Republic of Kenya who yearn for justice and who support the intervention of the Court in this country for understanding [sic] the following: there are, in law and in the existing systems of criminal justice in this world, essentially two different categories of crimes which are crucial in the present case. There are, on the one side, international crimes of concern to the international community as a whole, in particular genocide, crimes against humanity and war crimes pursuant to articles 6, 7, and 8 of the Statute. There are, on the other side, common crimes, albeit of a serious nature, prosecuted by national criminal justice systems, such as that of the Republic of Kenya.').

[4] Mulisch 2006:11 (translation from Dutch by present author).

attention and resources necessary for the fostering of agency and for the realisation of a broader vision of justice?[5] Worse, could it be that, in the pursuit of criminal accountability for some crimes, other injustices are unintentionally committed? Injustices in terms of entrenching inequality before the law, domestically and internationally, of foreign donors overruling those most directly affected, of the threat of criminal accountability of perpetrators postponing or ruining the prospects of millions of people being able to leave the camps for displaced persons and regain control over their own lives? Could it be that this amorphous concept 'justice' is not so much culture-specific, but dependent on context and time? That most people, no matter where in the world, would like to have accountability as well as security and prosperity and prospects, but that, if accountability threatens the other *desiderata*, they prioritise those other values?

These uncomfortable questions go beyond complementarity, beyond the Statute, beyond law and, indeed, beyond the scope of this book. But the story of complementarity's catalysing effect *does* raise them. In the field of international criminal justice, the prevalent response to these issues is to argue that, precisely because these issues transcend law, 'others' are responsible for them, for instance, the Security Council for 'peace', donors for 'rule-of-law promotion' and national authorities for the use of 'alternative justice mechanisms', whilst the ICC should just continue pursuing accountability on the ground that every extra bit of accountability is a gain.

However, if anything, the story of complementarity's catalysing effect has shown that this is not a world of endless 'complementarities' in which efforts for criminal, restorative, political and legal justice seamlessly 'complement' each other. This is a world of horrific constraint,[6] in which the promotion of one value often compromises another. More precisely, the absolute war on impunity succeeds in achieving some justice, but also produces, shapes and legitimates injustices. This is not the moment for concluding. It is the moment for more questioning.

---

[5] On the 'skewed, partial and piecemeal manner' in which practitioners and scholars have approached questions of justice in conflict and post-conflict situations, see Mani 2002:4 and *passim*. See also Clarke 2009.

[6] De Waal 2010a.

BIBLIOGRAPHY

LITERATURE AND DOCUMENTS FROM STATES AND INTERNATIONAL ORGANISATIONS

'A middle way for justice in Sudan' 2008. *Economist* (11 December)

Abbott, K. W. 1999. 'International Relations Theory, International Law, and the Regime Governing Atrocities in Internal Conflicts', 93(2) *American Journal of International Law* 361

Abdul Jalil, M. A., A. A. Mohammed and A. A. Yousuf 2007. 'Native Administration and Local Governance in Darfur: Past and Future', in A. de Waal (ed.), *War in Darfur and the Search for Peace* (Harvard University Press, Cambridge, MA) 39

Abu Al Gasim, H. A. 2005. 'A Report on the Work of the Committee for the Assessment of Damages and Losses in Darfur States' (26 May)

Abuelbashar, A. M. 2009. 'On the Failure of Darfur Peace Talks in Abuja: An SLM/A Insider's Perspective', in S. M. Hassan and C. E. Ray (eds.), *Darfur and the Crisis of Governance in Sudan: A Critical Reader* (Cornell University Press, New York) 345

Acholi Religious Leaders 1999. 'A Memorandum on the Amnesty Bill 1998 Submitted to the Minister of Internal Affairs and the Attorney General of Uganda by Acholi Religious Leaders' (April)

Adriko, M. J. 2008. 'The Role of Civil Society in Ensuring Justice with Reference to Uganda' (The ICJ-Kenya and the Institute for Security Studies Workshop on International Criminal Justice in Africa, Mombasa Continental Resort, 29–30 August)

Afako, B. 2002. 'Reconciliation and Justice: "Mato Oput" and the Amnesty Act', in O. Lucima (ed.), *Protracted Conflict, Elusive Peace* (Accord, Conciliation Resources, London), www.c-r.org/our-work/accord/northern-uganda/reconciliation-justice.php

2006. 'Traditional drink unites Ugandans', *BBC Focus on Africa* (29 September)

2007. 'Reckoning with the Past: An Anatomy of the Agreement on Accountability and Reconciliation Reached in Juba on 29th June 2007' (6 August)

2008. 'Country Study V: Uganda', in M. du Plessis and J. Ford (eds.), *Unable or Unwilling? Case Studies on Domestic Implementation of the*

ICC Statute in Selected African Countries (Monograph No. 141, March) 93

2009. 'No quick fix for the LRA', *Guardian* (16 April)

2010. 'Negotiating in the Shadow of Justice: The Juba Talks', in *Initiatives to End the Violence in Northern Uganda 2002–09 and the Juba Peace Process* (Accord, Conciliation Resources, London) 21

African Centre for Justice and Peace Studies 2009. 'An Opening for Expression or Shifting Tactics? Freedom of the Press and Freedom of Expression in Sudan' (Report on the Situation of the Freedom of Expression and the Freedom of Press in Sudan, 1 January–30 September)

2011. 'The African Centre condemns the use of death penalty against Darfur rebels' (29 November), www.sudantribune.com/spip.php?iframe&page=imprimable&id_article=40857

Agirre Aranburu, X. 2009. 'Gravity of Crimes and Responsibility of the Suspect', in M. Bergsmo (ed.), *Criteria for Prioritizing and Selecting Core International Crimes Cases* (FICHL Publication Series No. 4, Forum for International Criminal and Humanitarian Law, Oslo) 147

Ajawin, Y. 2001. 'Human Rights Violations and Transitional Justice', in A. H. Abdel Salam and A. de Waal (eds.), *The Phoenix State: Civil Society and the Future of Sudan* (Red Sea Press, Lawrenceville, NJ) 113

Akhavan, P. 2003. 'The International Criminal Court in Context: Mediating the Global and Local in the Age of Accountability', 97(3) *American Journal of International Law* 712

2005. 'The Lord's Resistance Army Case: Uganda's Submission of the First State Referral to the International Criminal Court', 99(2) *American Journal of International Law* 403

2010a. 'Self-Referrals before the International Criminal Court: Are States the Villains or the Victims of Atrocities?', (21) *Criminal Law Forum* 103

2010b. 'Whither National Courts? The Rome Statute's Missing Half', 8(5) *Journal of International Criminal Justice* 1245

AL Doc. 598-21d-29/11/2005 (2005). Arab Justice Ministers Council, 'Arab Model Law Project on Crimes within ICC Jurisdiction'

Al-Balushi, S. and A. Branch 2010. 'Africa: Africom and the ICC – Enforcing International Justice in Continent?', *Pambazuka News* (27 May), http://allafrica.com/stories/201005271324.html

Al-Mahdi, S. 2010. 'Contribution to the Consultation on Justice and Reconciliation during Sudan's Post-2011 Transition' (20 September)

Alai, C. and N. Mue 2011. 'Complementarity and the Impact of the Rome Statute and the International Criminal Court in Kenya', in C. Stahn and M. M. El Zeidy (eds.), *The International Criminal Court and Complementarity: From Theory to Practice* (Vol. II, Cambridge University Press, Cambridge) 1222

Ali, W. 2007. 'Sudan bans media from reporting on Darfur war crimes cases', *Sudan Tribune* (27 March)

2008a. 'Sudan contemplated extraditing Darfur suspects to ICC: official', *Sudan Tribune* (25 June)

2008b. 'Sudan offered to remove minister accused of war crimes: diplomat', *Sudan Tribune* (13 October)

Allen, T. 1991. 'Understanding Alice: Uganda's Holy Spirit Movement in Context', 61(3) *Africa* 370

2006. *Trial Justice: The International Criminal Court and the Lord's Resistance Army* (African Arguments, Zed Books, London; New York)

2007. 'The International Criminal Court and the Invention of Traditional Justice in Northern Uganda', (107) *Politique africaine* 147

2010. 'Bitter Roots: The "Invention" of Acholi Traditional Justice', in T. Allen and K. Vlassenroot (eds.), *The Lord's Resistance Army: Myth and Reality* (Zed Books, London; New York) 242

Allen, T. and K. Vlassenroot (eds.) 2010a. 'Introduction', in T. Allen and K. Vlassenroot (eds.), *The Lord's Resistance Army: Myth and Reality* (Zed Books, London; New York) 1

2010b. *The Lord's Resistance Army: Myth and Reality* (Zed Books, London; New York)

Allio, E. 2004. 'Sudan predicts Kony end', *New Vision* (17 February)

Alvarez, J. E. 2003. 'The New Dispute Settlers: (Half) Truths and Consequences', 38(3) *Texas International Law Journal* 405

Ambos, K. 2010. *The Colombian Peace Process and the Principle of Complementarity of the International Criminal Court: An Inductive, Situation-Based Approach* (Springer, Heidelberg; Dordrecht; London; New York)

Amnesty Commission 2008a. 'GoU Survey for Former Ugandan Combatants'

2008b. 'Overview of the Number of Amnesties Granted by Year between 2000 and 2008' (October)

2010. 'Letter from the Principal Legal Officer of the Amnesty Commission to the Director of Public Prosecutions re Suspects on Remand at Luzira Upper Prison' (19 March)

2012. 'Report: Rebel Group Percentages' (2 May)

Amnesty International 2004a. 'International Criminal Court: The Failure of States to Enact Effective Implementing Legislation' (IOR 40/019/2004, September)

2004b. 'Uganda: First Steps to Investigate Crimes Must be Part of Comprehensive Plan to End Impunity' (AFR 59/001/2004, 30 January)

2004c. 'Uganda: Concerns about the International Criminal Court Bill 2004' (AFR 59/005/2004, 27 July)

2005. 'Open Letter to the Chief Prosecutor of the International Criminal Court: Comments on the Concept of the Interests of Justice' (IOR 40/023/2005, 17 June)

2006. 'The International Criminal Court: Summary of Draft and Enacted Implementing Legislation' (2 IOR 40/041/2006, November)

2007. 'Uganda: Proposed National Framework to Address Impunity Does Not Remove Government's Obligation to Arrest and Surrender LRA Leaders to the International Criminal Court' (AFR 59/002/2007, 15 August)

2011. 'Uganda's Amnesty for LRA Commander a "Setback" for Justice' (23 September)

Amone-P'Olak, K. 2007. 'Coping with Life in Rebel Captivity and the Challenge of Reintegrating Formerly Abducted Boys in Northern Uganda', 20(4) *Journal of Refugee Studies* 641

Anyoli, E. 2010. 'Former LRA commander sent to War Court', *New Vision* (6 September)

2012. 'DPP rejects Kwoyelo amnesty', *New Vision* (5 February)

Aoun, E. 2012. 'The European Union and International Criminal Justice: Living up to its Normative Preferences?', 5(1) *Journal of Common Market Studies* 21

Aptel Williamson, C. 2006. 'Justice Empowered or Justice Hampered: The International Criminal Court in Darfur', 15(1) *African Security Review* 20

Apuuli, K. P. 2005. 'Amnesty and International Law: The Case of the Lord's Resistance Army Insurgents in Northern Uganda', 5(2) *African Journal on Conflict Resolution* 33

2011. 'Peace over Justice: The Acholi Religious Peace Initiative (ARLPI) vs. the International Criminal Court (ICC) in Northern Uganda', 11(1) *Studies in Ethnicity and Nationalism* 116

Arbia, S. and G. Bassy 2011. 'Proactive Complementarity: A Registrar's Perspective and Plans', in C. Stahn and M. M. El Zeidy (eds.), *The International Criminal Court and Complementarity: From Theory to Practice* (Vol. I, Cambridge University Press, Cambridge) 52

Arbour, L. 2006. 'Statement by the UN High Commissioner for Human Rights Following Visit to Sudan, 30 April–5 May 2006' (Khartoum, 5 May)

Arbour, L. and M. Bergsmo 1999. 'Conspicuous Absence of Jurisdictional Overreach', 1(1) *International Law Forum* 13

Arendt, H. 1977. *Eichmann in Jerusalem: A Report on the Banality of Evil* (Penguin, Harmondsworth)

Arsanjani, M. H. 1999. 'Reflections on the Jurisdiction and Trigger Mechanism of the International Criminal Court', in H. A. M. von Hebel, J. G. Lammers and J. Schukking (eds.), *Reflections on the International Criminal Court* (TMC Asser Press, The Hague) 57

Arsanjani, M. H. and W. M. Reisman 2005. 'The Law-in-Action of the International Criminal Court', 99(2) *American Journal of International Law* 385

Assal, M. A. M. 2009. 'Locating Responsibilities: National and International Responses to the Crisis in Darfur', in S. M. Hassan and C. E. Ray (eds.), *Darfur and the Crisis of Governance in Sudan: A Critical Reader* (Cornell University Press, New York) 285

'At five-year mark, Darfur crisis is only worsening – UN aid chief' 2008. *UN News Service* (22 April)

Atkinson, R. R. 2010a. '"The Realists in Juba"? An Analysis of the Juba Peace Talks', in T. Allen and K. Vlassenroot (eds.), *The Lord's Resistance Army: Myth and Reality* (Zed Books, London; New York) 205

2010b. *The Roots of Ethnicity: Origins of the Acholi of Uganda* (2nd edn, Fountain Publishers, Kampala)

AU Doc. PSC/AHG/2(CCVII) 2009. 'Report of the African Union High-Level Panel on Darfur (AUPD): Darfur – The Quest for Peace, Justice and Reconciliation' (October)

AU Doc. PSC/MIN/Comm (CXLII) Rev. 1 2008. 'Application made on 14 July 2008 by the Prosecutor of the International Criminal Court (ICC) to the Pre-Trial Chamber of the ICC for It to Issue a Warrant of Arrest under Article 58 of the Rome Statute of the ICC against the President of the Republic of the Sudan'

Aukerman, M. J. 2002. 'Extraordinary Evil, Ordinary Crime: A Framework for Understanding Transitional Justice', 15 *Harvard Human Rights Journal* 39

Ayugi, C. and P. Eichstaedt 2008. 'ICC calls for end to LRA aid', *Institute for War and Peace Reporting* (23 May)

Babiker, M. 2002. 'Research on Roots of Conflict and Traditional Conflict Transformation Mechanisms: Darfur, Kordofan, Sobat Basin' (UNDP, September)

Babiker, M. A. 2007. *Application of International Humanitarian and Human Rights Law to the Armed Conflicts of the Sudan: Complementary or Mutually Exclusive Regimes?* (Intersentia, Antwerp; Oxford)

2010. 'The International Criminal Court and the Darfur Crimes: The Dilemma of Peace and Supra-National Criminal Justice', 5(1) *International Journal of African Renaissance Studies – Multi-, Inter- and Trans-disciplinarity* 82

2011. 'The Prosecution of International Crimes under Sudan's Criminal and Military Laws: Developments, Gaps and Limitations', in L. Oette (ed.), *Criminal Law Reform and Transitional Justice: Human Rights Perspectives for Sudan* (Ashgate, Aldershot) 161

Baguma, R. 2009. 'LRA's Kwoyelo flown to Entebbe on drip', *New Vision* (4 March)

Baines, E. K. 2007. 'The Haunting of Alice: Local Approaches to Justice and Reconciliation in Northern Uganda', 1(1) *International Journal of Transitional Justice* 91

Baker, B. 2004. 'Twilight of Impunity for Africa's Presidential Criminals', 25(8) *Third World Quarterly* 1487

Baldo, S. 2007. 'The Impact of the ICC in the Sudan and DR Congo' (Building a Future on Peace and Justice, Nuremberg, 25–27 June)

Ban, K. 2010. '"An Age of Accountability": Address to the Review Conference on the International Criminal Court', Kampala (31 May), www.un.org/sg/selected-speeches/statement_full.asp?statID=829

Barends, M. 2007. 'Fighting Impunity: Legal Aid in Darfur', 28 *Forced Migration Review* 33

Barnett, M. N. and M. Finnemore 2004. *Rules for the World: International Organizations in Global Politics* (Cornell University Press, Ithaca, NY)

Bassiouni, M. C. (ed.) 2005. *The Legislative History of the International Criminal Court* (Transnational Publishers, Ardsley, NY)

2006. 'The ICC–Quo Vadis?', 4(3) *Journal of International Criminal Justice* 421

Baylis, E. 2008. 'Tribunal-Hopping with the Post-Conflict Justice Junkies', 10(2) *Oregon Review of International Law* (Symposium Issue) 361

2009. 'Reassessing the Role of International Criminal Law: Rebuilding National Courts through Transnational Networks', 50(1) *Boston College Law Review* 1

Becker, T. 2004. 'Address to the American International Law Association', 10(2) *ILSA Journal of International and Comparative Law* 477

Behrend, H. 1999. *Alice Lakwena and the Holy Spirits: War in Northern Uganda, 1985–97* (J. Currey, Oxford)

Bekou, O. 2009–2010. 'Rule 11 Bis: An Examination of the Process of Referrals to National Courts in ICTY Jurisprudence', 33 *Fordham International Law Journal* 723

Bekou, O. and R. Cryer (eds.) 2004. 'Introduction', in O. Bekou and R. Cryer (eds.), *The International Criminal Court* (Ashgate, Dartmouth) xi

2007. 'The International Criminal Court and Universal Jurisdiction: A Close Encounter?', 56(1) *International and Comparative Law Quarterly* 49

Bekou, O. and S. Shah 2006. 'Realising the Potential of the International Criminal Court: The African Experience', 6(3) *Human Rights Law Review* 499

Bensouda, F. 2009. 'Overview of Situations and Cases before the ICC, Linked with a Discussion of the Recent Bashir Arrest Warrant' (Pretoria, 15 April)

Benvenuti, P. 1999. 'Complementarity of the International Criminal Court to National Criminal Jurisdictions', in F. Lattanzi and W. Schabas (eds.), *Essays on the Rome Statute of the International Criminal Court* (il Sirente, Fonte di Sotto) 21

Benzing, M. 2003. 'The Complementarity Regime of the International Criminal Court: International Criminal Justice between State Sovereignty and the Fight against Impunity', 7 *Max Planck Yearbook of United Nations Law* 591

Benzing, M. and M. Bergsmo 2004. 'Some Tentative Remarks on the Relationship between Internationalized Criminal Jurisdictions and the International Criminal Court', in C. Romano, A. Nollkaemper and J. K. Kleffner (eds.), *Internationalized Criminal Courts and Tribunals: Sierra Leone, East Timor, Kosovo and Cambodia* (Oxford University Press, Oxford) 407

Bergsmo, M. 2000. 'Occasional Remarks on Certain State Concerns about the Jurisdictional Reach of the International Criminal Court, and their Possible Implications for the Relationship between the Court and the Security Council', 69(1) *Nordic Journal of International Law* 87

Bergsmo, M., O. Bekou and A. Jones 2010. 'Complementarity after Kampala: Capacity Building and the ICC's Legal Tools', 2(2) *Goettingen Journal of International Law* 791

Bergsmo, M. and P. Kruger 2008. 'Article 53: Initiation of an Investigation', in O. Triffterer (ed.), *Commentary on the Rome Statute of the International Criminal Court: Observers' Notes, Article by Article* (2nd edn, Beck; Hart; Nomos, Munich; Oxford; Baden-Baden) 1065

Bergsmo, M. and O. Triffterer 2008. 'Rome Statute of the International Criminal Court: Preamble', in O. Triffterer (ed.), *Commentary on the Rome Statute of the International Criminal Court: Observers' Notes, Article by Article* (2nd edn, Beck; Hart; Nomos, Munich; Oxford; Baden-Baden) 1

'Beshir brands ICC warrant "infringement" on Sudan' 2009. *AFP* (8 June)

Bitti, G. 2004. 'Two Bones of Contention between Civil Law and Common Law: The Record of the Proceedings and the Treatment of a Concursus Delictorum', in H. Fischer, C. Kress and S. R. Lüder (eds.), *International and National Prosecution of Crimes under International Law: Current Developments* (2nd edn, Bochumer Schriften zur Friedenssicherung und zum Humanitären Völkerrecht 44, BWV Berliner Wissenschafts-Verlag, Berlin) 273

  2007. 'Le principe de complémentarité dans le Statut de Rome: élaboration et mise en œuvre' (on file with author)

Blumenson, E. 2006. 'The Challenge of a Global Standard of Justice: Peace, Pluralism, and Punishment at the International Criminal Court', 44(3) *Columbia Journal of Transnational Law* 801

Boot, M. 2002. *Genocide, Crimes against Humanity, War Crimes: Nullum Crimen Sine Lege and the Subject Matter Jurisdiction of the International Criminal Court* (Intersentia, Antwerp; Oxford; New York)

Bos, A. 1998. 'The Role of an International Criminal Court in the Light of the Principle of Complementarity', in E. Denters and N. Schrijver (eds.), *Reflections on International Law from the Low Countries in Honour of Paul de Waart* (Martinus Nijhoff, The Hague; Boston; London) 249

Bourdon, W. 2000. *La Cour pénale internationale* (Seuil, Paris)

Bouwknecht, T. 2008. 'Sarkozy proposes Darfur deal', *Radio Netherlands Worldwide* (24 September)

Branch, A. 2004. 'International Justice, Local Injustice', 51(3) *Dissent*, www.dissentmagazine.org/article/?article=336

    2007. 'Uganda's Civil War and the Politics of ICC Intervention', 21(2) *Ethics and International Affairs* 179

    2008. 'Against Humanitarian Impunity: Rethinking Responsibility for Displacement and Disaster in Northern Uganda', 2(2) *Journal of Intervention and Statebuilding* 151

    2010. 'Exploring the Roots of LRA Violence: Political Crisis and Ethnic Politics in Acholiland', in T. Allen and K. Vlassenroot (eds.), *The Lord's Resistance Army: Myth and Reality* (Zed Books, London; New York) 25

    2011. *Displacing Human Rights: War and Intervention in Northern Uganda* (Oxford University Press, New York)

Broomhall, B. 2003. *International Justice and the International Criminal Court: Between Sovereignty and the Rule of Law* (Oxford University Press, Oxford)

Brown, B. S. 1998. 'Primacy or Complementarity: Reconciling the Jurisdiction of National Courts and International Criminal Tribunals', 23(2) *Yale Journal of International Law* 383

Brubacher, M. 2010. 'The ICC Investigation of the Lord's Resistance Army: An Insider's View', in T. Allen and K. Vlassenroot (eds.), *The Lord's Resistance Army: Myth and Reality* (Zed Books, London; New York) 262

    2013, forthcoming. 'Why Negotiating with War Criminals Is Sometimes a Bad Idea', in P. Wrange (ed.), *The International Criminal Court and the Juba Peace Process or Global Governance and Local Friction*

Burchard, C. 2011. 'Complementarity as Global Governance', in C. Stahn and M. M. El Zeidy (eds.), *The International Criminal Court and Complementarity: From Theory to Practice* (Vol. I, Cambridge University Press, Cambridge) 167

Burke-White, W. W. 2002. 'A Community of Courts: Towards a System of International Criminal Law Enforcement', 24(1) *Michigan Journal of International Law* 1

    2003–2004. 'The International Criminal Court and the Future of Legal Accountability', 10(1) *ILSA Journal of International and Comparative Law* 195

2005. 'Complementarity in Practice: The International Criminal Court as Part of a System of Multi-Level Global Governance in the Democratic Republic of Congo', 18(3) *Leiden Journal of International Law* 557

2008a. 'Implementing a Policy of Positive Complementarity in the Rome System of Justice', 19 *Criminal Law Forum* 59

2008b. 'Proactive Complementarity: The International Criminal Court and National Courts in the Rome System of Justice', 49(1) *Harvard International Law Journal* 53

2008c. 'The Domestic Influence of International Criminal Tribunals: The International Criminal Tribunal for the Former Yugoslavia and the Creation of the State Court of Bosnia & Herzegovina', 46(2) *Columbia Journal of Transnational Law* 279

2011. 'Reframing Positive Complementarity: Reflections on the First Decade and Insights from the US Federal Criminal Justice System', in C. Stahn and M. M. El Zeidy (eds.), *The International Criminal Court and Complementarity: From Theory to Practice* (Vol. I, Cambridge University Press, Cambridge) 341

Burke-White, W. W. and S. Kaplan 2009. 'Shaping the Contours of Domestic Justice: The International Criminal Court and an Admissibility Challenge in the Ugandan Situation', 7(2) *Journal of International Criminal Justice* 257

Cambridge International Dictionary of English 1996. (Cambridge University Press, Cambridge)

Cameron, I. 2004. 'Jurisdiction and Admissibility Issues under the ICC Statute', in D. McGoldrick, P. Rowe and E. Donnelly (eds.), *The Permanent International Criminal Court: Legal and Policy Issues* (Hart, Oxford) 65

Cárdenas, C. 2005. *Die Zulässigkeitsprüfung vor dem Internationalen Strafgerichtshof, zur Auslegung des Art. 17 IStGH-Statut under besonderer Berücksichtigung von Amnestien und Wahrheitskommissionen* (Berliner Wissenschafts-Verlag, Berlin)

'Carjackers in World Vision case convicted in Darfur' 2011. *Radio Dabanga* (5 May)

Carnero Rojo, E. 2005. 'The Role of Fair Trial Considerations in the Complementarity Regime of the International Criminal Court: From "No Peace without Justice" to "No Peace with Victor's Justice"?', 18(4) *Leiden Journal of International Law* 829

Cassese, A. 1998. 'On the Current Trends towards Criminal Prosecution and Punishment of Breaches of International Humanitarian Law', 9(1) *European Journal of International Law* 2

2003. *International Criminal Law* (Oxford University Press, Oxford)

Cayley, A. T. 2008. 'Recent Steps of the ICC Prosecutor in the Darfur Situation – Prosecutor v. President: The Prosecutor's Strategy in

Seeking the Arrest of Sudanese President Al Bashir on Charges of Genocide', 6 *Journal of International Criminal Justice* 829

Charbonneau, L. 2009. 'Darfur is now a "low-intensity conflict" – UN', *Reuters* (27 April)

Charney, J. 2001. 'International Criminal Law and the Role of Domestic Courts', 95(1) *American Journal of International Law* 120

Chayes, A. and A. H. Chayes 1993. 'On Compliance', 47(2) *International Organization* 175

  1995. *The New Sovereignty: Compliance with International Regulatory Agreements* (Harvard University Press, Cambridge, MA; London)

Chesterman, S. 2009. 'An International Rule of Law?', 56 *American Journal of Comparative Law* 331

Chung, C. H. 2007–2008. 'The Punishment and Prevention of Genocide: The International Criminal Court as a Benchmark of Progress and Need', 40(1–2) *Case Western Reserve Journal of International Law* 227

Ciampi, A. 2002. 'Other Forms of Cooperation', in A. Cassese, P. Gaeta and J. R. W. D. Jones (eds.), *The Rome Statute of the International Criminal Court: A Commentary* (Oxford University Press, Oxford) 1705

Cicero 52 BC. 'Pro Milone', in F. H. Colson, Cicero Pro Milone (Macmillan, London, 1929)

Clapham, C. 1977. 'Sub-Saharan Africa', in C. Clapham (ed.), *Foreign Policy Making in Developing States: A Comparative Approach* (Saxon House, Farnborough) 75

  1982a. 'Clientelism and the State', in C. Clapham (ed.), *Private Patronage and Public Power* (Frances Pinter (Publishers), London) 1

  1982b. 'The Politics of Failure: Clientelism, Political Instability and National Integration in Liberia and Sierra Leone', in C. Clapham (ed.), *Private Patronage and Public Power* (Frances Pinter (Publishers), London) 76

Clark, P. 2008. 'Law, Politics and Pragmatism: The ICC and Case Selection in the Democratic Republic of Congo and Uganda', in N. Waddell and P. Clark (eds.), *Courting Conflict? Justice, Peace and the ICC in Africa* (Royal African Society, London)

  2009. 'Grappling in the Great Lakes: The Challenges of International Justice in Rwanda, the Democratic Republic of Congo and Uganda', in B. Bowden, H. Charlesworth and J. Farrall (eds.), *The Role of International Law in Rebuilding Societies after Conflict: Great Expectations* (Cambridge University Press, Cambridge) 244

  2011. 'Chasing Cases', in C. Stahn and M. M. El Zeidy (eds.), *The International Criminal Court and Complementarity: From Theory to Practice* (Vol. II, Cambridge University Press, Cambridge) 1180

Clarke, K. M. 2007. 'Global Justice, Local Controversies: The International Criminal Court and the Sovereignty of Victims', in T. Keller and M.-B. Dembour (eds.), *Paths to International Justice: Social and Legal Perspectives* (Cambridge University Press, Cambridge) 134

　2009. *Fictions of Justice: The ICC and the Challenge of Legal Pluralism in Sub-Saharan Africa* (Cambridge University Press, Cambridge)

Coalition for the International Criminal Court 2011. 'Report on the first Review Conference on the Rome Statute, 31 May–11 June 2010, Kampala, Uganda' www.iccnow.org/documents/RC_Report_finalweb.pdf

Commission of Inquiry into Violations of Human Rights 1994. 'Findings, Conclusions and Recommendations' (October 1994, Kampala, Uganda)

Commission on Human Rights 2001. 'Report of the United Nations High Commissioner for Human Rights on the Mission Undertaken by Her Office, Pursuant to Commission Resolution 2000/60, to Assess the Situation on the Ground with Regard to the Abduction of Children from Northern Uganda' (E/CN.4/2002/86, 9 November)

Committee on Legal and Parliamentary Affairs 2004. 'Draft Report on the International Criminal Court Bill, 2004' (14 December)

Committee on the Elimination of Racial Discrimination 2000. 'Reports Submitted by States Parties under Article 9 of the Convention, Eleventh Periodic Report of States Parties due in 1998, Addendum, Sudan' (9 March)

Commonwealth Expert Group 2004. 'Report on Implementing Legislation for the Rome Statute of the International Criminal Court' (Marlborough House, London, 7–9 July)

Condorelli, L. 2008. 'Closing Remarks', in M. Politi and F. Gioia (eds.), *The International Criminal Court and National Jurisdictions* (Ashgate, Aldershot) 161

Condorelli, L. and S. Villalpando 2002. 'Referral and Deferral by the Security Council', in A. Cassese, P. Gaeta and J. R. W. D. Jones (eds.), *The Rome Statute of the International Criminal Court: A Commentary* (Oxford University Press, Oxford) 627

'Constitutional Court rejects petition against Bashir' 2000. *IRIN* (24 February)

'Corrections Column' 2008. *New Vision* (1 September)

'Court rules out Kony immunity' 2005. *New Vision* (18 April)

Crawford, J. 2003. 'The Drafting of the Rome Statute', in P. Sands (ed.), *From Nuremberg to The Hague: The Future of International Criminal Justice* (Cambridge University Press, Cambridge) 109

Crawford-Browne, S., S. Basha and K. Alexander 2006. 'Obstacles to Transitional Justice in Sudan', in B. Raftopoulos and K. Alexander (eds.),

Peace in the Balance: The Crisis in Sudan (Institute for Justice and Reconciliation, Cape Town) 139

Crook, J. R. 2005. 'President and Secretary of State Characterize Events in Darfur as Genocide', 99(1) *American Journal of International Law* 266

Cryer, R. 1998. 'Commentary on the Rome Statute for an International Criminal Court: A Cadenza for the Song of Those Who Died in Vain?', 3(2) *Journal of Armed Conflict Law* 271

2005a. 'International Criminal Law vs State Sovereignty: Another Round?', 16(5) *European Journal of International Law* 979

2005b. *Prosecuting International Crimes: Selectivity and the International Criminal Law Regime* (Cambridge University Press, Cambridge)

2006. 'Sudan, Resolution 1593, and International Criminal Justice', 19(1) *Leiden Journal of International Law* 195

2009. 'The International Criminal Court and its Relationship to Non-Party States', in C. Stahn and G. Sluiter (eds.), *The Emerging Practice of the International Criminal Court* (Martinus Nijhoff Publishers, Leiden; Boston) 115

2011. 'Darfur: Complementarity as the Drafters Intended?', in C. Stahn and M. M. El Zeidy (eds.), *The International Criminal Court and Complementarity: From Theory to Practice* (Vol. II, Cambridge University Press, Cambridge) 1097

Cryer, R. and N. D. White 2002. 'The Security Council and the International Criminal Court: Who's Feeling Threatened?', 8 *Yearbook of International Peace Operations* 143

Daly, M. W. 2007. *Darfur's Sorrow: A History of Destruction and Genocide* (Cambridge University Press, New York)

'Darfur crime prosecutor admits impact of politics on legal cases' 2010. *Miraya FM* (26 December)

'Darfur mediators hand compromise proposals to Sudanese parties' 2011. *Sudan Tribune* (2 January)

'Darfur rebel group says world must not turn its back on the ICC' 2007. *Sudan Tribune* (4 December)

'Darfur refugees named their children Okampo – Farrow' 2009. *Sudan Tribune* (6 June)

'Darfur's special prosecutor asks government to accept resignation' 2011. *Sudan Tribune* (13 April)

'Darfur war crimes suspect transferred to Khartoum' 2009. *Sudan Tribune* (18 January)

Darfurian Civil Society 2009. Doha I Declaration: Visions and Recommendations of Civil Society on Important Issues and Priorities that Must Be Included in the Terms of Negotiations to Achieve and Build Just and

Sustainable Peace in Darfur and the Role of Civil Society in All Stages of the Peace Process, Doha, 20 November

2010. Doha II Declaration: Visions and Recommendations of the Second Civil Society Meeting on the Key Issues of Priority to Be Included in the Terms of Negotiations to Establish a Just and Durable Peace in Darfur, and the Role of the Civil Society at All Stages of the Peace Process, Doha, 15 July

Dascalopoulou-Livada, P. 2008. 'The Principle of Complementarity and Security Council Referrals', in M. Politi and F. Gioia (eds.), *The International Criminal Court and National Jurisdictions* (Ashgate, Aldershot) 57

de Montesquiou, A. 2007. 'Sudan can prosecute atrocities, minister says: International Court is opposed', *Boston Globe* (1 February)

de Tocqueville, A. 2000. *Democracy in America* (translated, edited, and with an introduction by H. C. Mansfield and D. Winthrop, University of Chicago Press, Chicago; London)

De Waal, A. 2004a. 'Counter-Insurgency on the Cheap', 26(15) *London Review of Books* 25

2004b. 'Who Are the Darfurians? Arab and African Identities, Violence and External Engagement' (SSRC, Contemporary Conflicts, 10 December), http://conconflicts.ssrc.org/hornofafrica/dewaal

2007. 'Sudan: The Turbulent State', in A. de Waal (ed.), *War in Darfur and the Search for Peace* (Harvard University Press, Cambridge, MA) 1

2008. 'Darfur, the Court and Khartoum: The Politics of State Non-Cooperation', in N. Waddell and P. Clark (eds.), *Courting Conflict? Justice, Peace and the ICC in Africa* (Royal African Society, London) 29

2009. 'Mission without End: Peacekeeping in the African Political Marketplace', 85(1) *International Affairs* 99

2010a. 'The Humanitarians' Tragedy: Escapable and Inescapable Consequences', 34(2) *Disasters* 130

2010b. 'Dollarised', *London Review of Books* (24 June) 38

De Waal, A. and H. Young 2005. 'Steps towards the Stabilization of Governance and Livelihoods in Darfur, Sudan' (USAID, March)

Dealy, S. 2007. 'An atrocity that needs no exaggeration', *New York Times* (12 August)

Deen-Racsmány, Z. 2007. 'Lessons of the European Arrest Warrant for Domestic Implementation of the Obligation to Surrender Nationals to the International Criminal Court', 20(1) *Leiden Journal of International Law* 167

'Defiant Sudan expels aid agencies after Beshir warrant' 2009. *AFP* (4 March)

Degomme, O. and D. Guha-Sapir 2010. 'Patterns of Mortality Rates in Darfur Conflict', 375 *Lancet* 294

Delmas-Marty, M. 2009. 'Comparative Criminal Law as a Necessary Tool for the Application of International Criminal Law', in A. Cassese (ed.), *The Oxford Companion to International Criminal Justice* (Oxford University Press, Oxford) 97

Dicklitsch, S. and D. Lwanga 2003. 'The Politics of Being Non-Political: Human Rights Organizations and the Creation of a Positive Human Rights Culture in Uganda', 25(2) *Human Rights Quarterly* 482

Doherty, K. L. and T. L. H. McCormack 1999. '"Complementarity" as a Catalyst for Comprehensive Domestic Penal Legislation', 5(1) *UC Davis Journal of International Law and Policy* 147

Dolan, C. 2003. 'Collapsing Masculinities and Weak States – A Case Study of Northern Uganda', in C. Dolan and F. Cleaver (eds.), *Masculinities Matter! Men, Gender and Development* (Zed Books, London)

2005. 'Understanding War and its Continuation: The Case of Northern Uganda' (PhD thesis, Development Studies Institute, London School of Economics and Political Science, University of London)

2008. 'Imposed Justice and the Need for Sustainable Peace in Uganda' (Presentation to the Beyond Juba Project/AMANI Forum training, Transitional Justice for Parliamentarians, Entebbe, 18 July)

2011. *Social Torture: The Case of Northern Uganda 1986–2006* (Berghahn Books, Oxford)

Dolan, C., S. Tamale and J. Oloka-Onyango 2009. 'Prosecuting Crimes or Righting Wrongs: Where Is Uganda Heading To?' (Press Release, Refugee Law Project, 11 August)

Doom, R. and K. Vlassenroot 1999. 'Kony's Message: A New Koine? The Lord's Resistance Army in Northern Uganda', 98(390) *African Affairs* 5

'Dr Ghazi Salah El Din Attabani: "We have to pay an expensive political tax for resolving the Darfur crisis!"' 2008. *Al Intibaha* (17 August) 5

Drumbl, M. A. 2007. *Atrocity, Punishment, and International Law* (Cambridge University Press, New York)

2009. 'International Criminal Law: Taking Stock of a Busy Decade', 10(1) *Melbourne Journal of International Law* 38

2011. 'Policy through Complementarity: The Atrocity Trial as Justice', in C. Stahn and M. M. El Zeidy (eds.), *The International Criminal Court and Complementarity: From Theory to Practice* (Vol. I, Cambridge University Press, Cambridge) 197

2012. *Reimagining Child Soldiers in International Law and Policy* (Oxford University Press, Oxford)

Dugard, J. 1999. 'Dealing with Crimes of a Past Regime. Is Amnesty Still an Option?', 12(4) *Leiden Journal of International Law* 1001

Dunofe, J. L. and J. P. Trachtman 1999. 'The Law and Economics of Humanitarian Law Violations in Internal Conflict', 93(2) *American Journal of International Law* 394

Dupuy, P.-M. 2008. 'Principe de complementarité et droit international général', in M. Politi and F. Gioia (eds.), *The International Criminal Court and National Jurisdictions* (Ashgate, Aldershot) 17

Eckert, A. E. 2009. 'The Cosmopolitan Test: Universal Morality and the Challenge of the Darfur Genocide', in S. C. Roach (ed.), *Governance, Order, and the International Criminal Court* (Oxford University Press, Oxford) 205

Egadu, S. O. and J. P'Lajur 2008. 'Kony dares Museveni on Vincent Otti death', *Daily Monitor* (23 January)

Egeland, J. 2008. *A Billion Lives: An Eyewitness Report from the Frontlines of Humanity* (Simon & Schuster, New York; London; Toronto; Sydney)

'Egypt warns Sudan that Bashir not immune from ICC prosecution' 2008. *Sudan Tribune* (16 November)

Eichstaedt, P. 2008. 'Uganda: offensive against Kony backfires', *Institute for War and Peace Reporting* (8 January)

El-Gaili, A. T. 2002. 'The Politics of Judicial Independence in Sudan: The Equilibrium of Capture', unpublished paper, on file with author

El-Gizouli, K. 2009. 'The Erroneous Confrontation: The Dialectics of Law, Politics and the Prosecution of War Crimes in Darfur', in S. M. Hassan and C. E. Ray (eds.), *Darfur and the Crisis of Governance in Sudan: A Critical Reader* (Cornell University Press, New York) 261

El Zeidy, M. M. 2002. 'The Principle of Complementarity: A New Machinery to Implement International Criminal Law', 23(2) *Michigan Journal of International Law* 869

    2006. 'Some Remarks on the Question of the Admissibility of a Case during Arrest Warrant Proceedings before the International Criminal Court', 19(3) *Leiden Journal of International Law* 741

    2008a. 'From Primacy to Complementarity and Backwards: (Re)-Visiting Rule 11 Bis of the Ad Hoc Tribunals', 57 *International and Comparative Law Quarterly* 403

    2008b. *The Principle of Complementarity in International Criminal Law: Origin, Development and Practice* (Martinus Nijhoff Publishers, Leiden)

Elgak, A. M. 2008. 'The Darfur Consortium, the UN Security Council, and the International Criminal Court: Taking First Steps toward Justice in Darfur', (8) *Respect*, www.sudan-forall.org/sections/ihtiram/pages/ihtiram_issue8/pdf_files/Abdemoneim-Elgak_The-Darfur-Consortium.pdf

Ellis, M. S. 2002. 'The International Criminal Court and its Implication for Domestic Law and National Capacity Building', 15(2) *Florida Journal of International Law* 215

Eriku, J. and D. Livingstone 2011. 'Judges, Acholi leaders differ on LRA case', *Monitor* (8 August)

European Commission 2008. 'The ICC and the Fight against Impunity' (Programming Guide for Strategy Papers, Programming Fiche, November)

Farmar, S. 2006. 'I will use the ten commandments to liberate Uganda', *Times* (28 June)

Fernandez, A. M. 2008a. 'Iftar with the "Janjaweed"' (08khartoum1450, 25 September), http://cablegatesearch.net/cable.php?id=08KHARTOU M1450&q=hilal

2008b. 'Freed Human Rights Activist Describes "Ghost House" Detention' (Khartoum 1280, 2 December, http://wikileaks.org/cable/2008/12/ 08KHARTOUM1738.html

Fernández de Gurmendi, S. A. 2011. 'Foreword', in C. Stahn and M. M. El Zeidy (eds.), *The International Criminal Court and Complementarity: From Theory to Practice* (Vol. I, Cambridge University Press, Cambridge) xviii

Finnemore, M. and K. Sikkink 1998. 'International Norm Dynamics and Political Change', 52(4) *International Organization* 887

Finnström, S. 2006. 'Wars of the Past and War in the Present: The Lord's Resistance Movement/Army in Uganda', 76(2) *Africa* 200

2008. *Living with Bad Surroundings: War, History, and Everyday Moments in Northern Uganda* (Duke University Press, Durham, NC; London)

2010. 'An African Hell of Colonial Imagination? The Lord's Resistance Army in Uganda, Another Story', in T. Allen and K. Vlassenroot (eds.), *The Lord's Resistance Army: Myth and Reality* (Zed Books, London; New York) 74

Flint, J. 2009. 'Beyond "Janjaweed": Understanding the Militias of Darfur' (HSBA Working Paper No. 17, June)

2010. 'Rhetoric and Reality: The Failure to Resolve the Darfur Conflict' (HSBA Working Paper No. 19, January)

Flint, J. and A. de Waal 2008. *Darfur: A New History of a Long War* (revised and updated edn, Zed Books, London)

Franck, T. M. 1990. *The Power of Legitimacy among Nations* (Oxford University Press, New York; Oxford)

Freedom House 2011. 'Freedom of the Press 2011, Global Press Freedom Rankings', www.freedomhouse.org/sites/default/files/FOTP%202011% 20Tables%20and%20Graphs_0.pdf

Fricke, A. L. and A. Khair 2009. 'Sudan's Legal System and the Lack of Access to Justice for Survivors of Sexual Violence in Darfur', in S. M. Hassan and C. E. Ray (eds.), *Darfur and the Crisis of Governance in Sudan: A Critical Reader* (Cornell University Press, New York) 274

Gaeta, P. 2004. 'Is the Practice of "Self-Referrals" a Sound Start for the ICC?', 2(4) *Journal of International Criminal Justice* 949

Gaja, G. 2008. 'Issues of Admissibility in Case of Self-Referrals', in M. Politi and F. Gioia (eds.), *The International Criminal Court and National Jurisdictions* (Ashgate, Aldershot) 49

Gallant, K. S. 2009. *The Principle of Legality in International and Comparative Criminal Law* (Cambridge University Press, Cambridge)

Gallavin, C. 2006. 'Prosecutorial Discretion within the ICC: Under the Pressure of Justice', 17(1) *Criminal Law Forum* 43

Garang, N. A. 2011. 'SPLM officials pledge to take Abyei's war crimes to the ICC', *Sudan Tribune* (9 June)

George, A. L. and A. Bennett 2004. *Case Studies and Theory Development in the Social Sciences* (MIT Press, Cambridge, MA; London)

Geuss, R. 2008. *Philosophy and Real Politics* (Princeton, NJ, Princeton University Press)

Gioia, F. 2006. 'State Sovereignty, Jurisdiction, and "Modern" International Law: The Principle of Complementarity in the International Criminal Court', 19(4) *Leiden Journal of International Law* 1095

Glasius, M. 2006. *The International Criminal Court: A Global Civil Society Achievement* (Routledge, London)

   2011. 'A Problem, Not a Solution: Complementarity in the Central African Republic and Democratic Republic of the Congo', in C. Stahn and M. M. El Zeidy (eds.), *The International Criminal Court and Complementarity: From Theory to Practice* (Vol. II, Cambridge University Press, Cambridge) 1204

Glassborow, K. 2008. 'Uganda insists peace not at odds with ICC', *Institute for War and Peace Reporting* (14 April)

Glassborow, K. and P. Eichstaedt 2008. 'Ugandan rebels to appeal ICC warrants', *Institute for War and Peace Reporting* (18 March)

Goldstone, R. 1997. 'The United Nations' War Crimes Tribunals: An Assessment', 12(2) *Connecticut Journal of International Law* 227

   2008. 'For Peace's Sake: Should Justice Defer to Politics?', (1) *EQ: Equality of Arms Review* 4

Gordon, G. S. 2011. 'Complementarity and Alternative Forms of Justice: A New Test for ICC Admissibility', in C. Stahn and M. El Zeidy (eds.), *The International Criminal Court and Complementarity: From Theory to Practice* (Vol. II, Cambridge University Press, Cambridge) 745

Green, E. 2010. 'Patronage, District Creation and Reform in Uganda', 45 *Studies in Comparative International Development* 83

Greenawalt, A. K. A. 2009. 'Complementarity in Crisis: Uganda, Alternative Justice, and the International Criminal Court', 50(1) *Virginia Journal of International Law* 107

Greppi, E. 2008. 'Inability to Investigate and Prosecute under Article 17', in M. Politi and F. Gioia (eds.), *The International Criminal Court and National Jurisdictions* (Ashgate, Aldershot) 62

Gulu District NGO Forum and Liu Institute for Global Issues 2007. 'The Cooling of Hearts: Community Truth-Telling in Acholi-Land' (Justice and Reconciliation Project, July)

Hagan, J. and W. Rymond-Richmond 2009. *Darfur and the Crime of Genocide* (Cambridge University Press, New York)

Hall, C. K. 1999. 'Article 19: Challenges to the Jurisdiction of the Court or the Admissibility of a Case', in O. Triffterer (ed.), *Commentary on the Rome Statute of the International Criminal Court: Observers' Notes, Article by Article* (1st edn, Nomos, Baden-Baden) 405

　　2003. 'Suggestions Concerning International Criminal Court Prosecutorial Policy and External Relations' (Expert consultation process on general issues relevant to the ICC Office of the Prosecutor, ICC-OTP, 28 March)

　　2008. 'Article 19: Challenges to the Jurisdiction of the Court or the Admissibility of a Case', in O. Triffterer (ed.), *Commentary on the Rome Statute of the International Criminal Court: Observers' Notes, Article by Article* (2nd edn, Beck; Hart; Nomos, Munich; Oxford; Baden-Baden) 637

Hammersley, M. and P. Atkinson 1995. *Ethnography: Principles in Practice* (2nd edn, Routledge, London; New York)

Harlacher, T. 2006. *Traditional Ways of Coping in Acholi: Cultural Provisions for Reconciliation and Healing from War* (Caritas Gulu Archdiocese)

Hashim, F. A. 2009. 'Sudanese Civil Society Strategizing to End Sexual Violence against Women in Darfur', in S. M. Hassan and C. E. Ray (eds.), *Darfur and the Crisis of Governance in Sudan: A Critical Reader* (Cornell University Press, New York) 233

Hassan, S. M. and C. E. Ray (eds.) 2009a. *Darfur and the Crisis of Governance in Sudan: A Critical Reader* (Cornell University Press, New York)

　　2009b. 'Introduction: Critically Reading Darfur and the Crisis of Governance in Sudan', in S. M. Hassan and C. E. Ray (eds.), *Darfur and the Crisis of Governance in Sudan: A Critical Reader* (Cornell University Press, New York) 15

Hassanein, A. M. 2008. 'The Road to Resolve [the] Darfur Crisis' (on file with author)

Hathaway, O. A. 2002. 'Do Human Rights Treaties Make a Difference?', 111(8) *Yale Law Journal* 1935

Hauser, E. 1999. 'Ugandan Relations with Western Donors in the 1990s: What Impact on Democratisation?', 37(4) *Journal of Modern African Studies* 621

Hayner, P. B. 2011. *Unspeakable Truths: Transitional Justice and the Challenge of Truth Commissions* (2nd edn, Routledge, New York; London)

Heller, K. J. 2006. 'The Shadow Side of Complementarity: The Effect of Article 17 of the Rome Statute on National Due Process', 17(3/4) *Criminal Law Forum* 255

2012. 'A Sentence-Based Theory of Complementarity', 53(1) *Harvard International Law Journal* 202

Hernández, C. E. 2000. 'El principio de complementariedad', in J. A. Yáñez-Barnuevo (ed.), *La justicia penal internacional: una perspectiva Ibero-americana* (Casa de América, Madrid) 78

Hoge, W. 2005. 'UN gives suspect list to prosecutor', *International Herald Tribune* (7 April)

Holmes, J. T. 1999. 'The Principle of Complementarity', in R. S. K. Lee (ed.), *The International Criminal Court: The Making of the Rome Statute: Issues, Negotiations, Results* (Kluwer Law International, The Hague; London) 41

2002. 'Complementarity: National Court versus the ICC', in A. Cassese, P. Gaeta and J. R. W. D. Jones (eds.), *The Rome Statute of the International Criminal Court: A Commentary* (Oxford University Press, Oxford) 667

Hountondji, P. J. 1983. *African Philosophy: Myth and Reality* (Hutchinson & Co., London)

Hovil, L. and J. R. Quinn 2005. 'Peace First, Justice Later: Traditional Justice in Northern Uganda' (Refugee Law Project Working Paper No. 17, July)

Human Rights Center, Payson Center for International Development and International Center for Transitional Justice 2007. 'When the War Ends: A Population-Based Survey on Attitudes about Peace, Justice, and Social Reconstruction in Northern Uganda' (December)

Human Rights Committee 2004. 'Concluding Observations of the Human Rights Committee' (CCPR/CO/80/UGA, 4 May)

Human Rights Council 2007a. 'Final Report on the Situation of Human Rights in Darfur Prepared by the Group of Experts Mandated by the Human Rights Council in its Resolution 4/8' (A/HRC/6/19, 28 November)

2007b. 'Report on the Situation of Human Rights in Darfur Prepared by the Group of Experts Mandated by Human Rights Council Resolution 4/8' (A/HRC/5/6, 8 June)

Human Rights Watch 1998. 'Justice in the Balance: Recommendations for an Independent and Effective International Criminal Court'

2001. 'International Criminal Court: Making the International Criminal Court Work: A Handbook for Implementing the Rome Statute' (Vol. 13, No. 4(G), September)

2003. 'Abducted and Abused: Renewed Conflict in Northern Uganda' (Vol. 15, No. 12(A), July)

2004. 'ICC: Investigate All Sides in Uganda' (Press Release, 4 February)

2005a. 'The Curse of Gold, Democratic Republic of Congo' (26 April)

2005b. 'Uprooted and Forgotten: Impunity and Human Rights Abuses in Northern Uganda' (Vol. 17, No. 12(A), September)

2006. 'Lack of Conviction: The Special Criminal Court on the Events in Darfur' (Human Rights Watch Briefing Paper No. 1, June)

2007. 'Benchmarks for Assessing Possible National Alternatives to International Criminal Court Cases against LRA Leaders' (Human Rights Watch Memorandum No. 1, May)

2008. 'Uganda: New Accord Provides for War Crimes Trials; Prosecuting Rights Abusers Will Require Political Will, Legal Reforms' (Press Release, 19 February)

2009a. 'Open Secret: Illegal Detention and Torture by the Joint Anti-terrorism Task Force in Uganda' (April)

2009b. 'Sudan: Submission to the African Union High-Level Panel on Darfur' (29 June)

2009c. 'The Christmas Massacres: LRA Attacks on Civilians in Northern Congo' (February)

2011. 'Thomas Kwoyelo's Trial before Uganda's International Crimes Division: Questions and Answers' (July)

2012. 'Justice for Serious Crimes before National Courts: Uganda's International Crimes Division' (January)

Hume, C. 2006a. 'South Sudan VP Machar Outlines Talks with Lord's Resistance Army' (Khartoum 001484, Ref Khartoum 1396, June), www.leakoverflow.com/questions/418280/06khartoum1484-south-sudan-vp-machar-outlines-talks-with-lords

2006b. 'Sant'Egidio Returns from the Bush with Hope' (Khartoum 00001894, Ref Khartoum 01881, August), http://wikileaks.org/cable/2006/08/06KHARTOUM1894.html

2006c. 'LRA Talks Resume as LRA Assembles' (06Khartoum2161, Ref: Khartoum 2038, September), http://wikileaks.org/cable/2006/09/06KHARTOUM2161.html

Huntington, S. 1995. 'The Third Wave: Democratization in the Late Twentieth Century', in N. J. Kritz (ed.), *Transitional Justice: How Emerging Democracies Reckon with Former Regimes* (Vol. I, United States Institute for Peace, Washington) 65

Hurinet-U 2005. 'Analysis of the International Criminal Court Bill (No. 10/2004) in the Context of Uganda's Obligations under the Statute of the International Criminal Court' (17 January)

Ibrahim, F. 2005–2006. 'Strategies for a De-escalation of Violence in Darfur, Sudan', 4(1) *Global Development Studies* 29

ICC 2004. 'President of Uganda Refers Situation Concerning the Lord's Resistance Army (LRA) to the ICC' (ICC-20040129-44-En, 29 January)

2005. 'Delegation from Uganda Holds Talks with the Registrar of the ICC' (ICC-CPI-20050318-94)

2008. 'ICC Officials Discuss the Role of the Registry in Proceedings before the Court with the Lord's Resistance Army Delegation' (ICC-CPI-20080310-PR295-ENG, 10 March)

2011. 'Mieux comprendre la Cour Pénale Internationale'

ICC Weekly Update 2009. No. 15, 21 December

ICC-ASP/2/10 (2003). 'Official Records Assembly of States Parties to the Rome Statute of the International Criminal Court, Second Session' (New York, 8–12 September)

ICC-ASP/3/25 (2004)-a. 'Draft Programme Budget for 2005 Prepared by the Registrar'

(2004)-b. 'Part II, Programme Budget for 2005 and Related Documents'

(2004)-c. 'Reports of the Committee on Budget and Finance'

ICC-ASP/4/32 (2005)-a. 'Part II External Audit, Programme Budget for 2006 and Related Documents'

(2005)-b. 'Reports of the Committee on Budget and Finance'

ICC-ASP/5/6 (2006). 'Strategic Plan of the International Criminal Court' (4 August)

ICC-ASP/5/32 (2006)-a. '5. Proposed Programme Budget for 2007 Prepared by the Registrar'

(2006)-b. '6. Reports of the Committee on Budget and Finance'

ICC-ASP/6/WGRC/INF.1 (2008). 'Review Conference: Report on the Uganda Site-Visit' (4 June)

ICC-ASP/8/10 (2009). 'Proposed Programme Budget for 2010 of the International Criminal Court'

ICC-ASP/8/L.5/Rev.1 (2009). 'Draft Resolution on the Review Conference' (26 November)

ICC-ASP/8/Res.9 Annex 4 (2010). 'Stocktaking of International Criminal Justice: Complementarity', Appendix: Report of the Bureau on Stocktaking: Complementarity: Taking Stock of the Principle of Complementarity: Bridging the Impunity Gap (25 March)

ICC-OTP 2003a. 'Annex to the "Paper on Some Policy Issues before the Office of the Prosecutor": Referrals and Communications' (September)

2003b. 'Communications Received by the Office of the Prosecutor of the ICC' (pids.009.2003-EN, 16 July)

2003c. 'Informal Expert Paper for the Office of the Prosecutor of the International Criminal Court: The Principle of Complementarity in Practice' (December)

2003d. 'Paper on Some Policy Issues before the Office of the Prosecutor' (September)

2003e. 'Report of the Prosecutor of the ICC to the Second Assembly of States Parties to the Rome Statute of the International Criminal Court' (8 September)

2005a. 'List of Names of Suspects in Darfur Opened by the ICC OTP' (ICC-OTP-20050411-98-En, 11 April)

2005b. 'The Prosecutor of the ICC Opens Investigation in Darfur' (ICC-OTP-0606-104-En, 6 June)

2005c. 'Prosecutor Receives List Prepared by Commission of Inquiry on Darfur' (ICC-OTP-20050405-97-En, 5 April)

2005d. 'Statements by ICC Chief Prosecutor and the Visiting Delegation of Acholi leaders from Northern Uganda' (ICC-OTP-20050318-95-En, 18 March)

2005e. 'Joint Statement by ICC Chief Prosecutor and the Visiting Delegation of Lango, Acholi, Iteso and Madi Community Leaders from Northern Uganda' (ICC-OTP-20050416-99-En, 16 April)

2006a. 'Annex to the Three Year Report and the Report on the Prosecutorial Strategy'

2006b. 'Letter to Senders re Iraq' (9 February)

2006c. 'Report on Prosecutorial Strategy' (14 September)

2006d. 'Report on the Activities Performed during the First Three Years (June 2003–June 2006)' (12 September)

2006e. 'Draft Paper: Criteria for Selection of Situations and Cases' (June)

2007. 'Policy Paper on the Interests of Justice' (17 September)

2008a. 'ICC Prosecutor Presents Case against Sudanese President, Hassan Ahmad Al Bashir, for Genocide, Crimes against Humanity and War Crimes in Darfur' (ICC-OTP-20080714-PR341-ENG, 14 July)

2008b. 'OTP Statement in Relation to Events in Uganda' (4 March)

2009. 'Agreed Minutes of the Meeting between Prosecutor Moreno-Ocampo and the Delegation of the Kenyan Government' (The Hague, 3 July)

2010a. 'ICC Prosecutor Is Working with the Russian Federation to Promote Justice for All Victims of Georgian Conflict – OTP and Russian Federation Pledge Co-operation at Conclusion of Moscow Visit' (ICC-OTP-20100310-PR505, 10 March)

2010b. 'Prosecutorial Strategy, 2009–2012' (The Hague, 1 February)

2010c. 'Ugandan Director for Public Prosecutions Requests OTP Assistance to Prosecute LRA Commanders', OTP Weekly Briefing 65 (23–29 November)

2011a. 'OTP Meets with Ugandan Prosecutors in Preparation of First Domestic War Crimes Case against an LRA Commander', OTP Weekly Briefing 78 (8–14 March)

2011b. 'First Report of the Prosecutor of the International Criminal Court to the UN Security Council Pursuant to UNSCR 1970 (2011)' (4 May)

2011c. 'Report on Preliminary Examination Activities' (13 December)

2012. 'Deputy Prosecutor Bensouda Leads OTP Mission to Côte d'Ivoire and Guinea', OTP Weekly Briefing 117 (3–16 April)

ICRC 2008. 'Uganda: Status of International Humanitarian Law Implementation' (compiled by the communication department of the Uganda delegation of the International Committee of the Red Cross, August 2008)

International Bar Association Human Rights Institute 2007. 'ICC Monitoring and Outreach Programme, Second Outreach Report' (May)

International Bar Association ICC Monitoring and Outreach Programme 2008. 'Implementing Justice: Bringing the ICC Closer to Home', (1) *EQ: Equality of Arms Review* 11

International Center for Transitional Justice 2007. 'Reparation and the Darfur Peace Process: Ensuring Victims' Rights' (November)

2010. 'The Rome Statute Review Conference: Stocktaking: Complementarity', *ICTJ Briefing* (May)

2012. 'Building the First Line of Defense against Impunity: Podcast with Phakiso Mochochoko' (26 March), www.ictj.org/news/building-first-line-defense-against-impunity-podcast-phakiso-mochochoko

International Center for Transitional Justice and Human Rights Center 2005. 'Forgotten Voices: A Population-Based Survey on Attitudes about Peace and Justice in Northern Uganda' (July)

International Commission of Jurists 2007. 'The Administration of Justice in Sudan: The Case of Darfur' (June)

International Crimes Bill Working Document 2009, on file with author

International Crisis Group 2004. 'Northern Uganda: Understanding and Solving the Conflict' (ICG Africa Report, No. 77, 14 April)

2009. 'Sudan: Justice, Peace and the ICC' (Africa Report, No. 152, 17 July)

2012. 'Uganda: No Resolution to Growing Tensions' (Africa Report, No. 187, 5 April)

International Law Commission 2011. 'Fourth Report on the Obligation to Extradite or Prosecute (Aut Dedere Aut Judicare)', by Zdzislaw Galicki, Special Rapporteur (31 May)

International Refugee Rights Initiative 2011. 'A Poisoned Chalice? Local Civil Society and the International Criminal Court's Engagement in Uganda' (October)

'Interview: Deng Alor [Minister of Foreign Affairs], "There are two outlooks inside the ICC Crisis Management Committee"' 2008. *Al Ahdath* (24 August) 10

'Interview: Julian Hottinger – Perspectives of a Mediator' 2010. In *Initiatives to End the Violence in Northern Uganda 2002–09 and the Juba Peace Process* (Accord, Conciliation Resources, London) 15

'Invitation for Mato-Oput Cleansing Ceremony in Gulu' 2008. *Saturday Vision* (20 September) 18

Iya, R. 2010. 'Encountering Kony: A Madi Perspective', in T. Allen and K. Vlassenroot (eds.), *The Lord's Resistance Army: Myth and Reality* (Zed Books, London; New York) 177

Izama, A. 2008. 'Secret dealings that got LRA before world court', *Monitor* (18 May)

Jacobs, D. 2010. 'The Importance of Being Earnest: The Timeliness of the Challenge to Admissibility in Katanga', 23 *Leiden Journal of International Law* 331

Jensen, R. 2006. 'Complementarity, "Genuinely" and Article 17: Assessing the Boundaries of an Effective ICC', in J. K. Kleffner and G. Kor (eds.), *Complementary Views on Complementarity: Proceedings of the International Roundtable on the Complementary Nature of the International Criminal Court, Amsterdam, 25/26 June 2004* (TMC Asser Press, The Hague) 147

JLOS 2008. 'Draft Budget (000) Proposal for Establishment of the War Crimes Division' (September)

2010. 'JLOS Annual Performance Report 2009/2010' (September)

2011. 'Special Report: The Kwoyelo Trial Begins'

2012a. 'Community Dialogue on the Future of the Amnesty Act' (March)

2012b. 'The Amnesty Law (2000) Issues Paper, Review by the Transitional Justice Working Group' (April)

Johnson, D. H. 2007. *The Root Causes of Sudan's Civil Wars* (updated fourth impression, African Issues, James Currey; Fountain Publishers; Indiana University Press, Oxford; Kampala; Bloomington and Indianapolis, IN)

Jolie, A. 2007. 'Justice for Darfur', *Washington Post* (28 February)

Judiciary of the Republic of Uganda (undated). 'Establishment of International Crimes Division of the High Court', www.judicature.go.ug/index.php?option=com_content&task=view&id=117&Itemid=154

Judt, T. 2005. *Postwar: A History of Europe since 1945* (Penguin Books, New York)

Jurdi, N. N. 2010. 'The Prosecutorial Interpretation of the Complementarity Principle: Does It Really Contribute to Ending Impunity on the National Level?', 10 *International Criminal Law Review* 73

Justice and Reconciliation Project 2011a. 'Moving Forward: Thomas Kwoyelo and the Quest for Justice', *Situational Analysis* (15 November)

2011b. 'To Pardon or to Punish: Current Perceptions and Opinions on Uganda's Amnesty in Acholi-land', *Situational Analysis* (15 December)

Kakaire, A. 2006. 'Uganda: amnesty offer blow for rebel chief arrest plans', *Institute for War and Peace Reporting* (6 July)

Karadawi, A. 1991. 'The Smuggling of the Ethiopian Falasha to Israel through Sudan', 90(358) *African Affairs* 23

Kastner, P. 2011. *International Criminal Justice in Bello?: The ICC between Law and Politics in Darfur and Northern Uganda* (Martinus Nijhoff, Leiden)

Kaufman, Z. D. 2006. 'Justice in Jeopardy: Accountability for the Darfur Atrocities', 16(4) *Criminal Law Forum* 343

Kaul, H.-P. 2001. 'The International Criminal Court: Jurisdiction, Trigger Mechanism and Relationship to National Jurisdictions', in M. Politi and G. Nesi (eds.), *The Rome Statute of the International Criminal Court: A Challenge to Impunity* (Ashgate, Aldershot) 59

Kaul, H.-P. and C. Kress 1999. 'Jurisdiction and Cooperation in the Statute of the International Criminal Court: Principles and Compromises', 2 *Yearbook of International Humanitarian Law* 143

Kaye, D. 2004. 'ICC: Getting Down to Business?' (04thehague1885), http://wikileaks.org/cable/2004/07/04THEHAGUE1885.html

Keck, M. E. and K. Sikkink 1998. *Activists beyond Borders* (Cornell University Press, Ithaca, NY; London)

Kennedy, D. 2004. *The Dark Sides of Virtue: Reassessing International Humanitarianism* (Princeton University Press, Princeton, NJ; Oxford)

Keppler, E. 2013, forthcoming. 'Managing Peace and Justice in the Juba Process', in P. Wrange (ed.), *The International Criminal Court and the Juba Peace Process or Global Governance and Local Friction*

Ker Kwaro Acholi 2001. 'Law to Declare the Acholi Customary Law'

Khadiagala, G. M. 2001. 'The Role of the Acholi Religious Leaders Peace Initiative (ARLPI) in Peace Building in Northern Uganda' (Case Study Two of the Greater Horn of Africa Peace Building Project), http://pdf.usaid.gov/pdf_docs/PNACY566.pdf

Khagram, S., J. V. Riker and K. Sikkink (eds.) 2002. *Restructuring World Politics: Transnational Social Movements, Networks and Norms* (University of Minnesota Press, Minneapolis, MN; London)

Khalid, M. 2009. 'Darfur: A Problem within a Wider Problem', in S. M. Hassan and C. E. Ray (eds.), *Darfur and the Crisis of Governance in Sudan: A Critical Reader* (Cornell University Press, New York) 35

Kirchheimer, O. 1961. *Political Justice: The Use of Legal Procedure for Political Ends* (Princeton University Press, Princeton, NJ)

Kleffner, J. K. 2003. 'The Impact of Complementarity on National Implementation of Substantive International Criminal Law', 1(1) *Journal of International Criminal Justice* 86

    2006. 'Complementarity as a Catalyst for Compliance', in J. K. Kleffner and G. Kor (eds.), *Complementary Views on Complementarity: Proceedings of the International Roundtable on the Complementary Nature of the International Criminal Court, Amsterdam, 25/26 June 2004* (TMC Asser Press, The Hague) 79

    2008. *Complementarity in the Rome Statute and National Criminal Jurisdictions* (Oxford University Press, Oxford)

    2009. 'Auto-Referrals and the Complementary Nature of the ICC', in C. Stahn and G. Sluiter (eds.), *The Emerging Practice of the*

International Criminal Court (Martinus Nijhoff Publishers, Leiden; Boston) 41

2011. 'The Law and Policy of Complementarity in Relation to "Criminal Proceedings" Carried out by Non-State Organized Armed Groups', in C. Stahn and M. M. El Zeidy (eds.), *The International Criminal Court and Complementarity: From Theory to Practice* (Vol. II, Cambridge University Press, Cambridge) 707

Kobusingye, O. 2010. *The Correct Line? Uganda under Museveni* (Author-House, Milton Keynes)

Kor, G. 2006. 'Sovereignty in the Dock', in J. K. Kleffner and G. Kor (eds.), *Complementary Views on Complementarity: Proceedings of the International Roundtable on the Complementary Nature of the International Criminal Court, Amsterdam, 25/26 June 2004* (TMC Asser Press, The Hague) 53

Koskenniemi, M. 2002a. 'Between Impunity and Show Trials', 6 *Max Planck Yearbook of United Nations Law* 1

2002b. *The Gentle Civilizer of Nations: The Rise and Fall of International Law, 1870–1960* (Cambridge University Press, Cambridge)

2005. *From Apology to Utopia: The Structure of International Legal Argument* (reissue with a new epilogue, Cambridge University Press, Cambridge)

Kress, C. 2004. '"Self-Referrals" and "Waivers of Complementarity" – Some Considerations in Law and Policy', 2(4) *Journal of International Criminal Justice* 944

Kress, C. and K. Prost 2008. 'Article 93: Other Forms of Cooperation', in O. Triffterer (ed.), *Commentary on the Rome Statute of the International Criminal Court: Observers' Notes, Article by Article* (2nd edn, Beck; Hart; Nomos, Munich; Oxford; Baden-Baden) 1569

Kulayigye, F. 2009. 'Otunnu's notion of genocide in the North very absurd', *Monitor* (4 September)

Kurki, M. 2008. *Causation in International Relations: Reclaiming Causal Analysis* (Cambridge University Press, Cambridge)

Kwoyelo, T. 2010. 'Declaration Form' (12 January)

L/2773 (1996). 'Preparatory Committee on International Criminal Court Continues Considering Complementarity between National, International Jurisdictions' (2 April)

L/ROM/22 (1998). 'UN Diplomatic Conference Concludes in Rome with Decision to Establish Permanent International Criminal Court' (17 July)

Lacey, M. 2005. 'Atrocity Victims in Uganda Choose to Forgive', *New York Times* (18 April)

Lamwaka, C. 2002. 'The Peace Process in Northern Uganda 1986–1990' (Accord, Conciliation Resources, London), www.c-r.org/accord-article/ peace-process-northern-uganda-1986-1990-2002

Latigo, J. O. 2006. 'The Acholi Traditional Techniques of Conflict Management', 4(1) *Uganda Living Law Journal* 1

    2008. 'Northern Uganda: Tradition-Based Practices in the Acholi Region', in L. Huyse and M. Salter (eds.), *Traditional Justice and Reconciliation after Violent Conflict: Learning from African Experiences* (International Institute for Democracy and Electoral Assistance, Stockholm) 85

Lattanzi, F. 1999. 'The Rome Statute and State Sovereignty. ICC Competence, Jurisdictional Links, Trigger Mechanism', in F. Lattanzi and W. Schabas (eds.), *Essays on the Rome Statute of the International Criminal Court* (il Sirente, Fonte di Sotto) 51

    2001. 'The International Criminal Court and National Jurisdictions', in M. Politi and G. Nesi (eds.), *The Rome Statute of the International Criminal Court: A Challenge to Impunity* (Ashgate, Aldershot) 177

Lauwaars, R. H. 1984. 'The Interrelationship between United Nations Law and the Law of Other International Organizations', 82(5/6) *Michigan Law Review* 1604

Lerner, G. 2010. 'Ambassador: US Moving to Support International Court', *CNN* (25 March)

'Letter from Malick Coulibali, Minister of Justice of the Republic of Mali, to the Prosecutor of the ICC, "Renvoi de la situation au Mali"' 2012. (13 July)

'Letter of the President of the Democratic Republic of the Congo, Joseph Kabila, to the Prosecutor of the International Criminal Court "Renvoi de la situation au Mali"' 2004. (3 March)

'Letter President Ouattara to the Office of the Prosecutor' 2011. (3 May)

Liu Institute for Global Issues and Gulu District NGO Forum 2005. 'Roco Wat I Acoli, Restoring Relations in Acholi-Land: Traditional Approaches to Reintegration and Justice' (September)

    2007a. 'Justice and Reconciliation Project: Accountability, Reconciliation and the Juba Peace Talks: Beyond the Impasse' (Field Notes No. 3, October)

    2007b. 'Justice and Reconciliation Project: "Abomination": Local Belief Systems and International Justice' (Field Notes No. 5, September)

Llewellyn, J. J. and S. Raponi 1999. 'The Protection of Human Rights through International Criminal Law: A Conversation with Madame Justice Louise Arbour, Chief Prosecutor for the International Criminal Tribunals for the Former Yugoslavia and Rwanda', 57(1) *University of Toronto Faculty of Law Review* 83

Lomo, Z. 2004. 'The International Criminal Court Investigations: Implications for the Search for Peaceful Solutions to the Conflict in Northern Uganda' (Working Paper No. 2, July)

2006. 'Why the International Criminal Court Must Withdraw Indictments against the Top LRA Leaders: A Legal Perspective' (Refugee Law Project, August)

Lomo, Z. and L. Hovil 2004. 'Behind the Violence: Causes, Consequences and the Search for Solutions to the War in Northern Uganda' (Refugee Law Project Working Paper No. 11, February)

2005. 'Whose Justice? Perceptions of Uganda's Amnesty Act 2000: The Potential for Conflict Resolution and Long-Term Reconciliation' (Refugee Law Project Working Paper No. 15, February)

LRA 2006. 'LRA Position Paper on Accountability, Truth and Reconciliation in the Context of Alternative Justice System [*sic*] for Resolving the Northern/ Eastern Ugandan and Southern Sudan Conflicts' (Juba, 19 August)

MacMillan, K. E. 2007. 'The Practicability of Amnesty as a Non-Prosecutory Alternative in Post-Conflict Uganda', 6(1) *Cardozo Public Law, Policy, and Ethics Journal* 199

Mahmoud, M. e.-T. 2004. 'Inside Darfur: Ethnic Genocide by a Governance Crisis', 24(2) *Comparative Studies of South Asia, Africa and the Middle East* 3

Makubuya, K. 2008. 'Uganda's Statement Presented to the Working Group on the Review Conference' (Assembly of States Parties, sixth resumed session, New York, 5 June)

Mallinder, L. 2009. 'Uganda at a Crossroads: Narrowing the Amnesty?' (Beyond Legalism: Amnesties, Transition and Conflict Transformation, Working Paper No. 1, March)

Mamdani, M. 2004. *Good Muslim, Bad Muslim: America, the Cold War and the Roots of Terror* (Pantheon Books, New York)

2009. *Saviors and Survivors: Darfur, Politics and the War on Terror* (Verso, London; New York)

Mani, R. 2002. *Beyond Retribution: Seeking Justice in the Shadows of War* (Polity, Cambridge)

Maseruka, J. 2009. 'Traditional justice not applicable to war suspects', *New Vision* (30 June)

Matsiko, G. 2011. 'Uganda welcomes US troops to hunt rebel leaders', *AFP* (15 October)

Max Planck Institute for Comparative Public Law and International Law and Peace Research Institute 2010. Heidelberg Darfur Dialogue Outcome Document Containing Draft Proposals for Consideration in a Future Darfur Peace Agreement (Heidelberg and Khartoum), www.mpil.de/shared/data/pdf/hdd_outcome_document_rev.pdf

'Mbeki "outraged" over his panelist remark on Darfur mission' 2009. *Sudan Tribune* (9 November)

McCormack, T. L. H. 2006. 'Their Atrocities and Our Misdemeanours: The Reticence of States to Try Their "Own Nationals" for International

Crimes', in M. Lattimer and P. Sands (eds.), *Justice for Crimes against Humanity* (Hart, Oxford) 107

McDonald, A. and R. Haveman 2003. 'Prosecutorial Discretion – Some Thoughts on "Objectifying" the Exercise of Prosecutorial Discretion by the Prosecutor of the ICC' (Expert consultation process on general issues relevant to the ICC Office of the Prosecutor, ICC-OTP 2003, 15 April)

McDoom, O. 2008. 'Khartoum, Darfur rebels use child soldiers: UN rights', *Reuters* (10 July)

McGoldrick, D. 2004a. 'Criminal Trials before International Tribunals: Legality and Legitimacy', in D. McGoldrick, P. Rowe and E. Donnelly (eds.), *The Permanent International Criminal Court: Legal and Policy Issues* (Hart, Oxford) 9

2004b. 'The Legal and Political Significance of a Permanent International Criminal Court', in D. McGoldrick, P. Rowe and E. Donnelly (eds.), *The Permanent International Criminal Court: Legal and Policy Issues* (Hart, Oxford) 453

2004c. 'Political and Legal Responses to the ICC', in D. McGoldrick, P. Rowe and E. Donnelly (eds.), *The Permanent International Criminal Court: Legal and Policy Issues* (Hart, Oxford) 389

McGregor, L. 2008. 'International Law as a "Tiered Process": Transitional Justice at the Local, National and International Level', in K. McEvoy and L. McGregor (eds.), *Transitional Justice from Below: Grassroots Activism and the Struggle for Change* (Hart, Oxford; Portland, OR) 48

Mégret, F. 2004. 'Qu'est-ce qu'une juridiction "incapable" ou "manquant de volonté" au sens de l'article 17 du Traité de Rome? Quelques enseignements tirés des théories du déni de justice en droit international', 17(2) *Revue québécoise de droit international* 185

2005. 'In Defense of Hybridity: Towards a Representational Theory of International Criminal Justice', 38(3) *Cornell International Law Journal* 725

2006. 'Why Would States Want to Join the ICC? A Theoretical Exploration Based on the Legal Nature of Complementarity', in J. K. Kleffner and G. Kor (eds.), *Complementary Views on Complementarity: Proceedings of the International Roundtable on the Complementary Nature of the International Criminal Court, Amsterdam, 25/26 June 2004* (TMC Asser Press, The Hague) 1

2011. 'Too Much of a Good Thing? Implementation and the Uses of Complementarity', in C. Stahn and M. M. El Zeidy (eds.), *The International Criminal Court and Complementarity: From Theory to Practice* (Vol. I, Cambridge University Press, Cambridge) 361

Mekki Medani, A. 2008. 'Legal Opinion on the Judgment of the Constitutional Court Concerning the Case of Terrorism' (August, on file with author)

Méndez, J. E. 2011. 'Justice and Prevention', in C. Stahn and M. M. El Zeidy (eds.), *The International Criminal Court and Complementarity: From Theory to Practice* (Vol. I, Cambridge University Press, Cambridge) 33

Mercer, J. 1996. *Reputation and International Politics* (Cornell University Press, Ithaca, NY; London)

Merry, S. E. 2006a. *Human Rights and Gender Violence: Translating International Law into Local Justice* (University of Chicago Press, Chicago)

2006b. 'Transnational Human Rights and Local Activism: Mapping the Middle', 108(1) *American Anthropologist* 38

Mirghani, O. 2009. 'Al-Bashir at the scene of the crime', *Asharq Al-Awsat* (10 March)

Miskowiak, K. 2000. *The International Criminal Court: Consent, Complementarity and Cooperation* (DJØF Publishing, Copenhagen)

Mohamed, A. A. Z. 2002. 'Customary Mediation in the Sudan: Past, Present and Future' (UNDP Peacebuilding Center, June)

Montesquieu 1862. *Esprit des lois* (Whitefish, Kessinger Publishing, 2010)

Moreno-Ocampo, L. 2003a. 'Statement Made at the Ceremony for the Solemn Undertaking of the Chief Prosecutor of the International Criminal Court' (The Hague, 16 June)

2003b. 'Statement to the Assembly of States Parties to the Rome Statute of the International Criminal Court' (New York, 22 April)

2004a. 'Address to the Third Session of the Assembly of States Parties to the Rome Statute of the International Criminal Court' (The Hague, 6 September)

2004b. 'Remarks at the Council of Europe Committee of Legal Advisors on Public International Law' (Strasbourg, 18 March)

2004c. 'Statement to the Diplomatic Corps' (The Hague, 12 February)

2005a.'Statement on the Uganda Arrest Warrants' (The Hague, 14 October)

2005b. 'Statement to the Fourth Session of the Assembly of States Parties' (The Hague, 28 November)

2006. 'Keynote Address: Integrating the Work of the ICC into Local Justice Initiatives', 21(4) *American University International Law Review* 497

2007a. 'Address to the Assembly of States Parties' (New York, 30 November)

2007b. 'Building a Future on Peace and Justice' (Nuremberg, 24 and 25 June)

2007c. 'Statement at the Eleventh Diplomatic Briefing of the International Criminal Court' (The Hague, 10 October, ICC-DB11-ST-LMO-ENG)

2008a. 'Remarks by the Prosecutor of the International Criminal Court' (Chicago, 9 April)

2008b. 'Speech Given at Combating Genocide and Other Massive Crimes – The International Criminal Court's Contribution, Commemoration of the 60 Years of the Genocide Convention' (The Hague, 7 December)

2008c. 'The Tenth Anniversary of the ICC and Challenges for the Future: Implementing the Law' (London School of Economics, 8 October)

2009a. 'Press Conference' (Nairobi, Kenya, 7 November)

2009b. 'Working with Africa: The View from the ICC Prosecutor's Office' (Cape Winelands, 9 November)

2011. 'A Positive Approach to Complementarity', in C. Stahn and M. M. El Zeidy (eds.), *The International Criminal Court and Complementarity: From Theory to Practice* (Vol. I, Cambridge University Press, Cambridge) 21

Mueller, D. C. 2003. *Public Choice III* (Cambridge University Press, Cambridge)

Mugerwa, Y. 2012. 'House approves anti-torture bill', *Monitor* (27 April)

Mugisa, A. and H. Nsambu 2008. 'ICC clears UPDF in the North', *Saturday Vision* (30 August)

Mulisch, H. 2006. *De Zaak 40/61: Een Reportage* (De Bezige Bij, Amsterdam)

Murphy, T. and J. Tubiana 2010. 'Civil Society in Darfur: The Missing Peace' (United States Institute for Peace, Special Report 249, September)

'Museveni pledges to cooperate with ICC to probe Uganda war crimes' 2004. *AFP* (25 February)

Museveni, Y. K. 2010. 'Speech by H. E. Yoweri Kaguta Museveni, President of the Republic of Uganda at the Opening Ceremony of the International Criminal Court Review Conference' (Munyonyo, Commonwealth Resort, 31 May)

Musoke, C. 2011. 'Uganda: nation ready to try Col. Gaddafi', *New Vision* (11 June)

Musoke, C. and M. Oluput 2010. 'ICC boss rejects Otunnu's war case', *New Vision* (4 June)

Mutua, M. 2007. 'Beyond Juba: Does Uganda Need a National Truth and Reconciliation Process?', 13 *Buffalo Human Rights Law Review* 19

Muwonge, P. 2011. 'Uganda: EU to finance hunt for nation's LRA rebels', *EastAfrican* (12 December)

Mwenda, A. 2007. 'Personalizing Power in Uganda', 18(3) *Journal of Democracy* 23

2009. 'Who killed Gen. Kazini, and why?', *Independent* (24 November)

2010. 'Uganda's Politics of Foreign Aid and Violent Conflict: The Political Uses of the LRA Rebellion', in T. Allen and K. Vlassenroot (eds.),

The Lord's Resistance Army: Myth and Reality (Zed Books, London; New York) 45

Nakandha, S. 2011. 'Kwoyelo case: apply international fair trial principles', *Monitor* (18 July)

Nassar, A. E. 2003. 'The International Criminal Court and the Applicability of International Jurisdiction under Islamic Law', 4(2) *Chicago Journal of International Law* 587

National Commission on International Humanitarian Law (undated). 'Booklet on Implementation of International Humanitarian Law in Sudan'

Negara, K. 2011. 'Bitter Root', *Al-Jazeera* (*Witness*, 13 October)

Nehru, J. 1964. *Jawaharlal Nehru's Speeches 1949–1953* (Publications Division, Ministry of Information and Broadcasting, Government of India)

Nerlich, V. 2009. 'ICC (Complementarity)', in A. Cassese (ed.), *The Oxford Companion to International Criminal Justice* (Oxford University Press, Oxford) 346

'New native administration law for Darfur submits for presidency of the republic' 2009. *Sudan Media Centre* (16 September)

Newton, M. A. 2001. 'Comparative Complementarity: Domestic Jurisdiction Consistent with the Rome Statute of the International Criminal Court', 167 *Military Law Review* 20

    2011. 'The Quest for Constructive Complementarity', in C. Stahn and M. M. El Zeidy (eds.), *The International Criminal Court and Complementarity: From Theory to Practice* (Vol. I, Cambridge University Press, Cambridge) 304

Ninsiima, E. 2010. 'Lubega to take President to ICC', *Monitor* (24 December)

'Northern Uganda "world's biggest neglected crisis"' 2004. *Guardian* (22 October)

Nouwen, S. M. H. 2006. 'Sudan's Divided (and Divisive?) Peace Agreements', 19 *Hague Yearbook of International Law* 113

    2010a. 'Complementarity in Conflict: Law, Politics and the Catalysing Effect of the International Criminal Court in Uganda and Sudan' (PhD thesis, University of Cambridge)

    2010b. 'Traditional Justice: Improving Access to Justice in Darfur' (unpublished paper)

    2011. 'Complementarity in Uganda: Domestic Diversity or International Imposition?', in C. Stahn and M. M. El Zeidy (eds.), *The International Criminal Court and Complementarity: From Theory to Practice* (Vol. II, Cambridge University Press, Cambridge) 1120

    2012a. 'Justifying Justice', in J. Crawford and M. Koskenniemi (eds.), *The Cambridge Companion to International Law* (Cambridge University Press, Cambridge) 327

2012b. 'The ICC's Intervention in Uganda: Which Rule of Law Does It Promote?', in M. Zürn, A. Nollkaemper and R. Peereboom (eds.), *Rule of Law Dynamics* (Cambridge University Press, New York) 278

2012c. 'The International Criminal Court: A Peacebuilder in Africa?', in D. Curtis and G. A. Dzinesa (eds.), *Peacebuilding, Power and Politics in Africa* (Ohio University Press, Athens, OH) 171

2014a, forthcoming. 'The ICC and Complementarity Post Juba: Between International Imposition and Domestic Diversity', in P. Wrange (ed.), *The International Criminal Court and the Juba Peace Process or Global Governance and Local Friction*

2014b, forthcoming. '"As you set out for Ithaka": Practical, epistemological, ethical and existential questions about socio-legal empirical research in conflict', *Leiden Journal of International Law*

Nouwen, S. M. H. and D. Lewis 2013. 'Jurisdictional Arrangements and International Criminal Procedure', in G. Sluiter, H. Friman, S. Linton, S. Vasiliev and S. Zappalà (eds.), *International Criminal Procedure* (Oxford University Press, Oxford) 116

Nouwen, S. M. H. and W. G. Werner 2010a. 'Doing Justice to the Political: The International Criminal Court in Uganda and Sudan', 21(4) *European Journal of International Law* 941

2010b. 'The Law and Politics of Self-Referrals', in A. Smeulers (ed.), *Collective Violence and International Criminal Justice – An Interdisciplinary Approach* (Intersentia, Antwerp) 255

2011. 'Doing Justice to the Political: The International Criminal Court in Uganda and Sudan: A Rejoinder to Bas Schotel', 22(4) *European Journal of International Law* 1161

Ntanda Nsereko, D. D. 1999. 'The International Criminal Court: Jurisdictional and Related Issues', 10(1) *Criminal Law Forum* 87

2008. 'Article 18: Preliminary Rulings Regarding Admissibility', in O. Triffterer (ed.), *Commentary on the Rome Statute of the International Criminal Court: Observers' Notes, Article by Article* (2nd edn, Beck; Hart; Nomos, Munich; Oxford; Baden-Baden) 627

Nyakairu, F. 2008a. 'Joseph Kony's killing fields in Northern Uganda', *Sunday Monitor* (20 January)

2008b. 'Juba talks close as LRA tables fresh demands', *Monitor* (2 March)

Nyeko, B. and O. Lucima 2002. 'Profiles of the Parties to the Conflict', in O. Lucima (ed.), *Protracted Conflict, Elusive Peace* (Accord, Conciliation Resources, London), www.c-r.org/our-work/accord/northern-uganda/profiles.php

O'Brien, A. 2007. 'The Impact of International Justice on Local Peace Initiatives: The Case of Northern Uganda' (Building a Future on Peace and Justice, Nuremberg, 25–27 June)

O'Keefe, R. 2011. 'State Immunity and Human Rights: Heads and Walls, Hearts and Minds', 44(4) *Vanderbilt Journal of Transnational Law* 999

Ochola II, M. B. 2009. 'Spirituality of Reconciliation: A Case Study of Mato Oput within the Context of the Cultural and Traditional Justice System of the Nilotic Acholi/Central Luo People of Northern Uganda' (October, on file with author)

undated. 'The Relevance of Truth Telling and National Reconciliation Approaches in Promoting Accountability Leading to Genuine Reconciliation' (on file with author)

'Odhiambo won't face world court' 2009. *New Vision* (10 February)

Odongo, A. 2004. 'Acholi chief opposes Kony trial', *New Vision* (8 November)

Oette, L. 2010. 'The Repercussions of the Al-Bashir Case for International Criminal Justice and Beyond', 8 *Journal of International Criminal Justice* 345

Office of the Presidential Advisor 2010. 'Towards a New Strategy for Achieving Comprehensive Peace, Security and Development in Darfur', on file with author.

Ogola, F. 2010. 'Uganda victims question ICC's balance', *Institute for War and Peace Reporting* (16 June)

Ogoola, J. 2010. 'Lawfare: Where Justice Meets Peace', 43 *Case Western Reserve Journal of International Law* 181

Ogora, O. L. 2007. 'Traditional Justice: A Significant Part of the Solution to the Question on Accountability and Reconciliation in Northern Uganda: A Case Study of the Acholi Local Justice Mechanism of Mato Oput', 5(2) *Uganda Living Law Journal* 282

OHCHR 2007. 'Making Peace Our Own: Victims' Perceptions of Accountability, Reconciliation and Transitional Justice in Northern Uganda' (United Nations)

Okanya, A. and J. Akampa 2010. 'Suspected rebel given amnesty after 7 years', *New Vision* (19 February)

Oketch, B. 2010. 'Uganda set for first war crimes trial', *Institute for War and Peace Reporting* (14 July)

Okot, A., G. Lamunu and B. Oketch 2012. 'Contested lands in Ugandan North', *Institute for War and Peace Reporting* (26 March)

Okumu-Alya, F. 2006. 'The International Criminal Court and its Role in the Northern Uganda Conflicts – An Assessment', 4(1) *Uganda Living Law Journal* 16

Olásolo, H. 2005. *The Triggering Procedure of the International Criminal Court* (Martinus Nijhoff Publishers, Leiden)

Olásolo-Alonso, H. and E. C. Rojo 2011. 'The Admissibility of "Situations"', in C. Stahn and M. M. El Zeidy (eds.), *The International Criminal Court and Complementarity: From Theory to Practice* (Vol. I, Cambridge University Press, Cambridge) 393

Omach, P. 2009a. 'Demobilization and Reintegration of Former Combatants in Uganda: The Interplay of Domestic Politics and the International Contexts' (Rethinking Peacebuilding in Africa, Cambridge, 6 March)

2009b. 'Democratization and Conflict Resolution in Uganda', (41) *Les Cahiers d'Afrique de l'Est* 1

Oomen, B. 2005. 'Donor-Driven Justice and its Discontents: The Case of Rwanda', 36(5) *Development and Change* 887

Open Society Justice Initiative 2010. 'Promoting Complementarity in Practice – Lessons from Three ICC Countries' (7 December)

Osiel, M. 2009. *Making Sense of Mass Atrocity* (Cambridge University Press, Cambridge)

Otim, P. W. 2009. 'The Role of the Acholi Religious Leaders Peace Initiative in Uganda's Peacebuilding', *Beyond Intractability*, www.beyondintractability.org/casestudy/otim-role

Otunnu, O. A. 2006a. 'Saving our children from the scourge of war', *Monitor* (8 January)

2006b. 'The Secret Genocide', *Foreign Policy* (June)

Oulanyah, J. L. 2004. 'Proposed New Part to ICC Bill' (December, on file with author)

Pellet, A. 2004. 'Internationalized Courts: Better Than Nothing ...', in C. Romano, A. Nollkaemper and J. K. Kleffner (eds.), *Internationalized Criminal Courts and Tribunals: Sierra Leone, East Timor, Kosovo and Cambodia* (Oxford University Press, Oxford) 437

Perrot, S. 2005. 'La reconstruction d'un ordre politique dans l'Ouganda de Y. Museveni (1986–2001): de la réversibilité du chaos?', 27 *IFRA Les Cahiers*

2010. 'Northern Uganda: A "Forgotten Conflict", Again? The Impact of the Internationalization of the Resolution Process', in T. Allen and K. Vlassenroot (eds.), *The Lord's Resistance Army: Myth and Reality* (Zed Books, London; New York) 187

Peskin, V. 2009. 'The International Criminal Court, the Security Council, and the Politics of Impunity in Darfur', 4(3) *Genocide Studies and Prevention* 304

Pichon, J. 2008. 'The Principle of Complementarity in the Cases of the Sudanese Nationals Ahmad Harun and Ali Kushayb before the International Criminal Court', 8(1) *International Criminal Law Review* 185

Polgreen, L. and J. Gettlemen 2008. 'Sudan rallies behind leader reviled abroad', *New York Times* (28 July)

Politi, M. 1997. 'The Establishment of an International Criminal Court at a Crossroads: Issues and Prospects after the First Session of the Preparatory Committee', in M. C. Bassiouni (ed.), *The International Criminal Court: Observations and Issues before the 1997–1998 Preparatory Committee; and Administrative and Financial Implications* (Nouvelles Etudes Pénales, Chicago) 115

2011. 'Reflections on Complementarity at the Rome Conference and Beyond', in C. Stahn and M. M. El Zeidy (eds.), *The International Criminal Court and Complementarity: From Theory to Practice* (Vol. I, Cambridge University Press, Cambridge) 142

Politi, M. and F. Gioia (eds.) 2008a. *The International Criminal Court and National Jurisdictions* (Ashgate, Aldershot)

2008b. 'Round Table', in M. Politi and F. Gioia (eds.), *The International Criminal Court and National Jurisdictions* (Ashgate, Aldershot) 133

Prunier, G. 2005. *Darfur: The Ambiguous Genocide* (Hurst & Co., London)

Quinn, J. R. 2006. 'Comparing Formal and Informal Mechanisms of Acknowledgement in Uganda' (International Studies Association Annual Meeting, San Diego, 23 March)

2008. '"Accountability and Reconciliation": Traditional Mechanisms of Acknowledgement and the Implications of the Juba Peace Process' (Reconstructing Northern Uganda, Nationalism and Ethnic Conflict Working Group Conference, University of Western Ontario, 9 April)

2010. *The Politics of Acknowledgment: Truth Commissions in Uganda and Haiti* (UBC Press, Vancouver)

Quint, M. 2000. *Effroyables jardins* (Editions Joëlle Losfeld, Gallimard, Paris)

2004. *Et mon mal est délicieux* (Folio, Gallimard, Paris)

Rajagopal, B. 2003. *International Law from Below: Development, Social Movements, and Third World Resistance* (Cambridge University Press, Cambridge)

Rastan, R. 2007. 'The Power of the Prosecutor in Initiating Investigations' (Symposium on the International Criminal Court, International Centre for Criminal Law Reform and Criminal Justice Policy, Beijing, China, 3–4 February)

2008. 'What Is a "Case" for the Purposes of the Rome Statute?', 19 *Criminal Law Forum* 435

2011. 'Situation and Case: Defining the Parameters', in C. Stahn and M. M. El Zeidy (eds.), *The International Criminal Court and Complementarity: From Theory to Practice* (Vol. I, Cambridge University Press, Cambridge) 421

Ratan, A. 2012. 'Complementarity in the Emerging Admissibility Jurisprudence of the International Criminal Court: Balancing the Sovereign Rights of States against the Goal of Ending Impunity?' (unpublished thesis, University of Cambridge)

Ratner, S. R. 2003. 'The International Criminal Court and the Limits of Global Judicialization', 38(3) *Texas International Law Journal* 445

Razesberger, F. 2006. *The International Criminal Court: The Principle of Complementarity* (Völkerrecht Europarecht und Internationales Wirtschaftsrecht; Bd. 1, Peter Lang, Frankfurt am Main)

RC/11 Annex V(c) (2010). 'Stocktaking of International Criminal Justice – Taking Stock of the Principle of Complementarity: Bridging the Impunity Gap – Informal Summary by the Focal Points'

RC-4-ENG-04062010 (2010). 'Kampala Declaration' (Review Conference of the Rome Statute, Kampala, 31 May–11 June)

RC/Res.1 (2010). 'Complementarity' (8 June)

RC/Res.4 (2010). 'The Crime of Aggression' (11 June)

Refugee Law Project 2004. 'On the Announcement of Formal Investigations of the Lord's Resistance Army by the Chief Prosecutor of the International Criminal Court and its Implications on the Search for Peaceful Solutions to the War in Northern Uganda' (28 July)

2007. 'What about Us? The Exclusion of Urban IDPs from Uganda's IDP Related Policies and Interventions' (Briefing Paper, December)

2010. 'Greater North Parliamentary Forum Breakfast Meeting on Transitional Justice' (Imperial Royale Hotel, Kampala, 20 August)

2011a. '"Not only him is bright": A documentary on the National Reconciliation and Transitional Justice Audit', www.refugeelawproject.org/video_advocacy.php

2011b. 'Uganda v. Kwoyelo: Opening Criminal Session/Plea Taking; Gulu High Court, International Crimes Division, July 11, 2011' (Uganda's war crimes trial series, episode 1), http://refugeelawproject.org/kwoyelo_trial.php

Rice, A. 2009. *The Teeth May Smile but the Heart Does Not Forget: Murder and Memory in Uganda* (Picador, New York)

Risse, T., S. C. Ropp and K. Sikkink (eds.) 1999. *The Power of Human Rights: International Norms and Domestic Change* (Cambridge University Press, Cambridge)

Roach, S. 2005. 'Arab States and the Role of Islam in the International Criminal Court', 53(1) *Political Studies* 143

Robinson, D. 2003. 'Serving the Interests of Justice: Amnesties, Truth Commissions and the International Criminal Court', 14(3) *European Journal of International Law* 481

2006. 'Comments on Chapter 4 of Claudia Cárdenas Aravena', in J. K. Kleffner and G. Kor (eds.), *Complementary Views on Complementarity: Proceedings of the International Roundtable on the Complementary Nature of the International Criminal Court, Amsterdam, 25/26 June 2004* (TMC Asser Press, The Hague) 141

2008. 'The Identity Crisis of International Criminal Law', 21(4) *Leiden Journal of International Law* 925

2010. 'The Mysterious Mysteriousness of Complementarity', 21(1) *Criminal Law Forum* 67

2011a. 'The Controversy over Territorial State Referrals and Reflections on ICL Discourse', 9(2) *Journal of International Criminal Justice* 355

2011b. 'The Inaction Controversy: Neglected Words and New Opportunities', in C. Stahn and M. M. El Zeidy (eds.), *The International Criminal Court and Complementarity: From Theory to Practice* (Vol. I, Cambridge University Press, Cambridge) 460

2012. 'Three Theories of Complementarity: Charge, Sentence, or Process', 53 *Harvard International Law Journal* 165

Ruhindi, F. 2011. 'The Role of Specialised Courts in Prosecuting International Crimes and Transitional Justice in Uganda' (UNDP Policy Dialogue on Complementarity and Transitional Justice, New York, 12–13 October)

Ryngaert, C. 2009. 'The Principle of Complementarity: A Means of Ensuring Effective International Criminal Justice', in C. Ryngaert (ed.), *The Effectiveness of International Criminal Justice* (Intersentia, Antwerp; Oxford; Portland, OR)

Sabderat, A. 2008. 'Statement of the Minister of Justice of the Republic of the Sudan before the AU Peace and Security Council' (Addis Ababa, 21 July)

Sadat, L. N. and S. R. Carden 2000. 'The New International Criminal Court: An Uneasy Revolution', 88(3) *Georgetown Law Journal* 381

Said, E. W. 1995. *Orientalism: Western Conceptions of the Orient* (reproduced with a new afterword, Penguin History, Penguin Books, London)

Sands, P. 2003. 'After Pinochet: The Role of National Courts', in P. Sands (ed.), *From Nuremberg to The Hague: The Future of International Criminal Justice* (fourth printing, 2006, Cambridge University Press, Cambridge) 68

Sarooshi, D. 2001. 'Aspects of the Relationship between the International Criminal Court and the United Nations', 32 *Netherlands Yearbook of International Law* 27

2004. 'The ICC Takes Off – Prosecutorial Policy and the ICC – Prosecutor's Proprio Motu Action or Self-Denial?', 2(4) *Journal of International Criminal Justice* 940

Schabas, W. A. 2001. 'The International Criminal Court: Jurisdiction, Trigger Mechanism and Relationship to National Jurisdictions', in M. Politi and G. Nesi (eds.), *The Rome Statute of the International Criminal Court: A Challenge to Impunity* (Ashgate, Aldershot) 197

2003. 'Prosecution at the International Criminal Courts: Some Random Thoughts' (Guest Lecture Series of the Office of the Prosecutor, The Hague, 14 April 2003)

2004. *An Introduction to the International Criminal Court* (2nd edn, Cambridge University Press, Cambridge)

2008a. 'Complementarity in Practice: Creative Solutions or a Trap for the Court', in M. Politi and F. Gioia (eds.), *The International Criminal Court and National Jurisdictions* (Ashgate, Aldershot) 25

2008b. 'Prosecutorial Discretion v. Judicial Activism at the International Criminal Court', 6(4) *Journal of International Criminal Justice* 731

Schacht, J. 1964. *An Introduction to Islamic Law* (reprint 1991, Oxford University Press, Oxford)

Scheffer, D. J. 1998. 'US Department of State Testimony before the Senate Foreign Relations Committee, Developments at Rome Treaty Conference' (Washington, DC, 23 July), www.state.gov/www/policy_remarks/1998/980723_scheffer_icc.html

Schiff, B. N. 2008. *Building the International Criminal Court* (Cambridge University Press, Cambridge)

Schnabel, A. 2005. 'Preventing and Managing Violent Conflict: The Role of the Researcher', in E. Porter, G. Robinson, M. Smyth, A. Schnabel and E. Osaghae (eds.), *Researching Conflict in Africa: Insights and Experiences* (United Nations University Press, Tokyo; New York; Paris) 24

Schomerus, M. 2010a. '"A Terrorist Is Not a Person Like Me": An Interview with Joseph Kony', in T. Allen and K. Vlassenroot (eds.), *The Lord's Resistance Army: Myth and Reality* (Zed Books, London; New York) 113

2010b. 'Chasing the Kony Story', in T. Allen and K. Vlassenroot (eds.), *The Lord's Resistance Army: Myth and Reality* (Zed Books, London; New York) 93

forthcoming. *The Kony Campaigns* (Zed Books, London; New York)

Schomerus, M. and B. Acan Ogwaro 2010. 'Searching for Solutions in Juba: An Overview', in *Initiatives to End the Violence in Northern Uganda 2002–09 and the Juba Peace Process* (Accord, Conciliation Resources, London) 10

Secretariat-General of the Sudan Communist Party 2008. 'Statement on the Consequences of the Darfur Question' (22 July)

Seekers of Truth and Justice 2000. 'The Black Book: Imbalance of Power and Wealth in Sudan', www.sudanjem.com/2004/sudan-alt/english/books/blackbook_part1/20040422_bbone.htm

Seils, P. 2007. 'The Impact of the ICC on Peace Negotiations' (Building a Future on Peace and Justice, Nuremberg, 25–27 June)

2009. 'The Selection and Prioritization of Cases by the Office of the Prosecutor of the International Criminal Court', in M. Bergsmo (ed.), *Criteria for Prioritizing and Selecting Core International Crimes Cases* (FICHL Publication Series No. 4, Forum for International Criminal and Humanitarian Law, Oslo) 55

2011. 'Making Complementarity Work: Maximizing the Limited Role of the Prosecutor', in C. Stahn and M. M. El Zeidy (eds.), *The International Criminal Court and Complementarity: From Theory to Practice* (Vol. II, Cambridge University Press, Cambridge) 989

Seils, P. and M. Wierda 2005. 'The International Criminal Court and Conflict Mediation' (International Center for Transitional Justice Occasional Papers Series, June)

Seventh Parliament of Uganda Defence and Internal Affairs Committee 2006. 'Report on the Amnesty (Amendment) Bill, 2003' (April)

Shany, Y. 2012. 'Jurisdiction and Admissibility of Cases before International Courts and Tribunals' (Sir Hersch Lauterpacht Memorial Lectures, Cambridge, 28 and 29 February and 1 March), http://sms.cam.ac.uk/media/1221731

Sherif, V. 1999. *Het Land van de Vaders* (De Geus, Breda)

Sherif, Y. and N. Ibrahim 2006. 'The Internal Post-Conflict Dynamics', in B. Raftopoulos and K. Alexander (eds.), *Peace in the Balance: The Crisis in Sudan* (Institute for Justice and Reconciliation, Cape Town) 39

Shklar, J. N. 1986. *Legalism: Law, Morals, and Political Trials* (Harvard University Press, Cambridge, MA; London)

Simons, M. 2011. 'International Court Faces Key Test on Libya Captives', *New York Times* (20 November)

Simonse, S., W. Verkoren and G. Junne 2010. 'NGO Involvement in the Juba Peace Talks: The Role and Dilemmas of IKV Pax Christi', in T. Allen and K. Vlassenroot (eds.), *The Lord's Resistance Army: Myth and Reality* (Zed Books, London; New York) 223

Simpson, G. 2004. 'Politics, Sovereignty, Remembrance', in D. McGoldrick, P. Rowe and E. Donnelly (eds.), *The Permanent International Criminal Court: Legal and Policy Issues* (Hart, Oxford) 47

2007. *Law, War and Crime: War Crimes Trials and the Re-invention of International Law* (Polity, Cambridge)

Sivakumaran, S. 2009. 'Courts of Armed Opposition Groups: Fair Trials or Summary Justice?', 7(3) *Journal of International Criminal Justice* 489

Slaughter, A.-M. 2005. *A New World Order* (Princeton University Press, Princeton, NJ, Oxford)

SLM/SLA 2003. 'The Sudan Liberation Movement and Sudan Liberation Army (SLM/SLA): Political Declaration' (Press Release, 14 March), www.mathaba.net/sudan/SLM.htm

Sluiter, G. 2008. 'Obtaining Cooperation from Sudan – Where Is the Law?', 6(5) *Journal of International Criminal Justice* 871

2010. 'The ICC's decision informing the Security Council about the lack of cooperation by Sudan' (27 May), www.internationallawbureau.com/blog/?p=1424

Smith, A. M. 2009. *After Genocide: Bringing the Devil to Justice* (Prometheus Books, New York)

SOAT/Amel Centre 2006. 'Man convicted of rape in Darfur' (Press Release, 8 August)

Solera, O. 2002. 'Complementary Jurisdiction and International Criminal Justice', 84(845) *International Review of the Red Cross* 145

Song, S.-H. 2010. 'Keynote Remarks at ICTJ Retreat on Complementarity' (Greentree Estate, New York, 28 October)

'South Sudan's Machar confirms Bor "apology", calls for wider reconciliation' 2011. *Sudan Tribune* (29 August)

SPLM 2008. 'Statement: Indictment of the President of the Republic and Others Threatens Peace and Stability in Sudan and a Way of Understanding with the IC and ICC Is a Must' (14 July)

Stahn, C. 2008. 'Complementarity: A Tale of Two Notions', 19(1) *Criminal Law Forum* 87

2011a. 'Introduction: Bridge over Troubled Waters: Complementarity Themes and Debates in Context', in C. Stahn and M. M. El Zeidy (eds.), *The International Criminal Court and Complementarity: From Theory to Practice* (Vol. I, Cambridge University Press, Cambridge) 1

2011b. 'Taking Complementarity Seriously: On the Sense and Sensibility of "Classical", "Positive" and "Negative" Complementarity', in C. Stahn and M. M. El Zeidy (eds.), *The International Criminal Court and Complementarity: From Theory to Practice* (Vol. I, Cambridge University Press, Cambridge) 233

2012a. 'Libya, the International Criminal Court and Complementarity', 10(2) *Journal of International Criminal Justice* 325

2012b. 'One Step Forward, Two Steps Back?: Second Thoughts on a "Sentence-Based" Theory of Complementarity', 53 *Harvard International Law Journal* 183

Stigen, J. 2008. *The Relationship between the International Criminal Court and National Jurisdictions: The Principle of Complementarity* (Martinus Nijhoff Publishers, Leiden; Boston)

Strauss, A. L. and J. M. Corbin 1998. *Basics of Qualitative Research: Techniques and Procedures for Developing Grounded Theory* (2nd edn, Sage, Thousand Oaks, CA; London)

Struett, M. J. 2005. 'The Transformation of State Sovereign Rights and Responsibilities under the Rome Statute for the International Criminal Court', 8(1) *Chapman Law Review* 179

Sudan 2008. 'Progress Report from the Government of National Unity to the African Union Commission' (17 September)

2011. 'GoS's Observations on the Document Submitted by the Mediation' (27 February)

'Sudan appoints new Darfur prosecutor' 2011. *Sudan Tribune* (17 August)

Sudan Bar Association 2008a. 'Commission on Immunity of State's Presidents and Sovereignty of States' in Legal Studies of the Impact of a Memorandum Submitted by the Prosecutor of the ICC on Darfur (Sudan Bar Association, Khartoum)

2008b. 'The Legal Committee for the Study of the Repercussions of the ICC Prosecutor Memorandum: The Second Committee: The Jurisdiction Committee': in *Legal Studies of the Impact of a Memorandum Submitted by the Prosecutor of the ICC on Darfur* (Sudan Bar Association, Khartoum)

2008c. *Legal Studies of the Impact of a Memorandum Submitted by the Prosecutor of the ICC on Darfur* (Sudan Bar Association, Khartoum)

2008d. 'A Report on the Legality of Security Council's Resolution 1593 to Remit Darfur's Situation to the General Attorney of the International Criminal Court in the Light of International Law Fundamentals & Options of Counteracting the Rome Statute before International Judiciary' in *Legal Studies of the Impact of a Memorandum Submitted by the Prosecutor of the ICC on Darfur* (Sudan Bar Association, Khartoum)

2008e. 'Statement of the Sudan Bar Union to all People, 19 July 2008' in *Legal Studies of the Impact of a Memorandum Submitted by the Prosecutor of the ICC on Darfur* (Sudan Bar Association, Khartoum)

'Sudan detains militia leader wanted by ICC in preparation for trial' 2008. *Sudan Tribune* (13 October)

'Sudan fires Darfur war crimes prosecutor amid talk of "transitional justice"' 2010. *Sudan Tribune* (17 October)

'Sudan first VP pleads case against ICC arrest warrant for Bashir' 2009. *Sudan Tribune* (14 January)

'Sudan hires UK law firm to handle ICC indictment of Bashir' 2008. *Sudan Tribune* (10 November)

'Sudan minister criticized for slowness of Darfur massacre inquiry' 2010. *Radio Dabanga* (26 September)

'Sudan official report to UNSC in September shows no arrest of Kushayb' 2008. *Sudan Tribune* (15 October)

'Sudan on collision course with UN over Darfur trials' 2005. *AFP* (4 April)

'Sudan president lifts press censorship but warns from "exceeding red line"' 2009. *Sudan Tribune* (28 September)

'Sudan president says only DNA test can prove rape in Darfur' 2008. *Sudan Tribune* (10 October)

'Sudan reiterates opposition to try Darfur suspects before ICC' 2005. *Sudan Tribune* (18 October)

'Sudan reiterates rejection of AU plan for Darfur hybrid courts' 2011. *Sudan Tribune* (26 July)

'Sudan reiterates rejection of Darfur hybrid courts' 2009. *Sudan Tribune* (1 November)

'Sudan says ICC prosecutor "messenger of destruction"' 2009. *Sudan Tribune* (6 June)

'Sudan to establish special court for Darfur crimes and appoints new special prosecutor' 2012. *Sudan Tribune* (10 January)

'Sudan: judiciary challenges ICC over Darfur cases' 2005. *IRIN* (24 June)

'Sudan: National court to try suspects of Darfur crimes' 2005. *IRIN* (15 June)

'Sudan's former spy chief slams slow pace of Darfur crimes probe' 2011. *Sudan Tribune* (8 June)

'Sudan's Turabi jailed over Bashir remarks; family says no regrets' 2009. *Sudan Tribune* (15 January)

'Sudan's UN envoy invokes Macbeth to condemn ICC' 2009. *Reuters* (4 March)

'Sudanese ambassador to UN lashes at Ocampo' 2009. *China View* (6 June)

'Sudanese gets 17 years for "spying" for war crimes court' 2009. *AFP* (28 January)

'Sudanese Justice Minister on Darfur crisis, efforts to achieve peace, AU force' 2006. *Al-Sharq al-Awsat* (31 March)

'Sudanese police arrest 70 journalists over protest for press freedom' 2008. *Sudan Tribune* (17 November)

'Sudanese students wounded in clashes with government militia over ICC' 2009. *Sudan Tribune* (16 March)

Suliman, M. 1997. 'Ethnicity from Perception to Cause of Violent Conflicts: The Case of the Fur and Nuba Conflicts in Western Sudan' (CONTICI International Workshop, Bern, 8–11 July)

Swart, B. 2006. 'Comments on Chapter 5 of Rod Jensen', in J. K. Kleffner and G. Kor (eds.), *Complementary Views on Complementarity: Proceedings of the International Roundtable on the Complementary Nature of the International Criminal Court, Amsterdam, 25/26 June 2004* (TMC Asser Press, The Hague) 171

Swart, B. and G. Sluiter 1999. 'The International Criminal Court and International Criminal Co-operation', in H. A. M. von Hebel, J. G. Lammers and J. Schukking (eds.), *Reflections on the International Criminal Court* (TMC Asser Press, The Hague) 91

Tabaire, B. 2007. 'The Press and Political Repression in Uganda: Back to the Future?', 1(2) *Journal of Eastern African Studies* 193

Takemura, H. 2007. 'A Critical Analysis of Positive Complementarity', conference paper given at the XVth International Congress of Social Defence, Toledo, Spain, 22 September

Tallgren, I. 1998. 'Completing the "International Criminal Order": The Rhetoric of International Repression and the Notion of Complementarity in the Draft Statute for an International Criminal Court', 67(2) *Nordic Journal of International Law* 107

1999. 'We Did It? The Vertigo of Law and Everyday Life at the Diplomatic Conference on the Establishment of an International Criminal Court', 12(3) *Leiden Journal of International Law* 683

Tangri, R. and A. M. Mwenda 2003. 'Military Corruption and Ugandan Politics', 30(98) *Review of African Political Economy* 539

Tanner, V. 2004. 'Darfur: racines anciennes, nouvelles virulances', 4 *Politique étrangère* 715

    2005. 'Rule of Lawlessness: Roots and Repercussions of the Darfur Crisis' (Interagency Paper, January)

Terracino, J. B. 2007. 'National Implementation of ICC Crimes: Impact on National Jurisdictions and the ICC', 5(2) *Journal of International Criminal Justice* 421

Thomas, E. 2011. 'Reconciliation and the Consolidation of Peace – The Role of Civil Society' (Justice Africa meeting, Juba, July)

'Three human rights activists arrested in Sudan' 2008. *Sudan Tribune* (25 November)

Tisdall, S. 2008. 'Technicians in the workshop of double standards', *Guardian* (29 July)

    2011. 'Omar Al-Bashir: conflict in Darfur is my responsibility', *Guardian* (21 April)

Titeca, K. 2010. 'The Spiritual Order of the LRA', in T. Allen and K. Vlassenroot (eds.), *The Lord's Resistance Army: Myth and Reality* (Zed Books, London; New York) 59

Toga, D. 2007. 'The African Union Mediation and the Abuja Peace Talks', in A. de Waal (ed.), *War in Darfur* (Harvard University Press, Cambridge, MA) 214

Tolbert, D. and A. Kontić 2011. 'The International Criminal Tribunal for the Former Yugoslavia ("ICTY") and the Transfer of Cases and Materials to National Judicial Authorities: Lessons in Complementarity', in C. Stahn and M. M. El Zeidy (eds.), *The International Criminal Court and Complementarity: From Theory to Practice* (Vol. II, Cambridge University Press, Cambridge) 888

Tomlinson, J. 1999. *Globalization and Culture* (University of Chicago Press, Chicago)

Totten, C. D. and N. Tyler 2008. 'Arguing for an Integrated Approach to Resolving the Crisis in Darfur: The Challenges of Complementarity, Enforcement, and Related Issues in the International Criminal Court', 98(3) *Journal of Criminal Law and Criminology* 1069

Transitional Justice Team of the JLOS Secretariat 2011. 'Justice at Cross Roads? A Special Report on the Thomas Kwoyelo Trial' (5 October), www.jlos.go.ug/uploads/Special%20Report%20on%20the%20Thomas_kwoyelo_trial.pdf

Treves, T., M. F. di Rattalma, A. Tanzi, A. Fodella, C. Pitea and C. Ragni (eds.) 2005. *Civil Society, International Courts and Compliance Bodies* (TMC Asser Press, The Hague)

Triffterer, O. 2008. 'Article 1', in O. Triffterer (ed.), *Commentary on the Rome Statute of the International Criminal Court: Observers' Notes, Article by Article* (2nd edn, Beck; Hart; Nomos, Munich; Oxford; Baden-Baden) 49

Tripp, A. M. 2010. *Museveni's Uganda: Paradoxes of Power in a Hybrid Regime* (Lynne Rienner Publishers, Boulder, CO; London)

Tubiana, J. 2006. 'Le Darfour, un conflit pour la terre', (101) *Politique africaine* 111

2009. 'Lire entre les lignes d'un conflit: fractures locales et actions internationales au cœur du Darfur', (232) *Afrique contemporaine* 75

2010. *Chroniques du Darfur* (Glénat, Grenoble)

2011. 'Legal Limbo: How the International Criminal Court Is Freezing the Conflict in Darfur', *Foreign Policy* (23 February)

'Turabi calls on Sudan's Bashir to face ICC charges' 2009. *Sudan Tribune* (13 January)

Turner, J. I. 2005. 'Nationalizing International Criminal Law', 41(1) *Stanford Journal of International Law* 1

Uganda 1996. 'Core Document Forming Part of the Reports of the States Parties' (HRI/CORE/1/ADD.69, 7 March)

1999a. 'The Amnesty Bill 1999', *Hansard* (30 November)

1999b. 'The Amnesty Bill 1999', *Hansard* (1 December)

2003. 'Referral of the Situation concerning the Lord's Resistance Army Submitted by the Republic of Uganda' (16 December)

2004. 'Statement Defence Minister Mbabazi', *Hansard* (29 July)

2005a. 'Status Reports by Chairpersons on Pending Business in Their Committees in Accordance with Rule 182 of the Rules of Procedure', *Hansard* (26 May)

2005b. 'Address on the State of the Nation', *Hansard* (7 June)

2006a. 'Address on the State of the Nation', *Hansard* (8 June)

2006b. 'Communication from the Chair', *Hansard* (6 September)

2006c. 'Motion for a Resolution of Parliament on the Ongoing Peace Talks between the Goverment of Uganda and the Lord's Resistance Army in Juba, Southern Sudan', *Hansard* (7 September)

2006d. 'Government's Position on Reconciliation and Accountability' (date unclear)

2007. 'Question 14/1/08 to the Minister of Internal Affairs', *Hansard* (21 February)

2009. 'Question 73/1/08 to the Minister for Foreign Affairs', *Hansard* (16 July)

2010a. 'The International Criminal Court Bill, 2004', *Hansard* (10 March)

2010b. 'Request for Parliament to Approve the Declaration of Named Individuals as Persons not Eligible for Amnesty', *Hansard* (13 April)

'Uganda journalists held in raid' 2008. *BBC* (26 April)

'Uganda: 1,000 displaced die every week in war-torn north – report' 2005. *IRIN* (29 August)

'Uganda: former LRA combatants struggle for forgiveness' 2010. *IRIN* (10 November)

'Uganda: IDPs unlikely to meet deadline to vacate camps' 2006. *IRIN* (26 December)

'Uganda: interview with President Yoweri Museveni' 2005. *IRIN* (9 June)

'Uganda: Kony will eventually face trial, says ICC prosecutor' 2006. *IRIN* (7 July)

'Uganda: peace groups and government officials worried about ICC probe into LRA' 2004. *IRIN* (30 January)

'Uganda: US accuses LRA of abuses, calls for a quick peaceful solution' 2008. *IRIN* (18 June)

'UK, France agree to Chinese proposal on Darfur trials: report' 2008. *Sudan Tribune* (28 October)

UKMIL 2010. 'United Kingdom Materials on International Law 2009', 80 *British Yearbook of International Law* 661

'UN chief: Sudan president could avoid prosecution' 2009. *International Herald Tribune* (12 March)

UN Doc. A/49/10 (1994). 'Report of the International Law Commission on the Work of its Forty-Sixth Session: Draft Statute for an International Criminal Court with Commentaries'

UN Doc. A/50/22 (1995). 'Report of the Ad Hoc Committee on the Establishment of an International Criminal Court'

UN Doc. A/51/22 (1996). 'Report of the Preparatory Committee on the Establishment of an International Criminal Court, Vol. I (Proceedings of the Preparatory Committee during March–April and August 1996)' (13 September)

UN Doc. A/C.6/52/SR.11 (1997). 'Establishment of an International Criminal Court: Organization of Work' (Summary record of the 11th meeting of the Sixth Committee, 4 November)

UN Doc. A/CN.4/SR.2357 (1994). 'Draft Code of Crimes against the Peace and Security of Mankind (Part II) – Including the Draft Statute for an International Criminal Court' (Summary record of the 2357th meeting of the International Law Commission, *Yearbook of the International Law Commission* 1994, Vol. I, 194)

UN Doc. A/CONF.183/C.1/SR.4 (1998). '4th meeting of the Committee of the Whole', Extract from Volume II of the Official Records of the United Nations Diplomatic Conference of Plenipotentiaries on the Establishment of an International Criminal Court (Summary records of the plenary meetings and of the meetings of the Committee of the Whole)

UN Doc. A/CONF.183/C.1/SR.8 (1998). '8th Meeting of the Committee of the Whole, Extract from Volume II of the Official Records of the United Nations Diplomatic Conference of Plenipotentiaries on the Establishment of an International Criminal Court' (Summary records of the meetings of the Committee of the Whole)

UN Doc. A/CONF.183/C.1/SR.11 (1998). '11th Meeting of the Committee of the Whole, Extract from Volume II of the Official Records of the United Nations Diplomatic Conference of Plenipotentiaries on the Establishment of an International Criminal Court' (Summary records of the plenary meetings and of the meetings of the Committee of the Whole)

UN Doc. A/CONF.183/C.1/SR.12 (1998). '12th Meeting of the Committee of the Whole, Extract from Volume II of the Official Records of the United Nations Diplomatic Conference of Plenipotentiaries on the Establishment of an International Criminal Court' (Summary records of the plenary meetings and of the meetings of the Committee of the Whole)

UN Doc. A/RES/60/147 (2006). 'Basic Principles and Guidelines on the Right to a Remedy and Reparation for Victims of Gross Violations of International Human Rights Law and Serious Violations of International Humanitarian Law' (21 March)

UN Doc. CCPR/C/SDN/CO/3/CRP.1 (2007). 'Consideration of Reports Submitted by States Parties under Article 40 of the Covenant: Concluding Observations of the Human Rights Committee Sudan' (26 July)

UN Doc. GA/RES/2840 (1971). 'Question of the Punishment of War Criminals and of Persons Who Have Committed Crimes against Humanity' (18 December)

UN Doc. GA/RES/3074 (1973). 'Principles of International Co-operation in the Detection, Arrest, Extradition and Punishment of Persons Guilty of War Crimes and Crimes against Humanity' (3 December)

UN Doc. S/AC.43/2009/COMM.64 (2009). 'Communication Dated 17 December 2009 from the Permanent Mission of Uganda'

UN Doc. S/2004/616 (2004). 'Report of the Secretary-General on the Rule of Law and Transitional Justice in Conflict and Post-Conflict Societies' (3 August)

UN Doc. S/2005/60 (2005). 'Report of the International Commission of Inquiry on Darfur to the United Nations Secretary-General, pursuant to Security Council Resolution 1564 of 18 September 2004' (25 January)

UN Doc. S/2005/80 (2005). 'Letter dated 23 January 2005 from the Permanent Representative of the Sudan to the United Nations Addressed to the President of the Security Council' (26 January)

UN Doc. S/2005/403 (2005). 'Letter dated 18 June 2005 from the Chargé d'Affaires A. I. of the Permanent Mission of the Sudan to the United Nations Addressed to the President of the Security Council' (22 June)

UN Doc. S/2009/201 (2009). 'Report of the Secretary-General on the Deployment of the African Union–United Nations Hybrid Operation in Darfur' (14 April)

UN Doc. S/2009/352 (2009). 'Report of the Secretary-General on the Deployment of the African Union–United Nations Hybrid Operation in Darfur' (13 July)

UN Doc. S/2011/634 (2011). 'Report of the Secretary-General on the Rule of Law and Transitional Justice in Conflict and Post-Conflict Societies' (12 October)

UN Doc. S/PRST/2008/48 (2008). 'The Situation in the Great Lakes Region' (22 December)

UN Doc. S/PV.3453 (1994). Security Council Debate on the Establishment of the ICTR (8 November)

UN Doc. S/PV.5158 (2005). 'Reports of the Secretary-General on the Sudan' (31 March)

UN Doc. S/PV.5525 (2006). 'The Situation in Africa: Briefing by the Under-Secretary-General for Humanitarian Affairs and Emergency Relief Coordinator' (15 September)

UN Doc. S/RES/1192 (1998). 'Lockerbie Case' (27 August)

UN Doc. S/RES/1422 (2002). 'United Nations Peacekeeping'

UN Doc. S/RES/1556 (2004). 'Report of the Secretary-General on the Sudan' (30 July)

UN Doc. S/RES/1564 (2004). 'Report of the Secretary-General on the Sudan' (18 September)

UN Doc. S/RES/1591 (2005). 'Reports of the Secretary-General on the Sudan' (29 March)

UN Doc. S/RES/1593 (2005). 'Reports of the Secretary-General on the Sudan' (31 March)

UN Doc. S/RES/1970 (2011). 'Peace and Security in Africa' (26 February)

'UN hails lift of censorship on Sudanese press' 2009. *Sudan Tribune* (29 September)

UNDP and Ministry of Higher Education 2002. 'Conflict Survey and Mapping Analysis' (August)

UNHCR 2012. 'UNHCR Closes Chapter on Uganda's Internally Displaced People', *Briefing Notes* (6 January)

United Nations Secretary-General 2002. 'Depository Notification, Colombia: Ratification, C.N.834.2002. Treaties-33, Rome Statute of the International Criminal Court' (5 August)

University of Khartoum 2008. 'Memo of the U of K Work Group to Support National Efforts to Refute the Allegations of the ICC Prosecutor and Settlement of the Darfur Dispute' (16 September)

UNMIS Rule of Law 2009. 'Legislative Tracking Report, Updated: 18 August 2009'

Van de Wiel, A. 2011. 'Witness to the Trial: Monitoring the Kwoyelo Trial', Issue 1 (Refugee Law Project)

Van den Wyngaert, C. and T. Ongena 2002. 'Ne Bis in Idem Principle, Including the Issue of Amnesty', in A. Cassese, P. Gaeta and J. R. W. D. Jones (eds.), *The Rome Statute of the International Criminal Court: A Commentary* (Oxford University Press, Oxford) 705

Van der Vyver, J. D. 2000. 'Personal and Territorial Jurisdiction of the International Criminal Court', 14(1) *Emory International Law Review* 1

Van der Wilt, H. 2011. 'States' Obligation to Investigate and Prosecute Perpetrators of International Crimes: The Perspective of the European Court of Human Rights', in C. Stahn and M. M. El Zeidy (eds.), *The International Criminal Court and Complementarity: From Theory to Practice* (Vol. II, Cambridge University Press, Cambridge) 685

Van Oudenaren, D. 2008. 'US will veto attempts to defer ICC move against Sudan president: official', *Sudan Tribune* (25 September)

Verdirame, G. 2011. *The UN and Human Rights: Who Guards the Guardians?* (Cambridge University Press, Cambridge)

Verdirame, G. and B. E. Harrell-Bond 2005. *Rights in Exile: Janus-Faced Humanitarianism* (Berghahn Books, Oxford; New York)

Verrijn Stuart, H. 2005. 'Uganda file: a fruit ripe for the picking', *International Justice Tribune* (13 June)

Waddell, N. and P. Clark 2007. 'Peace, Justice and the ICC in Africa' (Meeting Series Report, Royal African Society, London)

Wainaina, B. 2005. 'How to Write About Africa', 92 *Granta*

Wallis, D. 2006. 'Uganda rebels want ICC arrest warrants scrapped', *Reuters* (6 September)

Wasswa, H. 2008. 'Kony lawyers to seek local trial: new legal team say they will challenge ICC's indictment against LRA leader', *Institute for War and Peace Reporting* (19 February)

Wastell, S. 2001. 'Presuming Scale, Making Diversity: On the Mischiefs of Measurement and the Global: Local Metonym in Theories of Law and Culture', 21(2) *Critique of Anthropology* 185

Weller, M. 2002. 'Undoing the Global Constitution: UN Security Council Action on the International Criminal Court', 78(4) *International Affairs* 693

Weschler, L. 2000. 'Exceptional Cases in Rome: The United States and the Struggle for an ICC', in S. B. Sewall and C. Kaysem (eds.), *The United States and the International Criminal Court* (Rowman & Littlefield Publishers Inc., Lanham, MD; Boulder, CO; New York; Oxford)

Wheeler, S. 2008. 'Ugandan rebels sign deals, walk out of talks', *Reuters* (1 March)

Widner, J. 2001. 'Courts and Democracy in Postconflict Transitions: A Social Scientist's Perspective on the African Case', 95(1) *American Journal of International Law* 64

Wierda, M. and M. Otim 2011. 'Courts, Conflict and Complementarity in Uganda', in C. Stahn and M. M. El Zeidy (eds.), *The International Criminal Court and Complementarity: From Theory to Practice* (Vol. II, Cambridge University Press, Cambridge) 1155

Willemse, K. 2009. 'The Darfur War: Masculinity and the Construction of a Sudanese National Identity', in S. M. Hassan and C. E. Ray (eds.), *Darfur and the Crisis of Governance in Sudan: A Critical Reader* (Cornell University Press, New York) 170

Williams, S. A. 1999. 'Article 17: Issues of Admissibility', in O. Triffterer (ed.), *Commentary on the Rome Statute of the International Criminal Court: Observers' Notes, Article by Article* (1st edn, Nomos, Baden-Baden) 383

    2008. 'Article 17: Issues of Admissibility', in O. Triffterer (ed.), *Commentary on the Rome Statute of the International Criminal Court: Observers' Notes, Article by Article* (2nd edn, Beck; Hart; Nomos, Munich; Oxford; Baden-Baden) 605

Wippman, D. 2004. 'The International Criminal Court', in C. Reus-Smit (ed.), *The Politics of International Law* (Cambridge University Press, Cambridge) 151

Wrange, P. 2008a. 'The ICC Bill, Complementarity and "Retroactivity"' (30 September)

    2008b. 'The Agreement and the Annexure on Accountability and Reconciliation between the Government of Uganda and the Lord's Resistance Army/Movement – A Legal and Pragmatic Commentary', 6(1) *Uganda Living Law Journal* 42

Wright, T. 2011. 'The Search for Transitional Justice in Uganda: Global Dimensions' (Master of Anthropology thesis, University of Canterbury, on file with author)

Yáñez-Barnuevo, J. A. 2000. 'El proceso en marcha para la ratificación y puesta en práctica del estatuto de Roma', in J. A. Yáñez-Barnuevo (ed.), *La justicia penal internacional: una perspectiva iberoamericana* (Casa de América, Madrid) 37

Yang, L. 2003. 'Some Critical Remarks on the Rome Statute of the International Criminal Court', 2(2) *Chinese Journal of International Law* 599

    2005a. 'On the Principle of Complementarity in the Rome Statute of the International Criminal Court', 4(1) *Chinese Journal of International Law* 121

    2005b. 'Some Critical Remarks on the Rome Statute of the International Criminal Court', in R. S. Lee (ed.), *States' Responses to Issues Arising from the ICC Statute: Constitutional, Sovereignty, Judicial Cooperation and Criminal Law* (Transnational Publishers, Ardsley, NY) 281

Yassin, A. M. O. 1998. 'Statement of the Minister of Justice of the Republic of the Sudan' (Rome, 18 June)

Yates, P., P. de Onis and P. Kinoy 2009. *The Reckoning: The Battle for the International Criminal Court* (Skylight Pictures)

Yongo-Bure, B. 2009. 'Marginalization and War: From the South to Darfur', in S. M. Hassan and C. E. Ray (eds.), *Darfur and the Crisis of Governance in Sudan: A Critical Reader* (Cornell University Press, New York) 68

Zahar, A. and G. Sluiter 2008. *International Criminal Law* (Oxford University Press, Oxford)

Zappalà, S. 2009. 'Judicial Activism v. Judicial Restraint in International Criminal Justice', in A. Cassese (ed.), *The Oxford Companion to International Criminal Justice* (Oxford University Press, Oxford) 216

CASES AND PROCEDURAL DOCUMENTS

African Commission on Human and Peoples' Rights
Democratic Republic of Congo v. Burundi, Rwanda and Uganda:

> Democratic Republic of Congo/Burundi, Rwanda, Uganda, Decision 227/99, May 2003

Inter-American Court of Human Rights
Barrios Altos:

> Barrios Altos (Chumbipuma Aguirre *et al.* v. Peru), Judgment, 14 March 2001, Series C No. 75 [2001] IACHR 5

International Criminal Court
Situation in the Central African Republic
Decision Requesting Information on Preliminary Examination CAR:

> Decision requesting Information on the Status of the Preliminary Examination of the Situation in the Central African Republic, ICC-01/05-6, Pre-Trial Chamber III, 30 November 2006

Notification Investigation CAR:

> Letter from the Prosecutor to all States Parties to the Rome Statute of the International Criminal Court, CAR/NOTIF/21052007/LMO, Office of the Prosecutor, 21 May 2007

Prosecutor v. Jean-Pierre Bemba Gombo
Decision Admissibility Challenge Bemba (TC):

> Decision on the Admissibility and Abuse of Process Challenges, ICC-01/05-01/08-802, Trial Chamber III, 24 June 2010

Decision Arrest Warrant Bemba:

Décision relative à la requête du Procureur aux fins de délivrance d'un mandat d'arrêt à l'encontre de Jean-Pierre Bemba Gombo, ICC-01/05-01/08-14, Pre-Trial Chamber III, 11 June 2008

Judgment Admissibility Challenge Bemba (AC):

Judgment on the Appeal of Mr Jean-Pierre Bemba Gombo against the Decision of Trial Chamber III of 24 June 2010 Entitled 'Decision on the Admissibility and Abuse of Process Challenges', ICC-01/05-01/-8-962, Appeals Chamber, 19 October 2010

Situation in Darfur, Sudan
Application Arrest Warrant Bashir:

Public Redacted Version of the Prosecutor's Application under Article 58, ICC-02/05-157-AnxA, Office of the Prosecutor, 12 September 2008

Application Citizens' Organisations of the Sudan:

Application on behalf of Citizens' Organisations of the Sudan in relation to the Prosecutor's Applications for Arrest Warrants of 14 July 2008 and 20 November 2008, Applicants, ICC-02/05-170, 12 January 2009

Decision Darfur Jurisdiction and Admissibility Challenge:

Décision relative aux conclusions aux fins d'exception d'incompétence et d'irrecevabilité, ICC-02/05-34, Pre-Trial Chamber I, 22 November 2006

Fifth Darfur Report:

Fifth Report of the Prosecutor of the International Criminal Court to the UN Security Council pursuant to UNSCR 1593 (2005), 7 June 2007

First Darfur Report:

Report of the Prosecutor of the International Criminal Court to the Security Council pursuant to UNSC 1593 (2005), 29 June 2005

Fourth Darfur Report:

Fourth Report of the Prosecutor of the International Criminal Court to the UN Security Council pursuant to UNSCR 1593 (2005), 14 December 2006

OTP Application Harun and Kushayb:

Prosecutor's Application under Article 58(7), ICC-02/05-56, Office of the Prosecutor, 27 February 2007

Prosecutor's Darfur Statement SC December 2007:

Statement of the Prosecutor of the International Criminal Court to the United Nations Security Council pursuant to UNSCR 1593 (2005), 5 December 2007

Prosecutor's Darfur Statement SC December 2009:

Statement by the Prosecutor of the International Criminal Court, Statement to the United Nations Security Council pursuant to UNSCR 1593 (2005), 4 December 2009

Prosecutor's Darfur Statement SC December 2010:

Statement of the Prosecutor of the International Criminal Court to the United Nations Security Council on the Situation in Darfur, the Sudan, pursuant to UNSCR 1593 (2005), New York, 9 December 2010

Prosecutor's Darfur Statement SC June 2007:

Statement of the Prosecutor of the International Criminal Court to the UN Security Council pursuant to UNSCR 1593 (2005), 7 June 2007

Prosecutor's Darfur Statement SC June 2009:

Statement of the Prosecutor of the International Criminal Court to the United Nations Security Council on the Situation in Darfur, the Sudan, pursuant to UNSCR 1593 (2005), 5 June 2009

Second Darfur Report:

Second Report of the Prosecutor of the International Criminal Court to the Security Council pursuant to UNSC 1593 (2005), 13 December 2005

Summary Prosecutor's Application Haskanita:

Summary of the Prosecutor's Application under Article 58, ICC-02/05-162, Office of the Prosecutor, 20 November 2008

Summary Prosecutor's Application Hussein:

Summary of Prosecutor's Application under Article 58 of the Rome Statute, ICC-02/05-238, Office of the Prosecutor, 2 December 2011

Tenth Darfur Report:

> Tenth Report of the Prosecutor of the International Criminal Court to the UN Security Council pursuant to UNSCR 1593 (2005), December 2009

Third Darfur Report:

> Third Report of the Prosecutor of the International Criminal Court to the UN Security Council pursuant to UNSCR 1593 (2005), 14 June 2006

Twelfth Darfur Report:

> Twelfth Report of the Prosecutor of the International Criminal Court to the UN Security Council Pursuant to UNSCR 1593 (2005), December 2010

Prosecutor v. Abdallah Banda Abakaer Nourain and Saleh Mohammed Jerbo Jamus
Confirmation of Charges Banda and Jerbo:

> Corrigendum of the 'Decision on the Confirmation of Charges', ICC-02/05-03/09-121-Corr-Red, Pre-Trial Chamber I, 7 March 2011

Decision Summonses Banda and Jerbo:

> Second Decision on the Prosecutor's Application under Article 58, ICC-02/05-03/09, Pre-Trial Chamber I, 27 August 2009

Joint Submission Confirmation Banda and Jerbo:

> Joint Submission by the Office of the Prosecutor and the Defence as to Agreed Facts and Submissions regarding Modalities for the Conduct of the Confirmation Hearing, ICC-02/05-03/09-80, 19 October 2010

Joint Submission Trial Banda and Jerbo:

> Joint Submission by the Office of the Prosecutor and the Defence Regarding the Contested Issues at the Trial of the Accused Persons, ICC-02/05-03/09-148, 16 May 2011

Prosecutor v. Abdel Raheem Muhammed Hussein
Decision Arrest Warrant Hussein:

> Public Redacted Version of 'Decision on the Prosecutor's Application under Article 58 Relating to Abdel Raheem Muhammad Hussein', ICC-02/05-01/12-1-Red, Pre-Trial Chamber I, 1 March 2012

Prosecutor v. Ahmad Muhammad Harun ('Ahmad Harun') and Ali Muhammad Al Abd-Al-Rahman ('Ali Kushayb')
Arrest Warrant Harun:

> Warrant of Arrest for Ahmad Harun, ICC-02/05-01/07-2, Pre-Trial Chamber I, 27 April 2007

Arrest Warrant Kushayb:

> Warrant of Arrest for Ali Kushayb, ICC-02/05-01/07-3, Pre-Trial Chamber I, 27 April 2007

Decision Arrest Warrants Harun and Kushayb:

> Decision on the Prosecution Application under Article 58(7) of the Statute, ICC-02/05-01/07-1, Pre-Trial Chamber I, 27 April 2007

Decision Non-cooperation Sudan in Harun and Kushayb:

> Decision informing the United Nations Security Council about the lack of cooperation by the Republic of the Sudan, ICC-02/05-01/07-57, Pre-Trial Chamber I, 25 May 2010

Request for a Finding of Non-Cooperation Harun and Kushayb:

> Prosecutor's Request for a Finding on the Non-Cooperation of the Government of the Sudan in the Case of the Prosecutor v. Ahmed Harun and Ali Kushayb Pursuant to Article 87 of the Rome Statute, ICC-02/05-01/07-48-Red, Office of the Prosecutor, 19 April 2010

Prosecutor v. Bahr Idriss Abu Garda (sometimes spelled Bahar Idriss Abu Garda)
Decision Confirmation of Charges Abu Garda:

> Decision on the Confirmation of Charges, ICC-02/05-02/09-243-Red, Pre-Trial Chamber I, 8 February 2010

Decision on Summons for Abu Garda:

> Decision on the Prosecutor's Application under Article 58, ICC-02/05-02/09-1, Pre-Trial Chamber I, 7 May 2009

Leave to Appeal Decision Confirmation Abu Garda:

> Decision on the 'Prosecution's Application for Leave to Appeal the "Decision on the Confirmation of Charges"', ICC-02/05-02/09, Pre-Trial Chamber I, 23 April 2010

Prosecutor v. Omar Hassan Ahmad Al Bashir ('Omar Al Bashir')
Decision Arrest Warrant Bashir (PTC):

> Decision on the Prosecution's Application for a Warrant of Arrest against Omar Hassan Ahmad Al Bashir, ICC-02/05-01/09-3, Pre-Trial Chamber I, 4 March 2009

Judgment Arrest Warrant Bashir (AC):

> Judgment on the appeal of the Prosecutor against the 'Decision on the Prosecution's Application for a Warrant of Arrest against Omar Hassan Ahmad Al Bashir', ICC-02/05-01/09-73, Appeals Chamber, 3 February 2010

Second Decision Arrest Warrant Bashir (PTC):

> Second Decision on the Prosecution's Application for a Warrant of Arrest, ICC-02/05-01/09-94, Pre-Trial Chamber I, 12 July 2010

Situation in the Democratic Republic of the Congo
Amicus Curiae Decision DRC (PTC):

> Decision on the Request Submitted pursuant to Rule 103(1) of the Rules of Procedure and Evidence, ICC-01/04-373, Pre-Trial Chamber I, 17 August 2007

Amicus Curiae Request Women's Initiatives for Gender Justice DRC:

> Request submitted pursuant to Rule 103(1) of the Rules of Procedure and Evidence for Leave to Participate as Amicus Curiae with Confidential Annex 2, ICC-01/04-313, Women's Initiatives for Gender Justice, 10 November 2006

Decision VPRS 1–6 DRC:

> Decision on the Applications for Participation in the Proceedings of VPRS 1, VPRS 2, VPRS 3, VPRS 4, VPRS 5 and VPRS 6, ICC-01/04-101, Pre-Trial Chamber I, 17 January 2006

Dissenting Opinion Judge Pikis Arrest Warrant Ntaganda (AC):

> Judgment on the Prosecutor's Appeal against the Decision of Pre-Trial Chamber I Entitled 'Decision on the Prosecutor's Application for Warrants of Arrest, Article 58', of 13 July 2006, made public in ICC-01/04-169, Appeals Chamber, Dissenting Opinion Judge Pikis, 23 September 2008

Judgment Arrest Warrant Ntaganda (AC):

> Judgment on the Prosecutor's Appeal against the Decision of Pre-Trial Chamber I Entitled 'Decision on the Prosecutor's Application for Warrants of Arrest, Article 58', Appeals Chamber, 13 July 2006, made public in ICC-01/04-169, 23 September 2008

Notification Investigation DRC:

> Fax from the Prosecutor to all States Parties to the Rome Statute of the International Criminal Court, OTP/20040621-Article 18 Notification, Office of the Prosecutor, 21 June 2004

Prosecutor v. Bosco Ntaganda
Decision Arrest Warrant Ntaganda (PTC):

> Decision on the Prosecutor's Application for Warrants of Arrest, Article 58, ICC-01/04-02/06-20-Anx2, Pre-Trial Chamber I, 21 July 2008

Decision Second Arrest Warrant Ntaganda (PTC):

> Decision on the Prosecutor's Application under Article 58, ICC-01/04-02/06-36-Red, Pre-Trial Chamber II, 13 July 2012

Prosecutor v. Callixte Mbarushimana
Decision Arrest Warrant Mbarushimana:

> Decision on the Prosecutor's under Seal Application for a Warrant of Arrest Mbarushimana, ICC-01/04-01/10, Pre-Trial Chamber I, 28 September 2010

Decision on Jurisdiction Challenge Mbarushimana:

> Decision on the 'Defence Challenge to the Jurisdiction of the Court', ICC-01/04-01/10-451, Pre-Trial Chamber I, 26 October 2011

Prosecutor v. Sylvestre Mudacumura
Decision Arrest Warrant Mudacumura:

> Decision on the Prosecutor's Application under Article 58, ICC-01/04-01/12-1-Red, Pre-Trial Chamber II, 13 July 2012

Prosecutor v. Germain Katanga and Mathieu Ngudjolo Chui
Admissibility Challenge Katanga:

> Motion Challenging the Admissibility of the Case by the Defence of Germain Katanga, pursuant to Article 19(2)(a), ICC-01/04-01/07-949, Defence, 11 March 2009

Admissibility Decision Katanga (TC):

Motifs de la décision orale relative à l'exception d'irrecevabilité de l'affaire (article 19 du Statut), ICC-01/04-01/07-1213, Trial Chamber II, 16 June 2009

Admissibility Judgment Katanga (AC):

Judgment on the Appeal of Mr Germain Katanga against the Oral Decision of Trial Chamber II of 12 June 2009 on the Admissibility of the Case, ICC-01/04-01/07-1497, Appeals Chamber, 25 September 2009

Decision Arrest Warrant Chui:

Decision on the Evidence and Information Provided by the Prosecution for the Issuance of a Warrant of Arrest for Mathieu Ngudjolo Chui, ICC-01/04-02/07-3/ICC-01/04-01/07-262, Pre-Trial Chamber I, 6 July 2007

Decision Arrest Warrant Katanga:

Decision on the Evidence and Information provided by the Prosecution for the Issuance of a Warrant of Arrest for Germain Katanga, ICC-01/04-01/07-55, Pre-Trial Chamber I, 5 November 2007 (decision taken on 6 July 2007)

Defence Appeal Admissibility Katanga:

Document in Support of Appeal of the Defence for Germain Katanga against the Decision of the Trial Chamber 'Motifs de la décision orale relative à l'exception d'irrecevabilité de l'affaire', ICC-01/04-01/07-1279, Defence, 8 July 2009

Observations DRC Admissibility Challenge Katanga:

Observations of the Democratic Republic of the Congo on the Challenge to Admissibility made by the Defence for Germain Katanga in the Case of the Prosecutor versus Germain Katanga and Mathieu Ngudjolo (ICC-01/04-01/07), ICC-01/04-01/07-1189-Anx-tENG, Democratic Republic of the Congo, 16 September 2009

OPCV Observations on Katanga Appeal on Admissibility:

Observations by the OPCV on the Document in support of Appeal of the Defence for Germain Katanga against the Decision of the Trial Chamber on the Motion Challenging the Admissibility of the Case, ICC-01/04-01/07-1369, Office of Public Counsel for Victims, 14 August 2009

OTP Response to Admissibility Challenge Katanga:

Public Redacted Version of the 19th March 2009 Prosecution Response to Motion Challenging the Admissibility of the Case by the Defence of

Germain Katanga, pursuant to Article 19(2)(a), ICC-01/04-01/07-1007, Office of the Prosecutor, 30 March 2009

Transcripts Admissibility Challenge Katanga:

Hearing – Open Session, Transcripts Admissibility Challenge, ICC-01/04-01/07-T-65-ENG ET WT, Trial Chamber II, 1 June 2009

Prosecutor v. Thomas Lubanga Dyilo
Confirmation of Charges Lubanga:

Décision sur la confirmation des charges, ICC-01/04-01/06-803, Pre-Trial Chamber I, 29 January 2007

Decision Arrest Warrant Lubanga:

Decision on the Prosecutor's Application for a Warrant of Arrest, Article 58, ICC-01/04-01/06-8, Pre-Trial Chamber I, 10 February 2006

Decision on the Practices of Witness Familiarisation and Witness Proofing:

Decision on the Practices of Witness Familiarisation and Witness Proofing, ICC-01/04-01/06-679, Pre-Trial Chamber I, 8 November 2006

Judgment Lubanga Jurisdiction Challenge:

Judgment on the Appeal of Mr Thomas Lubanga Dyilo against the Decision on the Defence Challenge to the Jurisdiction of the Court pursuant to Article 19(2)(a) of the Statute of 3 October 2006, ICC-01/04-01/06-772, Appeals Chamber, 14 December 2006

Judgment Lubanga (TC):

Judgment pursuant to Article 74 of the Statute, ICC-01/04-01/06-2842, Trial Chamber I, 14 March 2012

Transcripts Lubanga 2 February 2006:

Redacted Version of the Transcripts of the Hearing held on 2 February 2006 and Certain Materials Presented during that Hearing, ICC-01/04-01/06-48, Pre-Trial Chamber I, 22 March 2006

Situation in the Republic of Kenya
Decision Authorizing Kenya Investigation:

Decision pursuant to Article 15 of the Rome Statute on the Authorization of an Investigation into the Situation in the Republic of Kenya, ICC-01/09-19, Pre-Trial Chamber II, 31 March 2010

Decision Authorizing Kenya Investigation, Dissenting Opinion Judge Kaul:

Decision pursuant to Article 15 of the Rome Statute on the Authorization of an Investigation into the Situation in the Republic of Kenya, ICC-01/09-19, Dissenting Opinion Judge Hans-Peter Kaul, 31 March 2010

Decision Cooperation Request Government of Kenya:

Decision on the Request for Assistance Submitted on Behalf of the Government of the Republic of Kenya Pursuant to Article 93(10) of the Statute and Rule 194 of the Rules of Procedure and Evidence, ICC-01/09-63, Pre-Trial Chamber II, 29 June 2011

Prosecution's Response to Art. 93 Request in Kenya Situation:

Prosecution's Response to 'Request for Assistance on Behalf of the Government of the Republic of Kenya Pursuant to Article 93(10), Article 96 and Rule 194', ICC-01/09-80, Office of the Prosecutor, 6 October 2011

Prosecutor v. Francis Kirimi Muthaura, Uhuru Muigai Kenyatta and Mohammed Hussein Ali
Admissibility Challenge Government of Kenya:

Application on Behalf of the Government of the Republic of Kenya Pursuant to Article 19 of the ICC Statute, ICC-01/09-01/11-19, the Applicant, the Government of Kenya, 31 March 2011

Admissibility Decision Muthaura et al. (PTC):

Decision on the Application by the Government of Kenya Challenging the Admissibility of the Case Pursuant to Article 19(2)(b) of the Statute, Pre-Trial Chamber II, ICC-01/09-02/11-96, 30 May 2011

Admissibility Judgment Muthaura et al. (AC):

Judgment on the Appeal of the Republic of Kenya against the Decision of Pre-Trial Chamber II of 30 May 2011 Entitled 'Decision on the Application by the Government of Kenya Challenging the Admissibility of the Case Pursuant to Article 19(2)(b) of the Statute', ICC-01/09-02/11-274, Appeals Chamber, 30 August 2011

Admissibility Judgment Muthaura et al. (Dissenting Opinion Judge Ušacka):

Judgment on the Appeal of the Republic of Kenya against the Decision of Pre-Trial Chamber II of 30 May 2011 Entitled 'Decision on the Application by the Government of Kenya Challenging the Admissibility of the Case Pursuant to Article 19(2)(b) of the Statute', Dissenting Opinion of Judge Anita Ušacka, ICC-01/09-02/11-342, 20 September 2011

Decision Summonses Muthaura et al.:

Decision on the Prosecutor's Application for Summonses to Appear for Francis Kirimi Muthaura, Uhuru Muigai Kenyatta and Mohammed Hussein Ali, ICC-01/09-02/11-01, Pre-Trial Chamber II, 8 March 2011

Government of Kenya Admissibility Reply Muthaura et al.:

Reply on Behalf of the Government of Kenya to the Responses of the Prosecutor, Defence, and OPCV to the Government's Application Pursuant to Article 19 of the Rome Statute, ICC-01/09-02/11-91, 13 May 2011

Prosecutor v. William Samoei Ruto, Henry Kiprono Kosgey and Joshua Arap Sang
Admissibility Challenge Government of Kenya:

Application on Behalf of the Government of the Republic of Kenya Pursuant to Article 19 of the ICC Statute, ICC-01/09-01/11-19, the Applicant, the Government of Kenya, 31 March 2011

Admissibility Decision Ruto et al. (PTC):

Decision on the Application by the Government of Kenya Challenging the Admissibility of the Case Pursuant to Article 19(2)(b) of the Statute, Pre-Trial Chamber II, ICC-01/09-01/11, 30 May 2011

Admissibility Judgment Ruto et al. (AC):

Judgment on the Appeal of the Republic of Kenya against the Decision of Pre-Trial Chamber II of 30 May 2011 entitled 'Decision on the Application by the Government of Kenya Challenging the Admissibility of the Case Pursuant to Article 19(2)(b) of the Statute', ICC-01/09-01/11-307, Appeals Chamber, 30 August 2011

Admissibility Judgment Ruto et al. (Dissenting Opinion Judge Ušacka):

Judgment on the Appeal of the Republic of Kenya against the Decision of Pre-Trial Chamber II of 30 May 2011 Entitled 'Decision on the Application by the Government of Kenya Challenging the Admissibility of the Case Pursuant to Article 19(2)(b) of the Statute', Dissenting Opinion of Judge Anita Ušacka, ICC-01/09-01/11-336, 20 September 2011

Corrigendum Prosecution's Response Art. 93 Request Original Ruto et al.:

Corrigendum to the Prosecution's Response to 'Request for Assistance on Behalf of the Government of the Republic of Kenya Pursuant to Article 93(10) and Rule 194', ICC-01/09-01/11-83-Corr, Office of the Prosecutor, 11 May 2011

Decision Summonses Ruto et al.:

Decision on the Prosecutor's Application for Summons to Appear for William Samoei Ruto, Henry Kiprono Kosgey and Joshua Arap Sang, ICC-01/09-01/11-01, Pre-Trial Chamber II, 8 March 2011

Government of Kenya Admissibility Reply Ruto et al.:

Reply on Behalf of the Government of Kenya to the Responses of the Prosecutor, Defence, and OPCV to the Government's Application Pursuant to Article 19 of the Rome Statute, ICC-01/09-01/11-89, 13 May 2011

OTP Submission Art. 93(10) Request in Ruto et al.:

Corrigendum to the Prosecution's Response to 'Request for Assistance on behalf of the Government of the Republic of Kenya pursuant to Article 93(10) and Rule 194', ICC-01/09-01/11-83-Corr, Office of the Prosecutor, 11 May 2011

Prosecution's Response Art. 93 Request Original Ruto et al.:

Prosecution's Response to 'Request for Assistance on Behalf of the Government of the Republic of Kenya Pursuant to Article 93(10) and Rule 194', ICC-01/09-01/11-83, Office of the Prosecutor, 10 May 2011

Situation in Libya
Prosecutor's Application Arrest Warrants Libya:

Prosecutor's Application Pursuant to Article 58 as to Muammar Mohammed Abu Minyar Gaddafi, Saif Al Islam Gaddafi and Abdullah Al Senussi, Office of the Prosecutor, 16 May 2011

Prosecutor's Libya Statement SC May 2012:

ICC Prosecutor Statement to the United Nations Security Council on the Situation in the Libyan Arab Jamahiriya, Pursuant to UNSCR 1970 (2011), 16 May 2012

Prosecutor v. Saif Al-Islam Gaddafi and Abdullah Al-Senussi
Admissibility Challenge Libyan Government:

Application on Behalf of the Government of Libya Pursuant to Article 19 of the ICC Statute, ICC-01/11-01/11-130-Red, Government of Libya, 1 May 2012

Decision Arrest Warrant Muammar Gaddafi, Saif Gaddafi and Al-Senussi:

Decision on the 'Prosecutor's Application Pursuant to Article 58 as to Muammar Mohammed Abu Minyar Gaddafi, Saif Al-Islam Gaddafi and Abdullah Alsenussi', ICC-01/11, Pre-Trial Chamber I, 27 June 2011

OTP's Libya Trip Report:

Prosecution's Submissions on the Prosecutor's Recent Trip to Libya, ICC-01/11-01/11-31, Office of the Prosecutor, 25 November 2011

Postponement Decision Gaddafi:

Decision on the Postponement of the Execution of the Request for Surrender of Saif Al-Islam Gaddafi Pursuant to Article 95 of the Rome Statute, ICC-01/11-01/11-163, Pre-Trial Chamber I, 1 June 2012

Prosecution Response to Libyan Admissibility Challenge:

Prosecution Response to Application on Behalf of the Government of Libya Pursuant to Article 19 of the ICC Statute, ICC-01/11-01/11-167-Red, Office of the Prosecutor, 5 June 2012

Situation in the Republic of Côte d'Ivoire
Authorisation Investigation Republic of Côte d'Ivoire:

Corrigendum to 'Decision Pursuant to Article 15 of the Rome Statute on the Authorisation of an Investigation into the Situation in the Republic of Côte d'Ivoire', ICC-02/11-14-Corr, Pre-Trial Chamber III, 15 November 2011

Prosecutor v. Laurent Koudou Gbagbo
Decision Arrest Warrant Gbagbo:

Public Redacted Version of 'Decision on the Prosecutor's Application Pursuant to Article 58 for a Warrant of Arrest against Laurent Koudou Gbagbo', ICC-02/11-01/11-9-Red, Pre-Trial Chamber III, 20 December 2011

Situation in Uganda
Arrest Warrant Kony:

Warrant of Arrest for Joseph Kony, ICC-02/04-01/05-53, Pre-Trial Chamber II, 8 July 2005 as amended on 27 September 2005

Arrest Warrant Lukwiya:

> Warrant of Arrest for Raska Lukwiya, ICC-02/04-01/05-55, Pre-Trial Chamber II, 8 July 2005

Arrest Warrant Odhiambo:

> Warrant of Arrest for Okot Odhiambo, ICC-02/04-01/05-56, Pre-Trial Chamber II, 8 July 2005

Arrest Warrant Ongwen:

> Warrant of Arrest for Dominic Ongwen, ICC-02/04-01/05-57, Pre-Trial Chamber II, 8 July 2005

Arrest Warrant Otti:

> Warrant of Arrest for Vincent Otti, ICC-02/04-01/05-54, Pre-Trial Chamber II, 8 July 2005

Decision Arrest Warrants LRA:

> Decision on the Prosecutor's Application for Warrants of Arrest under Article 58, ICC-02/04-01/05-1, Pre-Trial Chamber II, 8 July 2005

Decision Status Conference Uganda:

> Decision to Convene a Status Conference on the Investigation in Uganda in relation to the Application of Article 53, ICC-02/04-01/05-68, Pre-Trial Chamber II, 2 December 2005

Judgment Proprio Motu Admissibility Assessment Uganda (AC):

> Judgment on the Appeal of the Defence against the 'Decision on the Admissibility of the Case under Article 19(1) of the Statute' of 10 March 2009, ICC-02/04-01/05-408, Appeals Chamber, 16 September 2009

Letter from the Chief Prosecutor to the President of the Court Uganda:

> Letter from the Chief Prosecutor to the President of the Court, 17 June 2004, attached to Decision Assigning the Situation in Uganda to Pre-Trial Chamber II, ICC-02/04-1, Presidency, 5 July 2004

Notification Investigation Uganda:

> Fax from the Prosecutor to all States Parties to the Rome Statute of the International Criminal Court, OTP/20040728-Article18 Notification Uganda, Office of the Prosecutor, 28 July 2004

OTP Submission Status Conference Uganda:

> OTP Submission Providing Information on Status of the Investigation in Anticipation of the Status Conference to be held on 13 January 2006, ICC-02/04-01/05-76, Office of the Prosecutor, 11 January 2006

Prosecutor v. Joseph Kony, Vincent Otti, Okot Odhiambo and
Dominic Ongwen
Amicus Curiae Brief Uganda Victims' Foundation and Redress Trust:

Amicus Curiae submitted pursuant to the Pre-Trial Chamber II 'Decision on Application for Leave to Submit Observations under Rule 103' dated 5 November 2008, ICC-02/04-01/05-353, Uganda Victims' Foundation and the Redress Trust, 18 November 2008

Decision Proprio Motu Admissibility Assessment LRA:

Decision Initiating Proceedings under Article 19, requesting Observations and Appointing Counsel for the Defence, ICC-02/04-01/05-320, Pre-Trial Chamber II, 21 October 2008

Decision to Terminate Proceedings against Lukwiya:

Decision to Terminate the Proceedings against Raska Lukwiya, ICC-02/04-01/05-248, Pre-Trial Chamber II, 11 July 2007

LRA Admissibility Decision (PTC):

Decision on the Admissibility of the Case under Article 19(1) of the Statute, ICC-02/04-01/05-377, Pre-Trial Chamber II, 10 March 2009

Observations GoU on Proprio Motu Admissibility Assessment LRA:

Report of the Registrar on the Execution of the Request to the Republic of Uganda for Observations on the Initiation of Proceedings pursuant to Article 19 of the Rome Statute, Annex 2, ICC-02/04-01/05-354-Anx2, Submission by the Government of Uganda, 18 November 2008

Observations on behalf of Victims Kony et al.:

Observations on Behalf of Victims pursuant to Article 19(1) of the Rome Statute with 55 Public Annexes and 45 Redacted Annexes, ICC-02/04-01/05-349, Office of Public Counsel for Victims, 18 November 2008

OTP Submission Information Status LRA Arrest Warrants:

Submission of Information on the Status of the Warrants of Arrest in Uganda, ICC-02/04-01/05-116, Office of the Prosecutor, 6 October 2006

Questionnaire Ugandan Victims on Admissibility:

Questionnaire Ugandan Victims on Admissibility, ICC-02/04-01/05-349-Anx1, Office of Public Counsel for Victims, 18 November 2008

Request Information Execution Arrest Warrants Kony et al:

Request for Information from the Republic of Uganda on the Status of Execution of the Warrants of Arrest, ICC-02/04-01/05-274, Pre-Trial Chamber II, 29 February 2008

Submission Information Lukwiya:

Submission of Information regarding Raska Lukwiya, ICC-02/04-01/ 05-97, Office of the Prosecutor, 14 August 2006

Submission Information Otti:

Submission of Information regarding Vincent Otti, ICC-02/04-01/05- 258, Office of the Prosecutor, 8 November 2007

Uganda Letter on Execution Arrest Warrants:

Letter from Jane F. B. Kiggundu, Solicitor General, Reply to Request for Information from the Republic of Uganda on the Status of Execution of the Warrants of Arrest, ICC-02/04-01/05-285-Anx2, Government of Uganda, 27 March 2008

International Criminal Tribunal for the former Yugoslavia
Ademi and Norac Referral Decision:

Prosecutor v. Rahim Ademi and Mirko Norac, Decision for Referral to the Authorities of the Republic of Croatia pursuant to Rule 11bis, IT- 04-78-PT, Referral Bench, 14 September 2005

Furundžija Judgment:

Prosecutor v. Anto Furundžija, Judgment, IT-95-17/1-T, ICTY, Trial Chamber, 10 December 1998

Hadžihasanović Judgment:

Prosecutor v. Enver Hadžihasanović Amir Kubura, Judgment, IT-01- 47-T, Trial Chamber, 15 March 2006

Stanković Referral Decision (AC):

Prosecutor v. Radovan Stanković, Decision on Rule 11bis Referral, IT- 96-23/2-AR11bis.1, Appeals Chamber, 1 September 2005

Tadić Defence Motion Decision (AC):

Prosecutor v. Duško Tadić, Decision on the Defence Motion for Interlocutory Appeal, IT-94-1-AR72, Appeals Chamber, 2 October 1995

Tadić Judgment:

Prosecutor v. Duško Tadić, Judgment, IT-94-1-A, Appeals Chamber, 15 July 1999

International Criminal Tribunal for Rwanda

Bagaragaza Referral Decision (AC):

> Prosecutor v. Michel Bagaragaza, Decision on Rule 11bis Appeal, ICTR-05-86-AR11bis, Appeals Chamber, 30 August 2006

Bucyibaruta Referral Decision:

> Prosecutor v. Laurent Bucyibaruta, Decision on Prosecutor's Request for Referral of Laurent Bucyibaruta's Indictment to France, ICTR-2005-85-I, Trial Chamber, 20 November 2007

Ntuyahaga Referral Decision:

> Prosecutor v. Bernard Ntuyahaga, Decision on the Prosecutor's Motion to Withdraw the Indictment, ICTR-98-40-T, Trial Chamber I, 18 March 1999

Permanent Court of International Justice and International Court of Justice

Anglo-Iranian Oil Co.:

> Anglo-Iranian Oil Co. (United Kingdom v. Iran), Preliminary Objection, Judgment, ICJ Reports 1952, 93

Application of the Convention on Genocide:

> Application of the Convention on the Prevention and Punishment of the Crime of Genocide (Bosnia and Herzegovina v. Yugoslavia), Preliminary Objections, Judgment, ICJ Reports 1996, 595

Armed Activities (DRC v. Uganda):

> Armed Activities on the Territory of the Congo (Democratic Republic of the Congo v. Uganda), Judgment, ICJ Reports 2005, 168

Armed Activities (DRC v. Rwanda):

> Armed Activities on the Territory of the Congo (New Application: 2002) (Democratic Republic of the Congo v. Rwanda), Jurisdiction and Admissibility, Judgment, ICJ Reports 2006, 6

Asylum Case:

> Asylum Case (Colombia/Peru), Judgment, ICJ Reports 1950, 266

Kosovo:

Accordance with International Law of the Unilateral Declaration of Independence in respect of Kosovo, Advisory Opinion, ICJ Reports 2010, 403

Reparation for Injuries:

Reparation for Injuries Suffered in the Service of the United Nations, Advisory Opinion, ICJ Reports 1949, 174

Reservations to the Convention on Genocide:

Reservations to the Convention on Genocide, Advisory Opinion, ICJ Reports 1951, 15

Rights of Nationals:

Rights of Nationals of the United States of America in Morocco, Judgment, ICJ Reports 1952, 176

Serbian Loans:

Payment of Various Serbian Loans Issued in France, PCIJ Series A. Nos. 20/21, 1929, 5

South West Africa:

Legal Consequences for States of the Continued Presence of South Africa in Namibia (South West Africa) notwithstanding Security Council Resolution 276 (1970), Advisory Opinion, ICJ Reports 1971, 16

Sovereignty over Pulau Ligitan and Pulau Sipadan:

Sovereignty over Pulau Ligitan and Pulau Sipadan (Indonesia/Malaysia), Judgment, ICJ Reports 2002, 625

Permanent Court of Arbitration
Eritrea–Ethiopia Boundary Delimitation:

Delimitation of the Border between the State of Eritrea and the Federal Democratic Republic of Ethiopia, Decision of the Eritrea–Ethiopia Boundary Commission, 130 ILR 1

Special Court for Sierra Leone
Prosecutor v. Morris Kallon and Brima Bazzy Kamara:

Decision on Challenge to Jurisdiction: Lomé Accord Amnesty, *Kallon and Kamara*, SCSL-2004-15/16-AR72(E), Appeals Chamber, 13 March 2004

Sudanese courts

Abdel Rahman Nugdallah:

Abdel Rahman Nugdallah and Others v. General Security Bureau of the Government of Sudan, High Court of Sudan, Constitutional Division, July–August 1998, unofficial translation

Farouq Mohamed Ibrahim Al Nour v. (1) Government of Sudan; (2) Legislative Body:

Farouq Mohamed Ibrahim Al Nour v. (1) Government of Sudan; (2) Legislative Body; Final order by Justice Abdallah Aalmin Albashir President of the Constitutional Court, 6 November 2008

Adam Abras Adam:

Sudan v. Adam Abras Adam, Special Criminal Court for the Events in Darfur, Nyala, 3 May 2006, unofficial translation

Syrian Arab Airways Corporation v. Khadeeja Mohammed El Shaekh:

Syrian Arab Airways Corporation (Applicant) v. Khadeeja Mohammed El Shaekh (Respondent), National Supreme Court Sudan, Civil Circuit, No. SC/Civil Cass./1208/2006

Ugandan courts

Abdalla Nasur:

Abdalla Nasur (Appellant) and Uganda (Respondent), Supreme Court, Criminal Appeal No. 1/82

Albertina Opio:

Albertina Opio and Others v. Attorney-General, High Court Gulu, Civil Suit No. HCT-02-CV-CS-0098 2004, file read in the Office of the State Attorney in Gulu, 17 September 2008

Celestina Odong Adyera:

Celestina Odong Adyera and Others v. Attorney-General, High Court Gulu, Civil Suit No. 0038 of 2006, file read in the Office of the State Attorney in Gulu, 17 September 2008

Charge Sheet Otti Lagony, Kony Joseph and Matsanga David (Terrorism):

Uganda v. Otti Lagony, Kony Joseph and Matsanga David Nyekorach, Uganda Police, Charge Sheet (Terrorism), E/31/99, 25 January 1999

Chris Rwakasisi:

Chris Rwakasisi and Elias Wanyama (Appellants) and Uganda (Respondent), Supreme Court, Criminal Appeal No. 8/88

Haji Musa Sebirumbi:

Haji Musa Sebirumbi (Appellant) and Uganda (Respondent), Supreme Court, Criminal Appeal No. 10 of 1989

John Magezi, Judy Obitre-Gama, Henry Onoria v. Attorney-General:

John Magezi, Judy Obitre-Gama, Henry Onoria v. Attorney-General, Constitutional Court, Constitutional Petition No. 10, 27 July 2005

Onynango-Obbo and Mwenda:

Onynango-Obbo and Mwenda v. Attorney-General, Supreme Court, Constitutional appeal, No. 2 of 2002, International Law in Domestic Courts 166 (UG 2004)

Otti Lagony, Kony Joseph and Matsanga David Nyekorach DPP Withdrawal Form:

Uganda v. Otti Lagony, Kony Joseph and Matsanga David Nyekorach, Director of Public Prosecutions, Withdrawal Form addressed to the Chief Magistrate in Buganda Road Court, 13 September 2001

Professor Isaac Newton Ojok:

Professor Isaac Newton Ojok (Appellant) and Uganda (Respondent), Supreme Court, Criminal Appeal No. 33/91

Susan Kigula:

Attorney-General v. Susan Kigula and 417 others, Supreme Court, Constitutional Appeal No. 3 of 2006, 21 January 2009

Warrants of Arrest for Otti Lagony, Kony Joseph and Matsanga David Nyekorach:

Warrants of Arrest for Otti Lagony, Kony Joseph and Matsanga David Nyekorach, Chief Magistrates Court of Buganda Road Court at Kampala, Warrants of Arrest for Criminal Offence No. 0221 of 1999, 4 February 1999

Kwoyelo Case
Charge Sheet Kwoyelo September 2010:

Uganda v. Kwoyelo Thomas alias Latoni, 6 September 2010

Kwoyelo (Constitutional Court Ruling):

Constitutional Petition No. 036/11 (Reference), arising out of HCT-00-ICD-Case No. 02/10, 22 September 2011

Kwoyelo Thomas v. Uganda (Notice of Appeal):

Kwoyelo Thomas (Applicant/Petitioner) v. Uganda (Respondent), Constitutional Reference No. 36 of 2011, Notice of Appeal, 23 September 2011

Thomas Kwoyelo v. Attorney General (Order of Mandamus):

Thomas Kwoyelo alias Latoni (Applicant) v. Attorney General (Respondent), High Court (Civil Division) HCT-00-CV-MC-0162-2011, Order by Judge Vincent T. Zehurikize, 25 January 2012

Uganda v. Kwoyelo Thomas (ICD Order):

Uganda (Prosecutor) v. Kwoyelo Thomas alias Latoni (Accused), HCT-00-ICD Case No. 0002 of 2010, Order, 11 November 2011

Uganda v. Kwoyelo Thomas (Indictment 2010):

Uganda (Prosecutor) v. Kwoyelo Thomas (Accused), Indictment, 21 August 2010

Uganda v. Kwoyelo Thomas (Indictment 2011):

Uganda (Prosecutor) v. Kwoyelo Thomas alias Latoni (Accused), Amended Indictment, 5 July 2011

Uganda v. Thomas Kwoyelo (Affidavit in Support of Application):

Uganda (Applicant) v. Thomas Kwoyelo alias Latoni (Respondent), Constitutional Application No. 50 of 2011, Affidavit in Support of Application, 31 October 2011

Uganda v. Thomas Kwoyelo (Attorney-General's Legal Arguments):

Uganda (Applicant) v. Thomas Kwoyelo alias Latoni (Respondent), Constitutional Reference No. 36 of 2011, Attorney General's Legal Arguments, 16 August 2011

Uganda v. Thomas Kwoyelo (Constitutional Directions Proceedings):

Uganda (Applicant) v. Thomas Kwoyelo alias Latoni (Respondent), Constitutional Reference No. 36/2011, Constitutional Directions Proceedings, 12 August 2011

Uganda v. Thomas Kwoyelo (Proceedings):

Uganda (Prosecutor) v. Kwoyelo Thomas alias Latoni (Accused), High Court Proceedings, 11 and 25 July 2011

Uganda v. Thomas Kwoyelo (Proceedings Kasule):

Uganda (Prosecutor) v. Thomas Kwoyelo alias Latoni (Respondent), Constitutional Petition No. 36/2011, Proceedings of Remmy Kasule, 16 August 2011

Uganda v. Thomas Kwoyelo (Reference to the Constitutional Court):

Uganda (Prosecutor) v. Thomas Kwoyelo alias Latoni (Accused), Constitutional Reference No. 36 of 2011, Reference to the Constitutional Court, 25 July 2011

Other national courts
AZAPO:

Azanian People's Organisation (AZAPO) and Others v. President of the Republic of South Africa, South African Constitutional Court, 27 July 1996

Gaddafi:

Gaddafi, France, Chambre d'accusation, Cour d'appel de Paris, 20 October 2000, 125 ILR 490

Ministry of Defence v. Ergialli:

Ministry of Defence v. Ergialli, Court of Venice, 5 February 1958, 26 ILR 732

Polyukhovich v. Commonwealth:

Polyukhovich v. Commonwealth, High Court of Australia, (1991) 172 CLR 501

LEGAL INSTRUMENTS

Treaties and other international legal instruments

1945   Charter of the United Nations, San Francisco, 6 June 1945 (UN Charter)

1948   Convention on the Prevention and Punishment of the Crime of Genocide, Paris, 9 December 1948, 78 UNTS 277 (Genocide Convention)

1949   Convention for the Amelioration of the Condition of the Wounded and Sick in Armed Forces in the Field, Geneva, 12 August 1949, 75 UNTS 31 (Geneva Convention (I))

Convention for the Amelioration of the Condition of Wounded, Sick and Shipwrecked Members of Armed Forces at Sea, Geneva, 12 August 1949, 75 UNTS 85 (Geneva Convention (II))

Convention Relative to the Treatment of Prisoners of War, Geneva, 12 August 1949, 75 UNTS 135 (Geneva Convention (III))

Convention Relative to the Protection of Civilian Persons in Time of War, Geneva, 12 August 1949, 75 UNTS 287 (Geneva Convention (IV))

1954   Convention for the Protection of Cultural Property in the Event of Armed Conflict with Regulations for the Execution of the Convention, The Hague, 14 May 1954, 249 UNTS 240 (Cultural Property Convention)

1966   International Covenant on Civil and Political Rights, New York, 16 December 1966, 999 UNTS 171 (ICCPR)

1969   Vienna Convention on the Law of Treaties, Vienna, 23 May 1969 1155 UNTS 331 (VCLT)

1973   International Convention on the Suppression and Punishment of the Crime of Apartheid, New York, 30 November 1973, 1015 UNTS 243 (Apartheid Convention)

1977   Protocol Additional to the Geneva Conventions of 12 August 1949, and Relating to the Protection of Victims of International Armed Conflicts, Geneva, 8 June 1977, 1125 UNTS 3 (Additional Protocol I)

Protocol Additional to the Geneva Conventions of 12 August 1949, and relating to the Protection of Victims of Non-International Armed Conflicts, Geneva, 8 June 1977, 1125 UNTS 609 (Additional Protocol II)

1984   Convention against Torture and Other Cruel, Inhuman or Degrading Treatment or Punishment, New York, 10 December 1984, 1465 UNTS 85 (Torture Convention)

1992   Convention on the Prohibition of the Development, Production, Stockpiling and Use of Chemical Weapons and on their Destruction, Geneva, 3 September 1992, 1974 UNTS 45 (Chemical Weapons Convention)

1993   Statute of the International Criminal Tribunal for the former Yugoslavia, UN Doc. S/25704 (1993), Annex, as amended (ICTY Statute)

1994   ICTY Rules of Procedure and Evidence, adopted on 11 February 1994, last updated 24 July 2009 (IT/32/Rev.43) (ICTY RPE)

Statute of the International Criminal Tribunal for Rwanda, UN Doc. S/RES/955 (1994), Annex, as amended (ICTR Statute)

Convention on the Safety of United Nations and Associated Personnel, New York, 9 December 1994, 2051 UNTS 363

1996   Protocol on Prohibitions or Restrictions on the Use of Mines, Booby-Traps and Other Devices as Amended on 3 May 1996 (Protocol II as amended on 3 May 1996) annexed to the Convention on Prohibitions or Restrictions on the Use of Certain Conventional Weapons which may be Deemed to be Excessively Injurious or to have Indiscriminate Effects, Geneva, 3 May 1996, 2048 UNTS 93 (Protocol II)

ICTR Rules of Procedure and Evidence, adopted on 29 June 1996, last updated 1 October 2009

1997   Convention on the Prohibition of the Use, Stockpiling, Production and Transfer of Anti-Personnel Mines and on their Destruction, Oslo, 18 September 1997, 2056 UNTS 211 (Anti-Personnel Mines Convention)

1998   Rome Statute of the International Criminal Court, Rome, 17 July 1998, 2187 UNTS 90 (RS)

Rome Statute of the International Criminal Court, Rome, 17 July 1998, 2187 UNTS 159 (RS French)

1999   Second Protocol to the Hague Convention of 1954 for the Protection of Cultural Property in the Event of Armed Conflict, The Hague, 26 March 1999, 2253 UNTS 172

2000   Constitutive Act of the African Union, Lomé, 11 July 2000, 2158 UNTS 3

2001   Articles on Responsibility of States for Internationally Wrongful Acts

2002   Statute of the Special Court for Sierra Leone, 16 January 2002 (SCSL Statute)

Rules of Procedure and Evidence, ICC-ASP/1/3, 9 September 2002 (RPE)

2003   Draft Regulations of the Office of the Prosecutor, 3 June 2003

2005   Agreement Amending the Partnership Agreement between the Members of the African, Caribbean and Pacific Group of States, of the One Part, and the European Community and its Member States, of the Other Part, Cotonou, 23 June 2000, *Official Journal of the European Union*, L 209/27

2006 Protocol for the Prevention and the Punishment of the Crime of Genocide, War Crimes and Crimes against Humanity and All Forms of Discrimination, Protocol to the Pact on Security, Stability and Development in the Great Lakes Region, 29 November 2006 (Great Lakes Pact Protocol for the Prevention and the Punishment of the Crime of Genocide, War Crimes and Crimes against Humanity and All Forms of Discrimination)

International Convention for the Protection of All Persons from Enforced Disappearance, New York, 20 December 2006, UN Doc. A/61/488 (Enforced Disappearance Convention)

2007 Statute of the Special Tribunal for Lebanon, attached to UN Doc. S/RES/1757

Colombia

2005 Definitive Conciliated Text of Law Bill Number 211 of 2005 Senate and 293 of 2005 House of Representatives (also known as the Peace and Justice Act)

Sudan

1954 Commissions of Inquiry Act

1966 Indemnity Act

1972 Addis Ababa Agreement

1977 Indemnity Act

1986 Judiciary Act

People's Armed Forces Act

1991 Criminal Act

Criminal Procedure Act

1995 Judiciary Headquarters, Criminal Decree No. 3/95, Trial of Accused Who Are Subject to Peoples Armed Forces Act

1997 Emergency and Public Safety Protection Act

1998 Constitution of the Sudan

1999 National Security Forces Act

Police Forces Act

2003 Ceasefire Agreement between the Government of Sudan and the SLA, Abéché, 3 September 2003

2004   Agreement on Humanitarian Ceasefire on the Conflict in Darfur and Protocol on the Establishment of Humanitarian Assistance in Darfur, N'Djamena, 8 April 2004

Presidential Decision No. 97 Establishing a Commission to Investigate Alleged Human Rights Violations Committed by Armed Groups in the Darfur States, 8 May 2004

2005   Comprehensive Peace Agreement between the Government of the Republic of the Sudan and the Sudan People's Liberation Movement/ Sudan People's Liberation Army, 9 January 2005 (CPA)

Minister of Justice, Decision No. 3/2005, 19 January 2005

National Judicial Service Commission Act

Sudan Armed Forces Act (Amendment)

Interim National Constitution (INC)

Chief Justice, Decree Establishing the Special Criminal Court on the Events in Darfur, 7 June 2005 (SCCED Decree)

Chief Justice, Resolution No. 702, 11 June 2005

Minister of Justice, Decision No. 9/2005 establishing a Committee of Prosecution for Special Criminal Cases in Darfur, 13 June 2005 (stamped), 12 July 2005 (signed)

Declaration of Principles for the Resolution of the Sudanese Conflict in Darfur, agreed upon by the Government of the Sudan, the Sudanese Liberation Movement/Army (SLM/A) and the Justice and Equality Movement, Abuja, 5 July 2005

Chief Justice, Resolution No. 981, 17 September 2005

Minister of Justice, Decree on the Establishment of a Specialized Prosecution for Crimes against Humanity, 2005, 18 September 2005

Chief Justice, Amendment of the Order of Establishment of Criminal Court for Darfur's Incidents, 10 November 2005

Chief Justice, Order of the Establishment of Criminal Court for Darfur's Incident, 16 November 2005 (Geneina)

Chief Justice, Resolution No. 1128, 20 November 2005

Chief Justice, Resolution No. 1129, 20 November 2005

2006   Darfur Peace Agreement, Abuja, 5 May 2006 (DPA)

Decree No. 114, 11/12 June 2006

Eastern Sudan Peace Agreement between the Government of Sudan and the Eastern Sudan Front, Asmara, 14 October 2006

2007 Draft Sudanese Armed Forces Act

Armed Forces Act

2008 National Police Forces Act

Decision No. 1 of the Emergency Session of the National Assembly: Rejection of the Accusations of the Prosecutor of the ICC against Leading Officials of the State Headed by the President of the Republic, 16 July 2008, unofficial translation

Decision No. 2 of the Emergency Session of the National Assembly to Refuse to Ratify the Rome Statute of the International Criminal Court, 16 July 2008, unofficial translation

Decision of the Minister of Justice, Appointment of Special Prosecutor for Crimes of Darfur, 3 August 2008, unofficial translation

Explanatory note to the Criminal Act Bill (Amendment)

2009 Agreement of Good Will and Confidence Building for the Settlement of the Problem of Darfur, Sudanese Government of National Unity and the Justice and Equality Movement, Doha, 17 February 2009

Criminal Procedures Act (Amendment)

Criminal Bill (Amendment)

2010 Framework Agreement to Resolve the Conflict in Darfur between the Government of Sudan (GoS) and the Justice and Equality Movement (JEM), Doha, 23 February 2010

Framework Agreement to Resolve the Conflict in Darfur between the Government of Sudan (GoS) and the Liberation and Justice Movement (LJM), Doha, 18 March 2010

National Security Act

2011 Doha Document for Peace in Darfur, as adopted by the Agreement between the Government of the Sudan and the Liberation and Justice Movement for the Adoption of the Doha Document for Peace in Darfur, Doha, 14 July 2011

Uganda

1950 Penal Code Act, *Laws of Uganda*, Chapter 120

1964 Geneva Conventions Act, *Laws of Uganda*, Chapter 363

1972 Decree No. 8, 8 May 1972

1987 Amnesty Statute, Statute 6

1994 Agreement between the Uganda Government and the Lord's Resistance Army (the Gulu Ceasefire), Gulu, 2 February 1994

1995   Constitution of the Republic of Uganda, as amended

1998   Amnesty Bill, XCL(58) *Uganda Gazette*, 22 September 1998

Ratification of Treaties Act, *Laws of Uganda*, Chapter 204

1999   People's Armed Forces Act, Amendment

2000   Amnesty Act, *Laws of Uganda*, Chapter 294 (Amnesty Act)

2002   Amnesty (Amendment) Act, 19 June 2002

2003   Amnesty (Amendment) Bill, XCVI(65) *Uganda Gazette*, 24 December 2003

2004   International Criminal Court Bill, XCVII(26) *Uganda Gazette*, 28 May 2004 (ICC Bill 2004)

2005   Uganda Peoples' Defence Forces Act, XCVIII(56) *Uganda Gazette*, 2 September 2005

2006   Amnesty (Amendment) Act

Agreement on Cessation of Hostilities between the Government of the Republic of Uganda and Lord's Resistance Army/Movement, Juba, Sudan, 26 August 2006

International Criminal Court Bill, XCVIX(67) *Uganda Gazette*, 17 November 2006 (ICC Bill 2006)

2007   Agreement on Accountability and Reconciliation between the Government of the Republic of Uganda and the Lord's Resistance Army/Movement, Juba, 29 June 2007 (A&R Agreement)

2008   Annexure to the Agreement on Accountability and Reconciliation, Juba, 19 February 2008 (Annexure)

Agreement on Implementation and Monitoring Mechanisms, Juba, 29 February 2008

Administrative Circular No. 1 of 2008, High Court Divisions and Circuits and Staff Deployment, 22 May 2008 (Administrative Circular No. 1 of 2008)

Amnesty (Extension of Expiry Period) Instrument 24 May 2008, Statutory Instruments Supplements No. 14, *Uganda Gazette*, 24 June 2008

2010   Amnesty Act (Extension of Expiry Period) Instrument 2010, Statutory Instruments Supplements No. 16, *Uganda Gazette*, 21 May 2010

International Criminal Court Act, 2010, *Uganda Gazette* No. 39, Vol. 103, 25 June 2010

2011   The High Court (International Crimes Division) Practice Directions, Legal Notice No. 10 of 2011, Legal Notices Supplement to the Uganda Gazette No. 38 Volume CIV, 31 May, 2011

2012   Amnesty Act (Declaration of Lapse of the Operation of Part II) Instrument, 2012, Statutory Instruments 2012 No. 34, Statutory Instruments Supplement No. 15, *Uganda Gazette*, 23 May 2012

Amnesty Act (Extension of Expiry Period) (No. 2) Instrument, 2012, Statutory Instruments 2012 No. 35, Statutory Instruments Supplement No. 15, *Uganda Gazette*, 23 May 2012

Prevention and Prohibition of Torture Act, 2012, *Uganda Gazette* No. 52, Vol. 105, 18 September 2012

2013   Amnesty Act (Extension of Expiry Period) Instrument 2013, Statutory Instruments Supplement No. 11, *Uganda Gazette* 24 May 2013

Amnesty Act (Revocation of Statutory Instrument No. 34 of 2012) Instrument 2013, Statutory Instruments No. 11, *Uganda Gazette*, 24 May 2013

INDEX

Abboud, Ibrahim
  pardon for human rights violations, 266
Abuja (Nigeria)
  Darfur Peace Agreement (DPA), 265, 291–3
accountability mechanisms
  catalysing effect of complementarity,
      179–87, 279–84
Accountability and Reconciliation Accords
    (A&R Accords) (Uganda), 133–6,
    139–40, 150–3, 160–1, 176, 179–80,
    201, 212–13, 223
Acholi, 125–7, 136, 143–59, 161, 206, 370,
    411
admissibility
  challenges 11, 22, 41, 49, 57, 80–1, 101–2,
      107, 122, 133, 261
  complementarity as rule of, 11, 14–15, 20,
      101, 334, 339, 409
    see also complementarity
  decisions not to prosecute, 61–2
  discretion of *proprio motu* admissibility
      assessment, 81–2
  gravity as rule of see gravity
  'investigation', requirement for, 59–61
African Union (AU)
  Darfur Peace Agreement, 265, 291–3
  High-Level Panel on Darfur (AUPD), 276–8,
      294, 297–8, 304, 315, 333, 343
  UNAMID, 265, 275, 278, 315
ajaweed
  and Darfur situation, 299–300, 302–6
al-Bashir, Omar
  admissibility assessment, 261
  arrest warrant, 23, 244, 251, 269–73, 276–9
  break with Hassan al-Turabi, 264
  opposition to ICC proceedings, 249–50
al-Turabi, Hassan
  break with Omar al-Bashir, 264
  on ICC, 273
amnesties
  catalysing effect of complementarity,
      206–27, 316–20
  prohibition?, 18–19, 41–3, 104
  in Sudan, 266–7, 295, 297, 316–20
  in Uganda, 128–9, 133, 142, 149, 159, 166,
      169, 177, 206–27, 232, 388–9, 411–12

Amnesty Act 2000 (Uganda), 128, 172–3,
    180, 206–27
Armed Forces Act 1986 (Sudan)
  amendment, 284–6, 289, 317
arrest warrants
  and admissibility assessments, 82
  admissibility challenge after issue, 80–1
  domestic proceedings initiated after issue of
      ICC warrants, 79
article 16, Rome Statute see deferral
article 17, Rome Statute see complementarity
article 21(3), Rome Statute
  human rights, 68–9
article 93(10), Rome Statute
  cooperation, 99–102, 379
  positive complementarity, 98–103, 109

Bigombe, Betty
  peace initiatives in northern Uganda,
      128–9, 138, 196
'bilateral immunity agreement'
  Uganda/USA, 119, 194

'case'
  case-by-case basis of assessment, 72–5,
      90–1, 106, 157, 292–3, 339
  'same case' requirement, 45–59, 61, 70, 106,
      121, 261, 298, 334, 351, 408–9
catalysing effect of complementarity
  assumptions as to, 24–6, 337, 397
  catalysing effect paradox, 14, 396, 400–3,
      408
  constructivist perspective, 25
  'cosmetic' reforms, 12, 336, 406
  cost–benefit analysis, 12, 23, 25–6, 177,
      235–6, 243, 273, 329–30, 337,
      367–98, 406
  cost of ICC intervention, 12, 26, 114, 234–5,
      273, 330, 367–9, 386–9, 398, 406–7
  domestic proceedings increased?, 12,
      228–33, 320–8, 337, 407
  dramatis personae, 21–4
  effect in Uganda and Sudan summarised,
      10–14, 233–43, 328–36, 337,
      406–10
  expectations as to, 8–10, 24–6

factors influencing, 86–104
normative assumptions, 25–6, 40, 104,
    234–7, 331, 337–8, 397–8, 407–8
paradoxes
    analysis of, 13–14, 396–405, 408
    catalysing effect paradox, 14, 396, 400–3,
        408
    normative paradox of complementarity,
        13, 345–51, 397–8, 408
    paradox of positive complementarity,
        395–6
potential for, 104–10
rational-choice perspective, 25–6
weakness, reasons for
    ambiguity of big idea, 338, 344–61, 397–8
    assumptions as to states' cost–benefit
        analysis, 367–96, 398–9
    generally, 337, 396–405
    ICC policy weaknesses, 399–405
    inhospitable domestic environment,
        338–9, 361–7, 398
    misrepresentation of principle and
        content, 338–44, 397
    no obligation on states to conduct
        proceedings, 338, 397
    see also domestic justice systems; Sudan;
        Uganda
Central African Republic, 31, 119, 173, 344,
    346, 400
Chad
    Chad–Sudan relations, 262, 264–5, 311–12
    Darfur mediation and peace talks, 264–5
China
    and Darfur, 248–9
'comparative gravity-test'
    alternative to same-conduct test, 59
complementarity
    actors involved, 21–4, 235–8, 329–35, 406
    admissibility see admissibility
    arguments for, 15–16, 56–8, 82, 108, 409
    assessment
        case-specificity, 72–5, 90–1, 106, 157,
            292–3, 339
        dynamic nature of, 79–83, 105, 339–40
        independence from trigger mechanism,
            75–6
    as 'big idea', 11, 13, 15–21, 110, 162, 226,
        338, 344–61, 378, 397, 399
    challenges to admissibility on grounds of
        see admissibility
    'complementarity obligations', 17–21
    as concept, 11, 14–21
    definition, popular shorthand description,
        17, 34, 43–5, 120–1
    'division of labour' concept, 11–12, 341–4,
        350, 360, 381–2, 397, 399–401, 407
    dramatis personae, 21–4

double life of, 11, 14–21, 104, 108–10
    as duty or obligation to prosecute see states
    and fair trial rights, 67–70, 104
    under fire, 410
    as 'foundational principle' of Rome
        Statute, 17
    and 'Global Criminal Justice System',
        19–20
    and human rights see human rights
    inadmissibility see admissibility
    institutions involved, 21–4, 406
    and 'international standards'
        see international standards
    literal concept of, ICC's use of, 11–12,
        340–2, 407, 409
    modified approach to, 410
    normative character of, 338–67
    normative paradox of, 13, 345–51, 397–8,
        408
    object and purpose, 56–8
    paradoxes see paradoxes of complementarity
    persons involved, 21–4, 406
    popular shorthand description, 17, 34, 43–5,
        120–1
    'positive complementarity', 12, 20–1, 25,
        97–104, 108–10, 122, 341–2, 344–5,
        378–85, 395–6, 399, 401
    primacy distinguished, 14–15, 31–2,
        49–51, 86, 97–8, 191, 205, 241,
        354, 359, 382
    as primary right see states
    as primary responsibility see states
    as priority rule, 11, 14–15, 20, 51, 107,
        409
    procedural aspects, 70–86
    and 'Rome System', 19–20, 25, 345–6, 359,
        397–8
    substantive aspects, 43–70
    as technical admissibility rule, 11, 14–15,
        20, 35–86, 409
    see also catalysing effect of
        complementarity; domestic justice
        systems; International Criminal
        Court (ICC); Rome Statute; states;
        Sudan; Uganda
Comprehensive Peace Agreement (CPA) in
        Sudan, 130–1, 161, 264, 267–8,
        273–4, 288
'comprehensive conduct-test'
    alternative to same-conduct test, 59
concurrent jurisdiction, 14–15
conflict paradigm
    catalysing effect of complementarity,
        171–9, 306–16
    inhibition on domestic proceedings, 362
Congo, Democratic Republic see Democratic
        Republic of the Congo (DRC)

cooperation
and admissibility assessments, 60–1, 69–70, 101
and domestic proceedings, 13–14, 97–8
facilitation by national law, 40–1, 104, 195–7, 201–2
ICC's dependence on, 14, 118–22, 171–2, 174–5, 250, 381, 389–403, 408, 410
lack of, 65, 274–5, 325, 330, 379–82, 393–4, 408
norm entrepreneurs and local actors, 22–3, 165
'positive complementarity' as policy of, 21, 97–9, 108–9
referrals and, 96, 118–22
Rome Statute, 41–2, 54, 98–110
'cosmetic' reforms see catalysing effect of complementarity
cost–benefit analysis see domestic justice systems
Côte d'Ivoire, 31, 344, 346
Criminal Act 1991 (Sudan)
amendment, 286–8, 291, 325
Criminal Procedure Act 1991 (Sudan)
amendment, 287
'culture talk'
risk of, 32

Darfur situation
African Union initiatives, 265, 276–8, 329–30, 356–7
ajaweed, 299–300, 302–6
conflict, 261–5, 369–77
Commission of Inquiry, 279–80
Darfur Peace Agreement (DPA), 265, 291–2, 373
deferral, hope for, 253, 276, 294, 328, 331–5, 391
Doha Document for Peace in Darfur (DDPD), 265, 283, 296–7, 301–3, 319
dominant conflict paradigm, 362
Haskanita war crimes case, 251–2, 261
Inter-Sudanese Peace Talks, 265, 291–2
'Janjaweed', 262, 308, 371–2
Judicial Investigation Commission (JIC), 280–1, 321–2
judiya, 268, 302–3, 305–6
Security Council referral of the situation, 31, 248–9, 357
Special Criminal Court on the Events in Darfur (SCCED), establishment and role, 280–1, 322–3, 342
Special Prosecutor, 282–3, 325–6, 374–5
Tabra market attack investigation, 282, 326

UNAMID, 265, 275, 278, 315
see also International Commission of Inquiry on Darfur (ICID); Sudan; referral; Justice and Equality Movement; Security Council
defendants
as actors with respect to complementarity, 22
deferral
article 18(2) basis, 77–9
ICC and other international criminal tribunals contrasted, 78–9, 83–6
by ICC Prosecutor, 77–9, 84–6
by Security Council request, 11, 90, 253, 328, 331–5, 357, 391, 398–9
Sudan context, 253, 328, 331–5, 357, 391
Uganda context, 135, 138
Democratic Republic of the Congo (DRC)
claims against Uganda, 111–12
conflict in eastern DRC, 111–12, 119
Katanga case see Katanga, Germain
Lubanga case see Lubanga, Thomas
referral to ICC, 31, 346
'division of labour' concept, 11–12, 341–4, 350, 360, 381–2, 397, 399–401, 407
Doha Document for Peace in Darfur (DDPD), 265, 296–7, 301–3, 319
domestic justice systems
cost–benefit analysis (domestic v. ICC proceedings)
assumptions as to catalysing effect of complementarity, 25–6, 367–9
combining of analyses, 392–6
costs of domestic action not reduced by ICC involvement, 378–85
costs of inaction
avoidance by use of alternatives to complementarity, 389–92
low costs, 385–9
expectation of benefit, 113–14, 171–5
high cost of action, 369–78
weak effect of complementarity on, 12, 337
'division of labour' with ICC, 11–12, 341–4, 350, 360, 381–2, 397, 399–401, 407
domestic proceedings and ICC
catalysing effect paradox generally, 14, 396, 400–3, 408
ICC as alternative, 13, 345
normative paradox of complementarity, 13, 345–51, 397–8, 408
pro-ICC ideology, 13, 352–61, 407–8
prosecutorial discretion lost to ICC, 52–3
'self-referral' to ICC, encouragement of, 13, 31, 407–8
in Sudan, 298–9, 320–8
in Uganda, 113–14, 120–3, 228–35, 238

weak effect of complementarity *see* catalysing effect of complementarity.
see also 'international standards'
ICC's jurisdiction where domestic proceedings initiated, 62–6
incorporation of Rome Statute crimes, 10, 12, 40–1, 194–206, 284–91, 406
mimicry/mirroring of ICC *see* International Criminal Court (ICC)
obligation to criminalise?, 40–1
primacy, 37, 53, 57–8, 61, 257, 337, 341–2, 348–9
same-conduct test and, 51–2
special courts as 'cosmetic' reform, 12, 406
see also states; Sudan; Uganda
domestic proceedings initiated after issue of ICC warrants, 79
donors
as actors in complementarity, 12, 24, 383–5, 406, 412
and human rights treaty ratification, 366–7
and 'international standards', 152
and NGOs, 24, 165–6, 190
in Sudan, 283
and 'traditional' justice, 149–50, 152, 154–5
and transitional justice, 164–8, 179, 181–4, 186–7, 190, 193, 237
in Uganda *see* Uganda
see also non-governmental organisations (NGOs)
dramatis personae, 21–4

'ethnophilosophy'
risk of, 32

fair trial rights
ICC overseeing compliance, 67–70
see also international standards; human rights
Final Peace Agreement (Uganda), 136–41, 158, 164, 168, 180, 182–3, 186, 189, 234, 237, 242, 383, 389

Gaddafi, Saif
admissibility challenge by, 22
'Global Criminal Justice System'
complementarity and, 19–20
gravity
'comparative gravity' test, 59
criterion for admissibility, 71, 82, 90–1
role in Uganda, 116, 390
'grounded theory'
methodological approach, 28–9

Harun, Ahmad Muhammad
admissibility assessment, 47–8, 260–1

arrest warrant, 250, 269
rejection of complementarity, 244
Haskanita (Darfur)
war crimes case, 251–2, 261
human rights
article 21(3), 69–70
human rights activists, 10–11, 23–4
ICC jurisdiction to review, 67–70
treaty ratification by Sudan and Uganda, 365–7
see also fair trial rights
Hussein, Abdel Raheem Muhammed
arrest warrant, 252

immunity
bilateral agreements, 119, 194
discouragement by ICC?, 316–20
and domestic proceedings, 65, 295, 328
ICC Act 2010 (Uganda), 199, 216–17
lifting of, 317, 369
upholding of, 309
impunity
anti-impunity agenda, 8, 19–20, 29–30, 42, 57–9, 106–8
inability to investigate or prosecute
absolute inability, 394–5
as admissibility criterion, 35–6, 43, 61–5, 191
avoidance of findings of, 351
claims as to, 121–3, 139, 259, 346, 387
fair trial rights and, 67–9
ICID's assessment, 260, 289, 292–3
paradoxes of complementarity, 392–6
as part of shorthand description, 17, 34, 43–5
partial inability, 395–6
reputational damage due to, 25–6, 347, 387
spectrum of, 393–4
subordination to patronage networks, 14
see also unwillingness to investigate or prosecute
'interests of justice'
no proceedings because of, 71, 91–2, 94–5, 159, 333
International Commission of Inquiry on Darfur (ICID)
assessment of inability to investigate or prosecute, 260, 289, 292–3
'list of fifty-one', 248, 280, 317
supports referral to ICC, 248
views on complementarity as to Sudan, 258–60, 289, 292–3, 333
international courts
primacy of jurisdiction, 14–15, 31–2, 86, 97–8, 241, 354, 359–60, 382
see also entries for specific courts and tribunals

International Crimes Division (Uganda)
  establishment, 179–87
  mimicry/mirroring of ICC, 185, 205
International Criminal Court (ICC)
  as actor in shaping complementarity's
    catalysing effect, 21–2
  admissibility *see* admissibility
  as alternative to domestic proceedings, 13,
    345
  civil-law/common-law divide, 120
  complementarity *see* complementarity
  cooperation *see* cooperation
  cost–benefit analysis, domestic v. ICC
    proceedings *see* domestic justice
    systems
  deferrals *see* deferral
  'division of labour' approach, 11–12, 341–4,
    350, 360, 381–2, 397, 399–401, 407
  expectations as to influence on domestic
    justice systems, 8–10, 24–6
  first referrals to, 31, 111
  first Prosecutor *see* Moreno-Ocampo, Luis
  inadmissibility *see* admissibility
  independence, 14, 174–5, 408
  intervention as stimulus to norm
    entrepreneurs, 362
  investigation
    opening, 60–1
    state's inability to terminate
      investigation, 70, 78
    state's influence on complementarity
      grounds, 76–8
  jurisdiction
    complementary jurisdiction, 14–15, 84,
      86, 205, 382–3, 394
      see also complementarity
    concurrent jurisdiction, 14–15
    to monitor human rights compliance,
      67–70
    primacy of domestic justice systems, 37,
      53, 57–8, 61, 257, 337, 341–2,
      348–9
    primacy of international court
      jurisdiction, 14–15, 31–2, 51, 86,
      97–8, 205, 241, 354, 359–60, 382
    of the state unaffected, 78–9
  triggers
    assessment independent of, 75–6, 86
    types of, 86–90
    see also proprio motu actions; referrals;
      Security Council; self-referrals
  mimicry/mirroring by domestic courts
    implications for international justice,
      413–14
    by SDHC, 185, 205
    story of, 10, 412
    Ugandan detention facilities, 189–90

Office of the Prosecutor (OTP)
  boat trip with Ugandan officials, 230
  prosecutorial discretion, 52–6, 59, 85,
    92–7, 108–9, 379–80
  prosecutorial policy, 92–7, 108–9, 389
  and Sudan, 245–7, 249–50, 260–1, 280–1,
    289–90, 300–1, 316, 327, 330
  and Uganda, 91, 112–16, 120–4, 138–9,
    173–4, 184–5, 213–14, 228–30,
    238–40, 379–80
  organs, 21–2
pro-ICC ideology
  emergence, 13, 345
  and political expectation on states to
    conduct proceedings, 352–61
  promotion, 407–8
  referrals to *see* referrals
  requests US military assistance for arrests,
    173
  'self-referral' by states to, 13, 31, 407–8
  subordination to patronage networks, 14,
    403, 408
  success, measure of, 2, 8–9, 404
  and Sudan *see* Sudan
  and Uganda *see* Uganda
  UK support for, 120
  US opposition to, 118–19, 248–9
  see also complementarity; international
    criminal justice movement;
    Rome Statute
International Criminal Court Act (Uganda)
  adoption, 194–206
international-criminal-justice movement
  as actor in complementarity, 23–4
  donors and, 24
  pro-ICC ideology, 352–3
  in Uganda, 192, 241
International Criminal Tribunal for the
    former Yugoslavia (ICTY)
  amnesty, 219
  catalysing effects, 31, 382–3
  complementarity, 97–8
  concurrent jurisdiction, 14–15
  conditional deferral procedure, 71, 83–6,
    191–2, 383
    see also rule 11 *bis below*
  conflation with ICC, 171–2, 190
  deferral to, 78
  human rights monitoring of domestic
    proceedings, 69, 85–6
  model, 189, 241
  ordinary crimes, 49–51
  primacy, 14–15, 31–2, 51
  rule 11 *bis*, 69–71, 86, 188, 192
    see also conditional deferral procedure
      above
  and state sovereignty, 16

International Criminal Tribunal for Rwanda
(ICTR)
catalysing effects, 31, 382–3
concurrent jurisdiction, 14–15
conditional deferral procedure, 71, 83–6,
191–2, 383
see also rule 11 bis below
conflation with ICC, 190, 342
deferral to, 78
human rights monitoring of domestic
proceedings, 69–70, 85–6
model, 185, 189, 205, 241, 342
ordinary crimes, 49–51
primacy, 14–15, 31–2, 205
rule 11 bis, 69–71, 86, 192, 205
see also conditional deferral procedure
above
and state sovereignty, 16
Ugandan judges, 181
'international standards'
attention to, 10, 12, 106, 141, 152–3, 157,
187–94, 234, 237, 241–3, 353, 412
investigation
article 17, 59–61
Darfur see Darfur situation
ICC see International Criminal Court
(ICC)
opening, 60–1
Uganda see Uganda
Israel
'unsigning' of Rome Statute, 251

Janjaweed
Darfur situation, 262, 308, 371–2
Juba peace talks
complementarity and, 56, 133–41, 176, 234,
388, 395
ICC and, 24, 129–33, 136–7, 155–62, 239,
355, 381
see also Accountability and Reconciliation
Accords
judiya
Darfur situation, 268, 302–3, 305–6
jurisdiction
ICC see International Criminal Court
(ICC)
ICTR see International Criminal Tribunal
for Rwanda (ICTR)
ICTY see International Criminal
Tribunal for the former Yugoslavia
(ICTY)
primacy, complementarity distinguished,
14–15, 31–2, 51, 86, 97–8, 191, 205,
241, 354, 359–60, 382
Justice and Equality Movement (JEM)
and Darfur conflict, 264–5, 269, 295,
318–20, 326

Justice, Law and Order Sector (JLOS)
(Uganda), 164–5, 172–3, 176,
180–1, 184–5, 188–90, 192–3, 203

Katanga, Germain
admissibility challenge by, 22, 52–3
case cited, 39–40, 43–8, 57, 60–4, 81, 89
'comparative gravity-test', 59
'comprehensive conduct-test', 59
DRC supports ICC prosecution, 51
Kenya situation
admissibility challenge, 48–9, 57, 107
Court's discussion, 48–9, 57, 60–1, 101–2,
108–9
ICC investigation initiated, 31
invocation of article 93(10), 101–2
invocation of positive complementarity, 108–9
invocation of sovereignty, 26, 57
proprio motu investigation, 31, 381
Ugandan reference to, 181, 232
Kony, Joseph
and Acholi, 124–5, 127
establishes LRA, 124–5
and Final Peace Agreement (FPA), 137–41,
158, 164, 168, 178, 180, 182–3, 186,
189, 234, 237, 242–3, 383, 389
ICC arrest warrant for, 115
ICC requests US military assistance to
arrest, 173
and mato oput, 150
quoted, 136, 160
reference to complementarity, 160
rejects amnesty offer, 128
Ugandan arrest warrant, 122, 238
Kushayb, Ali
admissibility, 47–8, 260–1
'case', meaning of, 48
Sudanese proceedings against, 260, 320–1,
332, 335, 377
Sudanese response to arrest warrant, 250,
269, 308–9, 320–1, 325, 332
Kwoyelo, Thomas
amnesty denied, 214–27
charges against, 205–6
and complementarity, 226, 231–3, 239–40
cooperation from OTP, 239–40
and patronage, 374
terrorism paradigm, 233

legal scholars
expectations as to complementarity, 9
Liberation and Justice Movement (LJM)
and Darfur peace talks, 265, 295–6, 318
Libya
Darfur peace talks, 265
degree of inability/unwillingness to conduct
domestic proceedings, 393, 402

Libya (cont.)
    Gaddafi (Saif) case, 22
    referral, 31
line-of-fire perspective
    challenges for research, 30
    choice of, 30–2
    complementarity under fire, 410
local justice practices
    ajaweed, 299–300, 302–6
    catalysing effect of complementarity,
        141–59, 299–306
    judiya, 268, 302–3, 305–6
    mato oput, 145–6, 148, 153–7, 174–5
Lord's Resistance Army (LRA)
    admissibility of ICC cases against members
        of, 120–4, 137–41, 188–9, 230–1,
        241–2, 360, 379–80, 388–9, 402
    agreement to Juba peace talks, 129–31
    amnesty for, 128, 159, 206–27
    conflict involving, 124–9
    deferral of proceedings against, 138, 334
    domestic proceedings against, 160, 179,
        186–7, 193, 205–6, 213–14, 231–3
    ICC investigation's focus on, 115–16,
        228–30
    ICC warrants issued against leaders, 115,
        142
    negotiations with, 116–17, 128–37, 159,
        196–7
    referral to ICC, 111–23, 171–2
    and Sudan, 119–20, 122, 128–32, 137,
        171–2, 174–5, 249–50
    see also Kony, Joseph; Kwoyelo, Thomas;
        Juba peace talks
low punishment
    admissibility on grounds of, 66
Lubanga, Thomas
    admissibility assessment, 46, 51–2, 60–1
    'case', meaning of, 46–8, 51–4
    DRC supports ICC prosecution, 51
    and Uganda, 111–12

Mali
    referral, 31, 346
mato oput
    and northern Uganda conflict, 145–6, 148,
        153–7, 174–5
'Meridionalism'
    risk of, 32
methodological perspective, overview, 28–30
mimicry/mirroring of ICC *see* International
        Criminal Court (ICC)
Moreno-Ocampo, Luis
    appointment supported by UK, 120
    on complementarity, 2, 8–9, 25, 111
    concerns over Uganda peace talks, 138–9,
        239–40

Darfur investigation, 248–50, 260, 280, 330
Haskanita war crimes case, 251–2
on ICC's success, 2, 8–9
on 'positive complementarity', 20, 25,
        344–5
on duty of states to prosecute, 19–20, 25, 37
requests arrest warrant for Sudanese
        President, 23, 244, 251, 269–70,
        273–4, 276–9, 289–90, 330
on 'Rome System', 19–20, 25
on situation in eastern DRC, 111
Sudan's opposition to, 244–6, 250–1, 284,
        289, 312–13
and Uganda's referral to ICC, 111, 122,
        239–40
and Ugandan state actors, 91, 230
see also International Criminal Court (ICC),
        Office of the Prosecutor (OTP)
Museveni, Yoweri
    on amnesty, 129, 207, 211
    and ICC, 112, 129, 171–2, 230, 386,
        388–9
    and situation in northern Uganda, 124–9,
        131–2, 169–71, 389
    and South Sudan, 131–2

N'Djamena (Chad)
    Darfur ceasefires, 264–5
Nehru, Jawaharlal
    on theory and reality, 26
networks
    inclusion into, 176, 182–3, 236–8, 314–15
    as actors in complementarity, 22–4
    theory, 176
    see also patronage
Nigeria
    Darfur peace talks, 265
non-governmental organisations (NGOs)
    as actors in complementarity, 22–4
    and donors, 24, 165–6, 190
    expectations as to complementarity, 9
    promoting complementarity as big idea, 11,
        20, 33, 195–6, 200–1
    and Sudan, 22–3, 275, 385
    and Uganda *see* Uganda.
    see also donors; international criminal
        justice movement
norm entrepreneurs
    as actors in complementarity, 12, 22–3
    changing conflict paradigm, 362
    in Uganda, 169–70, 177–8, 182–4, 235–7,
        241
norm hijacking
    literal over legal meaning of
        'complementarity', 340–1
    Uganda, 192–3
    see also 'division of labour' concept

normative perspective
  overview, 27–8
northern Uganda conflict see Lord's
      Resistance Army (LRA); Uganda

Office of the Prosecutor (OTP)
      see International Criminal Court
      (ICC); Moreno-Ocampo, Luis
ordinary crimes, 49–51
Otti, Vincent
  arrest warrant for, 115–16, 122
  and mato oput, 150
  reference to Lubanga case, 136–7
  referred to, 142
outreach
  by ICC, 199, 230, 343, 360
  as 'international standard', 190–1
  by NGOs, 190, 353

paradoxes of complementarity
  absence of paradox, 394
  analysis of, 13–14, 396–405, 408
  catalysing effect paradox, 14, 396, 400–3,
      408
  complementarity paradox, 392–3
  normative paradox, 13, 345–51, 397–8,
      408
  paradox of positive complementarity,
      395–6
pardon
  admissibility on grounds of, 66
  see also amnesties
patronage
  cover up, 389
  and domestic proceedings, 406–7
  entrepreneurs, 237
  impunity and, 373–8, 402
  institutional subordination to, 12, 14, 167,
      371–3, 408
  liberation from, 403–4
  maintenance of, 182
  potential for, 237
  price of, 371–2
  see also networks
political economy
  assumptions as to catalysing effect of
      complementarity, 25–6, 337
  see also cost–benefit analysis; norm
      entrepreneurs; patronage
politics
  head-of-state-driven politics, 168
  ICC politics, 357
  and law, 359
  Real Politics, 403–4
  rewards of international politics, 167
  transitional justice, 187
  see also patronage

'positive complementarity'
      see complementarity
primacy as to jurisdiction
  complementarity distinguished, 14–15,
      31–2, 49–51, 86, 97–8, 191, 205,
      241, 354, 359, 382
pro-ICC ideology see International Criminal
      Court (ICC)
proprio motu actions
  admissibility assessment, 81–2, 138
  interests-of-justice assessment, 92
  OTP investigation, 71–2, 77, 87–8, 94, 96,
      118
prosecution by states
  duty or obligation to prosecute, 11, 13,
      18–20, 25, 36–42
  responsibility to prosecute, 11, 13, 18, 25,
      36–40, 344–67, 410
  see also states
prosecutorial discretion
  of domestic justice systems, 52–3, 59, 74,
      107–8
  of ICC, 52–6, 59, 85, 92–7, 108–9, 379–80
prosecutorial policy
  OTP, 92–7, 108–9, 389

Qatar
  Darfur peace talks, 265

realism
  in study of complementarity, 26–30
referrals
  Democratic Republic of the Congo
      (DRC), 31, 346
  Mali, 31, 346
  by Security Council, 31, 75–6, 87
  by states, 3, 13, 87
  Sudan, 31, 248–9, 357
  Uganda, 31, 111–23, 171–2
  see also self-referrals
reputational damage, 12, 23, 25–6, 114, 172,
      235, 237, 368, 378, 386–8, 392–3, 398
research on present study
  approaches to, 26–30
  ethics, 30
  line-of-fire perspective
      choice of, 30–2
      conclusions as to, 406–10
  methods, 28–30
  scope of present study, 10–11, 27, 30–2
  structure of present study, 33
responsibility to conduct proceedings see states
right to conduct proceedings see states
Rome Statute
  complementarity see complementarity
  complementarity as 'foundational
      principle', 17

Rome Statute (cont.)
  gravity *see* gravity
  incorporation of crimes into domestic law,
      10, 12, 40–1, 194–206, 284–91, 406
  normative paradox of complementarity, 13,
      345–51, 397–8, 408
  object and purpose, 29–30, 39–40, 58
  prohibition of amnesties?, 18–19, 41–3, 104
  prosecutorial discretion, 52–6, 59, 85, 92–7,
      108–9, 379–80
  realism in analysis of, 29–30
  referrals *see* referrals
  states' responsibility to prosecute, 11, 13,
      18, 25, 36–40, 344–67, 410
  states' right to prosecute, 15–16, 25, 70,
      331, 408, 410
  'unsigning', 251
  see also entries at article; International
      Criminal Court (ICC)
'Rome System'
  complementarity and, 19–20, 25, 345–6,
      359, 397–8

scope of present study, 10–11, 27, 30–2
Security Council
  as actor in shaping complementarity's
      catalysing effect, 22–3
  complementarity as decision-making factor,
      11, 23, 259, 331–5, 344–5
  Darfur resolution, 31, 248–9, 357
  referrals, 31, 75–6, 87–90
  request for deferral, 11, 90, 253, 328, 331–5,
      357, 391, 398–9
  UNAMID, 265, 275, 278, 315
'self-referrals' 13, 31, 89, 111–13, 119, 228,
      238, 338, 347, 349–51, 386, 397,
      399–400, 407
Sirte (Libya)
  Darfur peace talks, 265
sovereignty
  benefits, 386
  complementarity in relation, 16, 27–8, 355,
      358–60, 409–10
  costs, 12, 25–6, 359, 367–9, 378, 385–9, 398–9
  international justice in relation, 27–8,
      56–7, 359–60, 409–10
  invocation, 26, 57
  recognition of, 365–6
Special Court for Sierra Leone (SCSL)
  amnesty, 219
  concurrent jurisdiction, 14–15
  primacy, 14–15, 359
  role model, 184, 241, 359
  Ugandan judge on, 181, 189
special courts
  as 'cosmetic' reform, 12, 406
  and human rights law, 281

Special Criminal Court on the Events in
      Darfur (SCCED)
  establishment and role of, 280–1, 322–3,
      342
Special Division of the High Court (SDHC)
      see International Crimes Division
      (Uganda)
Special Tribunal for Lebanon (STL)
  concurrent jurisdiction, 14–15
  primacy, 14–15
states
  as actors in complementarity, 22
  duty or obligation to prosecute, 11, 13,
      18–20, 25, 36–42
  expectations as to complementarity, 9
  inability to investigate or prosecute
      see inability to investigate or
      prosecute
  interaction with ICC jurisdiction
      see International Criminal Court
      (ICC), jurisdiction
  obligation to incorporate Rome Statute
      crimes?, 40–1
  responsibility to prosecute, 11, 13, 18, 25,
      36–40, 344–67, 410
  right to prosecute, 15–16, 25, 70, 331,
      339–44, 408, 410
  sovereignty *see* sovereignty
  'State' in article 17, 71
  see also domestic justice systems; Sudan;
      Uganda
Sudan
  al-Bashir case *see* al-Bashir, Omar
  catalysing effect of complementarity
    accountability on agenda peace
        negotiations, 291–9
    accountability mechanisms,
        establishment of, 279–84
    amnesties discouraged?, 318–20
    Armed Forces Act 1986 amendment,
        284–6, 289, 317
    conclusions as to, 328–36, 406–10
    conflict paradigm, expansion?, 306–16
    considerations underlying, 26
    context generally, 245–65
    Criminal Act 1991 amendment, 286–8,
        291, 325
    Criminal Procedure Act 1991
        amendment, 287
    domestic proceedings increased?, 320–8
    effect summarised, 10–14, 266, 328–37
    expected effects not experienced, 306–28
    immunities discouraged?, 316–17,
        319–20
    inhospitable environment for
        responsibility to conduct
        proceedings, 361–7

laws on international crimes, adoption of,
    284–91
local justice practices, promotion of,
    299–306
special mechanisms as ICC alternatives,
    279–84
transitional justice debate, 266–79
Uganda compared
    accountability mechanisms, 283
    accountability on agenda peace
        negotiations 293, 298
    effect summarised, 328–30
    expected effects not experienced, 306
    ICC's attention to complementarity,
        246–7, 330
    legal dimension included in conflict
        resolution?, 307–9, 314–15
    responsibility to conduct proceedings
        as norm, 361–7
    traditional justice practices, 301, 304–5
    transitional justice, 278
    unlikeliness of a catalysing effect, 244
    see also catalysing effect of
        complementarity
complementarity
    allusions to, 257, 342
    catalysing effect see catalysing effect of
        complementarity above
    denial of applicability, 244, 252–8, 261
    ICC's views, 260–1, 289–90
    ICID's views, 258–60, 289, 292–3, 333
    choice as case study, 31
Darfur see Darfur situation
donors and, 283
Harun case see Harun, Ahmad Muhammad
human rights treaties, ratification of, 365–7
Hussein, Abdel Raheem Muhammed, arrest
    warrant, 252
and ICC
    admissibility challenge?, 22, 261, 331
    deterioration of relations, 245–52
    ICC's views on complementarity, 260–1,
        289–90
    initial support for ICC's establishment,
        247–8
    legal response to ICC proceedings,
        246–7, 254–7, 261
    limited cooperation, 249–50
    political response to ICC proceedings,
        246–7, 252–4, 261
    'unsigning' of Rome Statute, 251
inhospitable environment for responsibility
    to conduct proceedings, 361–7
Kushayb case see Kushayb, Ali
NGOs and, 22–3, 275, 385
President see Abboud, Ibrahim; al-Bashir,
    Omar

South(ern) Sudan
    conflict 161, 256, 263–4, 266–8, 290,
        307–8, 321
    and ICC, 274–5
    and LRA, 125, 128–32, 137, 139, 175,
        225
    support for LRA, 121, 128
    support for Uganda against LRA, 129
    see also al-Bashir, Omar; Darfur situation
Sudan Liberation Movement (SLM)
    Darfur conflict, 264–5
Sudan People's Liberation Movement (SPLM),
    130–2, 161, 264, 273–5, 288, 307

Tabra (Darfur)
    investigation into market attack, 282, 326
'traditional' justice practices see local justice
    practices
transitional justice
    as alternative to international justice, 315,
        329–30
    catalysing effect of complementarity, 10,
        159–70, 242–3, 266–79
    donors and, 164–8, 179, 181–4, 186–7, 190,
        193, 237
    in peace agreement, 134–6, 159–60, 182–3,
        186–7, 223–5, 295–301, 329–30
    Transitional Justice Working Group
        (Uganda), 148, 164–8, 176, 180–1,
        198, 236
treaty interpretation, 29–30

Uganda
    Acholi, see Achdi
    Amnesty Act 2000, 128, 172–3, 180,
        206–27
    'bilateral immunity agreement' with US,
        119, 194
    catalysing effect of complementarity
        A&R Accords, 133–6, 139–40, 150–3,
            160–1, 176, 179–80, 201, 212–13, 223
        accountability on agenda of peace
            negotiations, 159–62
        amnesties discouraged, 206–27
        attempts to find alternatives to ICC,
            137–41, 237
        conclusions as to, 234–43, 406–10
        conflict paradigm expansion, 171–9
        considerations underlying, 26
        context generally, 114–41
        domestic proceedings increased?, 228–33
        effect summarised, 10–14, 141, 234–43,
            337
        expected effects not experienced, 228–33
        inhospitable environment for
            responsibility to conduct
            proceedings, 361–7

Uganda (cont.)
  International Crimes Division,
    establishment of, 179–87
  International Criminal Court Act,
    194–206
  'international standards', attention to,
    187–94
  local justice practices, promotion of,
    141–59
  Sudan compared
    accountability on agenda of peace
      negotiations, 293, 298
    accountability mechanisms, 283
    effect summarised, 328–30
    expected effects not experienced, 306
    ICC's attention to complementarity,
      246–7, 330
    legal dimension included in conflict
      resolution?, 307–9, 314–15
    responsibility to conduct proceedings
      as norm, 361–7
    traditional justice practices, 301,
      304–5
    transitional justice, 278
    transitional justice debate, 162–70
    transitional justice on peace talks agenda,
      159–62
  choice as case study, 31
  complementarity
    catalysing effect see catalysing effect of
      complementarity above
    downplaying of, 120–4
    see also and ICC below
  conflict in northern Uganda
    Agreement and Annexure on
      Accountability and Reconciliation
      (A&R Accords)
      see Accuountability and
      Reconciliation Accords
    Bigombe peace initiatives, 128–9, 138,
      196
    collapse of negotiations, 136–7
    conflict prior to referral, overview of,
      124–9
    dominant conflict paradigm, 171–9, 362
    Final Peace Agreement (FPA) see Final
      Peace Agreement
    government forces, 126–7
    see also Uganda People's Defence Forces
      (UPDF)
    Juba peace talks see Juba peace talks
    North–South political divisions, 125–7
    US support for government, 127, 173–4
    see also Kony, Joseph; Kwoyelo, Thomas;
      Lord's Resistance Army (LRA);
      Otti, Vincent
  detention centres, mirroring of ICC, 189–90

  donors in
    and Amnesty Act 2000, 222–3, 225–6, 236
    and human rights treaty ratification,
      366–7
    and ICC Act 2010, 200–1
    and ICC ideology, 356–8
    influence on government, 117, 194–5, 243
    and 'international standards', 152
    and outreach, 190
    and patronage, 373
    and traditional justice, 149–50, 152, 155
    and transitional justice, 164–8, 179,
      181–4, 186–7, 190, 193, 237
  and DRC see Democratic Republic of the
    Congo (DRC)
  first ever referral to ICC, 31, 111
  gravity test, 116, 390
  human rights treaties, ratification of, 195,
    365–7
  and ICC
    admissibility assessment
      ICC's position, 122–3, 138–40, 238–9
      Uganda's position, 121–2, 153, 157,
        190–1, 238–9
    admissibility challenge, 22, 122, 133,
      135, 140–1, 157, 190–1, 202, 237–9
    attempts to find alternatives to ICC,
      137–41, 237
    complementarity downplayed, 120–4
    convergence of interests, 114, 116–19
    ICC concerns over peace talks, 138–40
    inability/unwillingness to prosecute,
      121–2, 139, 387, 393–5
    Juba peace talks, 129–33
    referral, 111–14, 120–1
    right to withdraw referral assumed, 129
    scope of investigation, 114–16
  International Crimes Division
    see International Crimes Division
  International Criminal Court Act, 194–206
  Juba peace talks, see Juba peace talks
  Justice, Law and Order Sector (JLOS),
    164–5, 172–3, 176, 180–1, 184–5,
    188–90, 192–3, 203
  mato oput, 145–6, 148, 153–7, 174–5
  NGOs in
    capacity building, 165–6, 182–3
    and domestic proceedings, 192–3
    and ICC, 115, 133, 176–7
    and International Criminal Court Act,
      195–6, 200–1
    and Kwoyelo case, 223–4
    outreach, 190, 238
    and traditional justice, 147, 152–3, 176
    and War Crimes Court, 182–3
  norm entrepreneurs in, 169–70, 177, 182–4,
    235–8, 241

President *see* Museveni, Yoweri
securitisation, 178
Special Division of the High Court
  (SDHC) *see* International Crimes
  Division (Uganda)
support for South Sudan, 128, 132
Transitional Justice Working Group, 148,
  164–8, 176, 180–1, 198, 236
Uganda People's Defence Forces (UPDF),
  114–20, 124–32, 136–7, 141–2, 159,
  169–74
War Crimes Court *see* International Crimes
  Division (Uganda).
see also Lord's Resistance Army (LRA);
  Museveni, Yoweri
UNAMID
  265, 278, 278, 315
United Kingdom
  support for ICC, 120
United Nations Security Council *see* Security
  Council
United States
  'bilateral immunity agreement' with
    Uganda, 119, 194
  and Darfur resolution, 248–9
  ICC requests military assistance for arrests,
    173
  lists LRA as terrorist organisation, 119

opposition to ICC, 118–19, 248–9
support for Uganda, 127, 173–4
'unsigning' of Rome Statute, 251
unwillingness to investigate or prosecute
  absolute unwillingness, 394–5
  as admissibility criterion, 35–6, 43, 61–4, 66
  avoidance of findings of, 351
  claims as to, 121, 259, 387
  fair trial rights and, 67–9
  ICID's assessment, 260, 289, 292–3
  paradoxes of complementarity, 392–6
  as part of the shorthand description, 17, 34,
    43–5
  partial unwillingness, 395
  reputational damage due to, 25–6, 347, 387
  spectrum of, 393–4
  subordination to patronage networks, 14
  see also inability to investigate or
    prosecute

Vienna Convention on the Law of Treaties
  (VCLT)
  general rule on treaty interpretation,
    29–30, 241
  treaties and third parties, 38, 254–5

War Crimes Division *see* International Crimes
  Division (Uganda)